Americans
and Chinese

Americans and Chinese

Passage to Differences

THIRD EDITION

FRANCIS L. K. HSU

UNIVERSITY OF HAWAII
PRESS   *Honolulu*

02 01 00 99 98 97   10 9 8 7 6

THE UNIVERSITY OF HAWAI'I PRESS ACKNOWLEDGES
THE ASSISTANCE OF THE ANDREW W. MELLON
FOUNDATION IN THE PUBLICATION OF THIS BOOK.

Library of Congress Cataloging in Publication Data

Hsu, Francis L. K., 1909—
    Americans and Chinese

    Bibliography: p.
    Includes index.
    1.   China—Civilization.   2.   United States—
Civilization—20th century.   I.   Title.
DS721.H685   1981   951   81–10461
ISBN 0–8248–0710–3   AACR2
ISBN 0–8248–0757–X (pbk.)

University of Hawai'i Press books are printed on acid-
free paper and meet the guidelines for permanence
and durability of the Council on Library Resources

To my daughters
Eileen Yi-nan and Penalope Si-hwa
and their generation
in the hope that this book and their efforts
will help to lighten the burdens of those
yet to come

Contents

Foreword by Henry Steele Commager   *xi*

Preface   *xix*

Prologue. Culture and Behavior   1

PART ONE
IN SEARCH OF ORIGIN

    Introduction   17

1 *Mirrors of Life*   19
    ASPECTS OF ART   19
    FICTION   29

2 *The Sexes*   49
    ROMANCE   49
    WOMEN IN A MAN'S WORLD   60
    ROMANCE AND COMMUNISM   63
    A MULTIPLE MURDER CASE   70

3 *The Beginnings of Contrast*   76
    THE HOME   78
    PARENTS AND CHILDREN   79
    SCHOOL   92
    SOCIAL NEEDS AND VALUES   108

4 *Where Europe Ends and America Begins*   121
    THE RISE OF THE AMERICAN WAY OF LIFE   128

PART TWO
MEN, GODS, AND THINGS

    Introduction   141

5 *Marriage and Class*   144
    CLASS   156

6 *Success and the Hero*   165
    HERO WORSHIP   170

7 *Two Attitudes toward Government*   187
    THE PRESTIGE OF GOVERNMENT   187
    DISTANCE VERSUS IDENTIFICATION   197

8 *The Ills of Government*   209
    CORRUPTION   209
    HOW TO WIN FAVORS AND INFLUENCE OFFICIALS   216
    REVOLT AND SCHISM   225

9 *Two Kinds of Religion*   238
    THE CHINESE WAY IN RELIGION   240
    ANCESTOR WORSHIP   248
    POLYTHEISM VERSUS MONOTHEISM   253

10 *The Bases of Religious Faith*   270
    "WILLING TO BE A METHODIST"   270
    THE DIRECTION OF THE CHURCH IN AMERICA   276

11 *Two Approaches to Economic Life*   292
    THE CHARACTERISTICS OF THE CHINESE ECONOMY   293
    CHINESE GOVERNMENT AND CHINESE ECONOMY   304
    AMERICAN ECONOMIC ATTITUDES   306

12 *Industrial Failure and Economic Strife*   312
    WHY HAVE THE CHINESE FAILED TO INDUSTRIALIZE?   313
    COMPETITION: POINT OF UNITY OR DIVISION   320

PART THREE
DILEMMA

    Introduction   333

13 *American Problems*   335
    OLD AGE   335
    GENERATION GAP   343
    RACIAL CRISIS   351
    SEX CRIMES AND VIOLENCE   360

14 *Chinese Weaknesses*   372
    BONDAGE TO THE PAST   372
    REVOLT WITHOUT REVOLUTION   377
    LACK OF SCIENCE AND MUSIC   384
    LACK OF VOLUNTARY, NON-KINSHIP ORGANIZATIONS   394
    PRICE OF CONTENTMENT   399

15 *China under Communism*   403
    THE CHINESE FERMENT   405
    EARLY SOURCES OF COMMUNIST STRENGTH   412

CHANGE UNDER COMMUNISM   418

A RURAL COMMUNE   420

AN URBAN COMMUNE   422

WORK POINTS AND THE KINSHIP SYSTEM   424

CADRES, THE NEW COMMUNICATION SYSTEM, AND SOCIAL
TRANSFORMATION   428

16 *World Unrest: Communism and America*   439

THE AMERICAN DILEMMA   441

AMERICA'S ALTERNATIVES   445

THE ENEMY WITHIN   456

Epilogue: Purpose and Fulfillment   476

A Brief Chronology of China and the West   491

References   505

Indexes   523

Foreword

1

Francis L. K. Hsu's *Americans and Chinese* belongs in the great tradition of books by foreign observers interpreting the American character—the tradition of Crèvecoeur and Brissot, of Francis Lieber and Francis Grund, of Tocqueville and Bryce, of Münsterberg, and Santayana, and Denis Brogan. It shares their zeal to discover the significance and the portent of America for the world, and it shares, too, what the best of them have, a realization of how much is at stake for the whole of mankind in the fortune or misfortunes of America. "I confess," wrote Tocqueville in a famous passage in the *Democracy,* "that in America I saw more than America. I sought the image of democracy itself, with its inclinations, its character, its prejudices and its passions, in order to learn what we have to fear, or to hope, from its progress."

That strikes the note that has echoed, sometimes anxiously, sometimes confidently, but almost always with a sense of urgency, in a hundred interpretations, and that echoes, too, in the pages of Professor Hsu's original and penetrating book. But in three important respects *Americans and Chinese* differs from most of its predecessors in what we may call cultural sociology. First, almost all of the many commentators and interpreters of the past accepted without serious questioning the principle which Emerson had laid down for judging England, that the ultimate test of any nation is success. All were forced to concede that it was a material success—forty million immigrants to the New World were pretty conclusive proof of that; most conceded that it was a political success; some—the best among them like Tocqueville and Bryce—were prepared to maintain that it was a moral success. To many America was clearly the 'wave of the future, a wave already lapping European shores. A few critics looked upon the growth and the spread of America with alarm, more with resignation, the majority with qualified approval, and almost all with fascination.

Now, for the first time in over a century, Americans themselves are filled with misgivings about the success of their enterprise—no longer an "experiment"—and the rest of mankind is filled with forebodings. Not since the eighteenth-century philosophes solemnly debated the question, Was America a Mistake? has there been such a widespread questioning, such deep disillusionment as now resounds. Where a Crèvecoeur or a Tocqueville, a Dicey or a Bryce, looked upon the spread of American power and influence with enthusiasm, contemporary critics and observers look upon it with anxiety and even with fear. Where, in the past, much of the human race rejoiced in the progress of American institutions and social practices, especially in political and economic areas, now the term "Americanization" has become pejorative.

Professor Hsu's book is the first of importance to respond to this new situation and to articulate this new mood. In fact, an earlier and briefer version of the book some twenty years ago anticipated them and their diverse manifestations—from racial violence and the generation gap to militant dissension, government repression, and neocolonialism abroad. By contrast with its merciless analyses, its unflattering comparisons, and its sombre warnings, the animadversions of a Servan-Schreiber about "Americanization"—by which they mean chiefly the spread of American corporate interests—are trivial. In the eyes of Professor Hsu the spread of American economic interests or technological models to Western Europe is of little importance compared to the spread of American political and military power, social habits, and moral values over the entire globe.

The second thing that distinguishes Professor Hsu's analysis of American character from all previous interpretations derives from the book itself rather than from the circumstances that attend its appearance. Almost all previous interpretations of the American character started from pretty much the same premises about Western culture, and made pretty much the same assumptions about it. What we have in these classical essays by English, French, and German observers is a kind of family confrontation—sometimes a family quarrel, sometimes a family celebration, but always about problems and characters who are familiar. The observations, the questions, the predictions, all circulated within the framework of Western culture and sociology and were limited to matters of interest to those who participated in that culture and that society. If laws of history were ever to be formulated, wrote Henry Adams almost a century ago, it must be on the basis of American experience, for America recapitulated the past and predicted the future. He meant, of course, laws of Western history, for American experience could scarcely explain China, India, Africa, or even Russia. The objective to all this preoccupation with Western culture is not its parochialism; that was doubtless unavoidable. It is rather its cultural limitations. For European critics really took for granted what Americans themselves took for granted; they started from premises which, if not wholly American, were familiar enough to Americans; they came to conclusions which, if not wholly acceptable were rarely shocking and never wholly outside American experience—an experience often vicarious but none the worse for that. What Professor Hsu has done—of his predecessors only No-Yong Park (*An Oriental View of American Civilization,* 1934) anticipated him in any serious fashion—is to observe what Europeans missed because they took it for granted; to ask questions that Europeans failed to ask because they would have seemed eccentric; to make predictions based on three thousand years of history, not three hundred.

Tocqueville, incomparably the greatest of the foreign interpreters, was not unaware of the limitations imposed by these Western and therefore parochial assumptions, but unable to free himself from them. "The more I see the world of our day in greater detail," he wrote, "the more I consider the prodigious variety to be met with, the more I am tempted to believe that what we call necessary institutions are no more than institutions to which we have grown accustomed, and that the field of possibilities is much more extensive than men are ready to imagine." Just so. The field of possibilities is more extensive than most of our cultural anthropologists have imagined. Earlier generations of social critics had gone to the Orient for contrast: Montesquieu with the *Persian Letters,* for example, and Voltaire with the opening chapters of his *Manners and Spirit of Nations,* and Oliver Goldsmith with his entertaining *Sketches of London Society by a Chinese Traveller.* But all this was nothing but a game, for the oriental sages all turned out to be French philosophes wearing Persian or Chinese silks. Professor Hsu does not go to the Orient in this artificial way. China is not here merely for purposes of literary or dramatic contrast; it is as much the subject of inquiry and comparison as is the United States.

Here is a third quality that distinguishes *Americans and Chinese* from almost the whole vast library of literature interpreting America: that it is genuinely comparative, as valuable for the light it throws on the most ancient of nations and the most recent of world powers as for its illumination of the American scene. For what was said of America in Tocqueville's day, can be said of China in ours, that no student can be indifferent to its existence, no economist omit it from his calculations, no statesman ignore its immense potentialities, and no philosopher or moralist refuse to accommodate his speculations to its presence. It took perspicacity for a Tocqueville or a Lieber to see that the future of the Western world would be affected by the brash new nation that had sprung up overnight on the other side of the Atlantic, just as it took historical wisdom for Tocqueville and Henry Adams to predict the future greatness and power of Russia. But it should take no great leap of the imagination to realize that the fate of the whole world will be deeply affected by the future course of this vast nation with three thousand years of history crowding upon it, but new, and vigorous, even as the United States was new and vigorous when Europeans began to speculate upon it. Needless to say, Professor Hsu—himself Chinese born—does not fall into the error of supposing that we study China as a kind of foil to America. We study China and the Chinese character because it has much to teach us and much to teach the world.

2

Democracy in America has held its magisterial position in the literature about America for over a century in large part because Tocqueville seized upon a central theme and pursued it relentlessly into every nook and cranny of American thought and conduct. The principle of equality was indeed seminal; if it did not explain everything (slavery, for example) it illuminated everything. Professor Hsu, too, has seized upon a central theme: individualism. Individualism, as he portrays it, is perhaps not very different from equality, but it is fair to say that the passion for equality is more a manifestation of individualism than is individualism a manifestation of equality. And individualism, as a master key to the American character, has this merit, that far more clearly than equality it connects America with the rest of the Western world and distinguishes the Western world from the non-Western. For equality has not always been a common denominator of the West, nor is it everywhere now—in Spain, for example, or in Mississippi—but since the Renaissance individualism has been, and still is, a trait that more sharply than any other distinguishes the West from the Orient. Yet who can doubt that the circumstances of environment and of history have made America a kind of paradigm of an individualistic society, revealing its advantages and its ravages.

There is nothing surprising about this. The United States is, after all, the most nearly European of all countries, the only one whose population and whose cultural inheritance is *European*. Granted that, in language, law, literature, and politics the English inheritance has been predominant; in the realms of religion, education, social practices, moral and psychological values and attitudes, the German, Italian, Spanish, and Jewish have made significant contributions. If an anthropologist were to choose one Western people to contrast with the Chinese, the American is clearly the right choice.

Professor Hsu has traced the influence of the principle of individualism in the large and in the small. He observes it in the nature of the American political system, the workings of the criminal law, the attitude toward nature, the conduct of foreign policy, and the waging of war. He explores it in the relations of parents and children, the attitude toward ancestors and posterity, the cult of youth and the fate of age, the role of sex in literature and art as in life, in incidence of crime, the concepts of success and the ratings of prestige, the psychology of games and of sports, and many other areas of human endeavor. In all of these areas he contrasts American practices and malpractices with Chinese; American insecurity with Chinese security, American exclusiveness with Chinese inclusiveness, American worship of the next generation with Chinese veneration for the last. Individualism, he contends, explains why competition permeates every aspect of American life: the struggle of children for the attention and affection of their parents, and the struggle of parents to win the attention and approval of their children; the concern of the American woman for such beauty and style as will enable her to win her husband anew every day, the anxiety of the husband to prove that he is a success and thus deserves the respect and affection of his wife; the deadly competition for place and recognition within every organization from the corporation to the university; the readiness of churches to vie with each other for membership and contributions and for ostentatious displays of prosperity much as business enterprises vie with each other.

Individualism explains—so Professor Hsu affirms—the determination not only to keep up with the Joneses but visibly to surpass them, that supports the whole never-never world of the advertising industry; the passion for joining almost everything, and the readiness to abandon a club, a society, or a church and join another that proclaims a higher social status or promises quicker social and economic rewards; the constant moving about from one neighborhood to a better one, from one suburb to a more fashionable one. It illuminates the readiness of almost everyone to participate in politics and the conviction—doubtless at the very heart of democracy—that every man and woman can exert some influence and that every one has a right to be heard—even by the president who receives every day two or three thousand letters of advice and admonition. Nowhere is individualism more ostentatious than in the conviction that every one has a right to happiness, a right not only rooted in the very laws of nature, but actually guaranteed in the constitutions of state after state, and that happiness consists in the fulfillment of every individual wish—or whim. Inevitably all of this means constant pressure for experimentation, for change, for progress, for how could you attain happiness and success without these, and it carried with it, too, the notion that change was, inevitably, for the better.

Everywhere, as he surveys the American scene, Professor Hsu finds evidence of deep insecurity—the insecurity that comes from dependence on self, or on merely the nuclear family. What Americans lack—so he argues—is anchorage—the anchorage that comes from being part of something bigger than themselves, from a network of interdependencies and associations with family and clan and village and neighborhood, and with past and future. It is because Americans lack this that they are so restless, so discontented, so unfulfilled and unhappy, so ready to abandon home, family, religion, career, friends, and associates for the will-o'-the wisp of success—a success which, almost by definition—they can never wholly win. It is because they lack security that they feel compelled to prove themselves, over and over—the child to prove himself smarter or stronger or more popular than his playmates, the male to prove himself irresistible to the female, the White to prove himself superior to the Black.

3

For all his dour view of American individualism, Professor Hsu does not make the mistake of regarding individualism as an evil, not even as a necessary evil. Self-reliance is fraught with danger, but it has, too, palpable advantages—both to the individual and to society.

Thus the conviction that by taking thought men can improve not only their own lot, but the lot of society; thus the participation in politics—another term for democracy, this—which, for all its failings, has been a good deal more effective than anything the Chinese have worked out over the centuries; thus the principle of equality to which the Chinese paid the ultimate tribute of imitation in the revolution of 1911 and in the Communist revolution of our time. So, too, Mr. Hsu concedes the advantages of an education which fits the school to the child rather than the child to the school, and of a university system which, for all its drawbacks, has produced more than its normal share of scholars, scientists, and statesmen; or of a family life which, for all its hazards, recognizes the equality of women and encourages independence in the young.

These advantages may well outbalance the disadvantages—for Americans themselves. But what of the cost of unregulated, even anarchical, individualism to the rest of the world? For at this juncture of history the most ostentatious manifestation of American insecurity is, quite clear, not in the domestic but in the world arena. For the American is just as insecure collectively as individually, just as competitive, just as ruthless. Americans must be first in everything —first in wealth, first in power, first in armaments, first on the moon. Their system must not only be the best in the world, but must be acknowledged to be the best; preference for another system is regarded as a kind of treason and the rivalry of other systems a kind of lese majesty. It is American standards that must be accepted as the norm everywhere—in Europe, in Latin America, even in Asia. Thus it is normal and right that the United States should be an Asian power, but unthinkable that China should be an American power (or, for that matter, even a Southeast Asian power). Thus it is right that the United States Sixth Fleet should dominate the Mediterranean, but unthinkable that the Russian fleet should dominate the Caribbean. Thus it is right that American power should dictate the regimes in Guatemala and Santo Domingo, but wicked in the Russians to suppose that they have a right to dictate the regimes in Poland or Czechoslovakia. Thus it is right, too, that we explode our atomic bombs or dump our nerve gases in whatever oceans we select: Nature, after all, intended that the oceans should belong to us as God intended that the moon should belong to us. And just as the individual American spends a lifetime seeking a security which—given his commitment to individualism—always eludes him, so the nation is bankrupting itself materially, socially, and morally for a security which always eludes it, and which it can never attain because it seeks to win it not by equality and cooperation, but by superiority and the imposition of its will on much of mankind.

At this point Professor Hsu's vision takes on an apocalyptic hue. "Great armies and their deployment in worldwide conflicts," he writes, in words that conjure up the warnings of Erich Fromm, "are the final tragic evidence of Western insecurity. Unless social cohesion is restored . . . aimless individualism will surrender *en masse* to the totalitarianism which gives them in exchange for their freedom that purposefulness and emotional security for which they yearn. The task of Americans," he concludes, "is resistance through a reduction of self-reliance and a concomitant increase of mutual dependence among men."

Professor Hsu is too good an anthropologist to forget, for a moment, that social traits are deeply rooted; he certainly does not delude himself that Americans can, or would, exchange their deep-rooted individualism for an esoteric Chinese interdependence. But by contrasting, at every point, American with Chinese practices, he has brought to bear upon American social institutions and character traits a criticism radically different from that to which we have long been accustomed—a criticism not merely of departures from an idealized, or imagined, Old World norm, but one that proposes radical alternatives to that norm. He has made clear that the problems that glare upon America, and upon the Western world, are not fortuitous but a logical outcome of habits, standards, and values of the West, and that these problems are not to be solved by political incantations, or even by domestic therapy, but require a kind of moral surgery. If that diagnosis called for something new and alien to American experience, it would be desperate rather than helpful. Fortunately it does not. Professor Hsu does not himself belabor the point, but the abatement of selfish individualism, the revival of a fiduciary attitude toward natural resources, the abandonment of exclusiveness against neighbors, faiths and races, and the repudiation of the assumption of moral superiority over all other parts of the human race are, after all, not inconsistent with the religious creeds which almost all Americans profess. Perhaps what we need to do to save our resources of nature and of man is simply to return to our moral and spiritual inheritance.

HENRY STEELE COMMAGER

Amherst, Mass.
1970

Preface

I was born in a small village in south Manchuria. As a child I heard terrifying accounts from my elders of the crimes committed by Russian and Japanese soldiers during the first Sino-Japanese and Russo-Japanese wars, two wars which were fought largely in south Manchuria. As I grew older, I went to school in a small town, and traveled and worked amid banditry, famines, epidemics, student strikes and demonstrations, civil wars, Western brutalities, and Japanese invasions.

However strange it may sound, these obstacles did not at first prevent me or most of my contemporaries from leading, in our private ways, a normal and often joyful pattern of life. We feasted boisterously at weddings in which the bride's trousseau, each item colorfully decorated and transported by two carriers and heralded by musicians, was paraded the day before through the streets. We listened attentively to storytellers and singers at open-air markets. We were enthralled by the exploits of the heroes or heroines in operas or shadow plays. As teenagers some of us played truancy from school. Among our best times on such occasions was watching the express trains steaming in and departing from the local railroad station. The variety of passengers, the numerous hawkers of foods, and the uniformed railway police and officers fascinated us.

Best for us was the Chinese New Year when a grand time was had by all—including our deceased ancestors. We dined on fine dishes. We sported new clothes. Even the children were allowed to gamble a little—all youngsters had some ready cash on this occasion given us by parents, aunts and uncles, and other relatives. It was the Chinese equivalent of the American Christmas gift, except that the monetary gift went in one direction, from seniors to juniors.

Of course, there were other events not so joyful. We staged prayer meetings and affixed amulets to our doors when epidemics struck. We paraded the Dragon God during droughts. We huddled behind bolted gates and doors while bandits stormed our town or robbed families in the next street. Schools and shops closed for days or weeks when the fighting between warlords drew near, but they reopened when the victorious faction took over as pupils and teachers marched together in "welcome" parades. We went to the outskirts of town to watch the execution of murderous bandits or newspapermen who spoke too boldly just as later we flocked to witness the first automobiles carrying warlords with bodyguards on the running boards racing through the streets. Most of us slipped by life's hazards without being seriously scarred. We ate less when food was scarce. We ran from floods. We dodged rampant soldiers. We evaded corrupt officials or paid them for permission to exercise our legal rights. Our normal course was to step gingerly and maintain silence.

Then things grew tougher. Disturbances became more frequent, and outside pressures increased. The Sino-Soviet conflict burst into flames the year I graduated from high school in Harbin, north Manchuria. Two years after I entered college, Japan seized Manchuria, and I was no longer able to communicate with my parents. The following year Japan occupied part of Shanghai, our university was forcibly closed, and I assisted in the care of war refugees who streamed into the International Settlement. In 1933 I left Shanghai by boat for Manchuria, there to see my parents for the last time. On arrival at the port of Dairen, I was detained and grilled. Two weeks later, disguised as a laborer, I finally left Manchuria for Peking, arriving there just in time to witness Japan's final military infiltration of north China. For the next four years the Japanese, soldiers and civilians alike, together with their Korean protégés, exercised the most wanton "freedom." Student demonstrators protesting the Chinese government's lack of resistance were repelled by the clubs, fire hoses, and bayonets of the Chinese police. Thanks to a Sino-British Boxer Indemnity fellowship, in 1937, under a canopy of fire that signaled Japan's commencement of all-out war, I left Shanghai harbor on a British man-of-war.

The next two years I counted among the best of my life. I studied in peaceful and pleasant England, toured that country and Scotland, and passed my vacations in France, Belgium, Germany, and Denmark. But in 1939 the European war broke out and in 1940 the blitz came to London, presenting anew the same scenes of devastation I had witnessed in a land half a world away. Many of my waking hours were spent thinking of the night to come that would be passed, like the one before, sleeping in shelters or under staircases. In 1941 I returned to China via the Union of South Africa, India, and the Burma Road.

Besides the good fortune of having met my wife, Vera Y. N. Hsu, the next three years were intellectually productive. I did field work in a small town in the interior of Yunnan Province. I had a group of compatible friends and colleagues who stimulated me as I did them. I wrote the draft of two manuscripts which later were to become *Under the Ancestors' Shadow* and *Religion, Science, and Human Crises.* This, in spite of Japanese bombing raids, runaway inflation, epidemics, and food shortages which were the routine aspects of a life that I and millions of others shared. I came to the United States believing, like so many before me, that I was journeying to a land that war could never touch, where I could work in peace, and where my children would never witness what I had. That was nine months before the people of Hiroshima were introduced to the atomic age.

With this brief account of my experiences I hope to explain to my readers that this book was written, in the first place, for the personal interest of self-preservation. We are well into an era when war's front line is everywhere, and even a "limited" war may contain the seed of universal destruction. Moreover, as the sixties drew to a close we were already confronted with internal dangers which, according to the National Commission on the Causes and Prevention of Violence, under the leadership of Dr. Milton S. Eisenhower, were said to be equal to if not more than "any probable combination of external threats." If there is to be any realistic hope of betterment, every thinking person must without delay contribute whatever he can to uncovering those fundamental forces that have propelled us into our present situation.

I am a marginal man. I was born and raised in a culture—once wholly steadfast and where life for a majority was almost fully predictable—from which I have been uprooted. I live and work in a culture where change is desired because it is equated with progress, and where neither the physical nor the human scene is constant. The human being in whom two such contrasting cultures meet, moves, as it were, along the margin of each. He paces the border where they confront each other within himself, and he can reach out to touch them both. In that sense, this book is the report of a marginal man's life experience and his reflections upon it.

However, I am also a man of science. I strive to be objective in gathering, presenting, and interpreting facts about matters that concern me. This book is therefore neither a Chinese view of Americans nor an American view of Chinese. It is my sincere intent to present in the following pages a frank and unbiased analysis of both the American and Chinese ways of life. Drawing both from my life experience and the findings of organized research, I have attempted to relate the two broad sources of data in a manner that is meaningful in terms both of individuals and their societies.

In this task I am guided by a principle of basic importance to the study of human behavior which has yet to be well understood even by many social scientists. I believe that every student who deals with another society and culture and wishes to convey his understanding of that society and culture to others must self-consciously strive to become something of a marginal man. That is, he must not only be able to see the customs, institutions, and artifacts of the society and culture not his own as the natives see them, but also try to *feel* about these things as they do. Otherwise he cannot avoid projection of his own ethnocentric yardsticks and assumptions of what is important and unimportant. This is a most difficult process, especially for those who take the superiority of their own culture for granted. It is one of the reasons why some American Blacks claim that black studies cannot be taught by Whites, not even by well meaning and pro-Negro Whites.

Unless the student consciously cultivates what for want of a better term we shall call "marginal-man-ship," he is unlikely to *feel* for the object of his study. For even if his superiority does not get in the way, his deeply held cultural assumptions cannot but bias what he chooses to see and vitiate his understanding of what he does see. Thus many non-Hindus consider the Hindu sacred cow a pure waste without reflecting on the implications of the vast economic tentacles of their own Christian churches; and most Westerners look for religious persecution in China because Western history and contemporary life are replete with religious or church-connected strifes.

There is no simple formula for achieving marginal-man-ship. But a beginning can be made via the comparative method. That is to say the student must scrutinize his own way of life at the same time he seeks to understand one not his own. On the simplest level this involves, for example, not only examining Chinese behavior toward the United States and vice versa as interactions, but also determining how Americans would have conducted themselves if they had been in Chinese shoes.

On a more delicate plane, having both his own culture and one not his own systematically compared provides the proper perspective for the student. It may reduce the student's tendency to judge the actions of his own society realistically while at the same time judging those of other societies idealistically. For example, we eagerly seek reasons why the My Lai massacre might have occurred (such as battlefield hysteria) or why it could not have occurred (because our policy on the highest level is never to commit any atrocity). But have we been as eager to seek comparable reasons for the true or alleged atrocities committed by other peoples?

It may also help the student better to differentiate the culture-specific from the pan-cultural. For example, nearly all Western reporters saw the dispute over the shape of the conference table at the Paris Vietnam talks as an example of "Oriental" face in action. Had they engaged in a little historical comparison they would have realized that there is nothing Oriental about such disputes. At the end of the War of Grand Alliance, the Peace of Ryswick in 1697 took six months to sign because the representatives of France and the Holy Roman Empire disagreed on who should walk into the conference room first. They solved the problem by entering together. Exactly the same kind of wrangles occurred at the Congress of Vienna of 1815 and in the Potsdam Conference of 1945. In 1815 five monarchs entered the conference room simultaneously through five doors while in 1945 Churchill, Stalin, and Truman did the same through three doors.

However, even for the immigrant, who is a marginal man *par excellence,* the condition of his "marginal-man-ship" is subject to temporary eclipses with changing circumstances.

Once again I beg leave of my readers to relate some personal experiences. From the mid-fifties, after the guns on the battlefields of Korea became silent and the McCarthy hysteria ended, somehow I relaxed. Distractions were many. There was the delight of the newly emerged public medium—TV. It occupied quite a few of my waking hours. With my children's help I was even enjoying Milton Berle and Howdy Doody. The excitement of the first space explorations brought back many fond memories of my father during my grade school days in Manchuria. My father, before he died in 1943, believed the world to be round but stationary and in the shape of a dish. That was, according to him, how Columbus could sail westward and find America. His theory did not, of course, agree with what I learned in my school, so I would produce counterarguments accordingly. We usually came to some sort of a tie, however, since I could never convince him; but he did not want to squash me since he was committed to the new-style schools for my future. Secretly, however, I always wished for more overwhelming evidence on the subject so that my father and I could settle our argument once and for all. How nice it would have been for me to show him pictures from the first astronauts on the moon.

Outside of these excitements, I was in comfortable circumstances. I was getting ahead professionally. I published more papers and books setting forth some of my best ideas. I lectured everywhere to respectful and attentive audiences. I took my wife and children to Europe, India, Hong Kong, Japan, and back to the United States again. While away from the United States, I was disgusted with myself when sometimes I caught myself sharing certain common national gripes as an American traveler abroad. Upon my return my astonishment was great when I found how much I had become accustomed to this America, its people and its ways.

To be sure the shadow of the bomb was omnipresent—for we and the Russians, or the British and the French, were always testing, somewhere. But even the hair-raising Cuban missile crisis did not last long enough to disturb me.

How far my marginal-man-ship had lapsed was revealed to me abruptly but sadly. President Diem of South Vietnam and his right-hand strong man Ngu were assassinated in a coup on a November day in 1963. There was bloodshed all around. Diem's government fell, many of his cohorts fled or were killed, and many innocents died. Shortly after this news I was on my way from Northwestern University to San Francisco to read a paper at the annual meeting of the American Anthropological Association. All through the flight I felt deeply for the long-suffering Vietnamese common man but glad for myself that such a state of affairs could not possibly happen here. I was "watching a fire on the other bank of the river," as an old Chinese proverb went. My fool's paradise was rudely shattered on the second day of our convention when President Kennedy was assassinated. My feelings became indescribable as I watched with my own eyes on television the murder of Lee Harvey Oswald while officers of the law swarmed around him.

With millions of others, I had become so much an average and smug middle-class American that I took the security of my person, my family, my income, and my work to be part of the order of nature, like the sun's daily journey from east to west. One may stop to notice the journey now and then, inspired or intoxicated by the beauty of a particular dawn or a particular dusk. But one never doubts that the sun will rise and set again come another day, any day. In fact, my activities so occupied me at times that I even forgot some of the possible implications of what I had written in this book.

Then, suddenly, after the Dallas event, I was forced to stop and reflect anew on our difficulties as a nation—difficulties which have since 1963 greatly multiplied and become more intensified every passing day. The ugly Vietnam war is now behind us, but the psychological cost of this colossal failure will long haunt us, as will the recent debacle in Iran, not to speak of the decline in American prestige and the dollar. Internally, President Kennedy's assassination was followed by those of Robert Kennedy and Martin Luther King, and of numerous others of lesser fame, such as San Francisco mayor George Moscone. To avoid indictment a president and his vice-president were forced to resign from office. Students are no longer as restive as they were in the sixties, but the drug scene, racial tension, vandalism and interpersonal violence, and the troubled public school system are easily some of the obvious signs of our times.

The fantastic thing is that those who are concerned with our problems seem to be obsessed with the superficial. For example, to deal with vandalism and violence they seek more guards and more sophisticated surveillance devices. For combating racial tension and juvenile delinquency they look for more employment opportunities and recreational outlets.

The optimists say that all this turmoil merely portends greater things to come. Another name for turmoil is dynamism. In that perspective turmoil is symptomatic of change, or at least holds the potentiality of change. How can problems be solved without change?

On the other hand, the prophets of doom continue to predict final disaster. They quote Gibbon, the historian best known for his work *The Decline and Fall of the Roman Empire*. But in their minds this final disaster is curiously intertwined with the notion of the chosen man since the days of Noah and the Ark. In that Western psychology mankind will indeed come to a violent end except for those who know the only truth and others who faithfully follow the same one and exclusive truth.

I offer no panacea for the great troubles confronting us today as Americans. But I am deeply concerned that the thoughts and remedies foremost in the minds of our leaders, general public, and scholars do not include the most crucial element in *human* existence and well-being, namely, man's relationship with his fellow men.

Since I frankly see the root of our problems today as a crisis of inter-personal relationships due to runaway individualism, I invite my readers to journey through the following pages so that they may judge for themselves. Runaway individualism forces men to keep their thought but especially their feelings from each other. For fear of rejection they have no one except therapists to whom they can un-load their worst fears. Worse, to avoid being a victim they often have to draw first.

But a human condition in which one can be off guard, the oppor-tunity to unload one's anxieties and the need to receive succor— these are the true measures of human intimacy, and it is these that the American way of life discourages. Intimacy has become such a scarce commodity that many seek salvation in improved communi-cation or as participants in so-called sensitivity training sessions. The prior condition for communication is the willingness to communicate and be communicated to. When that condition is lacking, tools of communication are powerless. And under the same circumstances sensitivity training sessions are nothing but emotional massage for their participants.

Lacking the conditions for sharing intimacy, man tries to buy a way to relate to his fellow human beings, resorts to deadly weapons to defend himself against them, abandons them in disgust, or de-stroys them altogether in the hope of starting all over with his own privatized version of some utopian brave new world. Hence, he ex-tols the power of the dollar; he is obsessed with the need for economic development and expansion; he cannot wait for the construction of a nuclear Great Wall. Or he sounds the alarm of a final catastrophe for all mankind from which he the chosen man will rise again.

Diverse though these expressions appear, they are one and all based on the individualistic man's insistence on externalizing his re-lationship with his fellow men so that he does not have to surrender any part of his internal autonomy. If the externalized measures in one social context fail, he is always ready to go elsewhere. The indi-vidualistic man backs off from pursuing such questions as, How can the parent-child relationship be made more binding and durable? Is it possible to tailor our economic system so as to increase the chances of harmony rather than strife among men? Instead he speaks of the technological imperatives and asks, How can man be better trained to fulfill the machine's requirements?

Although this book is an attempt to take a close look at the human equation in two societies, its findings and conclusions have essential bearing on the rest of the world. After the first two American astronauts successfully landed on and returned from the moon, I heard more than once the sentiment, "If we can land men on the moon, we can solve any problem on earth." (I also heard the opposite, "We should have tried to solve some of our problems on earth instead of going to the moon.") The reader of this book will see how false this popular myth is. The scientific and technological problems behind our moon expeditions are indeed complex and difficult. Let us not make light of them. But the problems of *understanding* our human sources of tension and violence and especially of *doing something about them* are infinitely more complex and difficult.

Even innovators in the physical sciences did not always find easy acceptance of their discoveries and inventions. The difficulties Galileo had with the Holy Inquisitors and Pasteur with his fellow scientists forcibly remind us of that unfortunate fact. Although Western man had gradually emerged from the magical mode of thinking vis-à-vis the physical universe (since he no longer calls in the gods to control floods or believes in alchemy), he has yet to free himself from his primitive shackles with regard to human affairs (because he still acts as if undue privileges can last forever, without being paid for in the long run).

The term *modernity* has been naively defined by our present-day social scientists in terms of machines and organizational efficiency for economic and political purposes. Even where they speak of the quality of human life they still measure modernity by such things as mobility or consumption patterns. We have to realize that that is no more than semimodernity at best. Freedom from want does not lead to freedom from interpersonal anxiety and hostility. Unless man can dispense with the magical mode of thinking in human affairs as well, he is not modern. In fact, unless he achieves the latter freedom, much or most of what he has accomplished or will accomplish in the former sphere will be in vain, for he will only go through cycles of destruction, reconstruction, and bigger destruction, and more colossal reconstruction.

Over the years my sources of help or inspiration have been many. It is impossible to acknowledge them all here. In addition to those mentioned previously I wish to thank Mrs. Joyce Gruhn of the East-West Center, Mrs. Carol Chan and Mrs. Joy Stevenson of the University of San Francisco. They have each typed sections of the manuscript. Miss Jean Han of the Far Eastern Library of the University of

California at Berkeley has helped with numerous bibliographical items. Mr. Robert Lin kindly agreed to construct the two indexes even though his own graduate work and business activities keep him extremely busy. Professor Stuart Gerry Brown of the American Studies Department, University of Hawaii, Dr. Godwin C. Chu of the East-West Center, and Mr. Stuart Kiang, editor at the University Press of Hawaii, have separately offered their most valuable and constructive criticisms. Dr. John B. Tsu, director of the Multicultural Program of the University of San Francisco, has given me every encouragement both professionally and as a friend.

As always, I am indebted to my wife, Vera, who keeps me in perspective. When my zeal to pursue a given line of reasoning to its logical conclusion carried me too far, she would bring me back. When I was not able to see clearly the significance of some fresh data, she would suggest another way. In addition, she devoted many hours to constructing "A Brief Chronology of China and the West" appended to the end of the book.

Through my two daughters, Eileen Yi-nan and Penalope Si-hwa, I have come to experience (though still vicariously) what it is like to be born and grow up in America, with all its joys and frustrations, its hopes and despairs. Although this is a society where aged parents do not plan on being supported by their grown children, I cannot help but look to them for continuity, fulfillment, as well as improvement in the human condition. Hence, I dedicate this book to them and their generation.

Francis L. K. Hsu

Mill Valley, California
1980

Americans
and Chinese

Prologue: Culture and Behavior

There is no doubt that individuals differ as to temperament, taste, potentiality, and idiosyncrasy. Exceptional actions on the part of some individuals are not difficult to find. For example, a mischievous Chinese humorist, Hsu Wen-ch'ang of the Ming dynasty, did something that seemingly antedated the Russian Pavlov of the "conditioned reflex" fame by at least two hundred years. Hsu's maternal uncle disapproved of him in general, and the feeling was mutual. One day they had a particularly trying session with each other. While his older relative was visiting with Hsu's parents, Hsu went outside the house and bowed low toward the donkey on which his uncle had arrived. Before the animal realized what was happening Hsu whacked it with a stick several times on its head and body. Of course the donkey twisted and jerked wildly in pain.

When the time came for his uncle to take leave of Hsu's parents Hsu was asked to see the visitor off. As soon as his uncle mounted the beast, Hsu bowed low to the departing relative in the customary attitude of respect. The animal, remembering what had followed that gesture before, instantly jerked and twisted, throwing Hsu's uncle to the ground.

Beyond differences among individuals, every society exhibits variation within itself. Northern Chinese and Cantonese speak mutually unintelligible dialects. Clan temples were more numerous south of the Yangtze River than north of it. Some northern Chinese are prone to speak of their southern compatriots as superficial and "slippery headed" (tricky), or dishonest, while I often met southerners who told me that I did not look like a man from the north. I have, they would say, a southern complexion and a stature not quite tall enough for the north. The myth about northern stature is alive in spite of the fact that many Fukienese (the province opposite Taiwan) are giants of six feet or better.

As for the United States, some New Yorkers think, as one author put it, "Californians are adolescents with a surfboard under one arm and a guru under the other." On the other hand, some Californians see most New Yorkers as people too given to what's "in" and what's "out." They are "rigid with apprehension that they will die wearing the wrong sneakers."

It is well known that laws vary from state to state in the United States. But most Americans probably do not know that Mississippi is the only state in the Union that allows convicts in prison to receive regular conjugal visits; or that Nevada, besides having legalized gambling, did not post speed signs on its highways before the energy crisis, on the theory that motorists should be able to judge for themselves.

However, in spite of exceptional individuals and regional differences, a majority of the people of each society do act according to their society's accepted and usual patterns of behavior in their day-to-day business of life. The penalties for nonconformity vary. A departing male American who forgets to kiss his wife at the airport is in for trouble when he returns. A Chinese father who boasts to his friends about his son's good looks will be an object of derision. An American guest who brings someone else to dinner unheralded is not likely to be invited again. A Chinese visitor who compliments his hostess on her beauty comes close to being immoral. He can praise her cooking skills, or her kindness, or even the way she trains her children, but he must not mention her physical attributes, including her clothing. These do's and don'ts are but a few of the countless culturally prescribed rules of individual behavior so clear to the adults of each society that they seem to be part of the order of nature.

From this angle, the notion that each individual can "do his own thing" to the exclusion of others is unrealistic and nonhuman, for two reasons. First, all of us must live with some other human beings in varying degrees of affection. They are our spouses, parents and children, close friends, relatives, followers, and heroes.

The second reason we must have some other human beings is that they provide us with goods and/or services. We and they stand in role relationships to each other. We need not only basic utilities, garbage disposal, or medical attention, but also postcards, writing implements, and daily nourishment. Even Zen masters usually have to do their meditation in buildings which they did not build and guide or punish their disciples with tools which they did not produce. There are quite a few Hindu holy men who receive the adulation of their disciples while seated on tiger-skin-draped thronelike sofas or make use of the modern microphone as deftly as Billy Graham in Madison Square Garden.

Consequently, no matter how committed a society is to an individualistic philosophy, it cannot function without having to organize its members according to certain general principles of grouping: women as distinguished from men, adults from children, able-bodied from the unfit, atomic scientists from butchers, unskilled from the skilled, the qualified practitioners from the quacks, soldiers from civilians, and so forth. Individuals are placed in each of these categories for their commonality, not individuality.

As our society evolves toward greater equality and liberalization more women will enter occupations formerly thought to be male preserves, more children will break down more parental restrictions, and more "gays" will be accepted in the "straight" world. But it is unlikely, in fact impossible, for any society, including ours, to obliterate all categorization and consider every member as an individual in every way according to our individualistic idea. Can we stop certification of doctors and drivers so that anyone who wants to can practice medicine or drive a car? Can we forget about age and income differences so that anyone who so desires can collect Social Security and welfare payments?

Likewise, over and above differences based on class, national origin, sex, geographical region, age, and occupation, a majority of Chinese in China can deal with each other better than they can with the inhabitants of the United States, while a majority of Americans can do the same better with their own countrymen than with the Chinese in China. They may not approve of or understand all that their respective fellow countrymen do, but in the normal course of events they are less likely than foreigners to be surprised by them. For each people share a large body of basic, common ideas, attitudes, and expectations which provide the average man with his bearings in dealing with his fellow countrymen and which hold the society together, contemporaneously and over time.

In the 1953 edition of this book I related the following episode according to mid-1948 north China newspapers. A bundle containing the remains of a woman's body was found on the bank of a river which runs through the metropolitan city of Tientsin. More than ten years before, she and her husband, Chang, had left their north

China village and gone to Manchuria, where he worked as a coal miner. She died in 1946 and was buried there in a temporary grave. When the Nationalist-Communist civil war forced a shutdown of the mines, Chang decided to go back to his native village.

Not wanting to leave his wife's body in Manchuria, he dug its remains out of the tomb, packed them in a bundle, and started home with his three children, aged eleven, eight, and seven. Unable to pay for train fares all the way, they walked from Changchun, north Manchuria, to Shenyang, south Manchuria, a distance of about two hundred miles. From there they rode for forty miles west to Hsinmin, then walked for three hundred miles to the north China coal mining center of Tongshan, from which point they rode free in a coal train for another eighty miles to Tientsin.

Before beginning their last 120-mile walk home from Tientsin, the four passed the night at the bottom of a wall near the railway station. A thief, obviously mistaking the bundle for ordinary baggage, stole it and later abandoned it. As soon as Chang discovered the bundle was missing he begged a literate person to write a number of "lost" notices for him, and these he posted in streets around the station. When someone told him that the police had found a female body near the river, Chang went forward and identified it as that of his wife. But instead of agreeing to its local burial, which the authorities required for public health reasons, Chang insisted: "Burial here will never do. Even if I agree, my sons will object. I carried her over a thousand miles. I used the bundle as a pillow every night, but I am still not sick!" He was finally allowed to take the body. But before leaving, Chang asked that the lock of hair and a tooth, removed by the examiners for identification, be returned to him, saying "she must have her body intact for burial."

That Chang was a poor and illiterate man who could not afford to pay for rail transportation is easy for Americans to understand. They have heard that poverty was common in China. Americans who hear this story are also impressed by the intensity of Chang's devotion to his deceased wife, but they regard the form it took as bizarre and unnecessary since it might have imperiled the health of Chang and his children. Some of my American friends sympathize with Chang's insistence on the restoration of the tooth and the lock of hair, yet they cannot understand why Chang claimed to be acting on behalf of his children.

In the Chinese view both American objections are groundless. To be buried with body intact in the village of one's birth is, to the Chinese, part of the complete life, and it is a son's obligation to carry this out. Because the miner's children were too young to bury their mother, the father acted for them, regardless of whatever hardship this entailed.

Just as these customs baffle the average American, many American ideas and practices are equally alien to the Chinese. I first realized this in China in 1944 while watching the movie version of Marcia Davenport's novel, *Valley of Decision.*

The leading roles were played by Gregory Peck and Greer Garson. Peck, as the son of a wealthy industrialist in one of the great steel centers of the United States, had many new ideas concerning both production and labor relations which were contradictory to those of his parents and their associates. He was unhappily married to a woman whose ideas agreed with those of his parents and they had a child of about six. During a conversation with Greer Garson, a maid in the family's palatial home, whose father was a worker in one of her employer's plants, Peck became attracted by her views, personality, and sympathy. But she refused his love because he was a married man.

In the meantime, labor trouble erupted in the plant. The workers struck for higher wages and better work conditions. A group of strike breakers were then called in. Peck attempted to persuade his father and his advisers to call them off and to discuss terms with the labor leaders. But while his father, under pressure of the son's advice, was exchanging views with the labor leader, a battle started between the workers and the strike breakers. The father was killed, many men were injured, and the family's magnificent house was destroyed. Garson's father was killed also. After order was restored, Peck took over the management of the business and liberalized its labor policies. In conclusion, Peck's unsympathetic wife demanded a divorce and Peck and Garson were married.

To the American audience this was good drama, since every conflict was resolved in a way that is desirable from an American point of view. The production conflict was resolved in favor of new views on manufacturing methods over the old-fashioned ones; liberal attitudes toward labor won out in the social conflict with hard-fisted attempts to suppress the workingmen; Peck, the progressive son, replaced his conservative father; and true love triumphed where only marital misery had prevailed.

However, my Chinese friend who saw the film with me was far from pleased. He understood the gigantic size and extent of American industry and wealth, and he had some comprehension of the bitterness and violence of American industrial disputes. He was also aware that Americans are usually ready to experiment with new ideas or to introduce novel methods of production. But he considered both Peck and Garson villains. Peck was shamefully unfilial because he was opposed to his father and undid all that the elder tried to carry out. Garson was practically the sole cause not only of the breakdown of Peck's marriage but also of his family's ruin and his father's destruction. When the maid first entered the picture, the family was prosperous, dignified, and intact. If she had not encouraged her young master in his views, he would not have asked his father to negotiate with the laborers, the old man would not have been exposed to their fatal attack, nor would her own father have died in the melee.

To the Chinese audience, a son in conflict with his father was a bad son, and a maid who would help such a son in his ventures was a bad woman. Through the same Chinese lens, the daughter-in-law was regarded as an extremely virtuous woman who suffered in malicious hands. The question of the young master's own unhappiness with his wife as opposed to his possible happiness with the maid should never have been raised.

The contrasts epitomized in these two episodes arise out of the basic and characteristic ways in which people in each society see their past, present, and future, and define their problems and seek solutions to them. This common outlook has been variously termed "social character," "themes of culture," "life way," "ethos," "basic personality," or "philosophy of life." I shall not consider here the merits and demerits of these terms or enter upon a technical discussion of psychological anthropology. For the purposes of this book, I will simply call this common outlook the "Chinese way of life" or the "American way of life."

Does each way of life change over time? My answer is yes, but not in the usually understood sense of the word "change," especially as it has been applied to American society and culture. America has indeed undergone many changes since World War II and from the sixties to the seventies. In the sixties we saw the widespread use of drugs among youth, the hippie and yippie movements, the student unrest that challenged the nature and even the very existence of higher education, the racial violence that threatened to reduce our cities to ashes, and the sex explosion.

Since then and up to now we have witnessed a variety of new developments, which Christopher Lasch, Tom Wolfe, and others call the "new narcissism" or the "me generation." But is this trend really new? The shift from collective protest to the individual search for self-gratification and self-fulfillment was foretold in mass protesters' statements about their own mental condition while they were protesting. For example, "Pete" (not his real name), a philosophy major who turned to campus-wide protest to force his Ivy League university to divest itself of stocks of companies that did a primary amount of their business in South Africa, said, "Now that I'm actively involved in trying to change things I'm much happier than when I was feeling a lot of guilt—sex hangups and ambition hangups."[1] Pete's statement is echoed in the words of Susan Stern, another antiestablishmentarian of the late sixties. In her memoir of the Weathermen, she described her feelings during the demonstration at the 1968 Democratic National Convention in Chicago: "I felt good. I could feel my body supple and strong and slim, and ready to run miles, and my legs moving sure and swift under me."[2]

Seen in the longer-term context of the American culture, the trend toward individual fulfillment is but an escalation of that same American approach dramatized nearly a half century ago in *Valley of Decision*.

On the China side, tumultuous events after 1949 have seemed to signal to the Western world real breaks with the past. The avowed aim of the Communist government at Peking since 1949 has been no less than the total transformation of the entire Chinese society. The Great Leap, the Cultural Revolution, and now the fall of the Gang of Four and the drive for the Four Modernizations tell us something about the twists and turns of a giant revolutionary movement involving a huge society with a long and proud history.

But the Chinese character of the new developments has yet to be clearly understood even by Western visitors to the People's Republic who had known the country before 1949. For example, after a 1972 tour of China the columnist Joseph Alsop changed from a vehement critic of the new regime to a high praiser of its achievements. As he and his wife were leaving China by train from Canton to Hong Kong they discussed between themselves a question that puzzled them most. Both found the Soviet Union and other European Communist countries depressing in contrast to China, which they found during their month-long trip "neither suffocating nor depressing." "Rather than thanking God to be crossing the border (which is standard post-Russia trip response), we wished we could have had several months more." He and his wife asked themselves, "Why?"

Alsop's question was well posed, I think, for I had the same feeling about Russia when I was leaving that country in the summer of 1964. But I think Alsop's answer is confused.

On the one hand he said that "this new China *works* in Chinese terms," and that, in spite of the failures of the Great Leap and the devastation of the Cultural Revolution, "everywhere, you see the strong foundation for a better future being boldly, laboriously, intelligently laid. Whether in agriculture or industry, you find eye-popping achievements. So I suppose it is this sense of forward movement that answers the question we argued on the train to Hongkong."

On the other hand he could not but also note that "there was no hint of the more free life that goes on, under the surface, in the Soviet Union. A Chinese Solzhenitsyn is unimaginable. There is no underground art or literature. All march to the same drum, or they have their 'thoughts reformed.' "[3]

I suspect that neither of these reasons was what made the Alsops feel the way they did in that train leaving China. Achievement-wise we could say the same things about the Soviet Union. If we contrast Russia before and after the revolution, don't we also see eye-popping achievements? Don't we also see a sense of forward movement? In fact, Sir Alexander Eggleston, the Australian ambassador to China during World War II, once explained to my satisfaction in Chungking that he thought the Soviet Union *worked* because the Russians were Russians. The Australian envoy was not alone in this.

As to underground art and literature, why don't they exist in China? Why do all Chinese march to the same drum? Isn't it paradoxical that the Alsops found their journey in a society where there is "no hint of the more free life" neither suffocating nor depressing, while they thanked God each time they left another one where there is not only "the more free life" but which also produced writers like Solzhenitsyn whom Alsop and his countrymen have come to lionize?

The paradox will remain a paradox as long as we only see China and the Chinese in American terms. I think it is the human element that distinguishes the Chinese from the Russians as well as the Americans. I think China's forte, regardless of what else she is doing, is the way the people relate to each other and how that way of relating has been mobilized from the traditional to the new scheme of things.

The Alsops were not totally unaware of this. "Our countless hosts were friendly, interesting, and forthcoming. Our interpreter-manager, Yao Wei, was the most ideal traveling companion that either of us had ever encountered." But in the end the Alsops chose the typically American reason, the "sense of forward movement," as answer to the question why they wished to stay when they had to depart. Had the Alsops really understood the importance of that Chinese characteristic, they would have appreciated that the paradoxical facts sprang from the same source, that the lack of underground art and literature in China is an expression of the same human pattern where their "countless hosts were friendly, interesting, and forthcoming."

We shall use another example to illustrate the cultural continuity between what goes on in China today and what went on before. One well-known American developmental psychologist said after visiting some Chinese schools, "In a sense, the devoted support and affection Chinese adults give to children is, at once, more reliable, more general, and *less intimate than we are used to seeing among Americans* (italics mine). But the evidence that the visitor gives for this assertion is merely that Chinese teachers (in kindergartens) reward children "with verbal praise rather than touching or hugging."[4]

In my view less touching is poor evidence for less intimacy. Is public kissing and hugging between American spouses a good barometer of their marital intimacy? Touching and hugging are common American ways of expressing momentary emotional intensity, but they say nothing about the extent to which children will confide in their teachers. On the other hand, the "more reliable" type of support and affection Chinese teachers give to their charges may well be correlated with a greater intimacy in the truer sense of the term. Since more reliable support and affection mean that the support and affection will be more continuous and less sporadic, is it not reasonable to suppose that they will be more conducive to more intimate communication?

The whole question of fundamental versus superficial changes in the Chinese society and culture will be dealt with in Chapter 15 when we examine "China under Communism." The recent (fall of 1979) reports of trial and conviction of two sons of high ranking Party officials in Hangchow for the rape of over 100 girls have given us a glimpse of goings-on in the old China mode even through years of political spectaculars such as the Great Leap and the Cultural Revolution.

As to Taiwan, a recent event and its wider implications must give pause to those who claim that social and cultural changes necessarily follow economic development.

Concubinage is an old Chinese institution. Westerners often mistook concubines for mistresses, not knowing that they were legally "assistant" wives. The Confucian rationale for concubinage was to ensure having a male heir. But there was no scarcity of husbands who married concubines for desire. Concubinage was forbidden by law in 1935 but the practice continued extralegally in China until the establishment of the People's Republic. After 1949 those who were married as concubines were free to remain in that status if they chose to do so but no new husband-concubine relationship could be contracted.

Under the Japanese rule the inhabitants of Taiwan so disposed married concubines as their brethren did in China. But after the reassumption of Chinese power under the Nationalists the Chinese law of 1935 forbidding concubinage naturally prevailed. Yet recently the following news report appeared in a major Taiwan daily.

> With the coming of the warm spring and blossoming flowers, a local official, an old man of 62 years of age, will enter the third stage of his life's travel, a stage where birds chirp and flowers are fragrant. He will marry his third bride.
>
> This old community officer Mr. Huang is a VIP in San Feng Kung (a Taoist temple with a local *ke tsai* opera house). He is its long time patron, supporter and frequent donor of large sums. The bride is a famous opera star in that house.
>
> According to relatives of this old community officer, he first fell in love with this beautiful actress' performing skill. Then they became engaged because of his close connection with the temple and its opera house.
>
> The wedding date for this April-December marriage is set for March 25 [1977]. They will solemnize it in front of all the gods of the temple. Mayor Wang Yu-yun of Kao Hsiung municipality is among the invited guests.
>
> We heard that the old officer's wife and concubine at his home have kept themselves extremely busy with organizing this wedding—a rare and happy event, although each of them has already completed their fake divorces from their husband.[5]

The fake divorces satisfied the legal prohibition against concubinage. There is no doubt that the foursome expect to live in the same menage happily ever after.

The common element between this case and that of the laborer who carried his wife's body from Manchuria to Tientsin is the Chinese view that marital links depend far more heavily on duties and obligations among the related than on love and affection on the part of the individuals. That is why the news report said nothing about romance. But since these duties and obligations extend both vertically to one's progenitors and descendants and horizontally to the collaterally related, is it not natural for old Mr. Huang's wife and first concubine to help make his wedding with a second concubine a success? The fake divorces only show how far the old Chinese culture pattern is still alive and well and how great is the psychological distance between Chinese custom and modern Chinese law. Under Western influences Chinese law upholds monogamy. But Chinese custom still says there is nothing wrong with a plurality of wives. How else can we explain the fact that a newspaper would report the Huang event with its fake divorces so plainly without getting the participants in legal hot water and ostracized (or even persecuted) by the rest of their community, as they would have been were they inhabitants of the United States?

However, though this comparative analysis clarifies the Chinese and American happenings in terms of their respective customs, it offers but partial explanations. It does not tell us how these customs are related to or influence many other activities in their respective societies. For example, how do the Chinese marital and filial customs exemplified in the given episodes relate to the Chinese lack of interest in the affairs of their government and their resistance to Christianity? How do American generational conflicts and those between labor and management, portrayed in *Valley of Decision,* the student unrest and violence of the sixties, and the new narcissism of the seventies relate to American racial prejudice, the American way in politics, and American industrial and technological achievements?

On the other hand, our earlier analysis does not give any clue regarding the inconsistencies and even contradictions in individual behavior and group activities. For example, how can any American church community, while professing love of mankind through worship of God, refuse membership to Blacks? How can a society that emphasizes equality between the sexes have so far accorded its women so few high places in the professions and government? How could a nation founded on freedom and self-determination for all men have sent its soldiers half a world away to crush an internal revolution and support a hopelessly corrupt puppet regime? As for the Chinese scene, a major apparent inconsistency has been confronting Americans since World War II: How could a people well known for their formality, gentleness, love of family, and respect for tradition over the centuries suddenly turn Communist?

What we need to realize is that, like the spider's web, a people's behavior, infinitely complex though it may appear from a distance, has a common thread and a clear design. When that design and its ramifications are understood we shall find that its disparate elements may be interconnected by unsuspected links and its seemingly contradictory activities to be manifestations of the same substructure. It is the source of these links and this substructure and the behavior patterns they manifest in each of the two ways of life that this book will endeavor to trace.

In this task we shall focus on the lives, views, and activities of the common men in the United States and in China as much as on government policies and men and women of distinction or authority. It is especially upon the common men in both societies, masked to the world and to themselves as nations, that we shall fix not a telescope, but a microscope. We shall hope to help the reader to see through the abstractions "America" and "China," those misleading cloaks that cause people to think of one another as geographical terms or, at best, as nations housing masses of nameless men, women, and children. We shall show that behind the curtain of nationality move not formless and indecipherable masses, but persons with identifiable values, duties, and ideals; individuals who, however distinct the reasons, know sorrow, triumph, and devotion. It is not a recital of their vividly contrasting national histories, customs, forms of government, or economies that concerns us, though in our journey toward understanding the Americans and the Chinese these and certain other factors will serve as our guideposts and help us to answer this question: What are the root causes of these differences—so colorful, so sharp, and so many—between the two peoples?

The Chinese and American ways of life may be reduced to two sets of contrasts. First, in the American way of life the emphasis is placed upon the predilections of the individual, a characteristic we shall call *individual-centered*. This is in contrast to the emphasis the Chinese put upon an individual's appropriate place and behavior among his fellowmen, a characteristic we shall term *situation-centered*. The second fundamental contrast is the prominence of emotions in the American way of life as compared with the tendency of the Chinese to underplay all matters of the heart.

These two sets of contrasts are interrelated. Being individual-centered, the American moves toward social and psychological isolation. His happiness tends to be unqualified ecstasy just as his sorrow is likely to mean unbearable misery. A strong emotionality is inevitable since the emotions are concentrated in one individual.

Being more situation-centered, the Chinese is inclined to be socially or psychologically dependent on others, for this situation-centered individual is tied closer to his world and his fellowmen. His happiness and his sorrow tend to be milder since they are shared.[6]

These contrasting ways of life—the individual-centered American way and the situation-centered Chinese way—will, then, be our key to all the chapters that follow. We shall find also that this fundamental contrast is at the core of the unique and deeply embedded problems and weaknesses which plague each society, such as racial and religious intolerance in America and poverty and bureaucratic oppression in China. Then, in light of this contrast, we shall venture to project the implications of our findings into the world of tomorrow.

In doing so it will help us very much if we pause and ask ourselves: What is the human purpose served by each way of life and how far and how well is that human purpose fulfilled? What is the cost of the fulfillment? Is the cost too great? Is the cost going to escalate or can we hope to reduce it? For the world of tomorrow will be shaped, for good or evil, by each people's degree of self-knowledge, the extent to which they understand one another, and the manner in which they deal with the burdens and opportunities that the past has bequeathed to the present.

NOTES

1. As reported in *Newsweek,* March 17, 1969.
2. Quoted in Christopher Lasch, *The Culture of Narcissism.*
3. *Washington Post,* January 10, 1973.
4. William Kessen, ed., *Childhood in China,* p. 105.
5. Report from Kao Hsiung, in *Central Daily News,* March 19, 1977.
6. The individual versus situational contrast made in this prologue has nothing to do with the popularly known concepts of *introversion* and *extroversion.* Both Chinese and Americans may be introverts, persons who deal with reality by thought, or they may be extroverts, persons who deal with reality by action. But the Chinese tends to mobilize his thought and action for the purpose of conforming to the reality, while the American tends to do so for the purpose or making the *reality conform* to him. It also differs materially from David Riesman's notion of the inner-directed versus other-directed, as will become clear in Chapter 4.

Part One

IN SEARCH
OF ORIGIN

Introduction
to Part One

We have hypothesized that the Chinese have a situation-centered way of life while that of the Americans is individual-centered. It is now necessary to test this hypothesis in a common sense way—by examining the specific realities of life with which we are familiar.

For this purpose we shall examine art, especially painting, literature, and the patterns of conduct between the sexes.

There is a popular misconception that creative efforts of the individual may transcend time and place. (This concept, incidentally, is typically Western in its individual-centered origin.) No anthropologist will agree with this. In the first place, the creative individual, like others, is the product of a particular cultural context. In the second place, even if a practitioner of any one of the arts produces something totally foreign to this cultural context, such a creation has little chance of general acceptance. Anthropologists have found, through their study of many diverse societies, that among any given people both the form and the content of their art and literature show a high degree of consistency both historically and with reference to the total cultural context. Chinese and Americans are no exception.

Seen in this light, art and literature are much more than the cerebral-emotional products of creative individuals. They are fundamentally what may be described as mirrors—or, as the psychoanalyst says, projective screens—of the society to which the creative individual belongs. We shall look first at art and literature, for these mirrors register not only the surface concerns of the people in question, but also their deeper yearnings which often are not consciously recognized.

After viewing the pictures presented on the projective screens of art and literature, we shall scrutinize the conduct between the sexes among both peoples. I single out conduct between the sexes not only because it is a problem with which all organized societies have to deal, but also because it is one of the most popular subjects in the art and literature of the West. By examining how Chinese and Americans deal with this matter, both on the projective screens and in reality, we may gain a better understanding of their differing mental universes.

The final task of Part One is to determine the origin of the two people's differing ways of life. Here we must distinguish briefly between, on the one hand, the behavior of the individual Chinese or American and, on the other, the general patterns of life in China or the United States as a whole. How does the newborn baby become an adult Chinese or American, each speaking the language of his fellow men, sharing their common outlook, and behaving in general as they do? The most important agencies that set in motion this process, called socialization and enculturation by the anthropologist, are the home and the school.

The two ways of life have each a specific historical continuity. The Chinese way has been maintained for more than two thousand years, but the roots of the American way are even older, from the Middle East and Europe in general, and England in particular only a few centuries ago.

CHAPTER 1

Mirrors
of Life

Aspects of Art

The art form to be discussed here is restricted to painting. There are, of course, many technical differences between Chinese and Western painting. Western artists use a wider variety of media, such as oil, crayon, watercolor, pastel, charcoal, casein, and etching. Chinese artists have limited themselves more to watercolors or brush and ink. Western artists paint upon a variety of materials—canvas, cardboard, glossy papers, wood surfaces, walls, metal, and glass. The Chinese have resorted more exclusively to paper and silk. Perspective in Western painting is achieved by shading and by contrast; in Chinese painting, like that of the ancient Greeks, this is done by superimposing one object on another.

However, there is a far more basic difference that sets them apart from each other: human subjects are as conspicuous on Western canvases as they are relatively scarce on Chinese papers. Moreover, the conventional paintings that circulate widely in the West and in America seem to deal more with females than males, and they reveal, more than anything else, the mental state of the subject. Some, like the paintings of da Vinci and Van Dyck, often express a happy emotion. Others, like those of Van Gogh and Munch, tend to portray a bleaker side of life. In the majority of these paintings, the background on the canvas—such as a house, furniture, trees, or sky —is important only insofar as it adds color to the human beings portrayed. This pattern is so strong that even when a still life or a landscape is the subject, such as in Winslow Homer's and Andrew Wyeth's works, the painting—be it land- or seascape, grapes or bananas—contains an emotional quality that the artist instills in inanimate entities. Where the Western artist details the bustling human activities inside a bar (such as John Sloan's "McSorley's Bar"), the Chinese painter as a rule depicts the bare contours of a wine house topped with its customary sign board—a thin triangular flag.

Even when Chinese artists do portray the human form, they either treat it as a minute dot in a vast landscape, or so heavily clothe it that the body is hidden. The facial expression of such figures is nil. The viewer obtains a much better idea of the status, rank, prestige, and other social characteristics of the subjects portrayed than he does of their personalities.

Furthermore, Chinese painters throughout the last two millennia have excelled in depicting tigers, horses, flowers, landscapes, birds, fish, and even insects. But there are few indeed among the artistic greats who have focused their attention upon human subjects. The drama, the emotional vehemence, and the conflicts of the human heart, which are normal in paintings considered great in the West, are uncommon in Chinese art. In fact, when we do see human faces in Chinese paintings, their blankness bears a remarkable resemblance to the expressionless figures portrayed in *Daughters of the American Revolution*. However, the absence of expression in the Chinese faces results because the Chinese artist is not concerned with personality, whereas the very blankness of the features in Grant Wood's work is intended by the artist as a satiric representation of character.

The two life-styles are thus reflected clearly in the two nations' paintings. In Western art the focus is on man or woman as an individual. In Chinese art the important thing is the individual's place in the external scheme of things. In addition, American art often reflects the inner tension of the individual; this concern is practically absent from Chinese art.

However, the differences go much deeper. A basic search in much of Western art has been for the most beautiful or ideal female form in the person of the angel, goddess, madonna, wife, mother, prostitute, flower girl, or sea bather on a September morn. Yet, the Western artist, in his effort to realize this ideal, usually combines two opposing forces: the depiction of sexual temptation and the effort to partially conceal this very temptation. Western art abounds with suggestive sexuality.

Sexuality is almost totally absent from all Chinese art except pornography. In the latter genre, men and women do not appear in suggestive poses as is common in Western art; rather, they dramatize sexuality in the most minute detail. One may argue, of course, that pornography is not art. But, if by art one means a kind of visual reproduction of experience, whether literal, interpretative, or symbolic, there is little reason to exclude pornography. As in all categories of art, there are more artful pornographic pieces and less artful ones. It is certainly true that pornography is not absent in the West. Not only in France and the other Latin countries, but in England and the United States where such things were once legally banned, pornographic drawings are readily available to those who look for them. If the Western ones that I have seen are any indication of the whole, they are certainly not any less revealing than their Chinese counterparts.

Although both China and America have laws against pornography, the contrasting patterns of the two peoples' personal reactions to pornography are a true guide to their differing psychologies. No respected Chinese, especially the Confucian scholar-bureaucrat, and even the man on the street, would openly admit it, but few Chinese would have any qualms about privately viewing the frankest pictures together with their spouses, sweethearts, or prostitutes.

To a majority of Americans, with their puritan background, the matter is more complicated, for their personal guilt and social ostracism are forever associated with pornography. Even today, though pornography is much more openly flaunted than before in X-rated movies and adult books, I have seen quite a few letters to "Dear Abby" or Ann Landers written by irate, anguished, or perplexed wives or mothers who have unexpectedly discovered pornographic material hidden by their husbands or sons. Frequently these letter writers were told that their men need psychiatric help.

Every society must have rules to regulate behavior. In the individual-centered puritan tradition of America, sex is regulated more by restraints within the individual than by external barriers. Conversely, in situation-centered China, sex is controlled more by external barriers than by internal restraints. Where the emphasis is on internal restraints, man is enjoined not only to avoid sinful action but also to eliminate sinful thoughts. It is interesting that there is no Chinese counterpart to the biblical injunction, "But I say to you that every one who looks at a woman lustfully has already committed adultery with her in his heart" (Matthew 5:28).

Yet sex, being one of man's most fundamental urges, can hardly be eliminated from thought. Where attempts are made to eliminate it from consciousness by condemning it as bad, it merely takes refuge in the deeper layers of the mind, a condition Freud described as repression. Where the purpose is merely to regulate it, sex is simply channeled into specific areas of human association where one need not feel reserved. In the former approach, sex becomes a sin which may be justified by circumstances such as man's need for self-perpetuation. While this ideal is hard to live up to in actuality, it is interesting to note that the Virgin Birth and the Immaculate Conception remain active theological doctrines of the West. Furthermore, as we shall see in connection with our discussion of religion (Chapter 9), although the origin of the alleged founder of Taoism was also associated with a similar myth, the Chinese never made any virtue of it. For in the Chinese attitude, sex is a natural urge of man, like eating, to which, according to Mencius, expression must be given in the right place and with the right parties.

Consequently, repression of sex is correlated with the generalized interest in it in Western art, where sex appears very frequently in the form of diffused suggestiveness. Compartmentalization of sex, on the other hand, causes it to be practically absent from Chinese art in general, but concentrated without restraint in pornography. Except where sublimated, the desirability of sex increases in reverse ratio to its availability. Hence the emotional energy directed toward sex often outweighs that toward all other subjects of Western art while it is without comparable significance in Chinese art.

Those who are familiar with American developments may insist that the central characteristic of American art is its variety. Superficially, this seems to be true. Even a brief look will enable us at least to identify many American trends, most of which have their own well-known artists. The early portrait tradition (Gilbert Stuart, Thomas Sully, Samuel F. B. Morse, John Singleton Copley), the Hudson River school (Thomas Cole, John Kensett), surrealism (Yves Tanguy, Pavel Tchelitchew), cubism (Stuart Davis, John Marin), expressionism (Hans Hoffman, Willem de Kooning, Jackson Pollock), and reactions against emotionalism such as pop art, op art, conceptual art, and photorealism (Roy Lichtenstein, Andy Warhol, etc.) are but a few of the many examples. Different students may classify the artists and their works differently (and agreement is difficult) but there is no doubt about the variety.[1]

Although belonging to the same artistic tradition, European and American styles of art possess some noticeable fine differences. For example, American art makes less use of overtly sexual subject matter than its European counterpart. However, to my knowledge the following American artists are known for one or more paintings of nudes or of lightly clad women of evident sexuality: James McNeill Whistler, John Sloan, Willem de Kooning, Reginald Marsh, Yasuo Kuniyoshi, and Ivan LeLorraine Albright. Diffused sexuality, however, is by no means rare in the works of others.

Another more typically American development is the proliferation of new schools or trends, each of which seems to be a reaction to some more established school or trend: the precise realism of Grant Wood and Andrew Wyeth as reaction to expressionism; the pop and op art of Andy Warhol, Escobar, and Kenneth Noland as reaction to expressionism.

An earlier example of this trend would be the 1913 Armory Show in New York where the exhibition of paintings by Duchamp, Sloan, Glackens, Henri, and others, which had been gradually purged from the more acceptable exhibitions, created a furor so violent that police had to be called in to protect the more controversial pictures. But the following year a group later known as The Eight, under the leadership of Robert Henri, went on to exhibit in New York's Macbeth Galleries, thereafter exerting an enormous impact on the American art world. They "turned the eyes away from the niceties of the genteel tradition toward a more incisive and all-inclusive picture of the country and its people."[2]

A much later example of a trend based on reaction to more established ones is the minimal painters led by Ad Reinhardt, who, according to Mendelowitz, "was a mystic inspired to a degree by the Oriental philosophies . . . espoused by certain groups of American intellectuals who questioned the humane potentialities of our technological and material progress. Reinhardt sought an ultimate: to eliminate all the elements which create tension and to invoke a mood of hypnotic reverie."[3]

In fact, this tendency to proliferate is so great that charges of "that's not art" and extensive explanations of what makes this or that art are extremely common. In form and substance, Western art in general and American art in particular have undergone enormous changes through time. Between the works of Michelangelo and Jackson Pollock there does indeed seem to be no link.

However, if we examine the basic approach of Western artists we shall find in it no fundamental change in spite of a common assertion that "Modern art . . . differs radically from any art which has preceded it."[4] The cubists, the expressionists, the dadaists, the pop and op artists and others (in time there will be more innovators) concern themselves, as did their Western predecessors, with individual feelings. The difference between them and their predecessors is that, whereas the latter depicted the feelings of their individual subjects (or projected their own feelings into their individual subjects), they now tend to express the feelings (or the feelings against the expression of feelings) of their individual selves.

As early as half a century ago Edward Alden Jewell, in his book entitled *Have We an American Art?*, said:

> How, then, does one go about it to become a true American artist? . . . If we assume his necessary development on the craft side, the American, in order to become in the truest and fullest sense an American artist, has only to be himself. . . .
>
> For as I see it, the true objective is within, not without. It has to do with *being;* not with being, by some arbitrary extrinsic compulsion, forced to be what by nature one is not. . . . The artist who, caring, dares to look deeply into himself (for to do so calls for courage) will find there the precious stuff of which spiritual leagues are formed.[5]

Given this greater American intensification of the individual feelings of the artists themselves, their departure from their European antecedents becomes understandable. Thus, while human figures or landscapes by Western classicists or romanticists would, in the non-artist's eyes, bear some resemblance to these subjects, this need not be so in the case of the contemporary American artist. Since the artist seeks to express only his own feelings and imagery, which need not meet the requirements of objective requirement, the viewer will simply find his own meaning, very much as if he were reacting to an inkblot test. There is therefore no need to justify the validity of a square wheel (or a forest that looks like an empty tool shed, or a stenographer represented by a decimated notebook beside what looks like a deformed and dancing baby whale). Jackson Pollock's works seem to represent the most extreme American trend of atomization, since they aspire to freedom from all external restraints. It is said that many of his paintings are twenty-two feet long only because that is the length of his studio wall. The only difficulty is that much explanation is often necessary for many works of the newer Western art to be appreciated as art at all.

Such an intensification and elaboration of the artist's own feelings will inevitably lead to vitality and inventiveness without depth. Franz Schulze, an art critic, though noting correctly that vitality and inventiveness are "encouraged" in the American society while depth is "not so much discouraged as out of the question," interprets wrongly why most Western moderns have proceeded onto their present path:

> Perhaps because it is now so nearly impossible to find any steady, believable, profound, and clear-cut meaning in the contemporary world—hence it is impossible to interpret that world in depth—these artists seek to reproduce their only certain and reliable reaction to the world, which is that of undifferentiated sensation extracted from it. . . .
>
> That [Schulze is speaking of the works of Jordan Davies, Arthur Green and Raymond Siemanowski in Chicago] the symbols have more to do with comic strips and billboards than with apples, madonnas, sunsets, or even abstract volume analysis, suggests that when traditionally sanctioned subjects seem exhausted and meaningless, traditionally discredited ones appear at least worth a try, even if it is a tongue-in-cheek try.[6]

Had Schulze examined the real lives of diverse peoples outside America and Europe, he might have seen the error in his judgment. The truth is not that the contemporary world is so bereft of "steady, believable, profound, and clear-cut meaning," but that the intensification of each individual's feelings can only lead to his increasing isolation and lack of commitment to anything. Such individuals will inevitably find *their* world bereft of "steady, believable, profound, and clear-cut meaning." We shall return to this point in Chapter 13.

Chinese art, on the other hand, has undergone little change in historical times even after contact with the West, either in form and substance, or in approach. Historically, the northern school concentrated on exact details while the southern school used broadly expressionistic brush strokes. There were, of course, individual masters who differed in some minor ways from the others; but there were no innovations by some artists which were repudiated by other artists (much less which met with a kind of furor even remotely resembling that reported in the West) and there simply was no significant discussion on what was or what was not art. The similarity between Chinese masterpieces of the ninth century and those of today is so evident that they present no problem of understanding—in sharp contrast to the history of Western art.

The Western method of painting came to China with the introduction of Western schools, noticeably as early as the turn of the present century. Those who paint with that method use cardboard, canvas, Western watercolors, crayons, and oils. But for those who paint in the Chinese style the traditional media such as Chinese ink, color, paper, shell, and woodcut remain prominent. A sort of "marriage" between the two art traditions was effected when a few Chinese-style painters introduced Western-style perspective and a greater degree of expressiveness than their predecessors. In the main, a majority of Chinese painters stuck to their Chinese tradition, and the much smaller group of Western-style painters were assiduous disciples, at a distance, of Western Classical and Romantic masters.

Since 1949 the political imprint has been heavy on artistic as well as other activities of China. However, it is the *purpose* for which art is created that has changed, not its structure, content, or general approach. The traditional animals, flowers, and scenery are still common, but humans mostly in nontraditional situations now figure much more prominently than before. We now see *Eighth Route Army Soldiers Being Welcomed by Civilians, The Iron and Steel Plant at Paotow, Sheep and Shepherd on the Slopes of the Ningsha Hui Autonomous Region,* papercut figures of *Brother and Sister Planting Trees,* etc., as well as shell pictures of *Heavenly Angel Spreading Flowers* and a *Crane Standing Beside Pine Trees* (both the latter are traditional subjects). One most charming painting I know of is entitled *Commune Holiday,* featuring buildings and telephone lines and loudspeakers interspersed with trees and hundreds of men and women on bicycles, some with babies on their backs. Art is now used to propagandize for social and economic development under the guidance of an all-powerful state instead of being an object of mere enjoyment to the artist or consumer.

This same pattern has continued through political vicissitudes, including the recent fall of the Gang of Four. In December 1977 a collection of eighty paintings by the peasants of Hu county in Shensi Province toured United States cities, including New York, Chicago, and Los Angeles. Without exception all of them featured men, women, and children in politically but especially economically productive activity. Some titles tell us all: *Spring Hoeing, Joyful Cotton Harvest, Our Own Pharmacy, Digging a Well, Everyone Helps in Building Each Other's Houses, The Fragrance of Rice over the Threshing Ground, Sports and Games, Return from a Cultural Evening,* and *Announcement of the Two Great Happy Events in October, 1976.* The latter features a man returning home with his teenage daughter, each holding a copy of *Jen Min Jih Pao (People's Daily).* A red poster on the front door bears the following couplet:

Support Our Leader Chairman Hua,
Angrily denounce the Gang of Four.

Some peasants made a stab at the future and such efforts led to *Every Family Has Money in the Bank, New Look at the Weiho River Beach,* and *Artificial Rainfall.* A painting entitled *New Look at Hu County* gives us a view very much like that one may obtain from a low flying plane approaching Chicago from the west: rows of houses, factories and chimneys, neatly planted trees, and lines of tall office buildings and low residential houses. The only differences are that the well–laid out streets are teeming with trucks and buses but not cars, and a passenger train with smoke trailing from its engine is running through the middle of the entire scene. The man who painted *A Commune Fishpond* explains his vision of the future as follows:

> We artists paint the future and also the revolutionary ideal, not just things as they are. In our village the fishpond is not exactly like this; there's a wall around it. But in order to reflect the bright future I took out the wall. To express the bumper harvest, all the fish are jumping, all their scales are bright and shining. The little fish are escaping from the net. The net lets them through. The little fish are the new generation growing up. This is intended to show development; we don't eat up all the fish.[7]

A *New York Times Magazine* writer described the paintings as "examples of the Socialist Realist School of Art," and went on to say, "What many of the paintings evoke is a spirit of optimism and sheer delight. . . . The artist seems to be saying, 'work is light and sportive.' That is, after all, the brave new world of a Socialist countryside" (*New York Times Magazine,* December 11, 1977). A *Chicago Tribune* writer headlined his article "Chinese Turn 'Happy' into Sheer Tedium" and is far more critical of the exhibition: "Many of the works are lame or silly, though the same—and sometimes worse— may be said for much in Western painting. . . . To consider that centuries of Chinese art have come to this is a sobering thought" (*Chicago Tribune,* April 23, 1978).

I think to characterize post-1949 Chinese painting as constituting a "Socialist Realist School" is quite unnecessary, in fact misleading. And the *Chicago Tribune* man's adverse comments are simply due to his failure to see the Chinese artistic products in Chinese terms.

What the Chinese leaders claim is new, and what they are encouraging their people to see as new, are only two things. One, art must serve the society's need to move forward, not mere individual enjoyment. Two, all the people can now paint instead of the select few as before, and their artistic activity raises their fervor for the society's forward movement. Both of these artistic objectives, especially the first, are obviously unacceptable to the American critic.

What he fails to see is that, in spite of the new objectives, Chinese paintings today, by peasants and professionals alike, have an essential continuity with those of the past. They are very much Chinese. For one thing, all the human faces in the new paintings look alike, exactly as those in traditional Chinese paintings. The only difference is that while those in the traditional paintings resemble the expressionless faces in Grant Wood's *Daughters of American Revolution,* those in the post-1949 paintings have smiles. Furthermore, all of the new products portray specific events, an approach quite common in traditional Chinese works of art.

Finally, instead of initiating new approaches, new techniques, and new concepts as their American counterparts are fond of doing, most Chinese artists have been content to imitate the past greats. In fact it is the highest form of praise to tell a Chinese artist that his work is exactly like the famous original. For example, there are many versions of the famous *Ch'ing Ming Shang Ho (Spring Festival on the River),* none of which can be authenticated as the original, including the one at the Metropolitan Museum of Art in New York City. They vary in small details, and are located in Japan, Taiwan, and China. To a majority of Chinese artists there is nothing at all objectionable in conformity—a quality anathema to Western and American artists.

In Taiwan the question of the seeming stagnation of Chinese art in contrast to the proliferation of Western "schools" and trends has resulted in some heated newspaper debates. When David Kwok, a Chinese artist known in the United States, argued the need for change, other artists challenged him. As yet no real change is visible. There are, of course, well-known Chinese artists from Taiwan today, (and in China since the 1920s), such as Ch'en Huei-tung, who use Western media and paint in the Western idiom. Ch'en's works entitled *Vessel* (1978), with lively boats in a harbor, *The Nude, Imagining,* and *Poetry* have nothing Chinese about them.

Similarly, the Chinese artists who formed The Fifth Moon Group some twenty years ago seem to devote their talents entirely to the Western mode of modern art. Like those of their Western counterparts, the works of these artists cannot be understood without explanation. Thus a piece by Ch'en Ting-shih entitled *Peeping* features a series of black and red shapes with white holes in them. A piece by Hung Hsien named *Autumn Blaze* presents the viewer with pebbles and earth in multicolors. Only in some of the works by Liu Kuo-sung do we see any ordinary coincidence between the paintings and their titles, as in three entitled *Which is Earth?*[8]

However, a volume entitled *Sixth Art Exhibition of the Republic of China* (National Taiwan Arts Center, 1971) tells a fuller story of recent art trends based in Taiwan. Selected works are presented in ten categories, beginning with traditional Chinese painting, followed by watercolor, oil, flat paint, calligraphy, seals, sculpture, photography, crafts, and architectural designs. The traditional Chinese painting category contains sixty-nine works, or a little more than one-third of the total of some 180. A few of the pieces, such as one entitled *Rice Hulling* by Li Chi-mao, are indistinguishable from the new art from the People's Republic discussed above. Only two others (*Loneness of the Moon* by Liu Kuo-sung and *Eggs, Eggs* by Chao Chung-hsiang) show slight departures from traditional Chinese ways of art.

The works in the oil category are Western in motif and execution, both modern and classical. They present two interesting characteristics. The human figures depicted mostly look European or non-Chinese if they are portraits, and Chinese or Asian if they are faceless peasants in the field. Secondly, only a few of the buildings, where they occur, are Chinese; the rest are Western. They might easily be Spanish or Italian.[9]

Fiction

The basic contrasts in Chinese and Western art are equally obvious in fiction. Traditional Chinese novels usually concentrate on what the characters do in their roles as emperors or common men, while Western novels[10] are much more concerned with what the characters *do, think,* and *feel* as individuals. There are, of course, a few exceptions. But compare any Chinese novel which has remained popular throughout several centuries, such as *The Dream of the Red Chamber*[11] or *All Men Are Brothers,*[12] with any widely read American novel, such as *The Grapes of Wrath* or *Elmer Gantry* or *The Deer Park.* The absence in Chinese novels of excursions into the mind of a character is as pronounced as their abundance in American fiction. No traditional Chinese novelist tells the whole story from the point of view of one character, a common technique of his American counterpart.

Among the works of Chinese fiction with which I am familiar, the deepest an author has penetrated into the workings of a character's mind was when a hero, confronted by an enemy, calculated that if he did a certain thing he would surely defeat or outwit the villain. The height of Chinese imaginative authorship seems to have been reached in *Western Journey*,[13] a fantasy about an arduous trip to India by some Buddhist monks in the early seventh century A.D.; *Tale of the Mirrored Flower*, a satire on human relations; and *A Record of Adventures into the Western Ocean*, a fictional account of the historical exploits of the eunuch admiral, Cheng Ho, between 1405 and 1438.[14]

No less revealing is the way love is handled in the two types of novels. Chinese and American novels describe two very different kinds of romantic characters. With few exceptions the conventional American romantic hero and his lady are devoted to one another. In particular, there is a tendency for the male characters to exalt their female idols in thought, words, or action. In the American love story, the union of the hero and the heroine is usually the climax. Not infrequently, an entire book deals with the pursuit of romance, the agony, the misunderstandings, the stumbling blocks that must be hurdled before the two chief protagonists join each other and the book comes to an end. Even where love is not the primary emphasis, as in *The Grapes of Wrath* or *The Jungle* or *Of Mice and Men*, the American novel pulsates with strong emotions.

The Chinese novel, even when it deals with romance, does so with a casualness or frankness that may well be distasteful to many American readers. Sexual union usually occurs early in the narrative; it is never the climax of the story. The balance of the novel is concerned with how the hero goes about marrying the heroine properly, with the rectifying wedding ceremony tediously described to the last detail. Mutual attraction between a man and a woman is not enough. Their personal feelings are never more important than the sanctions and assistance of the family and the society. This Chinese cultural pattern remains true even in novels which superficially employ the complex plots common in Western novels.

A Chinese hero pursues his female love object and revels in her beauty in the same way that he strives to gain control of other worldly goods or prestige. In *The Dream of the Red Chamber*, the hero, although never sexually united with the heroine, has illicit relations with a number of other women, including maidservants, while never abandoning his ideal sweetheart. In addition, he also has erotic connections of varying degrees with other women and homosexual relations with an actor. To American readers such a characterization probably befits that of a rogue or villain unless he has other redeeming qualities or is able to repent. But Chinese readers do not condemn this character. Lacking the Western, individualized approach to sex, they have referred to him and his girl as great lovers for many decades.

Brief synopses of two Chinese novels of love—*Hao Ch'iu Chuan (The Story of an Ideal Marriage)* and *Yu Chiao Li (The Strange Romance of the Beautiful Pair)*—will give the reader a clearer idea of this contrast. Although the two plots involved appear to have all the complications —mistaken identity, odd coincidences, narrow escapes—of *Tom Jones* or *A Tale of Two Cities,* nevertheless it will be seen that the emphasis is still on family arrangements and approval rather than on individual romantic initiative and personal emotions.

In the first novel, the hero is the son of a member of the imperial censorate whose duty is to impeach corrupt officials. Worried that his father's strictness in his work is making him many enemies in high places, the hero urges his father to be more cautious. On the way to the national capital where his father has his official residence, he encounters the family of the beautiful heroine who through a forged imperial decree is nearly trapped into marrying a villain. The son exposes the plot and saves her, and she falls in love with him. When he falls ill, she nurses him back to health. After overcoming further difficulties perpetrated by the villain, he and the heroine are finally married with the emperor's approval.

The other novel, *The Strange Romance of the Beautiful Pair,* begins with an aged minister in the imperial court who is devoted to his only child, Red Jade, a beautiful poetess. Another high official asks for the hand of the poetess on behalf of his son, unsuccessfully because the latter failed the informal literary test given by the girl's father. In hatred, the boy's father arranges matters in court so that the poetess' father is ordered to embark on a difficult mission in Mongolia. The plot thickens with mistaken identities, plagiarism in poetry, the girl traveling disguised as a man, and a secret proposal of marriage until the hero Meng-li is happily married to Red Jade.

The familiar theme of love overcoming obstacles had made these two novels most appealing to Western readers. They were each partially or wholly translated into Western languages several times and commanded the attention of such notables as Goethe, Schiller, and Carlyle.[15]

These contrasts are not confined to only a select handful of Chinese and American novels. Among other popular Chinese novels are *The Romance of the Three Kingdoms; The True Story of Chi Kung, the Mad Monk; The True Story of His Eminence Pao, the Wonderful Official; The Golden Lotus (Chin Ping Mei); Western Chamber;* and *Strange Stories from a Chinese Studio.*[16] Any reader reasonably well acquainted with American fiction could prepare a similar and extensive list of novels. We are speaking primarily of the widely read "popular" novels found as book club selections and on paperback book racks in drugstores.[17]

Concern with what the characters do in their social roles as contrasted with what they do, think, and feel as individuals is only one of the Chinese-American differences. Another is the nearly universal preoccupation with sex in American fiction and its segregation into a separate area in Chinese fiction. Love today, as at all times, is the most important theme of native American novels as well as of other Western novels which have enjoyed wide acceptance in the United States. There are, of course, a number of great European and American works, such as Thomas Mann's *The Magic Mountain,* Thomas Wolfe's *Look Homeward, Angel,* Feodor Dostoevski's *Crime and Punishment,* John Hersey's *A Bell for Adano,* Sinclair Lewis' *Babbitt* or *Main Street,* Nordhoff and Hall's *Mutiny on the Bounty,* and Marjorie K. Rawlings' *The Yearling,* which have treated problems and situations that are not concerned essentially with love. Too, there are famous authors like Mark Twain, Herman Melville, and Jack London, whose writings have scarcely touched upon romance. I doubt, however, that anyone would choose to contend that the vast majority of Western novels do not deal with love.

With reference to love and sex, the most popular Chinese novels have been of three kinds. There are those which do not deal with the man-woman relationship at all, or only deal with it hurriedly as a minor matter; there are those which devote their entire attention essentially to one romantic affair like the two which were summarized, but which do not discuss sexual relations on a biological level; and there are pornographic novels.

The Romance of the Three Kingdoms is a typical novel in which romance is merely a bypath of the main route of the story. A synopsis of one brief section of this ten-volume work will indicate to what extent "romance" figures in Chinese novels of this variety. This novel was based upon that period of China's history, about A.D. 200, when the country was divided among three warring factions.

At one point, the mastermind of the Eastern faction, the kingdom of Wu, designs the following strategy to destroy the head of the Western faction, the kingdom of Shu. The ruler of Shu needs a wife, and the king of Wu has a beautiful sister. The story is spread that the former could marry this desirable woman if he came in person to the court of Wu. The strategist's idea is to kill the wife-seeker at a reception in his honor. The king of Shu, reluctant to accept the invitation, hesitates until his chief strategist advises him to go, accompanied by one lone warrior. What the Wu strategist fails to foresee is that the mother of the king of Wu would insist on attending the banquet to inspect her prospective son-in-law. The elderly dowager at once develops a liking for the king of Shu. She decides that he is the right man for her daughter. So he is married to the beautiful woman with all the ceremonial pomp due a king, against the wishes of the Wu strategist.

Having lost the first round, the unruffled Wu strategist works out a second plan. The king of Shu is showered with all kinds of gifts. A palace is built for him and his new bride, furnished with all manner of luxuries, and staffed with a host of servants and beautiful female attendants. Here he is entertained lavishly. The Wu strategist's idea is that, having lived in such ease and comfort, the king of Shu will be unwilling to leave his gracious surroundings. He also counts on the princess' persuading her husband to stay on indefinitely.

Unfortunately for the kingdom of Wu, the Shu strategist is one step ahead. He foresees this latter eventuality and provides his master with a plan to deal with it. The upshot is that the Wu princess, far from persuading her husband to stay, insists on going with him to his kingdom. A second attempt at assassination is out of the question because this would widow the princess. The pair could not be separated because the princess remained loyal to her husband. Result: the king of Wu loses the battle of strategy as well as a beautiful sister. The outcome so humiliates the Wu strategist that he eventually dies of anger, which, I suspect, is the common American disease—high blood pressure.

There are only a few other romantic episodes in this novel. The ruler of the Northern faction, the kingdom of Wei, is routed in battle because he neglected strategy while dallying with another man's wife. This is a typically Chinese piece of didacticism in which romance is no more than a vehicle for the moral—that the fulfillment of personal fancies runs a poor second to other considerations, and the failure to heed this injunction has disastrous consequences. In another instance, a great general, serving under the ruler of Shu, wins a wide expanse of territory after refusing romantic advances from an exquisite widow. But the remainder of the ten volumes is devoted to events that have nothing to do with romance.

Chinese pornographic novels do not portray romance, as Americans understand the term: the existence of a mutual devotion beyond the sexual plane, a situation where sexual congress between a man and woman is the catastasis. Chinese pornography describes the plain externalized pleasures of sex in blatant detail, and it is interspersed throughout with homosexuality and other forms of perversion. Until very recently one of the few American novels which could even faintly compare in frankness was Henry Miller's *Tropic of Cancer*. Even in this book (formerly forbidden in this country but since 1959 permitted to be sold in bookshops only because of a court decision), the author merely uses some artless four-letter words over and over again, relying upon the usual devices of shadow, sound, implication, or dialogue to portray the sexual act. Almost all other Western literary pieces, whether banned or not, deal with sex by nuance.[18]

Some illustrations will make this clear. For example, in James Jones's *From Here to Eternity*, the author describes a scene in which a soldier in Hawaii spends the night with a prostitute. The two are lying in bed, their nakedness covered by a quilt:

> "But why? Why will you remember me?"
> "Because," he said, "because of this." And smiling, he took a corner of her quilt and flipped it off her and looked at her lying there.
> She did not move and turned her head to smile at him. "Is that the only reason?"
> "No. Also because you touched me when Angelo was here."
> "Is that all?"
> "Maybe not all. But a lot."
> "But not because of talking to me?"
> "Yes, that too. Definitely that too. But this also," he said looking at her.
> "But the talking too?"
> "Yes. The talking too. Talking is important."
> "To me it is." She smiled contentedly at him and took a corner of his quilt that he was still lying under propped up on one elbow looking down at her and flipped it off of him, like he had done to her.
> "Why, look at you," she said.
> "I know. Ain't it shameful?"
> "I wonder what caused that."
> "Can't help it. Does it every time."
> "We really ought to change that."
> He laughed and suddenly they were talking, bed talking, as they had not been at all before. And this time it was different.
> Afterwards, grateful, he bent his head down for her lips.

Here not only the sexual act is veiled, but also feelings of love—"I know I'll remember you," "this time it was different," he was "grateful"—are added to the episode. Once the act of intercourse is completed, his attempt to kiss helps to sanctify the preceding, but unreported, coition. For in the American way of life, sex relations can only be justified within the terms of romantic love.

Henry Miller, in his *Tropic of Cancer,* is supposed to be more frank:

> As I watch Van Norden tackle her it seems to me that I'm looking at a machine whose cogs have slipped. Left to themselves they could go on this way forever, forever grinding and slipping without ever anything happening. Until a hand shuts the motor off. The sight of them coupled like a pair of goats without the least spark of passion, grinding and grinding away for no reason except the fifteen francs, washes away every bit of feeling I have except the inhuman one of sating my curiosity. The girl is lying on the edge of the bed and Van Norden is bent over her like a satyr with his two feet solidly planted on the floor. I am sitting on a chair behind him, watching their movements with a cool, scientific detachment: it doesn't matter to me if it should last forever. It's like watching one of those crazy machines which throw the newspapers out, millions and billions and trillions of them with their meaningless headlines. The machine seems more sensible, crazy as it is, and more fascinating to watch, than the human beings and the events which produced it. My interest in Van Norden and the girl is nil; if I could sit like this and watch every single performance going on at this minute all over the world my interest would be even less than nil. I wouldn't be able to differentiate between this phenomenon and the rain falling or a volcano erupting. As long as that spark of passion is missing there is no human significance in the performance. The machine is better to watch. And those two are like a machine which has slipped its cogs. It needs the touch of a human hand to set it right. It needs a mechanic.
>
> I get down on my knees behind Van Norden and I examine the machine more attentively. The girl throws her head on one side and gives me a despairing look. "It's no use," she says. "It's impossible." Upon which Van Norden sets to work with renewed energy, just like an old billy goat. He's such an obstinate cuss that he'd break his horns rather than give up. And now he's getting sore because I'm tickling him in the rump.
>
> "For God's sake, Joe, give it up! You'll kill the poor girl!"
>
> "Leave me alone," he grunts. "I almost had it that time!"

The language of the *Tropic of Cancer* is not any more explicit than in later examples such as Robert Grover's *One Hundred Dollar Misunderstanding,* which is also about a prostitute and her customers. Except for the added risqué element that the prostitute is black and the customers are white, Grover's description follows the same pattern of veiling the sex act with nonsexual phrases and nuances. This, in spite of the fact that the narrative of the sex act is given in two dialects: black American and white American, each being hardly intelligible to the speaker of the other. The following two excerpts deal with the same episode:

(1) I wash him real nice an soff, counta him bein so awful tickledingus, and then I gits t'work. Time I start in, I got me so many worryful considerins t'do, I can' hardly pay no mind t'teckneek. Workin an considerin, an wonnerin does this dum Whiteboy know what t'do wiff that thing fer the other haff o'his haff and haff, I find I done me too dam much considerin.

Nex, I ain been at him a minit, an pop, off he go!

Kee-ryess!

(2) But different—that's my point. For instance (and this will be difficult to tell without becoming obscene) this colored professional prostitute had the same inclination that Margie has, except she went about it. . . . Well, she went about it *more* so than Margie ever did. I mean, she just acted as if it was quite natural, as I suppose, in view of her status, it was. Though I found her manner of approach more than slightly disquieting. I mean, it was so professional, so undramatic and lacking in the necessary preliminaries. It was startling, almost sickening for gosh sakes!

I suppose, however, that never having been to a house of ill repute, I had acquired certain misconceptions about how such women behaved— based on my natural, normal experiences. Experiences unpaid for, is what I mean.

In fact, I was so surprised by her manner of approach (and also by a couple of unlikely intrusions by some other paid professional colored girl, who kept opening our door and sticking her head inside, first while mine was gone, and then later) that I reached my first (if you'll pardon the expression) climax a bit too hastily. (I should also add that the surroundings I found myself in had something to do with the above.)[19]

Tropic of Cancer and other novels such as *Lady Chatterly's Lover* are believed by many to be the extreme in literary directness, and a variety of "realism" over which writers, literary critics, police, judges, purity committees, and the general public all fiercely once contended (and in places still do). Yet these books as well as *The One Hundred Dollar Misunderstanding* do not compare in frankness with material to be found in the well-known Chinese novel, *The Golden Lotus*.[20]

Before it was light, Golden Lotus, still hungry for more, fondled his weapon with her slender fingers till it was ready once more for action.

"Darling," she said, "I want to lie on you." She climbed on to him, and played the game of making a candle upside down. She put her arms around his neck and wriggled about. She asked him to grip her firmly by the waist. Then she lifted herself up and dropped herself again: mox in mulierem penis capulo tenus iniit, nec ulla pars extra manebat nisi quam fibula tenuit.

"Darling," she said, "I will make a red silk belt for you, and you can keep in it the medicine the monk gave you. And I will make two supports which you can tie at the root of it and fasten around your waist. When they are tightly tied, molliserit et totus inibit. Nonne putas id praestare huic fibulae quae tam dura et molesta est?"

"Yes, my child, make it by all means. The medicine is in my little box. Put it in for yourself."

"Come back to-night," Golden Lotus said, "and we will see what it is like." (Vol. 3, pp. 318–319)

In spite of the fact that the descriptions of sexual intercourse in American literature are invariably much less bold than those in Chinese writings, American public reaction to these passages has consistently been more severe. The publishers of *God's Little Acre* were sued on the grounds of immorality by the New York Society for the Suppression of Vice. Whitman's *Leaves of Grass* was publicly burned in Philadelphia just before the turn of the twentieth century. The legal battles over the *Tropic of Cancer* are still comparatively recent. Some reviewers persistently charged that such works as *Two Adolescents* and *From Here to Eternity* were pornography in disguise. Many respectable libraries either do not keep such books as *Memoirs of Hecate County* or leave them in a locked press. On the other hand, *The Golden Lotus* is regarded in China as one of the greatest masterpieces of the empire. In the 1930s governmental organs, influenced by the West, attempted to have the franker paragraphs of this and similar works expurgated, but they met with little success.

So we see sex is more widespread in American than Chinese fiction but it tends to be less explicit. The reader's imagination is stimulated by suggestive words and phrases, just as it is aroused by certain lines or poses in art. In contrast, sex either receives but scant attention in a lengthy Chinese novel or it is relegated to a separate novel. The majority of novels are not concerned with the love lives of men and women, but those which do deal with sex do not do so by subterfuge.

Furthermore, in no Chinese novel is sex as such ever condemned. The sexual urge leads to undesirable results or punishment only if it appears in improper places and is indulged in excessively or between improper parties. Thus the previously mentioned ruler of Wei suffered defeat following his adventure with another man's wife. And the hero of *Golden Lotus* died of his wanton sexual escapades.

In the American novels where pornographic or nearly pornographic passages are present, they usually are accompanied by the message that the events described are matters for condemnation or are, as in the episode from *From Here to Eternity,* associated with affection approaching true love. Accordingly, bold descriptions are most often restricted to relationships outside of wedlock, often between prostitutes and their customers, or between notoriously "loose" women and their similarly unprincipled companions. Yet the majority of American popular novels exalt love, divorced from the sexual act, as something magnificent in itself. Individual feelings being most important, the moral or immoral nature of the affair usually depends upon whether the love is "true," or whether the partners are "happy." If it is "true," then love will find a way. If it is not "true," then separation between husband and wife is justified and so also is a liaison between a man and a woman either or both of whom are married to someone else.

The escalation of explicit sex in the printed pages and the movies since the middle sixties may seem to cloud this last observation. From Max Shulman's *Memoir of An Ex-Prom Queen* to Judith Rossner's *Looking for Mr. Goodbar* and Gay Talese's *Thy Neighbor's Wife,* already a best-seller even before it hit the stands, do we see anything but the dissociation of sex from love?

My answer to this question is twofold. The tendency to indulge in sexual pleasures per se is not new to Western literature. For example, Frank Harris's *My Life and Loves* was first published in Germany in 1922, and *My Secret Life* was first printed in an eleven-volume edition by the anonymous author at his own expense in Amsterdam around 1882. In fact, privately circulated erotica of this kind was known in the West for centuries before modern times. However, even in secrecy or under disguise it was in the main confined to the French and Italian languages. These books and others like them, published in the United States since 1959 because of court decisions, even surpass their Chinese counterparts in frankness.

The difference between such Western works and their Chinese counterpart is that, while Chinese writers treat erotica as part of a larger social context, Western writers see it as an end in itself, unrelated to other aspects of life. These Western writers are preoccupied with the variety of sexual conquest and sexual acts, with sexual sensations and details of sexual organs to an extent unknown among

Chinese brethren of comparable interest. *My Secret Life* is saturated with sexual episodes of every variety. Its author, a wealthy Englishman, not only takes pleasure in cunnilingus with his prostitute but also pays his prostitute's boyfriend so that he can do fellatio on the young man.[21] *My Life and Loves* is concerned with four things: adventure, ideas, men and events, and sex. But as its editor observes, "no matter what his subject, Harris' person and his vanity permeate every page" (p. xv).

The last observation, the fact that the author of neither book cared for any lasting intimacy (one of them mentioned brief marital interludes while the other never touched on marriage at all), and the preoccupation with varieties of sexual conquest as well as sexual sensation, betray the individual-centered approach very well. Frank Harris and the writer of *My Secret Life* merely exemplify the extremes to which some of those raised with that approach can go. But such extremes are even more interesting when we read about a more basic reason why Frank Harris wrote as he did. In his own "Foreword" to *My Life and Loves* Harris explained that several executive and judiciary decisions against his publications in the United States caused him financial embarrassment.

> If America had not reduced me to penury I should probably not have written this book as boldly as the ideal demanded. At the last push of Fate (I am much nearer seventy than sixty) we are all apt to sacrifice something of Truth for the sake of kindly recognition by our fellows and a peaceful ending. Being that "wicked animal," as the French say, "who defends himself when he is attacked," I turn at length to bay, without any malice, I hope, but also without any fear such as might prompt compromise. I have always fought for the Holy Spirit of Truth and have been, as Heine said he was, a brave soldier in the Liberation War of Humanity: now one fight more, the best and the last.[22]

It is clear that for Frank Harris, quite apart from his personal fondness for sexual variety and sensations, the frankness of his writing was the instrument of an antiestablishmentarian and a revolutionary, an attitude so characteristic of the individual-centered West and so alien to the situation-centered Chinese. Repression of sex in literature and blatant erotica are at once two sides in an irreconcilable tug-of-war in the West, in sharp contrast with China where no comparable polarization is discernible.

Liberalizing court decisions democratized pornography in books and visual media so that its enjoyment is no longer the exclusive privilege of the rich. This is one side of the picture. The puritan strain of the American psyche is bound to reassert itself. The recent and impressive successes of a flood of romances without explicit sex under the general trademark Harlequin (1978 sales: 125 million books) tell us that the reaction against explicit sex is already at hand. For twelve years these books, which are published in Canada, were distributed by New York's Simon and Schuster. But in 1979, the American firm initiated its own Silhouette series based on the same formula.

I have read only a few of these new titles which began to appear in the early seventies, but according to a news report the Harlequin books have brought in "big bucks."

> Authors Lamb, Donald and McLean are part of a stable of 100 women writers who collectively turn out twelve "romances" a month, twelve months a year.
> Together, they have written one of the most sensational success stories in publishing history—and they have done so without once getting down to the sexual nitty-gritty.[23]

The company's own publicity release describes their fiction exactly as I have characterized American popular novels before: "No matter how passionate the protagonists, the heroine's virtue remains intact until marriage. . . . While problems and misunderstandings delay the happy ending, there are no shocks to disturb the 'beautiful dream.' Along the way, not only is there no overt sex, there's no tragedy, no serious illness, nor the slightest hint of violence. Love conquers all."

Some readers may be wishing now for an opportunity to ask me this question: Since, as you yourself stated, the majority of Chinese do not read and write, how can the novels have anything to do with them? Isn't the contrast you have described here no more than one between what is read by a very small group of Chinese intellectuals and what is popular with the majority of the American people?

The question is not hard to answer. While many Americans learn about child-training, psychoanalysis, poetry, novels, drama, religion, and international affairs through schools, churches, clubs, and the mass media, the majority of their illiterate Chinese brethren are informed how ancient emperors ruled, famous warriors conquered, statesmen outwitted each other, and the handsome beggar married the daughter of the prime minister through storytelling, shadow plays, classical operas, and regional operettas.[24]

The themes of these stories, shadow plays, operas, and operettas are similar to those of Chinese fiction in general and in many cases may be the same, with the same plot and same characters. While most novels, movies, operas, and operettas which enjoy popularity among adult Americans are usually strung together by love affairs, Chinese themes can easily be classified into those which have to do with romance and those which do not. Romance is rare in the classical operas and in shadow plays, and it is only slightly more in evidence in the colloquial stories. In local operettas, romantic and non-romantic plots seem to be equally popular.

Storytelling is one of the most ubiquitous forms of entertainment in China. Storytellers are found in every market place and temple fair, and in all cities and towns. They are in great demand during the ancestral festival of the Seventh Moon and the Spring Festival at the end of the Chinese year. They are frequently hired to entertain guests at a wedding, funeral, or birthday celebration. They may recite a single episode or they may be commissioned to tell an entire novel from beginning to end. They tell their tales in different ways: some by talking; others by interspersing their talk with singing, since most of the popular novels are also available in lyric form.

As a matter of fact, storytelling most decidedly antedated written fiction in the vernacular in China. The first fiction was a kind of prompt book to aid the storyteller's memory, each containing a synopsis of the narrative, called *hua pen* or "story roots," which were the first rudimentary novels. The earliest surviving *hua pen* comes from the archives of the famous Buddhist caves in northwestern China, and probably was in circulation in the T'ang dynasty (A.D. 618–907). Five of the earliest specimens of these ancestors of Chinese fiction are today available in the government library in Japan. These prompt books retained their popularity with storytellers long after the full-fledged development of Chinese fiction.[25]

Shadow plays and colloquial operettas are always performed on a permanent or improvised stage. The average company's repertoire contains dramatized versions of the great novels, in whole or in part, and additional pieces based on unwritten folk tales often found in *hua pen*. The classical operas are much more formal than the shadow plays and operettas. They are more expensive to stage and to attend. Much of these troupes' repertoire is based on such novels as *The Ro-*

mance of the Three Kingdoms, and the opera may take from half an hour
to several days to perform.

Of these media, storytelling reaches the widest audience, for there
is no Chinese town or village unexposed to it in one way or another.
The classical operas, while less widespread, are performed in the
provincial capitals and other large cities, and are enjoyed by literates
and illiterates alike.

What has become of Chinese fiction since Western contact and especially since 1949? One big change is that, since about the 1900s,
the Western-style product has become more dominant in fiction than
in art. The traditional Chinese-style novels were still being written
and read: the historical, the detective, the "Robin Hood," the supernatural, the romantic, and the mixed forms. But it is of note that a
most important recent book on "modern Chinese fiction" deals exclusively with the Western-style Chinese novelists from Lu Hsün to
Eileen Chang, but entirely ignores, with some justification, modern
writers of traditional works such as Chang Hen-sui or P'ing Chiang
Pu Hsiao Sheng (pen name).[26] In these Western-style Chinese novels
the themes of individual struggle and the technique of first person
narrative have become prominent. However, with few exceptions,
notably Shen Ch'ung-wen, the modern Chinese novelists' chief concern has been the hypocrisy, decadence, cruelty, or oppressiveness of
traditional Chinese life, or the failure of the Republican Revolution.

The True Story of Ah Q[27] by Lu Hsün, one of the few modern Chinese stories to have attained an international reputation, is a good
example. Ah Q, the hero, is among the very poor in a village and
embodies all the characteristics of a Chinese national malady. His
time was about the end of the Ch'ing dynasty when China was suffering from one humiliating defeat after another at the hands of powerful foreign nations. Ah Q deceives himself about having gained
"spiritual victory" when he is bullied (which is often) and loses no
time in bullying those weaker than himself. He gets into the company of a gang of city thieves and becomes their fence for stolen
goods in the village. While doing this he brags about the anti-
Manchu revolution (of which he heard rumors) as though he were
personally a part of it. By this means he intimidates the village gentry and others who mistreated him before. However, the revolutionary forces that finally come to the village refuse to accept him as a
comrade. Instead they ally themselves with the village gentry and execute him for his alleged role in a robbery. During the trial the bewildered Ah Q can only profess his vague envy for the revolutionar-

ies. On the way to the execution ground he imitates a defiant shout like a traditional doomed convict for the benefit of the watching crowd because he feels this is expected of him.

Other modern Chinese novelists before 1949 said more about love or sex than did Lu Hsün in *The True Story of Ah Q.* But except for a few like Shen Ch'ung-wen they were preoccupied with the ills of the larger social and political situation. Even the works of Shen Ch'ung-wen, who is regarded as "the greatest impressionist in modern Chinese literature,"[28] exhibit, at one extreme, the need for "abiding by the wisdom of the earth and enjoying a realistic sense of contentment which redeems . . . [a man's] animal existence" and, at the other extreme, "a feeling of quietness, a mood of poignant sadness completely objectified in the helplessness of all the characters in their automatic motions of work and play, in the small talk which fails to dispel gloom, and especially in the contrasting views of the dingy house and the loveliness of spring outside."[29] This is not to say that there is no variation among noted modern Chinese novelists. Mao Tun is distinguished for his gallery of heroines and his psychological drama, while Lao She, who is best known to Western readers through his *Rickshaw Boy,*[30] eschews romance and devotes most of his literary energy to men and their actions. Pa Chin is especially famous for his massive *The Love Trilogy* (1936) and *The Torrent: A Trilogy* (in three separate books: *Family* 1933; *Spring* 1938; and *Autumn* 1940). He believes that the social system alone is to blame for the ills of the larger social and political situation. Chang T'ien-i is primarily a master of short stories and of satire. But he exercises his satiric skill on all individuals regardless of class: their tensions, snobberies, struggles, insults, and injuries. Eileen Chang[31] is a young author of *Romances,* unique for her "astonishing combination—a Chaucerian gusto for life and all its little enjoyments plus an adult and tragic awareness of the human condition."[32] But Ch'ien Chung-shu is "a stylist of unusual distinction"[33] and perhaps makes more use of symbolism than most other Chinese writers. Furthermore, instead of using satire as "a mode of protest against the evils of society," as is common in modern Chinese literature, "Ch'ien turns the tables on the writers and exhibits them as one of the major components of social and cultural decadence."[34]

Yet when all this is granted, three basic features mark most or all of the better modern Chinese fiction.

The first is the "inability" of the characters "to find in the purely erotic sphere any meaning as personal assertion or of self-indulgence." Ai-li S. Chin, who makes this observation, is speaking of three categories of modern Chinese short stories in her study sample: those between 1915 and 1949, those in Taiwan, and those on the mainland between 1962 and 1966. In the first group "romantic" love loses some of the romance as it is fitted into the lives of a generation intent on remaking society. Taiwan examples are marked by "intensity of negative feelings between father and son" but not by "the kind of emotional intensity which means positive individual satisfaction or personal indulgence." As for the Communist stories, "the underplaying of private emotions in the boy-girl and husband-wife relationship is obvious," and Chin concludes, "The Chinese self therefore has had his center of gravity more exclusively in social relations and less solidly in himself."[35]

A second basic feature of modern Chinese fiction is the tendency to scrutinize the ills of contemporary Chinese life, with strong emphasis on external realism but little interest in exploring the mind. Hsia, from whom we have drawn heavily in this discussion on modern Chinese fiction, characterizes this condition as "psychological poverty" and observes,

> In view of the absence of tragedy in traditional Chinese drama and of the strong satiric tradition in Ming and Ch'ing fiction (the distinguished exception is the tragic novel, *Dream of the Red Chamber*), one may legitimately wonder whether the study of Western literature has in any significant manner enriched the spiritual life of the Chinese.[36]

The third basic feature common to modern Chinese fiction is the nearly complete absence (with rare exceptions) of any influence from the Western symbolist movement. Except for Eileen Chang, nearly all the noted writers of modern Chinese fiction before 1949 were already involved in or sympathetic with the Communist movement in China. Most of them have been more or less active since then. The major change after 1949 has been the increasingly "rigid organization of writers into arbitrary regional units" and "the imposition upon them of harsh discipline almost immediately afterwards."[37]

According to some students, the literary products in China suffered both qualitatively and quantitatively even before the purges accompanying the Cultural Revolution wrecked the literary careers of some of the writers. Only recently (1979) have some of the writers who suffered from purges, such as Chou Yang (still living), Teng T'uo and Chang Wen T'ien (both already dead), had their position or honor restored.

The final basic feature of post-1949 Chinese fiction is the lack of concern with attachment or problems between the sexes. Romance seems even rarer than in the major traditional novels. So far I have seen none where it is not left to the faintest suggestion. With the fall of the Gang of Four and a new but limited policy of liberalization, sex may again take its proper place in literature in Chinese terms.

Whatever the future portends, it is clear that these new developments have not changed the basic common features of Chinese fiction outlined here. Under the new regime there will not be merely greater emphasis on depiction of external ills of contemporary Chinese life but on a uniform direction of their solution; not merely little interest in the individual mind, but stronger pressure for all minds to dwell on similar thoughts. The main difference between the purgers and the purged in the Cultural Revolution is not in the basic direction of Chinese fiction but in who has deviated from it and how deviously. In this framework the Western symbolist movement becomes even less relevant than before.

Hsia's explanation of the Chinese lack of interest in psyche and in Western symbolism leaves much to be desired. He is on sound grounds when he points out that ". . . in appropriating the Western tradition, it is only to be expected that Chinese writers should accept and make use of what they find most congenial and meaningful."[38] This principle is valid for all societies and cultures, including those of Americans and of Chinese. But he errs in believing it to be due to Chinese rejection of traditional religions in favor of nineteenth-century absolutes of democracy, science, and liberalism. The Chinese have never been interested in the deeper workings of the mind even when traditional religions were in full swing, as we shall see in Chapters 9 and 10. Hsia also errs in equating Confucian rationalism with Western rationalism, thereby alleging that, since traditional religions no longer "kept Confucian rationalism in check," Confucian rationalism precluded any possibility of Chinese interest in symbolist movement. There is no historical indication of Chinese interest in symbolist movement in the first place.

Religious creeds or scientific philosophies or political isms, no less than art and fiction, cannot as such cause the interest (or its lack) in mind exploration or symobolism in American fiction or modern Chinese fiction. Such creeds or philosophies or isms are subject to patterning by the approach to life of whatever people originate or receive them. They, too, will be accepted or magnified or rejected or modified by different societies and cultures depending on their congeniality and meaningfulness. The particular Chinese situation-centered approach to life makes particular patterns of art congenial and meaningful to a majority of the Chinese. These patterns emphasize external realism, not exploration of the mind; and the place of the individual in the environment, not the struggle against it. Similarly, in the particular Western (including American) individual-centered approach to life, the objectives tend to involve emotions, the seeking of the original and the unseen or unseeable, and the struggle of the individual to assert and find himself by way of anti-orthodoxy and proliferation of new trends. This focus on individualism occurs not merely in art and fiction, but also in business, religion, and political and social behavior.

NOTES

1. In *A History of American Art,* Daniel M. Mendelowitz mentions more trends: geometric abstractionism, symbolic abstract expressionism, minimal painters, the historical painters, the romantic allegorists, the genre painters, the mystics, the impressionists, the synchronists, the cubist-futurists, the social commentators, contemporary realism, contemporary expressionism.

2. Ibid., pp. 316–317.

3. Ibid., p. 454.

4. Kenneth Clark, "The Blot and the Diagram," *Encounter,* January 1963.

5. Edward Alden Jewell, *Have We An American Art?* pp. 151, 155–156.

6. Franz Schulze, "Scotch Broth, Chicago Chrome," *Chicago Sun-Times,* October 14, 1967.

7. *Peasant Paintings from Huhsien County of the People's Republic of China,* (pamphlet distributed at the exhibition by U.S.–China People's Friendship Association).

8. *Five Chinese Painters,* Fifth Moon Exhibition, Taipei, 1970.

9. These remarks pertain to the part of the volume designated "Invited Exhibits," but they are equally valid to the other two parts (those judged to be "Excellent" and all the rest of the works exhibited).

10. In this discussion we shall confine ourselves chiefly to novels of American origin except where noted.

11. Chan Ts'ao, translated by C. C. Wang.

12. Nai-an Shih, translated by Pearl S. Buck.

13. Ch'eng-en Wu, partially translated by Helen M. Hayes in *The Buddhist Pilgrim's Progress;* and by Arthur Waley in *Monkey* (New York, 1943).

14. *Western Journey* and *Tale of the Mirrored Flower* are Chinese fantasies comparable to *Alice in Wonderland* or *Gulliver's Travels.*

15. Fragmentary translations into English and Portuguese of *The Story of an Ideal Marriage* were first brought back to England in 1719. These were edited as *Hao Kiu Chuan* or *The Fortunate Union* by Thomas Percy and published in 1761. *The Strange Romance of the Beautiful Pair* was first translated into French in 1826, and later into English and Dutch. It was widely read and admired in Europe. (Shou-yi Ch'en, *Chinese Literature: A Historical Introduction,* pp. 493–497.) Ch'en's brilliant book provides more detailed synopses for most of the Chinese novels mentioned in our discussion. He suggests that the two romances were widely appreciated in the West because "there is usually a sufficient portrayal of the social usages and mores of the Chinese people to make a novel of this category interesting to foreign readers (Ibid., p. 494). Our interpretation of their popularity in the West obviously differs from Ch'en's

and is further supported by the fact that other novels such as *The Golden Lotus* or *All Men Are Brothers,* which also contain much "portrayal of the social usages and mores of the Chinese people," were not introduced into the West till much later and even then they never commanded as much attention. The reason for this differing treatment, I suspect, is that *The Golden Lotus* deals with physical sex too blatantly while *All Men Are Brothers* practically does not deal with love at all. Both are, consequently, less acceptable.

16. *The Romance of the Three Kingdoms* by Lo Kuan-chung was partially translated by C. H. Brewitt-Taylor. There are two translations of *Chin Ping Mei,* one being *The Golden Lotus* by Clement Edgerton in four volumes. An English translation by Bernard Miall, from an abridged version in German by Franz Kuhn, was published under the title *The Plum of the Golden Vase,* with an introduction by Arthur Waley (London, 1939). *Western Chamber* was also translated twice: Henry H. Hart (Stanford 1936), and S. I. Hsuing (London, 1936). *Strange Stories* was translated in part by Herbert A. Giles (Shanghai, 1908 and 1916), and also in part by Rose Quong, under the title *Chinese Ghost and Love Stories* (New York, 1946).

17. Those authors generally considered by university professors and other intellectuals to be of high literary merit and significance and which are the subject of classes in American literature—Hawthorne, Melville, Mark Twain, Faulkner, Hemingway, Nathanael West, Norman Mailer, James Baldwin, John Barth, Saul Bellow, etc.—do not necessarily conform to this pattern.

18. The hundreds of paperbacks found in newsstands, air terminals, train stations, and other bookstalls, in spite of their inflammatory titles and their often livid covers featuring nearly nude men and women, follow the same pattern. The relatively hesitant writers will leave a man and a woman at the chamber door. The bolder ones will step as far as the bed. But the Chinese authors who deal with this matter go relentlessly forward from that point where many of their Western brethren take leave of the scene.

19. Robert Grover, *The One Hundred Dollar Misunderstanding,* pp. 35, 45.

20. In the translation of *The Golden Lotus* by Clement Edgerton, all pornographic passages from their Chinese original are rendered in Latin, as in the paragraphs quoted below. The explanation for this is given by the translator in his introduction to the book. Referring to the novel's Chinese author, he said, "If he had been an English writer, he would have avoided some subjects completely, skated over thin ice, and wrapped up certain episodes in a mist of words. This he does not do. He allows himself no reticences. Whatever he has to say, he says in the plainest of language. This, of course, frequently is acutely embarrassing for the translator. . . . But it could not all go into English, and the reader will therefore be exasperated to find occasional long passages in Latin. I am sorry about this, but there was nothing else to do."

21. Such ways of pleasure-seeking came to me as a surprise because they are totally absent in Chinese pornography, either in pictures or in words. Status differences between a man and his prostitute as well as the latter's boyfriend would prevent them. In fact until I read *My Secret Life* such possibilities never occurred to me. It matches in sexual monotony any modern day X-rated movie playing in adult theatres. But it has no other content, such as a plot.

22. Frank Harris, *My Life and Loves,* pp. 1–2.

23. Lloyd Watson in *San Francisco Chronicle,* September 25, 1979.

24. Since 1949 the Peking authorities have consciously utilized a variety of mass media such as radio as well as group discussions, public confessions, operas, and newspapers for the dissemination and arousal of public enthusiasm for Maoist ideology and national goals. The many "anti-" movements, the Great Leap, and the now regrettable Cultural Revolution were for the same purpose. See Godwin C.

Chu, *Radical Change Through Communication in Mao's China;* and Godwin C. Chu, ed., *Popular Media in China: Shaping New Cultural Patterns.* Also see Chapter 15, "China under Communism." Under the power of the Gang of Four the traditional media were suppressed. For example, the entire traditional repertoire of the Peking opera was banned. After the fall of the Gang most of the traditional media have been revived, some with modification of the themes. In the meantime the literacy rate has risen from something less than 10 percent of the population in 1949 to about 75 plus percent in 1979.

25. Ch'en, *Chinese Literature: A Historical Survey,* pp. 467–497.

26. Chih-ts'ing Hsia, *A History of Modern Chinese Fiction.*

27. Lu Hsün, *Ah Q Cheng Chuan (The True Story of Ah Q),* translated by Wang Chi-chen, in *Ah Q and Others.*

28. Hsia, *History of Modern Chinese Fiction,* p. 208.

29. Ibid., pp. 201, 210.

30. *Luo-tuo Hsiang-tzu,* translated by Evan King as *Rickshaw Boy.*

31. Two of her novels have been translated by herself into English: *The Rice-Sprout Song* and *Naked Earth.*

32. Hsia, *History of Modern Chinese Fiction,* pp. 392–393.

33. Ibid., p. 459.

34. Ibid., p. 434.

35. Chin, Ai-li S., *Modern Chinese Fiction and Family Relations,* p. 88.

36. Hsia, *History of Modern Chinese Fiction,* p. 504.

37. Ibid., p. 470.

38. Ibid., p. 504.

CHAPTER 2

The Sexes

Romance

The contrasts in the art and fiction popular among the two peoples reflect their actual patterns of life. Americans "fall" in love without, in theory at least, rhyme or reason. One is at once "mad" or "crazy" about the other and both parties are pleasantly doomed. Their overt conduct makes no secret of their mutual affection. When two American lovers appear in public with their arms around one another, the rest of the world is excluded, if not ignored.

In the name of love, judges have refused to dissolve a marriage between underage youngsters which had been contracted against the wishes of their parents. Because of love, a school board retracted its decision to dismiss a teacher for romantic attachment with one of his pupils.

These attitudes and decisions are not surprising in a culture in which individual predilections are accorded the highest value and emotionality is given more and more of a free hand. Of all individual predilections and emotions, what could be more important than those connected with love for a member of the opposite sex?

In China the term "love," as it is used by Americans, has never been respectable. Up to modern times, the term rarely occurs in Chinese literature.

The Chinese term *lien ai* or romantic love is strictly a modern linguistic creation reflecting the need of an expression for its Western equivalent. The same is true of the term *ai jen* or lover. Before Western contact its Chinese equivalent was *ch'ing jen,* literally person of my feeling, or *yi chung jen,* person of my mind. In classical Chinese literature the two words *lien* and *ai* appeared separately, each meaning love or affection or attachment, not between a man and a woman but as corollaries to the concept of loyalty (emperor-subject) or of filial piety. Understandably, so far the Peking government has not succeeded too well in its call for husbands and wives to refer to each other as *ai jen*. Most Chinese we met in and outside the People's Republic, even the politically advanced cadres, are somewhat embarrassed, or at least hesitant, to use the term in this way.

This is not to say that Chinese culture denied or ignored the existence of sexual attraction—quite the contrary. But the American way of love would seem to the Chinese to be almost indistinguishable from what they term licentiousness. Since ancient times the Chinese emphasis in regard to man-woman relations has been that of procreation, and marriage is still referred to colloquially as taking a daughter-in-law for the parents of the husband.[1] For centuries Chinese have justified concubinage either on the ground that the husband's aged parents need help around the house, or, if the wife has not given birth to a son, because the family line must be continued. For centuries they have considered parental arrangement in betrothal and marriage to be part of the order of nature. For centuries Chinese lovers have avoided all public showing of affection, and they have not exhibited, either in public or in private, the familiar signs of love so common in the West.

In fact, when a man said that he loved a girl, the statement usually carried the implication that something irregular was afoot. If a woman told anyone that she loved some man, it would be tantamount to her downfall. This is probably why the word *ai* was used to describe the feeling of lovers in a few novels; in the vernacular it usually implied an illicit relationship.

These Chinese manners are the natural expression of a way of life in which individual feelings must be subordinated to the requirements of the group; sex and all activities associated with it must be restricted to the compartments of life in which it is socially appropriate.

To an American in love, his emotions tend to overshadow everything else, at least for the time being. To a Chinese in love, his love occupies a place among other considerations, especially his obligations to his parents. An American asks, "How does my heart feel?" A Chinese asks, "What will other people say?" Romantic love is such an important ideal in America that when a woman marries a man for support she rarely dares to admit it even to her family or her closest friends. But an age-old Chinese adage says of a woman's marriage:

She'll go, she'll go;
For meals, for clothes.

This contrast, although based on the patterns of old China, also applies to educated modern Chinese in the cities.

The idea of romantic love, it should be pointed out, did not originate in America or even in northern Europe; but a few centuries after it was given currency by the troubadours who flourished in southern France, northern Italy, and Spain between the eleventh and thirteenth centuries, it took deep root in all the West. Today romantic love is undoubtedly one of the most potent of those values that fires the imagination of American men and women. There is no mystery about this. Romantic love, with its emphasis on chance attachment, exclusive possession of the loved object, and complete ecstasy, is as much in harmony with the American individual-centered approach to life as it is discordant with the Chinese situation-centered orientation.

Accordingly, when the idea of romantic love reached China, it did not deeply affect the relations of Chinese young men and women. The letters to various American "Dear Abbys," no less than those to their counterparts in China, are interesting barometers of this contrast.

Americans write because they are troubled by difficulties with their boy- or girl-friends, husbands or wives, parents or children. A husband wants to know why his wife is so hard to please; a woman wants to know what she can do to keep her husband sexually interested in her after twenty years of marriage; a mother wants to know why, after she has done everything to make her daughter's friends feel at home, the girl refuses to bring her boyfriends to the house. Americans also write because of problems of personal popularity, especially with members of the opposite sex.

From the Chinese point of view, Americans write about extremely trivial matters. For example, one husband complained that his wife served his dinner "on a plate the dog had used the night before." When he objected, she told him not to be "silly, that the dish was thoroughly scalded." Another woman wanted to know whose job it was to take out the garbage, the man's or the woman's.

The Chinese letters[2] are colorful, but most of them deal with issues that are at once elementary and weighty, such as how to marry the desired man or woman. Not one of them alludes to the intimate emotional problems of adjustment between the sexes (or between parents and children in connection with sex) characteristic of American correspondences. Here are a few examples: a husband who received the consent of his parents and his barren wife to marry her younger sister was worried about the legal and financial complications; a man wondered if he could sue his fiancée's family because she married someone else on the pretext that he himself did not do well in the years following their childhood betrothal; a youth expressed dissatisfaction with his parentally arranged adolescent marriage and asked how he could get rid of the village wife to marry a city girl; a woman wanted to know how to silence a husband whom she left in favor of another male because the first husband married her by a ruse and because she subsequently found him to be a dope addict; a lover was at a loss as to what to do about his sweetheart who joined the ranks of the Communists and refused to come back to him.

The following Chinese letter is typical of the many that express anxiety about parental or other forms of interference with freedom of choice in marriage. Note that the letter is addressed to a male for, significantly, Chinese counselors are usually not females.

Dear Mr. ——:
The wheel of time marches on. Circumstances change continuously. I, too, am one of those who is looking for a way out. Sir, I am a seventeen-year-old school girl. Two years ago I made a friend of the opposite sex. In age and education he is equal to me. We saw each other frequently during the last two years. While our impressions of each other deepened, we remained on the level of platonic friendship. We never talked about the word love when we saw each other, therefore I trust him deeply and respect him very much. This last summer he proposed to me. I said yes. When I returned home I told my parents about it. Now my father is a conservative man; he absolutely refused. I have been living in a sea of bitterness for the last months.

Recently this man wrote me a letter in which he said, "You ought to break with this conservative family. For our future happiness you ought to be courageous and not weaken." Then this man walked back and forth in front of our house. When he saw me, he asked me to write an essay on "The Story of My Struggle." But who can understand? Physically my father is very weak, he is also bothered by high blood pressure. My reverend one cannot stand a big shock. I told this man about it, but he is not sympathetic toward this view. He comes around daily and gives me no peace.

I cannot think of any way out. I know of one way that will solve all the problems, which is suicide. Although I know that suicide is the road of the weak, I think I am a weak one. Sir, what do you think of this as a way out? If I do so, will that not be bad for the name of the family? If I do so, what will he do? Kindly point out to me a road bright and clear. If you can do that, my gratitude to you will last forever.

(Signed)——

The newspaper consultant replied as follows:

Dear ——:

Man is not a plant. He has emotions. Emotion has no limit. Young men and women too youthful in their outlook are usually troubled by emotions. However, when you talk about marriage as soon as your emotions are aroused, you are likely to run into many dangers.

If you really consider the matter rationally, you should realize that although your two hearts agree with one another and your emotions are deep, you do not have to marry right away so as to complicate matters. Marriage ought to be determined, of course, by the two partners concerned, but when you consider your unsatisfactory family environment and the high blood pressure of your father, you ought to take it easy in order to avoid a possible tragedy. Your thought that suicide will end all comes from over-narrow-mindedness, for which you will be adversely criticized by society.

My practical advice now is that, if you really love each other, and if you have both made up your mind on your common objective, you will do best by being engaged to each other secretly just between yourselves. After a period of time you can then ask someone to talk the matter over with your parents. You will find that then it will only be a matter of form, that the storm will die and the tides will ebb and all problems will be solved. I hope you will follow this advice and do not think of suicide.

Both letters speak the same language. The interesting point is not that the parents were a stumbling block to the girl's marital designs, a situation not uncommon in the United States, but the cool way in which she reacted to the situation and the very conservative nature of her counselor's advice. To Americans, the girl would seem to lack the determination of a woman in love. For even when she was thinking of suicide, she was still worried about the family name. And the counselor, although admitting the importance of romantic attachment, told her to wait patiently and indefinitely until the situation improved.

Some may say that much of the Chinese counselor's advice to the young girl might also be given by an American. But the Chinese counselor's advice was not typically Chinese, particularly in regard to his stand on the desirablity of individual choice in marriage. Throughout the newspapers surveyed, there were scores of other replies that maintained that the affections between a boy and his girl ran second not only to parental wishes, but also to the opinion of sisters and in-laws, and even to the demands of work and education.

Some may also wonder why the girl who worried about her father's high blood pressure was advised that "after a period of time you can then ask someone to talk the matter over with your parents." The idea that a girl should negotiate with her father through a third party (especially if the person suggested is not even a close relative) may seem ludicrous to Americans. But the situation-centered approach to life not only elevates parental reaction above personal feelings, it also makes direct individual-to-individual discussions on vital matters less satisfactory than those conducted through an intermediary. Since Chinese culture does not encourage strong expressions of personal feelings, discussion through an intermediary will reduce the need for direct, emotional responses. This Chinese desire to convert person-to-person matters into a broader group affair runs through all aspects of Chinese life.

Furthermore, the presence of an intermediary, especially if the latter is in a position of some strength (for example, social prominence), may strongly influence the outcome. The greater the superiority of the intermediary over the party to be persuaded, the greater the chances of success for the party who hopes to benefit from the persuasion. It is not at all uncommon, even among the college educated, for a boy, hoping to win over a girl who does not appear to be interested in him, to invoke the services of his or her professors for this purpose.

Besides, given the situation-centered approach, the superiority of the intermediary may also give the seemingly reluctant party the opportunity of accepting an outcome which he or she desired in the first place but was too timid to do anything about for himself. The following story related by a man in Taiwan illustrates that Chinese females are no less artful than the men in the use of superior intermediaries.

It was during the days of Nationalist-Communist conflict. As a young medic in the Nationalist army, J. set up temporary camp with his battalion in a village home one day. The moaning of the young daughter of the house kept the battalion commander awake all night. Upon inquiry the next morning, he learned that the young lady was suffering from an ulcerated growth, and thereupon he ordered J.,

the medic, to treat her. The mother of the girl declined the help because, she whispered, "The trouble is on her buttocks." The battalion commander overruled her objections, and J. successfully operated on the patient.

Twenty days later when the army detachment was getting ready to
leave the locality, mother and daughter came forward to say good-by
and express their gratitude, and J. saw that his former patient was
indeed beautiful. But they left in a hurry. While traveling, the battalion commander told J. that the mother offered his former patient to
him in marriage. According to their village customs, the mother told
the battalion commander, a maiden could not with honor remove
even her shoes and stockings in front of any male. Since in the
present instance the girl had exposed much more of herself than that
to J., she had no alternative but to marry him. Three months later,
battle exigencies led J. to another part of the country; his battalion
was stationed in a small city where he found his former patient, accompanied by her older brother, awaiting them. The commander,
having promised in advance to convince J., and having made some
suitable preparation for their wedding, now simply "ordered" J. to
marry her.

Twenty years later, in 1965, this man happily recounted the past
while preparing to send his eldest daughter to college.[3]

The idea that work and education should have priority over personal happiness shows itself to be more pervasive than even those familiar with Chinese patterns might think possible. For example, one
young lady, in a letter to the editor of a Peking paper, bemoaned her
misfortune in a piece entitled "Fellow Sisters, Beware of Men." She
was nineteen years old and in her last year of high school.[4] Her tale
of woe was this: She was introduced at a ball to a handsome, young,
college-educated army officer. Thereafter the two of them made the
rounds of the city. However, when sometime later she hinted at marriage, he made no response at all. Shortly afterward he stopped seeing her altogether. As a result she felt badly cheated—"everybody
laughed at me"—and she advised her female readers to beware of
such irresponsible wolves.

We see here an illustration of a fundamental pattern of thinking,
although the writer of this letter, being an urbanite, was less traditional than the village mother who thought her daughter could not
marry anyone except the army medic. The high school girl felt that
the attraction between her and the boy should have been a prelude to
marriage. We shall return to this point later. But here we must note

the extraordinary number of letters the paper received in response. These came from students and the general public, but the basic uniformity of their orientation was surprising. Some sympathized with her; some accused her of vanity and of forgetting that boyfriends are not for high school girls. Some said she had no business going out dancing when "only nineteen." Some defended army officers in general, even though they conceded that this particular one had been inconsiderate. But none of them questioned her right to expect marriage and all of them reiterated the theme: now that you have learned your lesson, be rational, give up pleasures, and concentrate on your studies. The consensus was that her goal should be to finish high school with flying colors, enter college, and work toward a great career. Some literally asked her to repent.

The American public would have responded very differently. Some Americans might say, "What can she expect!" if they thought she and her boyfriend were separated by wide socio-economic distances. But most would have regarded her as overdramatizing something that happens all the time. After all, a girl is not expected to marry the first man she meets. To Americans, dating is increasingly becoming a game of sex. The contest has few rules, but its course is determined in the main by personal ingenuity. It can occur between any man and any woman; it may take place anywhere; and it does not have to be anything serious.

Television commercials reflect and abet this tendency with full force. We see the undulating female rear designed to inspire its male viewers to buy tickets for some exotic island resort, or kisses that come to a girl as a result of using a certain toothpaste or mouthwash.

In fact, sex as a game seems to have achieved some currency at parties among married Americans, as suggested by the following letter to a newspaper:

Dear Ann Landers: I have always said your column does more harm than good. Now I have proof. Remember the woman who complained about the games that were being played in her social group? Someone had suggested that they play kids' kissing games just for the fun of it and then they graduated to more adult kissing games like, "Who have I Got?"

She described "Who Have I Got?" as a game played under a bed. The fellow is under the bed, blindfolded, and the girl crawls under the bed with him and kisses him. He is supposed to guess who she is.

Well, nobody in OUR crowd had ever heard of the game until they read about it in your column. Now it's all the rage. And my crazy husband is just wild about it. I wonder how many OTHER suburban parties have been pepped up by this new game Ann Landers has taught them? Would you like to hazard a guess?[5]

The extent to which letters to newspapers can reveal actuality is, of course, conjectural. But when such letters point in the same direction as other evidence, we probably can consider them seriously.[6]

This is in sharp contrast with the situation in Taiwan, where a college coed who goes out with different boys is usually branded as immoral though her American counterpart in similar circumstances will be considered popular and lucky. A distinguished visitor to the United States from Taiwan succinctly describes in his travel notes the American dating pattern as follows: "Superficially they [American girls] seem to be emancipated and equal with men. In reality, they have become objects of public recreation."[7]

The Chinese and American differences are no less striking when we consider the conduct of men and women who are already close friends, or who are engaged. Chinese girls and their boyfriends go to entertainment events together. They roam the fields, climb mountains, or attend ball games together. Some lovers even go so far as to hold hands in public. But they never indulge in other open expressions of intimacy. They consider praising the other before a third party in bad taste. No matter how much time they spend together, or how late it is in the evening, they rarely warm up to each other to the extent of forgetting themselves. Nor are these ways restricted to their public conduct. Their behavior away from the crowd seems likewise restrained. It is not uncommon to find today in Taiwan college men and women who did not go beyond handholding before engagement. I have even known educated men and women, now married with children, who did no more than see each other from a distance and exchange a few letters before they tied the marital knot.

It is in this social context that we can understand the contrasting Chinese and American reactions to the following episode. In 1943, when China was still at war with Japan, a college graduate in the then Free China set his heart on a young lady who did not care for him. Presently she fell ill and entered a hospital. During one of his visits an air raid alarm was sounded. Trying to make her feel better, he said, "Never mind it. If a bomb falls, we shall die together." The girl replied curtly, "Not I. I am not going to die with you!"[8]

It must not be supposed that all Chinese girls would have replied in precisely this fashion, but whenever my Chinese students and friends hear about the incident related above, their reaction is one of amusement at the naïveté of the boy, while the corresponding reaction of my American students and friends is one of shock and amazement at the rudeness of the girl. An American girl in similar circumstances would nonetheless have appreciated his romantic gesture and responded more gently than this. But to the Chinese girl who relegates sex to a specific compartment of her life, the young man's sentiments were unacceptable since she was not in love with him.

The conduct between Chinese males and females who have found mutual love seems equally aloof. This can be illustrated by a love song popular in Taiwan and Hong Kong during the late fifties. The hero has to go away and his sweetheart is accompanying him an extra mile to soften the mutual despair. The final dialogue in the song consists of the following:

> Woman: "My heart aches for you so much, I am willing to share with you the same pillow and sheet."
> Man: "A gentleman is known by his morals, how dare he indulge in private feelings?"

This aloofness is not even uncommon among Chinese students studying in the United States. In a midwestern city two Chinese students were engaged to be married. From time to time the young man wrote short letters to his girl to express his affections. In one of them he quoted some lines from a famous Chinese poem which read:

> As tree limbs entwine on the meadow;
> As birds wing together in the blue;
> So let us be.

However, instead of quoting the lines correctly, he made the mistake of putting the birds on the meadow and the tree limbs in the blue. The young lady amused herself by telling many of their mutual Chinese friends about his error. For some time afterward the friends chided him with the question as to whether it was not really chickens on the meadow instead of birds that he and his sweetheart wished to be.[9]

An American boy might have considered her behavior unforgivable, just as an American girl would have found the hero's response in the song to his sweetheart most unromantic. But once a Chinese couple is engaged, the lovers tend to take each other for granted since they are part of each other in a new relationship. After marriage, when the situation is even more definite, this pattern is more marked. And the Chinese hero in the song is not less attractive in Chinese eyes because of his response. For even if he would enjoy what she suggested, would he not gain stature by being mindful of propriety?

In the Chinese pattern of thinking, attraction between a man and a woman, outside of prostitution, should invariably be a prelude to marriage. Therefore Chinese girls who date, and especially those who become intimate with many boys, are considered to be merely practicing self-degradation, while American girls can justify sex relations within or without marriage by invoking love.

The Chinese approach to a man-woman relationship is a straight line. Sex relations (and for moderns, love) leads to marriage, which leads to children. The American approach tends to be in a straight line where love and sex are concerned; the latter must be linked with the former to be respectable, whether the couple begins with one or the other. But the roads to marriage and to children are not in that straight line because love and sex relations are not necessarily bound up with them.

For these reasons the conduct of unattached Chinese men and women toward each other must look tame to American eyes, just as American behavior in the same situation often appears careless and even lewd to the Chinese observer. The Chinese do not make a public display of sexual attraction because the requirements of the social situation tend to overshadow individual enjoyment. The latter must not, therefore, overflow its social boundaries; instead it must be kept contained by the two parties concerned. The Americans are, on the other hand, encouraged to enjoy themselves because in their way of life sex is individualized; socially defined boundaries are secondary. Consequently, there tend to be few limits beyond which individuals in love cannot go to express their state of ecstasy in public.

Yet it cannot be said that Chinese youngsters fail or have failed to live up to the American pattern of romantic love simply because it is of Western origin. For over a century the Chinese intelligentsia have enthusiastically received Western ideologies and technical achievements. For over a century the modernized Chinese young men and women have been most insistent in their demand to be free of parental choice in marriage. For over a century Chinese students have been known to be far more radical in their political and social views than are their American counterparts. We can only conclude that Chinese and Americans have not taken to romantic love with equal relish because of the distinct differences in basic life orientations.

These differences are vividly apparent in many matters between the sexes. Social dancing is one example. We have seen how some Chinese correspondents rebuked a nineteen-year-old girl for engaging in ballroom dancing. This is not at all atypical. Social dancing permits a high degree of diffused but disguised bodily intimacy between men and women who otherwise are not allowed such contact. Throughout Chinese history, there has never been social dancing as Westerners understand the term.

Consequently, Western-type social dancing can seldom occur between persons other than lovers or married couples at home, or prostitutes and their customers in a brothel. Under these latter circumstances, dancing either assumes a greater sexual intimacy than in the West or serves as a preliminary to intercourse, but *is not an end in itself* as in America. At times social dancing was tolerated in some cities, only to be banned when a change of administration occurred, and many viewed it as a sign of the society's downfall. This is why even today in Taiwan, social dancing is still by and large restricted to non-Chinese. In fact, not too long ago (1966) a government order provided that one dance hall was allowed per 460 *foreign* residents in metropolitan Taipei, and one in each tourist area, such as Sun Moon Lake, Peito, etc. (as reported in the *Central Daily News,* 1966); this, despite the existence of legalized prostitution.

For the same reasons, Chinese society has never accepted other Western practices that permit a diffused intimacy between the sexes while barring intercourse. Nothing akin to bundling has ever been suggested, and necking has always been condemned as lewd behavior. In brief, the Chinese view is that if a man and woman are not permitted complete sexual intimacy, they should be allowed no intimacy whatsoever.

Women in a Man's World

Chinese and American attitudes toward men and women differ even in situations in which sexual attraction theoretically should have no importance. Many American women today share in the public life of the nation. A majority of them have gone to school with men, worked in the same offices with them, shared identical or similar interests with them, and have even fought them on broad social, political, and economic issues. American women can count among their ranks doctors, lawyers, high government officials, professors, industrial and commercial executives as well as laborers, police, clerks, and members of the armed services.

One hundred years after the Opium War only a small minority of Chinese women enjoyed comparable distinctions. They also could name among themselves workers in various professions and occupations, no less than crusaders against social evils deeply embedded in Chinese tradition, but these few women towered above the illiterate majority who either did not hear about the privileged ones or looked upon them with idle curiosity. Up to 1949 the idea of equality between the sexes was unknown to the majority, and few women ever became aware of the fact that since the Revolution of 1911 a series of new laws was promulgated guaranteeing them extensive rights. Women were fed, clothed, and taught to sew. They learned to blush and run away from any young man, and finally they were shut up in a red sedan chair bedecked with flowers and carried from the family of their birth to the family whose name they and their children would bear. And then the cycle began again, for they expected to manage their daughters in the same way.

Yet, curiously enough, even before 1949 the relatively few educated Chinese women seemed to take equality with men as a matter of course and to carry on their business with complete self-assurance. After a tour of the Orient in the late forties, Dr. Irene Taeuber of the Office of Population Research, Princeton University, stated that the Chinese women's poise is unequaled by the vast majority of American women, professional or otherwise.[10]

Dr. Taeuber is not alone in holding this opinion. Nearly ten years earlier Pearl Buck made substantially the same observation when she wrote:

> My first surprise came when I asked for the name of a good bank, preferably a bank managed by women. Friends of mine had used a women's bank in Shanghai and liked the way women there had handled investments. They found women astute, daring, and cautious together. But in my own country, I was told, there is not a bank owned and managed by women. When I asked why, I was told that no one would put money in such a bank. To this day I have not found the reason for this.[11]

The reason for this lack of confidence is, however, not so obscure. To begin with, it is connected with the fact that many American women who work outside the home feel defensive. This is one arc of a vicious circle, for the more defensive women feel, the less confidence men will have in them.

Why do educated American women who have had lengthy experience in a man's world feel more defensive than their educated Chinese sisters who have but recently obtained equality and are only a small minority? The answer again lies in the underlying psychological patterns of the two groups. In the American individual-centered pattern of thought, sex, being diffused, appears whenever men and women meet. The boundaries defining when sex does or does not apply are simply not clear. Sexual attraction occurs without reference to time, role, and place. In the Chinese pattern, sex, being relegated to particular areas of life, does not pervade every aspect of life. Therefore, the Chinese male will react very differently to a show girl and to a woman professor. In the same way, the Chinese female will view different males from the standpoint of their diverse stations in life.

To put it more plainly, for Americans, sex differences tend to overshadow situation. For Chinese, situation tends to overshadow sex. An American woman is always prepared to use her womanly charms whether her business is with a store clerk, her landlord, or her husband. She is likely to be pleased by any sign that her beauty is appreciated, whether the complimentary word or glance comes from a bus conductor, her pupils, or a business associate. Even a modern Chinese woman is sure to bring humiliation upon herself if she copies her American sisters in this respect. For in her culture, female charms and beauty are sexual matters, and should therefore be reserved for a woman's lover or husband, or at least for a man whom she might marry.[12]

On the other hand, the American woman is, in male eyes, never separated from the qualities of her sex, even if her work has no connection with them. She feels defensive because the male resents her intrusion into what he considers his world, and he is resentful because she brings with her the advantage of her sex in addition to her professional abilities.

The Chinese woman's sexual attractions belong to her husband or fiancé alone. She can safely invoke them only in the privacy of her marital situation. But for this very reason, once she has achieved a new occupational or professional status, the Chinese woman tends to be judged in male eyes by her ability and not by her sex. With sex confined to the specific areas of marriage or prostitution, working females have no need to be defensive when entering into traditionally male activities, and males have no cause to view them as transgressors. A socially desexed female is just as good as a socially desexed male.

Sex differences are deepened in America by the presence of a heritage of chivalry—a concept unknown in China—which accentuates the psychological distance between masculinity and femininity. The self-assurance of the working woman will grow in inverse proportion to the extent to which men are appreciated for their brains and muscles and women for their desire to be supported by and dependent upon men. This is why the pride of the American male often is injured by any suggestion of gainful employment for his wife, while no such worries ever trouble a Chinese, high or low. It also explains why the American woman has had to fight for her economic and political equality inch by inch, but her educated Chinese sister covered miles of the same territory practically without a struggle.

Romance and Communism

Since 1949, the sphere of sex equality has expanded enormously in the People's Republic. Chinese women are entering into the nation's economic, professional, and public life at an unprecedented rate. The changes are not yet evident at the highest levels of leadership, however. For example, there are as yet no female commanders of the People's Liberation Army. But more women are seen in more capacities than ever before in schools, factories, banks, stores, government and commune offices.

For nearly thirty years Chinese women wore formless clothes nearly identical with men's and used few if any cosmetics. These and other facts, such as the absence of night life and emphasis on hard work, led many Western visitors to the mistaken notion that the Chinese have adopted puritanism.

Nothing is further from the truth. Puritanism involves repression of sex, which is commensurate with the individual-centered approach to life. The new Chinese pattern is merely a more widespread and striking expression of the compartmentalization of sex, which is today, as in centuries past, still rooted in the situation-centered approach to the problems of existence.

The utmost expression of sex repression is the great importance given to the myth of the Virgin Birth in the West. That myth says that sex is essentially sinful and the holiest of all holy is its eradication as a matter of fact. But the psychology of the myth of the Virgin Birth is not unlike that underlining an old Chinese tale of a villager who came to a sudden windfall of three hundred pieces of silver. Wishing to keep them for a rainy day and in order to avoid theft he buried them in his backyard, since banks were unknown in the village. But still fearful of discovery by others, he put up a sign on the spot where he buried his new found treasure: "There are no three hundred silver pieces here."

Seen in this light it is not hard to imagine how repression of sex has more psychological affinity with preoccupation with it. Thus most Western visitors to the People's Republic have been inquisitive about how Chinese are doing without sex. One Austrian journalist opines that Chinese men and women do not appear to care for romance, since their clothes are ill-fitted, their hairstyles lack variety, and the women use little makeup. He quotes the response of the principal of a Peking high school to his inquiry: "Our young people grow up in the spirit of the Revolution and social progress, and they have no time for love or the problem of sex."[13] Barbara Tuchman parroted the same line: "I can say that any overt interest in sex was simply nonexistent. . . . When the subject came up in conversation with one female interpreter, it produced a grimace of disgust as if we had mentioned a cockroach, and the same expression contorted the face of a doctor of mental health when he was asked about perversions and homosexuality."[14] The most direct reply that I have come across is that of a Chinese girl to a Western visitor's question about living together without marriage. "Why?" she retorted. "Is it so hard to get married in America?"

Many Westerners undoubtedly regard such Chinese responses as new developments under communism. The truth is that had Mrs. Tuchman, for example, been in a position to raise the question of sex with any college coed before 1949, she would not have gotten a more welcome response than the one she received from her female interpreter in 1972. To the situation-centered Chinese, Communist or otherwise, Mrs. Tuchman's and other visitors' inquisitiveness about sex was simply out of order. Chinese tend far less than Americans to discuss their personal worries and problems with strangers, including sex. They are never free of the social framework which gives them their individual importance and they rarely if ever dream of going it alone. In contrast, Americans are most fearful of being tied down by divulging themselves to those whom they may or will have to see again; they feel no comparable risk when they talk to strangers.

The zealots of the revolution did not create a puritanism in China but merely accentuated the age-old situational approach to sex. Under that approach women were spoken of as being either of the "good family" *(liang chia fu nu)* variety or of the "wind and dust" *(feng ch'en)* type. The former were "virtuous wives and kind mothers" *(hsien ch'i liang mu)* whose preoccupation was the home and children. The latter included females of easy virtue, such as actresses, singers, and streetwalkers. "Exposing one's head and face" *(p'ao t'ou lu mien)* was a colloquial expression depicting the involuntary condition of a woman being forced by adverse circumstances to be seen often in public. It is a phrase often heard in Chinese operas and songs lamenting the misery of an unfortunate female.

"Good family" women in households of modest means did appear in public in south and southwest China more often than in north China. In the latter region women went to the fields to bring the midday meal to their fathers, husbands, brothers, but they usually did not work there. In the south farmers' wives and daughters worked side by side with their men. A common sight was waterwheels being moved by the feet of men, women, and adolescents together. In Yunnan Province of the southwest, women not only were regular farm workers but were traders in markets with men. They often carried merchandise more than ten or fifteen miles on their backs or at the two ends of a pole.

In public these working women dressed themselves in blue or in other subdued colors; many wore trousers. They did not sport fancy hairdos, and unlike the "wind and dust" type, they conducted themselves with decorum, attracting as little male attention as possible. They did all this, it should be noted, without the influence of communism.

Since the early twentieth century and after the advent of Western inspired schools and colleges, it was not uncommon to see "good family" females in public wearing "war paint." Dating of a sort existed on college campuses and elsewhere. But such activities were restricted to a fraction of the population and to the so-called treaty ports such as Tientsin, Shanghai, Peking, and Canton. Even in these cities, the dating conduct of Chinese youngsters was far less daring than that of their counterparts in America at comparable times and places. In the 1930s, the deans of missionary women's high schools used to censor all incoming mail as a matter of regulation. A girl student found guilty of corresponding with a male would be reprimanded or expelled.

All this was in accord with the Chinese situation-centered and compartmentalized way of life. The high school students' business was to concentrate on their studies. They were not considered mature enough even to have a look at romance. Even the dating activities of those in higher education were merely tolerated, a sideline. It was expected that such activities would be suspended when the social situation demanded it. My Western readers will find the following episode incredible, but it happens to be true.

After Japan occupied China's northeastern provinces (Manchuria) in 1931, student demonstrations broke out all over the country. Classes were cancelled and students took to the streets demanding government action to fight the invaders. At the University of Shanghai, where I was a junior at the time, a group more militant than the others decided, in conjunction with those at other institutions of higher learning, to go to the Nationalist government at Nanking to press Generalissimo Chiang Kai-shek to mobilize for active resistance to the Japanese. Chiang's response was to make no trains available to the demonstrators, and the demonstrators' response to Chiang's response was to lie down on the tracks of the Nanking–Shanghai Railway lines so that all traffic stopped.

What was most interesting in light of our discussion here is that while the petitioners were on the railroad tracks the college militants decreed that no parties and no dating should take place among the students remaining on campus, even though all classes were cancelled. The militants held that during the period of national emergency and suffering (kuo nan ch'i chien) all enjoyment and self-gratification should cease.[15]

The action of militants at our colleges and universities during the Japanese invasion recalls the traditional Chinese way of mourning. A Chinese son used to be required by custom and law to observe mourning for three years after the death of either of his parents. Filial duties required that he and his wife not wear fancy clothes, eat elegant dishes, go to festivities, or have any marital relations. If one of their children was previously scheduled to be married during that period, they must postpone it till afterwards. If he was an important official in the government, he must resign his post and stay home for the period. Some famous Chinese who were more filial than others were known to have built little grass huts next to their fathers' or mothers' graves and lived there for three years to keep the deceased company.

Is it then farfetched to suggest that the extremists in the Cultural

Revolution led by the Gang of Four were not unlike the militant students on the University of Shanghai campus in 1931–1932, and that both types of behavior had their psychological and cultural roots in the traditional Chinese way of expressing grief? I think not.

It would be untrue, however, to say that romance is absent in the People's Republic, or was even before the fall of the Gang of Four. On one July 1972 evening (about 9:00 P.M.), I counted some 175 couples, mostly in their twenties or thirties, within a two-block area on the riverside of the Shanghai Bund.[16] However, even though the street lights were darkened by the thick foliage of trees and some lovers held hands or had arms around each other's waists, none showed any more external sign of passion than that. Reflecting on my student days in that same city in the thirties, I judge that those young couples were doing as much (or as little) in the art of romance as those of us who attended the then missionary-run University of Shanghai did in comparable circumstances.

In broad daylight Chinese young people are, of course, even more subdued by American standards. My family and I saw hundreds of couples in the Temple of Heaven and Summer Palace grounds of Peking, the East Lake of Wuhan, and the Botanical Garden of Shenyang. We even saw one couple perched inside a lookout on the side of the Great Wall facing Mongolia. But none of them even held hands, which fact certainly would have given most Western visitors the wrong impression. But another fact may have misled some visitors in a different direction. In a review of pictures of street scenes taken during our 1972 tour we found many in which men were holding hands with each other, had arms around each other's necks—and women likewise—but in which no persons of the opposite sex did the same. A picture taken by my younger daughter, Penny, shows six separate young couples strolling leisurely in Peking's famous Wang Fu Ching Street. Of the six, five unisex couples held hands, but the only male-female couple did not.

Could this be why some Western visitors make inquiries about homosexuality? Probably. Given an individual-centered way of life with its diffused sexuality, any physical intimacy between persons of the same sex naturally suggests homosexuality. On the other hand, given a situation-centered way of life in which the social context is more important, no such fear prevents two males (or two females) from close physical contact.

Consequently, when we look closer at individual cases of romance since 1949 we find no great surprises. In 1962, a thirty-two-year-old woman in a north China village was telling Jan Myrdal what was new in revolutionary China regarding marital choice: "[Formerly] if my parents had decided to marry me off with a cur, then I had to be content with a cur. But now you are allowed to see your husband before you marry, and you can refuse to marry him if you don't like the looks of him."[17]

The contrast here is very much exaggerated, for even before parents would not have been so oblivious of their daughters' wishes. Furthermore, long before 1949 educated men and women, as we already noted, saw each other before marriage. When this same villager spelled out the desired qualities in a husband, they were not so romantic by Western standards, and the final decision as to whom to marry was not made by the individuals concerned after all:

> Girls attach great importance to behavior: she looks for one who is strong and healthy and able to work well. . . . The boy . . . must be even- not quick-tempered. Appearance is less important.
>
> When a boy considers a girl, the first thing he asks himself is: "Can she look after a home?" Next in importance is that she should be even-tempered. Appearance plays a certain part, but not a great one.
>
> The person with the most say in the matter of a girl's marriage is her grandmother, then her grandfather, then her mother; what her father thinks is of least importance. . . ."[18]

Had this picture changed a decade later when my family and I toured China in 1972? Not much, as the case of Comrade Tung of Shenyang reveals. Tung and his wife were married in 1957, but as he related the following to me in the summer of 1972 both of us saw his story as part of current affairs. They first met in 1949 when working in the same factory. Then Tung was assigned to work in the party-sponsored labor union. They did not begin what Tung described as a "special relationship" until 1955.

> While working in the labor union, I went back from time to time to visit my old friends in my old factory. Please understand, *I did not go to visit her at first* [emphasis his], I must reiterate. But by 1955 she became older. I went one Sunday to see her. Then the next Sunday she came to my dormitory to see me. It was then that I became a member of the Party. She did the same about the same time. In 1956 I was assigned away to serve as Secretary of Youth Corps of a factory in Peking. I was elected by my co-workers to that post. We corresponded. We saw each other during summer and winter vacations. Always I came back to Shen-

yang to see her except once when she went to Peking to see me. Through all that correspondence and visits we never promised marriage to each other, but "our hearts knew the score" [*hsin li ming pai*]. The subject of our letters and conversations? They were about our work, study sessions, the good and worthy things we separately saw, and so forth. Even then we two only "understood each other in our hearts but never announced in our words" [*hsin chao pu hsüan*]. We never said "I love you" or "Will you marry me?"

But when she came to see me in Peking in the winter of 1956, we toured the sights and took a picture together. That was serious, you know. We never said so, but it was clear. Three or four months before that, I told my parents. My wife's parents died early; she was brought up by her older sister in Dairen [south Manchuria]. So she told her.[19]

Comrade Tung and his wife were married in Shenyang in the fall of 1957 at a simple wedding in her factory, attended by his former colleagues and her friends and coworkers, about forty-five in all. Our inquiries and observations in 1972, from north to south, revealed that romance in Communist China was not really so different from that in Nationalist China. It is still slow moving, and it often involves relatives, friends, and coworkers to an extent that most Americans would resent as intrusion. Given this, the tendency on the part of the Communist government to encourage subordination of personal or parental wishes to broader responsibilities, as indicated by the following example held up for people to follow, does not represent such a giant departure from the past:

> Yi Shih-ch'uan postponed her marriage even three times and opposed all the feudal wishes of her old mother, who longed to have a grandson. She was a model textile worker and head of her work district: "Whenever there was a movement she and her group were in the front row." Finally, she ended up marrying a Party member.[20]

Privately we found individuals whose conduct did not measure up to such high standards just as there were unfilial sons and fallen daughters throughout Chinese history. A girl we know in Shanghai vowed never to marry anyone who was a Party cadre. She could not forget how badly her father suffered in the hands of zealots during one of the antimovements. A Party member in a commune near Peking married a woman whose father was from the "wrong" class background. He did so in spite of having been warned, and, as a result, lost his alternate Party membership.

Since the fall of the Gang of Four in 1978 waves of letters to the
editor have appeared in the *People's Daily*. According to the Chinese
government this paper received 1,500 letters from readers in September 1977 and 40,000 in June 1978. "The paper is receiving as
many letters in a day as it used to in a month, and the curve is still
rising."[21] Two scholars have observed that "What has emerged is almost a direct confrontation with the leadership."[22] None of these letters, however, asks questions about personal problems between lovers comparable to those in America or in pre-1949 China. One letter
by a factory worker comes closest to the question of romance. He
"wanted to smash the spiritual bondage imposed by the Gang of
Four so that young men and women will develop a correct attitude
toward love and marriage. Under the Gang . . . , the word 'love'
was taboo."[23]

A Multiple Murder Case

In the October 20, 1979 issue of the *People's Daily* there appeared an
investigative report of a most spectacular case of multiple murder:
"What Caused Chiang Ai-chen to Kill?" Miss Chiang, a native of
eastern China, was a nurse in Regiment No. 144 Hospital in Sin-
kiang Province where her older brother was a military officer. She
became a member of Young Communist League (1973) and later of
the Communist party (1976). In the latter year she was elected
Branch Party committee member and concurrently secretary of the
League.

The vice-secretary of the Branch Party of the same hospital,
Chang Kuo-cheng (hereafter referred to as K. C.), was a comrade-
at-arms of Chiang's brother. When Chiang came to work in the hospital, her brother asked his old comrade-at-arms to look after her "as
an older brother would a younger sister." As a result they were
friendly with each other.

In the same Branch Party were members Li Pei-hua (hereafter re-
ferred to as P. H.) and Hsieh Shih-ping (hereafter referred to as
S. P.). They and several other cadres at the hospital had disliked
K. C. for some time and were looking for a pretext to demolish him.

In March 1978 Chiang was given leave to see her parents in Chekiang Province. On the evening before her departure K. C. and another worker visited her briefly at her on-call sleeping quarters in the
outpatient department. He "gave her some useful hints about her
forthcoming journey."

Suspecting that K. C. and Chiang were sleeping together, P. H. and S. P., with the consent of the assistant superintendent of the hospital, prepared to surprise them. At 2:00 A.M. they dispatched a nurse to Chiang's room on the excuse that her help was needed to secure some gauze in another building for an emergency case. As soon as Chiang left her bedroom S. P. entered it but did not find K. C. The six or seven of their cohorts, including a Chung Ch'iu, who guarded all the windows and doors of the night duty outpatient department and of K. C.'s home nearby, also did not find any trace of K. C.

Upon returning to the outpatient department, Chiang saw S. P. and they greeted each other as usual. But as she walked out she saw P. H. in a dark corner scurrying to hide himself. She at once thought of possible theft since she had $900 in her bedroom. So instead of returning there she decided to report her suspicions to the Branch Party secretary without delay. However, because the latter's home was not nearby, she knocked on K. C.'s door and roused him out of bed for help. As K. C. got to the outpatient department to make inquiries, P. H. and S. P. dashed in. When K. C. asked them what they were doing there, they responded: "We have come to catch a ghost."

At this K. C. immediately understood the real reason why they were there. According to Chinese usage "ghost" in this context could only refer to an adulterer. He sent for the Branch Party secretary as well as all Party committee members and personally explained to them the evening's happenings. After questioning all concerned the Branch Party secretary and Party committee members inspected Chiang's bed and failed to find any sign that two persons had been in it. At this P. H. and S. P. said: "We failed." But instead of admitting that they were wrong, they vowed to each other to redouble their efforts to vilify Chiang and K. C.

The article then goes on to relate how P. H. and S. P. and their cohorts spread the rumor throughout the hospital that K. C. and Chiang spent the night together. Later, the rumor that they were caught in *flagrante delicto* raged in the schools and stores outside the hospital. Three days later Chiang's accusers let it be known that some people saw K. C. escape from the hospital that same night and sneak into his own home next door. "More lies became more flagrant as the days went by" and such lies later were used as primary evidence by Yang Ming-san, head of the special investigative commission. Yang once had a bitter quarrel with K. C. so he favored

Chiang's accusers from the start. During the hearings P. H. and S. P. advanced what they said were "doubts" about the "relations" between Chiang and K. C. The head of the investigating commission required Chiang to explain every one of them. Later Chiang's persecutors also posted big character posters at many locations, "exposing" the so-called "K. C. and Chiang sexual affair." With these posters were even "extremely dirty" cartoons.

Some hospital members saw the injustice of the case and tried to defend Chiang and K. C. This group, numbering some thirty to forty, led by a cadre named Su, also posted big character posters detailing the truth and "clearing the name of the victimized youth Chiang." But before those posters were dry on the walls Cadre Su was reassigned to another city. A lady doctor who dared to listen to Chiang and to comfort her with a few encouraging words was required by Yang to explain herself in writing and verbally at a public meeting.

Chiang was harassed in diverse other ways and was totally isolated. Coworkers were afraid to speak to her. Yang even went to the home of the father of a young doctor who was romantically attached to her and ordered him to warn his son against having anything more to do with Chiang before she was cleared of the charge.

The rumors, accusations, forced public explanations, insults, and harassments went on for several months until August when all doors seemed to be closed for Chiang to clear herself. On August 29, 1979, with the rifle she was allotted for target practice, she shot to death P. H., and P. H.'s wife who got in the way, and one other of her tormentors. Before she was able to get S. P. and the head of the investigating commission she was arrested. K. C., accused without evidence of being an accomplice, was imprisoned for ninety-two days before being released. Chiang was sentenced to death for killing three persons. The Supreme Court of the Autonomous Region reviewed the case and changed the sentence to life imprisonment. But the chief justice of the Superior Court wrote to the editor of *People's Daily* which led the paper to send over reporters for the extensive investigation.

As a result of its publication Chiang's fate has taken a far better turn and the culprits are being punished in various ways, including dismissal and indictment. We will deal with the political and legal implications of the case later. For the present we must note that the facts of the case fit well with what we have said so far about relationship between the sexes in China today.

Men and women do meet romantically today as before the revolution. Their meeting is slow paced and premarital sex is taboo, so that they (but especially women) must guard against any suggestion that they have been so tainted. Not violating this taboo is the most serious element in the individual's reputation. Yang, as head of the investigating commission, obviously misused his public powers to avenge a personal grudge, but the fact that he and his cohorts could use an alleged sexual liaison between two unattached individuals as a pretext for doing so speaks volumes. Such a pretext will sound absurd to most or all Americans. The fact that they could get so many others to support or acquiesce in their persecutory activities on such a pretext makes it even clearer how the traditional Chinese morals in man-woman relations still prevail.

The fervor of the Communist revolution might have made the traditional conduct between the sexes more stringent, as when the militants among my University of Shanghai schoolmates during the Japanese invasion forbade dating and music. The situation—traditional, pre-Communist or Communist—takes precedence over the individual in China, whereas the order is reversed in the United States.

NOTES

1. At their children's weddings, American parents may say, "I haven't lost a daughter (or son), I have gained a son (or daughter)." But this expression carries neither the meaning of the Chinese thought nor is in reality the same as in the case of a Chinese marriage, as we shall see in Chapter 5.

2. The letters considered here were selected from several hundred which appeared between 1945 and 1948 in newspapers and magazines in north China.

3. *Central Daily News,* Taipei, August 3, 1965.

4. Until the Communist triumph there was no compulsory education in China. A nineteen year old in high school was not at all unusual.

5. *Chicago Sun-Times,* May 24, 1966.

6. Real estate developers in many parts of the United States are using the sex angle to sell new houses. The headline of one such recent report in the *Wall Street Journal* reads: "Three Bedrooms, Two Baths, and Wall-to-Wall Sex." The report goes on to say that one West Coast developer advertised a "Sex Pit" in each house. (August 1967.)

7. *Central Daily News,* Taipei, June 9, 1967.

8. The expression "Let's die together" is a well-known Chinese idiom between lovers, and also, oddly enough in American eyes, among those entering sworn or ritual brotherhood to indicate the finality of the bond. The human context will determine to which relationship it applies. The three famous heroes of *The Romance of Three Kingdoms*—Liu, Kuan, and Chang—reportedly swore together as follows:

"Though we could not be born on the same year,
the same month and the same day,
Let us die on the same year, the same month and the
same day."

The following dialogue between a college student and his girlfriend appears in a short story in a 1967 issue of the Literary Supplement of a Taiwan daily. They were barefoot together at the bottom of a waterfall at the time.

Girl (reciting two lines of a well-known poem):
   "How happy I am! I willingly die here!"
Boy: "No, let's die here together!"

9. The difference between the way Chinese regard chickens and birds is similar to the way Americans feel about pigs and horses.

10. Personal communication.

11. Pearl S. Buck, *Of Men and Women.*

In 1952 when I first read this passage, I was intrigued and decided to investigate. I did find a bank, the First Federal Savings and Loan Association of Akron, Ohio, incorporated in 1921, with assets amounting to $12,500,000 in 1952, where the staff was made up entirely of women—from teller to president. For many years the institution was known as the "Women's Federal" in the area. However, the board of directors, which is the usual controlling body in such institutions, was comprised of four men and the woman president. The sex ratio of the bank's clientele was not different from other banks. Some sixteen years later, the picture had changed somewhat. The lady president of this bank retired in 1961 and was replaced by a man, and most of the officers had since been replaced by men. A man was also hired as executive vice-president and manager, and the board of directors had since become all male. There was also a Women's Savings and Loan Association of Cleveland, Ohio, which had a history similar to the "Women's Federal" in Akron. However, the Cleveland institution is now also managed by a man.

Although two women's banks have passed into male hands, women bank officers have existed in the United States for a long time. According to the American Bankers Association, from 1936–1966 roughly one-tenth of the bank officers in the country were women. The male-female figures for 1950, 1960, and 1966 were as follows: 73,000 vs. 6,000; 104,200 vs. 11,600; and 126,000 vs. 14,000 (*Banking, A Career for Today and Tomorrow,* prepared by the Personnel Administration and Management Development Committee, the American Bankers Association, New York, 1967, p. 7). However, by December 31, 1967, only a fraction of these women (about 1 percent) held positions as president or chairman of the board (see Appendix I, "Analysis of Membership by Title of National Association of Bank-Women 1967"). Since then the percentages of women in banking and in executive positions both steadily risen. In 1975, 25 percent of bank officers were women (161,331 vs. 53,783, according to U.S. Treasury statistics). In 1978, the corresponding percentage was 30.4 (according to Bureau of Labor Statistics). However, according to a July 1979 release of the National Association of Bank Women (NABW), in which were quoted the last two figures, only 2 percent of bank women held "senior-level positions" in 1975. Upon inquiry by phone, a spokeswoman of the association said that "even today [November 1980] very few of the 2 percent are presidents or chairmen of the board." Today there are some nine women's banks in the United States. One of them is the Western Women's Bank in San Francisco, which began in 1976 and which recently (September 1980) changed its name to Golden Gate Bank. Some of the others are in New York City, Los Angeles, San Diego, and Denver. None of them is a giant. The Golden Gate Bank has assets of about $10 million or less.

12. During and since World War II a considerable number of American males have come into some sort of professional, social, or romantic contact with Chinese females, either in Asia or in the United States. Some of these Americans may have found Chinese females as adept as their American sisters in the art of generalized sex appeal, regardless of the situation.

These men receive the wrong impression because they are *Americans* and not Chinese. Being sensitive to the situation, Chinese females will act toward Chinese males with the situation-centered reserve, even when they are in the United States. But when Chinese females have to deal with males who are American, which fact alone drastically alters the interpersonal situation, they tend not to remain completely within their Chinese norm. For example, most Chinese friends in the United States greet each other with no more than a handshake, but quite a few of them will greet spouses of the opposite sex of their non-Chinese friends by closer body contact, including a kiss on the cheek.

13. Hugo Portisch, *Red China Today,* p. 36.

14. Barbara Tuchman, *Notes from China,* p. 11.

15. The main deprivation I suffered from at that time was not being allowed to play and practice my violin. All music was forbidden too.

16. See Eileen Hsu-Balzer, Richard Balzer, and Francis L. K. Hsu, *China Day by Day.*

17. Jan Myrdal, *Report from a Chinese Village,* p. 221. Myrdal's visit was made in 1962.

18. Ibid., p. 22.

19. Personal communication.

20. *Chung Kuo Fu Nu* [Chinese Women], no. 6, June 1, 1963.

21. *"People's Daily* and Letters from Readers," in *China Reconstructs* 27, no. 10 (October 1978):4.

22. Godwin C. Chu and Leonard L. Chu, "Letters to the Editor, They Write in China," *East-West Perspectives,* p. 2.

23. Ibid., p. 4.

CHAPTER 3

The Beginnings
of Contrast

How have Chinese and Americans acquired their contrasting ways
of life? I am convinced that the most plausible and probable answer
must be broadly Freudian. That is, these contrasts are nurtured in
the family, the first external mold of the vast majority of mankind.
The family is the human factory which manufactures the necessary
psychological orientation in individuals, preparing them to become
functioning members of their particular society.

The occurrences in the larger society, whether they are of external
origin such as natural calamities or conquests, or internal origin such
as rebellion or revolution, also help to influence the nature of the
family. What slavery did to the black family pattern in the New
World has been a subject of much scientific discussion. How far the
new political regime's efforts in China will seriously and permanently modify her age-old kinship system will be discussed in Chapter 15. For the moment we shall confine ourselves to the role of the
differing American and Chinese patterns of the family as it shapes
the majority of individuals in their respective societies.

All students of man today accept the general theorem that, except
in extreme cases such as geniuses and idiots, personality[1] is chiefly
the result of conditioning by culture. Personality is the sum total of
the individual's characteristic reactions to his environment, while
culture consists of the accepted pattern of behavior in every society.
The contrasts between Chinese and American ways of life may be
viewed, therefore, as contrasts between the sum totals of their respective patterns of personality and culture.

The personality of the individual and the culture of his society are
by no means identical. As we noted in the Prologue, no individual is
an automaton, just as no society is without variation. However, each
society offers rewards to those of its members who act according to its
accepted pattern of behavior and punishes those who do not.

There are, for example, role variations in any society, and ranges of conformity within the expected behavior pattern of any role. All human societies must have males and females, old and young, and most have doctors, lawyers, politicians, and soldiers, all of whom perform different tasks or maintain dissimilar interests. And in all human societies, those persons who have the same role do not possess the same interests, and may not even conduct their role activities in the same way. The personal interest of some businessmen may be night clubs, while that of others may be Platonic philosophy. However, not only do many roles and interests among members of any given society complement one another, but even those which seemingly contradict each other may turn out, upon closer inspection, to be functionally related.

Since cultural conditioning begins in the family, it is logical for us to inquire first into the broad contrasts between the family systems in which the two ways of life are taught and propagated.

In doing so, however, great restraint must be exercised. There is ample temptation to stretch Freudian theory to absurd lengths. British anthropologist Gregory Bateson, for example, suggested that British and American attitudes toward their respective colonies are rooted in the respective parent-child relationships in the two countries. The American parents encourage in their children "certain sorts of boastful and exhibitionistic behavior, while still in a position somewhat subordinate to and dependent upon the parents," but in England the parent-child relationship is characterized by "dominance and succoring." The American parent-child relationship "contains within itself factors for psychologically weaning the child, while in England, among the upper classes, the analogous breaking of the succoring dependent link has to be performed by . . . the boarding school." Since "colonies cannot be sent to a boarding school . . . England has very great difficulty in weaning her non–Anglo Saxon colonies, while these colonies have had corresponding difficulty in attaining maturity—in sharp contrast with the history of the Philippines."[2]

Geoffrey Gorer, another British anthropologist, is equally daring. He considers America's two houses of Congress as a sort of extension of a certain sibling relationship in the American family. The House, being the younger brother of the family, is erratic and less responsible in its actions, knowing full well that the Senate, its older brother, will come to its rescue.[3]

Neither of these are examples of true science or even of sound logic. To avoid such pitfalls, we shall, instead of concentrating on details (which tend to vary because of geography, class, occupation, and many other factors), look at the broader phases of the family pattern in which the two peoples differ greatly, but consistently.

The Home

Let us begin with Chinese and American homes. An American house usually has a yard, large or small. It may have a hedge, but rarely is there a wall so high that a passerby cannot see the windows. The majority of American houses have neither hedges nor outside walls. Usually the interior is shielded from exterior view only by window curtains or blinds, and then during but part of the day.

The majority of Chinese houses are, in the first place, surrounded by such high walls that only the roofs are visible from the outside, and solid gates separate the interior grounds from the outside world. In addition, there is usually a shadow wall placed directly in front of the gates on the other side of the street[4] as well as a four-paneled wooden screen standing about five feet behind the gates. The outside shadow wall keeps the home from direct exposure to the unseen spirits. The inside wooden screen shields the interior courtyard from pedestrians' glances when the gates are ajar.

Inside the home, the contrast between China and America is reversed. The American emphasis within the home is on privacy. There are not only doors to the bathrooms but also to the bedrooms, and often to the living room and even the kitchen. Space and possessions are individualized. Parents have little liberty in the rooms of the children, and children cannot do what they want in those parts of the house regarded as preeminently their parents' domain. Among some sections of the American population this rule of privacy extends to the husband and wife, so that each has a separate bedroom.

Within the Chinese home, on the other hand, privacy hardly exists at all, except between members of the opposite sexes who are not spouses. Chinese children, even in homes which have ample room, often share the same chambers with their parents until they reach adolescence. Not only do parents have freedom of action with reference to the children's belongings, but the youngsters can also use the possessions of the parents if they can lay their hands on them. If children damage their parents' possessions they are scolded, not because they touched things that were not theirs but because they are too young to handle them with proper care.

The lack of privacy within the home finds its extreme expression in many well-to-do families of north China. Here the rooms are arranged in rows like the cars of a train. But instead of each room having a separate entrance, all the rooms are arranged in sequence, one leading into another. Thus, if there are five rooms, the front door of the house opens into the center room, which serves as the kitchen, each leading into a room which has in turn another door opening into the end rooms. Beginning at one end of the house—call it room A—one can walk in a straight line to room B, into the kitchen-dining room C, into room D, and finally into room E. The parents will occupy room B, nearest the kitchen, leaving room A free for a married daughter when she and her children come for a prolonged visit. If the family has two married sons, the older brother and his wife and children will occupy room D, while the younger brother and his wife will occupy room E. The occupants of rooms A and E will have to pass through rooms B and D in order to go in and out of the house. Actual arrangements vary somewhat from family to family, but this simplified picture is generally true.

Such an arrangement in living quarters would be very offensive to Americans. But many Chinese adhere to a variation of the common linear arrangement even when they have more rooms and space in which to spread out. For they consider all within the four walls as being one body. The American child's physical environment establishes strong lines of individual distinction within the home, but there is very little stress on separation of the home from the outside world. The Chinese child's environment is exactly the reverse. He finds a home with few demarcation lines within it but separated by high walls and multiple gates from the outside world.

Parents and Children

The difference between Chinese and American homes reflects the contrasting patterns of behavior in the family. In no other country on earth is there so much attention paid to infancy[5] or so much privilege accorded during childhood as in the United States. In contrast, it may be said without exaggeration that China before 1949 was a country in which children came last.

The contrast can be seen in a myriad of ways. Americans are very verbal about their children's rights. There is not only state and federal legislation to protect the young ones, but there are also many voluntary juvenile protective associations to look after their welfare.

In China, parents have had a completely free hand with their children. Popular misconception notwithstanding, infanticide was never an everyday occurrence in China. It was the last resort of poor parents with too many daughters, especially during a famine. Certainly no parent would brag about it. In fact, there are stories about the grief of parents in such a predicament and quite a few jokes on the theme of how some irate parents deal with tactless clods who utter unwelcome expressions about the birth of a daughter.[6]

However, before 1949, infanticide by needy Chinese parents was never cause for public shock or censure. Parents who committed infanticide were seldom punished by the law. It is literally true that with regard to children, American parents have practically no rights; but from the viewpoint of Chinese parents, children have little reason to expect protection from their elders. If an American were to point with justifiable pride to his country's many child protective associations, a Chinese would simply counter with an equally proud boast about his nation's ancient cultural heritage in which Confucian filial piety was the highest ideal.

American parents are so concerned with the welfare of their children, and so determined to do the right thing, that they handsomely support a huge number of child specialists. Chinese parents have taken their children so much for granted that pediatrics as a separate branch of medicine was unknown until modern times. I know of no piece of traditional literature aimed at making the Chinese better parents, and even several decades after the fall of the Manchu dynasty there was hardly any scientific inquiry into what children might think or desire. Articles on how to treat children appeared only sporadically in a few Chinese newspapers and magazines, many of them translations or synopses of material from the West.[7]

But American do not only study their children's behavior—they glorify it. Chinese did not only take their children for granted—they minimized their importance. The important thing to Americans is what parents should do for their children; to Chinese, what children should do for their parents.

The extent to which some American parents will go to suit the convenience of their children is exemplified by a midwestern couple I know. To make their little ones happy, they installed a fancy slide in their living room. Guests entered the apartment by bending under it, and then they attempted to enjoy a conversation within reach of the boisterous sideshow provided by the young ones sliding up and down.

That this is unusual even for the United States is indicated by the fact that this couple felt compelled to justify their action every time they had a visitor and by the fact that their friends remarked about it. No Chinese parents could have kept the respect of the community if they permitted anything remotely resembling this indulgence.

For many centuries Chinese were both entertained and instructed by tales known as "The Twenty-Four Examples of Filial Piety." These tales were so popular that different versions of them are available. Following the traditional approach to literature of writing on some exalted model, the Chinese ancients have handed down to posterity at least two series of "The Twenty-Four Examples of Filial Piety."

These stories were illustrated in paintings, dramatized on the stage, and recited by storytellers in tea houses and market places all over the country. Here is one of these "examples":

> A poor man by the name of Kuo and his wife were confronted with a serious problem. His aged mother was sick in bed. She needed both medicine and nourishment which Kuo could ill afford. After consultation between themselves, Kuo and his wife decided that the only way out was to get rid of their three-year-old only son. For Kuo and his wife said to each other, "We have only one mother, but we can always get another child." Thereupon the two went out to the field to dig a pit for the purpose of burying their child alive. But shortly after the man had started to dig he suddenly struck gold. It transpired that the gods were moved by the spirit of their filial piety, and this was their reward. Both the child and the mother were amply provided for and the family thrived happily ever after.

To the Chinese this story dramatized their most important cultural ideal—that support of the parents came before all other obligations and that this obligation must be fulfilled even at the expense of the children.

Economic support is not, however, the only way in which Chinese children are obligated to their parents. The son not only has to follow the Confucian dictum that "parents are always right," but at all times and in all circumstances he must try to satisfy their wishes and look after their safety. If the parents are indisposed, the son should spare no trouble in obtaining a cure for them. Formerly, if a parent was sentenced to prison, the son might arrange to take that parent's place. If the parents were displeased with their daughter-in-law, the good son did not hesitate to think about divorce. In the service of the elders, no effort was too extraordinary or too great. In addition to parents, the elders in question could be a man's stepmother or a woman's parents-in-law.

Here again folk tales are useful indications of the actual values. One classical story tells how a man gave up his hard-won official post in order to walk many miles in search of his long lost mother. Another tells how a youngster of fourteen jumped on and strangled a tiger when the beast was about to devour his father. In a third story, a man cut a piece of flesh from his arm and boiled it in the pot with his father's medicine, believing that the soup would help the elder to recover from his long illness.

In a fourth story, a certain Wang Hwa who was married and had a son wanted a father of his own. His real father was presumed to have died during a civil war. He wanted to buy a father to whom he could be filial. When he met an old man who was searching for his long lost son, Wang made his offer and it was accepted. The newly installed father of Wang was really a rich man in disguise who could not refrain from his extravagant wining and dining. But Wang and his own son, being only of modest means, worked as hard as they could to satisfy the whims of the adopted father. Moved by his adopted son's filial behavior, the old man decided to give Wang all his riches, only to discover later that Wang was his long lost son after all.

Many Chinese stories were not seen only as ideal literature but were sometimes copied to the letter by daughters or sons. In the district histories and genealogical records to be found in every part of the country are many individual biographies of local notables. After a cursory reading of about fifty of them, I obtained at least five instances in which men and women were said to have sliced flesh from their arms to be boiled in the medicine pot of one or another of their parents. One man did this twice during one of his father's illnesses. Because the elder's condition remained serious, the filial son decided to take a more drastic course of action. He cut out a piece of what he thought was his "liver" instead. Both he and his father died shortly afterward.

In a 1966 autobiographical article, Mr. Keng-sheng Hao, the most important figure in Chinese Olympic affairs in China before 1949 and in Taiwan since, states that he knew his mother sliced flesh from her arm for reasons of filial piety. He describes her in the following way:

Mother was well known as a woman of charity and piety *(shan jen)*. She was also filial to the point of foolishness as well as superstitious. Before marriage she sliced flesh from one of her arms for my maternal grandmother's illness. After marriage, she once did the same for my paternal grandmother's recovery. Even today I still find it hard to imagine how she could do it in her rural conditions of life, with a pair of scissors but no anesthetic and no sterilizing agent.[8]

Hundreds of other biographies contain less dramatic episodes, but all are variations on similar themes.

American parents not only wish to help their children according to their own experiences, but they must also try to find out by elaborate research what the youngsters really want (so that the elders can better satisfy the youngsters' individual predilections). They feel compelled to reduce even the rudiments of a child's education to a matter of fun. I even came across two books advertised as *Playbooks That Teach Your Child to Dress*—one for boys and one for girls. We now find in many suburban communities hundreds of new programs for kids. In one California community there are three programs, "Kindergyms," "Side by Side," and "Kindersplash," all for children four years old or younger. In Kindergym, for those of three months to four years, mothers help their children to go at various loops, bars, and slides. Side by Side combines a parent/child nursery school experience with parenting workshops. Kindersplash is a "creative and positive water experience" for parents and child under the supervision of trained instructors.

By 1951, business catering to infant needs had already reached the colossal income of $5 billion annually. The toy industry alone rose from an annual business of a mere $150 million in 1939 to $750 million in 1951, and to the astronomical high of $2.1 billion in 1965.[9] Beatrice Judelle, who gave us these last estimates, states that since there were about 60 million children under the age of fifteen in 1965, the "average outlay per child" was placed at $35.15 annually. We may expect that this figure will increase continuously as the child population grows. Certainly the increasing number of commercially profitable events centered around children, the acceleration of learning by playing, and the coming and going of fashions in playthings as in other products cannot but spur on the toy industry.

The publication of children's books has always been good business in America, but it has become especially remarkable in recent years. In 1979, children's books cornered some 22 percent of total hardcover trade sales. Their variety is fantastic: books to "read aloud," beautiful picture books, photo essays, biographies, urban street novels, religious titles. "Some are to 'scratch and sniff', some have tough teen heroes who know much more than many parents. Especially remarkable is a new kind of children's book, the 'young adult' novel, which focuses on themes like rape, child abuse, death, and sex."[10]

One of ten best-selling young adult books is *After the First Death* by Robert Cromier. It is a "psychological thriller about terrorists who hijack a school bus in New England and hold a group of young children hostage." The *Newsweek* reviewer (July 16, 1979) says, "It is a marvellous story, written in crackling prose that weaves together the stories of the pretty teen-age girl bus driver, a teen-age terrorist who is attracted to her and another teen-ager who becomes the crucial messenger in the negotiations." Cromier's two other books, *The Chocolate War,* about mob violence in a prep school, and *I Am the Cheese,* about the perils of a family hiding under a false identity, each have more than 200,000 paperback copies in print.

According to the same report, several years ago The American Library Association, through its publication *Booklist,* attacked *The Chocolate War* for its violence and downbeat ending. But Cromier makes no apologies: "As long as what I write is true and believable, why should I have to create happy endings?"

The relationship between Chinese parents and children shows entirely different characteristics. Chinese parents are amused by infantile behavior and youthful exuberance, but the measure of their children's worth is determined primarily by the degree to which they act like adults. Chinese parents are rather proud of a child who acts "older than his age," whereas some American parents might take a similar child to a psychiatrist. What Chinese parents consider rowdiness in a child's behavior, American parents might approve of as a sign of initiative.

Also interesting is the approach of Chinese children to whatever toys they may have. When I was six years of age my mother bought me a cart made of tinfoil. Soldered above the door of the cart was an ornamental rectangle. Having seen movable curtains on real carts, I attempted to lower the "curtain" at the entrance of my toy cart and yanked the stationary ornament out of place. An American mother might have gloated over creative impulse of her "budding genius," but my mother was very much displeased because she thought me destructive and temperamental. Had I acted the model Chinese child and nursed one old toy for a couple of years, an American mother might have worried about the retarded or warped state of my mind.[11]

With regard to children's literature, there is nothing remotely comparable to the phenomenal success of books catering to American children either in Taiwan or the People's Republic. In fact not so long ago a writer in Taiwan asked, "What are our children's books?" Her story is as follows.

One day her nine-year-old nephew asked her: "Auntie, why is it that of ten books you bought me most say, 'rewritten after the original by So-and-so?' " She explained to the youngster that those are all famous works by foreign authors and must be translated and adapted for Chinese children. But her nephew persisted, "Why is it that foreigners could write such famous works but we can't?"

This youthful, blunt response hit her hard because she at once saw the painful truth of it. She realized that besides regular school curricula Chinese children have been flooded with stories of foreign origin from *Snow White and the Seven Dwarfs* to *Pinocchio*. She recalled having bought her little nephew some indigenous children's stories such as those based on *Twenty-Four Examples of Filial Piety* or those giving life sketches of great historical figures, but now admitted to herself that those "pure" Chinese children's stories were less interesting than the imported ones.

What this lady did was to make an intensive effort to search for pure Chinese children's stories. She was rewarded with the discovery of one set consisting of six titles by Prince Publishing House collectively called "Prince Chinese Children's Literature." Five of the six titles are: *The Case of the Olive,* the story of a preteen girl who solved the case of a headless body; *The Rooster and the Sun,* based on the old Chinese lore of a rooster who made the sun rise; *King of Chin Lung; Girl Who Herds Ducks Everyday;* and *The Pumpkin King.* The lady found the stories so interesting that she finished reading every one before passing them on to her nephew (*Central Daily News,* Taipei, August 22, 1978).

In order to understand the contrasting life-styles of the American and Chinese peoples, we must explore the long-standing parent-child bases that have nurtured them. Only then can we evaluate how far more recent developments have or have not altered the picture. It is true that a good many things have happened to the Chinese parent-child relationship since 1949.

To start with, when an American speaks of a family he refers to parents and unmarried children; a Chinese includes grandparents and in-laws. Even if Chinese grandparents and in-laws do not live under the same roof, they usually reside in the same village, a neighboring village, or, more rarely, a neighboring district. This is one of the traditional features which the government of the People's Republic has worked hard to alter by assigning places of work, by stimulating population movement, by the work-study program, and other measures. But as we shall see in Chapter 15, kinship and local ties remain important building blocks of the commune. On the other hand, Americans related by blood or legal bonds may live so far from one another that this broader group does not come together except on holidays.

These differences mark the point of departure in the early experiences of Chinese and American children. The Chinese child grows up amid continuing or frequent contacts with a number of related individuals besides his own parents and siblings, but his American counterpart grows up in much greater physical isolation. Thus very early in life the former is conditioned to getting along with a wide circle of relatives while the latter is not.

Far more crucial, however, is the manner of interaction between the growing child and individuals other than those belonging to his immediate family. American parents are the sole agents of control over their children until they are of age. The grandparents and in-laws do not ordinarily occupy a disciplinary role, whether they live in the same house or not. Even when grandparents take over during an emergency such as sickness or childbirth, the older people are supposed to do no more than administer things according to the laws laid down by the younger couple, most likely by the younger woman.

Chinese parents have much less exclusive control over their children. In cases where grandparents do not share the same roof with them, during a brief visit the older couple can do almost anything they see fit in regard to the children, even if it means going over the parents' heads. The liberty taken by most Chinese aunts, uncles, and in-laws would cause very severe stress in American families. Furthermore, while an American mother exhibits her displeasure with an overindulgent grandmother and is considered right by others, a Chinese mother doing the same thing would have been an object of censure rather than sympathy.

The inevitable result of the omnipresent and exclusive control of American parents over their children is greater and deeper emotional involvement. The American parent-child relationship is close and exclusive. To the extent that they are the only objects of worship, they also are liable to become the only oppressors. Accordingly, when an American child likes his parents, they are his idols. When he dislikes them they are his enemies. A conscious or unconscious attachment to one parent at the expense of the other, a situation which gave Freud ground for postulating his famed Oedipus complex, is the extreme expression of this configuration.

The mutual affection of Chinese parents and children is toned down compared to that of their American counterparts. Since parental authority varies with circumstances, the parental image in the mind of the growing child must necessarily share the spotlight with men and women held in much higher esteem, such as grandparents, and with those regarded as the equals of the parents, such as uncles and aunts. The feeling toward parents and other adult authority figures being divided and diluted, the child does not develop a paralyzing attachment to, or strong repulsion against, the elders. There is still less reason for the emergence of the Oedipal triangle in which the child is allied to one parent against the other. Consequently, when the Chinese child likes his parents, he fails to idolize them alone; when he dislikes them he vents his displeasure with great reserve.

These contrasting results flow inevitably from the respective kinship premises of the two cultures. Even though the biological family consists of parents and unmarried children everywhere, according to the American pattern of interaction it tends to become a collection of isolated dyads; according to its Chinese counterparts, no dyadic relationship is free from the larger network.

This contrast reveals itself with great clarity when pseudo-kinship is involved. The only pseudo-kinship relationship left in present day United States is that of godparents and godchild. Our older daughter Eileen's godfather, Mr. L. (an anthropologist and a native American), died in 1953. Some years later my wife and our two daughters paid a social visit to Mrs. L. While the five of us were having dinner, our younger daughter, Penny, then about twelve years old, casually declared to all of us that since Mrs. L. was Eileen's godmother, she was naturally also her godmother. This came to my wife and me as a surprise. Though born, raised, and partially educated in China, I had understood—intellectually at least—the American usage. Eileen was Mr. L.'s goddaughter, and he her godfather. But that relationship had nothing to do with Mrs. L. nor with any of Eileen's family members. Our Evanston-born second daughter, though she had never seen China at that time, had obviously picked up our implicit understanding of Chinese kinship logic. According to which, not only would Mrs. L. be Eileen's godmother and Eileen's sister would be Mr. and Mrs. L.'s second goddaughter, but all of Mr. and Mrs. L.'s children would be both of our daughters' godsiblings.[12]

The beginning of the contrasts between the two ways of life now become apparent. In America, the child learns to see the world strictly on an individual basis. Even though he did not have a chance to choose his parents, he can choose to prefer one more than the other. Extending from this basic tie outward, the American's relationship with other members of his kin group is strictly dependent upon individual preference. The American "must see early in life that a powerful force composed of many aspects of individual choice-making operates to create, maintain, or cancel out interpersonal relationships."[13] His parents, for their part, have to conduct themselves so that they will not lag in the competition for the affection of their children. This, and the fact that most American parents encourage their children very early to do things for themselves—to feed themselves, to make their own decisions—leads the American child to follow his own predilections. He expects *his environment to be sensitive to him.*

The Chinese child learns to see the world in terms of a network of relationships. He not only has to submit to his parents, but he also has little choice in his wider social relationships and what he individually would like to do about them. This, and the fact that Chinese parents are firmly convinced that elders know better and so never feel defensive about it, leads the Chinese child to appreciate the importance of differing circumstances. As to defending themselves, the characteristic advice to Chinese children is: "Don't get into trouble outside, but if there is danger, run home." The Chinese child is obliged to be *sensitive to his environment.*

There is experimental evidence for this difference. Godwin C. Chu, comparing his study of 182 Chinese high school students in Taiwan with an earlier study by Janis and Field of 182 American high school students, demonstrates that the Chinese are far more persuadable than the Americans.[14]

Though consciously encouraging their children to grow up in some ways, American parents firmly refuse to let the youngsters enter the real world of the adults. They leave their children with sitters when they go to parties. If they entertain at home, they put the youngsters to bed before the guests arrive. Children have no part in parents' regular social activities. There is a tendency on the part of a few ultra-modern American parents to take their babies or children with them to social gatherings, but this is not the generally accepted American way. At least not yet.

Chinese parents take their children with them not only to wedding feasts, funeral breakfasts, and religious celebrations, but also to purely social or business gatherings. A father in business thinks nothing of taking his boy of six or seven to an executive conference.

This pattern is still adhered to by the majority of second- , third- , and even fourth-generation Chinese-Americans in Hawaii, San Francisco, and New York. Like their Caucasian neighbors, Chinese organizers in Hawaii resort to "family" picnics and "family" evenings, and even athletics for the purpose of maintaining or increasing club or church enrollment. But unlike their Caucasian neighbors, Chinese parents take their very young children with them on many more occasions—for example, on social and business visits which last until late at night.

Some years ago the idea of "togetherness" between parents and children became fashionable, at least in some sections of American society. The central concern was that the parents and children should *do* things together, such as attend outings, shows, or church activities, and share hobbies. Some writers observed that television, for all of its faulty programming, at least brings members of a family together. Now we know that this isn't true. There is also no evidence that the togetherness which some progressive parents had hoped would solidify the family as a unit has achieved the desired effect. For the togetherness that progressive American parents looked for was *planned*—an activity-studded togetherness in which children and their elders would have each other but would define the rest of the world as outsiders and give it no part in their circle. So conceived, it was literally a honeymoon between parents and children. It was bound to get on the nerves of all, especially its commander-in-chief, the father. It failed because it was an artificial togetherness, not one nurtured in the American kinship constellation.

Chinese youngsters enter into the adult world unobtrusively in the course of their mental and physical growth. Their own infantile and youthful world is tolerated but never encouraged. On the contrary, they reap more rewards as they participate more and more in adult activities. From the beginning their elders share with them a community of interests, except relating to sex; they participate in real life, not in an artificially roped-off sector of it.

American parents, except for the very poor, proceed on quite the opposite assumption with their insistence on privacy for all individuals. The business of American parents—social and commercial—is their private reserve, and no trespassing by children is allowed except on those rare and eventful occasions when an explicit invitation is extended. By the same token, parents are also supposed to refrain from entering into the activities of their youngsters.

Not so among the Chinese. Chinese children consider it a matter of course to witness or participate in adult affairs, exactly as Chinese adults have no constraints about joining in their children's activities. This reciprocity goes so far that neither has any reservations about opening letters addressed to the other.

Nothing is more strikingly symbolic of these profound differences than the fact that American children celebrate their birthdays among themselves, their parents being assistants or servants, while Chinese children's birthdays are occasions for adult celebrations at which children may be present, as in wedding or funeral feasts, but where they certainly are not the center of attraction.

The line of demarcation between the adult and the child world is drawn in many other ways. For instance, many American parents may be totally divorced from the church, or entertain grave doubts about the existence of God, but they send their children to Sunday schools and help them to pray. American parents struggle in a competitive world where sheer cunning and falsehood are often rewarded and respected, but they feed their children with nursery tales in which the morally good is pitted against the bad, and in the end the good invariably is successful and the bad inevitably punished. When American parents are in serious domestic trouble, they maintain a front of sweetness and light before their children. Even if American parents suffer a major business or personal catastrophe, they feel obliged to turn to their children and say, "Honey, everything is going to be all right." This American desire to keep the children's world separate from that of the adults is also exemplified by the practice of delaying the transmission of bad news to children when their parents have been killed in an accident for example, or concealing certain facts from them, as when one of the parents goes to jail. In summary, American parents face a world of reality while many of their children live in the near-ideal, unreal realm where the rules of the parental world do not apply, are watered down, or may even be reversed.

It is this separateness of the children's world that makes the kind of hero found in J. D. Salinger's *The Catcher in the Rye* so meaningful to so many youthful American readers. Here is an adolescent who sees through the invisible walls around him. He denounces as phonies the people who act according to rules outside that wall, but he feels terribly lonely because most of those inside the wall are working so hard to be content with their place. However, even Holden Caulfield returns to the fold in the end. He decides not to run away; he goes back to school; and he reflects while his little sister, Phoebe, is on the carousel: "The thing with kids is, if they want to grab for the gold ring, you have to let them do it, and not say anything. If they fall off, they fall off, but it's bad if you say anything to them."[15]

In this context, too, we can understand why Eddie Seidel, Jr., a fifteen-year-old boy in Minnesota, jumped two hundred feet to his death from a bridge after the television series "Battlestar Galactica" was cancelled by ABC. "His father . . . described Eddie as a sometimes brilliant boy who couldn't find enough in life to keep him interested." The father "learned . . . the boy had been sniffing gas with friends so he sent him to a psychiatrist." The latter reported that the boy was "just kind of bored with life," because "there was nothing here for him to excel in. . . . There was no real challenge here on this earth." He "lived and died for television shows" according to the news story headline (*San Francisco Chronicle,* August 26, 1979). Eddie's is, of course, an unusual case in any society, but it is more in tune with what goes on in America than in China.

Chinese children share the same world with their parents, and the parents make little effort to hide their problems and real selves from their children. Very early in life, Chinese children learn that reward and punishment are not necessarily consistent with the established rules of conduct, and that justice and love do not always prevail. At the same time they are more likely than American children to become conscious of the power exercised by the environment—they see their parents' faults as well as their virtues. From the beginning, they see their parents as ordinary mortals succeeding at times but failing at others, following inevitably the paths marked by custom and tradition.

American children are not only increasingly convinced of the importance of their individual predilections, but they are equally sure that they can accomplish what they set out to achieve. In the American child's restricted and comfortable world, he experiences few irreparable setbacks and knows few situations in which he is entirely frustrated by reality. It is only parents who can impose restrictions that the child may see as barriers to his own advancement.

The Chinese child is not only fully aware that he should obey his parents and other seniors, but even when he succeeds in circumventing them, he still faces the hurdles presented by custom and tradition. Through his active observation of and participation in adult activities, he is already well acquainted with some of his own shortcomings and the real nature of his society. The foci of attention and power being many, the restrictions imposed upon the individual come not merely from the parents but from the society at large. Even if he resents these barriers, he can still see no point on which to center his attack, for they are too numerous and too diffuse.

Consequently, Chinese children's dreams are far less grandiose and their fantasies are far more down to earth. Being part of the adult world they tend to be too busy with adult or adult-linked activities to be left to their own devices. This explains, I think, why Chinese literature, regardless of political change, does not feature characters who will go it alone, and is not concerned with introspection —a condition that one scholar of Chinese literature characterizes as "psychological poverty."[16]

School

By school age, Chinese children have a fairly realistic world view. Most American children of the same age understand little of the world of human reality which awaits them.[17] The impact of the schools makes their differences even more pronounced. The traditional Chinese schools, which remained unchanged for two thousand years, and the American schools of today are different in every way imaginable.

Old-style Chinese schools carried forward what the growing children had learned from the preschool experience, just as modern American schools attempt to further the pattern of behavior that American youngsters learn at home. Chinese children learned at home to respect their parents and tradition. In school they had the same virtues impressed on them by Confucian classics. American children learn at home to follow their individual predilections. In school, it is true, they are taught to cooperate, to develop sportsmanship, and so forth, but the relentless emphasis on creativity, autonomy, and progressive teaching techniques reinforces the values learned in the home.

It is only since the beginning of the twentieth century that Chinese children have been confronted with ideas and activities in school that are different from those which prevail at home. In the newer schools, for example, they learned about the relationships between germs and disease; at home their elders, who might also have attended school, but the fully traditional school, spat on the floor just as their ancestors did. In the modern schools, youngsters engaged in physical exercise, arts and crafts, and band practice; at home their elders could not see any connection between scholarship on the one hand, and calisthenics, wielding a knife, and blowing a bugle on the other.

This is not to deny that the progressive teaching technique is relatively new, even in the United States. It began in the 1920s, and its principal proponent, John Dewey, believed that education should be related to a child's interests and experiences. Even so, many Americans today are not unfamiliar with the stereotype of the severe-looking schoolmarm in the one-room schoolhouse of early American history. But the progressive teaching philosophy and technique are indigenous American developments, and in terms of our analysis, a natural outgrowth of the American way of life.

Conversely, the old-style Chinese schools are truly of ancient origin. The philosophy of education on which they were based flourished in China without significant change for over twenty centuries. The new-style schools were introduced from the West from about the end of the nineteenth century and did not replace the old-style schools until about the end of World War II. The old-style Chinese schools are organic to the Chinese way of life, especially in view of their age, as much as the progressive teaching technique is to the American way of life, despite its recent origin.

Furthermore, although the new Western-style schools in China began to confront Chinese children with ideas and activities that were different from those which prevailed at home, the differences between them and the old-style Chinese schools are not so great as those between all Chinese institutions[18] as a whole and their American counterparts.

For one thing, American schools foster a desire and a skill for self-expression that is little known in the Chinese schools. Even in nursery schools American children are taught to stand up individually to tell the rest of the class about something they know—perhaps a toy or an outing with parents. When I compare American youngsters with those I have known in China, I cannot help being amazed at the ease and the self-composure of the former when facing a single listener or a sizable audience, as contrasted with the awkwardness and the self-consciousness of Chinese youngsters in similar circumstances. In old-style Chinese schools there was nothing like public performance at all. For purposes of recitation, the teacher listened to each pupil, standing beside him one at a time and facing the wall, as the pupil loudly repeated that section of the classics assigned the day before. The rest of the class, which might contain up to thirty boys, could not hear the performing pupil because they would all be busy reading aloud their own assignments. In fact, it was not uncommon for a lazy teacher to have two pupils reciting simultaneously, one on each side. In modern Chinese schools after 1911, public appearance came into vogue. But even then the responsibility usually fell on the shoulders of the selected few, and practically all of the public oratory in trade and high schools was performed by rote, prepared in advance, and corrected by teachers before delivery.

Since 1949, public exhibition of music, dance, sculpture, painting, and crafts has become far more common than before. Visitors in the seventies, my family and I included, have all marveled at the remarkable precision and, by American standards, advanced forms of the arts. Performers and exhibitors are no longer limited to the select few as before. Spontaneity, however, is not given priority. For the overriding emphasis, pronounced by large slogans everywhere, is on how the arts can serve laborers, farmers, and soldiers.

The American emphasis on self-expression not only enables the American child to feel unrestrained by the group, but also makes him confident that he can go beyond it. The Chinese lack of emphasis on self-expression not only leads the Chinese child to develop a greater consciousness of the status quo but also serves to tone down any desire on his part to transcend the larger scheme of things.

A second fundamental difference between American and Chinese schools is the importance of the progressive principle in the former and the lack of any indigenous development of it in the latter. Simply stated, the progressive principle has two facets: individuals learn at different rates, and individuals have different kinds of abilities.

While this principle is not equally endorsed or lived up to throughout the school system, there can be little doubt that no other single principle has had a comparable influence on American education. The rapid acceptance and widespread popularity of intelligence tests and various psychographs is one indication; the movement to provide special training to the exceptional child is another; and the many curricula in which more stress is laid on the pleasure of learning than on learning itself is a third.

To the extent that the Chinese tutor schools of old allowed students to proceed at different speeds, one might say that they also were partially progressive. But this scholastic liberty was a matter of practical convenience and not a matter of principle. Moreover, while American students began by taking different courses, ranging from those that were creative to ones that required some memorization, Chinese students in tutor schools had to concentrate on memorizing great literature from the past and practicing the art of handwriting. There was never any thought of devising methods to make the learning process more palatable; this scholastic route had but one immediate and long-term goal: imperial examination honors leading to official rank.

The modern Chinese schools, which came near and after the end of the Manchu dynasty, did open the door to different curricula and aimed at somewhat different objectives. They contained most of the subjects taught in American schools, and they no longer expressly prepared men for the now nonexistent imperial examinations. But in the majority of schools, there was no freedom to choose electives. Furthermore, while Chinese children in modern schools learned physics and chemistry and attended physical education and craft classes, they still concentrated on reading and writing, ethics and civics, and history and geography. Until World War II, the number of Chinese college students in the arts and humanities far outnumbered those in the physical sciences.

In other words, throughout the Republican years, there was no significant deviation from the Confucian ideal of education in which the individual should be concerned first and foremost with his place in the scheme of human relations: emperor-subject, father-son, husband-wife, brothers, and friends.

During and since World War II, the number of Chinese college students in the physical sciences and engineering has become much larger than in the arts, humanities, and social sciences. But new-style schools in Taiwan since 1945 have in many ways reaffirmed many of the educational practices and goals of traditional China. The most spectacular indication of this is what all Taiwan knows today as *ngo pu* which, for lack of a better translation, may be described as "evil-type supplementary instruction." All grade school students have to take entrance examinations to gain admission into the better high schools. The examinations are so competitive that all school work is keyed to passing them. Those who hope to succeed in these examinations (a majority) pay for supplementary instructions for several hours a day after school. Many of the supplementary instructors are regular school teachers paid by the parents of the pupils. As high school pupils have to pass entrance examinations for admission to colleges and universities, this practice is even more common for them.

Repeated popular outcries and governmental measures have failed to stem the rising tide of "evil-type supplementary instruction." In 1967 the Taiwan government decided to lengthen the period of compulsory education from six to nine years so that those who graduate from grade school will automatically be admitted to a high school, thereby eliminating the need for entrance examinations at that level and also, it was hoped, the "evil-type supplementary instruction." The effectiveness of the measure does not concern us. What we see operating here are two of the basic elements in traditional Chinese education: (a) the need to pass stiff examinations, and (b) saturation school work, a major part of which is rote learning, so that each generation follows in the footsteps of the last.

American schools not only give more and more prominence to physical science than do the Chinese schools, they also place more and more emphasis on individual creative skills—scientific, artistic, literary, or craft. Compared with Chinese youngsters, American children, even in kindergarten, amaze me with their exact knowledge about the physical universe and mechanical principles. One of my daughters, at the age of five, taught me a lesson in flying. Her teacher had taken the class to visit an airport, and she came home pariculary enthusiastic about the hangar and the windsock. I asked her what a windsock was for, and she replied:

> It is to tell the pilot which way to fly. If the windsock is blowing from Mommy to me (pointing to her mother at the other end of the room), then the pilot would fly the plane from me to Mommy.

The opportunities available in America for the exceptional child to develop his particular skills are rarely found even in other highly advanced countries of the West. But American young persons, even in high schools and colleges, equally amaze me by comparison with Chinese of similar ages, with their naïveté about human relations, past or present, American or foreign. In spite of the fact that United States history is required in all high schools, the ignorance of young Americans about even their own country's history and geography has been documented by many surveys and college entrance tests. And continuing efforts in test design seem only to escalate the attention on individual capabilities at the expense of ethics and interpersonal relations.

There are two problems. One is declining academic achievement in spite of many innovations. A 1979 report by the National Assessment of Education Progress, funded by the U.S. Department of Health, Education, and Welfare, indicates that SAT (Scholastic Aptitude Test) math scores have dipped "more than 20 points over the last decade." This report puts the blame on the back-to-basics movement in math curricula, alleging that the emphasis on addition, subtraction, division, and multiplication has been at the expense of giving students the ability to "effectively apply mathematics in the real world—solving everyday problems" (*Honolulu Advertiser,* September 23, 1979). But the back-to-basics movement (the "three Rs") was itself a response to declining academic achievement and an outcry against the escalation of educational frills such as extracurricular programs.

The other problem is that by magnifying what each child as an individual can achieve rather than his relationship with the world, American education minimizes the role of tradition in forming society or the impact of momentous events, however distant in place or time, upon the individual. The emphasis upon biography and autobiography in American schooling and the continuing popularity of this literary genre among adult American readers may at first glance appear as evidence to the contrary. However, these documents serve first and foremost as examples of what the unique individual can accomplish in spite of all obstacles. They say, in effect, "go and do likewise."

The rise of the so-called "progressive school" was and still is heralded as a "revolution" in education. Actually this was no more than an excellent adaptation of the basic psychological tendencies of American adults to the education of their children. Consequently, though this school of thought came from Rousseau in France, was developed by Pestalozzi in Switzerland, Froebel in Germany as well as New Englander Amos Bronson Alcott in the 1830s, Americans have seen it as an American phenomenon identified with John Dewey. Shortly after Dewey's death in 1952, Benjamin Fine, education editor of the *New York Times,* summarized the impact of Dewey's educational philosophy upon American schooling:

> Fifty years ago education was based on the authoritarian principle of "teacher knows best." Individual differences were neglected. The subject was the most important aspect of the classroom—and the child was the least important. . . .

Dewey believed that learning should be meaningful, that it should tie in with the interests and experiences of the child. The school, he stressed, should keep alive and direct the active inquiring attitude of the child. He emphasized the *interest motive:* a boy would want to go to school if he found there were things worth doing for their own sake. What the best and wisest parent wants for his own child, Dr. Dewey insisted, the community must want for all its children.

Among the main points of Dewey's influence on education might be cited the following concepts:

(1) The child is more important than the subject. Hence we now speak of *child-centered schools.*
(2) Learning should be related to its time. *It should not be bound by outworn tradition.*
(3) Schools should be based on democratic, not authoritarian principles.
(4) *Discipline comes from within not from without.*
(5) Learning can be taught by experience. This is the now famous "learning by doing" slogan that is one of the best-known catch phrases of the entire progressive-education movement.[19]

In addition to the emphasis on self-expression and the progressive principle there is a third facet: American schools seem to encourage a militant ethnocentrism. Many American school children entertain the idea that the world outside the United States is practically a jungle: China is a land of inscrutable ways and mysterious opium dens, and Africa a "dark continent" inhabited by cannibals and wild animals.[20] Even Europe is a backward place, its only export a decadent culture and its present inhabitants an unprogressive lot whose ancestors stayed behind when their more intelligent and ambitious fellows departed for America.

Once I met a youngster in a park who, seeing that I was Chinese and trying to be very nice, said in his boyishly exaggerated way, "The Chinese are great." I asked him if he knew what was so great about them. And he responded, after a long pause, "They fly kites and they invented gunpowder."

This boy's innocence is not accidental. He was first of all assisted by popular media such as movies and comics whenever the Chinese or other Orientals are included. For years we had Fu Manchu, the Chinese laundrymen and their broken English, and Harold Lloyd's movies featuring pig-tailed Chinese gambling their life savings away in opium dens. The best the Chinese have fared in American comics so far is in *Steve Canyon*. Occasionally he saved the hapless Chinese from the clutches of their own Communist schemers.

However, an even more massive source of the boy's innocence is to be found in American history texts. Older misrepresentations of China and the Chinese in these texts are legion.[21] However, it must be emphasized that in recent years movements have been under way to correct these inaccuracies. Some of the popular juvenile literature such as *Compton's Encyclopedia* has shown a steady evolution toward a fuller and more accurate presentation of non-Western peoples. But the photos depicting Chinese life in the fourteenth edition (1959) of the *Encyclopaedia Britannica* were confined to the following:

> Plate I, five photos: a street scene with barefoot carriers, hawkers, and slum-like buildings; a junk with sails; meal time for about ten coolies (all squatting around a table); a pagoda; a camel caravan in Inner Mongolia.
>
> Plate II, five photos: a barber giving a haircut to a boy on the street; interior of a Chinese fishing vessel used as a home; street fortuneteller and letter writer, three barefoot boys playing dominoes on the waterfront; an opium smoker in action.
>
> Plate III, six photos: a worker adjusting a modern generator; wood water wheels on the Yellow River; construction worker applying plaster to bamboo latticework on a house wall; six males outside a guard rail watching coke-oven batteries; bamboo rafts on a river; coolies carrying cargo on a water front.
>
> Plate IV, six photos: a harbor scene; a nearly nude coolie carrying loads with a pole; a soldier with a bayonetted rifle but bare head and upper body; a street scene with three buses and many tri-rickshas; mother and baby in front of a village shop; a laborer dining at a sidewalk restaurant.
>
> Plate V, five photos: two tribal women in rags grinding rice with primitive tools; farm women carrying produce to market; farmer transplanting rice; women grading coal by hand at a mine; a tri-ricksha man taking a nap in his vehicle.

By way of contrast, the section on the United States in the same encyclopedia not only was more than three times as long (143 versus forty-one pages), but the thirteen plates of photos, as against five plates for China, featured the following subject matter:

> Plates I to VI featured beautiful landscapes from Mt. Adams; immaculate wheat farms and lakes; Yosemite National Park; fauna and flora of the United States. Plate VII featured the main reading room of the Li-

brary of Congress; the Green Room of the White House; a joint session of the United States Congress. Plates VIII to XI featured all of the past presidents and vice-presidents of the United States. Plates XII and XIII gave us some famous landmarks in the history of the United States from the granite portico over Plymouth Rock to a restored cannon at Gettysburg. There were no pictures of American slums, ghettoes, black sharecroppers, migrant workers, or even common factory laborers.

In other words, China is a land where coolies, fortunetellers, opium smokers, and primitive water wheels predominate—a picture in substantial agreement with America's popular notion of that Asian land.

In the fifteenth edition of the *Encyclopaedia Britannica* (1974) all pictures in the two major articles have been eliminated. China occupies 50 percent more pages than the United States (146 versus 101 pages). It may be that its editors did this in response to criticisms such as I made above in the 1970 edition of this book. What they have done in the latest edition is not only to lengthen the coverage of China but also to eliminate social and cultural descriptions and analysis. There is no statement of Chinese cultural life in the half page devoted to it, except to say how China has changed as a result of the coming of Western ideas and commodities. In both articles the bulk of the space is given to history in terms of political vicissitudes.

The striking contrast in presentation between the sections on China and the United States in the 14th edition of the *Encyclopaedia Britannica* is not accidental. It is still being systematically reinforced by many high school history texts even today. One example is *Men and Nations: A World History* by Mazour and Peoples.[22] There is a total of ten parts in the book. It starts with "The Beginnings," "Greece: the Foundation of Western Civilization," and closes with "The Beginnings of the Modern World," "Adjustments to the New Age," and "The Global War and After." In a total of 822 pages, China is allotted no more than twenty-two pages (pages 506–525 in the main text, and two pages in the 1964 Supplement). Furthermore, not only have the authors disguised or neglected three hundred years of Western imperialism in all parts of the world, but the twenty-page chapter devoted to China is entitled: "The New Imperialism: China," which is followed by two chapters entitled "The Rise of Modern Japan" and "The United States Becomes a World Power." The slanted nature of these titles is obvious.

So strong and so deep-seated is the bias that even high school texts expressly designed to correct a lopsided view of the world cannot rise above it. This may be illustrated by a widely used book titled *A Global History of Man*[23] produced with the support of the Carnegie Corporation of New York. This text indeed tries to provide American children with a more adequate coverage of the cultures and societies around the world. However, even here certain prejudices are still obvious. For example, World War II was made to begin in September 1939, when Germany invaded Poland, instead of in July 1937, when Japan began her full-scale aggression against China. The authors' position cannot be defended here by the view that the latter date only marked the beginning of war between Japan and China. For September 1939 merely ushered in conflicts among Western nations and the United States stayed out of the Pacific conflict until December 1941.

With such a view of the world it is easy for the same authors to see the entire course of World War II as a *Western* accomplishment (Stavrianos et al., pp. 206–214). Not only is China scarcely mentioned in the text, but she and her leaders are also absent from the pictures. Besides plates of some bombed out cities, there is one showing Churchill, Roosevelt, and Stalin at Yalta, one of Churchill, and one drawing with an American girl offering milk to a Greek child. Chiang Kai-shek, who fought aggression before any of the Western leaders went into action, and who, by his refusal to come to terms, tied down three million Japanese soldiers on the mainland, did not even make a group picture.

A most warped view is given of the Korean conflict. "The United States brought this aggression [North Korea's] before the United Nations and obtained quick action in support of South Korea" (in fact, President Truman ordered American forces to intervene before he went to the United Nations)[24]; "troops were sent by more than a dozen United Nations members, and the North Korean armies were driven back over the old border almost to the Yalu River, the boundary between North Korea and China. At this point China entered the war and the United Nations forces were driven back" (in fact, the so-called Allied forces were almost entirely American and it was only after General MacArthur ordered his troops to march to the Yalu River, ignoring repeated Chinese warnings, that the Chinese entered the war).

At the end of many sections of the text is an exercise entitled "Explain, Identify, or Locate." There are up to fifty items (names, places, and events) which the student is supposed to recall after having worked on that section of the text. The following tabulation of the relative proportion of items pertaining to the West and those outside it is a good indication:

| | Items Pertaining to | | | |
Section of the Book	Asia or Asians	Africa or Africans	Middle East or Middle Easterners	West or Westerners
Classical Age	11		4	22
Medieval Age	3	1	7	21
Man Lives in Global Unity	20	5	3	106

Presuming that school texts will undergo continuous change and evolve toward a less ethnocentric view of the world, it probably will still be a long, long time, however, before the average high school honor student from the best equipped American institution will be able to associate much more than the name of Confucius, kite-flying, and gunpowder with China, and an even longer time, if ever, before American youngsters will concede that any other people on earth could have anything better than or even as good as what is to be found in America.

One reason for the above is that old prejudices die hard. The familiar ideas are bound to maintain their hold in spite of the best intentions. The other reason is more deep-seated. Can Americans afford to allow any other people, especially a non-Western people, to better them in any way? My conclusion is that they probably cannot because *active* superiority over others is essential to a people with the individual-centered way of life.

From this angle, the reason for America's insistence on its superiority over the rest of the world, especially the non-Western world, is both similar to and different from that underlying Peking's anti-United States posture in the recent past. In both cases the attitudes are functional and are dictated by felt needs. However, while the American need for superiority over others is rooted in the long-established national character of the people, the Chinese need to be anti-United States was based on temporary political expediency, generally unrelated to the aspirations of the people. It was Washington which rebuffed Chinese Communist leaders' friendly gestures, including Mao's and Chou's offers to visit the national capital shortly after they took power in Peking. Instead the United States adhered to the domino theory of John Foster Dulles and pursued a China encirclement policy. Such attitudes and acts were what led to Peking's militancy toward the United States. Consequently, Chinese militancy toward America could change in short order as new circumstances developed. The American approach toward the rest of the world, however, is likely to be longer lasting in spite of setbacks such as Vietnam.[25]

To the Chinese Confucian classics were, of course, the only important matters of learning, and history was written from the Chinese point of view alone. It is something of a surprise for many a present-day Chinese, including myself, to learn that Genghis Khan and his successors considered China only as a province of his much vaster empire, since the Mongol rule was presented in Chinese books simply as a dynasty, Yuan, in the sense that T'ang, Sung, and Ming were also dynasties. Many popular novels, either of the supernatural or the realistic kind, depicted victorious expeditions of founders of dynasties or their generals. Some of these dealt with battles between Chinese and "barbarians" but more often the opponents were all Chinese.

The most famous Chinese versus "barbarian" war was that waged by the clever tactician, Chu Ke Liang, of Three Kingdoms fame (A.D. 220–286) against a southern tribal chieftain, Meng Hu. In this campaign, Chu Ke Liang was supposed to have defeated and captured his "barbarian" opponent six times—each time the captive was released and each time he came back with a more formidable invading force. But when he was captured the seventh time and was once again released, Meng Hu vowed "eternal allegiance" to the Han people. In popular Chinese thought, Chu Ke Liang's actions were a great feat of "conquest of hearts" and it has ever since been eulogized in Chinese historical writings.

However, the Chinese, while always maintaining their own unquestioned superiority and conscious of their differences from others, never entertained the notion that their inferiors *should* change their ways of life. Some of the "barbarians" became "cooked barbarians" *(shu fan)* in that they took on Chinese speech and culture; they were welcomed. Many of them remained "raw barbarians" *(sheng fan);* they were also left alone. Some Chinese undoubtedly considered the latter unfortunate, but it was their own business.

For this reason, the Chinese attitude vis-à-vis the non-Chinese world must be characterized as *passive* superiority, in contrast to American and Western *active* superiority.

Neither attitude is an unmixed blessing, and we shall see the logical consequences associated with each as we journey through the body of this book. White Westerners in China were of course objects of curiosity to Chinese children and adults, as were Asians in the United States. The Chinese nickname for Westerners was "Ocean-born Devil or Ghost" *(yang kuei tze)* primarily because of their pale skin, and the frequent occurrence of blue eyes and blond hair. The Chinese associated these colors with death and funerals just as many Americans equate the color yellow with cowardice and white with purity and weddings. But because of their attitude of passive superiority, Chinese parents and teachers, far from encouraging their children to disregard all non-Chinese things and values, actually insisted on a relativistic view of the world.

Chinese, for instance, have for many centuries revered written characters, which they believe to have been created by past sages. There were many "societies for saving papers with written characters." These societies employed collectors who roamed around town, with forks in hand and baskets on their backs, gathering such scattered pieces. The bits were then burned at the local Confucian temple. It was believed that a person who used inscribed papers for toilet purposes would be struck dead by lightning. And one who accidentally stepped on a book must pick it up and place it on his head momentarily for propitiation.

We might imagine that Chinese parents and teachers would restrict their feelings to Chinese written characters, but this was not usually the case. I knew a number of parents and village tutor-teachers who advised their children or pupils to treat with equal reverence all pieces of paper on which there was writing, whether the words were Chinese or foreign. "After all," I heard one father say, "the foreign words must have been created by foreign sages." This seemingly minor episode is an expression of a basic aspect of the Chinese orientation to the world.

With the coming of the new schools and a new curriculum, the age-old injunction against defiling of the written character has been noticeably relaxed in many quarters. However, in this new curriculum, which prevailed until the rise of the Communist regime when jingoism and Mao's sayings began to overshadow everything else, school children learned not only about great men and significant events in Chinese history, but they also read and heard about the scientific investigations and statesmanship of Benjamin Franklin, Columbus and his discovery of the New World, Abraham Lincoln's efforts to emancipate the slaves, the Magna Carta, and the French

Revolution. As early as the first or second grade, I learned in an ethics course how George Washington when a small boy cut down a cherry tree and was honest with his father about it, how a famous French scholar by the name of Montaigne used all his spare time, including the few minutes before and after dinner, to write his thoughts down so that in ten years he accumulated a tremendous volume, and how the Scotsman, Robert Bruce, after disastrous defeats at the hands of his English adversaries, was inspired to victory by the actions of a spider which tirelessly and successfully built its web in spite of destructive winds. Some of these anecdotes are, of course, myths. But they are myths that represented the United States and the West in a favorable light.

It is no exaggeration to say that the average American high school graduate knows very little about the rest of the world, especially Asia and Africa. It is equally true that the average Chinese high school graduate, before the rise of the new regime in 1949, tended to have a fuller view of the world and its inhabitants.[26]

The usual Chinese description of things American is that they are different. This remains basically so in Taiwan today even though, since the country is under the pressure of so much American influence, the idea of American superiority often asserts itself. On the other hand, the usual and prevailing American view of the Chinese is that they do everything the wrong way. This does not deny the existence of a very small American minority of Sinophiles.

We have seen that American parents encourage a feeling of self-importance in their children who live in a world quite separate from reality; and the American educational system confirms this initial tendency. This belief in personal invincibility affects the belief in the invincibility of the country. This last conviction has an inevitable effect on internal politics and the conduct of international affairs.

The child's private world cannot, however, be kept distinct from that of the elders indefinitely. American children, when they begin school, for the first time come into close contact with persons, ideas, and activities over which the parents exercise little or no control. The children must submit some of their ideas about themselves and their environment to mild tests of reality.

The Chinese child, having never been set apart from the world of his elders, faces no such trial. He has always been in contact with a multiplicity of persons and he has few illusions about his own capabilities and how he may fare in the world.

Serious dislocations often result when the American child enters school life. These occur in two principal areas, the first of which is the religious. The majority of American children are raised in the Christian faith, learning its prayers, attending Sunday school, and participating in other church activities. As they are initiated into the wonders of science, with its mechanistic description of the universe, they cannot but apply the same mechanical principles to their conception of religion. For example, how can God watch over all of us at the same time? Who or what created God? How do we explain the miracles? Having been encouraged to be rational about things, American children will ask these and innumerable other questions. But finding no satisfactorily "scientific" answers to these questions, American parents and teachers have had to evade the issues. Some children will feel compelled to explain the supernatural in mechanistic terms. Recently I overheard one child say to his playmate: "Jesus is right in this room. We cannot see him because he is of every shape and color." This child was simply repeating the arguments I have heard in many a church and Sunday school. But his playmate extended the argument thus, to an extent not usually acceptable to ministers or Sunday-school teachers: "God must have very long, long legs, and He stands in the middle of the world. He can look this way or that way any time He pleases. That's why He is everywhere."

Are parents going to accept these explanations? Or are they to tell children that such ideas are wrong, that religious belief and the reality of life belong to two different orders? If they take the latter view, how are they to tell children that religion will have anything to do with a life and a universe which are increasingly described in scientific terms? If they take the former view, how can they face the question as to whether God is also in the ugly things that children of school age must have seen?

Most American parents I know tend to gloss over these questions, and have no effective reply to their children's mechanistic statements about God. Yet a child whose preschool years are marked by idealistic simplicity in which everything is consistently right or wrong, true or false, must be confused by the new situation in which the once authoritative and positive words of the parents become vague, facts are at variance, and ambiguity is everywhere. That is why a "God Is Dead" movement can arouse so much public attention. I have no figures to indicate whether its adherents are predominantly young, but this is probably the case. Theologians will undoubtedly be able to invent arguments showing that standard bearers of the "God Is Dead" movement do not mean God is dead. For our purposes this movement is merely another symptom of confusion and doubt.

Chinese children face no such problems. In the first place, religion in China, as we shall see later, is much more matter-of-fact than it is in America. Christianity and Judaism depend upon fixed dogmas which in turn must depend upon constant interpretation to relate them to the actuality of human existence. Chinese creeds have a few simple dogmas plainly tied to life's immediate problems, such as, if one has eye trouble the Goddess of Eyesight will help; or dogmas needing no extended argument to be convincing, such as, that ancestors and their own descendants have a community of interest. Chinese religion is nontheoretical, utilitarian, or based on self-evident truisms that require no defense. It is unlikely to come into conflict with other Chinese values or beliefs.

Secondly, the American child is from birth conditioned to attach himself to one parental authority, to one set of truths, and to one style of life that is absolutely right. To maintain this singleness of life, it is inevitable that he will want to synthesize his knowledge of science and religion.

The Chinese child is from the beginning conditioned to a multiple parental authority, to many points of view, and to the vicissitudes of a life in which circumstance dictates inconsistency, doubt, and compromise. It is almost inevitable that he should compartmentalize his experiences. Even if a medicine based on scientific experiments is proven to be more efficacious than offerings to gods, why should he not use both tools?

Finally, with their attitude of active superiority, most Americans who give themselves to science have a tendency to deny and to disprove all other avenues to truth. But with their attitude of passive superiority, their Chinese counterparts have no comparable concern. In exactly the same way, Chinese worshipers of one god did not care about the blasphemous. For the Chinese will say, "If you are bad the gods will punish you. Why should I usurp the gods' place?" For practical reasons, most Americans do live with conflicting standards. But I have not found any American counterpart of this kind of Chinese reasoning.

This attitude explains why, when the modern schools began to campaign against idolatry and superstition (meaning all traditional Chinese religious beliefs), few educated Chinese youngsters came into conflict with their parents. Nor do I know of any Chinese parents who withdrew their children from the schools that taught agnosticism or Christianity. In brief, there were no difficulties caused solely by the fact that the home and the modern school taught sharply different things.

The second difficulty facing the American child in school, at least among the middle and upper-middle classes, is the gap between his idealized childhood world and the real world. The latter is no longer the protective environment of the family nursery, with supportive parents to buffer the outside world. The new surroundings may be beautiful or ugly, comforting or cruel; the child discovers that some of his schoolmates have a lot and others little. Even if he is talented and very bright, he may still have trouble, for the exceptional child often faces social ostracism by his less gifted peers. But if he is not, his misery will be an entirely new experience. If he is from a lower class while his associates come from better circumstances, or worse still, if he belongs to a religious or racial minority, he is now in for wounds which he never thought God or Santa Claus would ever allow any human to inflict.

Social Needs and Values

The impact of these new forces on the American child is strong because of the values placed by the culture on self-reliance.

Very early in life the American child learns to think in terms of private property. He appreciates the difference between what is his and what is not. At school age he begins to become aware that what belongs to his parents is out of bounds to him. His basic needs are provided by the family, but he begins to earn some money, if only from his parents, or to handle a weekly allowance. Soon he is aware that after eighteen or twenty-one years of age his parents will have no obligation to support him in any way. This is the foundation of a businesslike relationship between American parents and children which assumes increasing clarity as the years go by.

We must outline the social needs of the human individual before we are able to see clearly the results of the two patterns of parent-child relationship. Although we are accustomed to think of human beings as entities, each human being is always tied to a web of fellow human beings. I use the word "tied" advisedly, for every human being must live in association with other human beings. This is why solitary confinement is one of the most severe punishments man can suffer and why, as we shall see later, rehabilitation programs such as

Alcoholics Anonymous, Alateen (for children whose parents are alcoholics), Al-Anon (for spouses of alcoholics), Encounter in Manhattan and Palmer Drug Abuse Program in Dallas (both organizations to combat narcotics addiction), are all based on dependence on some form of group affiliation for the client.

This kind of "cure" created the following predicament for the husband of a reformed alcoholic, described in his letter to Ann Landers:

> Through Alcoholics Anonymous my wife has been sober for nearly five years. My problem is an unusual one. When she was drunk she was home all the time. Now, I hardly see her anymore. When I come home from work she is getting ready to go to an AA meeting. She rarely returns before midnight. . . . (*Honolulu Advertiser,* January 22, 1980)

What do human beings seek among their fellow human beings? They crave satisfaction of one or all of three social needs—sociability, security, and status.

Sociability embodies the individual's enjoyment of being with other human beings: to see them, to rub shoulders with them, to hear them, to speak with them, to complain to them and to listen to their gripes, to gossip, and to engage in various degrees of body contact with them. The closest sociability is the intimacy between a man and a woman. The loosest sociability is New Year's Eve on Times Square. Between these extremes we have cocktail parties, dances, fox hunts, family gatherings, conversation between friends, seminars and conferences, coffee klatches, and psychotherapy sessions.

Security signifies the predictability of the individual's human environment, now or in the future. It has two components. First, every individual wants to be certain that an assured number of his fellow human beings are his intimates and share with him certain aims, thoughts, or action patterns. Second, in time of need he can count on their sympathy and support just as they can count on his. These are what we in daily speech express in terms of loyalty, faithfulness, fidelity, or devotion. Every individual needs to have some fellow men in whom he can confide his worst thoughts without the fear that they are going to despise him or draw away from him. When he speaks or expresses himself or acts, he needs to have a fair certainty regarding the kind of reaction he will receive. The highest security is that of the armed forces in peacetime, when the individual's movements and even recreation are well regulated. The lowest security is that of riots or war. Between these extremes are many human associations that affect one's sense of belonging to a group: friendship, clubs, cliques, political parties, church or temple, gang, honor society, or residential group.

Status provides the individual with his sense of importance among his fellow men. It is the rank or comparative position occupied by the individual in his group, and of the rank or comparative position of his own group vis-à-vis other groups, with the specific attitudes, duties, and privileges associated with it. Status can be seen in sports, in economic pursuits, in the professions, in academic achievements, in politics, among churchmen as well as hunters. It is felt by students no less than by warriors. The Chinese concepts of face and of propriety, and the American sensitivity to prestige and superiority are all familiar expressions of the same need. The utmost concern for status is to be found in a caste situation, where inter-dining or even sight of the lower groups carries pollution. An example of almost total lack of concern for status is to be found in some monasteries such as those of Trappist monks where all distinctions are conscientiously removed. But even the Trappist monks must regard their form of devotion as far superior to that of other orders.

The drug and alcohol rehabilitation groups mentioned before and those like them satisfy all three social needs. They provide ample company for the lonely. Their highly regulated programs make the human relation very predictable. And the more each such group distinguishes itself by size, by visibility or whatever, the higher the sense of status it confers on its members vis-à-vis the people outside it.

So far we have spoken about needs shared by Americans, Chinese, and human beings in all societies. Returning to our earlier discussion of the two differing patterns of parent-child relationships, we shall come to some interesting results. The first human group in which the American or the Chinese individual satisfies his social needs is the biological family consisting of parents and siblings. This is where, as every reader knows, he has so much of his siblings' and his parents'—especially his mother's—attention, that he sometimes wishes that they would leave him alone. This is where his every move and what he eats are so regulated that often he purposely does the opposite of what he has been told or refuses to eat food his mother offers him. And finally, this is where he first vies with his siblings for parental favors, but his parents, if they are wise, will make sure that failures are covered up and successes are praised, so that he may not suffer from an inferiority complex.

However, the self-reliant orientation makes it impossible for the

American child to continue satisfying his social needs in the kinship group. Even before school age the American child, because of the American customs concerning cribs, separate bedrooms, babysitters, and the American emphasis on peers, has already frequently and clearly led something of a separate existence from his parents. Still, since he is very much under the protective care and supervision of his parents, the best the American child can do at this stage of the game is to sometimes hide his activities from his parents and to unite with his siblings as a defense against his parents. The horizontal gravitation toward siblings is the beginning of opposition between the young and the old, which anticipates the generation gap to come later. The exclusive nature of the average American family makes it inevitable that, for the young child, his parents are the only great man and woman in existence. Therefore parents still figure greatly in the boastful world of youngsters. I once heard the son of a naval petty officer telling his playmates how absolutely useless the army and the air force were. More recently I saw a cartoon of two boys, the bigger of whom said to the other, "My father has been a father longer than yours." But by the time he is in second grade, the American child begins to realize that socially he and his elders are separate individuals.

Having been taught to rely on himself from the beginning, he is now ready to explore the wider world on the same basis. Yet his social needs prevent him from being independent of other human beings. When the American child, driven by independence training, wants to make it on his own, he must seek another group to substitute for the group at hand. This means that the American youngster, at school age, must learn to transfer his allegiance from the kinship (and kinship-connected) group to a group composed of his unrelated peers, the gang. Even siblings of the same sex cannot figure for long in this group. For, while siblings are better than parents, they are still connected with a group that he has not made on his own. The American child must, therefore, gravitate away from a group in which he has been deeply entrenched without trying, in favor of a group in which his membership is subject to change without notice. Furthermore, his place in the latter group is often adversely affected by the closeness of his relationship with the former. The net effect of his allegiance to the gang is the systematic undermining of his relationship with his parents.

This is not a question of love or lack of love for his parents. Even if he loves them, his needs for sociability, security, and status among his peer group must take precedence over his feelings for his elders. It is not even that he misunderstands his elders. Rather, the urgency of his own social needs precludes his acceptance of their communication. To make it on one's own is truly an all-pervasive American value. Currently (1980) even the superhero "Spider Man" of the comics is trying desperately to make it on his own, as Peter Parker, without the aid of his web-slinging powers.

Thus many American children give up music lessons despite parental protests, because the gang considers such skills to be sissified. Many American children shun foreign languages regardless of their ancestral background, because their linguistic prowess is derided by their playmates. I have known Chinese children raised in the United States who spat at anyone who dared talk to them in Chinese, and children of French origin who tearfully told their parents that they couldn't possibly continue to speak French. One wealthy German couple hired a German governess to speak German with their son, who was of course learning English in school. Soon the governess gave up because she could not make her charge follow any orders except in English. Conflict can develop over many matters— hair, dress, hours, sex, and drugs. The American child has to flout parental wishes because of his fear of rejection by his own peers. The more insecure he is about this, the more he must conform to the standards of his peer group at the expense of those of his parents.

The American school child's insecurity is easily matched by that of his parents. American parents, as we have mentioned, have complete control over their children. While consciously grooming them to be independent, they have unconsciously never doubted that the youngsters are inseparable parts of themselves. For by independence they really mean that the youngsters can do those things for themselves of which the parents approve but not others which the elders frown on. In this they are, of course, safe as long as the children are young; small children can be manipulated reasonably easily. They can coax the little ones to take care of themselves but at the same time be fully certain that such independence does not go far. Yet the situation is never stationary. The infant can be satisfied with a bottle or when he is picked up and held. At three or four, a male child may be placated by having a haircut like daddy's or a female child by being dressed like mommy. But at each successive age level, as his physical and mental powers grow, the increasingly autonomous little individual demands fuller freedom to do things on his own, and in his own way.

Sometimes after the child's entry into school, the American parents, having been used to confining youthful antics within a playpen, suddenly face a serious threat to their control. Their children have figured too largely as part of the satisfaction of their own social needs. They have seen and cuddled their children every day. They have watched and directed the youngster's habits and speech. They have praised and been proud of their progeny's performance. And in all this they have had an exclusive and strong hand. Now they are faced with the prospect of seeing little of the children, of having less to say about how they act, and even of being less proud of what they do. It is not unnatural that they feel threatened. The more they have been accustomed to having complete control, and the more their children have helped satisfy their social needs, the harder it is for parents to relinquish this control.

American parents feel threatened not merely because of reluctance to relinquish control. Their society is one in which each succeeding generation ruthlessly replaces the previous one; once the children become independent, parents have no honored place in their children's lives. School age gives the parents a preview of the children's future independence and of their own progressive decline from a position of dominance. This is a prospect or transition that few human beings can take with equanimity. The children's departure from the close, warm circle of the family thus creates a cloud of insecurity in the shadow of which both parents and children henceforth move.

Consequently, instead of welcoming the prospect of their children's ultimate independence, many American parents experience increasing anxiety as their youngsters progress. Some parents, as their children grow away from them, declare that they are glad to be free and that they would not have it any other way. Perhaps so, but such declarations are frequently necessary for the protection of parental pride. On the other hand, more American parents try, in one way or another, to hold on to the parent-child bond.

The results are not at all certain. In infancy, the simple formula of more attention–greater attachment and less attention–diminished attachment undoubtedly works in most cases. But children at school, under pressure to be both independent and to ally themselves with the gang, are a different matter. Some succumb to an increase in parental charm. Their love for their parents increases, and the calls of the gang go unanswered. These children are described derogatorily as being tied to their mothers' apron strings and if they continue this close attachment will in later life be known as "poor marital risks." Here American parents face a dilemma. Though wanting their children to be close to them, they are worried when their children are unpopular with their peer group. Most youngsters reject parental affection in favor of that of their own playmates, and they must do so with an ever-increasing sense of rebellion. Well-adjusted American children advance in a direction determined by their way of life much earlier: a way of life characterized by strong emotionality and the encouragement of individual predilection.

Chinese school children and their parents find life much easier in this respect. Having always been a part of the real world, the children are now prepared to deal with this same reality on a broader basis. They are not shocked by injustices, slights, or untruths, because they have already experienced or learned to expect these trials. At twelve or fourteen most of them are not merely acquainted with their future places and problems in society—they are already full-fledged members of that society.

This realistic orientation is furthered by the Chinese ideal of mutual dependence, which is the exact opposite of the American spirit of self-reliance. We have already noted that the Chinese son has to support his father; the Chinese father is likewise obligated to support his son. This reciprocity is a social contract that lasts for life. The idea of a legal will is alien to Chinese thought, for a Chinese father's assets, no less than his liabilities, go automatically and equally to his several sons before or after his death.[27]

The Chinese child learns about his permanent link with his parents in diverse ways. For one thing, he never has to manage an allowance.[28] He is free to spend whatever he can get out of his parents. The idea of earning money from one's parents is considered laughable by Chinese. Consequently, while necessity causes poor Chinese children to appreciate the value of money, youngsters from wealthier families rarely learn this.

The social tie between Chinese parents and sons is equally automatic, inviolable, and life-long. This proverb expresses the essence of the pattern: "First thirty years, one looks at the father and respects the son; second thirty years, one looks at the son and respects the father." That is to say, while the son is young the father's social status determines that of the son; but later the son's social status determines that of the father.

For this reason, the sons of the powerful, however young they may be, are as powerful as their fathers, while the fathers can, even after retirement, wield the authority and status they derive from the position of their sons. Once this is understood I think the reader will even more readily see why it would not have been possible for any Chinese son to write about his mother, famous or not, the way James Roosevelt did about Mrs. Eleanor Roosevelt.

This means that the Chinese child not only finds satisfaction of all his social needs in the kinship group where he begins life, but he is also under no compulsion to leave it as he grows up. Having been exposed gradually to the adult world, the Chinese child tends always to gravitate vertically. He plays games or gambles with his elders on festival occasions; he works together with them in the fields and markets. The automatically shared community of interests between him and his parents makes it unnecessary for him to go it alone. If the child has a few friends among unrelated peers it is condoned. But if he has many of them and their common activities interfere with his studies or family duties, his friends will be branded "fox friends and dog cronies" and he, a wastrel. On the other hand he will be much admired as an example of a good son and a good man if he has few outside associations and devotes his entire energy toward working and pleasing his parents. Popularity among peers is a condition which some Chinese youngsters may enjoy, but it is not an objective toward which they must strive.

Because of this, the Chinese have known neither the problem of the generation gap nor the fear of being known as a teacher's pet. Both of these situations reflect a horizontal orientation in which the young are pitted against the old, or the subjects of authority against its sources.

Consequently, while the American father who basks in his son's glory or the son who profits from his father's fame will always object to any suggestion that this is the case, a similarly situated Chinese father or son has no such desire to conceal his source of strength. In case the identity of such an individual is temporarily obscured, he is likely to reassert his position in just so many words.

Thus, the Chinese pattern of mutual dependence, as opposed to the American pattern of self-reliance, provides satisfaction in being under the protection of elders. For the parent-child ties are permanent rather than transitory. It is taken for granted that they are immutable, and so are not subject to individual acceptance or rejection. Secure in the shadow of their ancestors, Chinese youngsters of school age have no great psychological urge to seek any alliance outside the kin group.

For Chinese children, therefore, the call of their own age group possesses none of the dictatorial compulsion that it has for their American brethren. Chinese boys and girls are able to get along with their play groups without having to part with the things their parents represent. My own experience illustrates the point. When my parents moved their home from a south Manchurian village to an east Manchurian town, I was for the first time in my life confronted with a dialect difference. My first-grade schoolmates spoke a dialect considerably different from mine. Within six weeks, I had changed over to the speech prevailing in school when I was there, but at home I spoke in my original tongue, although my parents never suggested that I do so. This transition occurred again when I went to Peking and once more when I went to Shanghai. Each time I acquired a new dialect. But each new dialect was merely added to the list of those at my command. This pattern was true of all Chinese youngsters whom I knew, even with reference to entirely foreign languages, for Russian and Japanese were both widely known in Manchuria, French in Yunnan, and English in the rest of China. Furthermore, these added dialects and languages never prevented the individual from firmly retaining his original tongue, even though he took pride in his personal achievement in speaking them.

Chinese parents, on their part, have little reason for anxiety as their children grow older. First, never having been exclusive masters of their children, they do not feel rejected when the children become more independent. Second, the Chinese parent-child relationship is permanent. A father is always a father, whether or not he is loving or kind. A son is always a son; rarely is he disowned because he is not dutiful. Lastly, Chinese social organization is such that age, far from being a defect, is a blessing. Chinese parents have no reason to regret their children's maturity, for it assures not a lesser role but a more respected place for themselves.

The Chinese pattern of mutual dependence thus forms the basis of a mutual psychological security for both the old and the young. When children have little need to leave home, parents have little need to hold. The result is a life-style in which individual predilections are minimized not because there is strong restraint that demands conformity, but because the emotions of the individual are neutralized since he is satisfied with things as they are.

In Chapter 13 we shall see the relevance of this contrast to the problems of old age and juvenile delinquency. Here it should be noted that most American parents assert that their children present bigger and more complex problems as they grow older. The elders are most troubled when the youngsters draw near adolescence. Most Chinese parents see the situation entirely differently. Their children become less of a problem as they become older. Until the time of extensive contact with the West, the Chinese did not recognize adolescence as a specific period of human development, had no exact term to designate it, and had no literature on the subject.[29]

But the same contrast is sharpened by two more factors. For one thing, practically all Americans go to school until they are sixteen, while even in 1945 less than 30 percent of Chinese children received any formal education at all. Consequently, for the majority of Chinese, their transition from childhood to adulthood has been, up to recent decades, even less turbulent than the picture presented here.

Since 1949 many movements, some better known in the West for their involvement of youths in the form of Red Guards and Little Red Soldiers, have seemed to bring about drastic changes in this picture. They have certainly activated many sectors of the society formerly dormant and suppressed others formerly active. However, as we shall see in Chapter 15, even today the changes have not been that fundamental.

The other factor is the concept of equality as an active ideal, which has been as important in America as it has been insignificant in China. To evaluate the part played by this concept in the American way of life, we must first examine the differences between Europe and the United States.

NOTES
    1. The term *personality,* which has enjoyed so much currency in our discussions of human affairs, is, in my view, outmoded. It must be replaced by a concept which at once takes into consideration both the individual and his need for intimacy with others. This need is recognized by some scholars but continues to be given but lip service in most theories of human behavior. This need, the most tangible evidence of which consists of transactions between individuals, is an integral part of any personality. It is as indispensable to the functioning of the human individual as air and water are to human and animal physiology. Elsewhere I proposed the term *jen* (human being in Chinese, which corresponds to the same term in Japanese, but pronounced *jin*). See Francis L. K. Hsu, "Psychological Homeostasis and *Jen*," "*American Anthropologist* 73, no. 1 (1971):23–44. But a discussion of this proposal is beyond the scope of this book, in which use of the term personality will continue.
    2. Gregory Bateson, "Some Systematic Approaches to the Study of Culture and Personality," in *Character and Personality* 11:76–82, 1942; reprinted in D. Haring, *Personal Character and Social Milieu,* pp. 110–116.
    3. Geoffrey Gorer, *The American People.*
    4. Many streets are lined with houses on one side only. Where both sides of the street are occupied, it is still possible to erect shadow walls since home entrances do not as a rule directly face each other.

5. The attention-attracting value of children's photographs, recognized both by advertisers and the proverbial baby-kissing politician, is confirmed as well by newspaper readership surveys. In September 1947, the *Journalism Quarterly* published figures on reader reaction to 2,200 general news photographs published in newspapers from coast to coast. Among males, pictures in the "children and baby" category caught the attention of 59 percent, which was a slightly higher response than that produced by the photo categories of "beauty queens and glamour girls," "international and general news," "accidents and disasters" (each 58 percent), and even "sports" (57 percent). Among women, the children's photos attracted the attention of 77 percent, slightly lower than the "weddings and engagements" classification (79 percent) but somewhat above the "society and club news" category (76 percent). Judging by current newspapers throughout the country, the importance of children, babies, and girls has not waned since that time.

6. One joke goes as follows: In a large compound two women living in adjacent households gave birth to babies on the same day. Naturally the two households celebrated the Full-Month-after-Birth (a major celebration according to Chinese custom) at the same time. One of the guests, upon hearing "It's a boy" in the first household, congratulated its members loudly, "Well done! Well done!" When the same guest went to the second house and found it was a girl, he blurted out, "Too bad! Too bad!" The mother of the girl baby was very annoyed, but good manners prevented her from reacting at once. Just then a wedding procession noisily proclaimed itself outside the front gate and the adults (including the tactless guest) and children rushed out to see the sight. When all and sundry again returned to the second house, someone who did not rush out to see the procession asked what was going on. Before anyone could answer, the mother of the girl baby said, to the acute embarrassment of the tactless guest, "It was nothing! Only four 'Well dones' carrying one 'Too bad' in a sedan chair is all."

7. Comic books of a sort appeared in the streets of big cities such as Shanghai and Peking in the thirties. These were of two kinds: the Dagwood and Blondie type of Western origin and the serialized traditional Chinese stories.

8. *"Keng-sheng Hsiao Chi"* [A small autobiographical note of Keng-sheng], in *Chuan Chi Wen Hsueh*, [Biographical Literature] (a magazine) vol. 11, no. 4, 1966.

9. Beatrice Judelle, "Child Population Study: National Toy Market Analysis," *Toys and Novelties*.

10. Susan Ferraro, "A Primer for Parents (and Other Adults)," *American Way* (an in-flight magazine), (May 1979), p. 23.

11. My parents were no longer poor at that time. They could have afforded with ease many more toys than I ever received during my childhood and youth, but I never even had a respectable kite.

12. The Chinese do not have the "godchild" institution, though Chinese Christians practice it. The traditional Chinese custom closest to it is that of "dry-child" which has nothing to do with baptism (see note 5 in Chapter 5).

13. Helen Codere, "A genealogical study of kinship in the United States," *Psychiatry* 18, no. 1 (1955):79.

14. Irving L. Janis and Peter B. Field, "A Behavioral Assessment of Persuability: Consistency of Individual Differences," *Sociometry* 19 (1956):241-259; Godwin C. Chu, "Culture, Personality and Persuability," *Sociometry* 29, no. 2 (1966):169-174; Lily Chu Bergsma, *A Cross-Cultural Study of Conformity in Americans and Chinese*, pp. 64-74; and Lily Chu, "The Sensitivity of Chinese and American Children to Social Influences," *The Journal of Social Psychology* 109 (1979):175-186.

15. J. D. Salinger, *The Catcher in the Rye*, p. 11.

16. Hsia, *History of Modern Chinese Fiction*, p. 503.

17. In this connection we might note the large number of American novels which

devote themselves to the poignant problems of youthful adjustment to the real world, from James T. Farrell's *Studs Lonigan* and its social concern with "a world I never made" to Thomas Wolfe's autobiographical accounts of a youth's struggle to understand and be understood by others. The central theme of Wolfe's voluminous writings ("Which of us is not forever a stranger and alone?") is to be found with varying degrees of emphasis throughout Western literature, though it has become most explicit in contemporary American writing. Among others, the works of Sherwood Anderson and Carson McCullers are almost wholly concerned with the question of individual loneliness. J. D. Salinger's *The Catcher in the Rye,* and Hermann Hesse's *Steppenwolf* are examples of a similar theme. These writers all appear to assume that this is the *human* tragedy—that is, the condition of all mankind. In Chinese literature the one kind of loneliness expressed is that which occurs when lovers or families are separated. There is absolutely no expression of the idea that "aloneness" is the essential condition of man or of struggling youth.

18. Besides the old-style Chinese schools we may differentiate three kinds of modern Chinese schools inspired by the West: (1) new-style schools ca. 1900–1949 in China; (2) new-style schools in Taiwan ca. 1945 to date; and (3) new-style schools in the People's Republic of China since 1949.

The Cultural Revolution of 1966–1978 threatened to bring something new into Chinese schools but post-Gang of Four reports reveal mostly destructive effects. These effects were primarily confined to colleges and universities. When my family and I visited China in the summer of 1972 the institutions of higher learning were not really in operation. In most cases faculty outnumbered students most of whom were away from their campuses propagandizing the Cultural Revolution, planting trees, helping with communes, and digging archeological treasures. A huge number of new sites and new artifacts were discovered as a result of this digging, but regular university learning and research nearly ceased. Some students were vociferously against all grading and examinations. In one instance a college student handed in blank papers and became a hero.

Since the fall of the Gang of Four and the resumption of regular classes and examinations that hero is in disgrace. However, except for cursory observations by short-term visitors we lack systematic knowledge of the educational system in the People's Republic. See, for example, *Childhood in China,* ed. by William Kessen, and my review of the book in *American Journal of Sociology* 83, no. 2 (September 1977):521–524.

19. *New York Times,* June 2, 1952. (Italics mine.)

20. To be perfectly fair, recent generations of American children (especially since World War II) have not been taught these attitudes by their teachers. But the fact that American children continue to think the way they do shows how little the educational process has concerned itself with the correction of such misconceptions. Indeed as we shall see below, even most post-World War II history texts have not seriously attempted to present a truly balanced picture.

21. Timothy Tingfang Lew, "China in American School Textbooks," special supplement of the *Chinese Social and Political Science Review,* July 1923 (Peking) pp. 1–154.

22. Anatole G. Mazour and John M. Peoples, *Men and Nations: A World History* (with a 1964 Supplement).

23. Authored by Leften S. Stavrianos; Loretta Kreider Andrews; George I. Blanksten; Roger Hackett; Ella C. Keppert; Paul L. Murphy; and Lacy Baldwin Smith.

24. The quotes in this paragraph are from *A Global History of Man* (p. 214) and the remarks in parentheses are mine.

25. There is strong indication that Americans tend to dismiss the Vietnam War as a stupid mistake to be forgotten. For example, a history test used at Groveton High School in Fairfax County, Virginia "had a separate six-page section on Vietnam in

its 1969 edition," but only a two-and-a-half-page section in its 1975 edition entitled "Vietnam; The Black Revolt; The Student Protest." "Vietnam comes through to most students in terms that are stark and absolute—that it was all wrong, that it made no sense, that it was a grotesque failure totally at odds with American national purpose" (Martha M. Hamilton, "A Lesson Lost: Vietnam Becomes a Blur to High School Students," in *Washington Post,* May 20, 1979).

26. The reader who is planning a trip to the Far East is invited to make the following simple test. First, see if he can write on a sheet of paper from memory five well-known figures and events from Chinese history. Then find a Chinese who equals or is even *below him* in formal education to do the same with five well-known figures and events from American or Western history. My guess is that the Chinese will out-perform the experimenter.

27. This pattern survives today in Taiwan and Hong Kong despite laws to the contrary. Before 1949, villagers in China could not dispose of their property without the consent of their adult male children.

28. In some parts of China, married sons each have a yearly allowance from the head of the family called something like "clothes money." This sum meets the clothing and other pocket expenses of the man and his wife. But if there is only one son in the family, he may spend as much as the family can afford.

29. Chinese literati-poets occasionally but casually used the terms *ch'ing ch'un* ("green-ness of the spring") and *ch'ing nien* ("green-ness of years") for "youth" in general as distinguished from adulthood and old age.

CHAPTER 4

Where Europe Ends and America Begins

Throughout these first three chapters, many readers have probably asked: Isn't the way of life which the author designates as American fundamentally the same as the Anglo-Saxon, and isn't this itself but one floor of a European civilization which formed the foundation and framework for all later developments?

I must answer in the affirmative. When I speak of individual-centeredness as an American characteristic, I am reminded of the individualism of England. When I describe the emotional intensity peculiar to the people of the United States, I realize that I have characterized it by examples in art, literature, and romantic love which, without exception, had their origin in Europe.

But it is no less true that the American way of life has also departed considerably from that of England. Many writers have given lengthy consideration to the subject.[1] There is, however, one simple but central fact—while individualism is the basis of the English way of life, self-reliance has taken its place in America.

The initial differences between English individualism and American self-reliance are not obscure. English individualism developed hand in hand with legal equality. American self-reliance, on the other hand, has been inseparable from an insistence upon economic and social as well as political equality. The result is that a qualified individualism, with a qualified equality, has prevailed in England, but what has been considered the unalienable right of every American is unrestricted self-reliance and, at least ideally, unrestricted equality. The English, therefore, tend to respect class-based distinctions in birth, wealth, status, manners, and speech, while Americans resent them.

In the first place, there have been, and without doubt still are, more economic opportunities for the average man in the United States than in any other country in the world. In the second place, the many oil-strike stories, Hollywood-fame stories, and from-mechanic-to-industrial-tycoon stories constantly revive American imagination and vindicate American faith in the seemingly limitless economic possibilities that are open to the individual.

The effect that this emphasis on social equality has on the American way of life is all-pervasive, including, of course, the parent-child relationship. English children attain some independence after undergoing a long period of submission to parental authority. American children are encouraged to be independent from practically their first day of life. Not only do some American children tend to address their parents by first names—unthinkable in England—but also most American parents cannot discipline their children without fearing that they will hurt their feelings, a worry that rarely hampers an English parent engaged in such a task. This concern is illustrated by an interview with an American parent which David Riesman has reported:

Q. Do you think the teachers should punish the children for using make-up?
A. Yes, I think they should punish them, but understand, I'm a modern mother and while I'm strict with my daughters, I am still modern. You know you can't punish your children too much or they begin to think you are mean and other children tell them you are mean.[2]

While the English family relationship is still characterized by respect and authority, its American counterpart is based on friendship founded almost entirely on sentiment and utility. Respect and, especially, authority are implicitly based on the inequality between the old and the young. Under this English pattern, the good father is an adequate provider but he may also be a strict disciplinarian. He does not have to be very close to his children. In America, however, sentiment and utility are explicitly founded on equality between the old and the young. Being a good provider is no longer a sufficient criterion for a man to be regarded as a good father, and strict discipline is completely out of the question. Instead, the principal concern of American parents is to win the friendship of their children. They must constantly strive to be their children's good companions as well as providers; if they don't, their youngsters feel justified in treating them as strangers.

Admittedly these are strong generalizations that in fact vary from individual to individual. But it is only in the perspective of these attitudes that we can understand the following scene. A child does something naughty. His mother punishes him. The child becomes angry and sulks. The mother cleans up the mess, and asks the child, "Are we still friends?" The child grunts, "Humph." The mother is satisfied. Similarly it is not at all unusual for an American mother to be called a good mother because "she lives for her children," just as an American father may express his disgust with an ungrateful son by mournfully asking, "Haven't I done everything for him?"

The differences between the parent-child relationship in America and that in England are reflected faithfully in innumerable other areas of Anglo-American life: between employers and employees, teachers and pupils, ministers and their congregations, males and females, government leaders and their constituents, and different classes and different occupations. The most widespread expression of the American pattern is the tendency toward complete informality, which reaches its extreme in a desire to be free of all boundaries, restraints, and traditions.

A second look at art, literature, and conduct between the sexes, which were discussed earlier, will further clarify the Anglo-American differences. For example, American painting is undeniably in the European tradition—that is, both emphasize the individual and both revel in strong expressions of emotion. It is true, too, that modern art—whether cubism, dadaism, or futurism—either originated or was nurtured in France. But in every case these European-originated art trends have found their most fertile ground and most profitable market in the United States. Furthermore, in the work of American artists, abstraction becomes an expression of an uninhibited imagination, and emotion takes on an intensity that surpasses products from the Old World.

American art circles constantly buzz with talk of creating an art which will transcend all cultural forms and all time, and many American art students even resent being categorized into schools. If it is true that the artist, whatever his particular creative field, is both the mirror and the *avant garde* of society, I have no doubt that the works of Warhol, Marin, and Pollock foreshadow something characteristically American that is, perhaps, only faintly perceptible in the present time. This does not contradict the fact that American art is fundamentally European in origin. The two traditions are indeed highly similar to each other when they are compared with both ancient and modern Chinese art. But when they are compared with each other, the two Western art traditions differ considerably between themselves.

Just as American art faithfully mirrors the American drive to intensify the privatized feelings on the part of the artists themselves, American books and movies dramatize the same tendency. In 1953 I stated that two kinds of nonfiction books had become increasingly popular. Both kinds pointed in the same direction as American art. One group was represented by the writings of Fulton Sheen *(Peace of Soul* and *Life Is Worth Living)*, Harry Overstreet *(The Mature Mind)*, Joshua Liebman *(Peace of Mind)*, Gaylord Hauser *(Look Younger, Live Longer)*, Norman Vincent Peale *(The Power of Positive Thinking)*, and Fulton Oursler *(The Greatest Story Ever Told)*, all books emphasizing intensified feeling or a deepened search for the inner self. The second group was represented by such works as those of Immanuel Velikovsky *(Worlds in Collision* and *Ages in Chaos)*, Frank Sculley *(Behind the Flying Saucers)*, Thor Heyerdahl *(Kon Tiki)*, and Rachel Carson *(The Sea Around Us* and *Under the Sea Wind)*, all providing excellent vehicles through which the reader escapes from the world of man into a distant realm where he may ignore all boundaries and restraints, social and physical.

I observed also that there were similarly two developments in popular fiction. On the one hand there were those novels like Max Steele's *Debby* or Mary Jane Ward's *Snake Pit,* which delve into the mysteries of the individual mind, or those of the school of James Jones's *From Here to Eternity* which express the individual's revolt against the undesirable effects of army life, where the soldier loses his identity and his ability to reason, and eventually degenerates into an animal. On the other hand, there was the kind of writing best represented by Max Schulman's *Barefoot Boy with Cheek, The Feather Merchant,* and *The Zebra Derby,* Betty MacDonald's *The Egg and I,* and H. Allen Smith's *Low Man on a Totem Pole,* and more recently by James Herlihy's *Midnight Cowboy,* John Barth's *End of the Road,* or Judith Rossner's *Looking for Mr. Goodbar,* in which human life and relationships are reported in a pointless and frivolous manner so that individual pleasures are without reference to the actual problems of human existence.[3]

Some recent best-sellers would seem to indicate a change in these trends, but I think the shift is more superficial than real. The expressions of American popular literature as I saw them in 1953 exhibited really only two trends: (a) the search for inner self and revolt against the alleged undesirable effects of external regimentation or regulations; and (b) escape from the world of man either into distant realms where the individual may ignore all boundaries and restraints or into a view of life where individual pleasures are dissociated from human relationships and problems of human existence.

In the late 1960's, an intensified concern with one's real inner self seemed to be indicated by the popularity of various hallucinatory drugs and of Hindu musicians and priests who turned their followers on without drugs. But the popular literature seemed to be preoccupied with the inner selves of others. Hence we saw the popularity of autobiographies or biographies of murderers (*In Cold Blood* by Truman Capote), the culturally deprived (*Manchild in the Promised Land* by Claude Brown), dipsomaniacs (*I'll Cry Tomorrow* by Lillian Roth) as well as famous historical or literary figures (*Nicholas and Alexandra* by Robert K. Massie, *Tolstoy* by Henri Troyat, *Twenty Letters to a Friend* by Svetlana Alliluyeva, *Death of a President* by William Manchester, *Madame Sarah* by Cornelia Otis Skinner, or *Bertrand Russell: Autobiography 1872–1914*).

The need for escapism is now more and more being satisfied by the treatment of sex and violence for their own sake in literature, movies, and television. A Chicago film critic, Roger Ebert, writing about what he designates as a "good year" for films (1967), lists *Bonnie and Clyde, Ulysses,* and *Blow-Up* as the top three of the "Fifteen Best Films" (*Chicago Sun-Times,* December 31, 1967). *Bonnie and Clyde,* he says, tops all others because it is a "total movie," one that satisfies its audience on "every level," inspiring "the intellectuals in their cubby-holes" but also fascinating "people who want to see a good gangster movie." It is, he stoutly insists, a "message movie," in spite of the fact that the wanton killers are presented as attractive people in glamorous adventures, because:

> . . . the best movies are going beyond the old-fashioned story in which the moral is spelled out at the end. There is a more effective way to present a message, and that is by burying it in the method of the movie itself. Penn does this by deliberately placing humor side-by-side with violence, so that the audience is laughing whenever violence fills the screen. This is therapy of an excellent sort, and toward the end we do not laugh any more, not even when the jolly music on the sound track invites us to.

Ebert's thesis seems hard to defend because in the next two of his top movies, *Ulysses* and *Blow-Up,* the viewer cannot find any message except that they are "explorations" of illusion and reality, that in the human thought process fact and fancy are jumbled, as also are the relationships among facts. Other films high on critics' lists such as *La Dolce Vita, Never on Sunday, The Graduate,* and *I, A Woman,* which belabor sex or violence or both, hardly even fit the last mentioned type of justification.[4]

The reader should keep in mind that we have so far dealt primarily with highly praised films. Many very popular but not so well evaluated films confirm our point here with greater clarity. There are indications, however, that there is still interest in films that deal with the opposite of escape—commitment. But it is equally clear that the latter type of film production is far less common.

By the seventies some apparent changes had occurred. But when we look closer the newer phenomena can be seen merely as extensions of the same trends noted before. Andrew Sarris, one of the most respected film critics in the nation, says,

> Through the decade I had become increasingly reluctant to print my year-end lists. I was going one way, and the cinema another. More and more I was finding refuge in the past. The celebrated rise of the Hollywood cameroids left me cold. My own favorite films seemed eccentric and exotic, and I did not wish to argue about them at great length. Now, for once, I find it a genuine pleasure to record my choices for the past year (*The Village Voice,* January 14, 1980).

Sarris goes on to name the following films as his first five and then next seven favorites, separately in alphabetical order: *Kramer vs Kramer, Manhattan, The Marriage of Maria Braun, "10", The Tree of Wooden Clogs;* and, *Being There, Breaking Away, Don Giovanni, Newsfront, North Dallas Forty, Orchestra Rehearsal, The Shout.*

But only six of Sarris's choices coincide with those of Jeanne Miller of the *San Francisco Examiner* (December 30, 1979). When we add the choices of two other critics we find little agreement. As to the best films for the entire decade of the seventies, agreement among the critics is even scarcer. Sarris explains his views on the films of the seventies as follows:

> But when we get to the question of the best films of the decade, . . . we must . . . search for sublimity, immortality, and all that kind of stuff. The closest thing I have to a theory for the cinema of the '70s is a notion that we have gone beyond 'influences' and 'inventions' into a more com-

plex consideration of what constitutes a 'movie' in the first place, and what makes it endure both in the memory and in the repertory. All the easy rhetoric about 'expression' has yielded somewhat to the hard reality of 'communication' (*The Village Voice,* January 14, 1980).

It seems puzzling at first that "communication" should have become such a fashionable problem (and not only in motion pictures) in a society which prides itself on ultra-modern means of communication. However, the puzzle disappears when we realize that, as a result of the greater preoccupation with the self, far more people will want to communicate than to be communicated to. Naturally the problem of communication becomes both acute and widespread, because the more we communicate the less we tend to understand. No wonder Sarris laments in another article about the films of the seventies: "What is lacking is some spark that can momentarily illuminate our common condition. As it is, we all seem to go our separate ways in an increasingly fragmented world."[5]

The basic tendency to seek individual pleasures that are free from all social limitations has deeply invaded the conduct between the sexes. Here the American pattern has deviated so far from that of the British that the English once found the American custom of dating quite a novelty. The most important reasons for dating would seem to be (1) an increase in self-esteem because the more dates one has the greater the success in the eyes of one's friends; and (2) a desire to have a good time because having fun or not having fun is very important. Both reasons are as characteristically American as they are un-English, except for certain segments of the younger generation of English. In a culture pattern which enjoins the individual to seek himself, personal success is of primary importance. In a culture pattern which encourages unbridled emotionality, it is natural for romance to become an end in itself. Consequently, many American girls wish to date a boy not because of any feeling of affection, but because his desirability is enhanced by his successes with other girls. Similarly, many American teenagers are troubled because they cannot fully reconcile their puritanical background with their wish for completely egocentric pleasures.

Even the drinking patterns of Americans and British are different. Although drinking is noticeably more of a problem in Great Britain than in China, it is nevertheless very much regulated there, socially and ceremonially, while in America, even so-called social drinking is becoming more and more unrestrained.

The Rise of the American Way of Life

The American pattern of self-reliance and its concomitant demand for freedom from all restraints evolved because of three factors. First, in the environment of an undeveloped continent the pioneers found that self-sufficiency was an actuality, a prerequisite for survival that they had not experienced in their homelands. This is the basis of the famous Turner frontier theory.[6] The self-sufficiency of those who survived produced in pioneer Americans and many of those who came later an undeniable ruggedness of character, a degree of mastery over the environment, and a feeling of individual importance that provided the foundation for self-reliance.

But self-sufficiency alone, however complete, could not have been the touchstone of the American way of life. Many a Chinese farmer in China before 1949 could, and in Taiwan today can produce practically all he and his family need: food, clothing, housing, and even transportation. Many of his immediate ancestors migrated to Manchuria, where land was cheap, opportunities abundant, and where the conditions of life paralleled those in the American West in more ways than one. The Chinese in Manchuria never developed an outlook even remotely similar to that of the Americans because the self-sufficiency of the former was a result of circumstances, not of preference. As soon as he could lead the existence of a village landlord or an absentee landlord in some town or city, the erstwhile Chinese pioneer not only ceased to be self-sufficient in fact, but he consciously tried to forget the entire experience. He would hold on to his land, for land was his status symbol and his security. But the Chinese have never believed that all individuals *should be* self-sufficient.

The self-sufficiency of pioneer Americans was rooted in individualism, which is the second factor in the development of the American way of life. Their self-sufficiency was a channel into which their individualism could flow without restraint, and which was necessary if families were to survive in a hostile environment. And unfettered individualism became an ideal that they inculcated into their children and by which they judged the worth of all mankind.

However, even the emphasis on individualistic self-sufficiency is not enough to explain the American way. The pioneers who went to Australia, New Zealand, Canada, and Africa were also self-sufficient to varying extents, and most came from lands where individualism was a dominant ideal. But they did not evolve a way of life identical or even too similar to that of America. This does not mean that some

Americans may not find Australia or Canada more congenial than India or Malaya. There were apologists for apartheid who attempted to equate the situation of the Republic of South Africa with that of the United States. For example, Clarence Randall, former chairman of the board of Inland Steel Company, found white South Africans "lovable," "just like ourselves" (*Chicago Sunday Sun-Times,* February 3, 1963).

The fact is that in spite of grudging white concessions in recent years giving Blacks slightly more freedom and a subterfuge for racial equality in the planned so-called independent black states within its boundaries, the Republic of South Africa remains the most racially unequal society in the world. The laws of the Republic of South Africa and even much of its theology still openly propound and promote racial inequality, whereas in the United States, the racists and the religious bigots are everywhere on the defensive. Australia and New Zealand have never developed any internal movement for equality to their indigenous population.[7] Even today when the United States has already abolished the last vestiges of ethnic discrimination in her immigration laws, New Zealand and Australia still cling to their basically all-white policy.

The difference will be more understandable when a third factor in the American development, not present in the others, is considered. That is *revolution.* The English people who pioneered in the other lands made no sharp break from the political rule of Britain, however nominal, but the American Revolution, a violent political separation, permitted other significant developments.

In the first place, a break from the crown meant the brushing aside of all things for which the crown symbolically stood: differences in social privileges, inequality in wealth, and class or status-based distinctions in manners. Whereas the English upper and lower classes maintain their respective "public school" and lower-class accents, American speech differences are mostly geographic. Whereas the English look up to titles, American law requires that no immigrant can be naturalized unless he relinquishes them. The reverential attitude of the English toward their royal family contrasts with the buddylike atmosphere that surrounds the relationship between the American people and their president.[8] These phenomena are most illustrative of these profound Anglo-American differences.

Secondly, the American attitude toward the head of the government gave a tremendous impetus to the quest for equality and made it a much more obvious point of contention in America than in England. While inequality in principle has been attacked by various social and political movements in England, inequality in fact has always been accepted as a matter of tradition and custom. In England, the impact of inequality on the individual has been greatly mitigated by his psychological tie with the past. The American, having successfully broken with the crown for the express purpose of achieving equality and freedom, has found such inequalities to be emotionally unacceptable. This resultant intensity of American feeling about a self-reliant, equal system permeates all aspects of political, economic, religious, and social life.

This emphasis on self-reliance has caused Geoffrey Gorer to observe—mistakenly I think—that the psychology of the individual American is built on a rejection of the father just as the American society began by rejecting Europe.[9] Gorer errs for two reasons. First, there is little evidence that Americans reject their fathers or that the American society as a whole rejects its connection with Europe. On the contrary, there is, for example, a surprising degree of occupational continuity between fathers and sons, just as there is pride in kinship ties with England and in acceptance of European art, European fashions, and even European products. American aid to Europe was much more massive than that to other continents. Second, insofar as the psychological evidence permits, there seems to be more rejection of mothers in America than of fathers. American husbands, either because they hope to be friends with their children or because they are too busy at work, usually leave the disciplinarian aspect to their wives. This situation leads to a greater chance for possible tensions between mothers and children.[10]

However, what is evident in the United States is not rejection of the parents as such but an emphasis on the complete independence of the individual. This begins, naturally enough, between children and their parents, but it extends, in most cases, to all wider social relationships. This independence, although it has its origins in English individualism, has become more complete, pervasive, and, therefore, more obvious, in the New World. Thus, whereas English parents and children maintain a relationship of command and obedience, at least until the youngsters reach the age of puberty, very early in life American children are considered to be the equals of their parents; whereas English teachers still enjoy a great deal of disciplinary power over and social distance from their pupils, their American counterparts tend more and more to follow the interests and predilections of their charges; whereas Englishmen of lower socio-economic origin still find it possible to accept the status of their fore-bears without embarrassment, Americans in similar circumstances not only strive actively to better themselves, but feel positively superior to their elders.

This transition from English individualism to American self-reliance has brought about certain unforeseeable but far-reaching consequences. No individual can be completely self-reliant or completely independent. Human existence requires that the individual ego achieve an adjustment or balance between the inner and outer environments. The main elements of the inner environment are inborn drives, such as sex and hunger, and the principles of conduct that are instilled in childhood, the sum total of which Freud termed the superego. The main elements in the outer environment are other human beings, not only relatives, friends, and business associates, but all members of the society with whom the individual comes into direct or indirect contact.

The personal pattern of adjustment naturally varies from individual to individual. However, no matter what the variation, every individual must relate himself to these different categories of human beings according to the culturally sanctioned rules. An individual may feel closer to persons in one category rather than another, but he cannot dispense with all of them. When Mark Twain said something like, "The more I look at human beings, the more I like dogs," he was speaking from deep disillusionment. All human beings have social needs which cannot be satisfied except in association with their fellow human beings. Under these conditions those who are members of fixed and permanent human groups in which they may satisfy their social needs enjoy a higher degree of certainty of life than others reared in individualism and especially self-reliance who insist on being judged according to their individual merits.

The advantage or disadvantage of the contrasting ways, is, of course, strictly dependent upon the point of view of the observer. Those who emphasize self-reliance and deny the importance of other human beings in their lives will have greater social flexibility. They can exercise initiative unhampered; they can make decisions with speed. But the same people must experience a great deal of insecurity, for they must find their groups in which to satisfy their social needs and work constantly to maintain their places in them. The more self-reliance is stressed, the greater is likely to be the individual's social flexibility or insecurity.

The American school child faces a choice between allegiance to his parents and loyalty to the gang, or peer group. Only a relative minority wish to or can make a decisive and complete choice of one or the other. It is more likely to be a tug-of-war in which neither party overcomes the other. It may even be a series of compromises with which neither side is entirely satisfied.

But the lack of a permanent and continuing anchorage in the kinship group becomes manifest for the American adult. He must both set and achieve his own goals if he wants to maintain his self-esteem and avoid being branded a failure.

Facing the American adult is a large array of groups in which he can hope to satisfy his social needs: occupation, association, church, neighborhood, college, "race," and those revolving around interests, hobbies, and causes. Membership in one or more of these groups will serve as his anchorage which, however, is transitory, for the twin corollaries of self-reliance—the ideas of freedom and equality—remain primary. How will freedom and equality make this anchorage transitory? The answer is that, since these ideas are no respecter of fixed places and privileges, they tend to raise aspirations on all levels. Consequently, the individual who has made it on any level is still likely to be unhappy and dissatisfied because he envies those who have climbed above him and he fears the encroachment of those struggling below him. The greater the envy for those above, the more serious is the fear of encroachment from below.[11]

These envies and fears lead to a pair of American characteristics: conformity and the continuous proliferation of nonkinship associations and clubs. While the second of these characteristics is in line with self-reliance the first seems diametrically opposed to it.

Many observers have noted this and other contradictions. Some have avoided these problems by noting them without interpretation.[12] Harold Laski went hardly any further by observing Americanism to be inherently dualistic, that is to say, full of opposites.[13] Riesman is the only scholar who has thus far made a serious attempt to deal with the question of conformity. He has hypothesized three types of national character: tradition-direction, inner-direction, and other-direction.

Tradition-direction is a way of life in which the individual is almost irrevocably bound by age, sex, kinship, and local groups, and in which the social order remains relatively unchanged for many generations. This type of life, Riesman claims, is characteristic of peoples ranging in diversity from precapitalist Europeans to present-day Hindus, Chinese, North African Arabs, and Balinese.

Riesman describes inner-direction as a transitional way of life in which the individual selects his own personal goals and then unyieldingly drives toward achieving them, and in which the society is characterized by personal mobility, expansion in production, exploration, colonization, and imperialism. This type of personality, he claims, began to emerge in Europe during and after the Middle Ages and has been predominant in Western society since the Renaissance.

The term other-direction he applies to a way of life in which the individual is "shallower, freer with his money, friendlier, more uncertain of himself and his value, more demanding of approval" than an inner-directed person. Such an individual is capable of "a superficial intimacy with and response to anyone." Riesman claims that Americans have been changing from their European-based inner-directed orientation to an other-directed one.

This characteristic emphasis on conformity is, according to Riesman, the basic element determining the character type emerging in the larger American cities. The type is most noticeable among the "upper middle class," the "young," the "bureaucrats," and the "salaried employees in business."[14]

Riesman's inner-directed orientation roughly corresponds to our term, self-reliance, and his other-directed orientation is certainly central to what we generally see as conformity. What I disagree with is Riesman's notion that the American way of life has been changing from inner-direction to other-direction (or from self-reliance to conformity).

I believe that Riesman's interpretation suffers from two defects. First, he failed to see that the emphasis on conformity is an inevitable side effect of extreme self-reliance. Envy for those above and fear of the encroachment of those struggling below combine to make one extremely insistent demand on the conduct of the self-reliant man. This is that he must constantly attempt to climb not only in order to equal those above him but also as a matter of defense against those below him. The self-reliant man (the militantly inner-directed man) has to compete with his equals, has to belong to status-giving groups, and, as a means to these ends, has to conform to the customs and fads of the game whether he hopes to keep his existing status or to be accepted in a higher place. There is thus a direct relationship between self-reliance and conformity: the more militant the spirit of self-reliance, the greater the fear of nonconformity.[15]

The other difficulty in Riesman's position is that he mistakenly lumped together the Chinese way of life and that of preindustrialist

Europe. It is this failure to perceive the intimate link between self-reliance and conformity and the fundamental differences between traditional China and preindustrial Europe that prompted Riesman to observe that the differences between his three character types are "a matter of degree only." His tradition-directed Chinese and his other-directed American are similar insofar as both will take their "signals from others" but different merely because the signals sought by the Chinese "come in a cultural monotone" needing "no complex receiving equipment to pick them up," while those sought by Americans come "from far and near; the sources are many, the changes rapid."[16]

There are basic bonds between Europe and America which cannot be dissolved by an imaginative argument, just as there are deep gulfs between China and Europe, a bridge for which has yet to be found.

The differences between Chinese and Americans are a matter of quality. These differences are illustrated by American and Chinese attitudes toward conformity. The Chinese may appear to value conformity, but their conformity results from the relatively stable quality of their society. When they act opportunistically (as all conformists must do from time to time) *they are engaged in culturally approved behavior.* In fact, the Chinese have no exact equivalent for the English word conformity. A person doing what is expected is well versed in human sentiments, is understanding, has elegance, as distinguished from one who is clumsy, has no concern for others, or is obdurate.

The famous saying by a scholarly contemporary of Confucius that "high-class songs have few singers" has been more than overshadowed by the popular adage, "the tall tree is crushed by wind first." Throughout Chinese history there were, of course, brave men who spoke up or acted according to their convictions and risked torture and death. There were quite a few Chinese Sir Thomas Mores who dared to oppose the actions of quite a few Chinese Henry VIIIs. In the T'ang dynasty, Han Yu, whose famous ultimatum to the crocodiles we shall have occasion to discuss in Chapter 7, was demoted because he was opposed to the emperor's efforts to seek Buddha's relics from India. In the Ming dynasty, Yang Chi-Sheng was executed for bluntly advising the emperor (when all of his colleagues were silent) to dismiss and punish the favored, all-powerful, and corrupt prime minister.

However, the undeniable fact is that such Chinese acts were based on considerations of duty to the founder of the dynasty or for upholding Confucian ethical principles, but never for individual autonomy or freedom. Despite their erudition, the Chinese have produced no writings extolling self-reliance or attacking conformity. Their great literature deals with the means to achieve peace by wise government and by the elimination of causes of crime, corruption, and civil disturbance. Their problem has always been how to make the individual live according to the accepted customs and rules of conduct, not how to enable him to rise above them. The closest some Chinese came to being deliberate nonconformists was when a few of them removed themselves from active society by becoming monks or retiring to their paintings, calligraphy, gardens, or mountain retreats. At best this was passive nonconformity.

To Americans, by contrast, conformity is bad, is degrading, and a problem, for they are members of a society which holds self-reliance (and with it, freedom and equality) to be of the highest value. Consequently, when the American acts opportunistically by warping or shedding his principles, he cannot help suffering from feelings of guilt. And when he has no way of avoiding these feelings of guilt because the external circumstances make it difficult for him to be nonconforming, the least he must do to feel better is to voice some opposition to conformity. This is why *The Organization Man* by William H. Whyte, Jr., achieved such a wide readership.[17] It lambasts the tendency toward uniformity in living and thinking. It offers no solution to the individual American's problem of conformity, but it does express his resentment.

Moreover, in addition to directly voicing his resentment against conformity, the American can channel his feelings of guilt either against those who do not conform as he does, or by affirming all the more loudly the principles that he has broken. Either will give him a measure of peace and both express themselves as the American impulse to persecution. In the United States, all sorts of action groups spring up continuously among the common people, without political instigation or leadership. This force drove the Mormons to Utah, and has surfaced from time to time in groups extolling or enforcing white supremacy or segregation. This development contrasts sharply with avowed ideals of freedom and equality and is a result which Emerson overlooked when he wrote so brilliantly on the importance and necessity of self-reliance.

Faced with the necessity for conformity, the self-reliant man can defend himself in another way: join another organization he likes better or form an organization of his own. The "going into business for myself" ideology is at work here, but more is involved. At the end of his book, *The Organization Man,* Whyte advises his readers that the individual must constantly fight the organization. Whyte does not seem to realize that in order to fight the organization, the individual has to have more organization. With his ideology of self-reliance, the American is inevitably forced by his resentment against conformity to split ongoing organizations or to form new ones. Consequently, voluntary associations have proliferated in the United States to an extent unknown anywhere else in the world.

These developments are almost entirely absent in Chinese society and history. The difficulties and dangers facing Chinese nonconformists came from the political authorities, not the people. Their actions met with dire consequences because they challenged their rulers' decisions, but they did not concern the rest of the people. There were no organized protests by the people against them since resentment against conformity was not a significant factor in the situation.

If Americans had really discarded their inner-directed orientation and changed to an other-directed one, as Riesman claims, there would not have been any significant American resentment and protest against conformity or persecution for nonconformity. Quite the contrary, that Americans do resent conformity and have done so much to protest it and defend themselves against it is evidence enough that they have yet to give up their individual-centered way of life which stresses inner-direction or self-reliance.

The Chinese truly come much closer to Riesman's other-directed orientation. In their situation-centered way of life that values mutual dependence, conformity not only tends to govern all interpersonal relations, but it also enjoys social and cultural approval. Since Chinese can conform without resentment, they have no need to protest or to defend themselves against it.

This Chinese-American difference helps to explain why the Chinese before the influence of the West was introduced have never had any philosophical calls or significant struggles for individual liberties but at the same time have not felt any long-lasting need to persecute those who differed with themselves. This difference partially explains the fact that although Americans began their national life with a Bill of Rights, these constitutional guarantees have yet to be fully implemented, and those who work to realize or defend them are always in danger of violent attack on one pretext or another, Americanism or anticommunism.

Developments in China under the Communist government— from public confessions, group struggles, Red Guard rampages to the outpouring of sentiments at the death of Premier Chou, the fall of the Gang of Four, and the proliferation of the big character posters on the so-called "Freedom Wall" in Peking—would all seem to at least greatly modify the contrast outlined here. In fact this is hardly the case. The objectives of the Communist government were of Western origin. The course of revolution in any society is bound to be replete with ups and downs. But as we shall see in Chapter 15, both the forces for greater totalitarianism and those for greater liberalization are inspired by the West. We have yet to see how well the Chinese people at the grass-roots level are actively behind them in a sustained manner.

Our analysis compels us to see the differences between Europe and America as a matter of degree, in contrast to those between China and America which are a matter of kind. What distinguishes the United States from Europe is that the contradictory forces inherent in her ancestral cultures have in her way of life become exaggerated, more noticeable, and in many respects more violent.

In both cases the apparent contradictions are comprehensible when we dig into the common basis upon which each of them rests. The American contradictions stem from an individual-centered way of life that stresses self-reliance. The Chinese characteristics originate in a situation-centered way of life that values mutual dependence.

NOTES

1. See, for example, James Bryce, *The American Commonwealth;* Alexis De Tocqueville, *Democracy in America;* D. W. Brogan, *U.S.A.: An Outline of the Country, Its People and Institutions;* Harold Laski, *The American Democracy;* Geoffrey Gorer, *The American People;* Henry Steele Commager, *The American Mind;* David Riesman, *The Lonely Crowd;* Seymour Martin Lipset, *The First New Nation: The U.S. in Historical and Comparative Perspective;* Daniel J. Boorstin, *The Americans: The National Experience;* Lawrence H. Fuchs, *"Those Peculiar Americans": The Peace Corps and American National Character;* Michael Kammen, *People of Paradox: An Inquiry Concerning the Origins of American Civilization;* Daniel J. Boorstin, *The Americans: The Democratic Experience;* Gordon J. Di Renzo, ed., *We, The People: American Character and Social Change;* and Christopher Lasch, *The Culture of Narcissism.*

2. Riesman, *The Lonely Crowd,* p. 36.

3. Some may argue that Schulman's and Smith's works cited here contain an element of satire.

4. Of course, one can claim any and all such movies to be satires or revelations of some aspect of life; such claims are indeed being made more and more. But the tendency to hold nothing above satire or self-disclosure is in itself another expression of the individual-centered orientation of life.

5. Andrew Sarris, "Film Criticism in the Seventies," in *Film Comment,* vol. 14, no. 1, January 1978.

6. Frederick J. Turner, "The Significance of the Frontier in American History"

in his *The Fontier in American History*. For a brilliant application of the Turner thesis see Ray Allen Billington, *America's Frontier Heritage*. The Turner thesis has been criticized on various grounds, notably in George Rogers Taylor, ed., *The Turner Thesis*, and Henry Nash Smith, *Virgin Land*, pp. 250–260.

7. The Maoris, however, are treated better in New Zealand than the Blacks are in South Africa.

8. May I suggest that one of the many sources of Lyndon Johnson's unpopularity was his inability or unwillingness to be friendly with the people? Richard M. Nixon's attitude of remoteness from the people was even more pronounced. Shortly after his inauguration Nixon ordered for his White House guards glittering and gaudy uniforms more in tune with some medieval royal palace. Although they were soon discarded, the glittering uniforms were only one sign of Nixon's desire to remain distant from the people.

9. Gorer, *The American People*, pp. 23–49.

10. For example, this tension can be seen in the responses given by American college students to certain cards in the Thematic Apperception Test (TAT), as contrasted to those given by their Chinese counterparts in Hong Kong and Taiwan. This test consists of a series of cards depicting various human situations about which the respondent is asked to write a story. Card I shows a boy gazing at a violin on a table in front of him. Most Americans see the problem as one between the boy and his mother; the mother wants him to practice the violin, but the son wants to go out to play baseball with his friends. Most Chinese see, on the other hand, his parents on the same side as the boy. They want him to learn the violin and he wants to do so. The commonly mentioned problem is that the family is too poor to hire a tutor.

11. The interpersonal dynamics described here have been recognized by some who write on American manners. Russell Lynes noted that while books of manners circulating in eighteenth-century United States were "mostly translations of French books or importations from England," native American works began to appear in a "prodigious torrent" since the beginning of the nineteenth century. He observed: "The manners books coincided with a wave of gentility in America, a wave that, curiously enough, came along at the same time as a new spirit of Republicanism and a new emphasis on equality. When every man is as good as every other man, there is likely to be a scramble on the part of a good many people to be better than other people or, anyway, to emulate the manners of those whom they consider to be well established." ("Dining at Home" by Russell Lynes in *The American Heritage Cookbook and Illustrated History of American Eating and Drinking*, pp. 280–281.

12. John F. Cuber and Robert A. Harper, *Problems of American Society: Values in Conflict*, pp. 369–372, and Robin M. Williams, *American Society, A Sociological Interpretation*, pp. 287–288.

13. Laski, *The American Democracy*, p. 738, and "Religion, value-orientation, and intergroup conflict" in *The Journal of Social Issues* 12 (1960):14–15.

14. Riesman, *The Lonely Crowd*, pp. 11–26.

15. This link has since been recognized by Seymour Martin Lipset though, by a strange twist of the argument, he sees conformity as promoting inner autonomy after all. How strenuously, but precariously individual-centered American scholars hang on to their cherished notion of the individual individual! (Lipset, *First New Nation*, pp. 136–139).

16. Ibid., p. 26.

17. William H. Whyte, Jr., *The Organization Man*.

Part Two

MEN, GODS, AND THINGS

Introduction
to Part Two

Both the personality characteristics of the individual and the patterns of behavior of the society persist over long periods of time. We can all name idiosyncrasies which come and go. But if Mary is shy and ill at ease with people while Sally is bold and fun-loving, if John likes to read philosophical treatises while Peter goes for cheap fiction and Hollywood movies, if Lee is dexterous with his hands while Wong has a flair for poetry, we can be sure that these individual ways did not develop overnight nor will they vanish rapidly, if at all. Similarly, we can also name fads that appear and disappear. But if football and dancing are popular in America while t'ai chi and mahjong are popular in China, if representative government survives in England while autocracy persists in the Middle East, if Shintoism is the religion of all Japanese and the caste system remains strong in India, we can also be certain that these traits are not an artificial vogue subject to changes in fashion.

They reflect, instead, historical continuity of personality and culture. They are characteristics that persist through the vertical dimension of time. But both personality and culture also exist on the horizontal plane. Aggressiveness, or the lack of it, in a businessman is not confined to his commercial pursuits. If real—that is, if it is not something he has had to talk himself into—it cannot help reappearing in his other activities and interests, from his relations with his family and friends to his attitude toward domestic politics and international affairs. In the same way the cultural contrasts between China and America are not restricted to a few superficial aspects. They affect widely separate areas of endeavor and belief in each society, from art to philosophy, from religion to politics, and from race relations to the conquest of frontiers.

I have so far spoken of the individual's personality characteristics and the society's patterns of culture as though they were distinct realities. They are in fact inseparable—inseparable because individual characteristics are largely the result of cultural conditioning. Culture patterns are in turn affected and shaped by the individuals making up a society.

Of course, all individuals do not act according to the commonly understood patterns of the society. They may not wish to behave as their fellows expect. However, every society has definite mechanisms from mild ridicule to physical violence for eliminating the nonconformist or forcing him to change his ways. Similarly, in every society some aspects of life provide more room for deviation than do other compartments. Some societies are as a whole more elastic than others. Consequently, some societies have more internal impetuses for change than others. But there is no doubt that the personality characteristics of a majority of the members of a society must be congruent, over time, with the pattern of that society's culture.

In speaking of Americans or Chinese as tending to behave in certain ways under particular conditions we are dealing with probability, in much the same way as the forecasts of the National Safety Council before holiday weekends predict the number of Americans who will suffer traffic death or injury. These forecasts cannot specify which particular individuals will be among the victims, but they have usually been quite accurate in the overall figures.

Probability lies at the basis of all of our analyses of American and Chinese patterns of behavior. Thus we can safely predict that an American husband who constantly criticizes his wife in public will soon be in domestic trouble, just as a Chinese bureaucrat who habitually forgets to bring a gift when he pays a visit to his superior will soon find his rice bowl broken. Each of these individuals has behaved in a culturally inappropriate way. Conversely, it is evident that the highly demonstrative nature of American marital life is contributed to by the average wife's wish for public signs of husbandly affection. Likewise, the traditional pattern of corruption in government is fortified each time a Chinese bureaucrat undertakes to better himself by presenting a gift to his superior. The expectations of both individuals have accentuated the accepted culture pattern of their respective societies.

This may appear to be a circular argument, leading to the hen-and-egg kind of absurdity. But the hen-and-egg problem is embarrassing only if we attempt to determine which came first. If we arbitrarily begin with either the hen or the egg, then each is a good measure of the other. Given the hen, we will have a good idea of what kind of egg she is going to lay; given the egg, we may be fairly certain of the kind of bird that will hatch from it.

In Part One we saw how very different are the Chinese and American ways of life, and we examined the immediate origin of these patterns in the family, the school, and certain broader though less institutionalized patterns among the two peoples. In the next eight chapters we shall see how the behavior characteristics of the average person in China and America, not just the most powerful or creative few, merge with the diverse aspects of the two people's culture patterns. Here we have two interrelated tasks. We shall try to see how the characteristic attitudes, aspirations, and actions of the individual are encouraged by the existing ideals embodied in institutions such as marriage, the government, the church, and the economy. But we shall also undertake to determine how these very ideals and institutions are in turn modified or redefined by the efforts of the individual.

CHAPTER 5

Marriage and Class

Some years ago I went to a movie in which a young couple had a quarrel. The wife, in a huff, ran out of the apartment carrying a packed suitcase. The husband's mother, who lived on the next floor, then appeared on the scene. The elderly woman consoled her son by saying, "You're not alone, son. I am here." The audience roared with laughter. The sequence of events and that particular remark left little doubt in the minds of the audience that the older woman was the cause of the young couple's quarrel. The mother was committing the worst of follies because she did not have sense enough to stay away, especially after the trouble had flared into the open.

A Chinese audience would have found hardly anything amusing in these events. They would have seen the younger woman, and not the older one, as the culprit. A man's tie with his parents customarily has priority over his marital bond. Only a bad woman would leave her husband because of a conflict between these two responsibilities. Given this framework, the mother who consoled her son was doing nothing out of order.

The Chinese wife is, in the first place, selected by her husband's parents to become an additional member of a home which is founded on solidarity between her husband and his parents. The typical American wife, on the other hand, would never consider occupying a subsidiary position. She has claim not only to the bulk of her husband's earnings but also, after business hours, to his undivided attention as well. Parents-in-law are useful in an emergency, but the connection between the older couple and the younger one is a matter of friendship rather than kinship.

Chinese marital adjustment, instead of being exclusively a matter between a man and his wife, is very much the parents' business. In fact, some Chinese parents not only participate in quarrels between their sons and daughters-in-law, but it is not at all unusual for them to openly force a showdown between the younger couple. Most Chinese wives entertain the impression, usually with good reason, that their parents-in-law favor their husbands in any marital dispute. In self-defense, or if they really feel aggrieved, they often call in their own parents from another village. And not infrequently what begins as a minor ripple between the spouses soon develops into a battle royal between the two sets of parents-in-law, each reinforced by their other children. In this situation the husband and wife usually are divided by the battle line of the two sets of relatives.

No American parents would dare to interfere to such an extent. Even if they have strong feelings about their children's marital difficulties, they are obliged to do their manipulating behind the scenes. In fact, most family counselors do not hesitate to advise parents to keep out of their youngsters' affairs, difficulties or no difficulties.

"How can you cope with meddling in-laws?" asked a marital counselor in a big daily, and he continued:

> The answer to the problem of meddling in-laws usually lies within the couple themselves. If they show that they will brook no interference, they will usually get none. But they must present a united front!
>
> Each partner must come first with the other. Where either is made unhappy through in-law interference, first consideration should be given the partner rather than the parent.

The wisdom of this piece of advice is easily conceded anywhere in the United States.

These differences express something fundamental. To the Chinese, a man's relationship with his parents is permanent. It is so central and so important that all other individual relationships are overshadowed by or subordinated to it. American relationships are individually determined. The emphasis on marital happiness in America and the relative lack of attention to it in China is, therefore, another distinction between the two peoples.

The American ideal of marital life has three components: love, common living, and common life. Love means an ecstatic and exclusive attraction between a particular man and a particular woman; common living means that the spouses must be with each other nearly all of the time; and common life means that the husband and wife share the same interests and activities, completely understand each other, and have no secrets from each other.

The corresponding Chinese ideal is much different. It views sexual attraction only in terms of marital cohabitation; it considers common living necessary but has no objection to spouses being separated from each other for a long time; and it explicitly denies the need for common life, so that the wife's place is in the home as much as her husband's is outside of it.

Other distinctive modes of behavior are correlated with these patterns. Previously we saw that modern educated Chinese men and women behave toward one another in a manner far different from the romantic display exhibited by American lovers. But married couples in China are no less embarrassed by any public show of eroticism. American wives try to follow their husbands wherever they go, even overseas during a war. Chinese women usually stay behind when their husbands trade or work in another city. Some American wives engage in the same profession as their husbands or the two may even be partners in the same business. American wives discuss such topics as music, religion, and international relations with their husbands' associates, whom they know by their first names. The majority of Chinese wives know nothing, and care even less, about politics or government, business or professions. As they rarely meet their husbands' male friends, they never know them well. Some Chinese husbands are just as likely to entertain their cronies in brothels as in their homes. As late as 1929 I was present at a semimodern wedding feast in a north China restaurant during which the bridegroom called in some prostitutes whom he had known previously to pour the wine and sing for the guests. Some of those present thought the groom had gone too far, and the products of modern universities and colleges would regard him as vulgar, but nobody thought him crazy. And the bride did not even raise her eyebrows.

In the several decades immediately before 1949 college educated married men tended to look askance at prostitution. But even today prostitution is still legal in Taiwan and a visit to a brothel is not regarded as adultery. I am not, however, discussing whether Chinese men or American men have more to do with women of easy virtue. Judging by evidence of call girl rackets and the interesting adventures of some conventioneers, lawmakers, politicians, and union bosses in the United States, it is unlikely that American males lag far behind their Chinese brethren. But there is a point of contrast: while a majority of American males and females consider prostitution bad and sinful, most Chinese in pre-1949 China and in Taiwan today see it as part of the order of nature, or at worst as an unavoidable defect of that order.

Given the differing ways of life, these contrasts are as logical as they are inevitable. In the American way, marriage changes the entire social setting of the individual. In the Chinese way, marriage merely advances the social status of the male but changes the entire social setting of the female. While the bride has to adjust to her new surroundings, the husband's primary duties and obligations remain much the same as before.

In this context we can understand the following short piece from a Taiwan daily. This is one in a series, each by a different writer, illustrating a personal motto. This writer's motto is: "Ugly wife and nearby fields are family treasures."

I was not extremely handsome as a youth, but not hard to look at. Unfortunately I was (by parental arrangement) mated to a very ugly wife. Some friends and relatives sympathized with me.

I thought of running away from home on my wedding night, so revolted was I by the sight of her. But my grandfather saw through my intensions and he called me to his side. He bluntly asked me: "Ugly wife and nearby fields are family treasures. Do you know that?"

I replied that I did not know.

My grandfather explained: the most valuable quality of a wife is her virtue, not her beauty. Beauty may attract a lot of would-be adulterers. But virtue will cause her to be filial to your parents, faithful to you, besides serving as a good example for your sons. In the same way, nearby fields can be tilled conveniently, and easily cared for and guarded. These two treasures will bless you forever.

For years afterwards I travelled away from home and had few opportunities to be with my wife. But my wife dutifully served my parents and raised my children, with never a word of complaint.

Since we moved to Taiwan my wife supplemented my meager income by raising vegetables and pigs in our yard, and by sewing for others. In this way I have been happy and content.

Yesterday my eldest son told me, "Dad, do you remember that certain Mr. Wang who was married in the same group wedding when I was? His wife ran away with another man."

I certainly recall the admiring words and glances directed at that Mr. Wang's bride during the wedding. Boy, was she a beauty!

As I reflect on this incident, I am again reminded of my grandfather's teaching: "Ugly wife and nearby fields are family treasures." (*Central Daily News*, September 7, 1967)

Some American readers may point to a song (of Latin American origin) popular in the United States some years ago which begins with these lines: "If you want to be happy for the rest of your life, don't make a pretty woman your wife. . . ." And recently (1979) a man wrote to Dear Abby asking if a girl would make a good wife who gave him a questionnaire to fill out after he proposed marriage. The questionnaire "looked like an application for a job with the CIA," he said. Sample questions: "Where have you been for the last ten years? Have you ever been fired? If so, state reasons. . . . Have you ever had any communicable diseases? Do you have a police record? Give three character witnesses." But it would be hard to find an American man who would dare to author the Chinese gem quoted above and offer it, in all seriousness, as a personal success story. Evaluating a wife in terms of what she means to one's parents, equating her with easy-to-care-for fields, gloating over her earnings to supplement one's inadequate income—these and other obvious components of the piece are simply not acceptable things to the average self-reliant and self-respecting American man, to say nothing about the wife's reaction.

It must not be supposed that the contrasting patterns of marital life prevail with complete uniformity among the two peoples. It is not too hard to find instances in America in which duties toward a father or mother overshadow an individual's marital designs, or in which a marriage is not immediately endangered because a husband and wife live apart from one another more than they do together. Furthermore, one can find American marriages in which money, prestige, power, loneliness, or even that nebulous but ubiquitous thing called "compatibility," and not true romance, serve as the primary determinant for marriage.

Some evidence obtained by systematic inquiry lends support to the fact that as American married partners get older, the husband-wife bond tends to take second place to the importance of children and solidarity among siblings.[1] However, the importance of American children to their parents as the latter get older does not seem to be reciprocated by the children. American convalescent and old peoples' homes are full of aged parents longing for a phone call or a card that never comes, or a visit between Christmases from their loved ones.[2] For it is unavoidable that, in the individual-centered way of life, the self comes first. That self is usually expanded to include a spouse and children who, along with the self-reliant man's material acquisitions, are results of his work and signs of his success. On the other hand, the parents who protected, nurtured, and controlled the self in infancy and childhood tend to remind the grown-up, self-reliant man of his immaturity and helplessness.

Consequently, while not all Americans conduct themselves according to the romantic pattern indicated, the deviations from the expected patterns are often as revealing as the facts that conform to them. For example, the girl's detailed questionnaire to her suitor, mentioned earlier, did not include items about his relations with his own parents. And Abby's reply said nothing about this omission. On the contrary, it is obvious that Abby did not approve of her inquiry as a prelude to marriage: "she may make a good wife, but I think she'd make a better probation officer." Americans who are attached to their parents find it hard to achieve marital peace with their spouses (analysts brand them as poor marital risks), and American couples who live apart are usually objects of speculation by their friends and acquaintances ("When're they going to break up?"). I would guess that those who have met through a lonely hearts club would be highly reticent about their manner of introduction; they certainly would not be proud of it.

Similarly, it is possible also to find Chinese examples that are contrary to the general pattern. For instance there once was a famous Chinese poet who had to divorce his beloved wife because she did not please his mother. Years later, after both of them had remarried, he saw her at a fair and realized that he still loved her. Prevented by convention from speaking to her, he went home and wrote a poem for which he has since been known, expressing his lovesickness.

An anonymous but well-known Chinese ballad entitled "Southeast the Peacock Flies" describes a husband in the reign of Chien-an (A.D. 196–220) who went much further. While he was serving as magistrate away from home, his wife was driven away from the house by his mother. The young wife drowned herself as a result. When he heard about this, he hanged himself on a tree in the courtyard, rather than accepting a new wife the older woman picked out for him.

This magistrate certainly was not filial in Chinese terms; his behavior was highly individualized. But I suspect that this poem remained anonymous because the author or his descendants did not care to be publicly associated with such un-Chinese behavior.

Biographies found in the district records throughout China often betray sympathy for individual sacrifices, more or less in veiled form. One biography describes a man who had to divorce his wife because she was offensive to his widowed mother. But eleven years later, when the mother died, he remarried her. She remained single all those years, and the savings she had accumulated by spinning and weaving helped to finance his mother's funeral. Another biography describes a man who remained single for the remainder of his life after his wife died, as a consequence of which, the biographer implies, this widower scored successes in the imperial examinations.

Wealth or the lack of it also seriously affects marital behavior in China. China is usually described as a land of large families. Actually, the average size of Chinese families is only a little more than five members. There are, however, much larger well-to-do families which, in China before 1949 and in Taiwan today, like their counterparts in every land, have an upper-class style of life. In the United States some of the familiar symbols of upper-class distinction include membership in a club, a country house, a Cadillac, expensive furs or jewelry for the wife, and a prestige university for the son and the daughter. Among the Chinese the signs of a similar position have, for centuries, included a big family. Not only do two or three generations of direct descendants live under the same roof, but numerous collateral relatives are present as well. In imperial times, such families often received decorations, just as Americans are awarded medals for bravery in war. This traditional Chinese decoration was usually a wooden plaque five feet long, two or more inches thick, and three feet high, lacquered black, and inscribed with gilded characters.

To achieve such a distinction, the ideal Chinese marital pattern had to be strictly adhered to, the father-son tie prevailing over the husband-wife bond. The well-to-do Chinese husband could conform in this respect because he was not very dependent either socially or economically upon his wife. Some of his needs were satisfied by servants; others might be met by a concubine. Unity of the big family was insured at the expense of the individual desires of all but especially those of the wife.

The relatively poor families failed to enlarge themselves not because they did not wish to do so, but because poverty necessitated a different pattern of life. Here the husband was not only dependent upon his wife for all personal services, but he also had to rely on her to contribute to the economic and social welfare of the entire family. Under these circumstances the husband-wife tie tended to prevail over the parent-son bond, and when the husband took the side of his wife in tensions involving his mother, the big family broke up.

Since about 1900, changes in the traditional Chinese marital pattern have become apparent. These changes mostly occurred among persons educated in Western-style institutions of higher learning. There is now more emphasis on romantic love and on living away from the husband's parents. These conditions have led many to speak of the changing Chinese family, or to predict even more drastic developments in the Western direction.

What these scholars have done is to project their preconceived evolutionary theory based on limited Western experiences. The non-Western facts tell us differently. For example, nearly a quarter of a century after I first made the observation on the differential family size between the well-to-do and the poor, Myron Cohen's data from Taiwan unwittingly confirmed it. He says, "As of May 1965 the majority of Yen-lian's population were in fact members of joint families. The reason for this boils down to the fact that technological modernization has given customary tendencies greater opportunities of realization."[3] I found the same thing in 1975–1976 in the New Territories of Hong Kong where economic improvement and industrial spread had, instead of reducing family solidarity, actually increased the chances for related persons to live under the same roof.

Certainly all cultures change from time to time—some more rapidly than others. But I do not know of any culture which can reverse, in one century or less, a direction built up over many scores of centuries. We cannot find more eloquent evidence for this than the case of General Hu Tsung-nan's marriage according to an article in a 1968 Taiwan newspaper. The famous modern general of the Nationalist army greatly distinguished himself in Chiang's anti-Communist campaigns, including his pursuit of the Communist forces in their Long March as reported by Edgar Snow. The article in his memory after his death was entitled: "Ten Years as Fiancée; Three Days as Bride." The narrative goes as follows:

> The general was introduced to his wife twenty-five years ago by a fellow officer. They agreed on the wedding that very winter, but Japan's large-scale attack against China made the general decide that he would not think of a family till the enemies had been vanquished. The delay continued for the next ten years. During this time many friends and admirers were concerned. Their attempts to match him with someone else met with his rebuffs. The fact that many married high military officials of his time even had concubines led some to doubt the general's masculinity. Hu stuck to his original decision. After the Japanese surrendered in

1945 he delayed the happy date still further till he could present his future wife with a great victory on the battlefield as his wedding gift. He achieved the latter in February 1947, when he led the Nationalist forces and conquered Yenan, the Communist wartime capital. One month later, on March 19, 1947, he was married to his wife, née Yeh, in his field headquarters in Sian. They spent the next day together and parted a day later when she returned to Nanking. The couple did not see each other again until three years later, when the general and his forces were evacuated to Taiwan after the rise of Communist power on the mainland.[4]

It must not be supposed that Mrs. Hu was some illiterate woman of the traditional school. According to the author of the article she holds a Ph.D. in political science from the University of Wisconsin. Nor must it be supposed that the marriage did not last. Six years after the general's death his widow (who is much younger than he) and mother of his young children, remains devoted to his memory.

General Hu's protracted engagement and his selection of a wedding gift were certainly uncommon. But his approach to married life is not atypical of China since the coming of the West. For example, an appendix to an autobiography of Ts'ien Ch'ang-tsa provides us with different personal details but the same Chinese essentials. The appendix is entitled "Reflections on the Fortieth Anniversary of Our Marriage," and is in praise of his wife. He gives the following high points.

The marriage was arranged in the mid-thirties, with some pre-wedding social intercourse in the company of family or intimate friends. The betrothal and wedding ceremonies were traditional. Shortly after becoming man and wife the newlyweds each shared cabins with members of the same sex, to save money, in a ship between Shanghai and Tientsin en route to Peking where the husband was to assume a university professorship. In forty years of marriage she was a model daughter-in-law to his mother (adopted), she gave birth to sons who continued the family line, negotiated and oversaw his younger sister's marriage, stayed home during his protracted duties away (including two years in the United States), and never asked a single question about his work.

Being motivated by the ideal of mutual dependence, Chinese marital adjustment is influenced by a multiplicity of duties and obligations which buttress rather than replace one another, and which are definable by definite rules. The parent-child tie, therefore, does not explicitly conflict with the marital bond. In fact it is not uncommon even in Taiwan today to find cases in which, upon the death of his fiancée, a man takes his intended parents-in-law as his "dry parents."[5] But the ideal of self-reliance requires that American marital adjustment be achieved through individualized attraction and sentiments which in turn require constant efforts to sustain them and which cannot be shared. Marriage inevitably means the complete displacement of the parents by the spouse, which usually creates resentment, however concealed, on the part of the elders. Hence, while most Chinese spouses can take each other for granted, most of their American counterparts tend to worry constantly about the possible waning or loss of their partners' affection. In this connection the advice of many American family counselors is not very helpful. First they insist that spouses must have faith in one another, but on the other hand, they consider an ideal marriage as one in which the man and wife continue to court one another. This situation infuses real meaning into the serio-comic picture of the American husband and wife who battle when some aspect of the ritual is momentarily forgotten (a wedding anniversary or a good-morning kiss), for the unhappy partner takes this as a definite sign that the marriage is in trouble.

These differences between the two peoples' marital relationships are highlighted by the following episode. Two ladies, a Chinese and an American, shared a maternity room. The Chinese mother had a normal delivery, but the American had to undergo a Caesarean section. The Chinese mother received her husband until the last day of her stay without making any special effort to beautify herself. The American woman's activities were drastically different. Each time, just before her husband's arrival, she would get out of bed, dash back and forth between the bathroom and the bedside dresser—dressing, painting, and combing herself—while frantically repeating: "I can't let him see me like this!" Several times she finished her frenzied primping and crawled back into bed only a moment before he knocked on the door, and in obvious relief she smiled to her Chinese roommate: "Just made it!"

The Chinese mother commented to me: "She certainly makes her husband's arrival like that of a king. It seems that she treats him like an outsider. It is really foolish to exert herself like that only a few days after a major operation." These remarks were natural, for to the Chinese, the husband and wife are "insiders" to one another.

The consequences of these differences are far reaching. The Chinese, in spite of their complicated duties and obligations, have found their marital ties relatively lasting. The Americans, on the other hand, in spite of their simplified domestic situation, have developed a marriage pattern that is increasingly unstable. In the first place, marriages cannot be stable if the pattern of individual independence leads to competition even between the spouses. In the second place, marriages cannot be stable where the pattern of individual independence causes the partners to consider their individual interest first and foremost whenever any marital difficulty occurs.

Since 1949 a great deal has been said about how much marital and domestic life in China has changed. But these observers have only noted superficial aspects of interpersonal relations, not the fundamentals. We have seen in Chapter 3 how little the Chinese way of romance has changed since the Communist revolution and how such changes as have occurred are linked with the traditional. I do not wish to give the impression that the ways of peoples remain the same forever. Even in Taiwan some changes are occasionally visible. For example, in a 1968 divorce petition in P'ing-tung district, politics was the main grounds. The spouses could not get along with one another because each objected to the other's support of a competing candidate in the same local election. Some local people regarded this as highly improper. In their opinion political differences should be eradicated in the locality in the interest of local development and marital harmony. (*Lien Ho Pao,* February 29, 1968.)

However, I do wish to suggest that the Chinese in China are likely to change far less rapidly, in spite of the change of government, economy and leadership, than the Chinese who live and are raised abroad as minorities, especially in America. Already instances of divorce and separation among the Chinese in the United States are not rare.

For whatever it is worth I can also compare my own thoughts as a child in China with those of one of my daughters in America. In my childhood it never occurred to me or any of my playmates that our fathers might one day be separated from our mothers except by death. Their relationship was part of the unchangeable order of nature. My New York City-born and Evanston-raised older daughter seemed to have an entirely different outlook. At age five one day she was angry with me for some reason. "Mommie," she announced, "you and I can be very happy together." Her mother reminded her that she wouldn't do very well without a father. My daughter was not at all moved. "But you could be married to someone else," she replied, "and I'll have a new father!"

This is not meant to suggest that all American children are preoccupied with the instability of their parents' marital ties. But there is no denying that in the American social climate, where parental and marital bonds are chiefly a matter of individualized adjustment and choice, children as well as adults tend to think of separation or divorce as one easily available solution to domestic problems. In the Chinese cultural atmosphere, where the permanence of family ties is taken for granted, separation or divorce comes more rarely to anyone's consciousness.

The most recent statistics on *Divorce, Child Custody and Child Support* published by the U.S. Bureau of the Census (1979) shows that there indeed have been changes in the American marital and domestic picture. The divorce rate has more than doubled since 1940 when it was two out of every thousand people, to 5.1 per thousand in 1978. Whereas there were 361,000 children of divorced families in 1956, the corresponding number had risen to 1.1 million in 1976. From 1960 to 1978 there was a rapid rise in the number of one-parent families. In the former year 8.5 percent of families with children were headed by one parent (7.4 percent by the mother and 1.1 percent by the father), but eighteen years later the figure had risen to 19 percent (17 percent by the mother and 2 percent by the father). This, in spite of the fact that the total number of children living with one or both parents declined by 2 million (from 62 to 60 million) in the nearly two decades between 1960 and 1978.

In addition, quite a few American couples today cohabit without marriage (one 1979 estimate put the figure conservatively at 1 million). One such couple even wrote a book on the subject. Their main theme, discussed on a television talk show, was: We are trying to get rid of the idea of legitimacy.

These and other facts (such as the less frequent but noticeable number of unisex marriages sanctified by some ministers and the rising tide of gay liberation in general) have prompted some lawyers, sociologists, and futurists to suggest new forms of marriage. "When so many live in ways the law doesn't sanction, it's time for reform," says Judith Younger of Cornell University Law School.[6]

Younger proposes that law sanction three kinds of marriage: dress-rehearsal marriage, open to any one over the age of sixteen, requiring no license and carrying no economic and legal obligations; selfish marriage, for those twenty-two or older and self supporting who desire only personal fulfillment and mutual self-expression; and marriage for children. The second type would require simple registration to enter and to leave, but even the third type would no longer entail alimony from either spouse should the marriage end.[7]

Are such proposals new? Yes and No. They are new in that they suggest legal sanction for styles of cohabitation not now sanctioned. But they are old because they are merely further escalation of the individual-centered American way of life. The philosophy behind that way as it concerns marriage is aptly put by Professor Thomas E. Lasswell of the University of Southern California, a member of the board of the American Association for Marriage and Family Therapy and "a rock of conservation" in this discussion: "The impact on marriage is that persons stay together because they want to, primarily because they have affectual ties rather than because of economic or social need."[8]

Both systems possess advantages and pitfalls. The Chinese pattern definitely restricts freedom of action, but this very freedom in the American pattern makes mutual accommodation much more difficult and certainly much more complicated. Where there are definite and easily perceived rules, the individual finds his or her place in life with relative ease; but where family relations are left largely to personal manipulation, mutual adjustment entails constant vigilance and is accompanied by perpetual uncertainty. The ecstatic happiness of many American married couples is relatively rare in Chinese romances. But the reverse of the coin, the intense hatred and deep-seated pain that are often generated by disappointment in love between American husbands and wives, is equally rare in Chinese marriages.

Class

Before proceeding further, let us briefly recapitulate certain basic tendencies that we have so far discovered, for they are important to an understanding of the two peoples' contrasting attitudes toward the concept of class distinction. We have seen, for one thing, that the Chinese tend to retain the parent-child relationship as the foundation of their way of life, and that other duties and obligations that develop later in life must coexist with it. The Americans tend to move from one social setting into another, so that different relationships replace one another successively and, at least potentially, without end. Being situation-centered, the Chinese finds enough security in his basic human ties to allow him to relax or even to stop competing altogether, for he is embedded in a net of human ties. The removal or breakdown of any one of them does not lead to the collapse of his entire world. Being individual-centered, the American cannot take for granted any of his human ties and so must hold on to one of them hard (a pattern sometimes described as clinging) or be constantly on the move in search of new and more satisfying alliances. Consequently, while most Chinese are content to pause and enjoy what they have, most Americans feel compelled to march forward perpetually looking for further rewards or pleasures. These fundamental facts should be kept in mind in examining Chinese and American attitudes toward the idea of social class.

The class structures of Chinese and American societies differ in several respects. First, the relative sizes of the classes are different. At least four-fifths of the Americans are, by most definitions, "middle class" or higher, but over half, if not more, of the Chinese, even today in the People's Republic and in Taiwan, must be classed as "the poor."

Another difference between the two peoples concerns the criteria for class membership. Among Americans, wealth seems to be the most important single factor in determining an individual's class status. According to the studies of Richard Centers, this is especially true in the case of membership in the "upper class." And Lloyd Warner's studies make it clear that, of all types of wealth, that which is inherited ranks highest.[9] More comprehensive analysis shows that size of income and patterns of consumption are generally the most important criteria for class assignment in all strata of American society.[10]

Wealth is also important in China, but by itself could never place an individual in the highest class, whether his wealth came by inheritance or personal industry. The most important criterion for membership in the highest class was, until very recent times, scholarship, consisting chiefly of mastery of the Confucian classics, which in turn led to imperial honors and bureaucratic positions.

The literati-bureaucrats until recently served as standards for the rest of the Chinese society. Throughout the last twenty centuries not only did wealthy merchants buy titles in the government or send their children to schools as a means of improving their status via the imperial examinations, but even the aristocracy, who were one notch above the bureaucrats in power and wealth, and the military, who could sometimes seize the throne, were similarly affected.

The aristocracy of any dynasty consisted solely of the emperor and his relatives. The founders of Chinese dynasties were in some cases illiterate, such as that of the Ming, and in other cases they were of foreign origin, such as those of the Yuan (Mongol) and Ch'ing (Manchu). All of them, without exception, engaged literati-bureaucrats to tutor their male children, and even the illiterate founders of dynasties usually sought to improve themselves in this fashion. The result was that most rulers of China were masters of the classics and they were proud of it. The Emperor Ch'ien Lung of the Manchu dynasty was not only proficient in poetry and calligraphy but he personally supervised the editing (and some purging) of all Chinese works handed down from the past, an accomplishment that resulted in a colossal collection of more than thirty-six thousand volumes. These and many other similar historical facts show that the rulers eagerly sought to take up the stock in trade of a class over which they had full control and superiority.

The situation of the military is equally instructive. The common soldiers, despised or feared like bandits, were considered outcasts; even the officers enjoyed no equality with their civil counterparts of comparable rank. Yet those military officials who read the classics, wrote poetry, matched couplets, were fine calligraphers, and were known as "scholarly generals" ranked higher in social esteem than their fellow generals who knew strategy but lacked literary prowess. In time of chaos, the social importance of scholarship would be eclipsed temporarily by military power. This always happened in the past when one dynasty collapsed and another had not yet come to power; this condition also prevailed during the four decades after the fall of the Manchu dynasty in 1911. But in the long run the superior rating of scholarship was never challenged.[11]

We should note, too, that those who obtained their official positions or imperial titles by purchase were objects of contempt and ridicule by those who achieved distinction through examination.

Thus, although for many centuries the Chinese have spoken of themselves, in the order of their social ranking, as scholars, farmers, craftsmen and laborers, and merchants, the really important class division has always been between those who mastered the classics on the one hand, and the rest of society on the other.

There is nothing comparable to this in the United States. Here the factory wage earner does have a lower standing than a man with a college degree. It is true that among the elite, and many groups below it, a college education for the children has become one of the "musts." And polls still rank professors third in prestige professions. But for centuries in China the most important positions were filled exclusively by scholars who had attained the highest honors by examination. In the United States, such positions are open to a wide variety of individuals, and educational achievement, though more important at the national level since the New Deal, remains as a relatively insignificant qualification for positions in state and local administrations.

Furthermore, even at the national level, intellectuals have never enjoyed the kind of security their Chinese counterparts did for centuries. The importance of American intellectuals in the national administration fluctuates, depending upon who is president. Thus, their relatively high esteem under Roosevelt (and to a lesser extent Truman) sank low under Eisenhower; it rose under Kennedy only to plunge to new depths under Johnson and Nixon. Under Carter intellect seems to rate equally with personal friendship and political necessity.

The relationship between the intellectuals and the business community is always one of ambivalence. For certain specific objectives, business people seek the advice of the intellectuals, and there has been for some years a new emphasis on college degrees, often the master's in business administration (MBA), for top level executive positions. But the active elements in business do not hesitate to speak derogatorily of eggheads who meddle in practical affairs from ignorance.

In China, scholarship led to bureaucratic power, which in turn brought wealth and prestige. In the United States the sequence is reversed: wealth and consumption patterns by and large command prestige and bureaucratic power while scholarship is only a sideline.

These differences between China and America, though interesting, are not fundamental. The fundamental distinction is to be found in how each people reacts to the *idea* of class. To the situation-centered Chinese, class is a group matter. His class does not only belong to himself and to his immediate family, but the distinction is shared also by his clan, his wider band of relatives, and sometimes even his whole district. Since he is not insecure about his class position, he can aspire upward without anxiety and can mingle with those below without fearing that they may contaminate him.

For the individual-centered American, class is a personal attribute. His class belongs to himself; even the appearance of his wife and the achievement of his children are signs of his distinction.[12] His relatives and his community may try to claim him, but he has no psychological commitment to them. He strives mightily to enter the company of those above him and he is equally determined to avoid associating with those below lest they pull him down.

The distinction in China between the superior literati-bureaucrat group and the rest of society has always been clear-cut and without ambiguity. The external signs of class were rigid and obvious. The common people admitted their lowly status and deferred in speech and contact to members of the literati-bureaucracy, and the lower bureaucrats were similarly ceremonially obsequious toward higher ones.

In spite of these sharp distinctions, mobility between the two major classes has been both possible and without resistance from those very quarters in which one might expect it.[13] Most revealing is the Chinese attitude toward a change in status, for which they have two terms: "newly rich," and "recently prominent." The former is self-explanatory, and the latter describes those who have recently climbed the bureaucratic ladder. The first kind of people were sometimes slighted and ridiculed, but the second kind were accepted at once. In imperial times the most prominent families of the land, including that of the emperor, eagerly matched their daughters to men who had risen from complete obscurity to acquire the highest examination honors.

Class distinction is not at all clear-cut in the United States. It is true that, as a matter of probability, big businessmen, doctors, and affluent lawyers are likely to be seen in the public eye as members of the upper or upper-middle levels in the class structure just as factory workers and more especially janitors are seen as members of the lower levels of it. However, not only is there a tendency for most Americans to regard themselves as belonging to the "middle class," but also there is a great deal of overlapping between the classes.[14] In contrast to China and even to Europe, the external attitudes of different classes toward each other tend to be toned down rather than played up because of the overall emphasis on equality.

This American emphasis on equality leads to a mixture of attitudes toward class. On the one hand there is the popular notion that, if you only try hard enough you can reach any height you aspire to. Movies and magazines like *Reader's Digest* are replete with individual success stories. On the other hand, there is no lack of evidence that those in customarily low-ranking occupations tend to fortify themselves by status-raising tactics. For example, many janitors call themselves sanitary engineers. One farmer I know calls himself an agronomist. In a recent letter to Ann Landers (*Honolulu Advertiser,* August 22, 1979), a woman working in a dry-cleaning store was indignant because a customer had the nerve to ask her, " 'You seem to be a highly intelligent person. Why are you in such a low-class job?' . . . How many people realize that their dry-cleaners are specialists?" the writer complained. A Chinese customer could not have asked her such a question, nor could a Chinese dry-cleaning store operator have reacted in that way, because class distinctions would have been loud and clear.

Yet, in spite of the emphasis on equality, upward social mobility in America today is a much more strenuous proposition than in China, for two reasons. Obviously there are more economic opportunities in the United States than almost any other country in the world. But one recent publication issuing from a seven-year study by the Carnegie Coucil on Children has shown that, "although for more than a century we have tried repeatedly to reduce the inequalities that adversely affect millions of children, we have made virtually no progress in that effort."[15] The definitive findings are that, besides the effects of racial discrimination, and for a variety of reasons, those who are born to rich and well-to-do parents are destined to be rich and well-to-do, while those who are born to poor parents are destined to be poor.

The second reason upward social mobility in America is strenuous is that those more fortunately situated are very likely to oppose the self-elevating efforts of those below. This is done by refusing to admit the climbers into their residential areas, clubs, and even churches, or by snubbing them if they happen to get in.

This resistance to encroachment from below, at any point on the scale, is matched by the intense desire on the part of the subordinate classes to climb higher. Here is how Lloyd Warner and associates describe the efforts of two social climbers:

> Fred is only a skilled worker (rated 4) who punches a clock every day and receives a wage every week. When they came to Jonesville Nancy drove all over town and consulted everyone about a nice place to live. Several of her better-placed friends wrote notes to their friends in Jonesville and asked them to be nice to Nancy and Fred. Nancy says, "If you want something hard enough you can always get it. That's how I got our house and met the nice friends we have in Jonesville." Whatever the cause, the Fred Browns, with only a wage and a skilled worker classification, live in a house rated by us as above (3) in Top Circle (1). Their social equipment, their comparative youth, and their friendships with people who are better-placed than they, make it possible that Fred may move into a higher occupational and income bracket. The chances are better than even that Fred and Nancy will move into the upper-middle class. That's what they want, and they want it hard.[16]

There are obvious reasons why the "Freds" and "Nancys" of China would never have gone to such trouble. Finding security and con-

tentment in a definite place among their kinship and communal relations, they are not disposed to crash wealthier but unfamiliar neighborhoods. Conversely, once in a strange neighborhood, they need
not worry about being snubbed. One of the most popular axioms of
the Chinese is "harmony among neighbors," and this means regardless of status.

As in the marital situation, the Chinese attitude toward class is inclusive rather than exclusive, while the American attitude is the reverse. Since to the Chinese social relationships are merely additive
and mutually shared, the Chinese elite is less emotionally identified
with its high status than is its American counterpart, and its members see little personal threat in the rise of those below. On the other
hand, deprived of a permanent anchorage in the primary group relationships and determined to be independent of all, the individual
American is forced to guard the prerogatives of his social status with
greater vehemence than his Chinese brethren do; he fears discrimination from above no less than encroachment from below.

The result is one of the many paradoxes which distinguish the
Chinese and American peoples: Chinese openly admitted class differences and frankly symbolize them in custom, but there is less tension between the classes because there is less desire to change one's
assigned position which depends more on the kinship group as a
whole rather than on the individual. American class differences are
less evident in speech and behavior, but class barriers create strong
feelings because each level is directly threatened by the level above
and below it. In the society of China, we find, therefore, open neighborhoods and unrestricted educational facilities, clubs, associations,
and temples to which all are welcome, as contrasted to a professed
egalitarian America segmented into exclusive neighborhoods and
schools as well as clubs, associations, and even churches that are restricted sanctuaries for distinguished families.

Once the underlying reasons for these paradoxes are understood,
it becomes clear that racial discrimination in the United States is but
part of a larger general American tendency to exclude. Since that
tendency is founded on fears of losing one's place among a majority
of the individuals, attempts at integration will not lead to lasting results unless the source of that fear is allayed. This will be examined
in Chapter 13.

The Chinese Communist revolution, like its Russian counterpart,
had its inception in the Marxian theory of class struggle between labor and capital. Since large-scale industrialization formed only a

minor part of the Chinese economy, the Communist leaders shifted their emphasis to a struggle between the peasants, especially landless peasants, and landlords, especially absentee landlords.

After communization in the fifties the overall drive has been to elevate the worker, farmer, and soldier classes and depress the literati-bureaucrat, rich farmer, and capitalist classes. Under the Gang of Four sons and daughters whose forebears belonged to the wrong class could not enter college and were given no chance of advancement at all. At theatres, museums, and acrobatic shows everywhere the banners were the same: "Perform for Labor, Farmer, and Soldier." Since the fall of the Gang in 1978 the doors to institutions of higher learning are again open to all on the basis of merit.

What inroads have such vicissitudes due to high-level policy changes made on the fundamental Chinese approach to class? The situation-centered way of life is more conducive to accommodation than to struggle between the classes. Under the new government the hierarchical order of the classes has been switched around, not eliminated. We will touch on this matter again in Chapter 15. In the meantime we shall shift our focus to the exceptional or prominent individual in both societies: What makes him a success or hero? What does he do to symbolize success or hero status? How does he relate to the rest of the world after he has made it?

NOTES

1. Elaine Cumming and David Schneider, "Sibling Solidarity: A Property of American Kinship," *American Anthropologist* 63 (1961):3:498–507.

2. Such facts are so common and evident that it is quite superfluous to document them. Jules Henry has presented a clear (if pitiful) picture of the plight of the aged in his *Culture Against Man*, Chapter 10, "Human Obsolescence," pp. 391–474.

3. Francis L. K. Hsu, "The Myth of Chinese Family Size," *American Journal of Sociology*, pp. 555–562; and Myron Cohen, "Family Partition and Contractual Procedure in Taiwan," in David C. Buxbaum, ed., *Chinese Family Law and Social Change in Historical and Comparative Perspective*, p. 196.

4. Fen-yuan Chen, "An Everyman's View of General Hu Tsung-nan," in *Central Daily News*, February 20 and 21, 1968.

5. "Dry parenthood" is an old institution in China. It is slightly similar to Western "God-parenthood" because it is a pseudo-kinship relationship. But Chinese "dry" parenthood has nothing to do with baptism, can be arranged between two adults, and entails much more social responsibility than Western "God-parenthood."

6. Lawrence Van Gelder, "Does Marriage Have A Future?" *San Francisco Chronicle*, November 13, 1979, p. 19 (the article first appeared in *New York Times*).

7. Ibid.

8. Ibid.

9. Richard Centers, *The Psychology of Social Classes*, pp. 95–99; and Lloyd Warner and Associates, *Democracy in Jonesville*, pp. 33, 39–42, *et seq.*

10. Joseph A. Kahl, *The American Class Structure*, pp. 19–90. Lately, education has become as important.

11. With no great stretch of our imagination we may say that the emphasis on "Redness over Expertise" during some twenty years following 1949 was sort of a modern-day repetition of this age-old pattern. With the fall of the Gang of Four expertise (scholarship) has once again reasserted itself.

12. This is so up to the time that his children reach maturity but ceases to be true after this commonly understood point of cleavage between a child and his parents. A son may be divested of his father's class standing in short order when, once on his own, he moves in either an upward or downward direction.

13. See Francis L. K. Hsu, *Under the Ancestors' Shadow*, rev. ed., Chapter 12, pp. 297–317.

14. According to one study, 3 percent of "big businessmen" and 7 percent of doctors and lawyers are placed by the respondents in the working class, 2 percent of office workers, 2 percent of carpenters and 1 percent of factory workers in the "upper class," while 5 percent, 59 percent and 34 percent of janitors are respectively in the "middle class," "working class," and "lower class." Richard Centers, "Social Class, Occupation and Imputed Belief," *American Journal of Sociology* 58, (May 1953):546.

15. Richard de Lone, for the Carnegie Council on Children, *Small Futures: Children, Inequality, and the Limits of Liberal Reform*, p. xi.

16. W. Lloyd Warner and Associates, *Democracy in Jonesville*, p. 53. The occupational statuses and residences were each rated according to their locally felt desirability on a scale from 1 (the highest) to 7 (the lowest).

CHAPTER 6

Success
and the Hero

Within America's exclusive neighborhoods, schools, clubs, associations, and churches two forces are constantly at work. One is the individual's fear of slipping—that his social position or material achievements may fall below those of his status equals, his neighbors, or his fellow club members. Since one sure way to slip below others is to associate with individuals of a lower class, few individuals can afford to do so. This is at the root of the emphasis on conformity explained in Chapter 4. The other force operating within the restricted group is the pressure upon each individual to surpass his status equals, his neighbors, or his fellow club members. And as association with the next higher group is one avenue of social mobility, the inevitable American tendency is to climb or to create an additional elite within an already restricted group. In its extreme form, this exclusiveness reduces itself to an "elite" of one person, a reduction that obviously is a literal physical impossibility, and is only possible not through physical exclusion of others but through the development of a concept of one's own uniqueness. This is the essence of the American attitude toward success.[1]

The Chinese, in one sense, are as competitive as Americans, for among both peoples the "rags to riches" success story is popular. This is the theme of numerous Chinese novels, short stories, operas, shadow plays, and legends.

The Chinese underdog may appear first as an orphan, a child persecuted by his stepmother, an adolescent separated from his parents by war, an impoverished scholar of noble ancestry, or even a beggar. At the end of the story, the orphan eventually is adopted by a wealthy family, the evil stepmother is divorced by her husband, the adolescent finally is reunited with his parents, the impoverished scholar emerges from the imperial examinations with honors, and the beggar marries, through fortuitous circumstances, the beautiful daughter of the prime minister. The typical American underdog first appears as a poor immigrant, a young man with unrewarded talent, a Black, a misunderstood husband or wife, a child of the city tenements, or a dweller in a log cabin. These dramas also have happy endings.

But after they have "arrived," a Chinese and an American have profoundly different aspirations. Being individual in outlook, the American hopes to make a "pile" somewhere and to achieve a certain fame or even notoriety that is his to enjoy wherever he goes. A man who starts life in Jonesville, Ohio, may have some small interest in Jonesville after he has become successful; his home town may give him a noisy welcome if he returns briefly, and if there is a Jonesville College, he may receive an honorary degree. But there will be little further connection between him and his place of birth. He is likely to spend his active years in a great metropolis here or abroad, and when the time comes for him to retire, the fortunate spot to be graced by his presence is more apt to be Florida or California than his home state.[2]

For over ten centuries, however, the Chinese have reiterated this adage:

When fame and wealth flare,
To your home town repair;
For it is folly to wear silk
Where no one will care.

There are many tales in the repertoire of the Chinese storyteller and the stage that embody this theme. One is the historically based "Mr. Chu Divorces His Wife."

Chu, a poor scholar, had a very difficult time supporting his wife. He was only interested in studying the classics and was unable to provide food and comfort for the family with his own hands. His wife, far from being helpful and understanding, nagged him constantly for his ineptitude and derided him for his preoccupation with books. One cold day she was particularly incensed about the lack of heat, and forced him to go out into the hills to gather firewood. It was snowing hard and the wind blew furiously. After struggling and falling repeatedly on the slippery mountain roads, he returned with only a handful of twigs, the maximum effort of which he was capable. His wife was so infuriated that she made him divorce her right then and there. She married someone else, and Chu continued his studies.

Some years later Mr. Chu passed the examinations, received high imperial honors and was at once appointed to a prominent office. With an entourage displaying great pomp, he returned to his home town on a magnificent white steed. He was received by all levels of dignitaries, and his procession was hailed by an admiring throng that lined the streets.

Suddenly, the former Mrs. Chu came forth from the crowd. She knelt before him, asking to be taken back. Chu ordered a bucket of water poured in front of his horse. He addressed her thus: "Woman, if you can get the water back into the same bucket, I shall take you back." Unable to do so, she killed herself by beating her head against a stone wall. Chu's triumph was thereby complete, and the story came to an end. Both the adage and the story are truly expressive of the age-old Chinese desire to "shine oneself by returning to the home town."

In this connection, the way in which prominent Chinese and American names are linked with geography is most illuminating. In the United States it is customary for athletic stars to be announced as Dick Savitt, Orange, New Jersey, or Red Grange, Wheaton, Illinois.[3] If the individual is famous for achievements of a broader scope, his name may be chosen to grace a street, a park, the town of his birth, or even another locale. Thus we have Roosevelt Boulevard, Kennedy Airport, Jacksonville, Grant Park, and Washington.

In China the linkage is reversed. Instead of a famous man's place of birth being named after him, his name is overshadowed by the place of his birth. Thus Li Hung-Chang, an outstanding diplomat during the Manchu dynasty, was referred to by public consensus as Li Ho-Fei, the second part being his native district in Anhwei Province. Chang Chu-Cheng, a great minister in the Ming dynasty, was known as Chang Chiang-Ling, the latter part deriving from his native district in Hupei Province. Yuan Shih-Kai, who became the first president of the Chinese Republic in 1911, was referred to as Yuan Hsiang-Cheng, the second appellation coming from his native district in Honan Province. To translate this practice into American terms, instead of Milwaukee, Wisconsin, being named "MacArthurville" at some future date, the late soldier should be called "General of the Army Milwaukee MacArthur"; or instead of Plains, Georgia, being renamed Carter, Georgia, former president Jimmy Carter should be known as "Plains Carter."

In the case of Dr. Sun Yat-sen, whose formal name was Chung-Shan, the Western influence has become manifest. His home town, Hsiang-Shan, Kwangtung Province, has been renamed Chung-Shan after him instead of vice versa. Throughout China there are also various Chung-Shan boulevards, parks, and even uniforms and hardware. But the Western influence is only superficial. Dr. Sun's birthplace, instead of remaining one of two thousand districts in China, became a national shrine under the Nationalist government, supported by the national treasury. The town was rebuilt and made into a so-called "model district," administratively under the central instead of the provincial government.

Chiang Kai-shek, who did not cause his native district to be named after him, nevertheless spent large sums there to improve his own estates and the community in general. When I visited the area in 1933, I was awed not only by his magnificent town house, his huge ancestral temple, and his beautiful mountain retreat, but also by the macadam roads linking his houses and leading to the town. His private establishments towered over the hundreds of bamboo and mud-wall dwellings of the townspeople.

There was no reason why the Generalissimo should not have done this. He was a local boy who made good and all his fame, power, and wealth would have had no meaning in Chinese eyes if they were not visible to the humbler people to whom he was once just one more boy on the street. This practice is not restricted to the mightiest and most famous, but is indulged in widely by Chinese of lesser importance. Throughout China, including "West Town" in southwest China, where I did intensive field work between 1941 and 1943,[4] I found a number of beautiful but only occasionally occupied residences. These belonged to "West Towners" who resided in the provincial capital where they carried on their business or professional activities. They made good away from home, but their achievement, like that of the Generalissimo, would have had little meaning if it had not been visible to their home town brethren.

Again we see reflected the Chinese situational orientation in life as contrasted to the American individual orientation. When notoriety and wealth come to the Chinese, his first thought is to shine among, and share his success with, those who are related to him, parents, children, spouses, distant relatives, friends, neighbors, or by extension, residents of the same district. His glory is their glory, and he, in turn, is more satisfied because he has shone before them. The backbone of this situation-centered orientation is the same pattern, that of mutual dependence, which runs through all Chinese relationships.

No man, however great, is ever higher than his community. While he may have gained renown by personal ability, his efforts would have been futile but for the good accumulated by his ancestors and the excellent geomantic situation of the locality as whole.[5] A successful man who does not return to objectify his accomplishments in his home community has not only failed to transform his success into a meaningful entity, but by forgetting his origins, he is undermining the very foundation of his success.

To the successful American, the sense of his own greatness is quite unrelated to the people surrounding him, and certainly he does not feel that it depends at all upon the community of his origin. The dream of the ambitious person is to have the world at his feet, not at his side. In that world of hero worshipers he includes even his wife and his children. He may shower his wife and children with fine cars, glittering jewelry, and magnificent homes, but these, as Thorstein Veblen pointed out many years ago, are the outward symbols by which he shows the world how well he can provide for his family. They are, so to speak, expressions of his own personality. His parental family is not the cause of his greatness, for he is better than his parents, and has achieved success on his own.

The contrasting patterns also help us to understand why fan mail is so important in the United States but is an unknown phenomenon in China.[6] The Chinese would derive no satisfaction from fan mail, as his greatest triumph is to share his glory with his family and community. And most especially, the respect of those who knew him as a child is the true measure of his greatness. To the American, fan mail from whatever source is valuable. His success is his own, and the wider the impersonal audience the more impressive is his achievement. He is then, by the American definition of a personal success, in a class by himself.

The American goes through his life cycle by moving from one setting to another. He proceeds, as we have seen, from the parental to the marital relationship with a definite sense of ending and beginning. In the same fashion, he moves, or strives to move, from one class to another, the apex of which movement is to be considered in a class by oneself. Therefore his struggles are anxiety-ridden and his successes precarious. Lacking fellow human beings upon whom he can unquestionably rely, the person depends on such tokens as class and club membership or feats of individual accomplishment to bring him a sense of security that often is actually evanescent, for except for a few extraordinary people in each generation there is always one more summit to be topped.

The Chinese, in the meanwhile, goes through his life cycle retaining the same basic human relationships. He adds to them at successive stages, but he never replaces them. When he has obtained success, he purposely returns to where he began. He, therefore, never enjoys the intense, personal glory which crowns his American counterpart, but neither does he suffer deeply and alone should he slip or fail completely. The Chinese still retains his place in the primary groups in a mutually supportive situation. Consequently, social class, clubs, associations, and all other signs of personal achievement are of secondary importance to him. Having his place in the primary relationship, he has less psychological need to seek other symbols of position.

Hero Worship

Inequality exists in all societies. It may stem from heredity, caste or class distinctions, or from other forms of political, economic, or religious differentiation. Both among Chinese and among Americans this inequality becomes more apparent and more inevitable because of the concept of success.

But the failure to achieve success means one thing to the Chinese and another to the American. The Chinese is likely to find failure tolerable, not only because of his secure roots in his primary relationships, but also because his society takes the inequality of men for granted. The Communist revolution is rooted in the idea of future equality, but since 1949 the inequality of the formerly affluent with laborers, poor farmers, and soldiers has been very obvious. The American is prone to resent failure, not only because he lacks deep emotional anchorage in primary relationships, but also because one ideal of his society proclaims that all men are equal.

The Chinese tends therefore to be content even though he himself is not a success and has failed to reach the high goal he set himself. In fact, before modern times, most well-to-do Chinese fathers retired early and enjoyed leisure, their families, and their scholarship. Other Chinese found their *chi tuo* (spiritual refuge) in nature appreciation, calligraphy, poetry, or gardening. The Chinese male does not have to defend his personal failure by continuous acts of conquest. But the unsuccessful and even successful American must find some psychological defense behind which it is easier to continue his own struggles. Hero worship is one form of defense for both the successful man and the man who is a failure. The fact that the hero is a psychological necessity to Americans but not to Chinese causes the interaction between the hero and his public to differ widely in the two countries.

The American dignitary or celebrity is a man or woman of the people. He or she must maintain frequent contacts with the public, preferably by personal appearances, and secondarily through constant exposure in newspapers and magazines, and on radio and television. In the background, the press agent sets the stage and presents the hero, not as he is but as the public wishes to see him. Whatever the sex and whatever the field of endeavor, popular support is increased if the celebrity is good-looking and well groomed, and if he speaks well and has style. The most important thing is that he must be seen and heard often, and he must be sought after by autograph hunters, for the appeal of the outstanding American personality is founded on his actual contact with his fellow men. His popularity, especially if oe is a politician, will certainly increase if he also goes to baseball games, eats hot dogs, and enthusiastically shakes the hand of every anonymous well-wisher.

In contrast, Chinese dignitaries or celebrities seek to maintain their distinction from the public. This is done by ceremonial pomp, cloistered residences, and a battery of guards who are not so much protectors as symbols of rank. The wider his distance from the people, the higher is the hero's prestige.

Up to 1911 the emperor made an annual worship tour from his Forbidden City to the Temple of Heaven in the city of Peking. On this occasion the emperor's sedan chair, carried by at least thirty-two bearers, would be preceded and followed by numerous officials of high rank and at least a half-a-mile-long troop of resplendently uniformed horsemen and foot soldiers who carried all kinds of banners and other paraphernalia of state. The procession was at least as pompous and colorful as that attending the British monarch's opening of Parliament. The difference is that while the annual event in England is an occasion for the monarch and his subjects to renew a sort of personal acquaintance, the Chinese emperor was seen by no one except very high bureaucratic and aristocratic dignitaries. There was never any sign of recognition by his imperial majesty of the presence of any of the other people in his entourage, much less of any person outside it. In fact, the entire route between his palace and the temple was cleared of all pedestrians, and the windows of shops and houses along the way were ordered closed.

Older residents in Peking who lived under the Empress Dowager described to me a typical scene when she and the figurehead emperor

Kuang Hsu annually left the Forbidden City en route to temporary residence in the Summer Palace. The entire route was sprinkled with water, swept, and covered with the usual yellow sand. Five groups of guards marched along the route at successive intervals in advance of the progress of their majesties. These groups of guards were termed *T'ou Ch'ou* ("First Preparation"), *Er Ch'ou* ("Second Preparation"), all the way to *Wu Ch'ou* ("Fifth Preparation"). The presence of the imperial entourage was indicated by nothing except the clip-clop of the horses' hoofs in streets otherwise silent as tombs. My informants got their fragmentary glimpses of the event only by peeping through cracks behind closed windows or doors. The customary isolation of the emperor from his people explains also the ancient court rule that the emperor was not to leave the national capital except for reasons of extreme emergency, such as a foreign invasion.

These differences are fundamental to the two ways of life. Hero worship may be defined as the state of mind in which an individual reveres, respects, admires, seeks to possess all or part of, or tries to identify himself with, some other individual who for one reason or another is considered outstanding. But while the attitude of situation-centered Chinese toward their hero consists chiefly of reverence and respect, with the other elements playing but a minor role, that of individual-centered Americans is marked by admiration for the hero and a desire to possess or to be identified with the object of worship.

Chinese revere and respect the hero for his exalted station, but few of them entertain the active hope of one day being in his place. Americans admire, seek to possess, or identify themselves with their hero not only because they have incorporated the ideal of equality but also because they have a more urgent emotional need to succeed. They project their aspirations upon an individual who has achieved success. They want to be like him; and they look up to him for his individual attributes rather than because of his exalted station.

The Chinese pattern has changed very little in modern times. Generalissimo Chiang Kai-shek and Madame Chiang, during the many years of their political eminence, frequently appeared personally before organizations and the general public. Their photographs were everywhere in China and are still in Taiwan. But these deviations from the old pattern were only superficial. They attended public gatherings invariably to give *instructional* speeches. There were no questions, no discussions, and they were met with signs of extreme deference. Chiang's birthday was a national celebration which called for lavish praise from all high military, executive, and judiciary officials, and from schools and diverse people's guilds and associations.

Some years back, Taiwan celebrated the one hundredth other-worldly birthday *(ming shou)* of the Generalissimo's mother, and these groups offered profuse eulogies. In addition, they also received the Generalissimo's biography of his mother, and his other writings in praise of her, collected into a gilt-bound book. In the 1967 election for president in Taiwan, the "opposition" parties such as *Chung Kuo Ch'ing Nien Tang* (Chinese Youth Party), *Min Sheh Tang* (People's Socialist Party), and Independents, even "decided" not to "insult" the Generalissimo by putting up candidates to compete with him. Since the Generalissimo's passing in 1975 Taiwan has been celebrating his other-worldly birthday every year with typical ceremonial pomp. Chiang's son, Ching-kuo who is president of Taiwan today, has appeared in more relaxed circumstances before the public but the traditional Chinese aura of the ruler vis-à-vis the ruled remains unmistakable.

Under the circumstances, the scarcity of direct communication in the usual sense of the word between those Chinese who are in power and those who are not is hardly surprising. Americans are used to writing letters to public officials. Any American can also write to the nation's chief executive and frequently he will receive a reply. If he addresses a letter to a lesser official he usually receives a personally signed answer. I know of no Chinese who, without intimate connections with the inner circle of the Nationalist government, was able to obtain any kind of personal communication from Chiang's many Departments of Attendants, much less from Chiang himself. The common people, namely those who had no connections, could rarely expect to correspond with even lesser officials.

In Chapter 3 we noted the contrast between Chinese and American children's oratorical ability. An extension that closely parallels that of Chinese and American children's oratorical ability is the lack of verbal facility of most Chinese public men in contrast to their American counterparts. Even Dr. Sun Yat-sen, the fiery revolutionary whose untiring labors led to the fall of the Manchu dynasty in 1911, was no spellbinder. But compared with some of his best-known lieutenants he was an excellent orator. Chiang's speeches were noted neither for style nor lucidity. In fact, most Chinese themselves would agree that they were formal, laborious, or lifeless. I can think of not a single Chinese public figure in modern times who could even remotely compare in oratorical ability with his Western counterparts, even omitting such oratorical luminaries as Roosevelt, Churchill, and Stevenson.

Physical distance from the common people having always been a symbol of the status of the elite, Chinese public men never developed a tradition or skill in public persuasion nor felt the need to build any sort of public image that would equate the great men with the common people. To be kind and fatherly to the people and filial and dutiful to their own parents, yes. To laugh and jostle with or otherwise act like the ordinary populace, no.

It is in this context that Chairman Mao's Herculean feat of swimming across the Yangtze River—widely reported and ridiculed in the Western press—should be understood. It is a pity that Western newsmen, in their usual zeal to find fault with a country toward which they are hostile, took Mao's reported high speed in swimming so seriously. The real importance of the episode to the Chinese was that their leader, intent upon change, exposed himself to the torrents of the Yangtze unlike any Chinese leader before him. Common people had done this sort of thing from time to time, but not great leaders. Mao's feat thus served to reduce the psychological distance between the hero and the common man. In a very real sense, Chinese interest in Mao's swim across the Yangtze is comparable to American interest in Eisenhower's golf, Kennedy's touch football, Johnson's riding on his Texas ranch, and Carter's walking down the ramp of his presidential jet carrying his own garment bag.

But cultural tradition dies hard. The Chinese were enthusiastic about Mao's participation in a common man's activity; but Mao was, after all, their supreme leader. The unbelievable speed with which Mao crossed the world's fourth largest river was but a concession to a traditional pattern of distance between the hero and his public.

The pattern of maintaining physical distances has also affected the sex mores of the Chinese. It has often been said that socially determined sexual inequality imposed restraints upon the movements of Chinese women. The Chinese pattern has been compared with the purdah in India, the burka in Arabia, and the veil in Turkey. But this is another of the instances in which similarity has been mistaken for identity. The Hindu and Moslem countries maintain their usages for the sole purpose of segregating women. But the seclusion of a Chinese girl and her isolation from males with whom she has no bond of kinship or marriage is not only based on segregation of the sexes but also on her status. The same seclusion and social distance is also a mark of the Chinese man of distinction.

The reverse is true of America. Previously we noted that an American lady is highly complimented if a large number of men, known or unknown, gaze at her, and that she is even happier if an acquaintance tells her straightaway how much he is attracted by her beauty. A Chinese woman would be gravely insulted by such glances or expressions; and the higher the status of a Chinese woman's father or husband, the greater the insult. An American septuagenarian dowager might or might not be pleased if a male should take the liberty of whistling at her. If she had a sense of humor, she would probably be amused. But in dynastic days a Chinese would be punished as a criminal if he should dare to make similar gestures toward a princess or any other highly placed woman. The Chinese attitude has been somewhat relaxed in modern times, but it has not disappeared.

Since 1949, sex mores in Taiwan and in the People's Republic have diverged. The Western term "sex appeal" is sometimes found in Taiwan papers and magazines, but its undesirable connotation precludes its application to all but entertainers and a few others. Chinese college coeds enjoy attention from admirers but as noted earlier, any girl who dates many boys is branded immoral. Now and then a Chinese movie star is "mobbed" through publicity arrangement or otherwise, but one sees nothing of the American adolescent's hysterialike enthusiasm in similar contexts. In spite of obvious American presence and influence in Taiwan, the Chinese psychology that distance between the sexes is a status matter has changed but little for a vast majority of the population.

Under the Communist government, women in the People's Republic have come out of their homes in unprecedented numbers. They work in all aspects of the commune—shops, factories, schools, construction, transportation, and government. They dress so drably and seem to care so little for their feminine charms that some Western observers have been impressed by the "puritanical" aspects of the new regime.

This misreading is, as we noted before, based on Western projection. The Chinese have never had any idea of sex repression and do not have it now. But what Chinese culture has always emphasized is a situational view of sex, as observed in Chapters 1 and 2. To repeat, sex has its own private and socially approved domain but is irrelevant outside of it. That is why distance between the sexes is a status matter for the female, and at the same time why the Chinese have little tendency to discriminate against professional women in spite of their traditional culture pattern of inequality between the sexes. Now that many more women have come out of their homes under the new regime and rub shoulders with men in work, politics, and play (a non-Chinese phenomenon), Western observers expect a corresponding increase in Western-style public display of femininity in general. But the old Chinese pattern of lack of public display of feelings between the sexes also serves the new regime's goal of mobilizing more human resources for economic and political gains, since it minimizes the disturbing influence of sexuality outside the intimate family situation.

Seen in this way, it is understandable why actors and actresses have received the lowest social approval in China, and why conversely they enjoy the highest prestige in the United States. They were held in contempt in China because they exhibited their bodies as their principal asset; they are admired in the United States because they epitomize the success that can be achieved by the bare individual. This has gone so far that patrons of Hollywood productions do not condemn a star who is without talent if only he or she is glamorous.

One may be reminded, of course, that actors and actresses have not always mingled with presidents of the United States or the blue bloods of New England society. It is not too long ago that good hotels in many towns would have turned them from their doors. But the question of who is or who is not considered distinguished at any particular point in time is not relevant. Today's attitude toward actors and actresses is merely a more recent extension of a long and deep-seated cultural trend. The infusion of political campaigns with Hollywood names has already gone a long way in America. During the 1968 presidential election the trend reached a new high. Eugene McCarthy had in his corner prominent entertainers such as Paul Newman, Dick Van Dyke, Joan Bennett, Red Buttons, Frederic March, and Melvin Douglas. The late Robert Kennedy was able to count on an equally well-known list including Sammy Davis, Jr., Marlon Brando, Warren Beatty, Lauren Bacall, Marlene Dietrich, and Jack Paar. Richard Nixon's backers included Ginger Rogers and Rudy Vallee while former child star Shirley Temple Black appeared on behalf of Republican causes in general (*Chicago American*, April 15, 1968).

In 1953 in the first edition of this book I wrote: "It is safe to predict that, as time goes on, American show people, who in the very nature of their business are dependent upon the public and must encourage its adulation, will rise further in social esteem."[7] This prediction seems to have been borne out not only by the greater involvement of entertainers in helping aspirants to political office but even more by the successes on the part of entertainers such as George Murphy and Ronald Reagan to achieve high office themselves. In the 1980 presidential campaign opposing candidates and the media openly or covertly alluded to Ronald Reagan's age, but not as a rule to his career as an actor.

In China, exhibition of the person has always been frowned upon. During the last half century a few Chinese actors attained national acclaim and great wealth, but even as late as the 1930s when Mei Lan-Fang, the king of Chinese actors, was awarded an honorary L.L.D. by Pomona College, the news came to the Chinese reading public as a shock. Many Chinese students said then that they "know an American degree to be cheap, now it is cheaper." That is why, according to many Chinese inside and outside the People's Republic, Chiang Ch'ing, leader of the Gang of Four and Mao's widow, fell so soon after Mao's death. Chinese respect for Mao would have at least delayed the event for some time except for two reasons. One, she was an actress from Shanghai, a third-rate actress at that. Two, she opportunistically seduced Mao while his wife was in Moscow for medical attention.

On the other hand, Chiang Ch'ing came to power and stayed in power as long as Mao lived in spite of these facts. Being situation-centered, the Chinese see little difficulty in separating a woman's sex role from her other achievements, as we noted in our discussion of the sexes. Chiang Ch'ing as an entertainer and Chiang Ch'ing as the wife of Mao are, for the situation-centered Chinese, two separate and drastically different entities. As an actress she carried no weight, but as the wife of a national symbol and a powerful man, she could be as powerful as she chose to be. The source of her power was her husband. By contrast, the influence and power of the many famous American entertainers in political campaigns and politics derives directly from their own popular appeal.

It may seem incredible to American readers that the following incident happened in Tainan, Taiwan not so long ago. An entertainer by the stage name of Yi Roo was performing in a night club. She sang a tune entitled "Mama Asks Me to Marry." While rendering two of the phrases: "I won't marry big dope you" and "I won't marry ugly frog you" she playfully pointed twice at a young Mr. Ts'ai in the audience. Ts'ai was so angered that he grabbed a tea cup and threw it at the singer with such force that it lacerated her left leg (*Lien Ho Pao,* Taipei, February 23, 1968).

This incident literally dramatized what anthropologists have for years defined as culture conflict. In the West, a performer's familiarity with members of the audience during a performance has always been accepted. But it never has been, and still is not a Chinese custom. In this instance Mr. Ts'ai's anger might have had something to do with the nature of the lines directed at him, but it was not unrelated to the fact that female entertainers are still regarded in the Chinese view as only a small cut above women of easy virtue.

These differing attitudes seem to explain the different kinds of satisfaction Chinese and Americans derive from hero worship. Americans may occasionally honor a hero because of what he has done to benefit the worshipers. The tumultuous reception given to General Jonathan Wainwright and many other World War II heroes is of this kind. But more often Americans are stirred by heroes purely because of the glamour of the famous person's achievements and of the desire to participate, however indirectly, in this highly attractive ambience.

Glamour is amoral. Its mystique can be supplied by beauty, sex appeal, adventure, daring acts, big money, rebellion, defiance against authority, or even infamy. Some Americans can easily go from worship of South Pole explorers and heavyweight champions, to applause for a D. B. Cooper who hijacked a Northwest Orient plane and parachuted with $200,000 in ransom money, never to be heard from again; or a young man who climbed the World Trade Center Building in N.Y.C. and got a news conference with Mayor Koch; or a Willie Spann who violated his parole but got newspaper interviews and book contracts because he is President Carter's nephew; or a Clifford Irving who swindled some publisher of huge sums of money with a phony autobiography of Howard Hughes; or an Elizabeth Ray who told all after being on Ohio Congressman Wayne Hayes' government payroll as a sex partner.

The last scenes of the movie *The Great Train Robbery* express this very well. After lecturing the convicted robber on immorality, the presiding judge asked him why he did what he did. The robber replied: "I wanted money!" to the roaring laughter of all present. When the robber was led out by police in handcuffs chaos ensued. All hands tried to touch him. A young girl forcibly kissed him. And the camera then showed him mysteriously freed from police bondage and fleeing, to thunderous applause.

The mystique of glamour can even make life very pleasant for the survivors of the assassin of an American president. Lee Harvey Oswald's widow, after receiving $70,000 in donations from sympathizers, sold "pictures and personal stories to periodicals all over the world, generally at lofty prices," and later "instituted a suit against the federal government for $500,000, which she claims is the commercial value of some of Oswald's personal effects seized by the Justice Department."

Besides his letters (sold from $1,000 to $5,000 each, according to length), Oswald's mother offered his Marine shooting record, a toy organ he played (according to her) as a child, and a photo of Oswald in Marine uniform, each for several hundred to several thousand dollars. She also offered a paperweight for $250 incribed: "My son, Lee Harvey Oswald, even after his death, has done more for his country than any other living human being." When a prospective customer complained of the high prices, Mrs. Oswald snapped, "Are you kidding? This is Lee Harvey Oswald." (Quotes in the last two paragraphs are from *Newsweek,* December 4, 1967.)[8]

Of course, the souvenir-hunting motive is always at work, and many of those people who are fascinated by Oswald may be regarded as crackpots. But the astonishing thing, from the Chinese point of view, is that the personal effects of any American who did what Oswald did could enjoy such public demand, and his wife and mother could and would choose to profit from so much public interest.

Yet once the Chinese understands the basic premise of American culture, there is no need for him to be bewildered. In the Chinese situation-centered view of life which ties the individual to his web of social relationships, it is of course not possible to separate Oswald from his wife and mother. Consequently, a criminal's close kin must share at least some of his guilt, and the Chinese could never bear to see a criminal's kin benefit from his crime. But an individual-centered view of life leads one to evaluate his actions first and foremost in terms of their ability to enhance his own achievements. The tendency expresses itself in two directions. On the one hand, just as the individual-centered man's success is his own, so also is his crime. On the other hand, when the crime is of a spectacular nature such as that of Oswald's, spectacularity itself blurs the difference between fame and infamy—and amoral glamour takes over. Oswald raised himself from an obscure wastrel to one whose name has become a household word and whose deed has shaken the world. There is even truth (though some will call it perversion of truth) in the inscription Oswald's mother has put on his paperweight for sale. How many Americans have drawn world attention and sympathy to their country by a single individual deed? Isn't a man who succeeded so well a hero of some sort? He is at least an antihero of epic proportions.

Chinese usually justify their adulation of the greats on one of two grounds: because of the high moral example that they have set, or because of the real or imagined benefits that they have showered on the worshipers. Ancestors are objects of worship because "our fathers originate us and our mothers rear us." The emperor and his officials were deferred to because "they own the country and they enable us to lead an orderly existence and enjoy our occupations." General Kuan Yu of the three kingdoms became a popular god because of his loyalty to his sworn brothers and because of his unremitting struggle against usurpers of the throne. The image of another general of ancient times, Yueh Fei, adorns numerous temples throughout China because of his filial piety toward his mother and his efforts to save his country at great personal sacrifice. The T'ang emperor, Ming Huang, is worshipped by all actors and actresses because he amused himself in court with theatricals more often than did other emperors, even though he did not mix with the performers. Many old records describe how a good local official was given a hero's farewell when the term of his appointment ended. These always report how the populace turned out to express its gratitude to him and to emphasize the sorrow his departure brought to young and old. There are many cases in which, after an official's departure, his likeness was made into a statue and placed in a temple, where it was worshiped like one of the gods. But the distance between the worshiper and the worshiped remained, and the reasons for honoring the official were given as his "honesty and purity" and the tenderness with which he treated his charge as "wounds on his body."

The astonishing thing, from the American point of view, is how openly and abjectly the Chinese declared (and still declare) their submission to great men. Previously we noted that Generalissimo Chiang's birthdays, and those of his mother, are occasions for mammoth celebrations in Taiwan. It is hard to convey to readers who do not read Chinese an appreciation of the extent to which Chinese public communications media are preoccupied with them, but especially in what extreme terms Chinese sentiments are expressed.

These media do not merely report the Taiwan-wide celebrations. The papers and magazines are full of poems and serious articles authored by officials and scholars in praise of the great leader's learning, military thought, and philosophy of life. In 1966 a well-known scholar published on this occasion (when Chiang was seventy-nine years old) an essay on "Spirit of Righteousness and Longevity"

("Cheng Ch'i Yu Chien Shou"). It was written in response to an earlier piece by another authority on the subject but backed by more "concrete" facts and written from the truly "scientific" point of view. After analyzing nearly thirty Chinese expressions in which the word *ch'i* (or spirit, aspect, essence) is used, the author concluded that the "Spirit of Righteousness" of the Generalissimo was the "Spirit of Revolution." And it was this spirit *(ch'i)* which enabled the leader to achieve such longevity (*Central Daily News,* Taipei, October 31, 1965).

However, as soon as the premise of situation-centeredness of the Chinese culture is understood, Americans need not be puzzled by such Chinese activities. Under this premise the principal guide for behavior is whether it befits the role and the occasion, while individual predilections play a lesser part. Consequently, ceremonial and ritual activities tend to be escalated according to social requirements but not because of psychological necessity.

That is to say, Chinese who seem to go all out to adulate their hero are likely to be doing what is expected of them more than expressing true adoration, while far fewer Americans will do so for good form rather than as a genuine display of feeling for the man. Consequently the accent of American hero worship is more likely to be personal than ritualistic; Americans cannot go to the Chinese formalistic extremes without fear of being branded as insincere or even as bootlickers.

Thus Chinese hero worship, if indeed it might be called such, is built on the social relationship of the exalted to the inferior, the important to the insignificant, and the benefactor to the benefitted. It is but minutely characterized by psychological involvement. American hero worship, and in this case it is true worship, is based on the emotional tie between the great and the would-be great, the artist and the would-be artist, and the glamorous and the would-be glamorous. What the worshiper looks for in the hero is not an actual or imaginary contribution to the common good, but the fulfillment of his own unsatisfied ego and dreams.

This is why "men of distinction"—sports stars, movie stars, or any other big names—are such good advertising bait in America. One case of hero worship, in which situation the hero was an unwilling participant who possibly disappointed his public—and certainly disappointed those who hoped to profit from his momentary idolization—is supplied by the story of Henrik Kurt Carlsen. Carlsen was the freighter captain whose single-handed attempt to save his ship from the stormy waters of the North Atlantic made headlines here and in England for several days. During the height of his ordeal, as he later reported in *This Week* magazine ("It's Hell to Be a Hero," May 10, 1952), the battery radio, which was his only mode of contact with rescue ships, began relaying "hundreds of propositions asking me to endorse various products or causes . . . offers to advertise cigarettes, spark plugs, sweaters." His safe landing brought an avalanche of such offers, parades, civic honors, honorary memberships in various organizations, and all the other manifestations through which the hero worshipers celebrate not so much the hero but glorify themselves on their products. A reticent and apparently analytical man, Carlsen was grateful for the few tokens of sincere good will that he could distinguish from the blatant offers to capitalize upon his act. After discussing the matter with his family he decided not to endorse "beer, watches or any other commercial product because I do not want a seaman's honest fight to save his ship ruined." And Carlsen concluded that he hoped to return to the sea soon (as he did) and that "people will forget hero worshipping once and for all."

Conversely, even in the modern big cities of China before 1949 and Taiwan today, businessmen do not try to induce the public to smoke a certain brand of cigarettes, wear a certain style of sweater, or use a certain kind of cold cream because some Chinese big names smoke, wear, or use them. Revering or admiring their heroes and heroines for their statuses or those achievements that redound to the common welfare, the Chinese have little compulsion to imitate the great in personal details.

These differences between the heroes' roles in the two ways of life give rise to a curious paradox: the fame of Chinese idols is apt to be long-lasting while their American counterparts may find their popularity to be a mere fad. But at the same time a Chinese hero is practically finished when dethroned, while an American idol often regains his pedestal after a fall. Consequently, there are few heroes in China and the majority of them are men and women from the past, while American heroes may be numbered in the hundreds and the majority of them are men and women who are contemporaries of the worshipers. Emotions come and go, so each new generation of Americans tends to create its own heroes; but social bonds are much more durable, and so many generations of Chinese worship the same names.

Furthermore, since status differences always separate the Chinese hero and his public, few worshipers feel psychologically threatened

by the former's misfortune. Only the hangers-on whose very liveli-
hoods depend upon the resurrection of the hero will be really disturbed. Consequently, while Chinese will commiserate with those in
misfortune, they have little emotional urge to stand behind an underdog who once was great.

The Chinese pattern of hero-follower relationship has a relevance,
not usually understood, to the rise and fall of Chinese warlords, as it
did to dynastic changes of old. After the fall of the Manchu dynasty
in 1911, different parts of the country were occupied by warlords.
The strengths and territories of different warlords varied. Chang
Tso-lin (whose son later succeeded him and achieved international
notice as the "Young Marshal" who kidnaped the Generalissimo in
Sian in 1936) dominated Manchuria, a domain considerably larger
than Texas. Yen Hsi-shan dominated only Shansi, a single province
along the Yellow River valley. Sometimes a more powerful warlord
headed an alliance of warlords; other warlords enlarged themselves
by vanquishing weaker ones. Warlords had absolute power of life
and death over their domains and constantly waged wars against
each other. They were truly local kings except that the source of their
power was their armies, none of them dominated all of China, and
none was recognized as a legitimate king by the others and by the
people.

Not all of them were equally vicious or ignorant. In fact some,
such as the Christian General Feng Yü-hsiang,[9] were rather enlight-
ened while others, such as Yen Hsi-shan, even attempted planned industrial development. The domains of most warlords included their
own native places, so that they were not alien to the areas under their
control.

Yet none of the warlords achieved a significant following which
fled with him in defeat or helped restore him to power. Those who
followed a defeated warlord were the people who depended upon
him for offices. The only way a vanquished warlord could restore
himself to power was by raising an army (sometimes with Japanese
or European help) or by plotting to bring about the downfall of his
enemy. They had no grass-roots following and hence their comings
and goings, except for their negative consequences such as taxation
or destruction, were otherwise irrelevant to the common man. Few
came forward to welcome them when they arrived; even fewer shed
tears when they departed.

The lack of a sizable following on the part of any of the Chinese
warlords may not, of course, be unrelated to the fact that these char-

acters did more harm than good to China and the Chinese people as a whole. But I can hardly imagine that had they been Americans and had they played a comparable part in recent United States history, they would not have been adored by at least some segments of the American population.

Intimate psychological forces bind the American worshiper to his hero. As the hero's triumph is his triumph, so is his fall tantamount to that of the worshiper. Since his emotional security is threatened in this way, the American worshiper naturally is interested in ways and means by which his hero can be restored to his rightful glory. That is why Nixon—in spite of his many misdeeds that were revealed during the Watergate hearings and led to his forced resignation from the presidency—still enjoys a sizable following in America. Nixon has now abandoned his former "Western White House" and returned to New York. In the light of this analysis I will not be surprised if Nixon should again try for political office, even the highest office of the land.

Once this psychological link is understood it becomes easy to see why Americans are so interested in the intricate workings of the minds of their famous men and women but Chinese show no comparable desire. For example, Sigmund Freud and William C. Bullitt, a former American official who was part of President Woodrow Wilson's entourage at the Verseilles Treaty negotiations in 1919, wrote *Thomas Woodrow Wilson: A Psychological Study* in which they tried to explain the late president's character and actions on the basis of father identification. More recently, Doris Faber in her book *The President's Mothers* claimed that nearly all of the 38 presidents, including Lyndon B. Johnson and Teddy Roosevelt, were "Mama's Boys." There is no Chinese publication on any Chinese leader even remotely comparable. The Chinese, in their situation-centered relationships with their heroes, have simply not been interested in their leaders in such terms.

The unconscious transfer by American observers of the dynamics of American hero worship to the Chinese scene explains why American interpretations of Generalissimo Chiang Kai-shek's leadership were usually wide of the mark. Nor is their understanding of the position of his son, Chiang Ching-kuo, president of Taiwan today, a great improvement. In the early thirties, missionaries exulted when Chiang, then at the summit of his popularity, was baptized. Judging by the American advertising psychology and perhaps the memory of Constantine, it seemed only a small step from Chiang's baptism to the Chritianization of the majority of his followers. Nothing of the kind happened. Later in that same decade many Westerners were impressed by Chiang's New Life Movement, derived from a mixture of Christianity, Confucianism, the YMCA, and Nazism. But the result was merely another set of bureaucratic organizations overloading the never-balanced national budget. While expecting too much from the preceding, Americans were in turn unduly disturbed when Chiang started his Three Principles Youth Corps, patterned after the Hitler Youth Corps. Later, such persons were particularly alarmed when Chiang published his *China's Destiny,* modelled upon Hitler's *Mein Kampf.* Not one of these things had any important effect upon the Chinese, nor did they help to consolidate Chiang's position to any appreciable degree. When the end of his power was near, most of his one-time supporters went over to the other side with great haste. It should not be forgotten that this wholesale desertion of Chiang happened shortly after a tumultuous popular reception that was given him in Shanghai after Japan capitulated.

Not understanding the basic dynamics of Chinese hero-follower relationships, many Americans searched for familiar causes of Chiang's defeat. There must have been traitors in the United States government who sold Chiang down the river; or a different United States policy could have saved America from having "lost" China; or officials of the Nationalist government were at fault, though Chiang himself remained blameless. And finally there were those who were convinced that one day Chiang might be able to mobilize his previous followers and capitalize on his one-time popularity. They were, of course, disappointed.

NOTES

1. Perhaps two of the most outstanding acts of self-reliance in modern times, followed by nationwide acknowledgment of their success, were Lindbergh's solo flight across the Atlantic and Admiral Byrd's extended solitary investigations at the South Pole. Their respective books, which recorded these adventures, were properly and symbolically entitled *We* (the man and the machine *he* controlled) and *Alone.* Their *public* success, be it noted, had little or nothing to do with any advance in transport or science but resulted from the glamour of their individualized achievement. Lindbergh's *We* was echoed by William Willis when a hernia prevented him from completing his solo voyage across the Atlantic. "I put my hand softly on *Little One* (his eleven-foot six-inch boat) and said, "We'll come back." (*Life,* October 4, 1968).

2. In 1967 a high school reunion planned by the village of Red Granite, Wisconsin, hit the wires. An affair that was intended for alumni of the school was expanded greatly. "Invitations went to anybody who had ever lived here or who knew of the town" (*Chicago Daily News,* July 29, 1967). The reunion intended for four thousand guests (one thousand according to another report) turned out to be flooded by over

ten thousand. "They came from all over the country, and thousands more came just to enjoy the festivities" (*Chicago Tribune,* July 31, 1967). I interviewed one of the men upon his return to Evanston, Illinois. He had a good time in Red Granite, did not expect to go again, and had no thought that any of those who spent their youth in the town would return to live or retire in it.

3. This custom has nothing to do with lending importance to the stars' home towns since newspapers also similarly link names of criminals with their places of birth.

4. "West Town" is a pseudonym that I gave to a small semirural community that I studied during this period. The results were published in two books: *Under the Ancestors' Shadow;* and *Religion, Science, and Human Crises.*

5. In Chinese thought every housesite, graveyard, and wider locale has a certain quality, fortunate or unfortunate, known as the "wind and water" of the place. Specialists, called geomancers, are employed to determine the desirability of a location in respect to its wind and water. This practice will be touched upon again in Chapter 9.

6. This phenomenon is also rare in Europe.

7. *Americans and Chinese: Two Ways of Life,* pp. 156–157.

8. Not all of Oswald's relatives conducted themselves in a similar manner. Oswald's brother and close friend, Robert, who manages a brick company in Wichita Falls, Texas, completely refused to exploit his connection with Oswald for profit (*Newsweek,* December 4, 1967).

9. See James E. Sheridan, *Chinese Warlord: The Career of Feng Yü-hsiang.*

CHAPTER 7

Two Attitudes toward Government

For centuries Chinese have engaged in a pastime called "Advancement in Officialdom." The tools of this game consist of a die and a diagram showing numerous hierarchical positions, from that of the ordinary student to that of the prime minister. A throw of the die determines whether the token of each player is promoted or demoted on the diagram. The higher the token climbs on the official ladder, the more money its owner can collect from those whose tokens linger in the lower ranks. This game is played not only among the literati but also among illiterates with the help of one player who knows how to read the diagram.

The Prestige of Government

The universal popularity of this Chinese game is symbolic of historical reality. Chinese, until the turn of the twentieth century, could climb high socially and economically only if they were officials; it has always been possible for Americans to achieve fame and fortune in a multiplicity of fields. It is for this reason that when I discussed hero worship, I referred chiefly to Chinese government officials but selected American greats from many different lines of endeavor, including politics, sports, and entertainment. This was not an oversight; I did it of necessity. Except for the once a year dragon-boat competition in the south, traditional China had few public sports. But she could boast of many forms of entertainment, from the opera to the circus. American readers who visited Peking before 1949 will probably remember the area of that city called T'ien Ch'iao (Heavenly Bridge). It was a vast amusement and trading center where animal acts, child acrobatics, songs, classical operas, popular operas, peep shows, plays, boxing and wrestling, satires, and imitations were presented in different tents and open circles.

I never gave much thought to Chinese satirists and mimics until I came to the West. Those satirists in Heavenly Bridge combined the roles of orators in Hyde Park, London and militant newspaper editorialists in the West, except that some of their language was not so printable. But in retrospect, some of the mimics were remarkably comparable to the top box office stand-up comedians of the United States. Their misfortune was that they lived in a society where entertainers enjoyed little public esteem; hence they never figured among Chinese heroes.

In the last chapter we saw that for two millennia the literati-bureaucrats invariably stood first and foremost among the Chinese social classes. Lowly placed military men seeking to increase their prestige did so by mastering literature, while highly rated aristocrats maintained their respectability by following the same procedure.[1] But I know of no entertainers in pre-1949 China who ever became Chinese men of distinction.

For two thousand years the emperor and his bureaucrats were China's biggest spenders. The economic distinction of Chinese government officials from the people they governed was really striking. About A.D. 1700, the salary of a magistrate, depending upon the size of his administrative area, was between $800 and $1,500 per year, but by A.D. 1900, when prices were somewhat higher than in 1700, the average wage of those skilled workers in Peking who produced the exquisite rugs and carpets that today decorate many luxurious American homes was roughly $68 to $102 a year.[2] In other words, the difference between the earnings of the lowest officials and that of the best skilled workers was more than ten to one. The contrast was really much greater than the statistics reveal since the wages of the workers were all that they received, but the actual income of the magistrate was far above the known figures. Those officials who outranked the magistrate of course enjoyed incomes many times larger than his, but few individuals outside government offices earned more than a skilled laborer.

From time to time a few merchants who dealt in salt or silk or banking became millionaires, but they or their sons would seek an official connection or a place in officialdom as soon as it was practical. The contrast between the styles of life of the leading class and the common people has been highlighted in a few lines of an immortal poem by Tu Fu, a T'ang poet:

Behind the red gates of rich homes,
left over wine and meat rot
Frozen corpses of starving men litter
the roads.

The extravagance of the emperor and his court was legendary. Princess Der Ling, who served for two years as lady-in-waiting to the Empress Dowager, gave readers in the English-speaking world some glimpses of that extravagance in her book, *Two Years in the Forbidden City*. Even after being deposed, the late boy emperor Pu-yi (better known in the West as Henry Pu Yi) lived in unimaginable luxury and waste as long as he and his entourage were allowed to remain in the Forbidden City.[3]

This sharp contrast in income between the rulers and the ruled did not diminish with the advent of the Republic. There are no exact data on the extent of wealth amassed by officials, but in 1929 it was estimated that in the treaty port of Tientsin alone, property valued at no less than $300 million was held by various retired ministers, politicians, and warlords,[4] while in June 1931, the total amount of *working capital* of the eleven hundred registered Chinese-owned corporations in China was only $556 million.[5] There are no figures on property held by officials in the cosmopolitan center of Shanghai, where officialdom tended to concentrate after the removal of the national capital from Peking to Nanking. However, during the height of Nationalist power the International Settlement and the French Concession in Shanghai contained many magnificent residences belonging to government dignitaries including Chiang Kai-shek, T. V. Soong, and H. H. Kung, who traveled by special trains between their weekend resorts and the capital. A few modern industrialists like Yung Chung-Ching, who owned seven of Shanghai's huge textile mills, and Chang Ch'ien, who practically owned the important provincial town of Nan T'ung north of Shanghai, did lead a life of great leisure, but such entrepreneurs were few and far between.

In America the ratio of rewards is reversed. Here the industrial and commercial magnates or big time entertainers are at the top of the heap; the salary of the president of the United States is appreciably less than that of any vice-president at General Motors.[6] Compared with the pretentiousness and luxury of the residences of the late William Randolph Hearst of San Francisco and Colonel McCormack, publisher of the *Chicago Tribune,* the country houses of some big American industrialists and financiers, the glamour of the White

House is largely historical. Lesser officials, from cabinet ministers to justices of the peace, are outshone by tens of thousands of ordinary citizens in every walk of life. In fact, a laborer in the United States often makes more than persons in the lower echelons of the government. We may note, too, that wealth or private income from another source is often a necessity if an individual is to enter government service, as in diplomatic posts, and that occupancy of the chief executive's mansion may cost the tenant more than he earns. Thus, it is not by chance that the relatively few Chinese millionaires are usually present or former government officials like Kung and Soong, with industrialists like Yung a tiny minority, while most of the far larger number of American fortunes, like those of the Vanderbilts, Fords, and Rockefellers, are products of commerce or industry.

Official position in China brought such large economic returns that it was truly the most lucrative industry of the country; but official position in the United States is usually so inferior to other activities in its economic rewards that the government finds it difficult to attract talented persons. The social and economic importance of the government in China is correlated with the high prestige traditionally enjoyed by all functionaries from the emperor to the thousands of assistant magistrates. The respect accorded a few American political leaders, past or present, depends almost exclusively on their personal achievements, the mere occupancy of government position bringing little or no particular prestige to the thousands of average officials. The Chinese situation not only induced men of ambition to enter government service—in fact, to rush to and crowd it—but it also helped in the tendency of the Chinese people, as a whole, to obey their rulers so that their subordination was automatic both in deed and thought. Hence the Chinese peasant adage:

Whoever be the emperor,
He will get our taxes.

From about the third century B.C., to the early years of the twentieth century, rule by an emperor was the Chinese mode of government. His rule was absolute, and there was no pretense of popular representation or majority rule. The emperor "owned" the empire and his subjects were his "children." It was technically possible for the emperor to change unilaterally any point of law he wished, and death was often the punishment that awaited any person—court minister or peasant—who opposed his will.

The shabby and unjust way in which Emperor Tao Kuang of the Ch'ing dynasty treated Viceroy Lin Tse-hsu, chief opponent of British opium trade in China, is a flagrant illustration of this. Viceroy Lin was sent to Canton to deal with the British attempt to force the drug on China. The British merchants surrendered some two hundred thousand cases of opium which he consigned to a public bonfire, but they balked at the viceroy's demand that those who wanted to trade in China sign a pledge under penalty of death not to import opium into China. At this recalcitrance, Viceroy Lin strengthened the local defense and stopped all Sino-British trade. Finding no way of penetrating Lin's defenses, the British naval forces went north along the China coast, defeating the Chinese defenders as far as Shanghai. This was the well-known Opium War, which resulted in the Treaty of Nanking (1842) in which China suffered from the first of many defeats at the hands of Western powers. For his "crime" in leading to this defeat, Viceroy Lin was demoted and exiled to the desert in the northwest. Lin's official disgrace continued until after the death of Emperor Tao Kuang, when the next monarch (Emperor Hsien Feng) needed him to quell a rebellion.

The throne of the emperor was hereditary. In very ancient times, it is said, the line of succession was from the ruler to his next younger brother, and so on until the very last of the brothers, and with his death the throne passed to the oldest son of the oldest brother. Then the fraternal succession continued once again. But since 800 B.C., or thereabouts, each dynasty passed the throne from father to oldest son with few exceptions. When the dynastic continuity was broken by the emergence of a new ruler and a new line, as occurred many times, the pattern of succession remained the same, except during the last dynasty (Ch'ing or Manchu), when the will of the monarch determined the successor among his sons.

We saw in the last chapter that the emperor was inaccessible to the people and that this practice was not altered fundamentally during the reign of Chiang Kai-shek. In fact, after Chiang came to power it was decreed that in all newspapers, magazines, and other published material, Chiang was to be designated not by name but by official title, and that, as a sign of homage, this designation should appear one or more notches above the text. Chiang's distinction and distance from his subjects was derived from a heritage in which it was taboo not only to look upon the emperor's person but even to bear the same given name. For example, as recently as my father's generation, if the given name of a common citizen was Lan T'ing, and a newborn heir apparent was given a name which in part embodied such a lowly person's name, it was compulsory under penalty of death for the plebeian to change his name. It is as if all the citizens of Great Britain who bore the name of the royal heir Charles would either have to select a new name or corrupt it in some fashion, for instance altering it to "Char" or "Les." The highest officials knelt before the emperor throughout an audience, just as the common people knelt before all the officials even throughout a civil suit. It was in this social climate that the effigies of good officials were housed in special temples, there to be worshiped for many generations to come.

The avoidance of the emperor's name was extended to those of parents and in fact all superiors. A biographer of Dr. Wellington Koo[7] relates the following episode from the past of the famous juror and diplomat:

> When Dr. Koo was a young man serving as an official of medium rank in the Peking government, he had occasion one day to see the then Prime Minister Tong Shao-yi.[8] Before he left the senior man asked Dr. Koo his ceremonial name.[9] Dr. Koo said that he had not yet found a suitable one. After Koo left the Prime Minister remarked to his deputy that he was puzzled why such an able man as Koo should possess no ceremonial name. The deputy then told him the truth. It was not that Koo did not possess a ceremonial name. Koo's ceremonial name happened to be Shao Ch'uan and identical with that of the Prime Minister. Koo denied he had such a name out of respect for the elder. Upon learning this, the Prime Minister so appreciated Dr. Koo's qualities that he later gave Koo his daughter in marriage.[10]

The narrator of this episode says that he once asked Dr. Koo personally about the accuracy of this anecdote. He received neither confirmation nor denial. Whether or not the episode was reported accurately in all its details, there is no doubt of its complete acceptability in the Chinese cultural context. I know many lesser Chinese than Dr. Koo who increased their social esteem by similar behavior.

This distance and authority relationship between the leader of China and his people (and to a lesser extent between the higher officials and their subordinates) exercised a powerful but predictable influence on the conduct of the bureaucracy. For example, Chinese officials have always tended to concern themselves much more with how to please their superiors than with what the public thinks of them. Having so defined their goals as public officials, they not unnaturally paid little or no attention to whether or not their activities gave the taxpayers a fair return.

A few years back an official in the Nationalist government gave an account of his activities as commissioner of Public Works in the municipality of Nanking between 1935 and 1937. The following are excerpts from his book:

> I assumed the duties of my office in Nanking just after our Chairman Chiang[11] promulgated the eight principles of his New Life Movement. Four of the eight principles concerned our clothing, food, housing, and transportation, all of which must be simple, neat, frugal, and clean. As Commissioner of Public Works I was responsible for satisfying the housing and transportation needs of the citizens of Nanking.
>
> Our Chairman paid intensive and meticulous attention to the affairs of the municipality. During a moment of leisure in the late afternon he would, accompanied by only a few attendants, take a drive in some section of the city and inspect it carefully. His secretary wrote down his instructions on every need for improvement. Uncollected debris and broken-down buildings marred the municipal appearance in some places. Cracked roads and houses in violation of building codes were examples of other urban illnesses needing attention. The Generalissimo saw all. After every such trip he handed down numerous orders for correction. Sometimes two orders to correct the same trouble came in rapid succession. The earnestness of his concern and the diligence with which he supervised us were a great source of inspiration for all my colleagues in the municipal government.
>
> However, some of the corrections could not be made at once. Caught in the dilemma between our inability to act and the Generalissimo's urgent orders, we found a solution. Our Commission designed and made many huge and beautiful advertising boards. We placed them continuously on both sides of the messy sections of the streets and invited advertising subscriptions from business houses. In this way we often transferred extremely ugly municipal streets overnight into beautiful and attractive areas. It was like magic. The advertising fees we collected more than covered the expenses of making and installing these boards. Besides, the lights on these boards also benefitted vehicle and pedestrian traffic.
>
> Afterwards the Director of the Generalissimo's Secretariat commented: "A job truly well done! Swift, neat, beautiful, and economical!"[12]

The familiar picture of the relations between the American people and their government (and between those holding lower social positions and those in higher places) is, of course, quite the opposite.

American presidents and their lieutenants, in or out of office, appeal constantly for the support of the people, and a politician without the "common touch" is almost always foredoomed to defeat. Both elective and administrative officials are criticized constantly by the people, and controlled or checked through the press, pressure groups, the courts, and, finally, the vote.[13]

The contrast between the conditions of existence of the officials in China and those in the United States goes further. The American president and his fellow citizens worship the same god. The president has neither special spiritual powers nor a special place before that god. The powers of the Chinese emperor, however, extended beyond those applicable to his living subjects; they applied also to the dead and to all kinds of spirits under the Supreme Ruler of Heaven. The emperor not only represented the people in his annual worship of Heaven, but was himself popularly known as "The Son of Heaven," and was regarded as a sort of god himself. Not only did imperial decrees have to be received by the emperor's subjects with the same reverence and ritual as that accorded the gods, but the emperor could promote spirits if they pleased him or demote gods if he found them to have done something wrong. On many a historically verified occasion when the emperor visited a famous landmark, it was his pleasure to confer by decree an honorary title on the god guarding the particular mountain or river.

Even high ministers of the Chinese government, as representatives of the emperor, could exercise similar functions. About the middle of the eighth century A.D. a man named Han, who was a minister in the T'ang court and one of the best-known scholars of China, offended the reigning emperor, an enthusiastic convert to Buddhism who wished to establish a kind of Buddhist Mecca in China, by objecting to the latter's efforts to welcome the remains of Buddha from India to China. As a result, Han was demoted to the magistracy of Swatow, a port city on the extreme southern coast.

When Magistrate Han arrived at his post he found the local people very much troubled by crocodiles. These, they told him, emerged from the water and invaded the villages in packs, devouring men and animals. Because the people had no effective weapons to deal with this menace, they were unable to carry on their daily routine. Magistrate Han had an answer. He proclaimed to the people that he personally would deal with the crocodile epidemic. On an appointed day he led, from his official headquarters to a prearranged spot on the seashore, a great procession of civilians and police carrying a huge amount of religious paraphernalia. There his men set up a sacrificial table and placed upon it the usual incense burner, candles, and several sacrificial animals, facing the sea. With hundreds of local people looking on, he read aloud an ultimatum to the crocodiles. This piece has since become a classic in Chinese literature, and I read and recited it as a schoolboy. Briefly, it went as follows:

> Upon order of His Imperial Majesty, I, Han, have come to this region to take over the magistracy. It is my intention and duty to see that the people lead a normal and contented life. I have, however, found that you crocodiles have made it impossible for the people to attain this goal. This cannot be tolerated. I hereby petition to you, and with the petition, bring some sacrificial animals which will be thrown into the sea for your pleasure, that you leave my people alone. You can see that this petition is reasonable. However, if you should fail to heed this petition, I shall personally lead my people in a war of extermination against you with whatever weapons we have at our disposal.

The petition paper was then burned, and the ashes scattered over the sea. Magistrate Han next burned the incense sticks, performed the proper ritual and then prostrated himself before the sacrificial table and kowtowed the appropriate number of times. Then he and the crowd of villagers dispersed to their homes. Historical notes, quoting local testimony, say that a terrible thunderstorm raged that night over the village and the sea. The next morning the sea was calm, the water receded a considerable distance from the shore, and the crocodiles appeared no more. To attempt to dissect this tale with the tools of science would be beside the point. Whether or not the minister himself believed in his actions, the people were convinced of his supernatural as well as secular powers, and they regained their confidence in themselves as a result of his performance.

There is no indication that either Chiang or his high officials believed that they possessed godly powers. But once in the early thirties and again during World War II, Chu Cheng, president of the Examination Yuen, one of the five principal divisions of the Nationalist government, staged a tremendous prayer meeting, on behalf of all of the people, for the relief of drought. And local populations in every part of China held similar prayer meetings, usually supported by government representatives in their official capacity, which undertook to combat all kinds of disasters from drought to cholera epidemics. Everywhere in China, too, a number of operas, colloquial and classic, are based on the theme that a certain official, known for his integrity and sense of justice, not only straightened out the tangled affairs of ordinary men by entrance into and return from the world of spirits, but also executed certain gods because of some evil deed that they committed.

The Chinese emperor and the officials who served under him were thus much more than administrators in the Western sense of the term. The Chinese emperor, as we have said, was the owner of his empire and the people were his children. In the United States, however, the president and the ordinary citizen meet on a plane of equality. The Chinese officials were owners by authority of the emperor of whatever area was under their stewardship. The people of that locale were their wards, whom they would guide, punish, or protect, as they saw fit. The people were their children in a social, political, economic, and spiritual sense. These high officials not only ruled over the living, but they also possessed jurisdiction over the dead. Such a concept of the political executive's domain is of course totally alien to American thought.

Distance Versus Identification

Again, however, we come to an apparent paradox. On the one hand, the Chinese government has throughout history received far more respect and unquestioning obedience from its subjects than has its American counterpart. On the other hand, the Chinese have shown much less direct interest in the government and even less desire to identify themselves with officials than have their American brethren.

Apart from taxation, military service, and sometimes public works such as those connected with the control of the Yellow River, there has never been close contact of any kind between the common people of China and their government. The psychological bond between the two was tenuous. In the normal course of events, the people neither loved their government officials nor hated them, for the administrators and the people were not close. The religion and morals of government officials were their own business. The people asked no questions. In turn, the education and treatment of children were the people's private affairs and the government did not intervene. "Heaven is high and the emperor far away" is a centuries-old Chinese saying that expresses the people's contentment in their aloofness. One of the most important aspects of Chinese political life—the activities of local organizations—is difficult to understand unless seen as the formulation of this desire to steer clear of the government.

The types of local organizations most common in cities and towns are the craft and occupational guilds. One of their most important functions is to serve as the buffer between the workers and the government. The guilds organized parades of welcome or farewell for newly appointed or departing magistrates. Their officers were among the first persons consulted by a new magistrate upon his arrival. It was they who acted in the interest of the guild members to circumvent any prejudicial orders or levies emanating from the government.

Though the power of these town guilds was usually passive, it could also be coercive, as was demonstrated in Peking just before the beginning of World War II. For centuries, Peking had no proper sewage system. Even as late as the thirties, the majority of families in that city depended upon night soil collectors (the "honey wagon" drivers so beloved by the American GIs) for a daily solution to one of their most pressing problems. These men, depending upon pack mules or wheelbarrows for cartage, were organized in beats like garbage collectors in the United States. The difference was that they were paid monthly by each family and not, as in most American communities, by the government from taxes collected. Fully aware of their position as an indispensable evil, they often took advantage of their indispensability. On rainy days, the night soil collectors asked those they served for a special tip. On each festival they came for still another tip. And on the occasion of a family celebration, such as a birthday party or a wedding ceremony, they presented fresh demands to that particular family. Any family that became annoyed was free, of course, to discontinue their collector's services, only to find no other collector to take the absentee's place. The guild was so well organized that picketing was not even necessary.

In 1936 a courageous mayor took office in Peking. He decided that it was time for reform and organized a team of trucks and men with which he intended to displace the individual night soil collectors. The expenses were to be met by city taxes. No sooner had he completed his plans than a multitude of night soil collectors began demonstrating in front of the municipal building. Each demonstrator had his night soil bucket on his back and in his hands the regulation long-handled scoop and fork. The crowd loudly demanded to see the mayor in person. He, not unnaturally, declined. This went on for several days, until finally the majority of Peking's inhabitants became panicky and forced the mayor to call off his ill-starred reform. This incident was probably more dramatic than is usual, but it was not an uncharacteristic exhibition of the power that local organizations regularly wielded for their self-protection.

The village organizations were, as a whole, less dramatic in their activities and less well-defined organizationally than the city guilds, but their role in community life was nonetheless real. While these organizations varied from area to area, perhaps the best way for us to gain an understanding of their essence is to record a general description of those in one particular community, Ku Ch'eng, near Kunming in Yunnan Province, where I resided for extensive periods between the years 1941 and 1944.

Ku Ch'eng consisted of about two hundred households and had two kinds of local organizations. The government-sponsored organization divided it into two major units, each of which in turn consisted of ten minor units headed by local men who were approved by and responsible to the magistrate. The expressly stated functions of these men included assistance in the collection of land and other taxes, administration of schools, settlement of disputes, assistance to recruiting officers and others making military requisitions, and cooperation with the district police in the apprehension of criminals as well as in other matters of public safety.

The locally sponsored organization divided the same two hundred households of the village into twelve units headed by men who were neither approved by nor responsible to the magistrate. These men formed the village council, the function of which was, reportedly, to organize public worship for the purpose of giving comfort to the departed ancestors of the village and to invoke the aid of the gods in combatting epidemics, crop failure, or fire.

On the surface these two organizations were clearly defined, but in reality they worked together. For one thing, as in corporate interlocking directorates, numerous individuals served first as officers of one organization and then of the other. Occasionally an individual did so simultaneously. Work initiated by one group was often finished or joined in by the other. Since the personnel in both organizations was drawn from local people whose kinship, social, and economic ties were centered in the village, the two groups inevitably shared a common outlook: to protect the interests of the village against government encroachment.

For example, if the government imposed a levy, the heads of both organizations, not one, would get together to decide how much of it the villagers could afford to pay and how they could avoid paying as much as had been asked. Or the government might send a functionary to resurvey and regrade the land so that a person who in one year paid tax on five *mou* of land, or approximately one acre, might have to pay it on seven *mou* the following year; and land that had been on the tax record as low grade might be revised into the medium- or the high-grade category so that their owners would have to pay at a higher rate in the next year. These government surveyors were dealt with by entertainment, gifts, and other forms of hospitality. Again men from both organizations put their heads together and pooled their resources in this enterprise, their not unfounded hope being that the tokens of good will would be matched by a mitigated village tax burden.

With some variation in detail this dual local organization existed in most of China under the Nationalists before 1949. Since then the two sets of organizations have merged in favor of the central government through public election procedures, in both Taiwan and the People's Republic. Now a new organization has entered the village scene—the local branch of the ruling party organization (Kuomintang in Taiwan and Kungts'antang or Communist party in the People's Republic).

Communization in the People's Republic is today a firmly established and universal fact. Each commune is subdivided into several production brigades and each of the latter consists of several production teams which, in most areas, are the traditional villages. Each commune consists of from about two thousand to ten thousand households. The traditional more or less autonomous village administration composed of clan heads and other elders was swallowed up. At one time the duties remaining to the village heads were to register births and deaths and to mediate family quarrels.[14] In time such registration was taken over by the commune clinics, and now officers of the commune subdivisions mediate domestic and other disputes. The commune has become, in fact, the smallest unit of local government which controls its component districts, brigades, and work teams by means of a commune council responsible to a commune people's congress elected every two years. This organization is paralleled by the general branch of the Communist party and its subordinate branches all the way down to the party groups which parallel the work teams.[15]

In Taiwan, the government-sponsored system of local administration consists of district *(hsien)*, subdistrict *(hsiang)*, village, and neighborhood *(lin or li)*, as it existed in China before 1949. The new system of election enables villagers to elect their own village officials and the administrative heads of the districts as well as representatives to the subdistrict councils, to the district councils, and to the Taiwan provincial assembly.[16] But the ruling Kuomintang, which has parallel organizational branches down to the subdistrict *(hsiang)* level, has an important hand in local affairs. In Pu Yen subdistrict, where anthropologist Bernard Gallin did his Taiwan village study, "the Kuomintang office is virtually next door to the district Public Office. The Party office, staffed by several full-time people, serves as an unofficial mediating agent in local disputes, including domestic quarrels . . . and also offers its services free of charge to villagers who need assistance in the writing of formal letters of petition to the courts or some government office."[17]

Even more significant is the extent to which members of the Kuomintang hold the various elected offices. In the 1968 elections, sixty-one out of seventy-one successful provincial assemblymen and seventeen out of twenty successful district magistrates were members of the Kuomintang (as reported in *Central Daily News,* Taipei, April 22, 1968).

Thus both in Taiwan and the People's Republic the indubitable development has been the increase in centralization and control by a particular ruling party and, not unnaturally, a corresponding reduction of traditional influences for de facto local autonomy.

However, though the modern trend toward centralization is undeniable, it is important for us to realize that the traditional forces that run counter to it are still considerable. One of the most important of these forces is a group generally known among Westerners as *gentry.* Here a short digression is necessary. Although the term is commonly used by Western scholars on China, the nature of this group is very much misunderstood. The gentry are said to be landlords, officials, or others who are set apart in various ways as a distinct group in every Chinese town and city. Two well-known scholars, John King Fairbank and Owen Lattimore, as well as many others, have insisted that this group deals with both customary and legal rights to the use of the land and its taxation. Fairbank has stated that the land rights are "ordinarily . . . so incredibly diverse and complicated" that the gentry who as a group "are the landowners and the lowest rung of the great ruling class," are necessary to keep them straight.[18] Lattimore has maintained that since the "inadequacy of statistics is pathetic, and the confusion of land deeds and titles is fantastic," it is therefore "simply impossible to collect the land tax without the good will of the landlords."[19]

It is of course true that China lacks adequate statistics, and it is also correct that the land tax is often inequitably assessed. It does not follow, however, that the two facts are as closely related as these scholars and others believe. There are very fertile holdings that had been classified centuries ago as low-grade, just as there are others of lower fertility that had been classified too high. But I do not know of any district in China in which the records were so "confused" and the legal rights to the use of the land were so "incredibly diverse" that the government, in order to collect the land tax, ever had to call on the "gentry" to intervene.

These scholars are confused about the make-up and the role of the gentry because, first, they tend to regard it as a unitary group, and, second, they are convinced that it was an evil-doing group. The latter preconception makes it necessary to find the basis of the gentry's alleged evil power. But neither belief is correct.

To return to our Ku Ch'eng, who were the gentry of this rural community? First of all, nobody who lived in the village. Several citizens were landlords with fairly large holdings, but the villagers did not consider a single one of these a member of the gentry. The wealthiest of them was a man named Li, but he did not even dare to go near the headquarters of the magistrate unless he was forced to do so. However, there were certain individuals who lived in the next village and as far away as the walled town, Ch'eng Kung, about one mile away, whom the magistrate either called to his office for consultation or called on in person for the same purpose. Those whom the magistrate called to his office were less powerful than those whom he called on in person. These are the people whom villagers throughout China describe as *shen shih,* and whom some Western scholars have referred to as members of the well-organized, evil-doing gentry.

How did these persons attain their gentry status? They did so not by rising through the local ranks of officials, businessmen, or landholders, but primarily by their connections outside of the district. For example, one member of the gentry of Ku Ch'eng was a local man who rose to be a regimental commander in the provincial army. Another was a local man who attained official prominence in the national government. Such men, as well as their fathers, brothers, and male descendants, were considered members of the gentry. A member of the gentry, in other words, is a local man who has made good outside of the locality or who has powerful political or military connections beyond it.

When a man takes office in a locale far distant from his community, he may fatten himself, as the majority of office holders have done in China for twenty centuries, at the expense of the people. But when such a person is in his native village or town, a different set of considerations comes into play. There he is obligated by his primary kinship and neighborhood ties from which, unlike his American brethren, he has never been weaned. In fact, as we saw in the previous chapter, the successful man is not truly satisfied until he returns to his parental family and the community of his birth. For it is among these people that he finds the glory of his success most meaningful.

This being the case, it would be most unusual for a member of the gentry to be a ruthless exploiter of his fellow locals. On the contrary, he often tries his best to be on excellent terms with the local people, and there are many ways of doing so. In 1941, for instance, the head of a prominent family of a community in Yunnan Province died.[20] The funeral lasted more than two months. Not only were there much ceremonial pageantry and recitations of the sutras by hired priests, but the major feature of the event was a continuous open house for all the inhabitants of the town and its surrounding villages. Throughout the area, the family posted public notices specifying the dates on which inhabitants of different villages were invited. For over a month, men and women from localities within a radius of nearly a hundred miles came to the big house. There, at the expense of a token gift of condolence, the visitors were lavishly dined and wined. Those who wished were even provided with living accommodations for the night. The total bill came to well over a million Chinese dollars, which in the exchange rate of that year was approximately $50,000 in United States currency. As a consequence of this grandiose affair, the gentry family gained both in popularity and in prestige. They gained in popularity because so many people had a good time; they gained in prestige because those who came saw the scale of the ceremonial pomp and how many others were also present.

Members of the gentry can also do other things for the people who live in their locality. Early in 1944, the provincial government of Yunnan needed more recruits and assigned a quota to each district. When the provincial recruiting officer and his entourage arrived in district A, they entrenched themselves in one of the local houses. They issued numerous directives to the magistrate and the local organizations. They had to be provided with food and other comforts. But their demands did not end there. When recruits were sent to them, the recruiting officer raised all kinds of objections. At first the men were found to be "too short in stature"; next they were "too poor in health"; finally they were "underweight." But when a batch of recruits was accompanied by a suitable amount of money, the men were unhesitatingly accepted. For some time the local people and the magistrate paid as expected. But as time went on objections multiplied while local treasuries ran low. Still the quota was not filled. The magistrate then declared himself sick and entered a hospital. Coincidental with his retirement from the scene, the gentry and the officers of the local organizations got together and put on a tremendous thanksgiving show.

Now a public show for the prupose of expressing gratitude to the gods for a good harvest or for freedom from epidemics has long been traditional in all parts of China, but this show had a special meaning. Although it was put on within the customary framework, it contained an added gesture of gratitude to the recruiting officer and his entourage. All ranking members of the recruiting corps were invited to sit in specially designed boxes, where ranking members of the local gentry also sat. In the course of the show, members of the gentry praised the officers for efficiently discharging their arduous duties and thanked them for being so nice to the local populace. These commendations were followed by expressions of regret that the officers had now to worry over and concern themselves with the fortunate people of some other district.

The trick had two aspects. The members of the recruiting corps had been given a special honor, and according to Chinese usage they would be regarded as highly impudent if they did not appreciate it by departing. On the other hand, even if they were so impudent as not to take notice of it and remain, they could not in the future afford to refuse the suggestions of members of the gentry, who were not only important locally but also had powerful connections in the provincial and the central governments. As officials, the recruiting officers were at the mercy of the pleasure or displeasure of those who were above them. The possibility that they might offend the members of the local gentry, who had higher connections than they, was a chance that the officers did not care to take, especially after they had already made large financial collections. They left the district shortly afterward.

Other examples might be cited to show that a principal function of the local gentry is to check undue oppression in the locality to which it belongs. This is not to say that friendship and kindness invariably prevailed between the gentry and the local people. In some communities at least, members of the gentry were referred to as "evils" *(wo)* in the villagers' conversation with me. But it should not be forgotten that members of the gentry, like all human beings, cannot but vary in their behavior. For the same villagers who referred to them as "evils" also distinguished between "good evils" *(shan wo),* meaning those members of the gentry who were good to the populace, and "bad evils" *(ngo wo),* meaning those who acted otherwise. Members of the gentry, being bureaucrats themselves or deriving some manner of benefit from the government's operations elsewhere, usually do not care to shut all doors to exploitation. But they can and do soften its impact and limit its extension if only because of their concern for their own position and the welfare of their own community. In this, the gentry works—contrary to the usual conception—in conjunction with other forces such as the guilds and village organizations.[21]

Generally speaking, the pre–1949 village was one in which the locally rooted organization was counterpoised to the one controlled by the central government, with the gentry serving as a sort of interloper, mediator, protector, or sometimes exploiter, depending upon circumstances. After 1949, the Kuomintang in Taiwan and the Kungts'antang in the People's Republic entered powerfully into the village scene. Ostensibly the locally rooted organization has ceased its formal existence and the gentry as a group no longer has a function. In reality, at least in Taiwan, many former members of the gentry and others active in the old local organizations have simply become officeholders under the new alignment.[22] Changes in the People's Republic have been more drastic. The gentry was severely decimated during the initial onslaught of the Communist revolution. Many men once prominent locally were eliminated, and others dispersed to distant areas. Peking, even more than Taipei, aims at breaking up the age-old counterbalance between the village and the state. Instead, local organizations are more and more to become instruments of central government policies. However, as we shall see in Chapter 15, the communes and their subdivisions do not merely carry out policies from the higher levels; they also help to shape those policies by their feedback *(fan ying).*

In a superficial way the decentralized relationship between the American federal government and the state and local governments seems to bear a great deal of resemblance to that which prevailed in the past between the Chinese ruler and his officials on the one hand and the local organizations on the other. Each state of the Union has complete autonomy in respect to a wide range of affairs, having its own legislature, revenue, and courts. This pattern, to a lesser extent, is repeated at lower levels. Not only each state, but each city, each town, and even village in the United States is jealous of its own rights and resents any act or word it may characterize as interference from without or above.

Fundamentally, however, the various levels of officials and the American people maintain a pattern of communication and a degree of unity of outlook that, in their constancy and extent, differ greatly from the traditional relationships of the Chinese and their government. If we characterize the Chinese attitude toward government as checking it through respect and distance, we must note in contrast that the American attitude toward government is to control it through equality and identification. This difference is closely related to their differing ways of looking up to their heroes, which we noted in the last chapter. The Chinese, with his pattern of mutual dependence, maintains strong ties with his family, kin, and local group that necessarily overshadow all his relationships with the wider society. He has, therefore, little reason to look for his social and emotional security among personalities and objects in the wider world. However, should contact with government become necessary, as when he is involved in legal action or seeks a place in officialdom, the Chinese cannot, naturally, conceive of such contacts other than in that frame of mutual dependence experienced with his seniors. He expects financial benefits, but he asks for them in terms of his superior's generosity. He hopes to win a lawsuit, but he phrases that hope in terms of the official's good graces. For the officials possess the law and he, one of the common people, can gain only by subordination.

The American, with his pattern of self-reliance, must unflaggingly pursue individual advancements that transcend not only his ties with his primary groups but that also uproot most of his subsequent associations. His lack of security compels him to seek satisfaction of his social needs through some attachment beyond his kinship and communal scene or by identification with some hero or heroes, whether political or otherwise.

The American, therefore, does not try to keep away from government officials. On the contrary, he assumes a positive attitude toward them. He takes government subsidies, like those from his parents, for granted, but he resents his officials' interference, also like that of his parents, with his private affairs. What he wants the government to do or not do he announces through the ballot, pressure groups, and court action. Furthermore, this positive attitude is much more than a matter of external technique. Its most important component is identification: a compelling emotional involvement. Therefore, while the Chinese, as we noted before, tend to be indifferent toward their officials, Americans tend to love or hate their public men. Their love is expressed in the form of tumultuous public receptions, gifts of all descriptions, and letters filled with praise; and their hate is vented by public denunciations, letters filled with vituperation, and even violence.

In less than two hundred years of nationhood, four American presidents have been assassinated, and the likelihood of numerous attempts upon his life is an occupational hazard that an incoming president must accept. The assassination of Dr. Martin Luther King, Jr., led the Swedish sociologist Gunnar Myrdal[23] to fear that assassination is becoming an American way of life. In twenty centuries of Chinese history, no emperor was ever assassinated except by court intrigue. The emperor's seclusion and the guards surrounding him were not primarily protective in purpose, but symbolic of his prestige and power; the secret service men who surround an American president are there for the express purpose of protecting his person. Furthermore, violence directed against the lower officials in China was extremely rare. When it occurred, it was, as a rule, for reasons of personal revenge, such as when filial duty called upon a son to take the life of his father's murderer, whether an official or not, or when manly honor demanded that a husband kill his wife's seducer. Violence against American officials tends to be a consequence of something the officeholder did or did not do in his official capacity. A John Wilkes Booth assassinating an Abraham Lincoln in the name of freedom from tyranny or a Sirhan Sirhan murdering a Robert Kennedy because the latter proposed supplying new military equipment to Israel would be incomprehensible to the average Chinese.

The American grief following President John F. Kennedy's assassination was hard for most Chinese to believe. But the indifference and almost overt satisfaction on the part of the dead president's antagonists would have surprised them more.

Assassination, in which act is focused the powerful drives of hate for an official or his cause or love for his defeated opponent or a lost cause, epitomizes the emotional tie that characterizes the relationship between the commoner and the very highest of officials. But through the system of negative checks, which the Chinese imposed on their government for nearly twenty centuries, the people as a whole built bulwarks to separate themselves as completely as possible from their rulers.

It is understandable that American political cleavages usually occur when one section of the population (be it geographically, economically, racially, or religiously based) and its public leader take a stand against another section of the population and its offical spokesman, whereas in the Chinese political arena the contest is between the people and the officals. The Chinese have said for centuries that "officials will protect officials," meaning officials will unite with other officials against the people; but American political struggles find some officials allied with some of the people against other officials and citizens similarly united.

NOTES

1. In fact this pattern still holds true in Taiwan today. A little love story in the *Central Daily News* (February 6, 1980) of Taipei features a woman encouraging her first lieutenant lover not to neglect nonmilitary literature. "All the generals of renown in Chinese history," she explained, "were commanders well versed in both military and nonmilitary knowledge." As to the People's Republic, Chairman Mao's poems, written in his own calligraphy, were seen everywhere before 1978, in airports, hotel lobbies, and public halls. With the fall of the Gang of Four many such works have been replaced by Chinese paintings of rocks and trees. But as late as October 1980 when we last visited China, many of them still remained in hotels and public buildings in Changsha, Wuhan, and Kunming, though more rarely in Peking.

2. All dollars here and in subsequent paragraphs pertain to Chinese national currency unless otherwise specified, the value of which varied from one decade to another. However, from 1900 to 1935 the rate of exchange between the Chinese and the American dollar was 3:1. In 1935 the rate of the Chinese dollar was depreciated to 5:1. The beginning of the Sino-Japanese war in 1937 initiated a trend of inflation that, by 1942, had brought the Chinese-American exchange rate to somewhere between 20:1 and 100:1, and by 1944 the rate was no longer stable enough to be quoted.

3. Aisin-Gioro Pu Yi, *From Emperor to Citizen, The Autobiography of Aisin-Gioro Pu Yi*.

4. *Quarterly Journal of Economics* of the Chinese Economic Society, Shanghai, December 1932, p. 71.

5. Investigations of the Ministry of Industries, quoted in C. H. Lowe, *Facing Labor Issues in China*, p. 13.

6. In the March 1953 issue of *Reader's Digest* the following episode was reported by a mother. Her thirteen-year-old son came home telling her thxt he was the only one in his class who got 100 on the Social Living test. When she inquired about the questions the youngster said the only one he did not know the answer to was, "What is the salary of the Chief Justice of the United States?" However, the boy figured it out on his own. He knew that Ted Williams got $100,000 a year from the Red Sox and he "decided that a Chief Justice would probably get about a fourth as much." So he put down $25,000 and it was right. The annual salaries of the chief justice and many other government officials are now more than $25,000, but the rewards in the industrial, commercial, and entertainment worlds have since gone far higher.

7. Sometime foreign minister and prime minister in the Peking government since

1912; former Chinese ambassador at Washington, D.C., and later judge of the World Court at The Hague.

8. One time Chinese minister to Washington, D.C., during the late Ch'ing dynasty.

9. This was the name every literate Chinese would use for social purposes.

10. Yu-shou Kuo, "Events in the Life of Dr. Wellington Koo and the Secret of His Diplomacy" (*Central Daily News*, Taipei, August 30, 1964).

11. Generalissimo Chiang Kai-shek was then chairman of the Committee of Military Affairs in the Nationalist government. But that was only one of the several offices he held.

12. From Hsi-shang Sung, *"Chih Teh Hui Yi Ti Shih"* [Events Worthy of Reflection], reprinted in *Central Daily News,* Taipei, October 26, 1968.

13. For more on popular control of government, especially the administrative branch, see Charles S. Hyneman, *Bureaucracy in a Democracy;* for popular control through interest groups and their organizations, see Edward Pendleton Herring, *Public Administration and the Public Interest,* and David B. Truman, *The Government Process.*

14. Isabel and David Crook, *The First Years of Yangyi Commune,* p. 30.

15. Ibid., p. 196, and Lau Sui-Kai, "The People's Commune as a Communication Network in the Diffusion of Agritechnology," in Godwin Chu and Francis L. K. Hsu, eds., *Moving a Mountain: Cultural Change in China,* pp. 125–149.

16. Bernard Gallin, in *Hsin Hsing, Taiwan: A Chinese Village in Change,* p. 21, states that the district is "the highest level of government" in which the villagers "participate." His field work was done in 1957–1958. Since April 1968 the scope of the election has been raised to the provincial level. Since the 1970s the governor of Taiwan (province) has been a Taiwanese.

17. Ibid., p. 22.

18. John King Fairbank, *The United States and China,* p. 39.

19. Owen Lattimore, *Solution in Asia,* pp. 106–107.

20. Life in this community is described in Francis L. K. Hsu, *Under the Ancestors' Shadow.*

21. Our observations on the role of the gentry have now found additional support in the detailed life histories of prominent men in a southwestern China village. See Yung-teh Chow, *Social Mobility in China,* especially Chapter 2, "The Status Structure," pp. 46–94.

22. The works of more recent scholars in Taiwan do not speak of gentry *(shen shih)* as such. But the power features described here can be perceived. (See Chung-min Chen, *Upper Camp: A Study of a Chinese Mixed Cropping Village in Taiwan.*)

23. Well known in the United States for his study of the black-white racial problem, *An American Dilemma.*

CHAPTER 8

The Ills
of Government

The differing attitudes of the Chinese and the Americans toward their respective governments and officials do not explain all of the political behavior among the two peoples, for this, like all other aspects of human life, is subject to many variations and, at times, distinct departures from the usual. However, these deep-seated orientations do provide a norm or reference point that can help us to understand a great deal, including the widely discussed phenomenon of government corruption.

Corruption

Both before and since the fall of the Nationalist government in China, Americans have heard numerous reports, official and unofficial, of Kuomintang corruption.[1] From the fifties onward, similarly well-documented accounts have been presented detailing the corruption in their own government. Does this surface similarity warrant the conclusion that the Chinese before 1949 were hopelessly corrupt and that America is headed in the same direction?

Chinese government corruption was historically related to the great and time-honored discrepancy between the standard of living of the literati-bureaucrats and that of the people. Officials found they had to resort to nonlegal sources in order to maintain their status-determined standard of life. It was not sheer lust for extravagance that caused the average Chinese official to spend lavishly. The intense struggle to gain admittance to the bureaucracy, or to maintain one's place in it, forced many to spend beyond their means. To understand this clearly it is necessary to discuss the system of imperial examinations.

This system germinated at about the beginning of the Christian era and became definitely institutionalized about the sixth century. These examinations were open, with few exceptions, to all males. They were based on the Confucian classics and were conducted, on the whole, with remarkable impartiality and freedom from corruption.

The examinations took place on four successive levels: annually in every district, and triannually in the capital of each province, in the national capital, and finally in the imperial palace. A degree was conferred upon successful candidates in each examination, and success on one level was a prerequisite for candidacy on the next. An estimated thirty to forty thousand candidates annually emerged with a degree from the district examinations; one to three thousand from the provincial examinations; three hundred from the examinations held in the national capital; and three from the emperor's palace examination.[2]

However, while attainment of one or another of these degrees was the most important qualification for government posts, not all holders of these degrees actually secured office nor, when they did, were they automatically appointed to positions proportionate to the importance of the degrees they held. Therefore, between the time that a man received a degree and the time of his actual appointment to office, and between the occasion of his first appointment and a step upward in the hierarchy, many factors came into play.

Here we have two minor but interesting points of similarity between China and America. First, Americans talk about "getting the breaks" and the Chinese talk about "the working of fate," both phrases referring to those fortuitous combinations of circumstances which enable a man of talent to show, in the American idiom, what he has. The second similarity is perhaps more significant. For at least two thousand years there was one place in China—Ch'angan, Loyang, Peking, Nanking, or wherever the national capital was located —that was not unlike Hollywood.

In the film city and its environs there are thousands of aspiring men and women, young and old, who crowd the rooming houses, hotels, and bars of the area hoping for a chance encounter with one of the Hollywood greats or for the casting office to phone. If and when the break comes, fame and fortune may be achieved overnight. Exactly the same situation held true for the Chinese national capital even as late as the 1930s. There, thousands of office seekers, young and old, clustered around the many inns and the provincial and district guilds waiting for that long-desired interview with an important official or for the arrival of a messenger boy. Thousands of Americans die in or give up and leave Hollywood without ever getting a screen test for a bit part, just as thousands of Chinese who stagnated or departed from their nation's capital never secured title to even a minor post. But in both countries it is the dream of overnight success, made manifest by the fabulous stories of the fortunate few, that has given hope to the aspiring multitude.[3]

Being pressed by such competition, many Chinese necessarily resorted to any means they could use to reach the desired end. However, once on the ladder it was equally hard for an appointee to keep his post or to get himself promoted to a higher post. As all officials depended upon the pleasure of their superiors for security of tenure, any official could be dismissed arbitrarily—not only for incompetence but whenever someone else with better bureaucratic connections wanted his job, or because he had incurred the displeasure of a superior. Consequently he felt obliged to get all the money that he could, while at the same time doing his best to please his superiors by sending them gifts on such occasions as a birthday, a kin's funeral, a wedding, the New Year, or even when he was granted an interview. These gift articles, instead of being tokens of respect or loyalty, were often fantastically substantial. In *The Golden Lotus,* which depicts life in the southern Sung dynasty (about A.D. 1200), and from which we quoted in Chapter 1, the author described the visit of Hsi-Men Ch'ing, a local official, to the imperial capital to pay his respect to the Imperial Tutor, whom he had been cultivating.

"There will be no difficulty," said Chai [a friend of Hsi-Men Ch'ing]. "Though His Eminence is the most powerful of His Majesty's subjects, he is somewhat susceptible to praise and flattery. Let him but see the value of the present you have brought him, and not only will he accept you as his ward; he will see that you get a promotion."

Farther on we read this account of the interview with the Imperial Tutor:

"Your son," he [Hsi-Men Ch'ing] said, "has nothing to offer. I have brought no more than a few trifles in honor of your most illustrious birthday. It is as though one brought a feather for ten thousand *li.* But may Your Eminence live as long as the Mountains of the South."

"You are very kind," the Imperial Tutor said. "Please sit down."

An attendant gave Hsi-Men Ch'ing a chair. He bowed twice and sat down. Tea was brought. Chai went out and ordered the presents to be brought in. There were more than twenty loads. They were brought and laid before the steps. A small box was opened and the inventory taken from it. It said: One crimson dragon robe; one green dragon robe; twenty rolls of Han-figured satin; twenty rolls of Ssu-ch'uan silk; twenty rolls of foreign cloth; other rolls, forty, both plain and figured; a girdle of a lion's head in jade; another girdle mounted in gold of tagaraka wood; of jade goblets and horn goblets, each ten pairs; four pairs of golden wine cups with flowers for decoration; ten fine pearls and two hundred taels of gold. These were the presents.

The Imperial Tutor looked at the inventory and then at the twenty loads of offerings. He was pleased and thanked Hsi-Men Ch'ing.[4]

The fictional Hsi-Men Ch'ing was a wealthy merchant interested in climbing the official ladder, so his gifts, though impressive, did not strain his resources. But the requirements of self-protection forced the majority of real life bureaucrats, whose only legal source of income was their salary, to resort to corruption. This usage was so well established that it pervaded all levels of government. Money and valuables flowed continuously from the lower functionaries to the higher ones, and from the latter to members of the imperial household and to the emperor himself. It was professional suicide for an official to oppose this practice.

The account of a princess's experiences in the court of the Empress Dowager during the last days of the Manchu dynasty is most instructive. This woman, Princess Der Ling, was the daughter of a Manchu diplomat who served in various European capitals toward the end of the nineteenth century. After her return from Europe she spent two years as an attendant to the Empress Dowager, at the end of which period she wrote a fascinating description of court life (*Two Years in the Forbidden City*).[5] At one point she describes how, amid frequent military reverses in the Sino-Japanese War of 1894–1895 and despite the advice of her chief ministers, the Dowager successfully insisted upon celebrating her sixtieth birthday in the regular fashion. On this occasion, hundreds of thousands of gifts came from all levels of the bureaucracy. The old Dowager personally inspected every tribute, memorizing the names of those whose gifts she considered unsatisfactory.

Some observers have equated this Chinese practice with what American politicians refer to as "honest graft" and have declared that this gift-making cannot properly be termed corruption. This view is simply wide of the mark. Every single dollar, and every minute article which traveled from lower to higher officials and finally to the imperial court came from the common people. Under the strain imposed by insecurity of office and cutthroat competition, the literati and officials could neither choose their methods in the bureaucratic struggle nor set limits upon their use.

In 1943, for instance, a commissioner of civil affairs of the Yunnan provincial government celebrated his mother's sixtieth or seventieth birthday. Every one of the district magistrates under him sent her a message of congratulations in the form of a sixteen-ounce solid gold ingot. The idea of sending such a substantial gift began undoubtedly with one or at most a few of these officials. But once some did it, others had no alternative but to do likewise. In order to meet such heavy financial burdens, Chinese officials have for centuries sold justice, offices, and favors to the highest bidder; they embezzled so frequently that those who did not do so found it difficult to convince people that they were, in fact, impoverished.[6]

Corruption in the Chinese government is really another aspect of the basic Chinese pattern of mutual dependence. As children and parents depend on each other within the family, so in officialdom subordinates present their superiors with valuables while the higher officials provide the donors with government positions or promote those already in office. This dependence was in no way concealed, nor were the parties ashamed of their practices, for a feature which clearly distinguished Chinese corruption from the sub rosa deals of American political life is that such dependence was an expressly stated ideal. While Hsi-Men Ch'ing's gifts made it clear to the Imperial Tutor that extension of official favor was now in order, this was not a thing done in secret, but one that Hsi-Men Ch'ing openly discussed with his friends. Once the liaison with the Imperial Tutor was established, Hsi-Men found all doors open to him.

The ideal of mutual dependence makes it easier for us to understand why nepotism was so common in Chinese government. Tied almost inextricably to his primary group, the family and its wider kin relationships, it is a foregone conclusion that the individual will assist or be assisted by these people. The individual expects to do favors for those closest to him, and he expects them to do him favors in return.

It is for these reasons that the Chinese have never raised fundamental objections to the tradition that the officials possess the law while the people look to them for justice; nor did officials seriously contest the power that the emperors exercised over them, for, although he required much of them, they could ask and receive in their turn. It is also the reason why Chinese merchants, whose interests suffered for centuries because of the imperial policy of "emphasis on agriculture and discouragement to commerce," never thought of standing together to protect themselves. Instead, as soon as an individual merchant became wealthy, he sought to cultivate some high official. A place within the government, where he would inherit the prestige and power of the literati-bureaucrats, was his ultimate goal.[7]

Our analysis so far may strike some readers as a mere confirmation of the popular view that wholesale government corruption was something peculiar to China, or at any rate peculiar to the East. Shortly after Japan's capitulation, *Harper's* magazine published an article which concluded that the Chinese as people were "organizationally corrupt."[8] Such casual journalistic judgments were not uncommon then or since. A few years later no less a scholar than F. S. C. Northrop gave this popular view his philosophical sanction. He wrote:

> A very wise Christian missionary in Thailand said to me, "There will be no end to the corruption that accompanies the Asians' casual handling of Western reforms so long as the Asians retain their cyclical theory of time." This follows because of the nature of things of the determinate world, or the world of here and now which we know directly through our senses. These things are transitory and fleeting. Therefore they are not deserving of unswerving attachment on the part of man, himself in part a transitory phenomenon.[9]

One fault of Northrop's argument is his failure to see that there are important differences separating Asian societies. If, as Northrop claims, widespread corruption is peculiar to the Eastern way of life, it becomes at once necessary to make exceptions of the entire Japanese society and traditional Chinese businessmen. Neither the Japanese government nor Chinese business have ever been plagued by the kind of corruption that besieged the body of Chinese officialdom. The morality and integrity of Chinese merchants have long been proverbial among Western traders and, despite the power exercised by Japanese officials at home and abroad during the heyday of the Japanese empire in East Asia, there was never any indication that this power was to a significant degree offered up for auction. The recent case of a Premier Tanaka being forced to resign because of a bribery scandal was the exception rather than the rule. What Northrop overlooked is that corruption can exist in one area of the life of a people but not in another, or it can flourish among only one or two peoples sharing a similar way of life.

Secondly, and this is a more serious flaw in his case, Northrop appears to imply that corruption can only be linked to what he describes as the Eastern way of life, when in fact he must know that it has flourished and is flourishing today in America. Whatever the time theory of the West, it apparently has placed no limits on corruption. And we shall see that the American brand of corruption has been encouraged by the pattern of self-reliance.

It is obvious that most of the factors that cause corruption in the Chinese government have only limited application to the United States. To begin with, while government corruption in China is intimately related to the lack of lucrative economic opportunities in other areas of national life, it cannot be said that this is true in the United States. Previously we compared the Chinese national capital and Hollywood, each the harbor of many thousands of fortune seekers. But this similarity is only superficial. Americans who are unsuccessful in Hollywood frequently become successful in many diverse areas of life. Chinese who were unsuccessful in Peking or Nanking had few alternative outlets for their talents. The best such persons might do was to become teachers, a career which was truly a last resort for an aspirant to officialdom. In other words, failure in Peking or Nanking was a greater personal disaster to many a Chinese would-be bureaucrat than failure in Hollywood is to the majority of American would-be film stars. In the United States, the many possibilities of social and economic advancement are so superior to anything the bureaucracy can offer that most Americans, unlike the Chinese, have little desire to enter public office.

However, those Americans who do enter the federal bureaucracy find themselves in an organization that, though far from perfect, is much more efficient than that of pre-1949 China. First, it is held in check as a consequence of the clear separation of the three primary branches of government. Further, most of the administrative personnel are hired and fired according to, as a whole, objectively stated criteria so that they enjoy a degree of job security unknown to any of their Chinese counterparts. The fate of the relatively small number of federal, state, and city officeholders who occupy patronage positions may vary with the pleasure or displeasure of their superiors, but those under civil service are at least free from arbitrary dismissal, although their advancement may be impeded by a superior's frown or a lawmaker's unproven accusations.[10] For years, many Chinese reformers have clamored for the adoption of these particular American institutions as a possible means of eradicating corruption from the Chinese government.

How to Win Favors and Influence Officials

How then is self-reliance related to corruption in the American government? A clue lies in the differing nature of corruption as it is found among the two peoples. There are, roughly, five different kinds of government corruption: (1) embezzlement of funds; (2) intentional or careless misuse of funds and commodities; (3) extralegal levies on the people; (4) nepotism; and (5) the sale of influence by officials or the infliction upon officials of pressures either from within the government or outside of it. These categories are of course not mutually exclusive. All five kinds are found in China and all but the third occur in the United States. But while the most common misdeeds of Chinese officials are embezzlement, extralegal levies, and nepotism, the principal acts of misbehavior among American officials are the misuse of government funds and commodities and the sale of influence.

American officals are most often prevented from embezzlement by careful auditing and other mechanisms to detect fraud, and from extralegal levies by the people's widespread knowledge of their constitutional rights. Embezzlement, in the public mind, is little different from outright theft. In fact, legal statutes make it likely that a postal official convicted of embezzling a minor sum will be sentenced to a longer term than an influence-buyer who defrauds the government of many millions. "Public office," we say, "is a public trust," but the private interest group operates under no such ethical limitations. For the undeniable fact is that the misuse of funds or commodities and the manipulation of influence are two entirely different propositions.

Many Americans in both major parties complain against wasteful spending in government. (Others claim that such spending is absolutely necessary to keep America strong.) However, whether in the normal channels of government expenditure or in the emergency streams of defense spending, there are two kinds of waste. One is normal human failure, such as inefficiency, while the other comes closer to corruption, such as the practice of "empire building" so common in the American bureaucracy. The bureaucrat—civilian or military—who seeks to increase his power base by a needless expansion of personnel or by inflating his budgetary requirements is not merely inefficient, he is enhancing his own prestige and power at public expense.

But waste must be distinguished from government objectives, whether the objectives are in the realm of social welfare, military preparedness, or foreign aid. The impartial observer of the United States government, at home or abroad, will unhesitatingly admit that there is more conspicuous waste here than in perhaps any other government in the world. In fact we can expand the last statement without fear of exaggeration and say that Americans are the most wasteful of all peoples. The waste that can be laid at the doors of the empire builders is not basically attributable to what some persons call the necessary and inherent evils of a giant government. Charles S. Hyneman, a careful student of bureaucratic practices,[11] told me that a principal motivating force behind the activities of the individual bureaucrat in Washington, D.C., and elsewhere, is the desire "not to be made a sucker of." Every sectional chief, every committee chairman, and every bureau head wants his job to be the best and biggest job done, regardless of either the cost to the taxpayers or the extent to which it may limit or interfere with the other functions of the government. And these bureaucrats are not wrong in their assumption that if Chief Jones does not ask for a bigger budget for his outfit, Director Johnston surely will for his division. In this case Johnston may do a better job than Jones and that will surely make Jones look both inferior and foolish. On the other hand, the Congress, the executive higher-ups, and the people in general admire and commend administrators who perform great feats, and receive big publicity, often regardless of cost; but it is rare that a public figure receives bigger assignments or praise for his economy measures. In fact, in the mind of many, the sorry case of one time economy-minded Secretary of Defense Louis A. Johnson in the Truman administration, whatever its real pros and cons, will probably serve, for a long time, as an object lesson to most officials.

The Congress itself was recently stung by receiving Senator William Proxmire's Golden Fleece of the Month award (1979) "for the eruption in its spending over the past decade." Ten years ago the two houses employed 10,700 persons at $150 million a year; in 1979, the corresponding figures were 18,400 and $550 million (reported by James Kilpatrick in the *San Francisco Chronicle,* August 30, 1979).

The fear of being taken for a sucker is a manifestation of American self-reliance that penetrates deeply into all spheres of American life. Many universities, for example, have set up departments of research coordination. It is not unusual for such a department to ask its faculty for project ideas *after* it has located some possible sources for grants and contracts. The motto seems to be: if there is money, we will find projects on which to spend it.

And why not? It is also common for universities to circulate memos to their academic departments showing how different institutions have fared as recipients of federal grants for the last year or number of years. If comparable institutions have done much better than we have, isn't it time that we do something about it? It is only by moving up to bigger and bigger jobs that one can attain greater and greater success. The climb is strenuous; but failure is a far greater ordeal.

The fear that one may be a sucker relates to the important game of influence. Influence is not all bad. In fact, to be artful in the techniques of influencing others is highly desired by almost every American. Dale Carnegie soared to national prominence because he recognized the American's wish to be personally persuasive and undertook to show him how. Persuasiveness is the lifeline of every American salesman. Persuasiveness is equally the essence of all publicity organs and advertising agencies that promote any industrial or commercial product. Big profits, as any corporation head knows, depend not only on the quality of the product or its necessity to the public or to the general economy, but upon the total amount of influence that advertising salesmen and public relations experts can exert upon the potential consumers. In any particular corporation, the general ratio of wages or salaries favors these persuaders rather than the technicians, such as engineers or chemists, who created the product.

We all remember President Coolidge's dictum: "The business of America is business." If America's business is business then—and this is a proposition heartily endorsed by most Americans—government should be run like a business. In fact, one of the most damaging criticisms that can be leveled at a public servant is that he has had no business experience. Lincoln was forced to make light of his financial failure as a lawyer by saying that failures become teachers or politicians, and he chose politics. Wilson, both when running for the governorship of New Jersey and the nation's presidency, was often criticized for his professional background which presumably did not equip him to deal with the realities of state affairs. Franklin D. Roosevelt's family, it was charged by the most unrelenting of his critics, did not trust him to handle his own finances. Truman was frequently attacked because, during his less prominent years, he was conspicuously unsuccessful in business. Although both Roosevelt and Truman won the presidency in spite of such criticism, and Kennedy had no business experience, the frequency of such attacks reflect the importance and prestige of business in America. But if government is to be run like business, how can we expect to exclude influence—that most basic of business techniques?

Confused by this dilemma, most persons distinguish between two kinds of influence in government—that which is morally acceptable and that which is not. But this is actually no line of demarcation at all, for each person draws the line to suit his own convenience. If rackets go on unhampered because there is a liaison between public servants and gangsters, all honest citizens can argue that this situation should be eliminated. But suppose it is a question of conflict between interests which, each in its own right, has a real claim to legitimacy—oleomargarine producers versus dairy interests, coal versus natural gas, army versus air force, or marine corps versus navy? What is the real difference between influencing a congressman by word and letter or winning him over by charm and hospitality? Both are used by special-interest lobbyists and are standard equipment of public relations officers and salesmen of every corporation. For example, Congressman May of Kentucky was convicted of bribery in the early fifties on evidence that he associated with and accepted gifts from the Garsson brothers, who, with government contracts secured through the representative's help, fattened their corporation from a mere letterhead to a multimillion dollar combine. And what is the distinction between a lobbyist giving presents to a government official and the lavish wining, dining, and gifts that most buyers for big corporations receive as a matter of course from prospective sellers?[12]

Indeed this is the very kind of distinction which Bernard Goldfine (six years after I first wrote the above) said he could not see when the scandal about his vicuña coat broke. The reader may recall that Goldfine, a Boston industrialist, showered Sherman Adams, Eisenhower's right-hand man, with lavish gifts including the famous vicuña coat. Adams, on his part, reportedly interceded on behalf of Goldfine interests with the Federal Trade Commission and the Securities and Exchange Commission. Adams resigned under fire from the White House to private oblivion. Eisenhower merely said Adams had been "imprudent." But Goldfine, who died in 1967 an insolvent man who served prison terms for contempt of Congress and income tax evasion, was much more explicit in defending his actions:

"I don't feel in my heart it's wrong to do what I did. If I've erred, if I've done something I shouldn't have done, then I am sorry, and I'll right the wrong. I might have made a mistake."

Newsweek, which reported these remarks, explained the Goldfine philosophy: "Once, reviewing his climb to riches, Goldfine recalled that it had really started with a bribe back in 1897 to Cossack guards patrolling the Russian border. The first deal eventually enabled him to make it to America. ('See, there was graft even then, like there's graft around here today,' he explained.) Goldfine made no secret that methodical gift-giving had been a regular practice with him. It wasn't just the 'deals' that interested him, he also sought the companionship of New England's 'great' and 'near-great' and he collected politicians like postage stamps. 'I had the opportunity to meet people you can't in the old country,' he once said. 'I don't know any other way to show my appreciation,' he said of his bent for sending money and gifts to political figures. 'I'll continue giving until the end of time.' "

Goldfine's sentiments would seem to be acceptable to quite a few Americans. How else can we explain the fact that the Adams case was preceded by that of Major General Harry Vaughn and the deep freezer under President Truman and followed by that of Bobby Baker's entertainment activities under President Johnson? Vaughn, Baker, Adams, Congressman May, and others of their ilk were preceded by the Robber Barons of post-Civil War days. They will undoubtedly be succeeded by equally energetic seekers of influence who may be even more vehement in defending their acts.

However, their defense for such acts needs neither to be ingenious nor eloquent, for there is popular support all around them.

For example, Representative Charles C. Diggs (Michigan) was reelected in spite of his conviction on twenty-nine counts of mail fraud and receiving salary kickbacks from his staff. Representative Daniel J. Flood (Pennsylvania) is the object of tumultuous praise from his constituents in spite of his indictment on charges of criminal bribery. Only physical infirmity and the prospect of a retrial forced him to resign. Senator Herman Talmadge (Georgia) flamboyantly claims that he has done nothing wrong in spite of the fact that he had to pay back expense overdrafts to the Senate in the sum of $37,125 and was censured by the Senate Ethics Committee. Wayne Hayes, who lost his seat in the House because he put Elizabeth Ray on the government payroll for sex, did not think that he did anything wrong. "I think the people around here (St. Clairsville, Ohio) feel that if you locked everybody up who had a tumble in the hay there wouldn't be anybody left on the outside" (reported by Ellen Warren in *Chicago Sun-Times,* June 5, 1978). He promptly got elected to the Ohio House.

It is in this context that one can appreciate the possible significance of the FBI's recently surfaced two-year "sting" operation (nicknamed "Abscam") which implicated seven House members and one Senator. The undercover agents posed as businessmen and wealthy Arabs willing to pay bribes. They paid out some $700,000 during meetings that were taped or filmed with hidden cameras. The final verdicts in the case will not be in for months, perhaps for years. But we can hardly agree with the indignation shown by two California members of the Congress. Representative Don Edwards says that "reins are needed to prevent FBI" from using "entrapment" tactics to nab people for accepting payoffs. Senator Alan Cranston says that the FBI improperly dangled temptation before some of the lawmakers and that it should focus on known criminal activities instead of bearing in upon public officials in this way (*San Francisco Chronicle,* February 17, 1980).

As I see it the answer to these offended lawmakers is simple. Isn't entrapment a common way for local police and federal agents to catch drug pushers and other lawbreakers?

From the business standpoint, there is hardly any difference in principle between the gift of a skillet to a housewife from a salesman who hopes to induce her to purchase an entire set of cookware, and the big-time operator's gift of a mink coat to a White House secretary[13] in the hope that the government's multibillion dollar wheel of fortune might be influenced to stop at his number and disgorge a bit of its rewards. Lacking a clear distinction between corrupt and legitimate means of influencing others, few people know where to stop.

A book by Blair Bolles, *How to Get Rich in Washington,* is, in many respects, remarkably similar to that older landmark in the journalistic record of corruption in the American government, *The Autobiography of Lincoln Steffens.* Later books such as Walter Goodman's *All Honorable Men: Corruption and Compromise in American Life* and James Deakin's *The Lobbyists* discuss the same basic problem.

The world of Lincoln Steffens was one in which the man who

wanted something from the government went down to the city hall or the state legislature after the public utility franchises and other favors that local or state executives and legislators could bestow. In the world of Blair Bolles, all roads, or at least the main highways, lead to Washington and to men whose favors are defense contracts, industrial, commercial, or agricultural loans, and the thousand other benefits that the bureaucracy has to offer. For, as Bolles tells us and as Lincoln Steffens knew, both corrupter and corrupted are constantly seeking out the sources that can bring them personal advantages. The self-reliant individual strides forward on whatever paths to success present themselves.

We see then that the influence patterns in China and America have a high degree of similarity, but nevertheless, that their differences are more profound. The Chinese who cultivated influential government officals did so with the understood and expressed desire to be dependent upon them in the future. This, as we have seen, was the attitude of the fictional Hsi-Men Ch'ing. Just as revealing is the fact that in the real world of the Chinese bureaucracy the watchword of every official has always been "sound support from the higher-ups." Every time two Chinese officials came into contact, each lost no time in discovering the identity of the other one's backer or backers. It must be remembered that the tie between the backers and the backed was permanent rather than transitory; it was a relationship in which the bearer of gifts became the subordinate and the one who accepted them the superior.

But Americans cultivate government influence with the explicit purpose of controlling or influencing their political protégé's activities in those areas that impinge upon the interests of the sponsors. The tie between them is thus transitory rather than permanent; it is a relationship where the bearer of gifts becomes the superior and the one who accepts them the subordinate. This is why the techniques of government influence in China consisted chiefly of "gifts" in kind or in currency but their counterparts in the United States range all the way from an irate citizen's letter, a local group's petition, and the cloakroom warnings of the registered lobbyist (forms of influence unknown in China but accepted as legitimate "pressure" in America), to monthly protection money, mink coats, and pleasure rides in luxury planes (commonly called "corruption" in the United States and the same as Chinese "gifts").

Second, the majority of Chinese influence seekers hope to gain a place or an advancement in the bureaucracy. But Americans act to protect or advance their private interests outside of the government, often on colossal scales. American influence seekers do not merely go to the national capital as individuals. The interest groups are highly organized and most of them maintain permanent offices staffed by high-powered lawyers and publicity men. It is by such means that the National Association of Manufacturers protects or advances its interests with the Department of Commerce, the farm interests with the Department of Agriculture, the American Medical Association with the Department of Health, Education and Welfare, labor unions with the Department of Labor, the airlines with the Civil Aeronautics Board, and so forth. But often the lobbyists' activities are more generalized and not confined to specialized government agencies. For example, the target of the oil lobbyists, the real estate lobbyists, and the lobbyists representing gun manufacturers and merchants is the Congress as a whole.

Third, therefore, the influence game in China is limited by the number of government positions available and the extent to which the people come into contact with officials for specific purposes. During the latter part of any Chinese dynasty, for example, offices tended to be multiplied purely as outlets for office seekers and both the collection of taxes and the administration of law in general were abused to the extreme. Those who already had influence benefitted tremendously, often at the expense of those who did not. But this never went on for long, because these excesses became major contributing factors to the fall of the dynasty. A new aristocracy then stepped in and cleaned house. Furthermore, since success is shared by the family and the local community, and best measured by their admiration, the Chinese quest for influence is curtailed.

In contrast, the ceiling on the influence game in the United States is nowhere in sight. Since the benefit of political influence is not confined to jobs in the government, or even contracts from the government, it will tend to flourish and multiply as the country's total commerce and industries grow. Between 1946, when the law regulating lobbying was enacted, and 1965, a total of 4,962 individuals and organizations registered under the lobbying law.[14] This would make it about 500 per year. The late Frank Buchannan, chairman of the 1950 congressional committee investigating lobbying, estimated that the actual number in existence then was three times as large as those registered.[15] If we follow this estimate, we arrive at a figure of about 15,000 for the same period, or 1,500 per year. However, according to a later estimate, "there are at least 8 to 10 lobbyists for every member of Congress."[16] This estimate skyrockets the number of lobbyists to about 5,000 per year. However, since the number of lobbyists increases with the technical sophistication of their problems, this figure will rise markedly in the years ahead. Whatever the actual number, it seems safe to predict that the American government will increasingly be treated by private interests as though it were a natural resource, to be exploited by the best-organized pressure groups and those most skilled in the arts of human mechanics. One expression of this sophistication has led pressure groups to declare that they spend "millions for education—or public enlightenment—but not one cent for lobbying."[17]

This prediction is not farfetched in view of the fact that many lobbyists, instead of being the shadowy figures the Chinese would imagine them to be, are highly respected public men. Twenty ex-senators and more than seventy former representatives have registered as lobbyists since 1946. Among other former registrants were such figures as George Romney, formerly governor of Michigan and later secretary of Housing and Urban Development, George W. Ball, former under secretary of state and one time United States ambassador to the United Nations, Arthur J. Goldberg, former Supreme Court justice and former United States ambassador to the United Nations, and Charles S. Rhyne, a past president of the American Bar Association. In 1979 Billy Carter, the president's brother, was registered as a lobbyist for Libya. Furthermore, the interests that the lobbyists represent are not only diverse (from Iron Ore Lessors Association to the American Legion), but also include foreign governments. Thus former Secretary of State Dean Acheson was once an agent of the government of Venezuela; former governor of New York and twice Republican presidential candidate Thomas E. Dewey acted as agent for the Republic of Turkey; and Franklin D. Roosevelt, Jr., head of the federal commission on equal opportunity, was once an agent for the Dominican Republic.[18]

It is obvious that being a lobbyist is no bar to public office, although having held a public office makes one a better qualified lobbyist.

Many years ago Lincoln Steffens succinctly defined the nature of the problem to an audience of Los Angeles businessmen who, after hearing his prepared address, still felt that he had not come to the heart of the matter. A churchman present in the group asked, "What we want to know is who founded this system, . . . not only in San Francisco and Los Angeles, in this or the last generation, but back . . . in the beginning?" Steffens replied:

. . . Most people, you know, say it was Adam. But Adam, you remember, said it was Eve. . . . And Eve said no, no, it wasn't she; it was the serpent. And that's where you clergy have stuck ever since. You blame that serpent, Satan. Now I come and I am trying to show you that it was, it is, the apple.[19]

The Chinese apples are primarily places in the bureaucracy; but the American apples drop from the government tree into the private preserve. There are only a limited number of apples on the Chinese bureaucratic tree; but so long as the American government continues to be as crucial to the success or failure of private interests—industrial and commercial, agricultural and labor—as it has in the past, the apples will grow abundantly in the American orchard.

Revolt and Schism

A 1951 report of the Douglas Committee on Ethical Standards in the federal government quotes an old English quatrain:

The law locks up both man and woman
Who steals the goose from off the common.
But lets the greater felon loose
Who steals the common from the goose.

The cartoonist Herbert Block notes that this summarizes the contrast between gifts to executive officials (such as those of Bernard Goldfine to Sherman Adams) and influences of special pressure groups on Congress (such as that of the oil interests in their efforts to obtain the resources of an ocean floor). Block continues:

Much of the unethical conduct in the executive department struck me as being downright cheap—a mediocre kind of political immorality of mediocre men. . . . Its very cheapness, involving deep freezes, wholesale coats, and free hotel rooms, made it easy for everyone to grasp—easier than big-time political immorality, which involves higher mathematics and is difficult to visualize. . . . Figures running into hundreds of millions of dollars are just more big numbers. They aren't photogenic.

If a fellow is going to go in for unethical conduct, he's obviously better off to be big about it and stay away from the almost-familiar items.[20]

The old English quatrain finds a curious parallel in an old Chinese saying:

Steal a trinket
You're a thief.
Steal a country
You're its chief.[21]

Yet, in spite of obvious similarity between the Chinese saying and the English quatrain, the two have quite different applications. At most Chinese bureaucratic corruptors and influence seekers could be compared with stealers of the goose but they rarely had the opportunity of taking the village common as well. The only Chinese stealers, or would-be stealers, of the village common were the rebels. For traditionally, "any organized pressures or demands on the part of particular interests, if openly articulated, were treated as rude threats to public peace and order."[22] Consequently, mass grievances could be expressed primarily as open rebellion. When the leader of the rebellion succeeded in toppling the ruling dynasty and pacifying his rivals, he would become the new chief of a new dynasty.

The governments among both peoples possess certain internal forces that act to reform or readjust these governments when they fail to function adequately.

As stated previously, except for short periods of inter-dynastic chaos, the emperor and his officials in China received a degree of obedience and reverence from the people that would be unimaginable in the United States. The several decades of civil wars before 1949 have somewhat obscured the fact that, even during the alien Manchu dynasty, the emperor at Peking could decree suicide as penalty for an erring viceroy located at the farthest boundary of the empire, a man who usually had a large armed force at his command, and his decree would be carried out without fuss. In the same way, the authority of the governors and the magistrates was rarely even questioned within their own domains. The disappearance of the emperors did not basically alter this climate of opinion, and it has persisted up to the present moment. The scale of the turmoil in the People's Republic during the last two decades without leading to the fall of the regime may be a portent of something new, but we shall deal with that later. Furthermore, we have noted that the Chinese people, for their part, have protected themselves (a) by a system of negative checks through which they settle their own disputes and limit the government's power to that approved by custom and tradition, and (b) by a system of nepotism and favors through which the individual seeks to join the ranks of the elite or at least free himself from the burden of extralegal levies or other miscarriages of justice.

Occasionally, however, there were open attacks on corruption. In 1819 T'ao Chu, a censor of the imperial government, submitted to the emperor a most outspoken memorandum on "eight forms of bureaucratic corruption." About the year 1927 General Feng Yü-hsiang (known in the West as the "Christian General") started a "frugality-among-officials" movement.[23] He himself was a model of his movement's ideal. But these and other efforts to reform the system had little or no effect. For the Chinese, the desire was not for a change of system but for a mere substitution of bad individual officials by good individual officials, preferably oneself or one's kin.

In the literature of China we find no one work comparable to More's *Utopia,* Bellamy's *Looking Backward,* or other examples of the utopian literature so common in the West. Wang Ch'ung's *Lun Heng (A Discourse on Principles),* written approximately four centuries ago, was the only volume which raised fundamental questions concerning the structure of government and it never received widespread or serious attention. On the other hand, novels abound in which corrupt officials are punished by good officials or by supernatural figures. The most famous and probably most popular of these novels have been *Pao Kung An (The Story of His Eminence Pao)* and *Chi Kung Chuan (The True Story of Chi Kung, the Mad Monk).* Pao is a fearless man of complete integrity who is empowered by the emperor to deal out justice in any way he sees fit, even to the point of executing delinquent officials and aristocrats on the spot. In his attempts to detect the truth, he often goes among the people in disguise. Chi, the mad monk, is a god in disguise who brings comfort to the poor and oppressed but misfortune to the high and mighty. Another popular book in this vein is *All Men Are Brothers,* a Chinese Robin Hood-type novel that we remarked upon in a previous chapter. The essence of its approach to official irregularity is the same as the others—the punishment of evil persons and aid to the victims.

The relationship between the American government and its people is a far more dynamic affair. Its normal state is that of conflict, subdued or overt, between political parties and within parties, between levels of government, branches at any one level, policies, and personalities, between different organized interests, and between the latter and Congress or the chief executive and his lieutenants. Few regimes in the United States have ever represented much more than 50 percent of the popular vote at the time of their accession to office; and while public opinion tends to accept it as legitimate, the extent of this "popular mandate" may fluctuate violently during the regime's period in power. The executive offices and administrative sections of the federal government are not only under strict and constant surveillance by Congress (even if the majority of its members belong to the president's party), but only the judicial branch is substantially removed from the constant pressure that large sections of the general population exert.

This state of conflict and its results constitute, of course, the very substance of democracy. But besides the conflict between the executive and the legislative branches, the popular opinion of the people is of extreme importance. These expressions range from newspaper articles, which complain against a chief of police, through voluminous mail to Congress and the White House, to mass demonstrations and even open violence.

These cries of protest or outrage, if they are repeated often enough, help, at least in part, to bring about certain changes in the government organization itself. For example, the New Deal, which was the response to just such a nationwide cry for social reform, vitally influenced the relationship between the federal government and the total fabric of society.

These observations were first made over twenty-five years ago. Their soundness has since been proved by several outstanding developments. The civil rights movement for racial equality, which began in the fifties, is one such development. The 1954 Supreme Court in *Brown* v. *The Board of Education* abolished the legal basis for segregation in the schools, although schools are still not all integrated and residential patterns still betray a high degree of segregation. However, besides a black Supreme Court justice there are black judges, mayors, cabinet officers, corporation heads and directors, and presidents of major universities (e.g., Michigan State University, University of California at Sacramento, and New Jersey State College). Public media such as television have come a long way from the fifties and the early sixties when no black faces were to be seen except as servants or in all-black shows such as *Amos and Andy*. This would not have come about, or would have come about much later, had there not been lunch counter sit-ins, the Poor People's March on Washington, D.C., and numerous other acts of public protest which dramatized the need for basic changes in the social, economic, and even political fabric of the nation.

Another important development was the successful opposition to President Lyndon B. Johnson's conduct of the Vietnam War. In retrospect that war was an American disaster. As David Halberstam has shown in his book *The Best and the Brightest,* it was a war that most

Americans and their leaders did not at first want. They got into it bit by bit, and by the time they realized the larger implications they were already deeply into it. However, Johnson then cavalierly expanded the war at will and arrogantly told the Congress through his lieutenants Dean Rusk and Nicholas Katzenbach that he did not need any authorization from the legislative body because the Tonkin Resolution was a "functional equivalent" of such an authorization. This pronouncement was almost immediately followed by Senator Eugene McCarthy's decision to "take the issue to the people" by entering the New Hampshire primary where he scored an overwhelming success on an anti-Johnson platform. The antiwar sentiment became intensified and more widespread.[24] It is spectacular that a president who seemed resolved to settling all scores on the battlefield should abruptly decide to change that very course by taking himself out of politics and opening negotiations with his Communist enemies.

An even more spectacular event was President Nixon's resignation in disgrace as a result of the Watergate scandal.[25] Changes in government procedures and functions can be brought about by individual initiative, public demands, or even by a Watergate.

Some skeptics insist that the only good produced by the Kefauver crime investigations of the fifties or the Senate rackets investigations of the sixties or the Watergate hearings of the seventies was their entertainment value on the television screen, and that after a while the people and officials forgot all about such investigations. There is undeniably a measure of truth in such accusations, for the tendency to investigate, denounce, and then forget is not unknown in America. But this is not a peculiarly American failing.

Pressure groups may, of course, work for the maintenance of the status quo or for changes. The gun lobby has so far succeeded in squashing any attempt to legislate gun control laws. A 1978 national survey showed 84 percent of those polled, including gun owners, favored "stringent federal laws governing the registration of newly purchased handguns" (*Chicago Sun-Times,* June 4, 1978). But the chances for gun control laws to be enacted seem remote. When invited to address the Gun Owners of New Hampshire, of those on the ballot in the state's 1980 presidential primary who attended (six Republicans, one Democrat, and one Jack Carter representing his father), all except Representative John Anderson of Illinois cottoned up to the gun folks (*San Francisco Chronicle,* February 19, 1980). Jack Carter said, "My Dad has been a sportsman for as long as he has lived. He got his first quail when he was 10 years old." Such is the power of a pressure group in spite of its minority status. But it is also true that other pressure groups such as Common Cause and its older brother the American Civil Liberties Union have often been the impetus for reforms which might never have taken place without this widely supported mechanism for initiating change.

No comparable political processes existed in China, in spite of the many great emperors and famous censors who justly, but for different reasons, occupy a revered place in Chinese history. In China, as we noted before, when government oppression went too far, the people's last resort was always mass revolt. However, instead of altering the form and substance of the government, the new rulers would simply manage the national affairs in the same mode as their predecessors.

Somewhat like the rulers of England who, for symbolic reasons founded on the divine right of kingship, are crowned in Westminster Abbey at London, the Chinese emperors were explicitly said to receive their power from the Supreme Ruler of Heaven. This grant of powers was called the Mandate of Heaven. But unlike the monarchs of England, a Chinese emperor or dynasty did not permanently possess this mandate, even in theory. As long as the emperor maintained peace and prosperity in his empire he retained the Mandate of Heaven. As soon as he was unable to do so, he was in danger of losing it.

There were many circumstances under which the emperor might be regarded as having lost his Mandate of Heaven. There might be great floods and widespread famines from which he failed to rescue the people promptly, and as a result there might be uprisings that he failed to put down effectively. When the uprisings grew to serious proportions, especially if new leaders succeeded in seizing and consolidating most of the empire, the loss of the Mandate of Heaven was an accomplished fact. The mandate then descended upon the leader who restored peace and prosperity, or as an irreverent realist might say, the mandate is picked up by the new leader in the process of consolidating his power. Within this concept of government, the people were duty-bound to obey only so long as the imperial rule was more benevolent than despotic.

Furthermore, a European king or grand duke may have been thrown out by revolutionaries but the exiled ruler tended to retain his claim to his former domain. Many of his one-time subjects may have joined him in exile or continued to work within their native country in support of his possible return. The Chinese pattern is quite the reverse. An ex-emperor would never have been taken seriously except by some hangers-on with future profit in mind. For once a Chinese ruler lost his Mandate of Heaven he had very little chance of regaining it. In fact, in all Chinese history no fallen emperor ever regained his throne. Nor did his sons and grandsons apparently have any better chance than the next man. Royal descent in no way assured success, although during dynastic wars it was sometimes used as a convenient peripheral argument.

On the other hand, a man who emerged supreme after a period of dynastic rivalry had no difficulty in establishing the moral and legal foundation of his dynasty. The new ruler's origin was of no consequence. Thus a minor functionary in a local government rose to become the first emperor of the Han dynasty (206 B.C.–A.D. 8). And fifteen centuries later the founder of the great Ming dynasty (A.D. 1368–1644) started his public life as an apprentice monk in an unknown temple.[26] After he successfully defeated all adversaries it was not necessary for him to contest with his own past, and he soon became the object of many popular legends explaining his "unusual" birth. One legend had it that a dragon, the symbol of royalty, was seen hovering about his mother's maternity chamber. This was by no means an unusual legend in the lore of supernatural occurrences surrounding the birth of Chinese rulers.

Thus, the basis of Chinese governmental power has always been a matter of fact rather than of legitimacy or issues. The heir of an emperor had no inherent right to a throne lost by his forebears. Conversely, an ex-street urchin could with equanimity claim royal prerogatives if he was able to eliminate his rivals. Under these circumstances new Chinese dynasties, once established, rarely found themselves presented with continuing opposition. It was so customary for Chinese literati-officials to switch their loyalty readily that, although the very few who did not do so were hailed as the greatest of the great,[27] the overwhelming majority who chose to change their allegiance were never branded as persons of little character.

This pattern is intrinsically bound to the characteristic psychology of the individual Chinese. We have seen in the previous chapter that he is secure and will become more elevated in status in his primary relationships as he grows older and thus he has little need to irretrievably identify himself with wider alliances or associations. His concern with class, success, heroes, or the central government itself is limited by the extent to which they affect the security of his primary relationships, for it is within the web of the latter that he finds the triumphs or failures most meaningful. The liberty of the Chinese monarch to wield despotic power when he chose was basically a consequence of the relative lack of personal interest among his people in most of what he and his officials did. The Chinese government was a static arrangement in which there was no call for the people to follow the rulers in an active way. They revered and obeyed the rulers if the rulers ruled according to tradition and custom. But they did not hesitate to part with the rulers if the rulers lost control to their foes or tried to lead the people down untried paths.

Finding little or no permanence in his primary relationships, the American attempts to increase his own importance through wider commitments. Consequently, he attaches himself, with great anxiety and intense seriousness, to associations, class, success symbols, heroes, or the government itself. He does so in the conscious or unconscious hope that one or another of them will provide him with security, but especially status, the necessary ingredients of a sense of personal importance without which few human beings can exist. The basic strength of the American government thus comes from the personal interest and psychological involvement of the American people in most of what it does. Whatever unity exists between this government and the people is a positive and tenacious emotional bond.

There is a derivative affinity between American political behavior and the political traditions of Europe, and in particular, a very definite psychological similarity. American public figures may come and go, and the policies and structure of the American government may oscillate severely. But except during the exigencies of war those Americans who opposed the New Deal tended to continue their opposition even though, when running for office, they may have submerged their private antagonisms in order to "stay right" with the electorate. Once in power, the objective facts might have moderated their private feelings, but within these limitations they persisted in their attempts to reverse the decisions of history.

Likewise those who held isolationist views were perhaps forced to modify them; they did not abandon them. Those who do make an explicit break with their previous convictions or those of their party are regarded not only as irresponsible but as morally wrong. That is why an ex-isolationist, Senator Vandenberg, was condemned by many leaders of his party for his role in supporting the Democratic foreign policy, and why an ex-Democrat, the late Wendell Willkie, never secured the favor of the Republican party's regulars. It is a fair assumption that for whatever other reasons John Connally did not get the Republican nomination in 1980, the fact he is an ex-Democrat was certainly a factor. In regard to New Dealers, the charge that Roosevelt had "betrayed" his class was often voiced by the well-to-do. The grass-roots basis of such popular sentiments against political "betrayers" of their class is illustrated by the southern white vehemence against southern whites who dare to champion black causes.

Many persons, even today, find it extremely difficult to view ex-Communists as anything but highly questionable characters, not solely because they once committed themselves to a conspiratorial cause but because such conversions and reconversions are morally suspect. As for the facts of electioneering, while it is true that as a political bandwagon picks up speed it gathers additional supporters, it is equally true that when it slows down it usually loses but a few of its more opportunistic advocates. A Grover Cleveland can lose office yet be returned to power four years later; a William Jennings Bryan may never knock at the White House door successfully, but he may keep knocking for many years without a precipitous drop in his popular support; and a Richard Nixon who lost his first bid for the presidency, made it eight years later and resigned in disgrace, may yet come back to power at some future time.

Thus, when an American administration manages to remain in power for a long time, that administration and the people necessarily enjoy a higher degree of unity of outlook and action than that known in China either before or since its contact with the West. Where the leader-follower relationship is based on an emotional identification, the followers rise and fall with their hero, for his triumph is their triumph, his fall is their fall, and his fight is their fight. But for this very reason, the American government tends to be infused by divisive forces that are more numerous and more penetrating than those known to Chinese governments before or since the 1911 Revolution.

In the People's Republic events following the death of Premier Chou and later the fall of the Gang of Four did seem to pitch two camps of followers in spontaneous opposition to each other. Palace revolts were not unknown in Chinese history; but division on top which involves the voluntary support of the multitudes is a more recent Chinese phenomenon. Furthermore, the true measure of the depth of such division is its duration and the frequency with which it appears over long periods of time. Judging by the past and according to what we know about the situation-centered way of looking at man, gods, and things, Chinese under whatever ideology cannot develop in short order the deep forces for the kind of long-standing and irreconcilable schism characteristic of the West. This is not to say that they will never develop them.

Previously we cited examples of the unquestioned autocratic power of the Chinese dynastic rulers and their officials. But even Chiang's regime between 1927 and 1937—besieged as it was with the unremitting threat of Japanese aggression, disruptive tensions brought about by Communist opposition and warlords, and a crippling economy—could easily institute measures which a president of the United States and his supporters would have to work long and hard for with no assurance of success. The pattern of mutual dependence normally causes the Chinese to fall in line with relative ease. The pattern of self-reliance leads Americans into repeated schisms.

What has saved the Chinese from crushing oppression was their very weakness—that lack of emotional involvement between the people and their rulers which created a distance between them. This distance, as we have also observed, permitted the emperor to be autocratic but never totalitarian. For totalitarianism depends not only on a ruthless leader with a messianic message, it also must have the support of millions of little Hitlers or Stalins plus a general population that is emotionally involved in a most intense and lasting way with the despot.

What has prevented the American political system from crumbling into chaos is the fact that the individual American's lack of permanent human anchorage creates in him not only a fear of nonconformity but in many cases even an active hatred of it. These popular sentiments had at least in part to do with why the late Robert Kennedy did not decide on his candidacy before the 1968 New Hampshire primary, before he had clear signs of the turn of the popular tide. This is one of the basic reasons why a third party has never succeeded and, if this analysis is at all correct, stands very little chance of doing so in the foreseeable future. Americans often grumble because they see no presidential candidate satisfactory to them in either party. But they usually vote for the candidate of one of the two established parties anyway, because it is both realistic and respectable.

The two major parties of the present only grew out of the decline of two previously established parties. The fate of those political movements, which were conceived and born in isolation from the established parties, is well known. Those involved in many of these fringe movements are only too ready to return to the fold once a minor issue is settled or a personality they oppose disappears from the scene. One-party rule in the South is not likely to be terminated through the agency of a third party. George Wallace and his supporters did not succeed in that venture and I do not believe they would have succeeded even if Wallace had not been crippled by an assassin's bullet. John Anderson in 1980, too, failed to gain electoral votes in a single state in spite of his definite appeal to many liberals and those disaffected with the Carter presidency. The unexpected Ronald Reagan landslide in the 1980 election portends that a future candidate with Wallace's and Anderson's kind of aspirations will probably have to succeed through a swing of a sizable number of votes to the already established Republican party.[28] In fact, the Eisenhower victories in 1952 and 1956 seemed to portend this possibility, and the civil rights movement may once again sway the voting picture in the South.

NOTES

1. They have also read various news impressions by Canadians and Europeans that the functionaries on all levels of the Communist government, whatever their faults, cannot, by contrast, be accused of corruption.

2. There was no age limit to these examinations. However, it took at least seven or eight years of schoolwork before a candidate could even hope to succeed. The majority of candidates in the first examination were about eighteen to twenty-five years old. But there were instances in which a candidate emerged victorious from the palace examinations before thirty years of age. Some unsuccessful candidates kept trying until they were seventy or eighty years old.

3. After the 1930s, but especially after World War II, when the federal government entered into many more phases of American life and work than ever before, Washington, D.C., became the scene of more intense activity than ever before in American history. Even the American Anthropological Association, along with the American Psychological Association, and numerous other academic groups, set up its headquarters in the national capital in the fifties. But Americans who rush to Washington, D.C., are more likely to be well-paid lobbyists representing diverse interest groups than starving office seekers whose sole aim is entry into government service.

4. Edgerton, *The Golden Lotus,* p. 18 and pp. 20–21.

5. Princess Der Ling was later married to an American consul-general in China and spent her last years of retirement with her husband in Los Angeles, California. In 1944 I read a newspaper account of her death in an auto accident.

6. A point of high praise for any great man or former high official in Chinese obituaries has always been that "he died a poor man, containing but clear winds in his two sleeves and leaving his wife and children nothing."

7. The failure of the merchants to develop into entrepreneurial capitalists will be taken up in Chapter 12.

8. C. Lester Walker, "The China Legend," *Harper's,* March 1946, p. 239.

9. "The Mind of Asia," in *Life,* December 31, 1952, p. 41. This view derives from the thesis in his book, *The Meeting of East and West.*

10. Such as occurred in the fifties under the late Senator Joseph McCarthy.

11. See his *Bureaucracy in a Democracy.*

12. A prominent mercantile house gives these words of warning to its junior executives: "The buyer will find it advantageous to accord fair treatment to all sellers whether he buys from them or not. A buyer should be friendly but maintain *absolutely* independent relations with all sellers. The acceptance of personal favors, gifts or attentions of any kind is dangerous. Those who receive them are placed under obligation and often under pressure to give their business to the concerns that provide the favor. Buyers who are wise in their own interest as well as in the interest of their stores, decline *all* favors, even the most insignificant." (Italics in original.) To what extent such praiseworthy injunctions are followed in most business houses is left for the reader to judge in terms of his own knowledge of regular American commerical practices.

13. This occurred under the Truman administration and was the incident that led Richard Nixon to tell the public that Pat Nixon wore a simple cloth coat.

14. According to the *Congressional Quarterly*, as quoted by James Deakin, *The Lobbyists*, p. 5 (not counting duplications due to individuals and law firms who registered for several clients).

15. Quoted in Herbert Block, *The Herblock Book*, p. 107.

16. Deakin, *The Lobbyists*, p. 2. There is an apparent discrepancy between Deakin and the *Congressional Quarterly* on the number of registered lobbyists in 1965 or 1966. The former states, "More than 1,100 individuals and organizations are currently registered as lobbyists" (p. 1). Since Deakin's book was published in 1966, I presume that his figure pertains to 1965 or 1966. But according to the *Quarterly*, the number of "organizations" which "reported spending" was 304 in 1965 and 296 in 1966 (*Congressional Quarterly*, July 7, 1967, p. 1161). The discrepancy may be due to two factors and may be more apparent than real. First, Deakin's figure refers to "individuals and organizations" while the *Quarterly's* figure is for "organizations" only. Second, the former figure refers to registered lobbyists in general while the latter refers to those which "reported spending." Both factors will restrict the *Quarterly* figures to much smaller ones. There are a good many loopholes in filing rules, and "the Clerk of the House acknowledges receipt of each report and files it, but does not check contents" (*Congressional Quarterly*, p. 1161).

17. Block, *Herblock Book*, p. 108.

18. Deakin, *The Lobbyist*, pp. 3–5.

19. Lincoln Steffens, *The Autobiography of Lincoln Steffens*, p. 574.

20. Block, *Herblock Book*, pp. 213–215.

21. The actual Chinese saying is: "Stealer of hook will suffer execution, while stealer of a country will become its chief." Hook symbolizes a very inexpensive and common article of property.

22. Lucian Pye, *The Spirit of Chinese Politics*, p. 18.

23. See James E. Sheridan, *Chinese Warlord: The Career of Feng Yü-hsiang*.

24. In my view, too, Johnson's disregard of congressional opinion concerning the Vietnam War also led to the legislators' unusually protracted battle against his recommendation of a 10 percent surtax on income, and to the final withdrawal of the Abe Fortas nomination for chief justice of the Supreme Court. The delay of the former and the denial of the latter were Congress's way of reminding the chief executive that although he had much power, there are limits to that power.

25. A galaxy of books on the Watergate affair are available. One of the best is Carl Bernstein and Bob Woodward, *All The President's Men*. For an analysis of the Watergate affair in the context of the social and political development of the American society, see Henry Steele Commager, "The Significance of Watergate," in *Britannica Book of the Year, 1974*, pp. 709–710.

26. It should be noted that in China, monks have always been looked upon with disfavor. A monk soliciting funds from household to household was regarded as little

different from a tramp begging from door to door. The late Dr. Hu Shih, the foremost philosopher of China and one-time ambassador to Washington, D.C., wrote in his autobiography that on the street entrance to his parent's family home was the sign: "NO MONKS AND PRIESTS." In this action the senior Mr. and Mrs. Hu were being neither non-conformist nor even mildly peculiar. The entrances to many Chinese residences in all parts of China bore the same sign.

27. Such as Wen T'ien-hsiang of the Sung dynasty, who preferred execution to a high position under the Mongols who conquered China and established the Yuan dynasty.

28. This same conclusion was reached, for different reasons, by Samuel Lubell in his *Future of American Politics*. Chapter 4, "The Conservative Revolution."

CHAPTER 9

Two Kinds
of Religion

So far we have examined several of the most important human relationships that characterize the Chinese and American ways of life, and we found therein certain pronounced and consistent differences. The Chinese has close ties with his primary group, and this relationship is basic and the permanent core of all others. He has little active interest in wider entanglements except where the latter enhance his position among his family members, relatives, and fellow villagers or townsmen, or where they become necessary to protect himself or these same groups. The American participates in a wide variety of relationships, all of which tend to be transitory. The least personal of this multitude of relationships, such as his ties with his nation, can be of the greatest importance to him, but often none of these relationships is intimate.

The Chinese can maintain his primary relationships as the permanent core of all others because his ideal of mutual dependence decrees that human relationships should be multiple and additive. One relationship does not, or at least is not encouraged to, conflict with the others. Marriage, instead of cutting the parent-child bond, is supplementary to it. The American's relationships tend to be transitory and progressive because, within his ideal of self-reliance, human relationships are designed to be singular and exclusive. Because of this, many relationships tend to interfere with the others. The individual, facing a world of transitory relationships, develops a self-protecting rationale of desiring to reduce the number of restraints to a minimum and readily to abandon one set of relationships when he adopts another.

The Chinese finds his place without much effort; mutual dependence brings him satisfaction even when he personally does not better himself. Proceeding from one transitory bond to another, the adult American tends to be uncertain of his human relations at all times. Self-reliance demands that he travel alone on the road to success, and the rewards or failures are solely his. Further, the consequent insecurity makes for greater emotionality; his loves, hates, and particular anxieties are all accentuated because he stands or falls on his own.

This review helps set the focus for explaining Chinese and American conceptions of the supernatural. In the preceding chapter we saw that the Chinese have developed what is essentially a negative, or at best a neutral, relationship to their government and its officials. The people do not actively force the officials to behave in an acceptable manner, but keep their own distance from the government while passively accepting their fate so long as the officials stay within the bounds staked out by tradition. Consequently, for many centuries the Chinese government was able to maintain a despotic but benevolent autocracy. When the bureaucracy became too oppressive and corrupt, the people longed for good officials to remove the bad officials and then redress the accumulated wrongs. But the Chinese people as a whole never desired to change the structural arrangement of the Chinese society. It is for this reason that the Chinese have throughout their history enjoyed political peace for periods of time much longer than those known to their Western brethren. Civil strife, when it occurred, was a contest between men, not ideologies. Victory for one side brought a quick resumption of tranquility since it did not entail a reordering of the entire society.

The Chinese approach to the world of the supernatural is essentially the same as their approach to secular affairs. They look for a Buddha or some other divinity or spirit who can render immediate and specific assistance to those who are in trouble, but they do not seek a deity whose teachings are intended to save all mankind in all ways and for all time. So long as the chosen god or gods are willing to help, the Chinese is not reluctant to put himself at their mercy. He provides for them with ritual offerings; he praises them and expresses his reverence for them in chants and exaltations. Material offerings and spiritual reverence are the price of supernatural assistance, a price the Chinese considers to be both logical and natural. The Chinese attitude is epitomized in such sayings as "We depend upon Heaven for food," or "Heaven and fate will determine the course of events." These are in vivid contrast to Western mottoes such as "God helps those who help themselves," or "Pray to God and keep your powder dry."

These latter two sentiments reflect a way of life in which relationships among men tend to be exclusive but transitory, and in which
the self-reliant individual makes his own place by impressing others,
not by depending on them. Just as the Chinese attitude toward the
government is commensurate with their attitude toward the supernatural, the American approach to secular authorities and statutes
bears unmistakable similarity to that taken toward God and His
laws. The concept of monotheism is acceptable to Americans because their emotional need to identify themselves with a supernatural being is best satisfied when undiluted by sharing. They do not
wait for God to save them, for their insecurity compels them not only
to save themselves, but to serve as God's voluntary interpreters and
standard bearers. Self-reliant believers entertain little doubt that
what each of them wants as an individual must coincide with the will
of God. In this contest, "vox populi vox dei" is as meaningful in the
religious realm as in the governmental.

The Chinese Way in Religion

To appreciate the profound manner in which religious differences reflect the life of the two peoples, let us first take a close look at the Chinese idea of religion. The Chinese world of the spirits is essentially
like their world of men. In each, the mass of common men is governed by a hierarchy of officials. This hierarchy in the Chinese spirit
world consists of three interrelated domains: The Domain of Judgment, the Western Paradise, and the court of the Supreme Ruler of
Heaven. In the Domain of Judgment are found the courts of the ten
judges who keep complete records on the merits and demerits of all
human beings. The souls of all the dead are reviewed by each judge
successively. Those who committed evil deeds—such as licentiousness or unfilial behavior—in the world of humans are subject to all
manner of punishment; those who were blameless or meritorious,
the dutiful and the charitable, are given a variety of rewards.

The Western Paradise is a land of eternal happiness, thought by
some to be under the headship of Buddha and by others to be under
the Goddess Mother Wang. The Chinese are quite vague about this
domain. I am not aware of any Chinese quarrels about it, learned or
otherwise. Some observers say that belief in this paradise arose out of
the geographical relationship between India, Buddhism's place of
origin, and China, where Buddhism was introduced about A.D. 100,
some six hundred years after the death of Buddha. Whatever the

case, the Chinese do not seem to doubt that it is a highly desirable place for the soul of the dead. In a funeral procession anywhere in China "condolence banners" will be found. Upon these blue or white pieces of satin, held aloft by hired hands, are inscribed sentiments to the effect that the deceased has gone to the Western Paradise on the back of a stork. In north China, the farewell rite to the dead, which takes place the day before the funeral, is always performed with the participants facing toward the west. References to the Western Paradise also are common in scriptures recited by priests during those public prayer meetings in which the Goddess Mother Wang or Buddha is petitioned to bless the believers.

The Supreme Ruler of Heaven has jurisdiction over all men and all gods. As we have seen in the preceding chapter, even the emperor ruled by his mandate. But he is not omnipresent. In this regard he differs fundamentally from the Christian God. To govern both gods and men, the Supreme Ruler depends upon a large number of functionaries who have titles and ranks not unlike those of officials under the emperor. He is assisted not only by court ministers, commanders-in-chief, district gods, earth gods, judges, and armed forces, but his lieutenants also include the Kitchen God who watches over every household, and roving inspectors who travel from area to area. His orders are executed through these numerous functionaries, and he metes out reward or punishment on living individuals through them or on the souls of the dead through the ten judges in the Domain of Judgment.

It is not solely the structure of the Chinese world of the spirits that is similar to the world of men. The presumed attitudes of the gods toward men and the actual attitudes of men toward their gods are equally reflective of the relationship between Chinese dynastic rulers and their subjects. As in their dealings with worldly officialdom, the Chinese respect their gods, but they keep their distance from them—they feel neither identification with them nor emotional attachment to them. The best evidence for this is that the Chinese have never been very much concerned with nonbelievers or blasphemers against their gods. Some gods are believed to punish blasphemers; that is the problem of the blasphemers themselves. Their sons or daughters may try to rescue them from such consequences, as we shall see below, but no one else will worry about them.

The Supreme Ruler of Heaven and his lieutenants are believed to be wise, just, and firm. They need food and clothing, and express pleasure or anger just like their earthly counterparts, the emperor and his bureaucracy. It is not enough for the common folks who are their subjects to provide for them by ritual offerings; the people must also seek the gods' pleasure. In these propitiations, the people exercise a variety of techniques, for gods, like officials, are not infallible. If it is possible to bribe them, then they are bribed. Throughout China, for example, the Kitchen God and his wife are believed to ascend to heaven on the seventh day before the Chinese New Year's Eve, there to report on the conduct within each family during the past twelve months. On that evening, most families make offerings before the household altar dedicated to the pair. At the end of the ritual the mistress of the house takes pieces of sweetmeat from the offering dishes to smear the lips of the picture of the Kitchen God and his wife. The offerings please the deities while the smear sweetens their mouths, thus making it doubly certain that they do not report whatever improper conduct they may have observed throughout the year.

If the firmness of gods can be softened by pleading, the Chinese deities regularly have their ears filled. Disasters such as epidemics, drought, and earthquakes are thought to be indications of the gods' wrath or the work of evil spirits. In either case, only the Supreme Ruler of Heaven and his lieutenants can adjust the matter, and they are petitioned to do so when these calamities strike.[1] The typical Chinese petition to the gods is like the typical Chinese petition to the emperor and his officials. The gods are infinitely praised and exalted while the petitioners deprecate and demean themselves without reserve. Such gestures are designed to placate the angry gods or to have them intervene with the evil spirits in the petitioners' behalf.

Then, too, the deities may be cultivated by having their "birthdays" celebrated in luxury and pomp. Such celebrations are universal in China, and the festivities honor Buddha, the Dragon God, the God of Agriculture, the God of Wealth, the Goddess of Mercy, and many others. Some birthdays are celebrated at great fairs on the temple grounds and often last from three to five days. Others pass more quietly. In one of southwestern China's communities, I counted twenty-eight such days a year, but in northern towns eighteen is the average number.

In 1965 a new twist was added to this Chinese approach to gods. The gilded clay figure of the Earth God's wife disappeared from the local Earth God temple in a Taiwan community. The local people, taking pity on the deity, decided that he should "marry" a beautiful "concubine." The "wedding" was performed according to tradition: an auspicious day, fancy lights, colorful awnings, and musicians were provided. The clay statues of Kuan Yin (Goddess of Mercy), Ma Tsu (Goddess of Health), Kuan Ti (God of War or Wealth), and others—from a variety of other temples—were physically brought to the location of the "wedding" as witnesses, official matchmakers,[2] and honored guests. Relating the event, a reporter on the *Central Daily News* of Taipei commented as follows:

> Here is another example of Chinese feeling for human relations [*j'en ch'ing wei*] which has been the subject of much praise. . . . The villagers are proud of this happy event. Only in a prosperous society can there be so much sympathy and concern for the marital troubles of the unfortunate, including a god.
>
> In fact, to arrange a concubine for an Earth God is not less reasonable than to offer sweetmeat to the Kitchen God. Chinese gods are all "humanized." They may have supernatural powers but they possess the common man's elementary needs. Hence Westerners worship their God by genuflection, prayer, and hymn singing, while Chinese pay homage to their gods by offerings of wine, meat, opera—treating them as honored and fun-loving guests. In this regard we can only go to ancient Greece for comparability. Zeus and other gods on Mount Olympus were guided by their romantic desires much like the main characters of the Chinese novel, *Dream of Red Chamber* [see Chapter 1]. Consequently Greek mythology is much more interesting reading material than the Holy Bible.[3]

Yet in spite of their desire to obtain the gods' favors, the Chinese do not seek too close an association with them. In the normal course of events, gods are located in the temples or in special shrines. The closest the Chinese come to "living" with gods and spirits is in respect to the household altars. But this is no more than physical proximity, for the worshiper pays homage at appointed times before such an altar, and as soon as he leaves it, the gods are left behind. The same respectful distance that separated the people and the emperor, separates the people and their gods. The Chinese believe that those who have gods hovering about them are mediums or persons nearing death or in some way peculiar.

In the southern Manchurian village where I grew up, one man aspired to obey the daily will of the gods by seeking to live out his dreams of the previous night. Each morning he would wander around his yard and roam to other parts of his neighborhood to which he supposed the gods had directed him, turning up stones in search of money and other valuables which the gods said lay hidden there. His conviction that personal rapport with the gods would bring him wealth was generally regarded by the villagers as the idea of a ne'er-do-well or the slightly insane. The only other persons who could commune with spirits were the sick and women allegedly possessed by the essence of foxes. These persons were subjected to various treatments often involving physical torture.

This lack of intimacy with the supernatural has two important correlates: divination and polytheism. As for the first, having no sense of personal contact with the beyond, the Chinese resort to external means to ascertain the future. I do not know of a single city or town in China before 1949, or in Taiwan today that is without diviners or geomancy readers, physiognomists, phrenologists, mediums, and all kinds of fortunetellers. For a fee, these persons foretell the length of a person's life and his business prospects, or determine the marriageability of a boy and girl, or decide on the ritual suitability of a new housesite or graveyard. They will also often undertake to arrange a meeting or communication with the gods or with one's departed ancestors. There is literally no question they do not attempt to answer and almost no matter relating to the gods that they refuse to interpret. It is safe to say that no individual of prominence in traditional China failed to have his fate told, not once but many times, by different professional fortunetellers. One fortuneteller even became a minister briefly during the reign of an emperor in the Ming dynasty for no other reason than that his forecast happened to please the ruler.

The 1911 Revolution had little or no effect upon these practices, and the majority of the people as well as the warlords and many important persons in the Nationalist government regularly patronized diviners of one kind or another. Sometimes the results were amusing. In the early twenties a warlord of Hupei Province, Wang, sensed that he was fated to restore the empire and ascend the throne. Wanting to be sure that his feelings did not mislead him, he decided to consult a prominent phrenologist. Desirous of an objective report, he went in disguise. His lieutenants, however, did not wish to see their master disappointed, and so informed the phrenologist of the situation. Soon after, the warlord, convincingly clad as a poor man, appeared before the phrenologist. The latter, after a brief survey of the warlord's head, fell on his knees, saying that he was assuming this humble position because he was unquestionably paying homage to the future emperor of China. Greatly pleased, the warlord rewarded him with a fee nearly a hundred times the usual amount. Everyone was happy. The phrenologist received a fat reward, the warlord was convinced that he was destined to be emperor, and his underlings were pleased that they were able to satisfy their master.

In order to establish their "accuracy," these fortunetellers are not at all reluctant to provide the public with a sample of their wares. As "proof" of their ability, it has long been customary to display in their show windows their predictions of things to come in the lives of prominent persons. During the thirties, a pedestrian on the thoroughfare of Shanghai could see in the windows of fortunetellers' shops various interpretations of Chiang Kai-shek's life and fortune.[4]

The other correlate of the lack of intimacy between the worshiper and the supernatural is the polytheistic nature of Chinese religion. It is difficult to determine which is causal. That is, given a multiplicity of gods, an intimate relationship with them is impossible; but the absence of a sense of intimacy in turn contributes to the multiplication of gods. At any rate, when there are many gods, the worshiper's religious involvement is necessarily divided. Being divided, its intensity is reduced, and the worshiper is not likely to feel an overpowering attachment to any particular deity.

Consequently, in every Chinese village, town, and city we find a variety of temples all dedicated to the worship of many different gods. A typical village temple usually houses the Goddess of Mercy, who answers all kinds of prayers; the God of Wealth, who is indispensable to all businessmen; the Dragon God, who brings rain in times of drought; and the Earth God, whose wedding was recorded a few pages before, and who is the local emissary of the other world. The inventory of gods in city temples is much larger. There are temples housing the God of Literature; Confucius and his seventy-two famous disciples; the God of Agriculture; the God of Medicine; the Goddesses of Measles, Eyes, and other ailments or bodily parts; Ch'eng Huang or God of the District flanked by courts of the ten judges whose function is detailed below; and the gods who are said to be founders and patron deities of various crafts. Even Henri Doré's monumental ten-volume collection entitled *Researches into Chinese Superstitions* fails to exhaust the list of divinities. No one knows how many gods there are in China. There seems to be no limit to them, and most of them are unrelated to each other.

Implicit in the foregoing discussion is a recognition of the fact that there is no clear demarcation line between the Chinese world of the spirits and that of men. Naturally, the Chinese distinguish between life and death; they also speak of the difference between the workings of men and gods. But in the last analysis these distinctions become inseparably blurred because of the Chinese view that inhabitants of one world not only frequently and as a matter of course affect those of the other, but they can change places by design. One Chinese notion is that famous men (e.g., great generals or officials) are reincarnations of gods. Another Chinese notion is that meritorious men (and occasionally women) become gods after their deaths.[5] We saw in the previous chapter that the image of a popular district governor might be worshiped in a local temple even while he is alive, but usually after he was transferred to another area. This deification of humans occurred on a national scale. For example, from about the seventh century onward, various dynastic governments sanctioned the worship of a military counterpart to Confucius and his seventy-two disciples. At first it was Lu Shang (Chiang T'ai Kung as he was popularly known), a legendary chief minister in the Chou dynasty (1100–223 B.C.). However, later on, especially since the fourteenth century A.D., Kuan Yu (Kuan Kung as he was popularly known), a general during the Three Kingdom period (A.D. 220–280) took this place of honor. This is why it was necessary to include such practices as phrenology in a discussion of religion, although it may have struck many readers as inappropriate. Unlike the pseudo-science of Western phrenology which, like the practice of quack medicine, is a worldly matter, Chinese phrenology is in the realm of the gods, for the Chinese phrenologist purports to determine not the mental faculties but the spirit-determined fate of the subject.

As we noted in the previous chapter, Chinese emperors and the officials under them, by virtue of the emperor's Mandate of Heaven, exercised power over the spirits as well as the lives of men. The converse of this is equally true, and nowhere is the Chinese psychology more clearly demonstrated than in their concept of reward and punishment. The Chinese believe in a wide variety of rewards and punishments which the gods decree and which they may visit upon human beings in this world or the next. For example, a plentiful harvest for an entire district or province is a sign that people in the fortunate area have been good, just as drought, flood, epidemics, or earthquakes are an indication that the people have misbehaved.

On the individual level, the lack of a clear demarcation between the world of the spirits and that of men is much more evident. After death, the soul of every Chinese is subject, according to its deserts, to reward, punishment, or both. The courts of the ten judges, each of which successively reviews the merits and demerits of every newly departed soul, are well known among the Chinese for the tortures they may inflict. A soul may be sawed in half, restored, and then boiled in oil, next ground to mush, then slowly drowned in a river of blood, after which its eyes are poked out and its tongue cut off, and so on ad nauseam.[6] After all of these exasperating experiences, the soul may yet be banished to more suffering in one or all of the numerous hells. Some Chinese sources indicate that there are eighteen hells, one situated on top of the other, while other sources insist that there are many more.

A meritorious person's soul is treated very differently. Immediately after its departure from the body, it is met at the threshold of the world of spirits by a special reception party, playing music and bearing food, that has been dispatched by one of the judges. The newcomer progresses from court to court, residing in guest houses at each stopping place. On these occasions he is entertained lavishly for long periods of time and has various honors conferred on him. He may then be offered an appointment as a local god upon earth or as a higher official in the court of the Supreme Ruler. If especially deserving, he may ultimately be entitled to a place of eternal happiness in the Western Paradise.

However, the merits of the meritorious may be reduced because of a few misdeeds, just as the sinfulness of the infamous may be lightened as a result of good acts. The balance having been struck, both may be reincarnated in a form and with a fate that befits the evaluation of their previous existence.

The meritorious are reincarnated, according to the merits previously accumulated, into lives of various degrees of comfort and luxury. They may be predestined to pass the imperial examinations and enjoy the power, wealth, and prestige of an official, or to have filial sons and helpful friends who are especially diligent in the advancement of their welfare. The infamous are reincarnated, also according to the gradient of accumulated demerits, into a life of abject misery and poverty. They may be predestined to an existence marked by all forms of disasters, ending in violent death, or to lead the life of a beggar, an invalid beset by disease and constant pain, or an animal to be hunted and killed.[7]

These beliefs affect every area of Chinese life. A murderer being executed, a trader lost among wild tribes, or a concubine enduring the insults of her husband's first wife could all be suffering the consequences of misconduct in a previous existence, exactly as a scholar rising to the prime ministry, an official enjoying great wealth, or a father blessed with many sons are in part regarded as enjoying the rewards of exemplary behavior in their preceding incarnation.

In a way of life that values mutual dependence, the individual

never enjoys the sweets of life or drinks its bitter dregs alone. Therefore, those who do well may be reaping the fruits of their own previous life of virtue, or the blameless career of their parents or remote
ancestors, just as those who are in adverse circumstances may be
paying either for their own crimes and sins or for those of their forebears. Once this is understood, we are better prepared to compre-
hend why ancestor worship is fundamental to Chinese religious beliefs.

Ancestor Worship

Chinese ancestor worship should not be confused with what many
Westerners sometimes slightingly refer to as ancestor worship among
their Occidental fellows. This Western usage has reference to those
who, because of great pride in their pedigree, spare no effort or
money to trace their genealogy back to some early well-known pa-
triot or noble. These persons often add middle names such as Van-
derbilt, Astor, or Du Pont, which correspond to those of the famous
ancestor, or grace their own heirs with such honorifics. Or instead of
selecting new Christian names for their offspring, they prefer to in-
sure the continuity of the family name in full by calling the male descendants Stuyvesant Peabody IV or John R. Rutledge III. As for
the women, they join the Daughters of the American Revolution or
the Daughters of the Confederacy. Although these customs, so common in English and American life, superficially embody some sentiments similar to those found in Chinese ancestor worship, they
nevertheless are principally a token of social status not religious conviction.

Chinese ancestor worship is of an entirely different order from
such limited Western practices. I know of no Chinese, save the relatively few Christians and Moslems, who do not adhere to this cult. It
is literally the universal religion of China. More, it is the central link
between the Chinese world of men and their world of the spirits.
Ancestor worship not only specifically embodies all the general characteristics of the Chinese approach to the supernatural but, to the
Chinese, is itself positive proof and reinforcement of all their other
religious beliefs. Ancestor worship is an active ingredient in every aspect of Chinese society, from the family to the government, from local business to the national economy.

The Chinese have at least three basic assumptions about ancestor
worship. First, all living persons owe their fortunes or misfortunes to
their ancestors. A man may be a beggar because of his laziness, and

this fact may be well known to everyone in the community, but had his ancestors accumulated enough good deeds while they were alive, they probably never would have had such a lazy descendant. A great official may attain prominence by excellence of scholarship and strength of character, and everyone who knows him may testify to these virtues. But his very achievement is *de facto* evidence of his ancestors' high moral worth. Therefore, since the remotest times, the Chinese have said that their individual successes derived from the shadow of their ancestors and that their individual successes, in turn, shone upon their ancestors.

The second assumption of ancestor worship is that all departed ancestors, like other gods and spirits, have needs that are not different from those of the living. To prevent one's ancestors from degenerating into spiritual vagabonds, it is the duty of every man to provide for his departed ancestors just as faithfully as he provides for his parents while they are alive. Accordingly, the dead, to the limit of the male descendant's financial ability, must be offered food and life-sized paper models of clothing, furniture, sedan chairs, horses, donkeys, cows, and servants so that they may set up house in the other world. In the thirties, I saw paper rickshas and automobiles added to the age-old variety of offerings.

This concept explains why a Chinese man or woman who dies without male heirs is an object of public pity. For that person is doomed to an existence as a spirit tramp, depending entirely upon handouts from charitable families or consuming the leftovers of better situated spirits. The other-worldly presence of these spirit tramps is why those making offerings to their own ancestors on such occasions as the Ancestral Festival[8] also make a duplicate offering at public crossroads, so that their own ancestors may enjoy theirs in peace.

The third assumption is that the departed ancestors continue, as in life, to assist their relatives in this world just as their living descendants can also lend a hand to them. That is, a person's present lot may be improved by the spiritual efforts of departed ancestors, and the spiritual welfare or misery of a departed ancestor may likewise be enhanced or mitigated by the worldly actions of living descendants. The strength of this belief in a continuing "social tie" is attested to by many popular tales.

The following story is typical of those which indicate how the dead help the living. An imperial examiner was in his studio reading the examination papers of candidates for the great honors. As he reviewed them, he put the papers in two piles—those which he marked "consider again" and those which he decided to "flunk outright."

Beginning his perusal of the "consider again" pile, he picked up one which he was sure he had already discarded into the other group. He discarded it a second time. But a few moments later he came upon it once more in the "consider again" stack. Just when the annoyed examiner was about to discard it for the third time, a spirit appeared before him. They conversed, and the spirit convinced him that this particular paper, written by one of the spirit's great-grandchildren, deserved to be reconsidered. The examiner did so and passed the candidate. The burden of this tale was not that the examiner was forced to confer this imperial honor upon someone who was undeserving. On the contrary, the story made it clear that the spirit merely pointed out certain of the paper's qualities that the examiner had overlooked.[9]

More numerous than such stories are those depicting how ancestral spirits are assisted by their descendants. One of the most famous is entitled, *Mu Lien Rescues His Mother.* Mu Lien's mother was neither dutiful nor pious toward the gods. Even worse, she blasphemed the spirits and reviled monks and priests.[10] She ate meat on days when she had vowed to consume only fruits and vegetables. After death, following the infliction of every torture in the ten judges' courts, her soul lingered in one of the many hells. In the meantime, her son had become a monk and attained great spiritual power. Hearing that his mother was in trouble, he went to her rescue. After a search throughout the world of the spirits, he found her soul and eventually obtained its release from further torture.[11]

Evidence of this belief in interaction between the living and the dead is not confined to folklore. In all of the towns and villages where I visited or did research, it is the duty of the living to hire priests, monks, and nuns to perform elaborate services and scripture recitations in order to increase the spiritual welfare of the dead. Throughout the same communities, many men and women patronize mediums and attend seances to determine the situation and specific needs of recently departed relatives. Behind these investigations lay not mere inquisitiveness or an uncomplicated desire to communicate with the deceased. They wished to know about their departed ones' spiritual condition so that they could do something in the event it proved to be unsatisfactory.

The Chinese world of the spirits is, then, nearly an exact counterpart of the world of men. Structurally, the supernatural hierarchy is similar to that of the emperor and his bureaucracy, and the relationship of the living to the departed ancestors is akin to that which prevails in the intimate group of family members and relatives. Psychologically, the similarity is even more striking. The Chinese maintain a positive and close relationship with their departed ancestors just as they do with their living kinsmen, while their attitude toward the other gods is neutral and distant, reflecting their attitudes toward the emperor and his officials.

This projection of earthly relationship into the world beyond is highlighted by the fact that when an emergency of broad scope occurs—whether it be an epidemic, drought, or earthquake—the gods believed to be the source of the trouble, and other or stronger gods who may be of help, are placated with offerings, sacrifices, and prayers, but the ancestors are never appealed to on such occasions. Quite the opposite is the case. During any disaster, Chinese invariably ask the same priest who is pleading with the gods to perform additional rites for the benefit of those ancestors who may also be threatened by the same troublesome gods. The souls of departed ancestors are never thought of as being a menace to their own descendants, for the ancestral souls who are in a position to help will naturally do so without waiting for petitions from their descendants.

Therefore, while the Chinese attitude toward *all* inhabitants of the world of the spirits is characterized by a mutual dependence defined in terms of duties and obligations rather than of strong and individualized emotional involvement, that toward the departed souls of one's own ancestors and that toward all other gods and spirits are basically different. Two additional and recurrent customs symbolize this difference. Those readers who have visited a Chinatown in the United States or Canada on Chinese New Year's Day will undoubtedly associate it with firecrackers, dragon or lion dances, parades, and feasting. In China, only the first and last of these features are integral parts of this occasion, for the real significance is the reunion, not only among living members of the family, but also between the living and the dead. On this occasion, ancestral souls are ritually invited to the house while gods are not. A few days later they are ritually seen off. This ritual reunion with the ancestors is repeated on Ch'ing Ming, or what may be roughly designated the Chinese version of Easter, when members of all households visit the ancestral graveyards, clean the tombs, make offerings of food and incense, and share a picnic with the dead. This sharing of food is absent in the Chinese worship of other supernaturals.

Thus the Chinese dichotomizes his supernatural world in the same way he divides up reality. The souls of his ancestors stand apart from other spirits just as his kinsmen are distinct from all other humans, including rulers and heroes. It is for this reason that the worst imaginable plight for any Chinese is, while alive, to be without known parents and relatives, and, when dead, to be without living descendants. In the latter eventuality his position as a ghost will be like that of a Chinese who has no parents, no children, and no relatives.

As might be expected, mutual dependence runs through the Chinese idea of relationship with ancestral spirits and with other gods. A Chinese is as dependent upon his ancestors as the latter are upon him. He is also dependent upon the gods for protection and other forms of assistance which an authority can bestow, but the gods must look to him for provision and reverence. Many Chinese sayings imply how pitiable certain relatively minor and powerless gods must feel because for them the "incense and offerings are few and far between." But his ancestral spirits are in an inner circle with him far removed from the other gods, exactly as his parents and children are in an inner circle with him far removed from officials and heroes.

This Chinese conception is not usually understood in the West, especially by the naïve observer. For example, Colin Mackerras, an Australian who resided for two years in the People's Republic (1964–1966) as a teacher has the following to say about ancestor worship under communism:

> *I saw no trace of the survival of ancestor worship in the cities, but I am told that it is still found in the countryside. On the other hand, respect for the dead is still strongly encouraged by the Communists.* Indeed, Mao's most widely read article *Serve the People,* written in 1944, makes a special point of this. "From now on, when anyone in our ranks who has done some useful work dies, be he soldier or cook, we should have a funeral ceremony and a memorial meeting in his honour. This should become the rule. And it should be introduced among the people as well. When someone dies in a village, let a memorial meeting be held. In this way we express our mourning for the dead and unite all the people." Reverence for dead revolutionaries was very noticeable among my students.[12]

What Mao says here is not in support of ancestor worship as the Chinese have known and practiced it. In that Chinese practice *all* ancestral spirits will be honored and cared for by their *own* descendants *regardless of whether they were good or bad men.* In this instance, Mao's pronouncement goes directly counter to that Chinese view. Instead, it is entirely in line with Western attitudes toward the public hero, except that Communist heroes are likely to be "soldier or cook" rather than movie star or business tycoon. Mackerras quite correctly observes that "the Communists do not want to do away with the family"[13] but, as we shall see in Chapter 15, they are trying to achieve some important modifications of it which, if they are successful, portend far-reaching consequences.

The structural and psychological similarities between the two worlds are so great that the Chinese find their overlapping not at all bizarre. The absence of a clear-cut demarcation sometimes produces situations which to the Western mind are neither of a worldly nor godly nature, but which do not strike the Chinese as even "in-between" because of the interlinked nature of the two worlds in their minds. The ancestral tie involves more than just an association between the will of the spirits and the fate of a single human being, family, or kin group. The intrinsic principle of this tie even pervades the relationship between the individual and his community. The fortunes of the entire community, as noted previously, are not unaffected by the disposition of the gods who may be favorably inclined toward an entire district because of the special merit of one of its living or departed citizens. For example, an epidemic may be ended not only in response to mass prayer meetings but because of the merits of a highly virtuous individual who is a fellow townsman of the afflicted. In the same manner that the favorable wind and water of a locale contribute to an individual's success, so may his virtues and accomplishments be so magnificent as to raise the spiritual standing of his community.

Polytheism Versus Monotheism

Although studies in comparative religion have produced many classificatory systems in which to pigeonhole the religions of the world, the most basic and meaningful categories would appear to be monotheism, polytheism, and pantheism. Christianity, Judaism, and Islam are monotheistic religions; Hinduism and the Baha'i faith are pantheistic religions; while all other religions of the world are polytheistic. The characteristics of pantheism do not concern us here.[14] It is in the basic contrast between monotheism and polytheism that the profound differences between the Chinese and American approaches to the supernatural have their beginnings.

In a society where relationships tend to be exclusive rather than inclusive, where an attitude of "all or nothing" pervades every aspect of life, the worshiper finds in monotheism a religious doctrine compatible with secular life.

Christianity and Judaism, the two monotheistic religions most common in the West, are essentially individualistic religions that emphasize a direct link between the one and only God and the individual human soul. The more fervent the worshiper's belief in individual self-reliance, the stronger is his faith that there is only one omnipresent, omnipotent, and even omniscient (as in the tenets of the Christian Scientist's faith) God.[15] This being the case, by definition all other gods are false and evil idols to be eliminated at whatever cost.

On the other hand, in a society in which human relationships are inclusive rather than exclusive, and which are shared rather than monopolized, the worshiper finds polytheism to his liking. This religious outlook encourages not only a belief in many gods, but it emphasizes the coexistence of all supernatural beings. Taoism, Buddhism, and ancestor worship are essentially religions of the group. At one extreme, Buddhism preaches the negation of the individual. But the usual aim of the believer is to establish a satisfactory relationship will all spiritual forces, and the open and avowed reason is the achievement of specific human ends. Thus as man's activities extend and his purposes multiply, his gods become more numerous. In the minds of Chinese believers there is, therefore, no question of which gods are true and which false, and for this reason there are no grounds for religious contention.

Consequently, it is completely inaccurate to describe the Chinese —as social scientists, historians, and missionaries have done and still do—as Buddhists, Taoists, Confucianists, or ancestor worshipers in the same sense that we classify Americans as Jews, Protestants, or Catholics. The American *belongs* to a church or a temple, provides for its support, attends its services, and goes to its social meetings. Protestant differentiation, in turn, compels him to be a sectarian, such as a Presbyterian or a Baptist. Yet he must not only be a Baptist, but must choose between being a Baptist or a Southern Baptist. Finally he is not only a Baptist, but he is known also as a member of the First Baptist Church of Evanston, Illinois, or the Third Baptist Church of Jonesville, Ohio. For the American way in religion is to be more and more exclusive, so that not only is my God the only true God while all others are false, but I cannot rest until my particular view of God has prevailed over all others.

The Chinese tendency is exactly the reverse. The Chinese may go to a Buddhist monastery to pray for a male heir, but he may proceed from there to a Taoist shrine where he beseeches a god to cure him of malaria. Ask any number of Chinese what their religion is and the answer of the majority will be that they have no particular religion, or that, since all religions benefit man in one way or another, they are all equally good. Most Chinese temples, as we noted previously, are dedicated to the worship of many gods, and few family shrines are a sanctuary for only a single deity. There are many Chinese temples built expressly to house together Confucius, Buddha, and Lao Tze, the founder of Taoism. In "prayer" meetings to ward off a raging cholera epidemic staged by several southwestern Chinese communities during World War II, I saw included at many an altar the images of not only the numerous Chinese deities but also of Jesus Christ and Mohammed[16] as well. For the Chinese way in religion is to be more and more inclusive so that my god, your god, his god, and all gods, whether you or I know anything about them or not, must be equally honored or at least not be the objects of either my contempt or of yours.

These distinctive tendencies—the American tendency to exclude and the Chinese tendency to include—are fundamental, affecting as they do all other significant qualities in Chinese and American religious behavior. For example, the Chinese believer resorts little to prayers, but most pious Americans regard prayers as the essence of religious worship. Furthermore, even when a Chinese does pray, his utterances are little more then an express request for godly favors. On the other hand, the central focus of an American's prayers is introspection, a searching of the soul.[17] Given the Chinese type of polytheistic belief, in which the worshiper reveres and seeks the favors of the gods but does not link himself personally with them or regard himself as permanently committed to them, intensive personalized prayers are as incongruous as they are unnecessary.

By proceeding from our analysis of the two distinctive viewpoints we can also understand why in the Chinese religious conception, good and evil tend to be relative while to the religious American they are absolute. Of course, religion and ethics intertwine in China as they do elsewhere, and many gods will punish evil behavior among humans and reward the good. But although the polytheist holds some spirits to be evil, their evil is a matter of concern to him only if they hamper the work of the good spirits. Cholera epidemics are spread by *wen*-giving spirits that seek to enter every household. The great Wen God is then invoked to send the troublemakers away. In fact the *wen*-giving spirits and the Wen God may be one and the same. A drought is caused by demons called Han Pa. The Dragon God is then called upon to destroy them so that rain will fall. Once such practical ends are served, the Chinese has no further interest in the evil spirits until the next emergency occurs. Neither does he have any urge to wage an incessant war upon them. For all spirits, if propitiated in the right way, may be good to men, but any spirit, if displeased, may cause tragedy to befall them. This attitude is intrinsic to a belief system in which the worlds of the dead and the living are not only similar but overlap.

The monotheist holds one god to be good in contradistinction to all others who are by definition false and therefore evil. The followers of the one god not only refuse to compromise with that which is defined as false or evil, but his worshipers must seek out the false and evil and eliminate them. To the monotheist, being good is synonymous with fighting evil. Since the latter is a constant measure of the former, good and evil do not only coexist, but are at war with one another regardless of time or circumstance.[18] The wider context of this psychology is a life orientation in which the worlds of living and the dead are not only separate but also are completely different. This is in sharp contrast to the Chinese situation.

Yet all human beings, even monotheists, must of necessity explain their religious tenets in terms of thoughts and experiences that are familiar to the most humble of us. That is why terms like father, mother, children, marriage, or family are most commonly used everywhere in expressing man's relationships with gods, and in those of gods with one another. Polytheistic Chinese tend to go to one extreme in insisting on the similarity between the two worlds. That is why the inhabitants of a Taiwan village arranged a concubine for a local Earth God when the figure for the deity's wife disappeared from the temple. But monotheism, by its very nature, is further removed from such thoughts and experiences than is polytheism, and tends to lead to the other extreme of insisting on the total dissimilarity between the two worlds.

The Chinese believe that gods may be both good and evil, and that, while the wonderful things of the world are the gifts of the good deities, the illnesses and disasters that plague men come upon them either as punishments meted out by the good gods or through the maliciousness of the evil ones. A matter-of-fact belief like this is easily comprehended by even the least tutored and requires little explanation.

In contrast, Christians believe that God, who is the Creator of all things, is absolutely good, and while the kind, the virtuous, and the pure have their origin in Him, all evil, oppression, and strife result because men have failed to follow Him. Christ died to redeem all mankind yet waves of strife and atrocities have plagued and continue to plague followers of the same God or His only Son. In fact it is easy to see that many of the followers of God or His only Son have been and continue to be perpetrators of such strife and atrocities. These apparent inconsistencies are hard to reconcile even for the well educated. Faced with such basic difficulties, Americans (and Westerners in general) seek their solution through some single and simplified but all-embracing religious dogma. Once again their contrast with the Chinese is as pronounced as it is inevitable. Given the need for a constant war between the good and evil, the monotheist could not help but develop the perfect God at war with the irreparable demon; original sin hanging over all sexual love; and Immaculate Conception and the Virgin Birth symbolizing not only freedom from all biological constraints of life but also complete self-reliance.

Not being summoned to endless war between good and evil, the Chinese religious mythology pays little attention to antithetical forces. The well-known concepts of Yang and Yin underline the unity of the two, not their antithesis. It is true that according to one myth the Chinese people came from the incestuous marriage between the mythical ruler, Nu Wa, and her brother. Too, Lao Tze, the alleged founder of Taoism, was popularly supposed to have been conceived by a virgin mother who remained pregnant for eighty years. He was, therefore, very old when born and hence his name which means "the old master."

Folklorists have conjectured that Nu Wa was the same as Noah, and the Lao Tze's virgin birth and the concept of original sin had a common origin. But it is significant that, in spite of the fact that in China sexual misbehavior has for centuries headed the list of all evils and virginity has always been the most valuable asset of the unmarried woman, neither of these myths assumed any importance in Chinese religion.

The fact that the Chinese maintain a relativistic view of good and evil, virtue and sin, life and death, while the American view is absolutist, explains why the Chinese speak of "rescuing" *(chiu)* the soul, but Americans and other Westerners emphasize "saving" it.[19] To the Chinese, whose firm psychological and social roots lie in the primary groups, gods are needed only for specific and practical purposes. The

believer is not irretrievably committed to any or all of the gods and
he does not stand or fall with them. Since the god-worshiper relationship is temporary rather than permanent, and practical rather than
emotional, the Chinese tends to invoke his gods only when he needs
them. Because his gods are not omnipresent, the Chinese fails to
make a precise differentiation between crime, violation of the laws of
man, and sin, disobedience of the will of the gods. Offenses punishable by the gods tend to coincide with those punishable by the society
because the characteristics of the gods are akin to those of the emperor and his officials. According to Chinese belief, therefore, neither condemnation to hell nor elevation to paradise is permanent. A
good spirit can be demoted if he does the wrong thing, and a sinner
can be rescued from further torture if his descendants behave in the
proper way.

To the American, a permanent god, who provides the worshiper
with a source of support and a sense of security, is one way of solving
his dilemma caused by his lack of irrevocable social and psychological ties in life and every individual's inability to "go it alone." For
this very reason, the believer stands or falls with God. He is saved if
he has God, but he is lost if he does not. Crimes and sins tend to have
two centers of orientation because the former revolve around the
laws and customs of the group, while the latter are a matter intimately tied to the individual conscience. The hell in Western faiths is
therefore by and large a place to which a sinner's soul is irretrievably
committed in the same manner that the soul of the worthy resides in
paradise throughout eternity.[20]

Given the differences between soul saving and soul rescuing, between an irretrievable identification with one god and a generalized
relationship with diverse deities, and between believers who stand
and fall with one god and those who have no particular concern with
the fortunes of their deities, it is natural for Western monotheism to
be given to missionary activities, while Chinese polytheism has no
similar inclinations or venture.[21]

America, despite her presumed materialist outlook, has led the
West in this form of enterprise. There is, however, no contradiction
here, for where, as in the American way, God's success is necessarily
identified with the individual believer's success, the individual must
contribute to the overall success of God in order to protect his own
security but especially to enhance his prestige.[22] Conversely, where,
as in the Chinese way, the gods' success has meaning only with refer-

ence to specific needs such as relief when illness or disaster strikes, the individual's personal security and status are not threatened by other people's rejection of any or all of his gods. This is why the Chinese find it difficult to understand the exertions and commitment of Western missionaries. At great personal sacrifice and for many years, missionaries are thousands of miles from home, and in these far-off lands they often live under the most trying conditions for the sole purpose of bringing non-Christians into the fold. But the life stories of many great Western missionaries are impressive not only because of their dedication and self-sacrifice. Some contributed greatly to numerous advances among non-European peoples: better educational facilities, more measures for the protection of health, the alleviation of social evils (such as foot-binding in China), and a general awakening to the danger of being industrially backward in the modern world. No polytheists have ever labored in these ways to such an extent and with such determination.

But it is also unfortunately true that monotheistic missionaries have often resorted to anything but Christian measures when dealing with those who were not of their faith. For the "heathens," "pagans," or dissenters present a twofold threat to the missionaries' basic security and status. On one level, the superiority of their own Western culture and purpose is at stake, for the monotheistic missionary does not only assert the unquestioned superiority of his creed but of most, or even all, other aspects of his own way of life, from table manners and clothing to the conduct of education, marital arrangements, and business. This is not simply a superficial desire to see the heathen copy the outward aspects of Western culture; for if sex is evil then the Pacific islander must clothe his loins, and if cleanliness is next to godliness then the true believer must be sanitary as well as go to church.

This conviction that the missionary's total culture is superior has not been peculiar to those propagating Christianity. Ibn Fadhlan, a tenth-century Moslem missionary proselytizing among a settlement of Scandinavian merchants near the Baltic, described the behavior of his charges as that of "asses who have gone astray."[23] What he found particularly loathsome was their uncleanliness, their indiscreet sexual behavior, and their erotic rites of human sacrifice. But even missionaries who sincerely profess love and admiration for the peoples among whom they work rarely succeed in concealing their own sense of superior people being gracious to inferiors. And if the inferiors refuse to accept the monotheistic missionary's god, they are thereby repudiating the superiority of his very way of life—a situation which few monotheists can tolerate.

On a second level, the missionary's personal security and status are endangered by the nonbeliever's reluctance to accept the monotheistic god. For a monotheistic missionary's essential wish is to have others joined to him in that faith which is his psychological security and his social anchorage—mooring points that the polytheistic Chinese find in other spheres. Because the success of the missionary is inextricable from that of his faith, when the "pagans" or "heathens" refuse to heed the missionary's god, they are threatening the core of the missionary's psychological well-being.

However, this threat is a passive one because the polytheist has no desire to impose his beliefs on others or even to react violently to those who would impose their religious ways upon him. It is for this reason that the religious differences between the missionary and the pagan are rarely resolved by bloodshed, but those between different monotheistic creeds and denominations that worship the same god have often led to wars of extermination and prolonged periods of mass persecution.[24] The Christian-Moslem struggles, the Christian-Jewish struggles, the Moslem-Jewish struggles, and the Catholic-Protestant struggles have left their scars everywhere and today still inflict new divisive wounds throughout the world.

As for what happens when missionaries of diverse faiths attempt to convert a pagan land, the Catholic-Protestant strife in Hawaii is a graphic example. Protestants first came to these islands around 1820; the Catholics arrived about five years later. Because the Protestants were established with the Hawaiian royalty, between 1827 and 1850 there was a series of anti-Catholic measures and incidents in the islands. The Catholics claimed that these moves were instigated by the Protestant missionaries, and the Protestant missionaries tried to explain that the initiative lay entirely in the hands of Hawaiian natives who could not in good conscience reconcile their new-found beliefs with the Catholic faith. Perhaps more illuminating than the disputants' arguments is a resolution adopted by "The General Meeting of the Sandwich Island Mission" on January 30, 1830. In this resolution the Protestant mission declared that the Jesuits were dangerous to the islands' civil government, exerted a deadly influence in drawing souls away from God's word, hindered the progress of civilization and literature, and were enemies of sound morality and the true faith of Jesus Christ. The resolution then proceeded in the following vein:

We do not consider it persecution in the least degree when the chiefs ask our advice or opinion on the subject, fairly to tell them in our estimation the Jesuits as a body are dangerous to the civil, moral and religious prosperity of the Islands. But that we advised the chiefs not to inflict any punishment upon them or upon those who followed them on account of any part of their religion; but if they break the laws of the land, that they may be punished for that alone.[25]

Mr. Sidney Gulick, in whose book this was recorded and himself a Protestant missionary, declared that this resolution was solid evidence that the Protestant missionaries were not responsible for all the important anti-Catholic uprisings from 1827 until 1850. But the impartial reader of this very document cannot but come to a totally different conclusion. The Hawaiian chiefs, who looked to the early Protestant missionaries for religious guidance, were advised in this document that Jesuits were venomous creatures and then were told that if they chose to do so they could leave these dangerous men and their followers alone. There is little likelihood that any magistrate, civil or ecclesiastic, pagan or Christian, would sit on his hands after his trusted counselors had presented him with such a horrifying picture. The advice that the chiefs should punish anyone for breaking the law of the land is even more revealing. One is tempted to wonder what the chiefs did with those who broke the law of the land before such advice was given by the missionaries.

It must not be thought, however, that religious trouble has been altogether absent among the polytheistic Chinese. There have been conflicts between Chinese and Moslems at various times, and there was a great furor of Chinese opposition to Buddhism between A.D. 700 and A.D. 955. But when we analyze the Chinese-Moslem difficulties we usually find their source to be the attempt of Moslem leaders to aggrandize themselves or the expansionist ambitions of Chinese dynastic rulers. There was little tension among the common people who adhered to different faiths. In China proper, in Manchuria, and in Taiwan, Chinese Moslems and non-Moslems live side-by-side with no visible tension among them. They intermarry, with the usual proviso that a non-Moslem girl may marry into a Moslem household, but a Moslem girl may not marry into a non-Moslem household. This one restriction exists becuase it is possible for a non-Moslem girl to observe the food taboo in a Moslem household, but a Moslem girl entering a non-Moslem household would find it difficult to follow the dietary practices of her faith.

The nature of the objections to Buddhism in the T'ang dynasty are more instructive. They were three in number. First, the monks did not marry, and yet they had contacts with women worshipers. Therefore Buddhism was an invitation to immorality. Second, the monks did not work and had to be supported by others. Therefore they were an economic burden upon the community. Third, the monks forsook all family connections and did not practice ancestor worship. Therefore the spirits of their ancestors would become vagabond spirits, thus creating difficulties for normal souls. As is obvious, the objections had nothing to do with the question of the truth or falsehood of the new belief.

During the period in question, this opposition to Buddhism produced what might be called religious persecution. But this Chinese persecution had characteristics of its own wholly distinct from those of its Western counterpart. For example, at one time the reigning emperor was very much devoted to Buddha. When he decided to dispatch a special delegation to India to procure Buddha's relics, the great Han Yu, of whom we spoke in the previous chapter, was among the high ministers to oppose him. Han Yu was punished by demotion. Later, more furor resulted when another reigning emperor was opposed to Buddhism. But his reason for it was that rebels were using the new creed as cover and its temples as refuge.

The pattern of the emperor's persecutory actions followed that of his definition of the situation. First, he required all monks and nuns to be registered and regulated to make sure they were bona fide religious functionaries. Next, he stipulated that "only two temples with thirty monks each were permitted to stand in each of the two capitals, Ch'angan and Loyang. Of the 228 prefectures in the empire, only the capital cities of the 'first-grade' prefectures were permitted to retain one temple each with ten monks."[26] Finally, temples in excess of the permitted number were destroyed while monks and nuns in excess of the permitted number were forced to revert to civilian life. In this way, thousands of temples were destroyed and nearly a quarter of a million religious functionaries left the temples.

Thus in contrast to Western persecutors, the T'ang authorities did not attempt to stamp out Buddhism. They did not execute Buddhists or root out lingering Buddhist faith or practices by inquisition among those who had left it or were never part of it. The Chinese ruler's views and actions were neither followed up nor preceded by mob attacks against Buddhists or by mass revivals of other faiths to compete for the stray souls. Finally, and this is most important evidence of the Chinese approach to religion, the monks and nuns who were required to revert to secular life did not resist the governmental order, so that the ruler's wishes prevailed without the need for imprisonment, exile, or execution. The latter in particular signifies how profoundly the Chinese approach to religion differs from that of the West—where men have gone to the stake for much less than was required of these T'ang monks and nuns. Is there any wonder, then, that while religious tension and persecution are a continuing ingredient of Western culture, Chinese opposition to Buddhism was limited to four occurrences within a mere two centuries of her long history?

In the modern era, the Boxer Uprising of 1900, in which Western missionaries and Chinese Christians suffered a heavy toll, may be interpreted as a form of religious persecution. But this is not a full explanation. In the first place, the object of the uprising was not strictly religious, for it was aimed at all foreigners and all Chinese who were associated in any way with them. In the second place, the Boxer Uprising must be compared with its predecessor, the T'aip'ing Rebellion in the middle of the nineteenth century, and its successor, the revolution led by Sun Yat-sen in this century. The T'aip'ing event and the Sun Yat-sen revolution differed from the Boxer affair in that their aim was to overthrow the Manchu rulers and to restore China to the Chinese, while the Boxers sought to assist the Manchus in expelling the foreigners. All three were but a part of a long series of reactions that took place at a time when the people were under severe economic, social, and political strains. The missionaries were the scapegoats in 1900, but the Manchus were the principal targets of the other two struggles. In characteristic Chinese fashion, the Boxer storm blew over in an even shorter time than did the earlier anti-Buddhist episode.

When one compares this kind of persecution with the kind that has characterized the great monotheistic religions of the West, he is left with the feeling that if the latter are tragic dramas in the classic mold, the Chinese affairs are but one-act trifles.

Previously we mentioned the monotheist's need for a single, simplified, but all-embracing religious dogma to counterbalance the many apparent inconsistencies in his belief. However, the combative nature of all monotheistic religions is perhaps an even more important reason why they must be armored with an elaborate theology and why they are intolerant of other belief systems. Convinced that their religious concepts are the only true ones, and that truth must conquer not only other creeds that are wholly wrong but those heresies that develop within the same creed, monotheists must be equipped for attack and for defense. Under the impression that their own objects or forms of worship neither threaten nor are threatened by those of another people, even their national enemies, the polytheists feel no need for the armaments of theological battle. Thus, whether we look at Judaism, Christianity, or Islam, we find in each not only a definite group of scriptures as the Bible or the Koran, but also a large body of literature devoted to the extension, interpretation, and exemplification of the original dogmas, and all of these are elaborated in theological seminaries, universities, and elsewhere. Fierce sermons and other forms of dialectic exposition are indispensable parts of such a faith.

The polytheistic religions are not usually enriched by a systematic theology. Even the Chinese, who have a long written history and a highly developed written language, have but a fragmentary and meager theology. There were never any Chinese theological seminaries, nor were sermons or discussions ever intrinsic to Chinese religious activities. Confucianism is the only exception. The Analects of the sage have, it is true, been annotated, taught, and reinterpreted throughout the last twenty centuries. But, significantly for the scholars who thus engaged themselves, Confucius was not a god and Confucianism was not a religion. To the illiterate majority who paid homage to Confucius in the same manner that they honored other deities, the systematically interpreted Confucian classics possessed no meaning.

Furthermore, even when the founder of a polytheistic religion provides it with a systematic set of doctrines, his teaching becomes less and less systematic and more and more neglected as time goes on. This is what happened to Buddhism. Between the sixth and seventh centuries A.D., approximately three thousand Chinese believers traveled on foot to India for the sole purpose of obtaining the complete teachings of Buddha. The journey was so arduous that only a couple of hundred lived to reach their destination and only a handful of these eventually succeeded in returning to China with the treasured manuscripts. It was this journey that was the subject of the fantasy, *Western Journey,* which was discussed in Chapter 1. But the theology brought to China remained an object of study for a few sophisticated monks and lay believers. The refined doctrines never became generally known to the majority of Chinese who, in one way or another, have been affected by Buddhism. There was little effort on the part of the pious to pass them on nor was there any demand on the part of the public, literate or illiterate, to learn.

The Bible, however, has had a far different history. The battle to make the Bible and rituals accessible to all believers was a principal feature of the Protestant Reformation. For centuries, the Bible has been and is still a best-seller in Europe and America. It is published in a wider variety of editions than any other book.[27] The Bible is found in the majority of homes and even hotels; but it is a rare Chinese home which contains a copy of some Buddhist scripture. Chinese hotels, never.

All of these characteristics that differentiate polytheism from monotheism are interrelated. On one side stands the polytheistic Chinese with his continuing primary relations that even include the souls of his deceased ancestors as distinguished from all other supernatural beings, his nonintrospective prayers, his relativistic distinction between good and evil and between the living and the dead, his concept of rescuing the soul rather than saving it, his "live and let live" attitude toward other faiths and his lack of interest in theology and sermons.

Polytheistic Chinese rarely discuss religious unity because they see no need for such a religious concept, and they do not stress tolerance because intolerance is alien to their religious thought. The Chinese have no significant problems of unity or intolerance because their attitude toward the supernatural is essentially the same as the attitudes they traditionally assume toward their heroes and their government: their gods may be beneficial or harmful, good or bad, cooperative or hard to handle, but if one god is destroyed or falls out of favor, they simply select another. The Chinese react to the rise and fall of their gods as they do to the ascendancy or collapse of their dynasties. The Chinese philosophy is: whoever be the gods, we shall revere them and make adequate offerings. The great popularity of certain gods is the gods' glory; the Chinese believer has little sense of sharing the spotlight. Similarly the general neglect of certain gods is the gods' misfortune or the misfortune of those who neglect them. The pious Chinese is not threatened.

On the other side is the monotheistic American with his anxiety to achieve independence from his parents, which leaves each person to his own devices; his emphasis on individualized and introspective prayers; his rigid dichotomy between good and evil and between the living and the dead; his concept of the necessity for permanent conversion rather than a temporary change of heart; his missionary zeal, and his elaborate theology and eloquent sermons.

Further, an insistence on monotheism affects not merely the believer but generates agnosticism and especially atheism. The believer is absolutely committed to his god as the atheist is absolutely certain of the nonexistence of all supernatural powers. There is no possible ground for coexistence or accommodation between them. In the polytheistic way, the worshiper has little compulsion to decry the nonworshiper, but the nonworshiper's view is, why risk the wrath of gods and spirits?

NOTES

1. The reader may recall the case of Magistrate Han who ended a crocodile epidemic by a combination of pleas and threats addressed to these pillagers of his domain. As we noted then, his authority proceeded from the emperor. But, in turn, the emperor's authority came from the Supreme Ruler of Heaven. Thus in a roundabout fashion, Magistrate Han acted as the plenipotentiary of the Supreme Ruler. This consistency, however, was not necessarily reflected upon by the Chinese believer or nonbeliever who witnessed Han's ceremony.

2. An official "matchmaker" is included in most Chinese weddings whether or not the person actually introduced the bride and groom to each other.

3. Fang Ts'un, "The Wedding of a God," *Central Daily News,* Taipei, February 23, 1965.

4. No diviner, to the best of my knowledge, ever got into trouble with the law for having made such displays, and this practice is not to be confused with the American advertising psychology discussed in Chapter 6. The Chinese diviners wish to convince their prospective customers that their predictions were "accurate," and used Chiang as living "proof." They were not suggesting that these potential customers, by buying their goods, would somehow lead Chiang's life. On the other hand, American mouthwash or toothpaste advertisements are designed to suggest that the product will enable its users to be as fortunate as the girl on the television screen.

5. The Catholic church's custom of beatifying meritorious men and women to sainthood is similar to this, but the power of beatification in the Catholic church is a prerogative of the pope, while the Chinese custom is a popular matter. Any group of local people can decide to honor a meritorious man or official in this way. Another difference is that whereas sainthood was abolished by the Protestants, the Chinese custom has continued to this day. The only challenge to it has come from the West in modern times.

6. There is a display in the Chinese section of the Field Museum of Natural History, Chicago, of a partial representation of these tortures in papier-mâché.

7. There is evidence that ancient China lacked the notion of reincarnation, which came to the Middle Kingdom with Buddhism from India. But that is not the point. The idea took such deep root because it fits in with the Chinese cultural context. In contrast, the notion of Christian individual conversion never had much of a chance in that context, as we shall see in Chapter 10.

8. On the fifteenth of the Seventh Moon, according to the lunar calendar, somewhat similar to Western All Souls' Day.

9. Candidates who did not have such capable ancestral spirits to look after their welfare were simply the unfortunate ones.

10. Although monks and priests enjoyed no high social esteem, this woman's behavior was excessive.

11. The reader will note that I use the word "rescue" instead of the word "save." To the Chinese, Mu Lien was truly rescuing his mother from trouble, just as one would rescue a drowning person. There is no implication that his mother's soul was in any way converted and then saved. By virtue of the monk's great spiritual power, his mother was entitled to more favorable treatment regardless of the state of her soul.

12. Colin Mackerras and Neale Hunter, *China Observed*, pp. 18–19. (Italics mine.)

13. Ibid., p. 19.

14. Readers interested in the subject will find a discussion in my book, *Clan, Caste and Club.*

15. One common Western notion about religion is, of course, that man felt he was too weak to rely on himself alone. But this, as we shall see presently, becomes no more than a mental relic from the past and a euphony to hide the self-reliant man's immodesty as the American way of religion unfolds itself.

16. In spite of the fact that Islam forbids displays of idols or the images of the prophet. Over thirty years after I observed these prayer meetings in Yunnan Province I saw the same rituals lasting four days and five nights in the New Territories, Hong Kong, in the winter of 1975. In this instance the epidemic in question was bubonic plague, but it was a plague that had occurred many years before. The local population had promised the gods that, if they eliminated the dreaded plague, the people would stage one such prayer meeting in their honor every ten years. Nineteen seventy-five happened to be the tenth year of one such ten-year cycle. In the Western sense of the term these were not prayer meetings. The Chinese call them *chiao;* they embrace food and money offerings, the burning of incense and candles, reciting of scriptures, written and oral petitions, rituals to compel the evil spirits' departure, parades, and more, all done by hired priests (see Hsu, *Religion, Science and Human Crises*).

17. One branch of Buddhism, Zen, does emphasize meditation and introspection. But in this instance, meditation and introspection are for the purpose of reaching Nirvana, the highest goal of the religion, at which point the individual "removes" himself from all existence, sacred as well as profane. It is to be emphasized that this is a negation rather than a "rediscovery" of self. Only a few outstanding or learned Chinese devotees have ever taken Zen Buddhism seriously in the sectarian sense, and it has no meaning to the majority of Chinese who worship before any variety of Buddhist gods. In this and other respects China and Japan have developed along divergent lines. (These differences and their explanations are presented in my book, *Iemoto: The Heart of Japan.*)

18. In a post-Jonestown massacre press conference in the Peoples Temple at San Francisco Mark Lane, a lawyer of the Temple, said of Jones: "If you cannot be God, you don't fall back to the rank and file. . . . If you win, you're Moses, if you lose, you're Charles Manson." ("The Cult of Death," *Newsweek* December 4, 1978, p. 53.)

19. This basic distinction has not been understood by researchers on China. An example of this failure and consequent misreading of Chinese psychology is found in Wolfram Eberhard, *Guilt and Sin in Traditional China*, p. 20, *et seq.* The absence of this distinction in Western minds is underlined by the fact that, according to Webster's dictionary, "rescue" and "save" (the soul) are synonyms. The Chinese translators of the Bible coined the new term *teh chiu* for the Christian concept of salvation.

20. The difference between hell and the Catholic concept of purgatory will be taken up in the next chapter.

21. Judaism today has no missionary activities although it accepts converts. This, however, was not its original intent according to Rabbi Henry Fisher of Congregation B'nai Zion in Chicago, who explained:

"Ancient Judaism definitely believed in proselytization. The idea that is found in the beginning of the second chapter of Isaiah is found practically in all of the Prophets—that in the end of days, Mount Zion will be the world's religious center and all nations will draw unto it, and that the religion of Israel will be accepted by the whole world.

"Obviously, after the destruction of the second temple, when the Jewish people went into exile, it ill behooved them to talk about proselytization and missionary work. A minority scattered throughout the world, subjected to great persecution as they were, could not very well urge proselytization or engage in it.

"In the middle ages, the Church made it a penalty for any Jew to try and convert someone to Judaism. It is interesting that despite that, we had any number of instances of people who became Jews, and history records a whole group of people known as Khazrs in the seventh century converting to Judaism.

"There has been some expression on the part of some Jewish leaders that perhaps we ought to engage in active proselytization. The thesis there is: We lost six million, or one-third of our people as a result of the Nazi persecution, and perhaps we ought to replenish our number. So far it has been merely an expression and nothing at all has been done about it" (personal communication, 1953).

Rabbi Alexander Schindler, president of the Union of American Hebrew Congregations which represents 730 Reform synagogues, has recently (1979) come out more forcefully in favor of Jewish proselytization, and claims to have the support of many members of his group. Speaking at a news conference at the Fairmont Hotel in San Francisco he noted that while Judaism was a missionary religion before the Roman Empire, ". . . it was drummed out of us by repressive legislation. They would burn people at the stake who were Jews or who wanted to become Jews, and that cooled evangelical ardor pretty quickly." What Rabbi Schindler wants is for the Jews to reverse their centuries-old tradition against proselytization. Marc H. Tanenbaum, a Conservative rabbi who supports Schindler, says the missionary movement should concentrate on the estimated 60 million people in the United States who are not affiliated with any church or synagogue. Schindler believes Jewish missionary work will soon be accepted throughout the nation (reported in *San Francisco Chronicle,* October 27, 1979).

22. It is not unnatural that the reports of the missionary activities of any church board or council usually accentuate two things: (a) the number of missionaries and (b) the amount of money spent, with particular emphasis on the increase in both items for one year over the last year.

23. "The Vikings Abroad and at Home" in Carleton S. Coon, *A Reader in General Anthropology* (New York, 1948), p. 411.

24. These conflicts were, of course, not caused by religion. But the important thing is that the conflicts were publicly defined as religious, and wars and persecutions were carried out in the name of religion. In modern times Americans tend continuously to inject religion into the Cold War between the United States and the Soviet Union—so that it appears in the minds of many to be a struggle between those who worship God and those who are godless. It was no accident that President Eisenhower's book on his experiences in World War II was entitled *Crusade in Europe.*

25. Sidney L. Gulick, *Mixing the Races in Hawaii,* p. 140.

26. Hu Shih, "Ch'an (Zen) Buddhism in China: Its History and Method." *Philosophy East and West,* p. 17.

27. Since the first edition of this book saw print some thirty years ago, the Catholic church has changed much of its liturgy into English, Spanish, and other vernacu-

lars. In 1978 *The New International Version,* an American-inspired translation of the Bible, was published by Britain's 175-year-old Bible Society. This is the eighth new translation of the Bible into English since World War II. Nine months after its American publication the new version had sold two million copies in the United States. Reporter Gregory Jensen says: "Printing the Bible always has been profitable. It is a publisher's dream, producing sales figures which make Shakespeare and Agatha Christie and the biggest paperback heroes look like non-starters" (*Honolulu Advertiser,* August 18, 1979). The Episcopalians also came up with a modernized prayer book in 1979 (*Time,* August 13, 1979). Both the changeover in the Catholic liturgy and the new Episcopalian prayer book have led to much internal dissension within each church group.

CHAPTER 10

The Bases
of Religious
Faith

One key question remains to be answered: How can we be sure that the Chinese or American way in religion is not a consequence of the nature of the respective creeds themselves rather than an outgrowth of the two people's cultural orientation? In other words, isn't the Chinese tolerant of other faiths because his creed is polytheistic while the American is religiously intolerant because his creed is monotheistic? Perhaps the best way to determine the causal relationship, and so answer these questions, is to see what happens when a Chinese comes under the influence of some monotheistic religion and what occurs when a Westerner professes an interest in a polytheistic faith.

"Willing to Be a Methodist"

We have seen, in a previous connection, that Chinese opposition to Buddhism endured but briefly, and that Buddhist scriptures were never systematically studied and reinterpreted by any large number of Chinese believers. There were few translations of the original scriptures, and even this slight display of enthusiasm seems to have evaporated within two centuries of the scriptures' arrival in China. Furthermore, even professional Taoist priests think nothing of taking Buddhist roles in their ritual performances. This fate was not reserved exclusively for Buddhism. To varying degrees, this fusion of two or more religions occurred also with reference to monotheistic faiths when they arrived in China.

In ancient times, a small colony of Jews settled in China, mainly in the northern province of Honan. Very little is known about their origin except that they arrived via Persia and India in the Middle Kingdom long before the year A.D. 1163. They sinicized their names, adopted the Chinese language, clothing, customs, and learned the Confucian literature and philosophy with such proficiency that a disproportionate number of them achieved high honors in the imperial examinations and went on to hold important administrative posts in government. They intermarried with the Chinese, usually a Jewish husband with a Chinese wife, and all their women (according to photographs taken in the early twentieth century) had bound feet. One Jew, who lived about the middle of the seventeenth century, married six wives, five of whom were Chinese. Western missionaries, some of whom were sent by the "London Society for Promoting Christianity among the Jews," found them worshiping ancestors and participating in non-Jewish rites. Their synagogue was intact until the middle of the nineteenth century when a recurrent flood of the Yellow River destroyed it, and the Jews became either too poor or too uninterested to rebuild it. These facts led Reverend William Charles White, who lived in the city of K'aifeng for twenty-five years and was at one time Bishop of Honan (Canadian London Mission) to conclude:

> The one continuous disappointment in this association was the fact that no spark of interest in their history and in the divine heritage of Israel could be aroused in them; they were Jews no longer, either in a religious sense, or even as a community.[1]

Chinese Moslems, both original immigrants from the Middle East and their Chinese converts, are much more numerous. Large numbers of them are concentrated in the northwest but they are found also in every part of the country. They maintain certain customs of their faith such as circumcision, observe the taboo on pork, and worship in mosques but, in the words of a great missionary and scholar, K. S. Latourette, "they are not at all fanatical."[2] Many Moslem rituals have been modified to suit Chinese circumstances. During an epidemic or a drought, Moslems in many communities join in the non-Moslem population in various rituals that would be described as pagan by other Moslems and Christians alike. Chinese Moslems who became officials of the imperial government participated in the state religion, that of worshiping the Supreme Ruler of Heaven. Mohammed himself has often been represented as a sage of Confucianism and as a deity conforming to the Confucian values.

Christianity has had a far more ostentatious time in China than either of the other two monotheistic faiths. In spite of a thousand years of missionary work, backed up during the last century by gunboats and extraterritoriality, and despite the intense desire of many Chinese, principally the most influential, to imitate the West, Christianity has made little headway among the Chinese. According to the most optimistic estimates, including that of the World Council of Churches, less than 1 percent of the Chinese population was nominally Christian in 1949, the year of the ascension of Communist power in China.

It is true also that the deeply pious, by Western standards, do not form the majority of even this very small group of Chinese Christians. In 1947 a resident of Peking wrote a short piece on "how to conquer poverty" in response to the call of a newspaper for true experiences in regard to this always pressing matter. This respondent described in some detail how he did it by joining the Catholic church, where he found food and shelter for his family. With reference to another letter writer, he said, in part:

> I would like to offer my own experience. About twenty years ago I was in a similar plight. Then the times were good.[3] I had a big family, I had no selling skill and I was unfit as a heavy manual laborer. So a friend introduced me to the Catholic Church at————, where they have a Women's Home. I took my wife and three small children to this Home to pledge their faith in the creed [Catholicism]. I did some work elsewhere. I visited them once a week, bringing them some gift every time. In that enclosure they studied characters, learned the scriptures, and worshipped God. At first they were very unhappy and bored. But after some days they felt all right. They got to know other inmates and fell in with the routine. The children no longer craved for home, since they had lots of other children to play with. They had three meals a day. The food was not too good, but having lived in poverty, that was not unbearable. Those women who had nursing babies usually got a little more food. Generally a person could be eligible for Baptism three months after admission. There was no male in the home. All teachers and other officers were nuns. Boys over six years of age were not admitted. Those admitted did not have to bring their own bedding.
>
> In short, this is one of the ways of meeting an emergency. Just get baptized and don't worry about the rest. The proverb says: "The Supreme Ruler of Heaven will not starve even a blind sparrow." He will certainly not starve us, who are human beings, the most exalted of all living creatures, and are all children of God.
>
> Another way out is to go to the Relief Department of the Bureau of Social Welfare of the Municipal Government.
>
> P. L. Liu
> No. 68, Chaint Yang Fang
> Fifth Police Area, Peiping[4]

The important thing to be noted here is not that a certain Chinese by the name of Liu turned out to be a rice-bowl Christian, for it is not difficult to find Americans who take an active role in church out of ulterior motives. What is important is that Mr. Liu thought it perfectly natural to state his ulterior motives for joining the church, sincerely presented his case as an example for others to follow, and unabashedly gave his name and address at the end of his public communication. Furthermore, there was not a single subsequent denunciation of Mr. Liu.

Mr. Liu's realistic attitude toward the church was later paralleled by a Chinese student who applied for financial assistance to the scholarship committee of Northwestern University. She was deserving in view of both her scholastic record and her material need, but the thing that baffled the committee members was the fact that in the space on the application inquiring about the applicant's religion,[5] she wrote: "Willing to Be a Methodist." Because the university had been founded as a Methodist institution, the committee thought the girl was either being frivolous or, even worse, trying to become a rice-bowl Christian. But neither Mr. Liu of Peking nor the Chinese student at Northwestern was frivolous, nor were they ashamed of what Westerners would describe as their mercenary attitude toward Christianity. For their attitude sprang from the Chinese approach to religion; it has its counterparts wherever one looks among the Chinese. For example, most Chinese Christians think little of going through two wedding ceremonies, one to satisfy their church and one to please their parents and relatives, just as many Chinese families for similar reasons undertake two funerals for the dead.

This pattern survives among the Chinese in Hawaii. Many Chinese born and raised in Hawaii today are Christians. Yet, frequently members of the same family belong to different churches. A Methodist father may have a Catholic son, an Episcopalian daughter, and a "heathen" wife who worships at Chinese temples. Nor do differences in religion seem to hamper family solidarity. A Christian son does not hesitate to participate in the rituals at the Chinese temples if his "pagan" mother requests him to do so.

In 1978 my wife and I attended two New Year feasts in Honolulu. The first was marked by old Cantonese festivities though most of the participants and invited guests were second and third generation Chinese-Americans as well as members of various Christian churches. The other was marked by a mixture of traditional Chinese New Year rituals begun with a Christian prayer and nearly all of the assembled were recent immigrants from Taiwan or Hong Kong. The prayer was said by the president of the Taiwan College of Nursing. In both cases numerous children were present, another old Chinese custom.

In brief, when Chinese assume a monotheistic faith they tend to treat it in a polytheistic spirit. They do not absorb the hostility which characterizes the approach of Western monotheists to other sects of the same creed as well as to all other faiths.

When Westerners take up a polytheistic religion such as Buddhism, it is typical for them to describe themselves defiantly as Buddhists, but nothing else; they then consider Buddha as the only true god, all other gods being mere idols. Furthermore, they are in great haste to initiate religious controversies about Buddhism. One of these long-standing controversies has revolved around the problem of which of two versions of the Buddhist teachings is the "authentic" one.

It will be recalled that Buddha's teachings not only failed to arouse controversy in China but that they were of no interest to the majority of Chinese in a theological sense. In the hands of Western believers, however, the same teachings were highly systematized and elaborately interpreted. The Europeans could not be satisfied until they uncovered the "original" and "pure" teachings of Buddha. In rough form, the basis of their still undecided dispute is as follows. At the time when Buddha lived, the people of his native Indian state spoke two languages. Sanskrit was the learned language used by the elite, while Pali was the colloquial tongue of the plebeians. The situation was comparable to that of France under Charlemagne, when the learned Frenchmen spoke an undefiled Latin, while men on the street spoke a corrupted Latin, which later became the French language. So in India, Buddha's teachings were recorded in two languages: the Sanskrit texts conveyed what was known as the doctrine of Mahayana, and those in Pali became the doctrine of Hinayana. The Chinese Buddhists never doubted that *both* contained the true teachings of Buddha, but the few Western believers are still trying to decide which *one* of these contains the true teachings of Buddha and which one, therefore, is false.[6]

It is clear then that Chinese are indifferent toward other faiths not because they have been influenced by Buddhism or Taoism, but because their fundamental way of life makes such polytheistic religions attractive to them. And when a monotheistic creed is presented to them, the intruding faith, if accepted at all, tends to be transformed into what we must paradoxically term polytheistic monotheism. It is also clear that Westerners are intolerant toward other faiths not because they have accepted Christianity or Judaism, but because their fundamental way of life makes such monotheistic faiths satisfying to them.

But the principles underlying these observations are not restricted to situations wherein polytheistic and monotheistic faiths change territory. They are equally valid for predicting the future character of the dominant faiths among each people. Throughout the last two thousand years the Chinese have undergone little change in their basic religious orientation. Probably they have increased the total number of gods and spirits as well as the number of days and occasions on which the supernatural is to be feted and revered. But their attitude toward the supernatural, despite the invasion of radically different creeds, has not shown any significant evolution.

I believe this explains why, of the very small number of Chinese Christians, about 90 percent are Catholics. Catholicism, with its many saints, its complex rituals, and its priestly hierarchy which possesses the power to forgive, comes closer to the traditional Chinese approach to religion than does Protestantism. Even the Catholic purgatory, in which the punishment of the dead may be alleviated by the good deeds (including religious devotion) of living relatives is similar to the Chinese version of hell. To the Chinese mind, all this appears to be far more logical than what Protestantism offers—relatively simplified rituals, no secondary supernatural beings, a hell from which there is no return, and an emphasis on direct communion with God.[7] My guess is that, insofar as the Chinese take to Christianity, the great majority will continue to be Catholic rather than Protestant, and that the Protestant converts will tend to be Episcopalian rather than Unitarian.[8] And it is inconceivable that, without a drastic change in their psycho-cultural background, the Chinese should undertake to persecute each other for religious reasons.

This is in keeping with the nature of their basic web of human relations, which throughout twenty centuries has remained additive, mutually dependent, given to authority and submission, and permanently satisfying. Both as a group and as individuals the Chinese turn to the supernatural for specific forms of protection, but now as in the past they have few emotional requirements that cannot find gratification in those primary human contacts in the family, the wider kinship group, and, by extension, the neighborhood or local community.

Religion in the West has remained monotheistic because the characteristic Western human relations are singular, exclusive, and transitory, with each individual claiming or at least aiming for complete self-reliance. Western monotheism has been accompanied by disunity, tension, and violence precisely because the supernatural and the doctrine associated with it mean so much more to Westerners than to the Chinese. In Chapter 9 we noted how the "marriage" of a local Earth God still vividly expresses the Chinese approach to religion in modern Taiwan. No such traditional luxury is tolerated in China today. But the manner in which Chinese Christians and their clergy have fallen in line with the new regime should remind us of the course of events characterizing the so-called Chinese religious persecution of an earlier day. The T'ang emperors achieved their wish of regulating religion and reducing the number of Buddhist temples and clergy without bloodshed, just as the twentieth-century Chinese Communist authorities have secured the compliance of Chinese Christians without significant struggle. Chinese Catholic priests seem to simply take their role as People's Catholics in stride, which was noted with such puzzlement by returning Western Catholic missionaries.

The Direction of the Church in America

Thus far we have, in the main, spoken of European religion and American religion without distinction. This is, of course, incomplete and inadequate. So let us now inquire into the distinctions between the two. Harold J. Laski, in his book, *The American Democracy,* has contrasted a number of American religious characteristics with those of Europe. Laski says that in different areas of America the influence of religion is generally in inverse proportion to urbanization because technological advance permits more time for and creates new forms of leisure; that therefore the church is likely to be more important in the South and West, where the standard of living is lower, than in the North and East; that immigrants tend to be one of the mainstays of church power; that any church, to gain wide influence, must remain within the confines of accepted and prevailing ideas; that the majority of churchgoers tend to look upon church membership as a sort of traditional relationship which it never occurs to them to break; and that both branches of Christianity, the Catholic and the Protestant, in spite of their differences, strongly emphasize a general moral outlook and the importance of individual conversion rather than transformation of the society.

But while certain of these characteristics reach exaggerated proportions in the United States, none of them except the factor of immigration is absent on the other side of the Atlantic. And when Laski indicts American churches as being productive not of religion but of religiosity, he actually has little to say about any basic changes in the United States, and what he in fact does give us is an excellent exposition of the true monotheistic view of religion.

> For if by religion we mean that profound sense of an infinite universe so complex, so mysterious, so certain, as each of its immense problems are explained, to present us with new problems still more immense, its power to elevate is in the highest degree independent of historic dogma and the outcome of lonely meditation. Those who are able to reach beyond the petty cares of today or of tomorrow, who know that if faith gives comfort, reason leaves mystery beyond human penetration, know also, like Spinoza, that the fulfillment of the call to a deeper humility and a more profound elevation of spirit and of mind do not come from a participation in some formal ritual which is produced by some supposed history which, in the end, can never confront a critical analysis, nor from any temporary embodiment in a creed which has always to defend itself against some rival creed. The quality that is of the essence of a religion is the inner and passionate impulse which drives those who possess it beyond and above themselves to an elevation where they can conquer the immediate desire, and the temporary caprice, in their search for a fraternal relation with all who suffer and all who are broken by the tragedy of a pain they cannot face. Religion, in this sense, can never compromise with the world; it must be willing to break it or be broken by it rather than to yield the imperative passion in which it finds its supreme expression. It is not even a spirit which believes that fame or knowledge or power can ever compensate for the surrender of that inner vision which persists in those who present it by the fact that its call is never denied. This religion existed long before any of the historical religions were born, and it will live on long after many of them are dead. It has no institutions, no dogmas, no ritual, no priests; it is a spirit, something of which is in the character of those who possess it, something of which, also, breaks into flame as that character meets experience of the world.[9]

All the earmarks of true monotheism—the emphasis on the power of individual introspection, the contradictory attitude of humility joined with a militancy against that which it can define, often with realistic convenience, as abstract evil, the focus on passion, the determination to break or be broken, and the desire to transcend institutions, dogma, ritual, and priesthood—which Laski thinks that America has lost, are in fact more pronounced in America than they are in England. In fact, few other qualities are as characteristic of the American approach to religion as the desire to transcend institutions, dogma, ritual, and priesthood, and there is no better support for this observation than the distance between the very highly ritualistic Church of England and the almost completely informal Unitarian church of America.

American religion, instead of showing any basic departure from European monotheism, has actually become more centered in individual introspection, more militant toward other beliefs, and more a matter of personal passion. Laski failed to see that Americans have brought to the fore features which in retrospect were present below the surface when Christianity joined hands with European individualism, but which became evident when European individualism became American self-reliance.

The characteristic American approach to religion has three features. First, just as American education has been purged of the "authoritarian principle" and built on the "interest motive" so that we now speak of "child-centered schools," American religion is gradually shedding the authoritarian principle as it moves toward an interest motive orientation, so that we are, in a very real sense, moving from God-centered churches to churches in which the center of gravitation is the interest motive of the believers. This feature has two facets. On the one hand it helps to make Christianity or Judaism earthy, placing the two religions on a level where all their believers can understand. The popularity of ministers whose sermons deal with "everyone's daily problems" is also evidence of this development.

The trend toward popularization is also inexorable. The drive for individual success (on the part of the minister and his particular church) cannot but lead a majority of religious functionaries to make use of popular feelings in their creative efforts to enlarge the following of Christ. Hence the on and off struggles with the Soviet Union, the recently muted hostility between the United States and China, and the Vietnam War may all be given a religious stamp—the crusades of men of God against godless men.

Given the need for success, the other facet of the interest motive is inevitable. This is that American churches are compelled to make liberal use of the highly developed commercial art and media of persuasion. They have public relations officers to contact the gentlemen of the press, radio, and television media. Sometimes, before the church services, programs are mailed out to members of the congregation, questionnaires are distributed to parishioners to determine what the minister should preach. The necessity to please not only the congregation but also the general public has been remarked upon by Bishop J. Ralph Magee of the Methodist church: "I get letters criticizing a minister's neckties or table manners. Or, if the local Rotary and the Kiwanis like him, I get testimonials asking me to reappoint him—even though they don't belong to his church." This clergyman, who made the preceding statement just prior to retiring from the ministry after some fifty years of service, told his interviewer that he planned to write a book "on salesmanship as an indispensable part of a clergyman's equipment" (*Chicago Daily News,* June 20, 1952).

Further, churches have innumerable clubs, discussion groups, and athletic teams especially designed to accommodate both sexes, all age groups, and to appeal to many diverse interests. The most up-to-date have restaurants and parking lots to make religious life as convenient as possible. Some religious programs on television are practically indistinguishable from commercial shows, and at least one divinity school now has a course in television techniques.

We now have not only a full-blown "Truck Stop Congregation" which reportedly covered over 30,000 miles in six months during 1979 ("more miles than any other church in America"), but also a galaxy of radio and television churches and evangelical groups. "Some 250 radio stations in the United States and several overseas stations carry the Back to God Hour, which originates from a new $1.1 million center in Palos Heights" in western Chicago, reports the *Chicago Sun-Times* in an article headlined "Born-Again Evangelicals Make Chicago Their Hub" (February 27, 1979). The same report also mentions Domain Advertising Agency which describes itself as "specialists in Christian communications. . . . It has a staff of scriptwriters, announcers, engineers and account supervisors who buy time on radio for evangelical clients. One of its chief clients is the Chapel of the Air, whose broadcasts go from Chicago to 250 stations."

The television shows of Rev. Jack Van Impe and Rev. Oral Roberts reach vast audiences. Rev. Van Impe is impressive with his references to chapters and verses from the Bible in his every utterance throughout his entire show. But the most spectacular television Christian phenomenon in my opinion is Reverend Jerry Falwell's road show called "I Love America" and his "Old-Time Gospel Hour" seen on 324 television stations in the United States, Canada, and the Caribbean. Reverend Falwell has been described as one of the top stars of the "electric church." His enterprises employ 960 people with an annual budget of $56 million. He appeals to the jingoistic interest of Americans. "God loves America above all nations, and He has a message for Caesar," he says. In cooperation with Washington-based New Right political groups he recently organized his first purely secular enterprise, Moral Majority, Inc., with plans to hit all fifty states within eighteen months. He considers his new organization a necessary antidote to public interest groups such as Common Cause (*Time,* October 1, 1979). Although the factors leading to the 1980 Republican landslide are complex, Falwell and his Moral Majority have obviously played a part. Falwell and his followers must, in turn, be seen as the most recent and militant expressions of a people one in three of whom are said to have been "born again."

The second distinct feature of religion in America is its irreconcilable divisiveness. This result is sharply contrary to the expectations of Ralph Waldo Emerson, who proclaimed that "self-reliance, the height and perfection of man, is reliance on God," and that this self is "not the egoistic or 'selfish' self, but the universal and divine self."[10] When he spoke of self-reliance, Emerson undoubtedly was defining an ideal in which people would love each other for their love of God. Yet, as we have seen, one of the most striking characteristics of American society is the instability of human relationships. This instability, as we also noted before, is especially related to the American spirit of republicanism and a sharp emphasis on equality. When every man is as good as every other man there is likely to be a scramble on the part of most good people to be better than other good people. This instability cannot possibly lead human beings to love each other for their love of God. Instead, American church behavior has exhibited such divisiveness that, at first sight, we might feel compelled to deplore the fact that Americans have failed to live up to the ideal of their great thinker.

I do not think that Americans have failed to live up to the Emersonian ideal of self-reliance; in fact they have done so too well. But the notion that self-reliant men can unite permanently in love of God is unsupported rhetoric that needs to be examined. Our evidence points to the contrary—the greater the stress on self-reliance, the higher the tendency toward separatism in the church as in other spheres of endeavor. There are few other Christian countries where there is a more active interest in religion than in America. Not only has the Bible remained a best-seller, as we noted before, but any new book with a religious flavor is likely to receive wide circulation. Even movies with a religious theme are popular, for example, *In Search of the Historical Jesus*. Membership in organized religious bodies seems to increase a little every year.[11] Furthermore, not only can revivalists of the Billy Graham variety arouse great enthusiasm, but there is always ready publicity for the intellectual who, either in his capacity as an individual or as a scholar, reaffirms the dogmas of faith.[12] These certainly are not indications that American interest in religion is flagging or that it is merely a bond that most Americans would sever if the thought to do so came to mind.

The real difference between the Old World and America as far as the Church is concerned is that the United States has atomized the broader divisions which started in Europe. In spite of Emerson's glowing rhetoric, this is a direct result of self-reliance. Where European religious schism usually was rooted in dissimilarities in dogma, American sectarianism has often been a matter of personal differences. The latter trend, religious division on the basis of personal differences, was already noticeable in eighteenth-century Europe where the English Quakers, Methodists, Russian Dukhobors, and the French Jansenists all minimized dogma and emphasized personal "inner light" or conscience, or individual experience and emotion. When Christianity came to the New World, its divisive tendencies became even more pronounced. As long as the authority of tradition limited European individualism to the political much more than to the social and economic realms, religious schism could, on the whole, hardly achieve momentum unless based in theology—in dogma and rituals or their interpretation.

But in America, with a history of self-reliance founded on a firm belief in equality and freedom, and with religion increasingly given to the interest motive, the individual conscience as the way to God need pay no attention to restraints imposed by authority, tradition, or even the Bible. An educational pattern where "the child is more important than the subject" fits without difficulty into a religious pattern where the believer is more important than the Scripture.

Consequently, Americans have not merely sharpened the religious differences inherited from Europe, but they have subdivided them even more. There are already more than two hundred denominations within American Protestantism, many more than Europe has ever known, and the limit to this splintering is not yet in sight.

This is not to overlook the mergers of some denominations. In 1961 the American Unitarian Association and the Universalist Church of America merged into the Unitarian Universalist Association. That same year also saw the merger of the Evangelical and Reformed Church and the Congregational Christian Churches into the United Church of Christ. The Lutheran Church of America came into being in 1960 with the union of three churches. Later, in 1963, it was joined by one more denomination. But there are other attempts at merger that have failed. The Cumberland Presbyterian Church has continued as a separate denomination despite a merger effort in 1906 with the Presbyterian Church in the United States, and the National Association of Congregational Christian Churches was organized in 1955 by a group of Congregational Christian Churches that did not wish to enter the United Church of Christ.[13] Above all, an overwhelming majority of the denominations have remained separate.

Those impressed with the recurrent interest in the ecumenical movement may say that it is only a matter of time before a greater unity will develop among American churches. But the history and the characteristics of the self-reliant orientation are against such a prediction. New denominations, such as the Universal Life Church in California where one can be ordained by correspondence, will continue to crop up. On the other hand, objections to innovation, such as that of many Catholics against celebrating the mass in English or some Eastern Orthodox Christians against adoption of the Gregorian Calendar, cannot but add something to the force of separatism.

The foreseeable trend of this splintering process is a movement not only toward division between different denominations but between different churches of the same denomination, and even between different ministers of the same church, each of whom may enjoy a certain personal following. I also believe that even if the Protestants had not come first to America and had not been the majority of the early settlers, American religion would still tend to be more Protestant rather than Catholic.

This characteristically American tendency to desert the traditional and subdivide the divided was commented upon as far back as 1842 when Charles Dickens, reporting on his transoceanic visit, said in his *American Notes:*

> I cannot hold with other writers on these subjects that the prevalence of various forms of dissent in America is in any way attributable to the non-existence there of an established church: indeed, I think the temper of the people, if it admitted of such an Institution being founded amongst

them, would lead them to desert it, as a matter of course, merely because it *was* established.[14]

What the individual minister hopes to achieve, as do his lay brethren, is success. In American religion, the epitome of success is to possess the most radiant "inner light" or to be able to make the best interpretations of God's words. It is increasingly true that in this race, the measure of a minister's success is the size of his congregation. As for the lay believer, what he seeks in his religion is a complex of things that are increasingly functional. Some will attend churches as a matter of conformity, exactly as Laski observes, to "a traditional relation which it never occurs to them to break."[15] Many do so because of another molder of conformity, the fear of social censure. But more and more Americans will look to religion for personal mental health, and for a solution to their intimate, emotional problems. This search has led to two seemingly divergent developments. On the one hand there is an avalanche of religious books and newspaper columns keyed to the general formula of "you and religion" within the establishmentarian, Christian mold. On the other hand there is a proliferation in America of traditionally Far Eastern religions, from Zen Buddhism to the Hare Krishna variety of Hinduism.

One good example of the former is the famous book of Norman Vincent Peale, D.D., and Smiley Blanton, M.D., who together wrote *The Art of Real Happiness*. Here is a sample:

> Gilbert Dodds, one of the greatest track stars of our time, crouched at the starting line of the Wanamaker mile run.
>
> The flying parson took that brief moment to say a silent prayer. Letting his body relax in preparation for the tremendous effort to come, he prayed, "O Lord, in this glorious sport I pray that you will let me run well. Help each running against me to do his best, too. Go along with each of us. Amen."
>
> Free of any stress, moving ahead with an effortless grace, he went out in front of his competitors and came home an easy winner.
>
> Gil Dodds knew that a relaxed body and a quiet mind turned toward God can indeed draw on deep reserves of power when they are most needed.[16]

Working in combination, the interest motive and the ideal of self-reliance lead to a concept of God which is increasingly fashioned in the American image. Since most Americans are extremely active, He will be extremely active. Since most Americans possess certain ideals, He too will uphold these ideals. Since most Americans consider success in business the most important thing in their lives, the sign of His favor will be commercial reward.[17] Following is an Associated Press report which appeared June 20, 1952:

> He started out at the bottom. But now he is rich, successful, a top business executive.
>
> He stood before a microphone and said the "voice of God" led him there. Without God, he said, he was a failure.
>
> The intimately personal declaration came from _____, board chairman of _____ Inc., in a radio interview Friday with Dwight Cooke, CBS correspondent.
>
> The 61-year-old Minneapolis businessman said that when a vital, difficult problem arises, "I put it right up to God and then I watch for some sign—the voice of God."
>
> "I have found out by actual experience," he said, "that when I follow that hunch and follow what I believe to be God's prompting, that I have success in whatever I am trying to do. And in the times in the past when I have not followed it, I get confused and things don't come out right."

Is it then surprising that the likeness of Jesus is often depicted with a touch of the salesman's smile instead of His former serenity? Is it then surprising that we have Christian churches like that of Rev. Frederick J. Eikerenkoeter II (Rev. Ike), the United Church, Science of Living Institute in New York City, whose multimillion dollar operation to promote money power appears on a thousand radio and television stations and in magazines with 2 million-plus circulation (*Chicago Sun-Times,* June 30, 1978)? Is it then surprising that today we also have a Church of Hakeem (after Rev. Hakeem Abdul Rasheed, which with a slogan "Dare to Be Rich," offered its members 400 percent return on their donations) which grossed over $10 million between December 1977 and January 1979 (*San Francisco Examiner,* February 6, 1980)? Hakeem has now been convicted of fraud but the number of his followers is evidence of its popularity.[18]

Then there is the Jonestown phenomenon which resulted in the death of some 900 men, women, and children in 1978 and has been explained as a mentally sick man misleading innocents into suicide. If that was the case, why did so many Americans voluntarily fall into the trap? A more rational interpretation of it appeared in the *New Yorker* shortly after the tragedy. William Pfaff, the writer, calls the People's Temple a messianic cult, which commonly arises "in periods of trouble or social crisis." It can also occur "at any time among uprooted people, among marginal people without an assured place in society." He compared it with, among others, the Cargo Cult of the South Seas, the Ghost-Dance Cult among some American Indians, and the T'aip'ing Rebellion that convulsed China in the eighteenth century.[19] Several clinicians consulted by *Time* gave similar views on it (*Time,* December 4, 1978).

Of course there are similarities in the mental needs of the followers of all such cults. People who are well-off and well adjusted are less likely to seek drastically new paths. But it is significant that none of the other known messianic cults has called for voluntary mass suicide and not all followers of such cults, even those of the Reverend Jim Jones, are uprooted or marginal people.

We will come back to the T'aip'ing Rebellion in Chapter 15. It is important here to note that the interest motive and the individualized approach to religion in combination have led to privatization of God in America. God becomes the "hero" of every individual believer, and is behind the individual believer's joys or sorrows, successes or disappointments, loves or hates.[20] All human beings tend to seek affective links with other human beings; joining the People's Temple (or other religious cults) is one extreme solution to the individual-centered person's dilemma. He wants to be exclusive. But his exclusiveness has no bite unless other likeminded people combine forces with him.

In this light we can better understand the recent proliferation of traditionally Far Eastern religions in America. These not only include Zen and Hare Krishna but many others. For example, the Nyingma Institute under the Tibetan lama Tarthang Tulku Rinpoche is building a giant temple called Odiyan near Berkeley, California. The Tathagata Monastery was begun several years in Talmage, California, under the Buddhist monk Hsuan Hua, a native of Manchuria. It also inauguarated the Dharma Realm Buddhist University on November 4, 1979. Most of the devotees in these institutions are from the white middle class. In fact, many of them are not only college graduates but holders of advanced degrees, including the Ph.D.

However, it is not that the American followers of these sects and cults have gone "Asian," in spite of the outer trappings such as those of the Hare Krishnas we see in streets and airports. Individual-centered Americans must find creative ways of privatizing a god that is different from all others. In clinging to a deity from an Asian polytheistic pantheon, American devotees have simply made him an exclusive monotheistic object with typically un-Chinese fervor.

This brings us to the third distinct feature of the American approach to religion: a big businesslike pattern of competition between the individual churches of each sect. The number and size of material—and often novel—achievements are becoming the most important criterion by which to judge the success of a particular church— larger congregations, bigger budgets, better choirs, more clubs, and a wider variety of activities. A minister who can produce these results finds himself called to bigger and more lucrative assignments. One who falls behind is in danger of being without a place to preach.

The three dominant features of the American approach to religion —its appeal to the interest motive, its ceaseless tendency toward divisiveness, and its proclivity to judge its own success in material terms —were all dramatically illustrated by what the *Christian Century* magazine, after polling a hundred thousand ministers, described as the twelve "outstanding" and most "successful churches in the United States." One of them was the First Presbyterian Church of Hollywood which was given many accolades in another national magazine.[21] After noting this church must have "won through genuine competition," the writer went on to describe the crowded Sunday school, the overflowing services, the oversubscribed large budget, the eighty-six young people's groups built on their own interests,[22] the athletic activities, the radio and television programs originating from the church, the five choirs, and a "Cordon of Prayer" with fifteen hundred volunteers so organized that the entire Cordon can be mobilized instantly for continuous prayer in case a church member has to go to the hospital or suffers from other misfortune. Throughout the entire article depicting this "successful" church, the "happiness" of the parishioners revolves about social and material endeavors that redound to their benefit alone. This whirl of competitive activity seems inferentially equated with depth of spiritual faith, since the latter is not even explicitly mentioned. The quality of its ministers' teachings receives scant attention, and that in the parlance of a business directory.

The businessman's approach of the First Presbyterian Church of Hollywood to religion may be spectacular in intensity and scope, but it is not outside the mainstream of American church orientation. Fashions of American church activities have changed somewhat since the survey was made nearly thirty years ago. A few all-white churches have since opened their doors to Blacks and other minority groups. Some churchgoers have since asked themselves how their church activities could be made more relevant to the problems of peace, race, and poverty. The St. Francis Productions Telespots, selling "Love in Your Life" to the general public in the manner of commercials, have begun to appear on some TV programs. And finally, there is the kind of rebellion among church members represented by Father Groppi of Milwaukee, Wisconsin, which was certainly nonexistent in the early fifties, the time of the *Christian Century* survey.

But my view is that the *basic pattern,* as distinguished from the *prevailing fashion,* of the American's approach to his God, so closely linked to the American's approach to his fellow men, has not changed and will not change easily. I simply cannot believe that a reexamination of American churches and ministers today will reveal fundamental departures from the results of three decades ago. This evaluation is not based merely on personal observations and experiences (which are considerable), but also on more massive and systematic data which came after the first publication of my book in 1953. I refer to a book entitled *Popular Religion* by Schneider and Dornbusch, who have analyzed a total of forty-six best-sellers on religion over the years 1875–1955, of which most were written by Americans and all reached a large American audience.

The two sociologists set themselves four criteria in selecting the books for this analysis. The first is that the author must "assume the general validity of the Judeo-Christian tradition." Second, the "author must inspire with the hope of salvation on some terms." Third, the "author must offer his reader 'techniques.' " And a final criterion is that the "writer must address himself to the everyday 'problems' of 'everyday people.' "[23] On the basis of these criteria the forty-six books begin with Hannah W. Smith's *The Christian Secret of a Happy Life* published in 1875, E. Fosdick's *Twelve Tests of Character,* published in 1923, and E. Stanley Jones's *The Christ of Every Raod,* published in 1930, through Elton Trueblood's *The Predicament of Modern Man,* published in 1944, Norman Vincent Peale's *The Power of Positive Thinking,* and Fulton J. Sheen's *Life Is Worth Living.* The last two were published in 1952 and 1953 respectively.

The results of their analysis are too numerous to detail here; the interested reader will do well to read the book itself. But there is no doubt that the results confirmed the trends depicted in 1953 when *Americans and Chinese* was first published, and anticipated the subsequent developments through the later years, as we have seen in the foregoing pages. For example, there is the theme that religion will bring "our nation" leadership or victory over our enemies, which came to the fore during World War II and continued forcefully during the post-war anti-Communist crusade (p. 13). There is the theme that religion "will bring happiness, prestige, power, emotional security," and "easing of the pain of decision-making" (p. 14). There is the theme that you can change yourself through religion (p. 22), with a strong emphasis on psychology or psychiatry, especially during the depression period (pp. 24–25). There is the stress upon salvation in this life over that of salvation in the next (p. 25). While the theme that riches signify "goodness" is prominent (p. 30), the original Christian notion of a link between poverty and virtue is practically nonexistent. Another increasing preoccupation is that religion can be equated with health.

The two sociologists commented upon the trend of "declining emphasis on the theme of the love of Christ since about 1930, and with the exception of Catholic writers mainly, they suggest a tendency toward a more secularized outlook" (p. 34). The concept of hell has nearly ceased to exist for Protestants. In fact there is little stress on God "as a judge" (p. 22), which is compatible with Beatrice Jane Russell's characterization of God as a "livin' doll" (p. 109).

After a detailed analysis of both the constant and the variable trends, the two sociologists observed:

> Assuming that the expression of sincere religious feeling is a good thing, this good thing is not over-plentiful in the literature and is repeatedly counter-suggested. MacDonald writes: "There seems to be a Gresham's Law in cultural as well as monetary circulation: bad stuff drives out the good since it is more easily understood and enjoyed. It is this facility of access which at once sells *kitsch* on a wide market and also prevents it from achieving quality" (pp. 140–141).

The only point that I would disagree with is the answer the two sociologists give to the question, "Why is there not more expression of sincere religious feeling in the literature?" They believe that this is due largely to the fact of popularization among a public that is just barely literate (pp. 141–142). But I think the other part of their view, that "the administrators of the mint are experiencing some pressure not to produce good coinage at all" is really far more important (p. 142). In other words, what the American popular religious writers are doing is to give the customer what he wants; and the customers have so far seemed not to want God as much as they want individual happiness, success, wealth, health, prestige, and power.

It is this privatized orientation to God (on the part of the individual member of a church, of each church, and of each denomination) which is the fountainhead of the great wealth commanded by organized religion in the United States. According to reliable estimates, the value of the "visible assets"—land and buildings of all kinds—of American religious organizations is "approximately $79.5 billion— almost double that of the combined assets of the country's five largest industrial corporations,"[24] or "one and a half times the full value of *all* real property in the five sprawling boroughs of New York City."

The late James Pike, an Episcopal Bishop who made the last comparison and who proposed taxing of churches' income for "their own good," noted that churches "are presently in danger of 'gaining the whole world and losing their own souls.' "[25] "One hundred years from now, the present pattern of religious tax exemption . . . if continued, may present the state with problems of such magnitude that their only solution will be revolutionary expropriation of church property."[26] The question of tax exemption for churches is not our concern here. What is of note is that American ways in religion bear intrinsic resemblance to their actions in other endeavors, and the same can be said for the Chinese.

To some readers this privatized orientation toward God seems to contradict the recent participation of some American churches and churchmen in the civil rights movements. As we shall see when we come to dilemmas confronting each way of life in Part Three, and especially in Chapter 14, the contradiction here is more apparent than real. The separation of the individual-centered American from his primary group, which makes it imperative for him to seek nonkinship attachments, is the very source of the strengths of the American way of life in contrast to the weaknesses of its Chinese counterpart. Where the Chinese have been unduly bound to the past, Americans have felt much freer to seek change. Where the Chinese have developed few groupings unrelated to the kinship and community base, Americans have formed diverse and often enormous voluntary associations for the promotion of causes both just and unjust. In the meantime, we must turn our attention to another realm of human activity, and see how the two different orientations of the two civilizations bear on their respective ways of acquiring and enjoying material wealth.[27]

NOTES
1. William Charles White, *Chinese Jews: A Compilation of Matters Relating to the Jews of K'aifeng Fu*, 1:xiii. This book, from which the above facts on Chinese Jews are taken, speaks occasionally about Chinese prejudice against the Jews. However, it gives no concrete evidence for this. Instead it gives three assertions, two by the same

Catholic missionary. In view of the facts, these reports of prejudice seem to be no more than projection of a Western view. The stone incriptions found near or at the site of the synagogue of K'aifeng, first built in A.D. 1163, indicate that it was repaired or enlarged in the years 1270, 1421, 1445, 1461, ca. 1480, and 1512. It was rebuilt for the last time just after the middle of the seventeenth century. The work in 1421 was accomplished with a grant of incense from the reigning Ming emperor, Yung Lo.

2. K. S. Latourette, *The Chinese, Their History and Culture,* p. 557.

3. He was referring to the days before the Japanese invasion of Manchuria and north China.

4. From F. L. K. Hsu, "China," in Ralph Linton, ed., *Most of the World,* pp. 782–783.

5. Most American universities, including Northwestern, have omitted the category of religion since the early 1950s.

6. The Japanese, though polytheistic in comparison with Westerners, are nonetheless much more specific than the Chinese in their adherence to Buddhist creeds. Consequently while Buddhism went to Japan via China, sectarian Buddhism (such as Zen) has reached a height in that country never dreamed of by the Chinese. This and other differences between Japanese and Chinese ways of life are explained in Hsu, *Iemoto: The Heart of Japan.*

7. It is also possible to suggest that this difference in relative success between Catholic and Protestant missionaries was at least in part because the former came to China before the latter. But the logic of the situation is too obvious to be overlooked. Besides, up to 1949 there were at least nine Protestant universities (in addition to numerous YMCAs and YWCAs) in China but only two Catholic institutions of higher learning. Looking over modern Chinese leaders in education, government, and business who were also Christians, I find a preponderance of Protestants including, of course, Generalissimo Chiang and his wife.

8. Characteristic of the American divisive approach to religion, the Unitarian church was for years not recognized by other Christian churches as a Protestant or even specifically Christian body.

9. From Laski, *The American Democracy,* p. 320.

10. Norman Foerster, ed., *American Poetry and Prose,* pt. 1, p. 544.

11. Though that increase does not equal the increase in the population.

12. True to the spirit of self-reliance and free enterprise, there is also ready publicity for those like the late Bishop Pike who question and refute it.

13. The national Association of Congregational Christian Churches does not have doctrinal requirements.

14. Charles Dickens, *American Notes for General Circulation,* p. 125.

15. Laski, *American Democracy,* p. 305.

16. Norman Vincent Peale, *The Art of Real Happiness* (New York: Post-Hall Syndicate, 1951). A serialized condensed version was published in the *Chicago Daily News,* from which this quotation was extracted. A well-known earlier book in this vein is that of Henry C. Link, *The Return to Religion* (New York, 1936), which in five years went through thirty-four printings of its regular edition. It has been available in paperback since.

17. This is, of course, not a native American view. It began with the Reformation in England and on the Continent. See Richard H. Tawney, *Religion and the Rise of Capitalism.*

18. See also *Honolulu Advertiser,* January 5, 1979, for more details of its operation.

19. William Pfaff, "Reflections, The People's Temple," *New Yorker,* December 18, 1979.

20. This American attitude toward God is to be differentiated from that of the

Chinese toward the supernatural. Both may be utilitarian in design, but the pious in America tend to identify God with themselves and to consider God an intrinsic part of themselves. The faithful in China at best attempt to fortify their formal relationship with the gods by making bigger offerings and engaging in more elaborate rituals, but they never strive for an inseparable connection with the spirits. In one frame of reference, the worth and meaning of God are determined by the individual believer; in the other, the worth and the meaning of gods are determined by tradition. The American believer tends, therefore, to be touchy about his God, since he feels any slight to his God, or even neglect of Him, to be an assault on his ego. The Chinese tends, on the other hand, to be indifferent toward disbelievers or even blasphemers. Since he has little emotional involvement with any one supernatural being, he experiences no personal threat in the neglect or abuse of the gods by others.

21. Roger William Riis, "What Makes This Church Successful?" in *Reader's Digest,* February 1952.

22. This church outshone other churches by having not only "father-and-son affairs," but also "mother-and-daughter, father-and-daughter and mother-and-son affairs." The many interest groups included "Eager Beavers, Mustangs, Cathedral Choir, Women's Auxiliary" each with "its own constitution," "its own officers." Nearly all groups have their own publications, all meetings featured free-flowing conversations, topped "with coffee and cake," and talked "about Jesus as easily and simply as one might comment on the weather."

23. Louis Schneider and Sanford M. Dornbusch, *Popular Religion: Inspiration Books in America,* pp. 3–4.

24. Alfred Balk, "God Is Rich," *Harper's* (October 1967), p. 69.

25. Bishop James Pike, "Tax Organized Religion," *Playboy* 14, no. 4 (April 1967): 93.

26. Ibid., quoting Dr. Eugene C. Blake, Chief Executive of the World Council of Churches, *Christianity Today* magazine.

27. The tendency to see religion as a business, an expansionist business, is graphically depicted in a 1977 newspaper article. " 'In recent years,' Dr. Kenneth Kantzer, academic dean of Trinity Evangelical Divinity School in Deerfield, Illinois observed, 'the upsurge of evangelicalism (sic) has brought Chicago into an extremely prominent place as a center of evangelical activity.' Los Angeles . . . is Chicago's only serious rival for this distinction." Also, "Next summer *Christianity Today,* the leading journal of the nation's evangelical 'establishment,' will move its editorial offices from Washington to Carol Stream, a western suburb [of Chicago] where religion is a top growth industry" (Roy Larson, *Chicago Sun-Times,* February 27, 1977).

CHAPTER 11

Two Approaches
to Economic Life

The description in Chapter 7 of the Chinese game "Advancement in Officialdom" must have reminded some readers of its American counterpart, "Monopoly." Both may be classified as games of success. The difference in goals between the Chinese game and the American game truly reflects the social and economic importance attached, respectively, to government in China and to business in the United States.

"Monopoly" probably sounds ancient to many readers because its popularity dipped somewhat after the 1950s, but new games along the same line have since proliferated. One of the many newer American games is "Game of Life," in which the players can expect success or failure via the following chances: "meet future spouse, pay $500.00 for diamond ring," "add baby son, collect presents," "collect $1000.00 for scholarship," "weekend in Las Vegas, collect $50,000.00," "pay $500.00 for new set of choppers (artificial teeth)," "stock drop, pay $7000.00 of your own stock," "experiment pays off, collect $20,000.00," "lucky day, inherit real estate, collect $10,000.00; keep it or try for $15,000.00." The worst position for a player to possibly find himself in is "poor farm." In addition, players can also purchase insurance of all sorts, take luxury trips, and lose money in various ways.[1]

Also in Chapter 7 we saw that the Chinese bureaucracy has long been the road to economic as well as social betterment. One of the basic reasons why the Chinese aspired to the bureaucracy was that Chinese commerce and industry were so rudimentary that bureaucratic positions offered the most lucrative jobs in the entire society. This seems surprising when we recall that the Chinese have long produced some of the world's most beautiful goods, including Shang bronzes, Han jades, and Ming vases. Such items today add splendor and prestige to every important museum, and a vast number of private collections. Furthermore, the Chinese society has been one of the very few in history to enjoy a continuous civilization for over three millennia, and within this time it has been blessed by longer periods of internal stability and peace than those known to the majority of mankind. Why then did the Chinese not achieve an extensive development of their economy? This puzzle has aroused much speculation, most of it divorced from the basic realities of Chinese life. But if we apply the results of our analysis thus far, we must conclude that Chinese economic life has been restricted by the same factors that underlie other characteristics of their social life, government, and religion.

We have seen that mutual dependence is the outstanding Chinese characteristic, and that this deep-seated tendency to rely upon other persons, especially those within the primary groups, produces in the Chinese a sense of social and psychological security. Given this anchorage and the concept of the supernatural that derives from it, the Chinese feels less compulsion to seek other forms of material or psychological satisfaction. The self-reliant American, however, strives to eliminate from his life both the fact and the sense of dependence upon others. This unending struggle to be fully independent raises the constant and continuing threat of perpetual social and psychological insecurity. A close parental bond is severed early in life; the marriage that replaces it is often unstable; heroes come and go; class affiliation is subject to a constant struggle to climb from one level to another; and the alliance with God, though less ephemeral than the preceding relationships, is nevertheless affected by the same divisive forces. For, given the ideal of total self-reliance and its concomitant version of a god who helps those who help themselves, Americans cannot but seek their final anchorage in harbors other than men or the supernatural.

The Characteristics of the Chinese Economy

Viewed from any angle, business in traditional China has long shown itself to be stable, and without expansive or aggressive designs. Take manufacturing, for example. In addition to bronzes, jades, and vases, a myriad of other products and skills have made China famous: rugs, lacquer work, embroidery, silk, porcelain screens, cloisonné, ivory carvings, teakwood furniture, brass objects, silver and gold ornaments, fireworks, and boats. It was for some of these highly desirable items of commerce that Western explorers and traders have since ancient times undertaken hazardous trips to the East. But significantly few Chinese have ever made comparable attempts to seek a market for their goods in the West.

The majority of these products and many others whose listing could be extended almost endlessly are manufactured in homes or small family shops. The average Chinese craftsman usually handles the manufacturing processes of a single product from beginning to end. His hours are long, his efficiency is low, and his returns for the end result are meager.

The personnel of a typical Chinese handicraft shop consists of a master, his wife, one or more of his children, one or two journeymen, and one or two apprentices. The physical plant often is no more than two rooms, one fronting on the street. The back room provides the living quarters of the master and his family. During the day the front room is the workshop and sales department, the manufacturers doubling as salesmen, and at night it serves as the living quarters for the journeymen and apprentices. The master and the journeymen usually take their meals together, while the master's wife and children dine in the kitchen. The apprentices act as servants for all.

The craft guilds are not only local in character, having no ties with their counterparts in other communities, they also have as members both the owners and their employees. For, although the guilds fix prices, wages, and the terms of apprenticeship, and although their officers work to settle disputes within the craft or with other guilds, their primary concern is, as we saw in the chapter on government, the protection of localized interests against encroachment by political authority from beyond the local scene. Further, they stabilize the relationship between employers and employees as well as between one shop and another instead of in any way promoting competition or strife among these parties.

The workmanship, ingenuity, and artistry that go into many Chinese products amaze most Westerners, but these goods are by and large today still being produced with tools and methods that the Chinese have inherited from a time unknown. Consequently, the products of contemporary Chinese craftsmen bear close resemblance to many of their ancient antecedents, and changes in styles have occurred, if at all, only once in several generations.

This does not mean that the Chinese have been wholly devoid of new ideas in the field of production. The Chinese commonly are credited with the invention of gunpowder, printing, and paper, but it is not generally known that they were probably also the first to utilize the assembly line. The principle of the assembly line was employed as early as the sixteenth century in porcelain manufacturing plants supervised and operated by the imperial government. In such plants, some workers specialized in making the base, some in glazing, others in painting a decorative figure, while still others specialized in coloring the edges. Every teapot, cup, or plate thus went through a number of specialized departments before its completion. But this idea was never extended to other industries nor extensively accepted by private manufacturers of porcelain.

What is true of Chinese handicraft industries is equally true of Chinese commerce. Although Westerners think of the Chinese as good merchants, commerce has never been of great importance in China nor, as a rule, have its practitioners been highly esteemed. Nevertheless, commercial activities have flourished in local communities and between different regions of the country. But the bulk of China's trade has always been carried on by family enterprise.

Generally speaking, in addition to that typical of the craft shop, we may differentiate among three kinds of selling in China. The first is the periodic market found in a Chinese village or small town. These markets may be held in the towns or villages themselves or at a short distance from them in a traditional area. The markets may occur at intervals varying from once every three days to once a year. They may last for one day, several days, or several weeks. Though the periodic market was especially prevalent in southwest China, it was not rare elsewhere. Wherever held, these markets attract hundreds of men, women, and children; they stream to the market place carrying everything from fruit to furniture. A vendor's place of business may be a table, a tent, or simply a spot on the ground. Others, of course, merely come to buy. At the day's end, the seller of fruit may carry home a piece of furniture that he has purchased with his earnings, while some who came empty-handed may return wealthier but without goods, having profited by reselling commodities bought in the market. And, as with markets throughout the world, many persons come solely to look, inquire about prices, and visit with their friends and have a good time in general.

The largest of these periodic markets used to be held in Tali, Yunnan Province. This began during the third lunar month and usually lasted several weeks. My last visit to this market was in 1942. Then, as in the dim past, buyers and sellers were drawn there not only from nearby places, but they also came from a number of southern provinces and Tibet. Many aboriginal groups came in caravans, having camped all along the route. Present, besides those people directly concerned with buying and selling goods, were jugglers, tightrope walkers, magicians, storytellers, and diviners. The market was much like an industrial fair in the United States, except that the exhibitors represented no one but themselves and all buying and selling were done then and there.

The second type of retail commerce takes place in city and town shops. These range from one-room affairs, very much like the craft shops described before, to establishments employing thirty, forty, or even a hundred persons. Occasionally a firm may have two or more branches in different parts of the same community, or in two or three other cities. The smaller businesses are family affairs but the larger ones have stockholders, a managerial group, plus clerks and apprentices who are learning the trade. Goods at such well-established firms are never subject to haggling, a practice found only among traders at bazaars, periodic markets, and peddling stands. Western visitors thinking otherwise have often created situations acutely embarrassing to both themselves and the merchants. Most of the old retail houses in China have signboards which read as follows:

> Whether you are nine or ninety
> We sell at fixed prices.

The reason for this is much deeper than a desire to rise above the bargaining of the itinerant peddler. The majority of these establishments conduct much of their business, as do the craft shops, with long-term customers. All important customers are known personally to the management. In these firms a typical business transaction takes place as follows: upon entering the customer is received by the manager who sits on a long bench near the entrance. The two of them sit down and, while drinking tea served by an apprentice, they chat about the weather, the market, and local affairs. Eventually the customer may say that he wishes to look at a certain kind of cloth, and the manager asks one of the clerks to show him the goods, either on the counter or nearby. The customer examines the goods, and, if satisfied, the transaction is completed. He may pay cash or have the amount charged; if the latter, the clerk makes an entry in the purchaser's account. Whichever the case, there are no receipts. Finally, the customer may stay to have lunch or dinner with the manager and the assistant manager.

This manner of doing business may be described as friendship before trade. Therefore, most regular patrons of any shop expect to receive some token of appreciation on each of the three annual festivals when bills have to be paid. Even with the majority of customers who may only be acquainted with or unknown to the management and who deal directly with the clerks, business is done on the basis of good will and local respectability. No firm can expect to continue in business if, by unilateral action, its prices, which are often fixed by the guilds, fluctuate wildly or if it goes back on its word.

The third variety of business is conducted by independent entrepreneurs who transport goods from one part of China to another and distribute them to retailers on a wholesale basis. This has never been an easy task in China, and has always called for a liberal use of wits, energy, and initiative, especially in the days before railroads and insurance. The entrepreneur not only personally selects and oversees the packing of commodities, but he also accompanies the goods from their point of origin to their destination. He may not only have to direct the loading and unloading from one type of transportation to another, but he must negotiate with local officials and police for passage through their locality and even with bandits for certificates of safe conduct.

If the entrepreneur knows of a market for goods that are not available, he may commission a number of individual craft shops or families to produce the desired commodities. He himself furnishes the capital necessary for purchasing raw materials and often advances a part of the wages. Since the 1930s, many of these men also provide hand-operated machines to the workers they commission. Hosiery knitting in Hopei Province was such an example. Studies made by the Nankai University at Tientsin show that a sizable group of merchants maintain this relationship with a large number of rural households. The merchants furnish the yarn, the hand-operated machinery, and an advance in wages, which are on a piecework basis, and then collect the finished products for sale in urban markets. The exact extent of this type of enterprise is unknown, but it was found in all parts of the country.

In many instances, Chinese entrepreneurs—principally those dealing in such staples as rice, salt, or tea—became extremely wealthy. In the third century B.C., a businessman became the most successful government administrator of his time. District records speak of local merchants who counted their fortunes in millions of cashes.[2] Nevertheless the basic characteristic of Chinese commerce is the same as that of her manufacturing: the absence of expansionist designs. The role of commercial guilds is indicative. While these guilds may be more imposing structures than those of the craftsmen and, as a whole, are better endowed, their functions are not at all different from the manufacturers' guilds. The mission of the commercial guilds is to hold the line and to protect the merchants from excessive government exploitation, not to encourage or chart trade expansion. Like other guilds, they too are organized by locality and by trade. The salesmanship of their members, who are preoccupied with filling needs as they occur and holding their customers by friendship and good will, is as much in keeping with this approach as advertising on the American model is not. These businessmen feel no call to study retailing procedures, do exact cost accounting, or hold conventions to improve sales methods or promote new products.

Consequently, most manufacturers and merchants have been satisfied with a profit that would seem unreasonably low to Americans. What, we must therefore ask, keeps them from wishing to increase their returns? One answer is to apply the oft-reiterated East-West myth: the Chinese are more spiritual and therefore less interested in profit than Americans. This is completely false. Any American who has business experience with Chinese merchants can tell us that they try to obtain all the profit they can; there is nothing spiritual about them in this regard.

But if we abandon the misconceived spiritual-material dichotomy and look into the very real contrast in the two people's patterns of human relationship, we come closer to explaining the conservative tendency of the Chinese economy. The key fact is that, both within the shop and without it, the Chinese owner and his workers can find satisfactions that are not available to their Western counterparts. Within the shop the human relationship is again patterned on that of a family. Authority is in the hands of the master and his wife, while obedience is expected of the apprentices. The journeymen are like the big brothers or uncles who come in between the other two groups. Outside the shop the ambition of the master and his wife is to be able to buy a piece of land, rebuild the family home, and thenceforth enjoy the company of their fellow townsmen. The ambition of the apprentices and other workers is focused in the same direction.

The question may be raised, if the master and his wife can achieve their sense of social and psychological importance through shop ownership which, if it is at all profitable, brings other benefits, will not all merchants, assuming the same attitude, necessarily compete? Won't this force an all-around increase in business efficiency, scale of operation, and the exploitation of new markets with new products? The answer is an unqualified no. With a cultural emphasis on mutual dependence, the ceiling of competition is lowered in every sphere of endeavor. The individual Chinese desires the glory, wealth, and leisure that accompany success, but in his desire to climb he sees nothing wrong in settling for a position where he benefits by association, however marginal, with the more successful. He might become a servant in the big house; and as a servant he shares the social importance of the big house. He might become a secretary to an important person; as secretary he is far more fortunate than others who do not occupy a similar position. His daughter might marry into the family of a prominent person; as a relative of such a man he is treated by the rest of the community with more deference and respect than if he were not. Even making the successful one his "dry father" or a "sworn brother"[3] are all legitimate signs of his own success.

It has been plausibly argued for some time that commerce and industry cannot develop in a society where the majority of the people derive no more than a bare living from small farms. This observation appears to fit the condition of China where at least 75 percent of the population lived on farms and where even most of the so-called urban population had their roots in the villages or existed as absentee landlords. Such a picture is perhaps adequate for descriptive purposes, but it does not explain why those who have profited from commerce and industry, like all Chinese who attained a degree of success in any endeavor, desired to go back to their home community and invest in farms.

In 1959, nine years after the Communist revolution, the communization of all China was completed. Tenancy is a matter of history and farms are no longer as fragmented as before. But I shall describe the situation as it existed for centuries before 1949. It must serve as one of the bases for any generalization on long-range developments and how the Chinese economy evolved before the recent change.

The physical environment of the average Chinese farmer would not have been attractive to Americans. For one thing, the majority of Chinese farms were small, so small that with their ancient technological equipment only about 7 percent of them were suitable for optimum production. Though farms tended to be larger in the north than in the south, it remained true that four-fifths of the Chinese agriculturists derived their livelihood from farms that were less than five acres in extent.

For another thing, farming methods remained primitive—tools were crude, and even animal power, to say nothing of mechanical assistance, was often unavailable. The average farmer toiled twelve to fourteen hours a day during the summer. His winter work day was not much shorter because then he had to undertake other labors to eke out a living.

Both in the north and in the south, the women, when they did not go into the field, raised silkworms, pigs, and chickens, tended fruit trees or vegetable gardens, or wove. The products of these efforts supplemented the family income directly, or were sold or bartered in periodic markets.

The smallness of the farm and the primitive methods of land exploitation resulted in a third feature: poverty. At least one-third of the Chinese farmers existed on a calorie count that was below the minimum for subsistence. Further, in spite of the high rate of interest, which averaged 32 percent per year, more than one-third of the farmers covered in one nationwide survey had to obtain credit not, in the main, for productive purposes, but to purchase food for their families to eat and to meet ceremonial expenses.[4] The preceding figures related to owners and tenants. The lot of the farm laborer was even worse.

Logically, these features would seem to favor vigorous competition in agricultural pursuits and an exodus of persons from the farm into industry and commerce with a consequent expansion of these latter fields, thus producing a better balanced and more prosperous general economy. There is also the frequently propounded and widely accepted theory that military aggression often is rooted in overpopulation. In the recent past, the Germans and the Japanese spoke of the need for living space as a *raison d'être* for their actions. Even such self-proclaimed pacific nations as the United States and neutral Switzerland have lent a sympathetic ear to this argument. And bookshelves are crowded with works which support this thesis, an example of which is Josui de Castro's *The Geography of Hunger.*

But in China, necessity has been neither the mother of invention nor the father of aggression. For many centuries China has been overpopulated, land has been scarce, agriculture has been arduous, and malnutrition and even starvation have been the lot of untold millions. But instead of producing an inventive or even commercially aggressive spirit, these facts induced in the people who inhabited the villages an even greater desire to stay where they were in spite of the fact that it meant a further reduction of their already low standard of living.

This showed itself in several related ways. Perhaps the most pervasive evidence was the people's sentimental attachment to land, which often overrode all considerations of personal economic welfare. For to the Chinese, his land was not merely an investment; it was life itself. Accordingly, there was almost no sacrifice he was not prepared to make in order to avoid selling his land. When in dire need he was more likely to mortgage his land than to sell it, even though mortgage payments over the years often ran much higher than the actual price of the land.[5]

When a land transaction did occur in China, the scene was marked by a most revealing contrast of moods. For the seller's family the event was like a funeral, often marked by tears; for the buyer's family it was like a wedding, usually colored by laughter. For the same reason, the sale of land could not be final unless endorsed by the seller's grown sons and sometimes even by his brothers who were no longer living under the same roof with him. Furthermore, very often he could sell his land to someone who was not related only if his clansmen did not wish to buy.

The people's desire to remain in their own villages showed also in the large surplus of labor which remained on the land, especially in the south and southwest. During the many years of civil strife and the seven years of war against Japan, in spite of the tremendous demand for increased manpower by the military, Chinese farms and urban businesses that needed help never experienced any labor shortage. Migratory laborers did not all come from the ranks of the landless. Many originated from farms which were too small to maintain the number of people who had to live there. For this reason, though each acre of Chinese land produced 50 percent more rice or 15 percent more wheat (the two staple foods of the Chinese) than its American counterpart, each farmer in China produced less than one-fourteenth the annual average yield of the American farmer.

Why did such an abundant labor force stay on the small farms? Obviously the equal inheritance rule had something to do with it. Succession in the Chinese imperial line was mostly by primogeniture and sometimes by selection of the father before his death. For the common people, the rule was always equal division among the sons.

In some instances the eldest son would get a slightly larger share if he had the responsibility of taking care of the ancestral shrine formerly in the parental home. But his extra share was never significant and the custom was variable.

When I was preparing the 1953 edition of this book, I dismissed the importance of equal division to Chinese social development. I explained that while equal division might affect those whose parents left property, it would have no effect on those whose parents had nothing to leave. I have since that time spent a year in Japan (1964–1965) and am now forced to revise my view on this matter. For in contrast to China, one-son inheritance is the universal Japanese custom and is correlated directly with some of the basic differences between Chinese and Japanese social organizations. Under the one-son inheritance rule the noninheritors in Japan had to leave the families of their birth and enter into or form other groupings which, since their criteria for membership were other than kinship, became regional or national in scope. These regional and national organizations served as an effective infrastructure which materially helped the process of modernization when Japan came under intense pressure from the West.

On the other hand, with their equal-division rule, all Chinese sons were under no social pressure to depart from the families of their birth. Those whose parents left substantial property would of course have more incentive to stay than those whose parents left little or nothing. But even the latter would not be branded failures for remaining in the village since they also had their accepted places in it. The economic reality was hard on them but that fact was not cause for a sense of personal failure for which departure from the village was an established avenue of compensation. Consequently, the Chinese developed no nonkinship organizations strong, wide, or permanent enough to serve the needs of modernization when the West forced both Japan and China to open their doors.

However, though one-son inheritance added significantly to Japan's differences from China, it does not explain her differences from the West. In the absence of an egalitarian ideology, the noninheriting Japanese sons moved out of the households of their birth only to seek fixed places in hierarchically constructed wider groups after the kinship model, not horizontal associations of free and equal individuals. Once so affiliated, they usually remained for life. Consequently Japan arrived at the goal of modern industrialization via a course of social development quite different from that of the West.[6]

In fact, in contrast to the West the Japanese have shown little propensity to emigrate permanently *as individuals* from Japan proper, even in the days when the Japanese empire included Korea, Manchuria, and Taiwan. Some of them moved to these regions under government-sponsored organizations or giant semigovernment organizations *to work for these organizations*. But only a very few moved from Japan to stake out land and seek other fortunes as individuals. The same pattern can be seen today in the fact that Japanese college graduates prefer to work for Japanese corporations, not Western ones in Japan, even though the latter often pay much higher salaries than the former. They prefer the protective, hierarchical, and kinshiplike atmosphere of the former to the latter.

Under the custom of equal division, the Chinese sons tended to move away from their kinship base even less than did the Japanese. Over the centuries, only a very small percentage of Chinese migrated to areas adjacent to China such as South Asia. They have not even proved aggressive colonizers of Mongolia, Manchuria, Taiwan, the southwestern provinces, and the coastal islands. In Thailand, Malaysia, and Indonesia there are today, it is true, sizable Chinese minorities, but these represent no more than a fraction of the total Chinese population. Had the Chinese been as ready to emigrate as Europeans, it would not be difficult to imagine most of the world being Chinese.[7]

However, and this is an even more important point, granted that Chinese sons who received little or nothing from their parents were more likely to move away from their home villages, many of those who migrated to the Chinese frontier regions periodically returned to their old home towns or retired there after they had made their "fortune." Others sought at least to strengthen their ties with their ancestral communities through donations to clan temples, hospitals, and schools.

The pattern of Chinese emigration to the South Seas, Europe, and America followed the same pattern. In the first place, the majority of these emigrants, like their countrymen who went to Manchuria or southwest China, tended to maintain their home ties and have a desire to retire to their ancestral villages. In the second place, all emigrants had their origin in a few coastal counties of China. Most of the Chinese who settled in Europe came from a few counties in Chekiang Province; the majority of those in the South Seas came from a few counties in Fukien and Kwangtung provinces; and the ancestors of 90 percent of the Chinese in Hawaii were inhabitants of one

county in Kwangtung Province, while the forebears of over 90 percent of the Chinese in the continental United States came from four
adjacent counties in the same province. Admittedly the early contacts of the inhabitants of these coastal provinces with the West had
something to do with it. Then, too, some European emigrants to the
United States and elsewhere have also acted like the Chinese with
reference to their countries of origin, sending gifts, endowing
schools, and performing other good works. But early Western influence was by no means confined to the relative few coastal counties
from which some Chinese emigrated. And the poor in the vast non-
coastal areas of China did not seem to emigrate to any great extent.

If we look at China's history we cannot escape the conclusion that
the attachment of the Chinese to their ancestral communities is
matched by their reluctance to leave them. European emigrants may
entertain a sentimental regard for their homelands, but this has not
prevented their coming to America as individuals by the millions. At
the heights of China's dynastic powers, in Han (202 B.C.–A.D. 200),
in T'ang (A.D. 618–906), Yuan (A.D. 1260–1368), and in Ming (A.D.
1368–1644), the Chinese could have followed their conquering armies to many alien lands from Korea to Persia and eastern Europe
and become the pioneers of new domains. But they did nothing of
the kind.

If the simple fact of equal division had been the determining factor
in Chinese lack of desire to emigrate, poverty, famine, civil strife,
and repeated invasions by tribal peoples from the north and the
northwest would have driven many more Chinese away from China.

The fact turned out to be otherwise because equal division of inheritance and the reluctance to emigrate, instead of being cause and
effect, are actually common expressions of the same pattern—the
pattern of mutual dependence within the primary groups. This pattern is so deeply embedded and so satisfying socially and psychologically that the individual is prepared, almost without reflection, to
forgo material rewards that may be obtainable elsewhere or to lower
his material wants so that he can remain at home. His material welfare is relatively less important to him than his place of respect
among his primary social relations.

Chinese Government and Chinese Economy

The preceding analysis, it seems to me, clarifies the relationship between the Chinese government and the Chinese economy. Chinese

ruling houses, as we have observed, favored agriculture over commerce; in fact, they often went so far as to suppress the latter. The rulers never dared to challenge private ownership of land among the farmers, but they have always taken liberties with merchant wealth through special levies, commandeering, or outright confiscation. Because the agricultural tradition was of ancient vintage, its sanctity was respected by the tradition-bound government. Nor did the people, secure in this tradition, seek any change. But, for this same reason, the people did not develop an expanding and powerful industrial and commercial economy. And this, the absence of a countering force, permitted the government to assume an autocratic attitude in respect to these endeavors while permitting agriculture to proceed without significant interference.

Since the Chinese look to control over men as the principal source of wealth, there is a definite and traceable continuity that runs from the mutual dependence of parents and children, among relatives, between masters and disciples, between friends, and between big bureaucrats and small bureaucrats to that between the government as a whole and the people as a whole. For security in their old age, parents do not look to property ownership so much as they do to the filial piety of their sons. In the same way, the measure of a dynastic regime's success was not the extent to which it developed the country's natural resources but the degree to which it secured the obedience of its subjects and ensured their protection. In all cases the balance of power depended upon socially or politically defined relationships, not upon economic rights.

This autocratic behavior of the Chinese government was somewhat modified between 1929 and 1937 under the Nationalist regime of Chiang Kai-shek. This was the period when Chiang's rule was at the summit of its power and popularity. It was also during this period that China's modern commerce and industry reached their highest development since the time China's doors were knocked open by the West. A combination of three factors forced a modification of the traditional relationship between China's government and her economy.

First, much of China's commercial and industrial wealth was centered around or deposited in the banks located in the foreign concessions and in the International Settlement in Shanghai. Though some banks were Chinese, most were foreign-owned, and because of extraterritorial privileges the Nationalist government, though powerful, had no legal means of reaching this wealth.

Second, in its attempt to consolidate its power over the vestigial

warlords and the upcoming Communists, the Nationalist government had to depend upon foreign supplies of arms which it could not
manufacture within the country. These foreign arms had to be bar-
gained for through the regular channels and procedures of foreign
trade which only the financiers and the commercial people could
handle.

Third, the Nationalist government, in its bid for international
prestige and assistance, had to gain the confidence of the Western
powers. As commerce and industry are of primary importance in
these Western countries, the Nationalist government could not secure their confidence unless it also showed a certain degree of respect
toward its own merchants and industrialists. Consequently, industrial and commercial interests were more respected and favored by
the Nationalist government than by any previous regime in China's
history. In return, it was more ardently supported by these interests
than was any previous regime. The relationship between the Nationalist government and the commercial and industrial community was
so close that the Japanese militarists, in support of their expansionist
schemes in the thirties, launched repeated propaganda attacks charg-
ing the Nationalist government with a "subversive alliance with the
Chekiang financial lords."

When the ravages of war destroyed the bases of the Chinese commercial and industrial interests in the coastal provinces, the Nationalist government lost no time in reasserting its never questioned supremacy over them. The pattern was so much a part of the Chinese
tradition that the readjustment occurred without significant popular
protest.

American Economic Attitudes

Our purpose here is not to plow over the ground so thoroughly covered in numerous accounts of the structure of American business
and agriculture. Here we shall investigate the attitude of the self-
reliant American toward his economic activities. But absolute self-
reliance is an unattainable ideal. As explained in Chapter 3, every
individual has two environments—the external and the internal—
and he must balance these in a way that provides him with reasonable security. This security is made up of a sense of self-importance
and a feeling of purposefulness. The Chinese, who retains his primary ties to which he relates all subsequent bonds, finds his security
in human relationships. The American, who regards all human rela-

tionships as subject to severance or to being repatterned when personally convenient, must seek security outside the human fold. And since God helps him who helps himself, the one remaining source of security is the acquisition of material possessions or the conquest of the physical environment in other ways. The goal of their conquest may not even be desirable to him when it is attained but the art of conquering often becomes an end in itself.

American economic activities assume, therefore, a number of characteristics that are foreign to the Chinese. There is a divisiveness which, though somewhat restrained in politics and religion, is unbridled under the guise of the free enterprise tradition. New forms of economic enterprise keep emerging. Even though some industry observers insist that conglomerates (companies that diversify their production categories) are not as prevalent as people imagine them to be[8] and even though the federal government is ever watchful with its antitrust laws, mergers and diversification of products are clear facts of American economic life. Too, there is a constant change in production procedures and product styles, thereby introducing new kinds of goods and services or giving new appearances to the old. Intense competition makes such changes indispensable because the very existence of a manufacturing concern, and even the retail or service enterprises it supplies, depends upon its determination to expand and to create the new—and its success in doing so. It was for this reason that, when asked the secret of success, one of the leading businesswomen in the United States said, "Beat last year's record."

To assist businesses in reaching this goal, commercial and industrial firms must employ advertising agencies or public relations specialists to inform prospective consumers how necessary to their welfare is a new service or goods of whose existence, much less necessity, these consumers are perforce ignorant until the campaign begins. "Give me any product," I heard an advertising executive say, "and I can make it sell." The variety of clientele of some of the public relations firms makes fascinating reading. A report on one of the world's largest of these firms, Hill and Knowlton, for example, shows that its activities included "the job of staging the introduction of Svetlana Alliluyeva, Stalin's daughter, to the American public . . . ; representing the Bahamas Ministry of Tourism," under attack for gangster infiltration of the island's gambling concessions; besides helping "the Remington and Winchester companies beat off proposed curbs on sales of guns," and "the cigarette companies defend themselves against all the persuasive and widely reported evidence that smoking is unhealthy," and so on.[9] In this rush for higher profits, price-fixing and especially price wars to force competitors out of the market become inevitable.

However, while the American entrepreneur's efforts are directed toward maximizing his profit so as to achieve more material comfort, his ultimate satisfaction lies elsewhere. Many a Chinese has been puzzled by the unfaltering zeal of wealthy American industrialists and businessmen for whom greater monetary returns can have little material meaning. We do not have to cite the careers of the most famous, but just consider the case of any one of the vice-presidents of General Motors, each of whom, in the year 1949 alone, reportedly received a bonus of from $227,450 to over $500,000.[10] From the Chinese point of view any one of them could stop worrying about profit right then and there. Most wealthy Chinese bureaucrats or merchants have always chosen to retire early in life. The characteristic Chinese attitude is summed up in the saying, "When currents are swift, bravely stop at the suitable moment."

The careers of H. H. Kung and T. V. Soong are interesting to examine in this connection. Both are millionaires whose wealth was derived from political power. But following Chiang's defeat, both chose a life of ease and silence in the United States. Neither has participated in any activities, such as the China Institute or the Committee for Free Asia, aimed at promoting faith in the Nationalist administration.

The majority of Chinese bureaucrats would have stopped long before Kung and Soong did. For to the Chinese, money is important to obtain the needed comforts of life, and as a means to conspicuous consumption for maintaining or increasing his status in the community. The successful American who has more money than he needs to ensure the comforts of living nevertheless continues his quest because money is the most significant sign of his importance—his control over things.

Here the American faces a dilemma. He has greater control over more things than anyone else on earth. But such control is not as a rule emotionally satisfying unless it leads to closer or more permanent relationships with men. In obedience to the ideal of self-reliance, it is precisely this need—common to all mankind and an inevitable consequence of human life, into whatever society a man may be born—that the American has sought to deny.

For all human beings begin life in a state of dependence. The child's physical needs are supplied by his elders. As the once completely dependent individual grows progressively more independent and moves beyond this first set of relationships, the pattern that he has learned in these formative years becomes the basis of his reactions to the wider society and the other individuals who compose it. All humans—Americans, Eskimos, Chinese, or Hottentots—have a compelling need to be in the company of other human beings to satisfy their needs for sociability, security, and status. Control over the physical universe is meaningless unless that power can in some ways be transferred to the human scene so as to further the individuals' desire for association with his fellow men.

The Chinese, by retaining permanently a close relationship with those persons he has known in infancy and childhood, meets easily the need for intimate human association. He therefore feels little compulsion to extend his control over the physical world, since he achieves a sense of self-importance and purposefulness by the direct route available to him in the primary groups. His self-importance is assured through his seniority and the respect due him. His purposefulness perpetuates itself because his kinship and communal obligations and responsibilities never end. The American, however, follows a circuitous path in his search for emotional security. He strives to separate himself from his previous ties, but his conquest of the physical environment is propelled, consciously and unconsciously, by his search for the same humanly satisfying rewards sought by the Chinese. Yet when he has arrived at a position where he possesses much more than is needed for his material comfort, he is rudely awakened by the temporary and superficial nature of his relationships with other men. To strengthen his sense of self-importance and to ensure his place among his fellows, he intensifies his acquisitive activities and creates more material devices.

But material devices, however fancy and ingenious, are lifeless. They do not reciprocate with love and affection. Here is where pets, especially dogs come in. Dogs provide plenty of affection when and where and how the individual-centered person wants it, but ask for very little in return, also when and where and how the individual-centered person wants it.

Consequently, the American attitude toward dogs (and secondarily cats) is in sharp contrast to that of the Chinese. In fact this is among the most spectacular of the contrasts between the two ways of life. The pet food business today is more hefty than the baby food business. The increase in pet food sold (4 percent a year) has been higher than the gross national product for several years. It is a $3 billion-a-year industry with an added $310 million a year for breeders. Dog and cat dinners fill an average of 210 feet of shelf space in the supermarket, more space than any other grocery category. The variety of flavors and ingredients and the amount of television advertising are simply fantastic (see Paul Ingrassia and David P. Garino, "There is a Bull Market in Dog and Cat Food," in *Wall Street Journal*, reprinted in *San Francisco Chronicle*, March 4, 1979). We have not only national groups such as the National Association of the Pet Industry, the American Humane Association which has some 750 local affiliates, and the American Society for the Prevention of Cruelty to Animals which has an even larger number of local branches, but also numerous local organizations such as Pet Pride, Cat Charity, Cat Care, the Good Shepherd Foundation, the Pet Assistance Foundation, the Mercy League and the Voice of the Voiceless in Los Angeles and, in New York City, the Save-A-Cat League, Friends of Animals, Inc., American Feline Society, and the Institute of Human–Animal Relationship. In addition there are magazines such as *Show Dog* and *The Poodle Show Case* and many special events such as the Cat Week International at Yonkers and the annual Animal Kingdom Ball in New York City. One writer entitles a chapter in his book on pets, "The New Religion."[11] Is it any wonder that we see pet cemeteries and pet restaurants and hotels? In at least one instance recently, a woman in the midwest secured the change of a cemetery rule so that she could be buried with her cat.

All this would make the average Chinese giddy, if he only knew. To most Chinese dogs are for warding off prowlers and cats are for eliminating mice. That was why the Communist government of China met with high compliance among the people when it moved to eliminate dogs and cats. The success of this centrally directed campaign was in sharp contrast to other centrally directed campaigns which were failures, or at best not so successful.

NOTES

1. Some other games are: "Swap, the wheeler-dealer game," ("buy cheap, trade smart, out swap everyone"); "High Society," in which the players try for entry into the blue book of society via estates, property, status symbols, liquid assets, country club lane, etc., and numerous games of war strategy and of dating and love.

2. The Chinese "cash" was a metal disk which had a square hole in its center to permit stringing. This ancient medium of exchange was discontinued during the 1920s in favor of coins based on the Western model.

3. For explanation of these and other ritual or pseudo-kinship relationships, see Chapter 5, note 5.

4. J. L. Buck, *Land Utilization in China*, p. 439.

5. Pearl S. Buck, in her novel, *The Good Earth,* has, in my view, captured this Chinese sentimental regard for land as no other author has ever done. The protagonist, Wong Lung, even after having become wealthy, rigidly opposed the attempts of his modern educated sons to liquidate the family's landed property and move into the city. Americans can also get a glimpse of how the Chinese farmer feels about his land by reading the story of Widow Nellie McCall and Tom Moser, the last two holdouts to be evicted from their houses to make way for the $116 million Tellico Dam in Tennessee (one account appeared in the *San Francisco Chronicle,* November 14, 1979).

6. This difference between China and Japan is explained in detail in my book *Iemoto: the Heart of Japan.*

7. See Eileen Hsu-Balzer, Richard J. Balzer, and Francis L. K. Hsu, *China Day by Day,* pp. xiv–xv.

8. Thomas O'Hanlon, "Odd News about Conglomerates," *Fortune* (June 15, 1967), pp. 175–177.

9. T. A. Wise, "Hill and Knowlton's World of Images," *Fortune* (September 1, 1967), p. 98.

10. According to *Buiness Week* magazine (June 1, 1968), 133 top executives in various corporations each received total salaries and bonuses of $100,000 or more. The largest salary was $331,470 for 1967, paid to the president of Distillers Corporation Seagrams, Ltd. But the three top salaries and bonuses combined were received by the chairmen of Proctor and Gamble, International Telephone & Telegraph, and Johnson & Johnson, each of whom received about $500,000 for the year.

11. Berkeley Rice, *The Other End of the Leash: The American Way with Pets,* p. 19. Also Iris Nowell, *The Dog Crisis.*

CHAPTER 12

Industrial Failure and Economic Strife

Perhaps the most evident and consequently the most widely appreciated fact about the pre-1949 economy of China is that, despite the urgent necessity to do so, the Chinese, after a century of intimate contact with the West, failed to join the mainstream of industrialization that swept up every other major noncolonial nation. Up to World War II the largest plants, the most up-to-date machinery, and the majority of China's industrial laborers were employed in the textile industry. Yet as late as 1930, hand looms consumed about 78.5 percent of the cotton yarn on the Chinese market. In 1933 the most reliable estimates showed that China had less than two million industrial workers and of this number, less than one-tenth were employed in plants hiring ten or more workers and utilizing some form of mechanical power. But even this insignificant industrial labor force was mostly employed by foreign capital. Before World War II, the total capital invested in modern industries in China was estimated at $1.3 billion of which only one-fourth represented Chinese investment.

The nature of Chinese cities also clearly reveals the relatively somnolent mood of the Chinese economy. In 1937 the provincial capital was the most populous city in twenty-one of the twenty-six Chinese provinces. In five provinces, the capital was smaller than or was matched by other cities. But of three of these, one province contained the former national capital, Peking, the second contained Nanking, the capital of the Nationalist government, and within the boundaries of the third was Shanghai, a city developed under the pressure of the Western powers and whose swampland foundation was laid only a century ago. In the United States, however, as of 1947 there were only fifteen states of the Union in which the state capital was the largest city, while in eighteen states the capital was outranked in size by from one to three cities and in the remaining fifteen by from four to ten cities. According to the 1970 Census the picture remained much the same. In eighteen states of the Union the capital was the largest city while in thirty-two the capital was outranked in size by at least one or more cities. It is obvious that Chinese cities were founded on a political rather than a commercial and industrial base and that exactly the reverse is true in the United States. Although during the past century some Chinese cities have been the harbor of several business firms of some magnitude and wealth, considering the size and population of the country as a whole, these are hardly worthy of comparison to the business giants of the Western, and particularly American, urban centers.

Why Have the Chinese Failed to Industrialize?

The lack of capital has been regarded as one obvious reason for the failure of the Chinese to industrialize their country. The absence of a system of primogeniture means that all inheritances, instead of growing in size, tended to become smaller and smaller as they were divided among many. However, this is far from being the entire story. For history shows that wealthy Chinese instead of entering into a new business or expanding existing businesses tended to expend their money on conspicuous consumption and land. Even when, during the last hundred years, before 1949, industrial enterprises were founded by the government on state capital or with cash borrowed from foreign powers, such ventures were soon bankrupt. The absence of one-son inheritance rule is probably a secondary rather than a primary aspect of the Chinese economy.

The culture pattern of mutual dependence is a far more comprehensive explanation of China's failure to industrialize. It was because of the emphasis on mutual dependence that the Chinese failed to pioneer in the frontier areas just as they refrained from emigration. And again it was this pattern that caused the Chinese either to be without capital resources or not to use them for business adventures. All are part and parcel of the Chinese lack of aggressive designs toward the world of things, an attitude that is not a bit "spiritual" in origin but patently "human"—an emphasis upon mutual dependence among men. It is for this reason that Chinese parents never teach a son to "go it alone," for what his parents possess is his and what he later comes to own is then at the disposal of his parents.

Therefore, instead of considering personal savings as the most important element of old-age security, the Chinese depend upon male descendants to look out for their welfare.

Herein lies the difference between conspicuous consumption in China and in America. In America, it is largely personal and only incidentally ceremonial. It brings to the individual himself an aura of prestige, and is not only a token of his class standing at any point of time but also an index of his movement upward. The indices—whether Christian Dior gowns for his wife, the season's most gala debut for his daughter, or his own collection of Renaissance art—are all acknowledgments of his personal worth. Consequently, he is precise about his expenditures that do not contribute to this sense and cautious about gift-making in general.

While the American engages in conspicuous consumption because he owes it to himself, the Chinese does so because he owes it to others —parents and relatives, friends and fellow townsmen. Consequently, he has less leeway in determining the extent to which he disburses his surplus. And even if he possesses no surplus, he still is forced to engage in conspicuous consumption because of its characteristically Chinese form. For the Chinese variety is essentially ceremonial in nature, not personal, and the character and degree of the individual's expenditures are commanded by his established place in the community. This is so because, while no one expects to raise his class standing in this manner, the respectable person must fulfill his obligations to others. For the living, he builds a house too big for the family, and spends lavishly for such things as birthday celebrations, gifts on festive occasions, and entertainment in general. For the dead and the yet unborn, he constructs a stately ancestral graveyard, refurbishes the clan temple, enlarges the many volumes of genealogical records, and spares no expense on his parents' funerals. This is the price he pays to ensure a respectable place among his relatives and within his community. Budgetary considerations are minor compared to that, since to surrender his position in the primary group is to forsake the true determinant of importance.

When a wealthy American deems it necessary to reduce the sums he expends in conspicuous consumption, he finds it relatively simple to make excuses for his economy measures. There may be knowing neighborhood gossip about the fact that he did not take his midwinter trip to Florida, that his wife is now assisted by only one servant instead of two, or that the daughter's wedding was a rather minor affair. But an explanation that business comes before pleasure, that the son's departure for college made two servants unnecessary, or that the doctor advised a quiet wedding because of the wife's well-known nervous condition is usually sufficient to subdue the rumors. Once in a more secure financial position the trips are resumed, the servant rehired, and the next family wedding is a spectacle. The point is that conspicuous consumption, since it involves individual expenditures for individual aggrandizement, is individually determined.

Not so in China. Since the forms of conspicuous consumption relate mostly to ceremonial matters they are, therefore, of serious concern not only to an individual or his family, but to his entire kinship group, friends, and neighbors. Take funerals, for example. In America they are outside the realm of conspicuous consumption. Services at a particular funeral home and the kind of casket and grave marker do raise the cost of a funeral, but there is no reception and no other way in which a funeral can be made more elaborate. But the family pattern and ancestor worship require that Chinese dead be honored and buried with great ritual and ceremonial pomp.

The lavish expenditures connected with a Chinese funeral would dismay the average American. Among the wealthy the coffin is kept in the house for long periods while hired monks and priests recite sutras. The home is filled with life-sized papier-mâché images of commodities, livestock, and servants, all of which are eventually burned to provide for the comfort of the dead. An overflowing crowd of guests is served expensive feasts and entertained by storytellers. The less well-to-do and even the relatively poor often make similar stupendous efforts. Since filial piety requires a man, rich or poor, to consider the welfare of his parents before all else, it follows that the living should spare no effort to assure the comfort of the dead. But it is equally imperative that an auspicious funeral meet the definitive expectations of the living. A man who fails to make his best efforts on such an occasion soon finds himself handicapped and slighted on all sides. Here there can be no excuses, for in this social environment, a person's worth is known to practically everyone. Tradition determines the form and extent of most conspicuous consumption, and the individual must perform his part accordingly or suffer the social consequences.

Of course, even where tradition dictates everything there is always room for idiosyncratic interpretation by ambitious individuals who want to outdo their fellow men. In the Chinese context, if such individuals break the economic backbone of their families because of lavish funerals for their parents, no one would say they were wrong. Instead, they would become known as outstanding examples of filial piety.

These same expectations also apply to birthday celebrations for aged parents, family weddings, and gift-giving in festivals. An individual can, therefore, save himself economically only at the price of self-respect. As previously noted, agricultural surveys showed that many farmers obtained credit to purchase food and to meet the cost of birthdays, weddings, and funerals. The average cost of a wedding was about four months' net family income, while the customary funeral cost about three months' net family income.[1] There is no American ceremonial that is the counterpart to this expenditure.

It is only in such a framework that we can understand certain facts that, to the American, appear irrational. Consider the case of a widowed schoolteacher who for fifteen years provided for her three children. In the melee of the Sino-Japanese War the family lost its house and furniture and took what refuge it could find in Free China's crowded wartime capital. In 1943 one of her sons became a clerk in a factory and she was able to stop teaching. When the son became betrothed, the mother decided on a very elaborate wedding. The clerk's income barely kept the family going, and their only other resource was a share in some real estate which the mother had saved for many years to purchase. She sold this property in order to pay the son's nuptial expenses.

The wedding was a great success. Those relatives and friends who also had taken refuge in Chungking attended and everyone had a good time. All concerned were happy and satisfied. Two months later, the son lost his job and the family was without support. The heartbreaking sequel wherein disaster followed disaster is not important for us here. The question is why, under war conditions with all their uncertainties, did the widow give up for such a cause the one material source of security she possessed?

Although Americans would consider her actions unwise, it all seemed logical to the Chinese. Having almost singlehandedly raised her children to adulthood, this gay wedding of her eldest son signified the successful completion of her duty. Also, throughout the previous years when her children were young and helpless, the relatives had lent some assistance, and the wedding was her announcement that she had a grown son upon whom she could henceforth fully rely.

Such elaborate ceremonial activities express and strengthen the social bonds among men and encourage them to stay together; a relative lack of ceremony indicates independence, and an implicit acknowledgment that the bonds between men are temporary. When an individual finds security in human relationships, there is no less need for hard work and competition, but it is the rare speculative spirit who deviates from the established path. It is precisely this spirit and this desire that are encouraged by independence from other human beings. Thus the Chinese pattern of mutual dependence not only cuts down the accumulation of savings, large or small, but it also discourages ventures into the unknown and the untried. It was this that prevented the rise of large-scale industrial development.

Many Americans conclude that since the Chinese are well known as inveterate gamblers, they must therefore possess the speculative spirit. There is indeed a great deal of gambling both in China and among the Chinese who have settled in America. But it is erroneous to say this means the Chinese are speculative. Besides, there is no reason to suppose that the people of China gamble more than Americans, and for the Chinese in America, gambling seems to be largely a recreational outlet for those separated from family and country. Under the harsh exclusionist laws of immigration (abolished since 1942) the Chinese in Chinatowns were in this respect like American soldiers in Vietnam. The difference is in their substitute activities for loneliness and boredom. But of deeper significance is the fact that while Americans bet on practically anything from sports to presidential elections, the Chinese prefer games with familiar and well-defined situations, such as mahjong or *tien chiu.* American gambling usually is individually conceived and individually engaged in; it can occur with no tools and on the spur of the moment. Further, organized gambling in America is a highly impersonal affair, carried on with or without equipment and between strangers, many of whom may do "business" with one another once but never again. The Chinese rarely engage in offhand betting. The most popular Chinese gambling games are invariably played with certain tools; the participants sit in definite positions, know each other, and meet together regularly.

In America, the outcome of comparable games, such as bridge or canasta, is rarely thought of as a gambling proposition. Chinese wager on just such games of skill; Americans usually gamble on games or events the outcome of which is wholly or largely a question of chance, such as dice games, or over whose outcome the bettor has little or no control, such as sports. The Chinese form of gambling is truly competitive, but the American brand is essentially speculative. From the office baseball pool through the casino roulette table to

what is about the most humanly isolated, noncompetitive, and purely speculative gamble imaginable—a coin and an arm pitted against
a slot machine—American gambling is primarily a privatized business proposition. To be sure, many Americans also play poker and go
to the racetrack for the sociability these gatherings afford. But these
persons are not real gamblers, nor do they handle the bulk of the
money that changes hands through gambling. Conversely, though in
the thirties horse and dog racing as well as lotteries were introduced
to China by way of the treaty ports, they never spread beyond these
partially Westernized zones and even there never attracted widespread interest. Neither have the Chinese ever gambled on the outcome of such events as the ancient dragonboat race in south China,
nor in modern times have they seen fit to bet on their favorites in
athletic events such as wrestling matches, track and field meets, or
soccer, basketball, and volleyball games. Gambling on sports strikes
the Chinese as highly immoral. In brief, even when gambling, Chinese feel no desire to deviate from the familiar, no compulsion to risk
the unknown.

Since the person outside the bureaucracy could hardly better himself by engaging in agriculture and since he had little wish to develop
or control other physical resources, the ambitious person of the modern day followed two new avenues of advancement. Many young
Chinese became protégés of missionaries, either as students or assistants, thereby learning English and something of Western ways. This
prepared them for positions with the Chinese branches of such foreign firms as Asiatic Petroleum, Standard Oil, or General Motors.
Others became compradores, the middlemen between Western producers and traders and the Chinese consumers. For a hundred years
after the Opium War many of these men attained great wealth and,
through it, political prominence. Neither of these routes deviated
from the principal direction of Chinese economic effort: to meet
one's needs through dependence upon the human element, not
through the exploitation and control of physical resources.

We can now better understand why China failed to respond to
the challenge of Western economic pressure. The essential problem
was not the absence of capital; whatever capital became available
through the government was in turn the object of corruption. The official regarded public funds as a legitimate source of private income,
for this income was necessary to ingratiate himself to a superior.
When such bureaucrats interfered with entrepreneurs, the latter ac-

ceded not solely out of weakness, but mainly because their culture patterns encouraged them to accept dependence upon the throne and its representatives as more profitable than conflict.

One scholar, Max Weber, has come closer than any other to understanding why China did not fit itself into the pattern of Western capitalism. Weber saw that China possessed nearly all the factors favorable to capitalist development. The restraining influences, Weber declared, were certain "irrational" elements basic to the social and political structure. He cited as the most important of these, magical animism and ancestor worship. The latter, he continued, cemented fraternal harmony and, in the form of filial piety, implemented all human relations of superior and subordinate.[2]

Weber was clearly on the right track in asserting that these relationships impeded the growth of Chinese commerce and industry. But he did not see that ancestor worship, fraternal harmony, and filial piety are all manifestations of the same orientation that held back economic development. The relation is not one of cause and effect, but extensions from a common source. In the same way, it is not essentially a causal relationship that exists between the ethics of Protestantism and the growth of capitalism.[3] Rather, the two are twin consequences of an individualistic orientation fundamental to Western life, another outgrowth of which is American self-reliance.

Further, it is unfortunately true that many Western scholars are sometimes guilty of ethnocentricism. Weber made the ethnocentric error of relating Western capitalism to "rationality" and Chinese economic behavior to the "irrational," magical, and animistic elements of Chinese culture. The exclusion of Blacks from many white churches and schools in the United States appears very "irrational" to the Chinese. The attitude which supports that exclusion is tied up with certain American myths concerning Negro sexual behavior and racial purity. Each society has its own cultural premises; some of these are held by a section of the population while others are held by all. No matter what the case, members of one society behave in accordance with its premises with just as much logic as do members of another society who are conditioned to a different set of premises.

Whatever the society's premises, its members look out for their personal security within the cultural framework embodying them. The personal security of the individual American lies in his conquest of the physical environment, staking out a world of his own in which he can exclude others if he so wishes, because of his premise of self-reliance. His Chinese counterpart finds security within the kinship and primary circles, helps his relatives and shares his troubles with them, because of his premise of mutual dependence. This is the basic reason the Chinese never developed a capitalistic system on their own, and why they did not adopt it when challenged by the West. Since economic gains are not their primary source of security, Chinese do not emphasize them. This is also the basic explanation why Westerners, and particularly Americans, overrode authority and the restraints of tradition; by stressing complete freedom and equality, economic success or control over things becomes the principal foundation of an American's personal security.

Competition: Point of Unity or Division

Chinese competitiveness, to which we have referred at several points, may seem similar in spirit to American competitiveness but its effects are not at all comparable. For, instead of being divisive, Chinese competitiveness tends to bring men together. Filial piety is an area of such competition. Two men of comparable status try to outdo each other in the care and attention they give to their parents. An extreme expression of competitive filial piety was related in Chapter 3: the son who, instead of cutting from his arm the flesh thought to be needed to cure his father's illness, opened his abdomen to extract a slice of his liver. This is indeed competitiveness, but of a kind that strengthens the parent-son relationship at no expense to a third party.

Similarly, Chinese families strive to surpass their equals in ceremonial activities: bigger and better funerals, weddings and birthday celebrations, and larger and finer residences, clan temples and genealogical records. But all of this is directly related to obligations to parents, relatives, and even the community at large. The initiators gain face and the participants share the glory. Competitive victories of this order do not depend on the success of one person being based on the failure of another. This remains substantially true even where competition is, in the first instance, an individual matter. Imperial examinations are a case in point. There were, of course, great numbers who failed to pass, but these "losers" could always try again. More important, what the successful candidate looked forward to was the day when his family, his clan, or his community would all be bettered because of his achievement.

Even economic conflict must be examined in terms of mutual dependence. In an agricultural country, such as China, these conflicts largely center about land ownership.

Many Westerners and Chinese revolutionaries and reformers, stunned by Chinese poverty and the small size of the average farm, assumed that all tenants must hate the landlords intensely, particularly the big landowners. The actual relationship of the two groups was by no means so simple. It is undeniable that a few giant absentee landlords turned over the management of their properties to harsh and unscrupulous agents. In addition, many officials and warlords, who were absentee owners themselves, were guilty of torturing tenants to extract exorbitant rents on land. These abuses were among the reasons for the many outbursts against landlords in the early years of the Communist revolution. The Communists' initial appeal was to the landless. A life-sized model of the "rent collection courtyard" of a tyrannical landlord in Tayi County, Szechuan Province was exhibited throughout the country in the sixties. I saw it in Canton. It depicts how landlord Liu, in partnership with local warlords, engaged in blackmail, corruption, bribery, and torture to traffic in drugs and extract rent from helpless tenants. In the first years after 1949 many landlords and rich peasants were publicly tried and then imprisoned or executed.[4]

However, much of the traditional Chinese landlord-tenant relationship must be characterized as personal, paternal, and, therefore, often cordial. Since most landlords resided in the area of their properties, they and their tenants visited each other and exchanged gifts at festival times or on ceremonial occasions. Having reviewed in Chapter 5 the conditions and relationships that prevented the gentry from becoming the exploiters of their fellow townsmen, we need only add here that these same factors operated also to restrain many landlords. Because of the patterns of mutual dependence it was not unusual to find landlords who took great pride in their benevolence, and tenants who felt a similar pride in being the objects of the owner's generosity.

Additional evidence as to the true nature of the landlord-tenant relationship is revealed by the apparently irrelevant fact that the intelligentsia were among the chief supporters of the Communist movement before and after it gained power. Western news media had a great time reporting how badly the Chinese intellectuals were crushed after the "Let Hundred Flowers Bloom" episode of the fifties, but they failed to note how many of the criticisms leveled against the new regime were in a *constructive* vein. We now have much more graphic details about the far greater atrocities—during the Red Guards' rampage and later when the now fallen Gang of Four was in control—perpetrated against musicians and artists, writers, scholars, medical practitioners, and many others. Many of the victimized had devoted their lives to the revolutionary cause yet there is no evidence that a majority of the Chinese intelligentsia would have substantially changed its view regarding the need and potentiality of the regime. Throughout the crises they argued vehemently about techniques, methods, and approaches involved in reaching the goals, but they never disagreed about the goals. Furthermore, I have met scores of such victims or their relatives in Hong Kong and elsewhere, some of whom were able to leave because of the late Premier Chou's intervention. I have yet to meet one who held greatly different views on this.

For years some scholars and journalists maintained that the Nationalist government failed to push land reform because the majority of its officials and their relatives were landowners. But they failed to realize that the economic foundation of the intelligentsia was no different. Since most of its present-day members are products of the modern schools in China or abroad, since this education was not available to the poor, and since the purchase of land has always been the preferred form of investment by the well-to-do, it should be evident that the main body of the intelligentsia comes from landed wealth. Yet this privileged background did not prevent their adherence to the Communist cause. In reshaping the land tenure problem, the Communist government at first did not have a clear program except the belief that, as Dr. Sun Yat-sen's slogan maintained, "Tillers of the soil must own their land." As soon as they took power, the Communists broke up all of the larger estates and embarked upon a thorough program of investigation preparatory to eventual land redistribution. They did not decide on communization on a national scale until much later. In all this, members of the intelligentsia were active participants.[5]

It appears that among the Chinese, differences in economic interests did not prevent the intelligentsia, as a whole, from substantially supporting the revolutionary cause.

American competitiveness, in spite of many rules and attitudes concerning sportsmanship and chivalry, never brings men together because its basis is "each for himself." One individual's gain invariably means some degree of loss to others. Consequently, if Mr. White is promoted from the position of a foreman to that of a plant superintendent, Mr. Brown finds absolutely no comfort or pleasure in that fact because he lives on the same street or is related to White. If Brown is himself a foreman, he is likely to feel much worse. Because the goal of the individual is complete self-reliance, economic differences, almost by definition, divide men. The more successful need the inferiority of the less successful to make their triumph more absolute; the less fortunate resent both the privileges of the better situated and their help, however benevolent, when proffered. To accept the assistance of others is to confess weakness, and, if the assistance verges on charity, it is a source of humiliation. Whatever one individual accomplishes or receives must come through his own efforts. This is the most important reason for industrial unrest in the United States and the reason why overall peace between labor and management is unlikely to be attained in the foreseeable future. The double-digit inflation of recent years has only exacerbated this unrest, but has not created it. It will continue even if the inflation is under control.

The history of unionism in China bears certain external resemblances to the struggles of organized labor in America, but once again these surface similarities are deceptive. Chinese unions of the American type first appeared about 1910. Among them, to mention a few, were the Railway Worker's Union, the Postal Worker's Union, the Textile Worker's Union, and the Seamen's Union. Unlike the guilds, these were national or at least nonlocal organizations, and their membership ranged from several thousand to nearly a hundred thousand. The unions had paid officials, retained lawyers, investigated labor conditions, and staged strikes for higher wages and better working conditions. Between the middle of the thirties and 1949, these unions were represented in the People's Assembly, an advisory body to the Nationalist government.

But the forces undermining these unions were tremendous. The unions themselves were small and unimportant in a country where factory industry was rudimentary. Because the economic situation was precarious for the majority, the workers either did not care to join or were afraid to. Besides, and more typically Chinese, the Nationalist party, with the power of government behind it, either infiltrated the unions or clamped down on them from without. Union leaders were often arrested and tortured in the name of anticommunism. Finally, those foreign powers, especially the British and the Japanese, who had a large industrial stake in China, were even more adamant in their opposition to organized labor than was the Nationalist government.[6] When the government did try to legislate against child labor in factory employment and to establish minimum conditions of work, it was unable to secure the cooperation of those who controlled the greatest portion of industry and who were protected by concessions and extraterritoriality—the foreign investors.

The strength of the forces—economic, government, and foreign—opposed to what American labor leaders call "militant unionism" may appear sufficient to explain why, despite their depressed condition, the workers shied away from union activities. In the Western world, such difficulties and acts of repression have often served to unite and inflame the workers. But even the messianic message and tireless efforts of the Communist organizers during the Nationalist rule failed to move the Chinese city workers. Says Benjamin Schwartz, a keen student of the vicissitudes of the Chinese Communist party: its "long series of attempts . . . to beat down the *iron wall of proletarian indifference* . . . were finally to end in complete failure."[7] The demoralization of the unions that followed the suppression of the Peking–Hankow Railway Worker's Union strike in 1923 brought forth this somewhat exasperated commentary from Ch'en Tu-hsiu, a founder of the Chinese Communist party:

> The Chinese proletariat is immature both quantitatively and qualitatively. Most of the workers are still imbued with patriarchal notions and their family ties and regional patriotism are extremely strong. These former handicraft workers carry over the habits of their previous existence even when they become industrial workers. They do not feel the need for political action and are still full of ancient superstitions.[8]

Ch'en's Marxist explanation of the Chinese workers' reluctance to commit themselves to economic struggle in the pattern of Western communism echoes the same argument that Max Weber used to explain the failure of the Chinese to devleop their economy in the model of Western capitalism. Weber scored Chinese "irrationality"; Ch'en denounced the workers' "immaturity," but Schwartz came closer to the truth when he let the matter pass as "indifference."

This attitude, as we have seen in the case of the businessman, and for that matter the bureaucrat or the farmer, is not one of total indifference to economic success as such. Instead it is indifference to and rejection of the idea that personal security can be obtained through competition and bitter strife with others for the control of the physical environment. The pattern of mutual dependence directs all men —laborer and businessman, tenant farmer and landowner—to seek their security and advancement through persons, through the alliance of superior and subordinate. This means that when there is conflict, the tendency is to compromise rather than to adopt a unilateral position.

It is for these reasons that Chinese workers have never been militant supporters of large-scale labor movements and have not, in the Western sense of the term, proved to be good or persevering fighters in an economic struggle. The individual does not fight with the owners and managers for higher wages or better working conditions, but tries to achieve these goals by joining their ranks or influencing them through family connections, friendship, and neighborhood or communal ties. In the small factories, which in 1933 employed approximately 90 percent of the labor force, this could be accomplished directly. In the larger factories, such as the Shanghai textile mills, the workers were isolated from management. But this did not stop the individual from exercising the same ingrained Chinese tactics in dealing with such managerial representatives as superintendents and foremen. The Chinese labor movement had never gotten under way when the Communists took power in 1949. The latter event made unionism in American terms impossible in the country. But unionism has not flourished in Taiwan since 1949 under the Nationalists either.

The bounty of the American land and economy today is more fully shared by all segments of the population than in any other nation. Compared to his fellows elsewhere, and particularly in China, the American laborer can be ranked among the most privileged of men. He is better paid, works shorter hours, lives and plays in more healthy surroundings, and is more adequately protected against sickness, unemployment, and the material hazards of old age than is the average factory hand of any other nation. In addition, there seem to be more economic opportunities in America than in any other society of comparable size. "With 600,000 new businesses starting every year, it's obvious the American Dream is alive and kicking."[9] These contrasts have only become more pronounced, not lessened, since I first drew them in 1953. Some attribute them to the benefits inherent in a capitalist economy; others say it is the direct result of the strength of unions and the federal legislation of the past decades. There is undoubtedly truth in both positions.

What remains unaccounted for, however, is that despite the superior economic position of the American worker, industrial peace in these United States is nowhere in sight. In the years since the uneasy wartime truce it appears that labor-management clashes have been growing in frequency, duration, vandalism and violence, and the extent of damage they do to the economy. In addition, the struggle for power within labor has seemed to heighten and become more severe, as indicated by the murders of labor leaders Yablonsky and Hoffa. To say that the increased number of unions and the expansion of their membership fully explains this, or to charge labor leaders with "dictatorial" tendencies and "power-bloated" intransigence is only to skim the surface of the problem and substitute partisanship for analysis. The average person's sense of dismay and concern with this question was expressed by the late Eleanor Roosevelt in 1952, but the former First Lady's remarks are even more meaningful today.

> Thousands of Long Island commuters to Manhattan underwent a couple of pretty difficult days this week when, with little warning, the Long Island Railroad, on which most of them depend for transportation, halted operation as the engineers went on strike.
>
> At the same time there is a steel strike going on. As it drags on day after day, there is mention that certain plants doing defense are not going to be open and continue production.
>
> There is food for thought in both these situations.
>
> If we, living in a country where there is no real reason for bitterness or tension between various groups, cannot work out a pattern under which disputes of various kinds are worked out without the stopping of production or of services which are vital to great numbers of people, then I submit that we show a lamentable poverty in the art of human relations.
>
> It is evident to anyone as they look about the world that it is to the advantage of peoples to settle their difficulties.
>
> For instance, Israel and the Arab states would be far better off if bitterness and tensions could become a thing of the past and normal cooperation could exist. The same situation holds good for Pakistan and India. The same is true on a far larger scale where the Soviet Union and the United States are concerned.
>
> But how can we expect to iron out difficulties in these situations where so many different questions of nationality, of creed, of customs enter into the picture if here at home we cannot settle our simple labor problems?[10]

Such sentiments, while morally attractive, run afoul of a condition that cannot be brushed aside by denying its existence or stating there is no reason for it—the very real "bitterness or tension between groups." The crux of the American labor problems is to be found in the pattern of self-reliance. For self-reliance forces owners, managers, and workers alike to equate control of things with personal security and, therefore, happiness. Since executives and workers, like all Americans, desire ever-increasing control over more and more things, their struggles will be increasingly frequent and bitter. Self-reliance implies also that a person's happiness is relative, subject to comparison with the happiness of others, and has little to do with absolute standards of comfort. In this perpetual race for happiness, all victories are temporary: the triumph of one only spurs greater efforts by the defeated to crush the victor.

Among the factory-level weapons in labor struggles are the closed shop or the lockout, the picket line or the strikebreaker, not to speak of sabotage and violence. Since these weapons are themselves subject to reforging by federal action, the increasingly crucial factor in determining which group emerges triumphant, particularly in struggles involving basic industries, is not what occurs at the factory entrance or the conference table but what happens in the nation's legislative chambers and administrative departments. These government bodies have in their power the weapons, laws, and rulings that can determine the present or future success or failure of either side.

The battle thus transfers itself sometimes even before it begins at the factory level, to the political arena—to party conventions and national elections—and the interminable struggle introduces new forces of instability into both the governing and the industrial process. For here also victories are temporary: a biennial congressional election, by bringing to power representatives of an opposite viewpoint who proceed to alter the rules under which the battle was previously fought, can shift the balance of power at the factory level. Thus personal security and happiness—who controls what and how fully—become increasingly dependent on forces and factors beyond the family and the local group.

To improve relations, some of the best industrial psychologists recommend not the remedy of increased wages, but the desirability of admitting the workers into the ownership of the means of production. Many firms have followed this advice by rewarding their employees with stock. More recently the spectacular performance of Japanese industries such as steel, shipbuilding, automobile, and electronics have led some American observers and a few American companies to reconsider the management process. "Unlike American workers, the Japanese are given enormous freedom to both plan and execute their work and solve problems alone without help or interference from managers. The plants are not from the 'top down' like ours where managers deliver orders, but from the 'bottom up' where the workers make crucial decisions."[11] Without reference to the Japanese model, The American Center for the Quality of Work Life at Washington, D.C., with which my son-in-law Richard Balzer has been associated for a few years, is also working along similar lines in helping its client companies.[12] In view of our analysis, the wisdom of such steps is undeniable. For, as we have seen, it is precisely this sense of belonging that the self-reliant American misses. It is this same feeling of belonging that other students of American industrial life hope to see restored by programs and procedures that will give the worker a sense of participation in a "factory family." It is this same need that Americans seek to satisfy when they answer the call to join "our university family," "our church family," or "the great family of our political party."

The Chinese, whose pattern of life enables them to retain their primary human relations permanently, regard such ideas with amusement. The president of my university in China, a man who received his doctorate in education from an American institution, was laughed at and derided by the students and faculty when he attempted to promote esprit de corps by describing the university as "a big family." The Chinese do not even employ the word "home" for organizations that have a more natural claim to the title. A "foundling home" in America is a "foundling institute" in China.

A greater sense of participation by labor may indeed contribute to industrial peace in America; it will certainly strengthen the laborer's feeling for the plant. The chief stumbling block is that the share of control granted labor will at best be too nominal to make labor happy. The inevitable impulse will be to demand what Samuel Gompers always demanded—"more."[13] This will be intolerable to owners and managers because their security and their happiness depend on this very control. "You cannot," says a Chinese proverb, "consult a tiger about giving you his skin."

NOTES

1. See Buck, *Land Utilization in China*, pp. 466 and 468.

2. Max Weber, *The Religion of China*. (First published as essays in 1915 in *Archiv fur Sozialwissenschaft und Sozialpolitik*. Before his death in 1920, Weber revised these for book publication. English translation is by Hans H. Gerth.)

3. See R. H. Tawney's *Religion and the Rise of Capitalism*, an able exposition, for the English-reading public, of Max Weber's thesis as it pertains to European life.

4. A photographic book entitled *Rent Collection Courtyard: Sculptures of Oppression and Revolt* (Peking, 1968), is available for English readers.

5. Robert C. North's detailed analysis of Kuomintang and Communist party leadership groups confirms these conclusions. His book, one of the Hoover Institute Studies, is *Kuomintang and Chinese Communist Elites* (Stanford, 1952). In his chapter on the social characteristics of Chinese party elites, North states: "We find ourselves forced to concede that a major portion of the elite of both movements came from

quite similar high social strata, and responded to similar Western and native influences during their years of growth and education. . . . In both parties, he leaders have been drawn most frequently from a relatively thin upper layer of the Chinese population. In both parties these men were often the sons of landlords, merchants, scholars, or officials, and they usually came from parts of China where Western influence had first penetrated and where the penetration itself was most vigorous. All of them had higher education, and most of them had studied abroad. . . . Despite plebeian protestations of the Communists, the relatively smaller mass of proletarians have continued to enjoy only limited access to the elite. . . . About half of the Communist elite [was] drawn from upper-class and middle-class families, and another quarter from the prosperous section of the peasantry" (pp. 46–48). The fact that many revolutionary leaders tend to emerge from among the elite is not confined to China. A recent report on the Colombia guerila group known as M-19 which seized the Dominican Embassy and fifteen ambassadors (including the United States ambassador) tells us a similar story. Its leaders are "young intellectual elite, many of whom come from some of the country's leading, most respected and richest families" (Tad Szulc in *San Francisco Chronicle,* February 29, 1980). The reporter characterized the situation as a "generational revolt." In China, it is of course true that the crushing of the "Hundred Flowers," the Red Guards' rampage during the Cultural Revolution, and the nearly terrorist period of the Gang of Four combined to reduce the active role of the intelligentsia and greatly increased the participation of formerly voiceless sections of the population. How much the fall of the Gang and the new emphasis on expertise under Hua and Teng has changed the picture remains unknown. This speculative question is dealt with in Chapter 15. For a discussion of the situation up to the Cultural Revolution see Tang Tsou, "Reintegration and Crisis in Communist China" (in *China in Crisis,* vol. 1, ed. by Ping-ti Ho and Tang Tsou, pp. 308–315). See also John W. Lewis, "Political Aspects of Mobility in China's Urban Development," *American Political Science Review* 60 (December 1966): 899–912.

6. The "May 30th Affair" of 1925 was the most serious and aggressive act of anti-unionism ever taken by a foreign power. This clash with British police is remembered as one of China's "National Humiliation Days." The trouble began when workers in the British-owned textile mills in Shanghai went on strike. A sympathy strike was undertaken by workers in other mills, some of them Japanese-owned. Led by thousands of Chinese students in the city, a general demonstration in support of the strikers occurred several weeks after the first walkout. When their clubs failed to halt this procession, the British police opened fire. Several hundred demonstrators were killed or wounded. Following the subsequent nationwide series of demonstrations and a boycott of British goods, the British relinquished some of their control of the International Settlement to the Chinese.

7. Benjamin I. Schwartz, *Chinese Communism and the Rise of Mao* (Cambridge, Mass., 1951). (Italics mine.)

8. Ibid., p. 48.

9. Chris Barnett, "Owning Your Own Business," *TWA Ambassador* (an in-flight magazine), June 1977, pp. 21–25.

10. *Chicago Sun-Times,* June 24, 1952.

11. Jean Carper and John Naisbitt, "Revolution in the Workplace," *San Francisco Sunday Examiner and Chronicle,* November 4, 1979. The authors drew their sources from an article by John Hird, an engineer, in *Assembly Engineering* magazine.

12. See Ted Mills, *Quality of Work Life: "What's in a Name?".*

13. With a slight variation, the labor leader's name could be John L. Lewis, Walter Reuther, George Meany, or many others.

PART THREE
DILEMMA

Introduction
to Part Three

Part Two has shown us that the individual's search to satisfy his social needs has a profound effect upon his attitudes toward and relationships with other human beings, the supernatural, and material
things. The Chinese finds security within the primary groups and
has less interest in other attachments, while the American finds no
assurance of permanence in human relationships and therefore seeks
satisfaction elsewhere. These are the differing points of psychological
orientation from which the two peoples have proceeded in fundamentally different social, political, religious, and economic directions.

But these differences have further consequences. All human societies are confronted with certain common problems: the maintenance of internal order, protection from external dangers, the production and distribution of goods, the development of means to cope
with natural disasters, and the like. Yet we find that each society
tends to be plagued by different aspects of such common problems or
even by difficulties that are uniquely its own. These peculiar problems can be shown to have their origin in the particular strengths and
weaknesses of each people's way of life.

The most serious problems of American life tend to occur in the
domain of human relationships: their atomization and explosiveness.
The most tenacious Chinese problems tend to center upon the natural environment: the lack of incentive to control it and the relative
absence of internal impetus to alter the status quo. American problems are, therefore, generally characterized by bitter struggles between individuals and between groups. Chinese problems develop
from the absence of any significant or sustained compulsion to
change existing institutions, however problem-ridden, to alter the

material environment, in spite of the hardships it may cause, or to labor in the realm of the abstract, even though it may be interesting. Not only are the weaknesses of each people the price of their strengths, but the weaknesses of the Chinese tend to occur in the sphere of American strengths and vice versa.

CHAPTER 13

American Problems

The United Press once reported from France that "Bernard Mac-Fadden parachuted from a plane at 6:03 P.M. Friday and landed on the left bank of the winding Seine River. . . . The American physical culturist was 85 [and] made the parachute jump to 'prove to everyone that I am young.'" MacFadden's fame was more than matched by the Englishman, Chichester, who sailed around the world alone in his boat, *Gypsy Moth,* but even more so by the septuagenarian, William Willis, who set out for the last time into the Atlantic from a New England port in a tiny eleven-foot six-inch boat christened, *The Little One.* After Willis perished in this voyage, *Life* magazine's feature article about him was entitled, "An Ancient Mariner Who Defied Age and the Oceans" (October 4, 1968). Willis never let his wife voyage with him and reportedly always commanded his own resources—and no one else's. MacFadden and Willis were, of course, unusual men but their activities were not, in fact, outside the American pattern of behavior as old age approaches.

Old Age

At middle age, Americans turn to regimens that give them a sense of continuing youthfulness. Men undertake activities that purport to sustain physical strength and vigor; women seek the beautician and the masseuse who promise to maintain their waning glamour. For the average American, the approach of old age means the end of almost everything that gives life meaning. To the average Chinese, however, it marks the beginning of a loftier and more respected status.

At the threshold of old age, the self-reliant American faces problems rarely known to his Chinese brethren. The first consequence of old age is the loss of economic independence, or at least the likelihood of a lowered standard of living. At sixty-five, although a person may still be physically and mentally sound, he finds most, if not all, doors to employment closed. Even long before reaching this age, if he has not worked in the same job continuously or does not have something special to offer, he may already have been shunned by employers. If his savings, pension, and Social Security are substantial, he can engage in charitable, religious, or communal activities. But the self-reliant American finds these poor substitutes for those social and business activities which once occupied his time and energies.

Overshadowing his economic weakness is the average American oldster's problem of social isolation. His children, whether single or married, have drifted away from him. Even if they are physically near, he has little place in their lives. He might be useful to them in an emergency, or a welcome occasional guest in their household. But if he resides with them permanently, he is likely to be an object of toleration or pity. The grown-up children have their own friends, who don't usually enjoy his company, and their own activities in which it is often impossible for him to participate. Far from being able to retain what authority he exercised in his active years, he is reduced to social oblivion. His advice, especially if it goes contrary to the inclination of the young, is unsought and unheeded.

The Chinese elder has no fear of unemployment. Long before he is physically unable to work, he is likely to have retired to live on the fruits of his children's labor. An older man who does seek employment not only is not handicapped by age, but, if equally qualified otherwise, is in fact preferred to a younger person. Lest some scholars should say that this contrast is not cultural but one between agricultural and industrial societies, we must note the recent American trend, both legislative and social, toward pushing back retirement age, and the active recruitment of retirees in business and industry.

The relative economic security of the Chinese elder is surpassed by his social importance. Instead of restricting their associations to persons of their own age level, Chinese men and women continually seek the counsel and company of their elders. Even in recreational activities, of which social gambling is a very important form, the old regularly join the young. Furthermore, the elders enjoy a degree of authority over the young that is unheard of in the West. When living under the same roof, the former tend to exercise full control. If sons live separately from their elders, the authoritative position of the old is somewhat modified, but not surrendered, for their advice is sought on important matters.

A recent letter from a friend brought home to me the contrast between Chinese and American attitudes toward old age. In the course of describing a vacation visit she and her family had with her grandmother, who was ninety-seven years old, she said:

> Her mind is so clear that it is a lot of fun to talk with her. The thing that pleases her most is the fact that the children enjoy her company and are not afraid of her. I don't know why they should be afraid, because she is gentle and sweet, but, being a true American, I guess she thinks age is ugly.

My reaction to this letter was one of amazement. In spite of my close contact with American ways, the idea that age can inspire fear in a child, particularly one related to the aged person, remains unimaginable to me. But, as my friend implied, this is not unusual in America. Another friend told me of the following episode. A four-year-old boy, his parents, and his grandparents were dining out when an elderly couple entered the restaurant. The two were obviously bent and crippled with age. The four-year-old, mouth agape, stared at them until his sixty-three-year-old grandfather reprimanded him for doing so. Whereupon the child asked:

"What's wrong with those people, Grandpop?"
"Nothing, they are old, that's all."
"We don't have any old people where we live, do we?"

These episodes are symptomatic of the fact that, in the normal course of American life, the old and feeble do not enter the orbit of the very young. When they do, the young tend to regard them with curiosity and probably apprehension. More important, those who are advanced in years tend to decline admitting that they are old—the very word is taboo. The boy's last remark to his aging grandfather exemplifies this common attitude. Lastly, these episodes also indicate the psychological difficulties of the old: the painful self-consciousness that the American oldster experiences in his struggle to carry on and come to terms with his new situation.

None of this appears in the Chinese scene. Chinese infants are likely to have grown up in their grandparents' arms, and many children share their elders' beds. Chinese oldsters do not dolefully admit they are old, they proudly announce the fact. Tombstones, inscribed with inflated ages, are often commissioned by the elderly. In Chinese families, grandparents, as originators of the parents, fill the elevated role of super-parents. Just as "a son is never ashamed of his mother's lack of beauty," so no grandson finds the physical awkwardness of his grandparents distasteful.

The aspirations and expectations of the old therefore differ widely in America and in China. Undoubtedly many aged Americans accept the inevitable with grace, but nevertheless it is rare to meet an old person who does not refer to his age without a definite sense of either regret or bravado. The usual American reaction to old age is an open refusal to recognize it. Some, though financially able, refuse to retire while many of those who cease to work still go back to their offices day after day because they do not know what else to do.[1]

Other Americans who refuse to admit that they are past middle age seek to carry on through the antics of youthful exhibitionism. In this, Messrs. MacFadden and Willis whom we met in a previous paragraph, have ample company. There are eighty-year-old grandmothers who hit the headlines by riding a motorcycle or by racing ancient autos between New York and Chicago. There are equally ancient males who achieve an evanescent fame by making a singing debut or climbing the interior steps of the Washington Monument on their hands. When the *Life* writer described the ocean-conquering Willis as an ancient mariner who defies age, he was merely giving the public what it wants. For the standard news peg for interviews with those who have become newsworthy simply by reaching a ripe old age is their answer to the question of how to stay young though old. A typical response is that of a woman who, at one hundred years, attributed her long life to a "firm refusal to grow old."

The artificiality of the principal "solution" of the American old-age problem has been apparent for some time. The tenuous security of money—whether in savings, pensions, stocks and bonds, private insurance, or government benefits—disappears as economic forces chip it away bit by bit. As the index of inflation mounts, the index of security vanishes. The individual who has looked away from persons and to money for his salvation finds that he has made a losing gamble on one of the most unstable of life's rewards. In China, far more disastrous inflations than any America has ever known have periodically left the aged without individual economic resources. Within the last hundred years many currencies have been inflated out of existence, taking with them nearly all personal savings. But although this caused difficulties, it was not catastrophic, for the real security of the aged Chinese lay elsewhere. Also the American half-measures of employment in menial tasks, however worthy the aim of the employer may be, and maintaining the illusion of youth, however satisfactory it may at first appear, face two drawbacks in common. Neither course of action brings the desired happiness or sense of fulfillment, and both must be abandoned at some point.

It is for such reasons that the relatively recent science of geriatrics cannot be expected to produce significant results as long as it treats the old-age problem in America in terms of (a) more Social Security or fuller employment, (b) more thorough medical attention or more recreational facilities, or (c) maintaining the youthfulness of the aged. The need which these stopgaps cannot supply is one that is required by all humans: the feeling of belonging, of being an accepted, normal, and integral member of society, and of having some importance among his fellow human beings. As the number of Americans sixty-five years and over increases,[2] the aged find it increasingly difficult to integrate themselves into a divisive society. As the pace of normal society accelerates, the aged find it harder to keep up. Furthermore, a lengthened span of physical survival is no substitute for an abbreviated life of social worth. At the same time, since the whole approach of geriatrics is one of outsiders helping secondary citizens to be useful and happy, it cannot but be intolerable to the aged who wish to keep their self-respect, particularly when we recall that these persons have always lived by the ideal of self-reliance.

Some sociologists may take issue with the Chinese-American contrast drawn here. In particular they can point to a body of survey data in the United States since the 1950s showing that mutual aid (including physical and social care of the aged) and social activities (including visitation, joint recreational, and ceremonial activities) among kin members outside the nuclear family are not at all rare.[3] However, what these sociologists have not sufficiently taken into account and what they have certainly failed to understand is the fact that economic and social aids given the old are based on the donor's *choice.* Instead, one of these sociologists concludes that "the alienation from their families of most old people in America" is a "myth," and that this myth is "created and perpetrated by professional workers in the field of aging and by old people themselves."[4]

If alienation of the aged from their families is nothing but a myth, why do social workers and the old people themselves continue to operate on and entertain it? The sociologist's answer is that the old people who believe in neglect by children are most likely to be without children and the social workers see only the problem cases.[5] My view is that the first half of the explanation is untrue and the second half misunderstands the evidence.

In the first place, even results of attitude studies used by sociologists attacking the so-called "myth" indicate a strong desire for complete independence on the part of all parties concerned. "Young couples, when asked about accepting aid from parental families, almost universally reject this as an acceptable source of income." "Middle-aged parents are equally adamant in stating their expectation that they will never receive support from their children."[6] "These elderly people, products of the 'Protestant ethic' (or immigrants into it), *must* be independent in order to maintain their self-esteem. To many, even death is preferable to 'becoming a burden.' "[7]

It is clear that the nuclear nature of the American family is not simply a concept in the minds of old people without children or social workers who only see problem cases. Both groups do no more than express the general American orientation, which is amply confirmed by other inquiries.[8]

In the second place Americans do not merely see the independence of the nuclear family and of the self as a remote ideal. They actively live it. This is where the social workers find the data in support of their working principles. In their study of the aged in San Francisco (both healthy and sick) Margaret Clark and Barbara Anderson conclude that,

> A good relationship with children in old age depends, to a large extent, on the graces and autonomy of the aged parent—in short, on his ability to manage gracefully by himself. . . . The parent must remain strong and independent. If his resources fail, then conflict arises.[9]

What happens when the parent's resources fail? A visit to any institution for the aged will bear out Jules Henry's conclusion on "Human Obsolescence":

> As for the patients [in one public and two private institutions], they live out their last days in long stretches of *anxiety* and *silent reminiscing,* punctuated by outbursts of *petulance* at one another, by TV viewing, and by visits from their relatives. There is no inner peace, and *social life* is *minimal.* Meanwhile the patients *reach out* to the researcher and would engage her endlessly in conversation if she would stay. There is yearning *af-*

ter communication but no real ability to achieve it. In this we are all very much like them.[10]

Finally, it is in the United States, but not in China that the aged have become a specialized minority group with identifiable interests and formalized characteristics. In the 1953 edition of this book I wrote:

> Instead of resorting to geriatric agencies the aged in America increasingly flock to old people's homes where they can find some emotional security in relative equality, in contrast to their position in the society at large, among their aged fellows. In addition, instead of being able to relax during their last years, for the purpose of public education and legislative action in their interests, they are more and more compelled to give organizational form to the separate segment of society which they presently compose. Already the word "minority" has been applied to the aged in America.

We must note that both anticipated trends have become more evident than before. It is no accident that Ellen Goodman, speaking about the jokes and comments of Republican nominee Ronald Reagan's age made by rival candidates and the media during the 1980 presidential campaign, entitled her article, "Few Contented Guides for Old Age" (as it appeared in the *Honolulu Advertiser,* January 11, 1980). The aged form or join old people's colonies. California, Florida, and Arizona are among three of the most popular states for retirement communities. Residents of most of these colonies "voluntarily" segregate themselves from the outside world, develop clubs of their own centered entirely inside the community, and then sever connections with organizations in which they were active before. They claim a preference for their own company or allege that voluntary segregation has enabled them to enjoy "more contact with younger people" than others who did not. They patronize a whole group of magazines designed for the aged.[11] Since the early 1960s, they have been active in age associations that stand on the platform of "positive recognition to send aggressive demands for change across the age border."[12] Outstanding among these associations is the National Council of Senior Citizens formed to fight for Medicare. It now has over two million members.

> They continue to demand respect, income, housing, and better medical care as the rights of all retired people. NCSC does not place polite requests for benefits before a benevolent society. Assuming a partner's

place in the process of change, the Council argues from its members' experiences with using a retired constituent in their lives to the adjustments America must make to use a retired constituent in the culture.[13]

In other words, the older people have decided to "organize around their independence and their needs at the same time, instead of having to choose between admitting dependence in order to ask for assistance . . . or claiming independence by denying a need for assistance."[14]

The aged in the United States have voluntarily segregated themselves and become so well organized for positive demands precisely because they have no respected place in the self-reliant American culture. On the other hand, the aged in China did not have to segregate themselves and get organized (and still do not) because they automatically enjoy high esteem in the mutual dependence framework of the Chinese culture.

One can, of course, see that not all Chinese sons are filial to their parents just as there are American cases where the old are well taken care of or never lose their status. The company of wealthy oldsters often is prized by relatives and friends; they are sought after by directors of charities and the heads of endowed institutions; their names frequently appear in the social columns. American elders who possess special talents which do not disappear with age, and those who have achieved national fame and distinction, are often equally fortunate. But the neglected oldsters in China and the pampered septuagenarians in the United States are both relative minorities among the aged in their respective societies. The many American epithets such as the "old fogey farm," the "vegetable patch," and the "freeloaders," for retirement communities and their residents,[15] are indicative of the deep-seated American attitude toward the aged.

There will be little reason for the Chinese to regard age as a problem so long as they maintain their pattern of continuity between the generations, whereby age brings not penalty but honor. And we should not forget the ancient teaching that the individual must be prepared for a fall even when at the summit of his power. Hence the proverb says:

No human can abide in health and peace for
    three years
Any more than a flower can retain its bloom
    for a hundred days.

Generation Gap

"Teen-agers Tell of Arson on West Side"; "Son of Victim Held as Bandit"; "Boy Attacker of Four Women Gets 2–24 Years"; "Two Boys Admit They Tried to Wreck Trains"; "Sex Orgies Involving Four Teen-age Girls"; "Boy, 16, Kills 3 Kin over Use of Car." These were familiar items of each day's newspaper when this book first saw print in 1953. Most people would unhesitatingly term these to be instances of juvenile delinquency. In the sixties when student riots were common on university campuses, including famous ones such as Columbia and California, the papers were flooded with another kind of headline: "Black Students Call a Boycott"; "NYU Head Says Students May Picket"; "U. of C. Students Tent-In to Protest Housing Policy"; "Pot Party at a University"; "Student Radicals Agree to Back Mexican Revolt"; and "Hippie Victim Buried in Suburban Dignity." The term juvenile delinquency was not applied in most of these incidents. Instead we spoke of the generation gap.

Today the college campuses are quiet and many immediate problems such as inflation, runaway oil prices, and Iran flood the news media, but juvenile delinquency is an ever-pressing problem.

Did the massive student protests, the hippie and yippie movements, and the waves of dropouts and runaways of the sixties constitute new developments? I submit that both what happened in the sixties and the persistent and increasing juvenile delinquency are manifestations of the same generation gap. Self-reliance cannot but sharpen the demarcation between the generations. The problem of the aged is one facet of that sharpened demarcation; adolescent and youthful turbulence, dissatisfaction and revolt are another.

Many causes have been attributed to adolescent crimes: physical growth leading to the ability to defy parental control, glandular disturbances, poverty, release from school, lack of legal responsibility, occupational uncertainty, confusion of values, and many more. For a time, many writers, educators, parents, and welfare workers attacked the "danger" of comic books. Of late, violence on television has been blamed.

Some of these explanations appear reasonable until we consider the fact that, though all of these alleged causes of youthful crimes were to be found in China, the Chinese traditionally had no problem of adolescent criminality. In truth, many of the "causes" attributed to adolescent criminality in this country were present in China to an even greater extent. All human beings are subject to the same biological changes; all reach a point where they can physically defy their parents. Furthermore, before 1949 not all Chinese youngsters of school age were in school; most of them never went to school. During the first half of the twentieth century, Chinese young men and women in urban centers suffered from worse than occupational uncertainty; most of them knew long periods of unemployment or were exploited as apprentices in blind-alley trades. Since late in the nineteenth century, youths in China, both educated and uneducated, were confronted with every confusion of values and ideas imaginable. The educated in particular were forced to wrestle with foreign "isms" coming from every direction, and most were simply caught between knowledge acquired in school and old mores still practiced at home.

Chinese youngsters in urban areas were also exposed to comic books. These were purchased or rented at a fraction of a cent per day. On many streets of Shanghai were rows of bookstands purveying "Small Folks Books." Among the themes were murder, robbery, mayhem, and kidnaping. Though lacking in ultrascientific adventures, Chinese comic books contained gory accounts of the supernatural. In place of Western characters like Hopalong Cassidy, they had female vigilantes such as "The Thirteenth Sister." Both Chinese and American comics share one additional trait—crime does not pay.

Despite these seemingly basic similarities, adolescent behavior among the two peoples has been very different. American parents and educators consider adolescence as a period marked by numerous forms of behavior difficulties including even the tendency to criminality. The Chinese did not even have a term for adolescence, and were not plagued by the problem of the youthful offender. Crime statistics can never tell us the full, or perhaps not even a completely accurate story, but as symptoms they are useful. For example, during the most efficient years of the Nationalist government—1931 to 1933 —when police records were fairly accurate, statistics show that Chinese males between thirteen and twenty committed fewer crimes than all other seven-year groups under fifty-one. Of these juvenile crimes, minor offenses predominated.[16]

In the United States violent crimes seem more prevalent among juvenile offenders than crimes such as those against property. Furthermore, granted that the crime statistics in the United States also leave something to be desired, there is insistent evidence that youths under eighteen years of age outpace older age groups in most categories of serious crimes. From 1960 to 1974 urban police arrests of suspected offenders for crimes of violence doubled for all ages but tripled for ages eleven to fourteen and fifteen to seventeen. In 1960 the rate was 70.3 and 273.0 per hundred thousand of the urban population respectively for eleven to fourteen year olds and for fifteen to seventeen. But for 1974 the corresponding figures had jumped to 195.3 and 674.7 respectively for the same two age groups.[17]

Three other observations need to be made about juvenile crime in America. First, between 1968 and 1977 arrests among youths under eighteen years of age showed higher rates of increase than those among either the population as a whole or those eighteen years of age and over in criminal homicide, robbery, and aggravated assault.[18] Second, during the same period rates of increase in arrest among females under eighteen years of age were spectacularly higher than those among males of that age group for the same offenses, except rape. Third, there is strong evidence that juvenile crime in America is now also a suburban problem. While the arrest rates for violent crimes among those under eighteen years of age had decreased in cities between 1976 and 1977, they had increased far more in suburbs.[19]

The problem of narcotics addiction is equally illuminating. The usual view is that juveniles fall victim to the habit because of the pusher, the foreign smuggler, the uncertainties of an "era of crisis," or poverty. But the truth is that juveniles do not simply fall victim to external inducements any more than good boys can get girls pregnant simply because of unscrupulous female charms. For nearly a century China suffered from dope pushers, foreign smugglers, and political and economic crises. Even the Japanese and Korean narcotics dens protected and promoted by powerful invaders in the middle thirties did not create a juvenile addiction problem in China.

The occurrence of juvenile delinquency or its absence is in each case part of a larger cultural context. Neither can be understood by resorting to these myopic explanations. Instead they must be examined in terms of overriding influence exerted by a people's way of life.

Speaking from different points of view two scholars have converged on the same ground that is consonant with but not identical to ours. Marvin Wolfgang maintains that "any overall increase in juvenile delinquency can be largely attributed to the population increase in the ages from 14 to 18." He argues that "a certain amount of delinquency has always existed, will continue to exist, and perhaps should exist." He notes that the "attributes associated with the delinquents sound similar to descriptions of the Renaissance Man who defied the authority and static orthodoxy of the middle ages, who was aggressive, richly assertive, this-world rather than other-world centered, and was less banal, more innovative, than his medieval predecessors."[20]

Kenneth Keniston blames youthful alienation on "the growing bankruptcy of technological values and visions. If we are to move toward a society that is less alienating, that releases rather than imprisons the energies of the dissident, that is truly worthy of dedication, devotion, idealism and commitment, we must transcend our outworn visions of technological abundance, seeking new values beyond technology."[21]

Both scholars see juvenile turbulence in terms of the wider social and cultural context but neither comes to grips with the essence of the problem of the generation gap by going the necessary extra mile. Wolfgang does not tell us why, in spite of better schools, better counseling services, better recreational facilities, and better prevention and detection measures as well as unprecedented material prosperity, the "overall increase in juvenile delinquency" should still keep pace with the increase in population (in fact the former has outstripped the latter). Keniston fails to show how we are going "to transcend our outworn visions of technological abundance" and to develop "new values beyond technology."

Both of these gaps will be more fully illuminated when we deal with Chinese weaknesses in the next chapter. In the meantime we must note, as we already detailed in Chapter 3, very distinct differences between the social atmospheres breathed by Chinese and American children. The world of Chinese children is not divorced from their parents' world. From the first, they are in contact with the Janus-face of mankind; they have impressed upon them the importance of obedience to social conventions; they learn the distinction between what their parents say and what their elders in fact do. By adolescence, they have learned most of the ropes.

Except among the very poor or immigrants from southern and eastern Europe, American children generally lead an existence quite distinct from that of their parents. The self-reliance that is emphasized in family training undeniably encourages behavior superficially imitative of adult life. But this simulation of adult roles is a totally ineffective substitute for a real initiation into adult life, since the sole concern of the former is with the surface aspects of the latter. There is little to give the adolescent an awareness of human frailties and strengths, a realistic introduction into what are commonly called the ways of the world.[22]

This becomes difficult or impossible because the teaching of self-reliance has another and far more significant consequence: as children grow, the gulf between them and their parents progressively widens. From the first, the elders have interests and activities that they pursue while the child remains with a sitter. Having no integrated place in their parents' doings, the youngsters soon find in their playmates a society that is equally exclusive and in turn unconcerned with the world of its elders. It is therefore vain to hope, as some educators and parents presently do, that television may restore that family unity which they say has been undermined by the attractions of nonfamily commercial amusements. It is plain that the American family bond has not been weakened or destroyed by the lack of home entertainment, and its cohesion will not be restored by such artificial solutions.[23]

It is thus not surprising that the majority of Americans enter adolescence with a romantic concept of life. Unprepared for the imperfections of the real world, they tend to be easily disillusioned. Humanity's inconsistencies and weaknesses, especially when discovered in those whom they have idolized, confuse or shock young persons whose idealized view of life proves no guide to its true nature. These experiences come as no surprise to Chinese adolescents.

Furthermore, while Chinese parents, reflecting the pattern of mutual dependence, welcome their children's progress toward adulthood, the American pattern of self-reliance causes parents to erect barriers to their offspring's independence. The first direct presentation of this conflict occurs at school age, but when children enter adolescence the struggle becomes more pronounced. For at this point American parents see before them the threat of being completely relegated to the background. They tend, naturally enough, to react by intensifying their efforts to delay or prevent their children's full independence. In this campaign, the elders have a variety of resources at their disposal: love, money, persuasion, and personal or legal force.

This leads to a situation often unbearable to the American adolescent. Having been raised to be self-reliant, he is now resentful toward efforts to turn him back from his self-seeking activities. In addition, the highly competitive American society demands that the self-respecting individual achieve success as quickly as possible. Even the boundary of legality need not restrain him. For, like the successful and therefore respected businessman who prides himself on operating "just within the law," the adolescent reduces himself to the principle of "anything goes" so long as you don't get caught. Furthermore, society tends to applaud extraordinary feats whether legal or not, as we saw in our discussion of hero worship. Hence, a D. B. Cooper (who successfully got away with $200,000 by hijacking a plane) and his like are never short of admirers. Disillusioned by the inconsistencies of the real world, innocent of its intricacies but pressed by the desire to achieve success in a hurry, the American adolescent finds himself in far greater difficulties than he experienced during his grade school days. His parents' concern over him now only seems authoritarian, and more a stumbling block to his freedom than before. But, standing alone, his insecurity vis-à-vis reality seems greater than before. He cannot retreat from this dilemma without losing his self-respect.

The result is emotional agitation. Since individuals differ widely in their temperament, intelligence, and circumstances, this emotional turbulence expresses itself in diverse ways, which include idealist activities such as the Save the Whales and animal rights movements, antipollution and antinuclear power sit-ins; mild behavior such as sulky moods, quarrelsomeness, incorrigibility, hostility to parents; and the more drastic forms of misconduct such as drag racing, joy rides in stolen autos, robbery, rape, narcotics addiction, and apparently unmotivated murder.

However, we shall never unearth the root of juvenile delinquency in America as long as we regard it as a matter of youth being led astray by a few bad influences or due to unfortunate individual circumstances that may be locally adjusted. In the 1953 edition of this book I wrote:

> For, quite apart from those forms of misconduct usually described as crimes, there are other and sometimes more ominous phenomena which are rarely pointed out as a juvenile problem. For example, in the St. Louis, Mo., riot of June 21, 1949, when public swimming pools were opened to Negroes, *Life* magazine (July 4, 1949) reported that "teenagers made up a surprisingly large percentage of the rioters." In the Cicero, Illinois, affair of 1951, when a Negro family moved into an all-white apartment house, all Chicago newspapers reported a preponderance of youthful rioters.

What we saw in the early 1950s were minor samples of what we have since witnessed on a grander scale: riots and sit-ins on the campus, the hippie and yippie love-ins in the streets, the proliferation of the use of drugs, the drop-outs and the cop-outs, the "student power" antidraft and anti-Vietnam demonstrations, the violence of the civil rights movement, and the bloodshed of the Chicago Democratic Convention—all of which were predominantly youth-oriented.

The reader will probably at once note that, in this brief account of disturbances involving youth, from robbery to civil rights demonstrations, I have combined the lawful and the illegal, those with lofty purposes and those that are antisocial by any definition, and those in support of racial prejudices and those that aim at bringing about justice. This I have done advisedly. For the American youth, in his search for independence, is confronted with a complex of possibilities, none of which is very close to him but all or any one of which may become urgent at any particular time. The central thing is some action to give meaning to the needs of the self. As one youth put it:

One year I joined in to "ban the bomb"; another year it was stylish to demand "civil rights"; this year the call is for "peace in Vietnam." But where is the real immediacy of any of these causes for me? It is difficult to act on an abstraction. It has taken the exclusiveness of black power for me to realize that my battle with society also must be concrete and personally direct; conviction can only be sincere when the battle is to improve your life and not your soul. As I see things now the only real issue for me at this time is draft resistance. I can meaningfully express my general outrage about the war in Vietnam by specifically resisting the immediate threat of being drafted to serve in that war. Protest without some personal investment, without putting something on the line, becomes hollow; it becomes no more than a caricature of itself.[24]

The particular goals and methods used are, then, far less important than the stresses facing the identity-seeking youth in a self-reliant way of life. These stresses cannot be pinned on a single source (such as "identity crisis"), but come from a concatenation of circumstances. On one side is the transitory and insecure nature of all the individual's human relationships. On the other side is his parents' increased interference (real or imagined) with his freedom and independence because they are also threatened by the same transitory and insecure nature of their human relationships. Finally, these opposing forces operate in a culture that sanctifies success for the sake of success. Under the circumstances, the American youth defends himself against the instability of his human relationships by making sure of his acceptance in some peer group. He furthers his needs for success by attaining some position of achievement in the group that accepts him. He also has to accomplish his efforts without consistent direction other than that of the dictates of his group.

Hence, even though the college campuses are quiet and the Vietnam debacle is behind us, those who think that such disturbances will not recur and those who hope for "new values beyond technology" are bound to be disappointed. As long as the individual-centered American way continues to dominate our family and social relations in general, the sources of youth agitation will remain, for better or worse. But "new values beyond technology" cannot possibly emerge from an individual-centered way of life. Instead, we will see more and more widespread externalization of measures for preventing antisocial behavior and of inducements for socially acceptable behavior. When more and more human relations are externalized the end results cannot be otherwise. [25]

The misconduct of the Chinese adolescent is more of an individual matter; his behavior is rarely dictated by his peer group. For the one group to which he is closely attached, and consequently the one group whose rules or commands have any real meaning, is the kinship group. If he gets into trouble, he not only incurs the displeasure of his parents and relatives, but he receives little moral support from most persons his own age. Those who support his misconduct will surely be termed by society as "fox friends and dog comrades." [26]

The American adolescent's misconduct is likely to be the price of his belonging to his own age group. Trouble with the law merely hurts his parents, whom he often intentionally disregards, but it may earn him a firmer place among his own, and it is their rejection he fears. Under this compulsion, he is likely to do anything dictated by his peers. The dictates of the group range from the literal to the abstract. Two widely publicized killings are illustrative. On June 27, 1952, two New York City youths, aged sixteen and seventeen, after accepting a "dare" to kill someone, murdered a man they had never seen before. In their confession, they said they killed the stranger to prove they "weren't chicken." Three days before this, a twenty-nine-year-old war veteran walked into the office of the American Physical Society at Columbia University and shot and killed an eighteen-year-old stenographer, the only person present at the time. The reason? The Society had repeatedly refused to publish a treatise he had written, and so he decided to murder "a lot of physicists" to secure publicity for his views. In these two crimes, one committed by youths who apparently had no previous record of delinquency, and the other by a young man with a lengthy history of psychiatric disorders, there is a common factor: the desire for recognition. To obtain or retain the esteem of others, two "normal" youths killed a stranger; seeking revenge upon those who had denied him a place of respect, who had prevented his success, an "abnormal" youth committed the same act. Whatever distinctions psychiatrists might draw between these two cases, it is plain that society's demands upon the individuals concerned were different only in the degree of their literalness.

Racial Crisis

Racial tension is not new in the United States. It only became more obvious and assumed critical proportions since World War II, but especially in the sixties. Yet despite much concern about racial violence, there is only superficial understanding of racial tension. The *Kerner Report*[27] links mass violence fundamentally with "the racial attitude and behavior of white Americans toward black Americans." This "white racism" expresses itself in (a) a mixture consisting of "pervasive discrimination and segregation," (b) "black migration and white exodus," and (c) "black ghettos." The report then goes on to detail the "three powerful ingredients" that "have begun to catalyze the mixture": (a) "frustrated hopes," (b) "legitimation of violence," and (c) "powerlessness."[28] These findings cannot but be salutary, since they have at least admitted that there is a very real racial problem in America. For as late as 1963 and in a book aimed at understanding "the United States in historical and comparative perspective," Seymour M. Lipset, a well-known sociologist, saw the racial problem as a Southern problem, and made no more than passing mention of race relations in the American South which, in his view, "has constituted a major source of the instability in the American polity."[29]

However, if the *Kerner Report*'s findings are no more than descriptive, they have merely echoed the results of American sociologists that went before them.[30] What American students have so far failed to see is that job discrimination, segregation, and racist attitudes in general are simply the outward expression of factors which go deeply back to the very root of the self-reliant way of life.

Separation between the generations is the common denominator of the problems of old age and juvenile delinquency. This separation, however, is but one product of the temporary nature of human relationships in America. Since their human relationships do not endure, Americans look to the control of *things* for their personal security and for predictability in their environment. But control of things, however masterful, falls short of its goal because it cannot rest on or create that which is dearest to men—trustworthy human relationships. Consequently Americans, rich or poor, though professing self-reliance, are constantly groping for some meaningful human relationship to which they can cling. This accomplished, and tenuous and artificial though the relationship may be, they take a militant attitude toward those who are outside the charmed circle, whether it is an exclusive neighborhood, a restricted club, a religious sect, or a band of hero worshipers. In a society in which no human relationship is permanent, such defensiveness is inevitable. The greater the insecurity, the greater the need to defend oneself against the outsider. And it is this deeply ingrained defensiveness that is the mainspring of racial tension in the United States.

The sociologists and other scholars, having themselves been brought up consciously or unconsciously to regard control of things as the chief means to personal security and happiness, see poor housing, job discrimination, and related matters as causes of black unrest. They fail to see that, by offering Blacks material advantages they are merely tendering half a loaf, so to speak, which would not have satisfied themselves in the first place. Perhaps it is because economic advantages are more amenable to change than other aspects of the society where it is a question of taking immediate and concrete steps. Or perhaps the sociologists and politicians who think about racial problems do not really care to have their own charmed circles invaded by mentioning solutions other than economic.[31] The fact is that our political and social scientists dealing with the racial problem have been unusually concerned with correcting economic inequities which, as our analysis reveals, fails to get to the root of the matter.

Perhaps sensing the inadequacy of the economic inequity thesis, some scholars take refuge behind the inevitability misconception. They maintain that discrimination occurs wherever different races with identifiable physical and other traits live in the same society, especially if one of them is a numerical minority as in the United States or because of undemocratic control of power as in the Republic of South Africa. This misconception is even repeated in textbooks as an established fact.[32] American newspaper dispatches and other travelers' accounts often reiterate the canard that high-caste Hindus have fairer skins than their low-caste countrymen. The fact is that identifiable physical characteristics or differences in language and manners are not cause for racial tension, any more than differences in economic rewards. The Nazis required the Jews of Germany to wear special armbands precisely because most German Jews were not different from other Germans physically, linguistically, or culturally. If there is the need for discrimination, artificial differences must be created where none exist.

Because they have little security in their human relationships, Americans cannot be satisfied with an implicit acknowledgment of their superiority. First of all, they must constantly impress the minority groups with their superiority. The three ingredients of "white racism" mentioned by the *Kerner Report*, namely, "pervasive discrimination and segregation," "black migration and white exodus," and "black ghettos" are all ways in which white Americans demonstrate their superiority to Blacks and, with less emphasis but in the same vein, to other minority groups.[33] The most extreme of these ways, namely white violence against Blacks and other minority groups, is not even mentioned in the *Kerner Report* but nevertheless was and is very real.[34]

This is not to deny that organizational, legal, and extralegal efforts to combat racial injustice and to right some of the accumulated wrongs have appreciably changed the conditions of race relations in America. The Supreme Court school desegregation decision of 1954, civil rights legislation, the various enforcement interventions by the Justice Department, the marches, demonstrations, picketings, and even the riots from one end of the country to the other have all achieved something in the right direction or at least have shaken some people from their inertia.

However, one wonders if the commitment of labor union executives to equal employment opportunities for all can persuade most union members to welcome social contacts with Blacks or to live in the same neighborhood with them. We must also ask the northern white intellectuals who denounce southern discrimination as undemocratic, how many of them are ready to treat non-Whites without reference to their race? And of the social and civic leaders who sponsor educational programs directed at eliminating racial bias (not to speak of those who are opposed to such programs), how many are ready to admit into their clubs the Black who possesses professional attainment and the pecuniary wherewithal? Even a Dr. Ralph Bunche—a man showered with honorary degrees, praised in newspaper

editorials and acclaimed in church sermons because of his service to
his country and world peace—could not find an appropriate place to
live in the nation's capital not so long ago when he was offered the
post of Assistant Secretary of State. In the end he had to refuse the
honor for that very reason.

"Such things take time," say many. Undoubtedly social changes
cannot be achieved in one stroke. Even political revolutions, after
the initial bloodshed, take years to accomplish their professed aims.
But our mention of the resistance to change is not simply to signify
the distance to be traveled, but to illustrate a curious paradox between Chinese and American behavior in these matters. The Chinese, lacking concern for "the" individual, tend to stress the quali-
fications of "a" man as the most important determinants of his
acceptance; Americans, in spite of their emphasis on "the" individual, do not hesitate to erect social and occupational barriers to "a"
man's progress regardless of his achievements and the thoroughness
with which he is Americanized.

These barriers do not exist solely where the minority group is so
large that tension is produced by the very fact of the minority's size
and its proximity to the majority; neither does racial animosity occur
only where the sight of a Black is so uncommon as to arouse in children a fear of the strange, a fear that allegedly is the source of an in-
eradicable prejudice; nor, finally, is the problem confined to areas
where the economic situation of the "poor Whites" produces tensions that find release in racial violence. These explanations—the
theories of "pressure," "color shock," and "frustration-aggression"
and others like them that have filled our sociological works on race
relations, are obviously mutually exclusive and rationalist in character because they merely justify white racist attitudes and can at best
do no more than elucidate certain factors that may accentuate tension *when the tension is already there.* They are descriptive of the underlying trouble, but are in no way causal.

Just as factors justifying white racist attitudes fail to touch the root
of the matter, the *Kerner Report*'s list of ingredients for black violence,
such as segregation or job discrimination, represent no more than an
about face but *in the same vein.* They, too, merely justify black riots
and can at best do no more than explain certain specific grievances
that may increase violence *when the seeds for it* are already there.

Racial aggression in America is not the outgrowth of any temporary condition resulting from any specific pressure, fear, or frustration, but a consequence of the permanent insecurity of a way of life

in which human relationships are evanescent. In its deepest form this insecurity expresses itself not in the assertion of superiority but in the *fear of inferiority*. This fear does not always reveal itself in spectacular ways, rather it often appears in devious and unspoken but persistent fashions. In its most superstitious phase, biased Americans share with their nonliterate brethren the world over a fear of contamination. Many southern department stores, for example, used to bar Blacks from trying on hats or shoes preliminary to purchase. In its usual cloak, this fear is allied to snobbishness. The person who meets Blacks on a basis of real equality is branded a "nigger lover" and is thenceforth suspect to others or is an outcast.

But this fear can take yet another diffuse form—an apprehension that the minority may infiltrate the dominant group or raise itself to a position from which to challenge that dominance. Chinese and American attitudes toward interracial marriage are a case in point. Parents all over the world interfere or wish to interfere with their children's marriages. In one respect, Chinese are more sensitive on this score than Americans. They not only frown on marriage with foreigners—Japanese as well as Mongols, Europeans and Americans as well as Lolos—some of them even object to marriage between Chinese from two different regions. I know of some Cantonese parents who disowned their children for marrying Hakkas, who are Chinese but speak a dialect different from that of the Cantonese.

However, a Chinese does not object to an interracial marriage unless one of his children should be a party to it. This is not, as it might first appear, a bit of hypocrisy. It simply means that Chinese opposition to an interracial marriage is personalized and concrete. It has nothing to do with any notions about maintaining "racial purity," but is concerned almost entirely with the possibility of social inconvenience. "Think of it," one of my friends advised another who was contemplating marriage with a Japanese girl, "she will not be able to converse with your guests, and will be a drag on your professional relations." Rarely do Chinese objections deviate far from the attitude expressed in that remark. And again, it relates to the close, reciprocally dependent primary group.

When I ask first generation Chinese workers and merchants in the United States why they do not seek a mate among white girls or American-born Chinese girls, the replies are similar: "They are too independent"; "They think having fun is everything"; "If they are not satisfied in every way, they want a divorce. Pay! Pay! Pay!" For such practical reasons many of these Chinese-Americans prefer to travel across the Pacific to marry a girl from China, or, with the aid of photographs, to arrange a match through a middleman.[35] Perhaps the best clue to the Chinese attitude is found in the fact that if a non-Chinese spouse or the offspring of a mixed union can speak Chinese and behave like a Chinese, other Chinese, including close relatives and friends of the Chinese member of the union, are usually eager to accept the newcomer. Furthermore, never in Chinese history has there been a legal ban on interracial marriage, except by the Manchu government in the early days of the Ch'ing dynasty. One of the first Manchu empresses even issued a perpetual decree against any Han girl being part of the emperor's harem. If discovered, the decree went on sternly, the girl and those responsible for bringing her to the court would be subject to decapitation. But such is the power of the Chinese world view that this ban was relaxed after a few decades. Intermarriage simply is not a Chinese public issue.

The existence in many American states of specific legal prohibitions to interracial marriage reflects the underlying general pressure against it. Not until 1976 were such laws declared unconstitutional by the Supreme Court in the case of *Loving* v. *Virginia*. This pressure expresses itself in social ostracism, organized popular movements, and personal crusades. The best-known, supposedly unanswerable question to many white Americans is, of course, "But would you want your daughter to marry a Negro?" But a variety of other indications of the widespread and deep-seated nature of the feeling can be observed by anyone who cares to look. Even without any deliberate effort on my part, I personally happened upon many of them. There was, for example, the instance of two of my white students' mixed marriages. Both were trained to be Christian missionaries. One married a Japanese girl, and the other married a Hindu. The family of the former bears an old and distinguished name. When all opposition failed to change the young man's mind, his mother told the Japanese bride, "I would never forgive you if you have a child." My white student who married the Hindu girl (who is much darker than he) fared better with his parents but she was several times spat on by women pedestrians who muttered the epithet, "You bitch," while she walked hand in hand with her husband on the streets of Chicago.

Then, also, there are the offhand remarks of some fellow professors in some universities when we were talking about the future of some colleagues. At least three times in the past years, when the subject of our talk was nonwhite, a fellow professor would say something to this effect, "You know, he would have trouble finding a permanent job anywhere, married to a white wife and all that." The words were different each time; the substance was not.

But my sharpest experience on this first came in the winter of 1949, when my wife and I made the shipboard acquaintance of a charming elderly couple while traveling between the West Coast and Hawaii for the first time. The pair radiated graciousness and charm. At one of the bingo sessions the lady brought up the subject of interracial marriage. Under no provocation whatsoever, she told us how badly she felt about the mixture of races in Hawaii, and how glad she was that my wife and I had married our own kind. She was not the only one who held that attitude. During our seven-month stay in Hawaii, we came across at least half a dozen Whites who privately campaigned on the same subject. The same kind of Whites have continued to pop up ever since that time in our many visits to the Islands, a beautiful place but sometimes mistakenly described as a paradise of racial harmony. None of these people except the parents in the very first case had any immediate personal stake in the question, but they still condemned interracial marriage no less an evil for that. Though the Whites in Hawaii often said that they were worried about the disappearance of pure Hawaiians, their real fear was the threat to the purity of white blood.

This fear of loss of race—the fear of any alteration of the general racial picture—and therefore of some unknown state of group inferiority as cause enough for campaigns by the common man, is wholly without a counterpart among the Chinese. But, most important, it has its counterparts in many other facets of American life. For example, the fear of loss of membership in peer groups spurs juveniles into all forms of misconduct, including race riots, and directs their elders, who are similarly insecure, to struggle ceaselessly for like tokens of position. This is so basic that it does not occur to the average person to make any reckoning of cost in money, ideal values, or contravention of laws, either God-given or man-made.

The hierarchy of factors underlying racial tension in the United States is then as follows: the evanescence of human relationships gives rise to fear of loss of group status and resulting inferiority; the alleviation of this fear requires constant protests of superiority but especially active and forceful demonstrations of it. It is the latter two kinds of white American behavior, namely implicit or explicit protestations of white supremacy and enforcement of legal, economic, and social inequality, which have engaged public attention and the *Kerner Report*.

During the racial crisis of the sixties, it was naturally the black unrest and violence that was most noticeable. And the *Kerner Report* rightly regards this unrest and violence as reaction to white racism. It must be made clear that there have been, and there still are, at least three simultaneously discernible trends of black reaction. First, many Blacks hate to be Blacks and want to be like Whites. Besides the well-known fact of passing, many Blacks have simulated white appearance (hair straightening for example), a white style of living (there are middle-class Blacks who share white values and are psychologically as distant from other Blacks as the Whites), and success in white terms (for example, the many prominent and wealthy Blacks regularly publicized in *Ebony* magazine). But as this route did not move fast enough for many Blacks, the active sit-ins (in universities and elsewhere), marches (including the Poor People's March to Washington, D.C., in the spring of 1968), and riots occurred. Finally, just as white extremists contended that all that has happened to the Blacks is the result of black innate inferiority,[36] or would advocate total suppression of or sending the Blacks back to Africa, so black extremists insisted on separatism—"Black is beautiful" slogans, black Santa Claus, rejection of white assistance in the black movement, a "psychological revolution" so complete that "black kids can walk all over in the streets and the white man is invisible to them, like we have been all these years,"[37] or the establishment of a black nation comprising most of southern United States. Outside of these trends are, of course, those Blacks, perhaps a majority, who neither wish to be White nor espouse black separatism. Many participate in the civil rights movement in general but quite a few of them wish to be left alone, much like their brethren among other ethnic groups.

Many white Americans were understandably shocked by what they considered to be extravagant black demands. What they may not be aware of is that their own self-reliant culture is a hotbed for such excesses, especially the separatist kind. The late Kurt Lewin, an eminent Jewish-American social psychologist, long ago spoke of the necessity of a "strong feeling of being part and parcel of the [Jewish] group and having a positive attitude toward it" in order to reduce or avoid self-hatred on the part of Jews in Europe and America.[38] In the case of American Jews who have felt discrimination but not oppression and who have a cohesive, written tradition, the sense of belonging is more easily achieved with less militancy than in the case of Blacks. But their basic need as minorities in the individual-centered way of life is the same. The fear of inferiority makes it impossible for white Americans to live up to their ideal of universal love and equality. They are forced to reject the minorities as much as the minorities are forced to organize themselves for legal and social but especially psychological protection.

Current programs to better race relations in the United States, therefore, face a far more formidable barrier to the accomplishment of their objectives than can be removed by a Fair Employment Practices Act, massive educational and job opportunities for Blacks and other racial minorities, desegregated housing and schools, civil rights legislation, and other similar measures. Laws, ethnological exposés, and social contacts will not change the minds of those who want to— indeed need to—believe in permanent white superiority. What is deeply rooted in a way of life cannot easily be eradicated by legal provisions or policy or economic prosperity.

It is not difficult to obtain support for this contention. For example, heads of government agencies and presidents of industrial and commercial companies may agree to desegregate or to offer equal employment opportunities; and they may actively support such measures. But their first obstacles are the lower-echelon functionaries in charge of personnel. Another example is that while television, comic book writers, and movie makers are now busy giving favorable (and even herioc) roles to Blacks, they continue to cast Chinese as slant-eyed, opium-spoking white slavers. Or Chinese appear on the periphery as laundrymen and restaurant operators with queer accents. If they do not fall into these two convenient slots, they are hapless figures oppressed by native Communists, eventually to be rescued by an American like Steve Canyon in the comic strip.[39] And when a Chinese is featured as anything but a servant, the basic Chinese facts are so wrong that they might have come out of *Gulliver's Travels.* The Chinese wife of the Irish hero in a 1967 Western could not even take one step because of her bound feet.

Not only do makers of these programs, their sponsors, and most consumers see nothing wrong with this, but often even the very people who are working against prejudice fail to realize the direct connection between maligning Asians or Indians and the unfair treatment of Blacks that they are working so hard to eradicate.

As long as the American way of life fosters a general insecurity which perpetually breeds in each new generation the fear of becoming inferior, the majority of Americans will *need* prejudice in order to maintain self-esteem. For if one cannot advance upward, one must at least find someone else to push down, in order to achieve the illusion of going up. Hence racial tension is only one aspect of a general tension pattern that underlies all of American society. Individual feelings against Blacks are, therefore, easily turned against Jews or Catholics, or other minority groups. It is not uncommon for members of the white Protestant majority to be violently prejudiced against all three, and for Jews to be as anti-Negro as Blacks may be anti-Semitic. For this reason, when we approach prejudice against Blacks as a racial matter and no more than that, when we look at anti-Semitism only as a religio-ethnic question, and when we interpret anti-Catholic feeling as simply an outcropping of religious intolerance, we immediately limit the possibility of eliminating these prejudices and of even understanding them. It is only at the surface, like separate springs of water bubbling from the earth, that they appear distinct. But beneath the crust of society lies their common reservoir, the basic insecurity of the American way of life. Herein lies the potentiality for new inundations. Until this fear of inferiority is reduced, the danger of a resurgent and violent flood of intolerance, racial or otherwise, will be ever-present.

Sex Crimes and Violence

Fear of inferiority or insecurity not only underlies tensions between groups, it also gives rise to irreconcilable differences between individuals or groups. In an individual-centered way of life, the chances that such differences will be resolved by violence are immeasurably escalated.

Given the need to protest on the part of those who fear inferiority, the maintenance of differences between individuals or groups tends to assume a significance beyond reality. Small concessions are likely to be defined as total surrender. In this situation, strong entrenchment behind individual or group differences, however minor in an objective sense, is a foregone conclusion.[40] For to accept compromises is to surrender the self—the one thing the individual-centered American most abhors. When man is caught in such a trap he will not avoid using violence to secure his ends. Violence is the individual's (or group's or nation's) instrument for imposing his will on another person (or another group or another nation) for his own purposes but without regard for the convenience or feelings of the victim.

This is not, of course, to say that all violence erupts from the same basic cause. There are forms of insanity that express themselves in violence no matter what the cultural context. Personal grudges and vendettas have resulted in violence historically as they do today. Wars and revolutions always bring about individual violence over and above the military or political necessities. And black rage and anger in the twentieth century in the United States is, as we noted before, linked directly to centuries of oppression and frustration by Whites.

However, what I have tried to show is that, over and above factors that may operate among a particular group at any time and in any place, the American way of life is particularly conducive to violence because it fosters a fear of inferiority which makes compromise so devastatingly deflating to the individual's ego. Different individuals react differently to this danger. If personal good looks, athletic achievements, killings on the stock market, and professional or business successes and achievements become all-important in defense against insecurity for some, sexual conquest may fill the same need for others. Here the sources of violence and sex crime merge together; rape is simply violence applied in man-woman relationships.

Violent sex crimes are occurring with increasing frequency in the United States.[41] A widely read newspaper advice columnist had this to say, to my great surprise: "The number of children who are molested and raped every year is appalling, and the guilty party is usually not a stranger, interestingly enough, but a family friend or a relative."[42]

The remedies proposed such as stricter laws for incarceration of the offender, or more psychiatric services for early identification and confinement of "constitutional psychopathic inferiors" (and other external devices such as community watchfulness) will not remove this threat. Those in favor of harsher laws need only remember the failure of Prohibition. That unsuccessful experiment proved that the most thorough police methods will fail to enforce any law to which great numbers of people do not wish to submit. Those who emphasize the early discovery and treatment of "insanity," so often a defense in murder trials, ignore the fact that actual criminal psychopaths are responsible for only a fraction of all sex crimes. Here is how Dr. Edward Kelleher, chief of the Municipal Court Psychiatric Institute of Chicago, stated the matter:

> Our experience shows that the sex offender can be anyone, or any kind of person. Only one-half of one per cent were found to be actual criminal sexual psychopaths. The group of sex offenders as a whole varies as widely in intelligence and stability as any other segment of society.[43]

Such facts were probably among the considerations that prompted the late Alfred C. Kinsey to propose what he must have regarded as a most radical remedy: the elimination of sex laws because "the most important factor in the origin of sex offenders is that we have a law against it" (sic) (*Chicago Sun-Times,* May 24, 1952). In 1973 Billy Graham suggested a more radical remedy in response to a newsman's query, namely castration of the rapist as a way of stopping sexual assaults on women. "That would stop him pretty quick," he said.[44] The evangelist's remedy reminds us of another era when some kings and tribal chiefs punished pickpockets by chopping off their hands. But Kinsey's proposal is simply contrary to known facts. The problem of alcoholism might have been accentuated by Prohibition, but repeal of the law has not solved it.

Without seeing a paradise where the police are idle and the jails are empty, we must realize that law and enforcement agencies, no matter how detailed and efficient, can never cope with the problem of lawlessness if the number of potential offenders is large. The actual and potential offenders will simply find more loopholes and resort to new ways of evasion and escape to match the ingenuity and thoroughness of the law and its enforcers. Like the wage-price spiral, legal provisions and lawlessness will simply mutually escalate to new heights. The net result is that the cost of law and its enforcement will skyrocket with the damage of increased crime. It is sad that the latest President's Commission on Law Enforcement and Administration of Justice, composed of a large team of high government experts and professors, which was responsible for volumes, including *The Challenge of Crime in a Free Society,* failed to produce significant departures from the age-old, law-connected recommendations.[45]

On the other hand, if more laws and better enforcement measures cannot prevent the increase of crime, will understanding and cultivation of the individual through education and the clinical disciplines be able to do it? Again I have grave doubts. Quite apart from Kinsey's and Graham's kind of absurd recommendations, the view of Bruno Bettelheim, an influential psychologist on the subject, is worth examining:

> We have abolished the red-light districts and outlawed prostitution. I am all for such progress, mainly because it offers the girls more protection from being exploited. But for those who cannot afford the call girl, we have closed off an easy way to discharge both sexual and violent tendencies. Worse, by asserting that there is no place for sex outside of marriage, and none for violence in our society, we force each individual to suppress his violent tendencies till they build up to a pitch where he can

no longer deny them or control them. They suddenly erupt in isolated acts of explosive violence.[46]

This view contains many fallacies. First, cheap prostitution, premarital sex, and extramarital affairs are in most cases available for any male who wants sex badly enough without resorting to physical attack. The abolition of red-light districts has not eliminated prostitution or other extramarital sexual outlets.

Second, Americans have an "image" of themselves as "peace-loving and rational beings," but they have historically used violence to achieve their individual or group ends. Dr. John P. Spiegel, Director of the Lemberg Center for the Study of Violence at Brandeis University, who made these observations, went on to remind us of a few of the many instances of violence in which the *white users of violence* nearly always got what they set out to get. Spiegel called violence "an American heritage."[47]

In fact the American society does not even assert that violence has no place in it and that it forces "each individual to suppress his aggressive tendencies. . . ."[48] American fathers coach their children in self-defense. Americans usually praise a "good" fight. American children imitate karate experts as often as they play cowboys. The devastation of Vietnam that was shown daily on our television screens was perfectly acceptable to many Americans because it was in the "national interest." In addition there are thousands of other established channels through which Americans can transfer their aggressions: via boxing and other sports, hunting, fishing, movies and television, as well as a myriad of legitimate and illegitimate money-making activities.

But the emphasis on law and law enforcement or the search for answers in some simple-minded psychological theory of frustration are but twin expressions of the dilemma of an individual-centered way of life. Given the flimsiness and transient nature of human relations, steeped in a cultural ideal committed to individualistic separateness of man, even the best brains of the society fail to lift their sights above the traditional approaches: more external control or more psychic exploration. No wonder American women are reduced to more individual devices for self-protection. The latest of these is "Rapel", an inch-long cylinder that contains a glass ampoule of a fluid with a skunklike odor. It can be clipped to the inside of a dress, bra, or nightgown (*Time,* March 10, 1980).

We have so far discussed sex crime and other crimes of violence without distinction. All crimes possess the potentiality of violence, and sex crimes, like the varied faces of racial tension, are not as distinct as their overt manifestations have led us to believe. They share a common denominator with hundreds of other crimes of violence: the murder of a girl by her jealous twin sister; the torture of a woman by her sadistic lover; the strangulation of a father by his angry son; the nailing of a girl by her outstretched hands to an oak tree because she offended members of the Outlaws Motorcycle Club; the bludgeoning to death of a fifteen-year-old girl by two men and one girl because she either refused to join or tried to leave a sex club; the ninety-minute shooting spree of Charles Whitman from on top the Administration Building of the University of Texas which killed fourteen persons including his wife and mother, and wounded thirty-one persons; the shooting of a baseball star by a girl he had never met but who decided that, if she could not have him, "nobody else will"; the Hillside Strangler of Los Angeles; or the "Son of Sam" murders in New York City. The assassinations of well-known political figures such as President John Kennedy, Senator Robert Kennedy, and Dr. Martin Luther King, Jr. are other tragic examples. The common denominator is the fact that these crimes occur when the emotions of the insecure get out of control.[49]

The connection is not obscure. The emotions of the insecure tend to overshadow all other considerations. Those who are madly in love have a deep and abiding fear that they may lose the love object. Should the love object slip away from such an individual, the emotion of love is likely to become hatred which may be even more intense than the love it replaces. In any such situation, insecure individuals driven by the fear of inferiority consider only themselves: their defense against the threat or the fact of inferiority is to take immediate action to satisfy their own wants without regard for the wishes or even the lives of other persons. This attitude is no less true of the person whose grudge leads to violence directed against his adversary than it is of those who commit rape and sex murder. In both the dominant factor is emotion; in both the perpetrators' only consideration is to impose, at any cost, their own emotional demands on others.

However, our analysis leads us to suspect another dimension underlying sex crime in America. This is the American male's fear of inferiority. Rape may be seen as one defense against this fear by asserting his masculinity. For "maleness in America is not absolutely defined, it has to be kept and reearned every day, and one essential element in the definition is beating women in every game that both sexes play, in every activity in which both sexes engage."[50]

For this reason, even if we revive legalized prostitution and open red-light districts, we still will be far from making any significant dent in the problem. The male tormented to prove his maleness is not going to be satisfied with easy access to sex by purchase. He must convince himself that he has conquered by his own efforts. He wants to fish and hunt by his own marksmanship; he does not want the fish and the fowl that he can obtain by walking into any supermarket. The extreme expression of this is that of "The Old Man" in Hemingway's *The Old Man and the Sea.*

This is perhaps why gun control is such a problem and why it has become such a highly charged issue. This is why eleven jockeys at Tropical Park, Miami, boycotted a race to keep Barbara Jo Rubin "from becoming the first girl jockey at a major thoroughbred track."[51] Of course, the merchants of firearms have had a strong lobbying hand in preventing gun control legislation, but in both cases the feeling on the part of males who feel their maleness is under attack is no small stumbling block.

Once this is understood, an often discussed "Negro problem" falls into perspective. This is that "women rule the roost" in many more black families than in white ones and consequently, black husbands and sons feel inadequate, which facts add much fuel to the need for riots.[52] From our analysis we can easily see that this so-called "Negro problem" is part of the general problem of fear of inferiority. Blacks, having been old Americans for many generations, have not been left untouched by the pressures felt by the white majority. Blacks have many of the same problems besetting Whites plus other special ones of their own.

So it is that insecurity casts its protean shadow into nearly every corner of the American society, for it moves with the self-reliant individual throughout most of his days. This is essentially what Erich Fromm describes as man's "helplessness, isolation and insecurity" following upon the disintegration of European medieval life.

. . . All human relationships were poisoned by this fierce life-and-death struggle for the maintenance of power and wealth. Solidarity with one's fellow men—or at least with the members of one's own class—was replaced by a cynical detached attitude; other individuals were looked upon as "objects" to be used and manipulated, or they were ruthlessly destroyed if it suited one's own ends. The individual was absorbed by a

DILEMMA

passionate egocentricity, an insatiable greed for power and wealth. As a result of all this, the successful individual's relation to his own self, his sense of security and confidence were poisoned too. His own self became as much an object of manipulation to him as other persons had become. We have reasons to doubt whether the powerful masters of Renaissance capitalism were as happy and as secure as they are often pictured. It seems that the new freedom brought two things to them: an increased feeling of strength and at the same time an increased isolation, doubt, scepticism, and—resulting from all these—anxiety.[53]

Fromm, as a psychoanalyst, advises us that in this situation man can be helped by "spontaneous activities" such as "love" or "work." No one would deny that individual differences mean some persons are more deeply affected by this state of anxiety than are others, and that, therefore, spontaneous activities may help them to achieve an increased measure of individualized security or at least to forget about insecurity or to rechannel it temporarily. But given the general culture pattern, few can entirely escape the trap of the fear of inferiority. The results of spontaneous activities can at best be but a remote match for the consequences of the group pattern. For insecurity, it should again be underlined, is not peculiar to a few individuals who may be in need of psychiatric care. It affects the majority of Americans because it stems from the culturally sanctioned transitory nature of their human relationships. Further, Fromm did not distinguish between the insecurity of the twentieth-century American and that known to the postindustrial revolution European. The latter, individualist though he was, still retained many of the human associations of earlier days; the former, in striving to escape all bonds and all dependence, has purchased more freedom at an even higher cost in emotional security.[54]

When men are insecure, they are afraid. And it is neither God nor the physical universe the American fears, since he sees himself as the associate of the one and the master of the other. What he fears is his fellow man; for among self-reliant men, bound neither by custom nor other lasting ties, there can be no permanent common accord. The best to be hoped for is a series of truces of convenience. Each signatory to the truce is suspect to the other, each party either expects or works toward the accord's dissolution, and then both resume their feverish search for a human relationship that will be emotionally satisfying. The cycle is endless, insecurity is deep-seated, and each person's consequent fear of other men is constant though it may be expressed in diverse ways.

The expressions of this fear can range from the witch hunts of early New England to those which characterize the American society during a crisis. Either individuals or groups are sought after as the threat incarnate—the German minority became the embodiment of the "Hun" during World War I; the bearded, bomb-throwing Bolshevik was the prey of that postwar era; Herbert Hoover and "Wall Street" were the ogres of the depression period; during World War II the Japanese minority took the place of the Hun, and was extraordinarily victimized in consequence; in post-World War II and for decades later Communist China was used again and again as justification for aggressive activities such as the "thin" defense by ABM in the midwest and the war in Vietnam. No one would question the fact that in each of these periods there were individuals guilty of sympathy for the enemy or of bad judgment, bad judgment either in respect to stock exchange practices in 1929 or the objectives of Communist Russia later. But between treason and naïveté there is a gulf, and between a proved case against one guilty individual and a frenetic broadside attack on an entire group or class there is an even wider abyss.

It is not enough to say that hysteria is induced by election-minded politicians or overzealous publicists. For the politicians' or the propagandists' slogans ("labor union Reds," "Fascist big businessmen," "merchants of death") appeal to a basic fear—the fear of other men, even though these unseen threats may be wholly anonymous. And society responds by erecting barriers to domestic criticism, "un-American influences" in American life, and men from Mars or elsewhere in space. Publishers grow ever more cautious, the liberalization of immigration laws and visa regulations—made more restrictive and stringent in the forties and fifties under the late Joseph McCarthy—is accompanied by the biggest war to stop communism abroad, and radar and jets search the skies for flying saucers.

But external fortifications cannot placate this fear of men. When insecurity is deep and fear is rampant, the need for self-protection also expresses itself in a demand for taking militant action, and any act is satisfactory so long as it is militant. When militancy passes beyond its comparatively mild expression in individual or group competitiveness, it may erupt, as we have seen, in unmotivated assault and murder or group action such as prison, race, and other riots.

In brief, the spawn of insecurity and fear are violence and bigotry. These are projected against racial, religious, and political minority groups whose attack upon the majority—either by overt action or through infiltration—is deeply feared. Or they are projected against individuals and groups in authority, often vaguely termed "The Establishment," whose unfair advantage over the young and the underdog is strongly resented. White violence generates black violence in retaliation. And violence by the young and the underdog touch off such deep fears in the adult world that even law enforcement officers were said to have "rioted" against the Chicago Democratic Convention demonstrators.[55] Violence in fiction, from comic strips to best-sellers, movies, and television, is no longer an aspect of many stories —violence and/or sex, too, is the story. "The medium is the message." One of the most spectacularly successful purveyors of violence in fiction is Mickey Spillane, a former comic book writer whose six novels—wherein forty-eight persons were disposed of, all in a particularly brutal fashion—had sold a record-breaking total of thirteen million copies by 1953. His popularity is now matched if not surpassed by writers of violent international thrillers such as Frederick Forsyth, Robert Ludlum, and Ken Follett. It is not surprising to read that people who knew Spillane in his younger days "feel that the violence was there all along, the stronger for being repressed," that they suspect in him "a deep distrust of people," and that "one old acquaintance says, 'he has been running all his life, trying to catch up with security.' "[56] Mickey Spillane was made for his audience, and they for him.

NOTES

1. Long before the latest trend in delayed retirement a few organizations had already ventured to hire aged persons. In the fifties Northwestern University of Evanston, Illinois hired a retired mathematics professor as an on-campus mail carrier. Later, others were hired as consultants or part-time faculty members. In 1952, the Washington National Insurance Company, also of Evanston, hired five former executives as clerks. Their preretirement salaries were three times their postretirement salaries (*Chicago Daily News,* June 12, 1952).

2. In 1900 only 4.1 percent of the population was sixty-five or older. In 1940 the figure reached 6.8 percent. The figure for 1970 was 10 percent. And the projected figure for the year 2000 is 11.6 percent (according to the U.S. Department of Commerce, *Social Indicators 1976,* p. 22).

3. The best summary I know of these findings is given by Marvin B. Sussman, "Relationships of Adult Children with Their Parents," in *Social Structure and the Family: Generational Relations,* ed. by Ethel Shanas and Gordon F. Streib, pp. 68–70.

4. Ethel Shanas, "The Unmarried Old Person in the United States: Living Arrangements and Care in Illness, Myth and Fact," paper prepared for the International Social Science Research Seminar in Gerontology, Markaryd, Sweden, August 1963. Quoted in Margaret Blenker, "Social Work and Family Relationships in Labor Life with Some Thoughts on Filial Maturity," Chapter 3, in *Social Structure and the Family: Generational Relations,* p. 50.

5. Shanas and Streib, *Social Structure and the Family,* p. 49.

6. Sussman, "Relationships of Adult Children with Their Parents," p. 79.

7. Margaret Clark and Barbara Gallatin Anderson, *Culture and Aging: An Anthropological Study of Older Americans.*

8. Helen Codere, "A Genealogical Study of Kinship," *Psychiatry* 18, no. 1, (February 1955): 65–79; and David Schneider, *American Kinship: A Cultural Account.*

9. Clark and Anderson, *Culture and Aging,* p. 275.

10. Jules Henry, *Culture Against Man,* p. 474 (author's italics).

11. For example, *Modern Maturity, Senior Citizen, Dynamic Maturity,* and *Harvest Years.*

12. Jennie-Keith Hill, *The Culture of Retirement,* (Ph.D. dissertation, Northwestern University, 1968), p. 194.

13. Ibid.

14. Ibid.

15. Some other epithets are: the "elephant farm," "old people's Russian roulette," "foyers to the tomb," "waiting rooms for death," "public housing for well-to-do," "geriatric ghettos," "geriatric capitals," and "sunset skyscrapers." Ibid., Appendix.

16. From the police files of fourteen capital cities. (*Ministry of the Interior Year Book,* 1936, Shanghai.)

17. U.S. Department of Commerce, *Social Indicators 1976,* p. 250.

18. FBI, *Uniform Crime Reports,* p 174

19. Ibid., p. 187–196. For example, between 1976 and 1977 arrests for criminal homicide and rape for this age group had actually decreased in cities but greatly increased in suburban areas.

20. Marvin E. Wolfgang, "The Culture of Youth," Office of Juvenile Delinquency Welfare Administration, U.S. Department of Health, Education, and Welfare, 1967. Reproduced in *Task Force Report: Juvenile Delinquency and Youth Crime,* President's Commission on Law Enforcement and Administration of Justice, p. 152.

21. Kenneth Keniston, *The Uncommitted: Alienated Youth in American Society,* p. 429.

22. Some scholars see this contrast as between agricultural (or "primitive") and industrialized (or "modern") societies. The fact is that the parent-child relationship even among second and third generation Chinese in Hawaii is still close to the Chinese pattern described.

23. The unpopularity of the Vietnam War did not create the generation gap. The inconsistency between forcing youths to die for a colonial-type struggle when they have been brought up to side with the underdog merely aggravated the gap that already existed. The ending of the Vietnam War did not, therefore, end or even reduce it.

24. Richard Lorber and Ernest Fladell, "The Generation Gap," *Life* magazine, May 17, 1968.

25. For an analysis of the significance of externalization of human relations see Francis L. K. Hsu, "Individual Fulfillment, Social Stability and Cultural Progress" in *We, the People: American Character and Social Change,* ed. by Gordon J. DiRenzo, pp. 95–114.

26. Some readers may regard the Red Guards' eruption in 1966–1969 as conflicting with these observations. But as we shall see in Chapter 15, the Red Guards were instigated as a new political movement designed to induce youths away from their parents.

27. *The Kerner Report,* Report of the National Advisory Commission on Civil Disorders.

28. Ibid., pp. 203–206. An earlier report, *Toward an Understanding of Mass Violence* (Contributions from the Behavioral Sciences) by Gordon Globus, Peter Knapp, Jr., and Donald Oken, prepared by the staff of the NIMH, August 1967, p. 58, came to

the same general conclusion, ". . . the Negro's conviction about his victimization by the system of deprivation is the major cause of riots."

29. Lipset, *The First New Nation,* pp. 214-215.

30. See for example, Harry C. Brademeier and Jackson Toby, *Social Programs in America,* pp. 39-46, 47-53, 180-182.

31. I do not believe that either of these is a conscious motive behind the scholarly approaches to the racial question.

32. See for example, Kimball Young and Raymond Mack, *Sociology and Social Life,* pp. 190 and 204.

33. Describing John Kennedy's consultation with Robert A. Lovett after Kennedy became president-elect, David Halberstam said: "And when Lovett told Kennedy that he had not voted for him, Kennedy just grinned at the news, though he might have grinned somewhat less at Lovett's reason, which was Lovett's reservation about old Joe Kennedy. In a way, of course, this would have made Lovett all the more attractive, since much of the Kennedy family's thrust was motivated by the Irish desire to make these patricians, who had snubbed Joe Kennedy, reckon with his sons; this meeting was, if anything, part of the reckoning. ('Tell me,' Rose Kennedy once asked a young and somewhat shocked aristocratic college classmate of Jack Kennedy's back in 1939 as she drove him from Hyannisport to Boston, 'When are the good people of Boston going to accept us Irish?' " *The Best and the Brightest,* pp. 8-9). Rose Kennedy's problem at the time might have been one of class as well as race. But it is obvious that even great wealth and political prominence neither lead to social acceptance nor erase the need to climb.

34. Probably this oversight was unintentional, for we were confronted with so much violence by Blacks at this time, and the Kerner Commission was charged with the task of diagnosing that violence. But it is still not excusable.

35. The first generation Chinese male's reluctance to marry an American-born Chinese girl seems to be reciprocated by the latter's view of the former. The girl's most common derogatory remark about the former is that "he has no sex appeal."

36. See for example, Carleton Putnam's books, *Race and Reason: A Yankee View,* and *Race and Reality: A Search for Solutions.* Also his regular Putnam Letters.

37. From a speech by Claude Brown at a Northwestern University Symposium, and quoted in the *Daily Northwestern,* January 9, 1969.

38. Kurt Lewin, *Resolving Social Conflict,* pp. 198-199. Like others, Lewin, whose vision was confined to the Western world, did not see that Jews and other minority groups in China did not need the same kind of defense as Jews in the West.

39. A 1968 movie *Thoroughly Modern Millie,* featuring Julie Andrews, has every American device for defaming the Chinese. All the numerous Chinese in this film are little shadowy and sly figures who smoke opium, wear pigtails, walk like puppets, besides being white slavers. On top of all this they are also cowards to be repeatedly bested by a gangster-type white woman. To find the nearest Chinese counterpart to it, one would have to go to the worst anti-American diatribe under Communist regimes.

40. This, for example, we saw was the case with many so-called religious differences among Christians.

41. There are still many unsolved problems in measuring the volume of crime in the United States as elsewhere. However, there is no question that crime growth in general has far outpaced the population growth no matter how we look at the facts (crime rate increased by 42 percent from 1948 to 1957, and 63 percent from 1958 to 1964). Property offences grew half again as fast as crime against persons between 1958 and 1964 (65.7 percent versus 46.2 percent). The rate of rape increased from 7.6 percent per 100,000 population in 1958 to 10.7 percent in 1964, an increase of 40 percent. See Ronald H. Battle and John P. Kenney, "Aggressive Crime," *The*

Annals of the American Academy of Political and Social Science, special issue on "Patterns of Violence," pp. 73–85. Also Task Force Report: *Crime and Its Impact—An Assessment,* (Task Force on Assessment, The President's Commission on Law Enforcement and Administration of Justice), pp. 19–21. Although the same sources are used in both studies, Battle and Kenney conclude that there has been "no substantial increase in aggressive crime during recent years" (p. 84). This conclusion is hard to defend in view of the facts. Their view of "no substantial increase" may be the fault of what they regard as "substantial." For they also describe the increase in robbery and rape rates as "moderate" (p. 84) when the increase rate for the former is nearly 50 percent between 1957 and 1964 and 40 percent for the latter. If we go back farther, the rate for rape has tripled between 1933 and 1965 (see *The Challenge of Crime in a Free Society,* a report by the President's Commission on Law Enforcement and Administration of Justice, p. 23). The picture has not changed since. Between 1968 and 1977 the rate of rape went up 57.2 percent (see FBI, *Uniform Crime Reports,* p. 174).

42. *Chicago Sun-Times,* January 11, 1969.

43. *Chicago Tribune,* April 9, 1950.

44. See Francis L. K. Hsu, "Kinship is the key" in *The Center Magazine,* p. 5.

45. *Challenge of Crime in a Free Society,* pp. 279–291.

46. Bruno Bettelheim, "Violence: A Neglected Note of Behavior" in *The Annals of the American Academy of Political and Social Science,* special issue on "Patterns of Violence," p. 53.

47. Such as Shay's Rebellion against the courts of Massachusetts in 1786, anti-Catholic riots of the 1840s and 1850s, the Civil War draft riots in 1863, anti-Chinese riots in California during the 1870s, and the anti-Negro riots of 1919, 1920, and later (*Chicago Daily News,* October 31, 1968).

48. Ibid.

49. Some of these culprits may be psychotics, or at any rate their attorneys may use insanity as an argument for their defense.

50. Margaret Mead, *Male and Female,* p. 318.

51. As reported in the *Chicago Sun-Times,* January 17, 1969.

52. See Lloyd Shearer, "Negro Problem: Women Rule the Roost," *Parade* magazine, August 20, 1967. The article gives statistics and discusses the Moynihan report (1965) and other sholarly findings.

53. Erich Fromm, *Escape from Freedom,* pp. 260–261.

54. That is why we have books on America entitled *The Temporary Society* (Warren G. Bennis and Philip E. Slater) and *The Pursuit of Loneliness: American Culture at the Breaking Point* (Philip E. Slater).

55. *Kerner Report.*

56. Richard W. Johnston, "Death's Fair-haired Boy," *Life,* June 23, 1952.

CHAPTER 14

Chinese Weaknesses

Virtues, says the moralist, can produce grievous faults when they are carried to excess. Without passing judgment in quite the moralist's manner, we can at least conclude that a people's basic outlook, while it can be a source of strength in certain areas of life, can also produce distinctive problems and weaknesses. This is true of the Chinese way of life no less than of the American way. Just as self-reliance and its associated attitudes have given rise to difficulties that are uniquely American or have exaggerated problems found to a limited extent elsewhere, so in China mutual dependence has had deleterious as well as beneficial consequences.

Bondage to the Past

The solidity of the kinship group has its price in the resignation with which the average Chinese accepts life as he finds it. Situated securely in their primary human relationships, the Chinese have no urge to embark upon crusades. This means not only that the Chinese, throughout their long history before massive Western impact, showed no desire to make the world safe for ancestor worship. Nor did they exhibit any determined zeal to reform their own society, make over the lives of their neighbors, or change the style of the government of the peoples they had defeated and conquered.

The local hubbub that a cigar-smoking youngster created some time ago in Portland, Oregon, would be impossible in China. The Portland child started smoking before she was two, and when newspapers published photographs of her puffing upon a cigar, she and her parents immediately became a civic issue. A group of irate citizens saw to it that the family was haled before a juvenile court judge.

There, the child agreed to give up smoking, and her father agreed to do the same in order to set an example for her.

Admittedly, Portland's infant cigar smoker was unique. The reaction of the community's aroused citizens was not. The agitation of Samuel Adams and the Committees of Correspondence, the thundering editorials of William Lloyd Garrison and the work of the American Anti-Slavery Society, the busy hatchet of Carrie Nation and the labors of the Anti-Saloon League, and the flow of pamphlets from the pen of Gerald L. K. Smith and the Christian Front are of course distinct in point of time and objective. And, according to one's own views, these activities are surely of differing social merit. Similarly, unlike the night riders of the Ku Klux Klan, the Society for the Prevention of Cruelty to Animals and the League of Women Voters are not apt to produce social discord or open violence in their efforts to adjust situations which they feel require attention. Civic reform groups are responsible for many real improvements in American life, and missionary societies have likewise contributed to the welfare of other peoples. On a broader international scale, millions in foreign lands owe their lives to the American Red Cross, organizations such as CARE, the Peace Corps, and other programs that Americans have instituted, staffed, and paid for either privately or through their government.

As assuredly different in many respects as these and countless other activites may be, their supporters meet on a common ground with the citizens of Portland: all are zealously determined to accomplish a social end. They are joined together in behalf of a *cause,* whether its unity of purpose is brief or relatively long lasting, whether its theatre of action is at home or abroad, and whether the goal is moral, religious, economic, or political.

This sense of resolute committal to a cause is missing from the Chinese social conscience. There is no crusading spirit among the Chinese because they have no emotional need for it. Their acts of charity and other contributions to social welfare are good deeds that take care of an immediate need. When the necessity arises, a well-to-do person pays for the construction of a bridge across a local stream or for the repair of a section of a road passing through his village. Such persons also donate coffins to poor families, distribute free rice or open free meal centers in time of famine, and provide medicines to the needy during an epidemic. But few if any of these persons or their less prosperous neighbors would think of organizing a movement dedicated, say, to the improvement of China's road system or to the founding of a permanent organization for disaster relief. When the hopeful few have sought to initiate such movements, their conceptions have died aborning.

This is the fate not only of such programs of rejuvenation as Generalissimo Chiang's New Life Movement. It has been equally impossible to interest the Chinese in a sustained attack on specific social evils just outside their own doors. "Sweep the snow in front of your own dwelling," says a Chinese maxim, "but don't bother about the frost on the roof of other homes." The Chinese who pays for a new bridge in his locality is taking care of the snow at his own threshold, for by doing so, he and his neighbors expressly understand that he is accumulating merits in the world of the gods for himself and his family. But this same man guards himself against imposing his will on others in the name of their salvation. If another man sells his daughter into prostitution, that is the particular family's affair. If prison wardens mistreat those in their charge, the wise man conducts himself in such a way as to avoid imprisonment.

One of the results of this *laissez-faire* position is that slavery existed in China until recent times, and Chinese prisons not so long ago were a match for history's infamous Black Hole of Calcutta. Other evils like infanticide, opium addiction, and the frequent exploitation and inhuman treatment of coal and tin miners and trade apprentices have never aroused popular outrage or been combatted by social pressure. It was solely on the initiative of the Nationalist regime and through its resources that any effort was made to eradicate narcotics addiction.

It is, in fact, precisely this quality that is common both to Chinese who join organizations and those who do not: there is practically no individual or group effort to alter the behavior or beliefs of others and little impetus from any direction to upset existing institutions or usages. In this bed of social inactivity and of personal philanthropy, injustice, poverty, and corruption flourish.

Here, too, is the explanation of why footbinding remained a universal Chinese custom for so long. Footbinding probably began late in the southern T'ang dynasty when a favorite concubine of the sovereign-poet Li Yü (A.D. 961–975) wrapped her feet in white satin in an effort to make her dances more pleasing.[1] For nearly a thousand years thereafter, the willowy walk and the tiny perfume-spreading slippers of famous beauties enchanted the aristocracy and literati. The more frivolous took great pleasure in drinking wine from cups inserted in the "bowlike" shoes, and in poetry and prose writers

composed paeans to the custom and its loveliest servitors. Lin Yutang rightly debunked the contention that footbinding was a measure
for the suppression of women. His explanation is that it was "sexual
in its nature throughout. . . . Its popularity with men was based on
the worship of women's feet and shoes as a love fetish and on the
feminine gait which naturally followed, and its popularity with wom-
en was based on their desire to curry men's favor."[2] Lin Yutang observed further that footbinding in China therefore served much the
same function as did the whalebone corsets of Victorian England,
and the European ballerina's wooden-toed footbinding slippers. And
we may add here that in both Europe and America to drink from the
slipper of his evening's companion was one of yesterday's pastimes
for many a gentleman of means.

But Chinese footbinding cannot be fully understood if we stop at
sex and fashion. Western ladies have been no less anxious to be in-
triguing to men, and no less mindful of fashion. Why was Chinese
footbinding permitted to go so far toward deforming the female person, and why did it persist for so long, while the erotic attraction of a
woman's foot and walk never went beyond alcoholic frivolities in the
West?

One obvious influence is the Western artistic sense which finds in
the naked human body the highest expression of beauty. The Westerner naturally objects, therefore, to any drastic alteration of the
body's natural form. The Chinese, whose artistic ideal is so far removed from the human body that they seem almost oblivious to it,
would not share this reluctance to tamper with the human frame.
But behind the persistance of footbinding is a much deeper trait: the
unwillingness of Chinese to initiate or become involved in a fight for
or against any cause, including footbinding. This does not mean that
some individual Chinese did not condemn footbinding. According to
Lin Yutang, at least three scholars of the eighteenth and nineteenth
centuries did so. But we should note that these objections came one
thousand years after the practice began. And theirs were lone voices
among a people who were too securely placed in their primary
groups and too preoccupied with their own private duties and privileges to either interfere with the life and conduct of others or to chart
new paths for themselves.

It is therefore no surprise that those who instituted the movement
to end footbinding were either Western missionaries, men whose way
of life instilled in them the perseverance necessary to the success of
such a campaign, or young Chinese who came under Western influ-

ence and then carried the antifootbinding message back to their native villages or to the areas where they went as doctors, teachers, and the like. The propelling force was Western in origin, and we can safely say that Chinese inertia would have won the day for footbinding had not Western influence continued to penetrate deeper and deeper into Chinese life.

Thus the individual's strong attachment to the primary group, while it has saved China from the problems that arise in America in consequence of the individual's isolation, has been responsible also for the inability of the Chinese to cope with many aspects of their national and personal life that have long been in need of drastic reform. In America, the instability of human ties bears the greatest measure of responsibility for juvenile delinquency, racial tension, interpersonal violence, and other problems. But let us not forget that the generation gap, so vexatious and puzzling to many adults, has its positive as well as its negative effects. Having been brought up to eschew traditional ways, in contrast to his Chinese fellows, the American youth is more ready and far better prepared to challenge his world. If properly directed, this individual—self-reliant and instilled with the idea of progress—is capable of attacking wrongs in his society with a determination unknown to the Chinese.

This internal pressure for change in America is one of the secrets of the strength of the American way of life. Its complete lack, until after the nineteenth century and Western impact, was the basic weakness of the Chinese way of life. Famine and gross injustice led to many peasant uprisings and regional revolts in China, but never to student unrest. Because of their continuity with the older generation, Chinese youths, educated and otherwise, tended to follow the beaten paths, to talk wisely, and to compromise.[3] This fact completely negates the notion on the part of many present-day American parents that their daughters and sons reject the Establishment because, while the parents knew the hardship of the Great Depression, the youngsters were born with silver spoons in their mouths. In China, children of the wealthy and the highly placed were especially reluctant to challenge the past. The American generation gap and the Chinese lack of it are founded on cultural differences. They have little to do with economic facts.

The idealism of youth results from the individual-centered way of life almost in spite of the parents. And that youthful idealism, which does not necessarily fade with the years, is the germ of social reform. The eldest are not always the wisest, and the old ways are not always the best. The Chinese society has long been an aged and ailing witness to this. It is those idealists who have challenged the ways of yesterday, often quixotically but always with resolve, whom their more "practical" and "realistic" fellows may thank for many of the benefits the American society enjoys. The elevation of such practicality and realism to a dogma of social wisdom has dug the grave of Chinese reform. Some American skeptics are wont to say that yesterday's radical is today's conservative. That may be, but the fortunate fact is that today's conservative often has accomplished the radical task that he undertook yesterday. In China, for centuries the conservative has simply produced more conservatives for tomorrow, and the result has been a static society.

Revolt Without Revolution

The absence among the Chinese of those qualities and motives that produce peaceful reform meant also that they had little motivation toward social or political revolution. A revolution in the West—however short it may fall of its goal—is usually an attempt to completely destroy the existing order and to substitute in its place a new design of life. It is not just the theoreticians, pamphleteers, and leaders—whether their names be Rousseau and Robespierre, Jefferson and Paine, or Lenin and Trotsky—who see in the travail of revolution the birth of a wholly new world. This is also the hope of the ordinary people who take their positions at the barricades. If they did not want the old uprooted, as the ideologists say it should be, and if they did not believe that it could be done, as the organizers of revolution say it can, they would not be found on the firing line. They respond to the promises of the prophets and the slogans of the orators because these strike a responsive chord in their own hearts.

But to the Chinese, revolt had no such overtones. They dethroned their rulers many times. This done, they then allowed an exact model of the fallen dynasty to take charge of the government. For, until the dawn of the twentieth century, few Chinese—high and low, intellectual and peasant—ever actively sought to destroy established customs, however evil, and they never attempted to seize for themselves the reins of government. Instead, they fought to eliminate unjust rulers and then returned to their regular tasks, quite willing to obey the newcomers until the day the new regime in turn became too oppressive and corrupt.

It is usually explained that Confucianism was responsible for this dynastic cycle. It is true that China's rulers promoted Confucianism in the belief that it was the most effective means of insuring the people's obedience. Reformers and revolutionists of the modern day, from the early Republican years to later under communism, have vigorously denounced Confucianism, seeing in it the biggest obstacle to the success of their programs. In a limited way, these views are correct. There is an obvious similarity between the themes of Confucianism and the actualities of dynastic rule.

Confucianism holds that the good society is one in which each individual occupies his proper place. It teaches that when the individual is right his family will be right, when the family is right the nation will be right, and when each nation is right all under heaven will be right. To achieve this end, one must fulfill the duties and obligations inherent in the five cardinal relationships. These are the relationships between emperor and subject, between father and son, between husband and wife, between brothers, and between friends. Confucianism also emphasizes the rule of the superior man, a principal task of the governors being to set a high moral example for their subjects. Only when the rulers fail to govern wisely do the people have the right to revolt, not for the purpose of changing the system, but to place in power a new group who will govern as rulers should. This is certainly no philosophy of revolution or even reform. Confucianism is a philosophy that teaches the preservation of things as they are; it upholds the status quo of the society and its institutions. Revolt is regarded not as a weapon of destruction but as a tool of restoration; revolt is a lever to restore the balance of society, not to upset it.

However, Confucius was no more responsible for the Chinese way of life than was Ralph Waldo Emerson the initiator of the American way. Adam Smith's *The Wealth of Nations* did not create *laissez-faire* capitalism, and the Confucian Analects did not establish the pattern of Chinese government. It perhaps may be said that in making a brilliant summary of Chinese ways, Confucius gave those ways new emphasis and lucidity. But no individual and no body of writings can construct out of air a pattern of living that generations will slavishly observe. It is a forgivable failing of philosophers of all degrees and of their commentators, either pro or con, that they are apt to attribute more power to the weapon of organized thought than it probably deserves. For men heed those precepts that most closely correspond to their needs and desires, not those that are farthest removed from such feelings.

Tyrants may force an unwilling people to submit for a limited time to arbitrary dictates and innovations that have no roots in the society upon which they are imposed. But they can never successfully generate enthusiasm in their subjects for a pattern of life that is contrary to their wishes. When the founder of the Ming dynasty discovered in the writings of Mencius, the chief disciple of Confucius, an exposition of the right to revolt and the contention that the people were most important and the ruler least, this emperor had these "undesirable" thoughts expurgated from the philosopher's works. His success was of brief duration, and the suppressed elements were soon restored.

Conversely, when the tenets of Confucianism failed to agree with those forces that were actively shaping the Chinese society, it was of no use for the rulers to call upon Confucianism for support. Thus though Yuan Shih-kai, the first president of the Chinese Republic, revived Confucian rites as a state worship, he was catapulted from office when he made himself the emperor a few years after the Revolution of 1911. By then the urge to Westernize, at least in form, was too strong to be withstood by an appeal to a strict interpretation of the ancient ideology.

But having been imbedded in the Chinese social fabric for thousands of years, the tenets of Confucius are by no means dead and they will not die easily. Even under the Communists since 1949, many elements of Confucian ethics found their proper places in the scheme of things, or were too imbedded in the Chinese way of life to be eradicated in short order, as we noted in Chapter 2. That was why, not so long ago, the ideas of Lin Piao, the fallen heir-designate to Chairman Mao, and the legacy of Confucius were criticized in the same movement *(P'i Lin P'i K'ung)*. In Taiwan, as an ideological defense against communism, the government recently launched a Movement for the Renaissance of Chinese Civilization *(Chung Kuo Wen Hwa Fu Hsing Yun Tung)*, the essence of which is to combine Confucian virtues such as filial piety, harmony, and compromise with scientific and technological florescence.

Confucianism became dominant in traditional China not merely because the ruling groups promoted it, but because it was in deep agreement with the ways the Chinese have followed from time immemorial. Nor did Confucianism gain its hold upon Chinese thought by entering into an intellectual void. More or less contemporaneous with the rise of the Confucian school there arose a variety of other philosophies, all of which vied with Confucianism for supremacy.

The Legalists, for example, concerned themselves with the ordering of society by a rigid system of law. Said the Legalists, man, being imperfect in nature, can only be improved by education, and he should be controlled by a fixed and firmly administered body of universally applicable law. This law should, of course, be changed as circumstances and study warranted, but the aristocracy and the state should always remain supreme.

Another school was the Taoist. Their philosophy centers around the idea of the Tao, or "the way," which is the ultimate reality back of and permeating the universe. Within the Tao, all things are equal, and the one and the many need not be distinguished. Men will be freed from their worldly difficulties if they conduct themselves according to Tao. They can conform to the Tao only if they cease to excel, to conquer, to compete, to love, to hate, to inquire, and if they make every effort to do nothing. On the individual level, this has often been interpreted as a philosophy which if widely accepted would lead to universal inaction or even anarchy. But as a philosophy of political economy its emphasis on noninterference bears a remarkable similarity to the doctrines of the most extreme expositors of Western capitalism.[4]

The Mohists, whose school constituted the third main competitor to Confucianism, proposed wholehearted conformity to the will of Shang Ti, the supreme deity. This dedication plus the use of reason would lead to an improved society. Believing in the inherent goodness of human nature and the existence of spirits, the Mohists held that if men would love each other as the supreme deity loves them, then peace and prosperity would prevail without the help of ceremonies and other external restraints—a doctrine essentially similar to certain branches of the Christian faith.

To the Taoists, Confucianism would appear much more positive than is warranted by the Tao. To the Legalists, Confucianism would appear much less positive than is necessary to the operation of impersonal law. To the Mohists, Confucianism would appear overly narrow in its conception of social life since it excludes the active participation of an all-embracing supreme deity.

But there are discernible reasons for Confucianism's triumph over these and several other philosophies. Confucianism is not concerned with ultimate reality. Mutual dependence leads the Chinese to reason that order exists in the universe in consequence of the order among human beings. Confucianism is not concerned with the meaning of life after death. A people whose religious life centers around ancestor worship find it easy to assume that the nature of all spirits and gods is similar to that of men and, therefore, need not be the object of protracted curiosity or discussion. Confucianism does not endorse an absolutist concept of the supremacy of the state and the aristocracy. No people whose orientation in life is derived from mutual dependence can fail to link the rulers' privileges with the fulfillment of their duties and any delinquency in this regard with a loss of respect.

In brief, the philosophies rivaling Confucianism were founded on what appeared to the Chinese as extremist doctrines, and it was to the Golden Mean of Confucius that their way of life bade them turn. This rejection of extremist doctrines in favor of a middle of the road philosophy and the lack of determination to refashion the existing order either through reform or revolution is also reflected, as we have noted previously, in the absence of utopian Chinese literature. It is inconceivable that the genius of a Plato or even a Saint-Simon could have come to fruition in China. For such men are not so much creators of thought as they are products of a way of life. Even though there be variations from the mean, as were Taoism and the other philosophies, most men turn for sustenance to those foods that best suit their own particular palates and digestive tracts. The ideal Republic of Plato, preaching the search for the absolute, still nourishes Western thought more than two thousand years after the philosopher's death; the Confucian Analects, counseling moderation in all things, have remained the philosophic staple of Chinese society for a similar span of time.

These considerations help us to understand also why a body of impersonal law, based on the idea of human rights, has failed to develop in China. In the Chinese philosophy, the interpretation of law is based upon human feelings and situations not upon absolute standards. Disputants do not turn to lawyers who argue a client's case in abstract terms joined with appeals to legal precedent. Instead, they look to a middleman or peacemaker.[5] A concept of law that defines justice in human terms has no place for abstract or absolute notions of right and wrong. Each case is different, and it is always right or wrong that is relative: what is right for the father may be wrong for the son, or what is permissible in one situation may be punishable in another. Nor does this relativistic approach stop even here. The Chinese middleman does not uphold one party against another or insist that one is completely right and the other wholly wrong. His mission is to smooth ruffled feelings by having each disputant sacrifice a little, whether the sacrifice involves principles or not.

So it is that in matters of law, as in all spheres of Chinese life, the individual has little emotional urge to pursue one objective or one principle or one enemy to the bitter end. This does not mean that there have been no Chinese martyrs. Throughout China's history many persons have sacrificed much, including their lives, for causes whose success could bring no direct profit to themselves or to their children.

In 1519 the reigning Ming emperor desired to leave his capital at Peking and take a pleasure trip to the southern part of his domain. The very thought of an emperor leaving his capital except during an emergency, such as invasion or rebellion, was without sanction. He was soon bombarded with a succession of petitions from his officials. Grossly offended, the emperor ordered severe punishment for the two officials who initiated the first petition. But this did not dam the flood of protests. More officials began to speak out against the proposed journey. Exile, flogging, imprisonment, and death were meted out to the various petitioners. And the emperor made the trip.

This was not a singular event. Many officials, at different times, opposed the emperor's will and suffered in consequence. Some protested an emperor's wish to confer titles upon undeserving persons or to depose the heir apparent and replace him with the son of a favorite concubine. Others paid with their lives when they incurred the wrath of an emperor's favored minister or eunuch by opposing the latter's misuse of power. All of these cases have one thing in common: the objectives which Chinese martyrs opposed were those that violated traditions established by the forefathers and which they sought to uphold.

Chinese emperors were, of course, severe in their measures for eradicating any threat or sign of a threat to their power. Working on the Chinese cultural assumption that the individual is part and parcel of his kinship system, many emperors even punished rebels or would-be rebels by wiping out the culprits' kin to the extent of the ninth degree. But Chinese did not make martyrs of themselves, and Chinese emperors did not make martyrs of persons who merely held or lived according to nonorthodox ideas. Therefore rebels who used Taoist ideology to build rebel states or communities were ruthlessly suppressed, but Taoist ideas and practices were always left alone. In fact, "their utility as an expressive outlet for the populace was acknowledged. . . . The central government never made any real effort to wipe out these 'heretical' beliefs."[6]

Consequently, no list of Chinese martyrs could match in length a similar Western compilation. Legion are those in the West who have suffered or died for their religious belief, political thought, scientific conviction, and numerous other reasons. But I know of not one Westerner who resolutely drank hemlock so that the world might remain precisely as an ancient philosopher, ruler, or custom had ordained it should be. Many battles have been fought to uphold the American Constitution, but, characteristically, the defenders of American tradition fought not for tradition's sake but in the name of freedom for themselves and for the well-being of the generations to come. In other words, the Chinese have most often interpreted the present in terms of the *concrete* past, while Americans express their feelings about either the present or the past in terms of an *imagined* future.

Nevertheless, we often hear that mediocrity is encouraged by American disapproval of noncomformity. There are, as we have seen, certain areas of thought or activity where the American society is extremely sensitive to noncomformity. But this may also be said of all societies, for the noncomformist finds his way difficult in any organized group. But on this problem the American society differs from its Chinese counterpart in two respects. First, because of the individual-centered person's all-or-none approach, the nonconformist is not likely to be left alone. In fact, he is hated and often attacked. Such hatred and attack threaten the nonconformist so that the latter tends to fortify himself or take the road of offense as the best defense. This sets the stage for a struggle in which each side expects complete victory. The gay liberation movement and the opposition to it are a good example of this.

The other difference is that under the individual-centered way of life, many people who have conformed all along may be willing to come to the rescue of the nonconformist or even rally around him. His nonconformist views may snowball as a result. Thus the critical points are the extent to which the exceptional individual may depart from established ways without severe punishment and the readiness with which society is prepared to follow him upon the trail he has broken.

With this in view I think it is a most important truth of the world in which we live, and most clearly seen perhaps by those who recently have come from other lands, that the American society as a whole presents more opportunities for the exceptional individual to realize his potentialities than he could dare to hope for elsewhere. The tendency is, of course, to encourage talent in the natural and applied sciences, commerce and industry, and art and entertainment, the emphasis throughout being on individualized technical skills.

However, a Chinese child endowed with special inclinations and capabilities, of whatever sort, had, until China came into contact with the West, no real opportunity to put them to use. His only chance for true distinction lay at the terminus of the examination road—official position. The strength and durability of this single-lane prestige pattern must certainly have kept many a potential scientist, entrepreneur, and artist from following his natural inclinations. How many entertainers in China would have been Bob Hopes, Gary Coopers, Mae Wests, or Barbra Streisands? We will never know. We will never know because their society and culture never gave them a chance. No wonder Chinese visitors to the American pavilion in the Montreal Expo of 1967 were amazed to see Clark Gable as its centerpiece. To date I know of no Chinese exhibition anywhere under whatever political persuasion which included portraits of famous Chinese actors and actresses. On the other hand, we also cannot guess how many inefficient officials, unsuccessful scholars, and custom-bound teachers might have made China a better place in which to live and been happier themselves had the society been attuned to welcoming them as carpenters, scientists, novelists, or entertainers.

The American society consciously encourages individual differences, even though it is more and more distressed by some of the end results. The Chinese society is one that has never encouraged such differences, the consequence being that it has known twenty centuries of cultural and political stagnation.

Lack of Science and Music

The relatively static condition of the Chinese society and particularly its failure to pursue new trails when once opened—to follow up the multifold implications of discoveries—is clearly evident in the history of Chinese science. Chinese folklore attributes the development of the compass to Huang Ti, the Yellow Emperor, a sovereign said to have ruled four or five thousand years ago. This invention was followed by the development, allegedly by another ancient ruler, of the trigrams, which was the starting point of Chinese mathematics.

Though the antiquity of these inventions is probably wholly legendary, their native origin is not. The monumental work of Joseph Needham in collaboration with Wang Ling and later Lu Gwei Djen, which is still in progress, has enabled us to see much more clearly than ever before the depth and variety of Chinese science and technology throughout historical times.[7] As early as 1751 B.C., the Chinese had worked out a 365¼-day year and a refined metallurgy involving copper, tin, and bronze. Later (1111 B.C.) they had a close calculation of the ratio of a circle's circumference to its diameter *(pi = 3)* and knew *(x^p - x)* to be divisible by its exponent *(p)*.[8] By the middle of the third century A.D., the Chinese already possessed the Pythagorean theorem; computations of the distance to and orbit of the sun; distinction of odd and even numbers and of positive and negative numbers; operations with fractions, including a rude method of division; extraction of square and cube roots; and linear, simultaneous, and quadratic equations. During the same approximate period, the densities of many metals became known, some calculations being very accurate and others much less so.

Later, in the fifth century, Chinese scholars reestimated the previous calculation of pi, determining its value to lie between 3.1415926 and 3.1415927. It should be noted that the accurate value of pi (3.14159265) was wholly unknown to the Greeks, and was rediscovered in Europe only in 1585. And the method of dividing fractions, namely, multiplication after inversion of the divisor, was not known in Europe until that same century.[9]

In the latter part of the thirteenth century the Chinese developed an original system of algebra containing what the West knows as Horner's method for extracting the roots of equations, and the Heronic formula.

The ancient Chinese were accredited with many other discoveries and inventions, notably a seismograph, a spherical model of the universe, printing, an accurate calendar, the water clock, hormones, anesthetics, and the principles of aerodynamics, besides the well-known gun powder. In physics, the Chinese discovery of "the declination, as well as the polarity, of the magnet," antedated European knowledge of it by some six centuries. The Chinese were theorizing about the declination before Europe knew even of the polarity.[10]

Characteristically, however, the Chinese were not much interested in principles apart from their practical utility. According to Needham, "until the middle of the seventeenth century Chinese and European scientific theories were about on a par, and only thereafter did European thought begin to move ahead so rapidly."[11] Why did the West move forward while China, which antedated the West on so many discoveries and inventions, did not?

F. S. C. Northrop explains the poverty of scientific thought in the

"Orient" as the result of an aesthetic and indeterminate approach to life, arising out of a

> . . . positivistic conception of human knowledge, restraining it solely to the realm of the immediately apprehended, denying any component in the nature of things of which the immediately apprehended is the epistemic correlate or the sign, and tending to reject all postulationally designated, indirectly verified, theoretically known factors which mathematical and logical methods alone can determine in a trustworthy manner.[12]

This explanation is fair enough on the descriptive level. Those who have no interest in the theoretical certainly do not become scientists. Chinese indifference to the elaboration of the unseen is also not obscure, as evidenced in their art and literature. In both they avoid the introspective and the deeply imaginative, concerning themselves almost wholly with men's dealings with nature or with other men. Even their religion is a nearly complete extension of the content and the form of their human relations. They are satisfied with gods or spirits who, like men, are greedy or generous, or temperamental or dependable, kind or unkind, bribable or absolutely just. To these persons, the idea of a one and only infallible god, different from and independent of all men, is inconceivable.

This matter-of-fact attitude toward the supernatural makes it almost inevitable that the Chinese should fail to define the natural world in terms of atoms, gravitation, parabolas, and geologic strata, all of which are extremely remote from that which is open to the senses and experience. It is far more reasonable for them to explain nature's bounties and catastrophes in terms of the rewards or punishments that they deserve in respect to how fully they have observed or flaunted the rules of conduct codified by Confucius as the five relationships.

But the point is not just that the Chinese have exhibited little interest in the unseen or the imaginative. The essential characteristic is that even when they are on the right trail they do not seem to pursue their subject of inquiry remorselessly. Here the basic error of Northrop's definition of the characteristics of the East and of the West, besides mistakenly lumping China and India together,[13] becomes obvious. Northrop rightly points out that the unseen, or the theoretical, is emphasized in the West while the immediately apprehended, or the positivistic, is emphasized in the East in societies such as China. But it is not correct to term the Chinese attitude "aesthetic" or to equate this with the emotional factor.

The foregoing chapters have revealed that emotionality is as uncharacteristic of the Chinese as it is pronounced among Americans and Europeans. It is this basic error that led Northrop to represent the Eastern way of life with Georgia O'Keefe's "Abstraction No. 3."[14] In the typical features of the Chinese way of life there is simply no evidence of such free-flowing emotion as that which Miss O'Keefe tries to convey to her viewers.

This same misinterpretation led Northrop to state that ". . . the logic of the verification of all doctrines, such as those of Western science, philosophy and religion, which refer to unseen factors" does not give absolute certainty, and therefore, ". . . no Westerner is ever entitled to be cocksure about that portion of his moral, religious and social ideals which refers to or derives its justification from unseen, inferred factors not given with immediacy."[15] Yet we have seen that it is exactly about "that portion" of "moral, religious and social ideals" which refer to the "unseen" that Westerners are most adamant—willing to ostracize or be ostracized, to imprison or be imprisoned, to kill or be killed. In fact, Westerners have also been overweeningly confident about the unknown in science: for example, the contempt heaped upon Pasteur and his germs, or Freud and his psychoanalysis. I submit that this assurance about the unseen and the inferred —whether it be the nature or existence of God or the question of geocentric or heliocentric interpretation of the universe—is impossible without strong emotional commitment. This audacious certainty is also an *inevitable* expression of the very psycho-cultural foundation that is responsible for the growth and flowering of Western science.

Needham does not agree that the Chinese were weak in postulation and scientific hypothesis. He thinks "there is no good reason for denying to the [Chinese] theories of Yin and Yang or the Five Elements the same proto-scientific hypotheses as can be claimed by the systems of the pre-Socratic and other Greek schools."

> What went wrong with Chinese science was its ultimate failure to develop out of these theories forms more adequate to the growth of practical knowledge, and in particular its failure to apply mathematics to the formulation of regularities in natural phenomena. This is equivalent to saying that no Renaissance awoke it from its "empirical slumbers."[16]

But since the Chinese had the mathematics and since they had shown no lack of interest in natural phenomena, why did they never link the two through a Chinese renaissance? Needham believes the answer is to be found in "the specific nature of the social and economic system" and he at once speaks of the commonality among the livelihood practices, basic legal concepts, and views of the supernatural. Nomads beat and command their beasts, but agriculturists can only follow the natural growth rhythm of their plants. So the Confucian *li* (禮or propriety)[17] is only applicable to human society while Western natural law is rooted in *universality* which governs both men and things. Finally, "in order to believe in the rational intelligibility of Nature, the Western mind had to presuppose (or found it convenient to presuppose) the existence of a Supreme Being who, himself rational, had put it there." On the other hand:

> The Chinese world-view depended upon a totally different line of thought. The harmonious co-operation of all beings arose, not from the orders of a superior authority external to themselves, but from the fact that they were all parts in a hierarchy of wholes forming a cosmic pattern, and what they obeyed were the internal dictates of their own natures.[18]

To a certain extent Needham's approach is consonant with ours. A people's pattern of behavior with reference to science and technology certainly does not exist in a vacuum. The same pattern tends to appear again and again throughout different aspects of their culture. But the burden of our analysis in the foregoing chapters is that man's relationship with his fellow human beings, beginning with life under his parents, is dominant over his dealings with gods and things. If the Chinese developed the notion that gods and men "were all parts in a hierarchy of wholes forming a cosmic pattern" because they grew plants which cannot be beaten or given commands, what happened to their notion when they were food gatherers or nomads before they developed agriculture (unless we accept the unlikely assumption that the Chinese always were agriculturists)?

On the other hand, the individual-centered and self-reliant Americans, as we saw in Chapters 11 and 12, not only are determined to control and accumulate things, but they also have taken steps to shape their theoretically omnipotent, omniscient, and omnipresent God in their own image. For this reason I cannot agree with Needham when he says that the earliest Chinese had "the [indigenous] ideas of a supreme being . . . who soon lost the qualities of personality and creativity."[19] The Chinese certainly have always entertained the idea of a Supreme Ruler of Heaven, but there is absolutely no evidence that the Chinese ever attributed to this being "qualities of personality and creativity" which they later discarded. The Chinese Supreme Ruler of Heaven was always part of the hierarchy of wholes in the same cosmos with men. But as time went on, the Chinese merely elaborated this relationship so that the Chinese Supreme Ruler of Heaven was not even the god who separated heaven from earth.

Western Judeo-Christian tradition always had a god who was the creator of all men and things and who stood apart from the results of his creation. It was therefore perfectly in keeping with the individual-centered orientation that God could decide on His own to erase all His creatures except the chosen few by a terrible flood. The Chinese Supreme Ruler of Heaven could never do this. If he did, he could not hold his position as the Supreme Ruler any more than could a Chinese reigning monarch. In fact the ancient flood of Chinese myth was neither created by any Chinese god to punish men nor eliminated by any supernatural being (see "Epilogue"). The cultural pattern of mutual dependence extends from men to gods, and would thus make such a step impossible. With the passage of time, Western individualism became intensified into self-reliance, and Westerners often tended to abrogate some of the attributes of God by their need to control men via the control of things.

This contrast is then the foundation of why the Chinese, in spite of their good head start, were surpassed by Westerners in the development of science and technology. For what distinguishes China is not what Northrop calls the aesthetic component which he equates with emotion, but the mutual dependence among men which makes attachment to the unseen needless and strong emotions inappropriate. For this reason what Northrop says Westerners *ought* to do— restrain their cocksureness—is not done by Westerners as a rule. Westerners are so cocksure of their religious beliefs and ideologies that they not only proselytize on a grand scale, but they have not hesitated to resort to force to convert unwilling subjects of their proselytization. On the contrary, the Chinese have been doing exactly what, according to Northrop's analysis, they should not do. The Chinese do speak of "breaking one's own cooking pot" and "sinking one's own ship" as symbolic expressions of an all-out effort from which there is no retreat. The trouble is that the majority of Chinese never feel themselves to be in a social situation where there is no retreat.

The Chinese, like Americans, love success. But if worldly success is unattainable for a man, his wife—and especially his children—and fellow men within the kinship and communal circles are always ready to accept him. His place among them is inalienable. Similarly, the Chinese attack those they consider their enemies, but even when motivated by a desire for revenge, they caution themselves not to push an opponent to the wall. There are many expressions that voice this attitude: "if given an inch, don't take a foot"; "do not mistake retreat for weakness"; and "leave living space for even your worst enemy." That is why, while the Western Gulliver in *Gulliver's Travels* made his fantastic journeys alone, his Chinese counterpart in a comparable Chinese fantasy, *Tale of the Mirrored Flower (Ching Hua Yuan)* which we briefly touched on in Chapter 1, was accompanied by a friend and a brother-in-law. The Chinese simply do not go it alone, even in fantasy.

It is this spirit which, as already noted, permits the middleman to become the key figure in Chinese legal disputes while barring the way to Western-model lawyers and the rule of impersonal law wherein one party must win and the other must lose. It is this reluctance of the Chinese to "shoot the works" or "go the limit," joined to an interpretation of the supernatural in natural terms, that has prevented the growth of Chinese science. What kind of science can a people develop if they avoid extremes, choosing always the middle road, and if their scientists have so little conviction of the ultimate truth of their own theories that they are willing to change them at the first sign that these convictions do not agree with what is experienced by the senses? For while dedication to science is extremely difficult without depth of imagination, often verging on the fantastic, it will be impossible without a fervent determination to pursue the inquiry, however foolish it may appear to other men and however violently the rest of society may oppose it.

This lack of intense interest in the imaginary and the absence of any emotional need to commit oneself to it also go far toward explaining why Chinese music is by Western standards considered so primitive.[20] Two characteristics distinguish Chinese music from its well-developed Western counterpart: the absence of harmony and an emphasis on the programmatic. No matter how many instruments perform at the same time, Chinese music is always in unison. Musical theory is unelaborated, musical instruments are never standardized, music scales are not variegated, and the total musical repertoire is extremely small in view of both China's size and its long history.

However, this evaluation of Chinese music was not always true. As in the case of science and technology, the Chinese achievement in music (instrumentation and theory) also antedated its Western counterpart by centuries. For years, some Chinese historians spoke about a sort of "paradise lost" of Chinese music. They said that the ancient Chinese possessed a much larger variety of musical instruments than is known today, that the imperial courts of the distant past featured large orchestras—sometimes a hundred musicians played together—and that Chinese music theory was very elaborate. Music was one of the Six Arts[21] and was regarded by Confucius as a most important means for cultivating the individual. Circulating in China for centuries were a number of well-known stories in which music played a prominent role. A scholar Yu played the lute amid the lush scenery of a deep valley. A farmer Chung was so moved by the music that he determinedly sought out the musician. The two became lifelong friends. In another tale a bachelor-scholar-houseguest began to play the lute in the stillness of the night. The music so overcame a young widow that she went to him and the two eloped.

Thanks to the labors of Joseph Needham and his collaborators, we now also have a much more thorough idea of the theory and technology of music in ancient China.[22] The ancient Chinese had highly precise musical instruments made of wood, reed, metal, and stone. They left records indicating that as early as the Chou dynasty (about 1100 B.C.), the ritual of the three great sacrifices included six changes of melody using three modes in the winter solstice, eight changes of melody with four modes at the summer solstice, and nine changes of melody with three modes at the sacrifice to the ancestors.

The ancient Chinese had the five-note pentatonic scale, but they also were quite aware of the semitones and heptatonic scale and had the twelve-note gamut resembling the Pythagorean scale probably by the fourth century B.C. They dealt with the changes in "character in music caused by the displacing of the semitones in heptatonic modes, and also with the subtler changes in character caused by transposition of a melody from one key to another within the same mode."[23] The appreciation of these changes required knowledge of the absolute frequencies of the notes and the precise differences in frequency among the intervals. To deal with the problem of the subtler changes caused by transposition, Prince Chu Tsai-yü invented, about A.D. 1584, the equal temperament method of fixing the intervals.[24] This method, which is still the basis of tuning in Western music today, is commonly credited to the European Andreas Werkmeister. But Needham, after considering all sorts of evidence, infers that "an independent invention of equal temperament in Europe" is most unlikely. Needham thinks the invention went from China to Europe by way of the Flemish mathematician Simon Stevin. He concludes:

> In any case it is fair to say that the European and modern music of the last three centuries may well have been powerfully influenced by a masterpiece of Chinese mathematics, though proof of transmission be not yet available. The name of the inventor is of less importance than the fact of the invention, and Chu Tsai-yü himself would certainly have been the first to give another investigator his due, and the last to quarrel over claims of precedence. To China must certainly be accorded the honour of first mathematically formulating equal temperament.[25]

However, after such high spots of development, Chinese music went the same way as did Chinese science. The equal temperament invention of Chu Tsai-yü, so crucial to the development of Western music, "was put into practice but little in his own country" because his accomplishment was out of tune with his society and culture. By the end of the Manchu dynasty, Chinese music was little more than what the West called programmatic. It was primarily tied to the stage, the musical scores of operas and operettas being synchronized with the movements of the performers. Among the storytellers, music was only incidental to narration. There was no concern with absolute pitch or the role of their mathematical properties; all tuning was relative.

Furthermore, in spite of the historical high spots, the Chinese never developed harmony, and I doubt if Chinese music ever reached any depth or gave the artists room for artistry and virtuosity comparable to its Western counterpart. It is well known that much ancient Chinese culture survived in Japan. The Japanese *goto* is probably the ancient lute lost to modern Chinese. It is not without charm and some scope for virtuosity. But I cannot say as much about other lost ancient Chinese instruments.

In the 1968 International Congress of Anthropological and Ethnological Sciences at Tokyo, the Japanese government included a performance of ancient "Japanese" music in its National Theatre in the opening ceremony. The explanatory notes in the program indicated that ancient "Japanese" music came from many sources, including Indo-China, China, and Korea. The instruments were *sho* (a small pipe organ with seventeen bamboo pipes), *hichiriki* (a kind of primitive oboe), *ryuteki* (a long flute with seven finger holes), the *komabue* (or "Korean" flute, a short instrument with six finger holes), three different drums, and a small gong. Some fifteen uniformly costumed musicians moved slowly around in formation as they played. It was a series of seemingly endless notes in unison; and if the music had accents or nuances or great variety, they escaped me.

This restricted musical development is in marked contrast to the Chinese plastic and graphic art heritage, which both as product and model, has made its influence felt throughout the world. In an attempt to determine the source of this contrast, some critics have pointed out that Chinese painters occupied a relatively high social position, while musicians were classified with common laborers. However, this low status was also accorded to the Chinese plastic workers who produced exquisite masterpieces in porcelain, jade, and ivory. Too, the composer and the musician have not always enjoyed a position of respect in the West. Paganini and Chopin were treated like entertainers and ate with servants of the big houses, and Mozart and Beethoven were accorded little more deference than court jesters.

A truer reason for this contrast is to be found in the nature of the beast. The plastic and graphic arts are visual and concrete while music is auditory and illusory. Visual experiences tend to be more permanent than auditory stimuli. That is why the Chinese say "the hundred times heard is not as good as the once seen." Western composers emphasize the need for repetition of a work's thematic melody. The Chinese, with their situation-centered orientation and their lack of concern for the introspective and the emotional, could not propel an already fleeting auditory impression to greater depths. They have always moved within the limitations of the familiar and what can be perceived by the senses. They have never overly interested themselves in high abstraction.

Consequently, Chinese music is nearly always tied to the interpersonal scene—the stage, the storyteller, or the female entertainer—because the interpersonal element is the preoccupation of the Chinese mind, and this element is likewise limited and circumscribed by convention. Even the ancient Chinese musical achievements, fantastically rich and complex in view of their antiquity, were always tied similarly to the ritual and social activities of the society, as for example the sacrifices to the solstices and to ancestors. There is no Chinese desire to penetrate the mind's inner layers or the world's outer boundaries. In such an atmosphere, the musical imagination is as fully stifled as is the scientific, while the graphic and plastic ideal is essentially conventional and static. But because of the concreteness of their inspiration—the familiar world of trees and mountains—and their expressed form—the visible object—the Chinese graphic and plastic arts have advanced further than the musical art.

With his individual-centered orientation, the Western composer, like the Western graphic or plastic artist, turns to his inner being for that interpretation which is felt to be singularly his and for that particular vision which he then fixes upon the natural and familiar object. This is the reason for the modern intentional distortion of form and the deliberate rejection of the commonly agreed upon criteria. This conscious and perpetual striving to see beyond the immediate, to penetrate the unknown, to discover the essence or create the unique is common to both Western science and Western art. No artist, as was remarked much earlier, can ever completely liberate himself from his cultural heritage or the pressures of his own epoch, but it is precisely the *effort thus to liberate himself* that characterizes the Western composer, as well as other artists and scientists, and accounts for the richness and multiformity of Western artistic creation and scientific thought.

There is, however, another reason why Chinese graphic and plastic arts have enjoyed such a worldwide esteem while Chinese music is hardly appreciated by the non-Chinese. This reason is linked with the difference between visual and auditory stimuli but quite unrelated to the level of complexity or sophistication. The matter-of-fact reproduction of ordinary sensory experiences is easier to appreciate across cultural lines when the artist's material is visual rather than auditory. For example, the famous *Ch'ing Ming Shang Ho,* on a scroll more than twenty feet long, portrays several hundred different human activities.[26] This polychrome panorama records a festival in the capital of the northern Sung dynasty; the artist simply put down everything as he saw it. There was no attempt to combine the multitudinous elements into any kind of a whole possessing unity and theme. I am afraid the auditory elements of this event, if abstracted on the same matter-of-fact basis, would not have commanded the same Western attention, for they would then have been a cacophonic clamor of human voices and animal calls mixed with the clang and throb of cymbals and drums.

The Lack of Voluntary, Nonkinship Organizations

In connection with the Chinese approach to economic activities (Chapter 11), we have already seen the relative lack of desire to emigrate to foreign lands. Given their centripetal adherence to the security of their primary kinship organizations, the Chinese did not care to follow on the heels of the expansionist military and politcal powers of their rulers abroad. Nor did the Chinese provide any sufficient mass basis as a forerunner for such expansionist powers. There were a few famous Chinese explorers to the far west, such as Pan Ch'ao and Chang Ch'ien in the Han dynasty (206 B.C. to A.D. 220). But they were few and far between, and their adventures did not prompt others to follow their trails, nor were they even elevated to the status of gods—in the common Chinese way (see Chapter 9) as were some of the heroes from the Three Kingdoms and other periods. The Chinese have ancestral gods for cooks, for actors, for masons, but they simply do not have one for travelers. The pilgrimage to India by the famous monks Hsuan Tsang and Fa Hsien in the T'ang dynasty (A.D. 618–907), and probably by several thousand others who left behind no records, was not for Chinese expansion. Their mission was to bring back to China the original and most authenticated teachings of the Buddha.

These examples are symptomatic of a basic peculiarity of the Chinese and the Chinese civilization: the lack of voluntary, nonkinship organizations. Given our analysis in the foregoing chapters, this peculiarity should cause no surprise. In this the Chinese society and the American society (as well as any other Western society) present another basic contrast.

In both cases there are the nuclear organization of parents and children and the territorial organization such as villages and towns. In both societies an overall national organization is headed by a central government. But while in China a near void exists between the two levels of organization, in America, an enormous number and variety of volunteer, nonkinship organizations mediate between them. A voluntary, nonkinship organization is used here to denote one that draws people together on some common interest for its promotion or prevention across territorial, communal, or kinship connections. The Ku Klux Klan, the White Citizens Council, the NAACP, the Salvation Army, the American Civil Liberties Union, the Potato Chip Makers Association, the American Federation of Labor, Common Cause, and missionary societies are all examples of American voluntary, nonkinship organizations, as also are the Society for the Prevention of Cruelty to Animals, the Association of Odd Fellows, the UFO watchers, spirit writers, and stamp collector groups. Over the centuries, the Chinese society developed none of these.

The following diagrams illustrate the two contrasting situations:

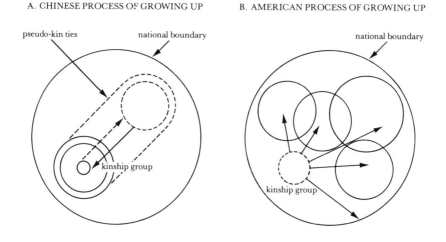

A. CHINESE PROCESS OF GROWING UP

B. AMERICAN PROCESS OF GROWING UP

The Chinese individual will leave his family and kinship group for specific purposes, but he always returns to them or else he develops pseudo-kin ties in the new nonkinship groups that he enters. Consequently, the kinship group tends to be large, and nonkinship groups tend to be small and unimportant. The primary importance of the kinship ties prevents the individual from wholehearted or even effective participation as a member of nonkinship groups or a citizen of the national state. The American individual is reared to leave the family and kinship base; he must find nonkinship groups in which he will find satisfaction of his social needs. Consequently the nonkinship groups proliferate, and the kinship group remains amorphous and permanently small. Being freed from the supremacy of the kinship principle, the individual has the potentiality of wholehearted devotion to nonkinship groups and nonkinship causes including those of the national state.

The few traditional Chinese voluntary, nonkinship groups included "societies for saving papers bearing written characters," "societies for giving away free coffins," and "association of teetotalers." The first group hired men to roam the streets with bags on their backs and pointed sticks in their hands. They collected any piece of waste bearing written characters in the gutter or on the ground and burned what they collected at the end of the day in the specially provided urn in the local Confucian temple. The written word is sacred to the Chinese and it must not be defiled. The second group provided coffins for the poor and unfortunate who died without children and relatives to care for their remains. The teetotalers gathered together to socialize among themselves and to discuss the benefits of abstention from alcohol.

However, even these Chinese organizations were typically localized affairs, confined to each village, or part of a district, but never federated nationally or even provincially. Furthermore, and this is more important, none of these Chinese organizations showed the slightest tendency toward expansion or centralization. Consequently, the free coffin givers, for example, did not campaign to "educate" the public, make membership drives, or hold annual conventions to discuss ways and means for giving away bigger and better coffins. In fact, even the localized organizations were not too well organized. They were likely to be the pet projects of a few learned or well-to-do local citizens.

The other nonkinship groups were occupational guilds, community clubs, and secret societies. These were semivoluntary guilds such as butchers' guilds, silk merchants' guilds, and others composed of owners and employees. These small groups were so localized that a district town might have two butchers' guilds located in two different sections of it.

The community clubs, called in Chinese *hui kuan*, might have a larger membership. Up to 1949 there were still old club houses for many of the provinces in Peking. Thus there would be a Chekiang *Hui Kuan*, a Kwangtung *Hui Kuan*, and so forth, where sojourners in Peking from Chekiang and Kwangtung provinces could respectively find temporary lodging, contacts, and other forms of assistance. But there were also Ningpo *Hui Kuan*, Wu Hsi *Hui Kuan*, and so forth in Shanghai, which served the same purpose for inhabitants from particular cities. In American terms there might be a club of Chicago traders in New York City called "Chicago *Hui Kuan*," or one of North Dakota and South Dakota office seekers in Washington, D.C., called "Two Dakotas *Hui Kuan*." Throughout China there were hundreds of such organizations, but none of them was ever consolidated on a national scale. Their growth or decline was generally dependent upon the increase or decrease of the needs of the local travelers.

The secret societies were the only voluntary, nonkinship organizations on a seminational scale (for example, the *Ch'ing Pang* [Blue Gang] operated all along the Yangtze River), with some expansionist tendencies. From time to time the secret societies involved them-

selves in political movements—for example, in support of the Manchus against Westerners through the Boxer Rebellion of 1900, and
on behalf of Dr. Sun Yat-sen's revolutionaries against the Manchus.
But their organizational principle was familistic, the bulk of their activities was extortive and predatory, and they were not part of the
regular social system.

These facts once more underline the basic conclusions of our analysis, that the situation-centered Chinese were too tied to their kinship and local groups to involve themselves in wider alliances and
nontraditional objectives, and that those who did so were a minority
—they were either outlaws or had other good reasons to stay away
from legitimate society.

This conclusion finds additional support in a bit of biographical
material from the life of Prince Chu Tsai-yü who, as we saw in the
previous section, was credited by Joseph Needham with "first math-
ematically formulating Equal Temperament" in music. Why did a
Chinese prince choose to devote himself to such a subject?

> In + 1536 was born one of China's most distinguished mathematical
> and musicological scholars. He was the son of Chu Hou-Huan and a de-
> scendant of the fourth Ming emperor Chao. When his father was unjus-
> tly reduced in rank by the emperor, he signified his filial grief by living in
> an earth-walled cottage for nineteen years. This time was spent in re-
> search into mathematical, musical and calendrical matters, the results of
> which were published at intervals and finally as a collected work.[27]

Prince Chu Tsai-yü was outside of the regular society in a different
sense from members of the secret societies, but he and they certainly
had something in common. It is useless to speculate on how many
other discoveries and inventions the Chinese might otherwise have
contributed to the world. It is also typical that Prince Chu's formulation "was put into practice but little in his own country." The prince
suffered from the same lack of popular support for his lead which be-
fell distinguished Chinese explorers, conquerors, inventors, astrono-
mers, and other original thinkers.[28]

This lack of voluntary, nonkinship organizations is rooted in the
Chinese lack of zeal for causes. It is also central to what the Chinese
Communist government hopes to change by many drastic measures
widely reported and misunderstood in the West; that question will be
taken up in the next chapter. In the meantime it is necessary to point
out that this lack was what Dr. Sun Yat-sen meant when he com-

plained that the Chinese were like a "tray of loose sand." The reader of this book will realize that the Chinese are not like a "tray of loose sand" everywhere. As far as kinship and localized organizations are concerned, they adhere together like the strongest of clays. The "loose sand" character appears where the issues involved go beyond the limits of loyalty to the primary group.

This weakness still persists as indicated by the results of a survey in a subdistrict of Taipei, Taiwan, by students of sociology in 1964. The subdistrict, Ku T'ing, had a total population of 139,107, nearly equally divided between old Taiwanese and recent immigrants.[29] They were 90 percent literate (15 percent with college education, 32 percent with high school education, and 45 percent with elementary school education); and judged by the investigators as being predominantly "middle class" ("upper class" 22 percent, "middle class" 50 percent, and "lower class" 28 percent).[30] The investigators found a variety of civic organizations, the purposes of which included farm, labor, employment information, women, old age, scholarship, and common local origin. Their sample survey showed (a) at least half of the inhabitants were not aware of the existence of these organizations; (b) the other half knew of their existence but did not participate in or use them; and (c) only a fraction of 1 percent of the people had anything to do with most of them. The only exceptions occurred with reference to Christian churches, traditional temples, common local-origin associations, and the library, each of them enjoying active participation or use by about 10 percent of the people.[31]

Price of Contentment

Chinese society has paid dearly for this lack of enthusiasm for cause-oriented organizations; for failure to develop movements to question the orthodoxy; and for not supporting those unusual or talented individuals who conceived new thoughts, discovered new theories, or conquered new worlds. Too much personal security has retarded the development of the society and prevented it from coming up with an adequate and early response to challenges from the West. What is not always so apparent but equally true is that the Chinese form of security often proves to be a mirage in some individual cases and in fact is the direct cause of great personal suffering. An illustrative example of this occurred in my wife's home town.

A widow, having raised her only son to maturity, was looking forward to her offspring's marriage, his assumption of adult responsibilities, and her retirement into the security of the new household. But just about this time a cholera epidemic struck the region; her son was one of its first victims. The night following his sudden death and each night for many months thereafter, the mother claimed she heard the sound of chains clanking outside her window. Her grief-stricken interpretation, in which the neighbors concurred, was that a spirit, bearing a grudge, had snared her son.[32] By enchaining him, the spirit had obtained its own freedom from the world of the departed. The clatter of the chains was caused by the son's struggle to free himself and return to her.

There are two interrelated tragedies in this story: the mother's sudden and absolute loss of security and the intensification of her psychological distress because of her inability to deal with this disaster in worldly terms. With no one else to turn to, without material security other than her few possessions, her misery was more intense and immediate than would be that of most American elders who would not have counted on such support in the first place. In displacing upon the spirit world the cause of their human misery, the Chinese have found additional reasons for not seeking to correct or ameliorate those evil or unfortunate conditions created by nature or man.

The pattern of human relationships being what it is, salvation is sought for in men, and the concrete, immediate situation is all that concerns the average person. Although this outlook often produces harmony, it is necessarily accompanied by contentment and opportunism. The Chinese are content because their personal security under normal conditions is assured and wholly satisfying. They are opportunistic because, being so irretrievably tied to their primary relations, they are prone to think of right or wrong, truth or untruth, justice or injustice, in relative terms. The only absolutes are those that revolve around concrete duties toward specific individuals. Those who are content with things as they are have no urge to establish mechanisms that may assist them in time of crisis. Those who possess a highly liquid concept of right and wrong which is always defined in personal terms see little reason to combat social injustice. Morality inside the family group is structured by clearly understood reciprocal obligations that are not subject to change.

It is obvious that conflict is inevitable when people hold that everything in this world is either black or white. But it is equally obvious that if you view the world as uniformly gray, the result is that you are too ready to compromise and too mindful of social restraints. For conflict brings in its wake not only human tragedy but human progress as well. But compromise and devotion to social propriety, while they do evade the evils of persecution and wars of annihilation, result also in little personal vision and social and intellectual advancement. In its widest and most general aspect this amounts to shackling all spontaneous impulses, noble or ignoble. This quiescent quality is what gives the Westerner his impression that the Chinese are "inscrutable," while the Chinese regard Western spontaneity as "unpredictability."

The Chinese have an excessive faith in men which is apt to be betrayed by men. And nature is ever ready to undo what men have made. Neither of these pitfalls can be avoided if the acts of man and nature are interpreted as the will of the spirits. Man-made calamities can be averted or fought only if men are conditioned to an abstract standard of values more absolute than the Chinese have known; nature's power can be understood and channeled for man's benefit only if men are taught to look beyond the immediate and the concrete. As long as the Chinese rely wholly on mutual dependence, their society will be one in which poverty prevails because they fail to look to nature's bounties for economic reward; social atrocities will persist because the Chinese have no abstract reasons to fight them; the individual will lack the initiative to attempt what has not been tried before; and the culture as a whole—its arts, science, economy, and government—will remain relatively stagnant.

NOTES

1. Howard S. Levy, *Chinese Footbinding,* p. 39. This is a well-documented account of the custom through Chinese literature and some field inquiry.

2. Lin Yutang, *My Country and My People,* p. 165.

3. Student demonstrations did not appear in China until after the 1911 Revolution, although some of Dr. Sun's supporters who made the revolution possible were students.

4. The kind that economist Milton Friedman still goes around preaching today. His theories have apparently been put to practice in Britain by Prime Minister Margaret Thatcher. A big political storm is raging because the economic woes of Britain have since become worse (see *San Francisco Chronicle,* March 7, 1980).

5. Until less than a century ago China had no lawyers who could argue a client's case before a judge, only solicitors, as in Britain, who prepare cases for clients but do not appear in court.

6. Albert Feuerwerker, "Comments" on "Nineteenth-Century China: The Disintegration of the Old Order and the Impact of the West" by Kwang-ching Lin in Ping-ti Ho and Tang Tsou, eds., *China in Crisis,* p. 188.

7. Joseph Needham (with the collaboration of Wang Ling), *Science and Civilization in China.*

8. For example, $(2^5 - 2) = 32 - 2 = 30$; the resulting figure is divisible by 5.

9. The reader who cannot wade through the many volumes of Needham's work can gain a briefer but nonetheless accurate idea of Chinese achievements in science in A. L. Kroeber, *Configurations of Culture Growth*, pp. 183–199.

10. Needham, *Science and Civilization in China*, vol. 4, pt. 1, p. 333.

11. Ibid., vol. 2, p. 303.

12. Northrop, *The Meeting of East and West*, p. 338.

13. See Francis L. K. Hsu, *Clan, Caste and Club*, p. 1. There are also large psycho-cultural differences between China and Japan. See Francis L. K. Hsu, *Iemoto: The Heart of Japan*, pp. vii–x.

14. See Northrop, *Meeting of East and West*, pl. XI, captioned by the author "the Aesthetic Component—The Differentiated Aesthetic Continuum."

15. Ibid., p. 297.

16. Needham, *Science and Civilization in China*, vol. 2, p. 579.

17. But when the Neo-Confucianist philosophers spoke of *li* (理 or principle), its meaning is the *Tao* of Taoists, "neither of which had juristic content" (ibid., p. 579).

18. Ibid., pp. 576–579 and 582.

19. Ibid., p. 582.

20. Hindu music is also far more advanced than Chinese music, but in a direction different from its Western counterpart. But this question cannot be dealt with here.

21. The others are *li* (禮 or propriety), *she* (射 or archery), *yu* (御 or riding), *shu* (書 or calligraphy or writing), and *shu* (數 or mathematics).

22. Ibid., vol. 4, pt. 1, pp. 126–228, Section H "Sound (Accoustics)."

23. Ibid., pp. 168–169.

24. According to which "every fifth without exception is one eleventh of a comma, or V(vibrations)1 in 885 too flat, and every major third, without exception, is seven elevenths of a comma, or V 1 in 126 too sharp." Ibid., p. 216.

25. Ibid., p. 228.

26. This piece is highly valued by the Metropolitan Museum of Art of New York City, which not only purchased it for a very high price, but also reproduced it in sectional form to instruct the public. There are many versions of this painting, none of which can be authenticated as the original, including the one at the Metropolitan Museum. They vary in small details, and are located in Japan, Taiwan, and The People's Republic of China. These numerous copies are another indication of the Chinese lack of incentive to depart from the known and accepted. The Western art student may legitimately copy originals as part of his training or illegitimately fake them as a matter of art thievery, but he intends to go beyond this to create what is peculiarly his own. The Chinese artist intends to continue following the ancient mold, and it is the highest form of praise to tell him that his work is exactly like the famous original. The bondage to the past is obvious.

27. Ibid., p. 220.

28. For another Chinese scholar whose scientific and technological labors fell to oblivion, see E-Tu Zen Sun, "Wu Ch'i-chun: Profile of a Chinese Scholar-Technologist," in *Technology and Culture* 6, no. 3, (1965): 394–406.

29. "Old Taiwanese" are like "old Americans"; their Chinese ancestors moved to the island centuries ago. "Recent immigrants" are Chinese who moved to Taiwan since World War II.

30. Lung Kuan-hai (director and editor of project), *Tai Pei Shih Ku T'ing Ch'ü She Hui Tiao Ch'a Pao Kao* [A social survey of the Kuting District of Taipei City], pp. 45 and 80.

31. Chu Ch'en-lou, "Civic Organizations," in ibid., pp. 115–128.

32. A natural death from age gives the Chinese no cause for such suspicion, but sudden death is thought to be caused by the intervention of a spirit.

CHAPTER 15

China under Communism

The international struggle since World War II has had many interpretations. One school of thought holds that the struggle is basically geographical-racial, that it is a contest between East and West. This view won new adherents after China came under Communist rule in 1949; even before that time, many maintained that Russia is essentially Asiatic. I have heard well-educated Europeans and Americans state that Stalin's physical appearance was definitely Oriental, the implication being that this supplied an important clue to contemporary affairs. Though the last assertion may seem fantastic to some Americans, it is quite in tune with others—especially those given to racism. White Christian Americans attempted for years to block Jewish immigration to the United States on the grounds that they were nonwhite; the United States immigration laws remained racist until the 1960s; well-known columnists have written implicitly or explicitly that Russia should come together with the United States rather than with China since Russia is white; the still prevalent white view of Blacks has been discussed in one of the foregoing chapters. To racists, for whom physical race explains nearly everything from intelligence to moral behavior, the extension that it governs international relations is but a foregone conclusion.

A second approach is social-philosophical. Those people who hold this conviction, because of their own predilections, usually attach varying degrees of importance to what is termed the economic struggle between free enterprise and national planning and ownership, the religious struggle between Christianity and atheism, and the political struggle between freedom and tyranny. The basic difficulty of this view is that many of the societies that have been shining examples of economic free enterprise have become more and more involved in national planning every day; that the religious violence of Christians against themselves (as during the Inquisition and in Northern Ireland today), and between Jews and Moslems (who worship the same God), was and is more intense and long-lasting than that between them and those whom they contemptuously call heathens or infidels; and that the United States is still trying to be the best friend of all kinds of dictators, even after they appropriate American investments, seize fishing boats, and take diplomats hostage.

Another school finds refuge in the doctrines of power politics—that the Soviet Union, the United States, and China are engaged in a fight for world hegemony. Therefore in the name of stopping Soviet expansion in Europe or preventing Chinese conquest in South Asia, the United States has encircled those two peoples with global political alliances, missle bases, and military personnel supporting a collection of dependent regimes regardless of their popularity with their own peoples or of their leaders' morality or ability.

The events and international developments of the world since 1945 have been, of course, complex. But two psychological factors basic to them must be kept in mind if we are not to be blinded by their complexity. The first is the spread of nationalism. Whether it is an expression against colonial domination or against being inferior, every identifiable people, however small in size, wants independence and equality. Symptomatic of this general aspiration is not only the continued proliferation of the minuscule nations of Asia, Africa and the Pacific Ocean, but also the United States and Russia have to exchange ambassadorial representatives with these small countries; diplomatic ministers are no longer satisfactory even to such small nations as Tuvalu and Barbados.

The other factor is the desire to industrialize in Western terms as a means of buttressing the claim to independence and equality in face of Western superiority. Consequently, many of the so-called underdeveloped nations have preferred guns to food, and steel plants to textile mills, usually at the expense of the material comforts and welfare of their people. China's determined march toward possessing nuclear weapons in spite of her people's material needs is but one of many examples. Once we understand the basic psychological factors, the Chinese pattern of priorities becomes no more bizarre or irrational than that of the United States where the federal government devotes nearly one third of its annual budget to its armed forces but only a fraction of that to education, and in 1974 as in 1966 continued to allow over 10 percent of its citizens to languish below the poverty line.[1]

However, nationalism and industrialization, though basic factors that initiate change in the twentieth-century world, are broad generalizations. They do not help us much unless we succeed in showing how they are relevant to the life of the average man. For most people, whether literate or illiterate, neither think nor act in abstract terms. They view the world, and their places in it, in terms of a concrete past and an even more concrete present. They want to know how what is happening in the world affects their daily lives. It is from this angle that we shall attempt to assess the reasons for the rise of communism in China and the American reaction to it.

The Chinese Ferment

In the welter of charge and countercharge, in the heat of partisan contention about the fall of China to communism, Americans, with their individual-centered preoccupations, have tended to fail, indeed have often refused, to see the need to pay attention to the conditions of the Chinese themselves *before* communism. They have therefore been startled and bewildered by the drastic political change in China since 1949. Many of them have wondered, "How can the Chinese, with their deep ties to family, kin, and locality, accept communism or become Communists?"

My answer is severalfold. First, communism as an ideology and as a form of government could not have developed out of the Chinese situation-centered way of life. Communism is an ideology of Western origin and it clearly came to China from the West. Second, the Chinese did not welcome any form of Western ideology willingly. We have seen how successfully they resisted Christianity over a long period of time. But third, by the end of the 1940s, the Chinese had hardly any alternative to communism. And finally, the Chinese have accepted communism as a form of government much more than they have communism as a way of life. Individual-centered Americans have to seek causes and creeds to satisfy their emotional need for commitment, in contrast to the situation-centered Chinese whose lives are embedded in their kinship framework, and whose goals are colored by it.

Why did the Chinese have little alternative to communism at the end of World War II? First were the traditional ills, one of which was poverty.[2] Because of the values placed on mutual dependence, the Chinese regard relationships with fellow human beings but not control of things as the principal avenue for the solution of life's problems. Consequently, China has suffered from a stagnant economy and retarded technological development.

The second traditional ill was oppression. This oppression, as we have seen, was not an innovation of the Kuomintang hierarchy but a direct corollary of the traditional Chinese way of life in which appropriate place among fellow human beings is the chief aspiration of the individual. Since the human network is seen as the principal avenue for dealing with one's problems, authority and exploitation tend to escalate themselves to a level from which the individual can hardly extricate himself.

These traditional ills were interrelated and aggravated each other. But they were also ameliorated by traditional remedies. Fatalism is a belief that conditions of life and significant events of society are predestined. In Eastern thought, it is also tied in with reincarnation and retribution. Thus today's poverty may be seen as punishment for misbehavior in one's last life, just as its sufferance now may lead to a more rewarding life in another future reincarnation. But when life became truly unbearable for a majority, the Chinese from time to time revolted. As we have also related in detail, when the burden of oppression became too great, when the governmental elite became too corrupt, when the entire structure deteriorated to the point where benevolence disappeared and only despotism remained, the Chinese revolted and permitted a new governing group to take charge. In the days when the tools of warfare were swords, spears, and bows and arrows, the ruler's forces, no matter how well trained, could not succeed in quelling a really determined popular revolt. One dynasty reportedly was overthrown by a population wielding wooden poles, the monarch having confiscated all metal implements.

This once self-perpetuating dynastic cycle was broken by the impact of the West upon China, which is the third and most devastating fact to be borne in mind when searching for the causes of communism's success in China. China was no longer able to continue as she had for ages. She could no longer solve her problems in the old ways, for the ancient ills of the country were now worsened, and new burdens were added which were a direct consequence of Western infiltration.

The wholesale invasion of China—military, political, economic, and cultural—began in 1840, and was led by Britain, France, and

America. These three countries were joined by other Western powers and eventually by Japan. This invasion drastically altered China's internal situation.

For one thing, once her doors were battered ajar, China almost immediately became the victim of an unfavorable balance of trade. Industrially backward, she never succeeded in exporting enough to offset her imports from economically advanced nations. This meant that much of the wealth of tribute and graft extracted by the officials from the people flowed out of China by way of treaty ports and foreign concessions. Many Americans in the 1960s and the 1970s are greatly concerned with an occasional trade imbalance in the neighborhood of a few percent but the Chinese suffered for nearly a century from excessively unfavorable balances of payment, often as large as 70 percent.

Besides severe economic difficulties, the weight of oppression itself was increased. Chinese princes and officials were joined and even outranked by representatives of the Western nations and Japan. Ordinary citizens from other nations were elevated above Chinese police and most officials, because the foreigners were protected by extraterritoriality and gunboats. And with the advent of modern weapons, a ruthless minority with access to the guns, cannon, and planes which could not be manufactured locally was able to suppress any revolt of the traditional Chinese variety. In addition, the interminable strife among the many warlords, each of them a little emperor in his private preserve and most of whom secured backing from one or another of the Western powers or Japan, brought ruin throughout the country. Whole provinces were razed, the routes of commerce were severed, and the people were bled by taxes and confiscation. To make matters even worse, the corrupt officials and the ruthless warlords now had privileged sanctuaries in the Foreign Concessions in China.

Before 1842 any erring Chinese could only escape the consequences of his deeds by working within the Chinese system or by the much more difficult path of escape to border regions or by sea. Now an official who went too far or a warlord who overestimated his strength simply retired to a comfortable villa in one of the Foreign Concessions in the heart of Tientsin, Shanghai, or elsewhere where he took his family, including his concubines, and his wealth. Not only were his money and his relatives out of reach of any Chinese law, but he and his cohorts could scheme and conspire in safety for a comeback. Many Chinese officials and warlords used to maintain regular residences in these Foreign Concessions where their women and children could reside in safety. Wandering around the streets of the British Concession of Tientsin and the French Concession and International Settlement of Shanghai in the 1930s, my friends and I used to make a game of identifying which houses belonged to whom.[3]

It was in this situation that the deposed Manchu boy emperor Aisin-Gioro Pu Yi (better known in the West as Henry Pu Yi) was able not only to keep much of the imperial wealth, but also to finance various warlords and foreign swindlers with the hope of restoring his dynasty's control over the country. His favorite sanctuaries were Peking's Legation Quarter and Tientsin's Japanese Concession; and his crowning glory came later when he was made the puppet emperor of "Manchukuo" under Japanese guns.[4] Not satisfied with partial colonization of China, Japan then decided to conquer the whole of China. This ignited the Sino-Japanese War in 1937, which spelled the absolute finish of the ancient Chinese society. The old mechanisms of readjustment were no longer sufficient to grapple with the problems of the era, problems that owed either their deepening or their origin to Western penetration.

Societies and individuals are alike in that if they are to survive they both have to deal with unplanned-for problems of external origin. A driver, however careful, may be hit by another car from the rear, or the company in which one has invested his life as a competent employee suddenly goes bankrupt. These and many other eventualities are beyond his control. The individual can only exercise a degree of control over his destiny in how he deals with the unexpected contingency after it has arisen; this is where he shows his character.

A whole society may be overrun by the military might of another country and be devastated or vassalized. The less alike the conquered and their conquerors, the more sudden and accute the problem. The Indians of the two Americas vis-à-vis the Spanish and the English, the Middle Eastern peoples vis-à-vis the forces of Alexander, the Chinese vis-à-vis the Mongols and the Manchus—in each instance, the conquered had no control over the events. But the victimized society does exercise a degree of control in how it deals with the unexpected predicament. And the very response reflects its way of life.

Having thus been forced to deal with the Western challenge, the Chinese began to examine their way of life in the light of its obvious incapacity to prevent other nations from exploiting China. But it took them a long time. A people so tied to the glories of a course set by the past found change too painful. Having been keyed to the security of family, kin, and local community, the Chinese were unable to organize and give themselves to cause-oriented groups that were removed from kinship and local bases. Borrowing pages from their history, some Chinese thought China could in time outlive and absorb the conquerors. Confident that the Chinese heritage was not unequal to the new challenge, others suggested the combination of "Western learning as function and Chinese learning as structure."

These courses of action (or inaction) obviously could not meet the exigencies of the times. For through the open door flowed goods, gunboats, and missionaries, and with them came that most potent of stimulants, new ideas. These were first of all objectified in the very fact of Western material superiority. A British gunboat on the Yangtze was often a far more potent ambassador or germinator of ideas than a visiting lecturer from Oxford. And when Western teachers, missionaries, and books propagated, often unintentionally, ideas that were hostile to the very poverty and oppression that had been deepened and broadened by Western contact, the first faint stirrings of discontent began to find a focus. In addition, Chinese students returning from studying at Western universities brought back with them not only ideas and eyewitness accounts of Western life, but also something of the Westerner's resolution to discard that which is no longer sufficient to the needs of the time and to adopt that which promises to be so. Fatalism was questioned, and many of the young intellectuals insisted that officials did not all have to be corrupt.

The rallying point where most could meet was under the standard marked "change." But agreement upon the direction that this change should take was another matter. It would have been difficult enough simply in terms of the Chinese situation, but the confusion was accentuated by the fact that the West was itself at this time entering upon a period of extensive reexamination, a period of both intellectual ferment and social upheaval. Consequently, the ideas that came to China from the West were diverse and contradictory. Adam Smith and Karl Marx arrived as contemporaries, as did John Calvin and Charles Darwin, John Locke and Immanuel Kant, Plato and Peter Alexeivich Kropotkin. Every variety of Western ideology from anarchism to the corporate state flooded the collective Chinese mind in one great stream. Ideas from the whitest white to the reddest red were discussed among the intelligentsia and thence spread in one guise or another to other sections of the population.

The several major and numerous minor political uprisings and movements of a whole century tell us something of the grab-bag character of this mélange of Western ideologies that besieged China. In 1851 the T'aip'ing rebels conquered nearly one third of China and with great speed established themselves in Nanking; they were not defeated until 1864. The Western powers gave serious consideration at one point to recognizing the T'aip'ing regime as the legitimate government. That uprising was initiated by a missionary protégé who sounded the call to arms with the assertion that he was the younger brother of Jesus Christ and charged by God to rid the country of its oppressors, the Manchus. The T'aip'ing government restored the traditional long hair for Chinese males (instead of the pigtails worn under the Manchus), and they emphasized the emancipation of women by making them eligible for the traditional imperial examinations.

The Boxer Rebellion came in 1900. This was led by groups of physical culturists, secret society members, and gangsters who claimed to be in possession of certain supernatural weapons that would clear China of all Westerners. The leaders supported the power of the Manchu dynasty, and even they advanced equality between the sexes since many of their numbers were women.

Then, in 1911, the Manchu dynasty was overthrown and China became a republic under the leadership of Dr. Sun Yat-sen. His Three Peoples' Principles contained some Chinese elements but were largely an adaptation of Western democratic and socialist thought. In spite of his declaration, upon acceptance of the office of president of the Republic of China in 1912, that the Chinese people were "continuing the historic struggle of the French and American peoples for republican institutions,"[5] Sun later cooperated with the Communists. His Republic of China was first usurped by royalists bent on restoration of the Manchu dynasty, and later by Yuan Shih-k'ai, who declared himself emperor. When Yuan died shortly afterward, the Republic was decimated by warlords whose activities we have mentioned before. Chiang Kai-check purged the Kuomintang of Communists and in 1927 led his Northern Expedition to bring political and military unity to China. He followed closely the teachings of Dr. Sun but the New Life Movement he initiated and propagated contained elements of Confucianism, Christianity, the YMCA, and Socialism.

Why did the Chinese, less than 1 percent of whom were Christians, follow the T'aip'ing rebels? Why did the Chinese, who despise physical culturists and find execution a suitable punishment for gangsters, support the Boxers? Why did the Chinese, to whom American-style democracy is as alien as class warfare, follow the standard raised by Sun Yat-sen? And why did they support Chiang Kai-shek, whose secret police killed thousands and imprisoned untold numbers?

There is a single answer to all these questions. To the Chinese multitude, reacting to intensified poverty and oppression under Western impact, all of these movements offered an immediately available avenue of expression and action which appeared plausible. Patrick J. Hurley, one-time United States Ambassador to Nationalist China at Chungking, is reported to have told a National Press Club audience that "the only real difference between Chinese Communists and Oklahoma Republicans is that the Oklahoma Republicans are not armed." His was a perfectly natural American reaction. From the American point of view, if the Democrats do not behave, then it is time for the Republicans to take over. The only trouble is that the Chinese did not have two well-established alternatives, but suffered from a plethora of confusing and unequal options. The objectives of these movements did not need to be consistent, their methods and their leaders did not need to be similar, and their consequences might be temporary or lasting. The essential point was that each promised to do something, anything, to lift the people's burdens.

The total picture of China in the first half of the twentieth century, or those aspects of it that the average Chinese experienced, remained both confusing and profoundly discouraging. As the Western powers and Japan grew mightier, the Chinese—with their new dreams of equality, freedom, economic development, streamlined government, and powerful armed forces—seemed to be sinking lower and lower. Indeed, the existence and spread of these new hopes served to etch in their minds all the more clearly the increasingly pitiful condition of their individual existence and the progressive decline of their nation.

This then was China's dilemma when her way of life was forced into a contest of strength with the West; however advantageous or satisfactory the traditional Chinese way may have been, it could be saved at all only at the cost of almost completely transforming it. Or, to state the Chinese dilemma in another fashion, the price of survival seemed to be the acceptance of ways and ideas that might ultimately undermine much of what the Chinese hoped to preserve. Once this is understood, the Communist triumph must be seen simply as the culmination of a long series of Chinese revolutionary movements along similar lines and reacting to the same problems which became ever more serious since 1840.

Those problems were incredibly augmented, but China's ability to deal with them infinitely reduced, by Japan's total war of conquest on China. Quite apart from Japanese atrocities, which matched if not surpassed Nazi atrocities against the Jews, the war devastated the country, decimated the economy, and created a body of refugees conservatively estimated at seventy million. The end of World War II eliminated Japan's domination of China, but the country was in shambles, with runaway inflation and heightened general aspirations among a long-suffering population for a strong and unified China capable of standing up to the world and befitting her Big Four membership status[6]—but without the means of satisfying them. The stage was set for communism.

Early Sources of Communist Strength

One popular misunderstanding is that communism became entrenched in China because its leaders offered land to the landless. There is no question that Chinese poverty was related to the land, for with antiquated methods of agriculture and a large population there was not enough land to go around. It is also undeniable that some landlords possessed enormous property holdings. However, in spite of Mao's own emphasis on the land tenancy problem,[7] Dr. Sun Yat-sen's slogan, "All tillers must own their soil" before him, and the chorus of scholars and journalists in support of this view, the Communist movement had not made appreciable showing on the equitable redistribution of land by the time it gained political ascendancy in China. For one thing, as we have seen in Chapter 12, the actual landlord-tenant relationship was not so universally strife-ridden as popularly imagined. Mao's notion of the extent of tenancy ("Over eighty percent of our population are peasants living on small plots of land, most of which belong to big, unscrupulous landlords"[8]) also did not correspond to reality. According to the research of J. L. Buck at Nanking University, only about 30 percent of all Chinese farmers were tenants. The percentage throughout the country was highly varied, being higher in the south and lower in the north.[9] In the province of Shensi, which served for many years as the Communist base of operations, the known tenancy rate was but 18 percent.

However, although the percentage of tenancy was not as high as

Mao thought, the hidden element in the situation was the miserable lot of the many who simply had to hire themselves out as farm laborers. They generally owned no land, and they were too poor or otherwise unable to find acceptance as tenants by landowners. The lucky ones among them found long-term employment, usually several years for the same employer. Others simply had to roam from farm to farm working for one to a few days at a time. Still others flooded the urban areas for the same purpose.

The exact percentage of such farm laborers in the total population before 1949 is not known. It could easily amount to a quarter of the adults in rural China and it certainly augmented the ranks of the land hungry.

Yet the Communist leaders were not quick in dealing with the land problem. As a matter of fact, it was shortly after their arrival in Shensi, following upon the famous Long March, that the Communists made "drastic changes in Soviet Land Policy" for "reasons of national political maneuver."[10] Furthermore, as late as 1950, at which time the Communists were in complete domination of China and Hainan Island, they were still busying themselves with *plans* for a *general* redistribution of land. When the first edition of this book was published, more than three years after their conquest, the Communists had simply gone through preliminary motions in response to the question which was said to be so harrowingly pressing, so crucial to the farmers, and over which so much ink had been spilled.

Within the context of post-World War II China, I am convinced that the Communists offered at least three immediate attractions which the Nationalists lacked: first, involvement of a majority of the poor and the voiceless in doing something about their condition of life; second, reduction of the cost of government; and, third, an uncompromising attitude toward the West.

The questioning of the traditional, fatalistic belief only produced intensified dissatisfaction. But it was the Communists and not the Nationalists who showed the common people how to translate this new state of mind into some concrete and meaningful action.[11] As soon as they came into power, the new government at once jailed or executed notorious landlords or officials. The common people identified the culprits and participated in the trials. The new government at once organized communal autonomy and activities to be part of a larger social structure and not as its antagonist. It was the common people who chose the new local functionaries and decided on the programs. The new government also abolished the crushing taxes, which would not have been possible without fundamental changes in the philosophy and behavior of officialdom. This was the second source of strength.

As pointed out before, corruption in government, though an ancient Chinese pattern, had become more of a problem since the nineteenth century both in its extent and in its effect on the nation's economy. And that corruption was made even worse by a runaway inflation which led officials to redouble their efforts to grab what they could whenever they could.[12]

In contrast to this, as the Communist functionaries emerged to assume positions of responsibility in the areas that came under their control, they did a most un-Chinese thing; they lived like the common people. Testimony to this most fundamental fact comes from every source, whether Chinese or foreign, and whether written by persons sympathetic to the Communists or not. The Communists permitted neither themselves nor their followers and soldiers the luxuries and the excesses that were the stigma and the symbol of previous governments and their armies. This practical equalization of consumption meant that both the legitimate costs of government and the incentive for corruption were reduced. The economic burden was thus drastically lightened for peasants and city people alike.

By decreasing taxes and eliminating graft at the precise time that these two evils were increasing throughout Nationalist China, the Communists gained an immeasurable base of popular support. In a land where the visit of the tax collector could mean the difference between whether one's family would or would not survive through the winter, these changes became the people's very important measures of the rulers' true benevolence or worth.

The Chinese Communists' third source of strength was their militant attitude toward the West. For one hundred years, the Chinese common man had bowed before two superiors, the Chinese government and the foreigners. Of the two, it was clear enough that the Chinese officials were second-class masters. One did not have to be profound or unusually aware to understand the nature of the situation. The foreigners were explicit. Until 1925 the entrance to the public parks in Shanghai's International Settlement and French Concession bore the sign: "Chinese and Dogs Not Allowed."[13]

Western nationals and Japanese regularly stormed Chinese police headquarters or the official residences of magistrates to demand and receive immediate attention to their complaints. The Chinese people were lucky to obtain a hearing after waiting for months and making use of every connection they had. Nor did the conduct of the higher reaches of the bureaucracy contravene this pattern. At the height of Nationalist power, almost any American, whether a government official or private citizen, could secure an interview with the Generalissimo or Madame Chiang. But, as reported earlier, no Chinese national could do so, for whatever purpose, without the closest of connections with the inner circle.

The Nationalist government, indeed any Chinese government of modern times, had good reasons to be so docile and amenable to Western pressures. As late as 1925, Great Britain dispatched warships nine hundred miles inland up the Yangtze River from Shanghai to Wanhsien, the approximate Mississippi River distance from New Orleans to Dubuque, and bombarded that open city in reprisal for the local population's anti-British demonstrations and their boycott of British goods. In 1928 a Japanese expeditionary force was sent to Shantung to interrupt Chiang's military campaign to unify the country. This Japanese venture was unsuccessful, but it was followed in 1931 by her seizure of Manchuria, in 1932 by the invasion of Shanghai, and in 1937 by the initiation of full-scale war to conquer all China.

Few if any Chinese failed to link the signs in the Shanghai parks with the government's deference to foreigners and such overt brutalities as the preceding. Literate and illiterate, rich and poor, however different may have been their other viewpoints or aspirations, shared a common opinion about foreign domination.[14] Consequently, during World War II, it was not unusual to see many Chinese, despite their intense hatred of the Japanese, applauding their invaders when the latter humiliated the once haughty Europeans by submitting them to all sorts of indignities. When Europeans were stripped in public, supposedly in a search for concealed weapons, or beaten and otherwise cruelly manhandled in prison camps, the average Chinese, though he may have honestly deplored such extremes, felt himself and his country in part avenged for a century of inferiority, maltreatment, and humiliation.

The end of World War II found the Nationalist government more fully tied to the West's apron strings, particularly America's, than at any previous time. The Nationalist government was so abjectly dependent upon Western military and economic aid that it was made to appear as the steward of foreign interests in China. In the following three years, Chinese newspapers of all political allegiances leveled a barrage of criticism against Westerners that was unequalled in any preceding period.

In contrast, the Communists were evidencing their militant opposition to Westerners not only in barrages of propaganda, but by backing them up with deeds. Their prestige climbed precipitously when in 1949 they did something that no Chinese government had ever been able to do—they blasted British warships out of the Yangtze River. Their stock rose even higher when, for the first time in a century, they cleared Shanghai harbor of all foreign men-of-war. From the American point of view, the Communists' undiplomatic treatment of Consul-General Angus Ward and his party was absolutely uncalled for. And from the British point of view, the humiliating cold shoulder that the Communists showed the first British Ambassador after his government had promptly recognized the new regime, might seem little better than insane.

But the Communists knew themselves to be on stage, and it was to the home audience—not foreign opinion—that they were playing, and playing successfully. All of these acts buttressed the Communists' position to an extraordinary extent. Their successful intervention on behalf of North Korea against the United States served the same end, although there is evidence that the Chinese did not ask for that venture.[15]

This anti-Western attitude was not at odds with Sino-Soviet cooperation until the fifties but it is easily commensurate with the rift between the two Communist powers since that time. Their cooperation was not due to the fact (as suggested by some Western observers at the time) that Russia is "Asiatic." This proposition, other than in the geopolitical sense perhaps, is completely without foundation. Racially and culturally Russia is Western, and the Stalinist system is not only founded in a patently Western set of dogmas, that is, Marxist thought, but, as I shall endeavor to show in the next chapter, is in its own right one of the essential denouements of other Western cultural tendencies and attributes.

The committal of China's new government to Marxist theory and its early history of close connection with the Soviet Union would probably not in themselves have been sufficient to rescue Russians from the anti-Western flood if they had not already escaped it on their own. During the latter half of the nineteenth century, Russia's position of privilege in China was no different from that enjoyed by other Western powers. She, too, was feared and denounced as one of the "foreign devils." The 1917 Bolshevik Revolution caused a twofold change in the relations between Russia and China.

First, by formal declaration, Soviet Russia abrogated all her privileges and possessions in China. Consequently, throughout the 1930s, when the Nationalist government was futilely attempting to abolish

China's unequal treaties with various Western powers and Japan, Soviet Russia was not a stumbling block and was itself able to make political capital of its unilateral withdrawal. The second factor in the Chinese change of opinion about Russians was the emigration to China of refugees from the Bolshevik state. Deprived of their property at home or of their privileged position in China, these pathetic persons dispersed into all occupational levels. The status of most was such that the popular Chinese caricature of a Russian was that of a bearded peddler notable for his nose, bearing a bundle of blankets on his shoulder. An image of this sort is far removed from that of a proud overlord, and it prompted sympathy, not fear or hatred, in spite of the Nationalist government's policy of relentless suppression of communism and elimination of proven or suspected Communists.

How very different the Chinese feeling about Soviet Russia was from that about the West may be illustrated by an experience I had as a student at the University of Shanghai in the early thirties. I served as a member of an intra-University debating team of three on the subject: "Resolved: that Red Imperialism is Even More Vicious than White Imperialism." Our team happened to have drawn the positive side of the debate. Each team spent nearly three months preparing for the event and our team performed valiantly, and, if I may be egotistical, exhibited more brilliance than the opposing team. But we lost. Afterward various faculty members and fellow students congratulated us for our brilliant performance and comforted us with the thought that, but for the fact that the weight of reality was so "obviously" against our position, we would have won. They assured us that we were simply on the greatly disadvantageous side of the debate.

Our acceptance of such consolation was understandable in terms of the urgent desire of losers to find some comfort in defeat. But that is beside the point. The fact is that the term "Imperialism," whether it is preceded by the adjective "English," "American," "Western," "Red," or "White," had been well known in China for over a century. No one had a serious misunderstanding of it. It was not a Communist creation; it was based upon large and persistent facts of Western and Japanese aggression well known to the average Chinese.

Even in the 1930s Soviet Russia represented to the Chinese no less than "Red Imperialism." She was the lesser of two evils, but an evil nonetheless. And when circumstances changed, when she appeared to cooperate with the United States in the sixties, the Chinese had no difficulty in being as anti-Soviet as they were anti-United States.

The foregoing analysis will enable us to appreciate why a majority of the Chinese, despite their emphasis upon the primary human relationships and their essentially nonaggressive attitude toward the world, should have acquiesced in an ideology that is completely alien to Chinese thought and embraced a political, economic, and social pattern of organization in which regimentation, persecution, and even outright murder are inherent aspects of the whole. There is a Chinese saying that when a man is dying of thirst he may choose to drink poisoned water. His immediate need overshadows all else.

Change under Communism

Accepting Communist leadership in government is not, however, the same as being converted to communism as an ideology.[16] In their situation-centered way of life the Chinese have always tended to treat any nontraditional ideology or involvement as a means and not as an end. Christianity was never popular in China. A few Chinese became genuine converts, and many affiliated themselves with Christian churches or church related institutions such as YMCAs, schools, or orphanages for the advantages they offered. As we saw in the chapters on religion (Chapters 9 and 10), the Chinese who did so were not even apologetic about their attitudes. The church and its related institutions are means and they did little or nothing to the individual's basic linkage with his kinship group and its values.

Similarly, the relationship of the Chinese with their rulers was always one of submission and distance but not one of control and identification. A holder of the Chinese Mandate of Heaven was secure in his rule so long as he was able to keep peace and order, but it was not part of the Chinese way of life to be committed to a particular ruler, a particular dynasty, and especially an exogenous ideology.

The Chinese had little urge to espouse causes and develop voluntary nonkinship groups because the individual is part of a permanent social network. That network satisfies all his social needs; it binds the individual by defining his place as a human being in terms of his duties, obligations, and privileges within and with reference to it. Herein lies a basic stumbling block to national solidarity under a democratic or Communistic ideology, which led Dr. Sun Yat-sen to lament, as we noted before, that Chinese are like a "tray of loose sand." Most of the major developments in China since 1949 must be understood as attempting to overcome this obstacle.

Take the "Great Leap," for example. There is no doubt that economically it was a failure. The backyard furnaces yielded iron and steel that could not be economically and efficiently used. In addition, farm production suffered terribly because manpower was diverted to nonagricultural activities. Although the "Great Leap" was not entirely to blame for the severe crop failures of 1959–1961, it certainly had something to do with them. The crop failures were followed by enormous purchases of wheat from Australia, Canada, and elsewhere.

Individual-centered Americans, with their emphasis on things, not unnaturally have paid sole attention to the economic aspect of the phenomenon. They do not realize that the "Great Leap" was an important mechanism toward a psycho-social revolution. For the first time in the long history of China, the common people were able to experience some intrinsic and positive relationship between what they did as individuals and the overall purposes of the state.

Another example is the commune. Few subjects concerning the People's Republic have been so sensationally and even deliberately misunderstood as the commune. As first reported, not only were children taken from parents, but also husbands were permanently separated from wives. There were juicy and titillating reports in American communications media of how husbands and wives contrived to meet in privacy for two hours on Saturday night. Sympathy was showered on the "poor Chinese" who were deprived of romantic love and a normal sex life by the harsh dictates of an "inhuman" government.

Anyone who has read this book, and especially Chapter 5 regarding romance and marriage patterns among the Chinese, will have already realized that the American pattern of romance and marriage is a far cry from even the "modernized" Chinese of the thirties and forties. For a vast majority of Chinese who were not fortunate enough to have gone to schools and universities, or who were illiterate, separation of husband from wife because of employment was common. Chinese tradesmen traditionally worked in their places of employment away from their families for "three years and a festival" (three and one-third years in duration) at a time. At the end of this working period, they would return to their homes for a period of two or three months before departing once again for a similar cycle. Chinese farm laborers, too, often left their home villages for several years at a time, or for as long as they found suitable employment in order to maintain their families back home. It is in this context that we must understand how thousands of Chinese could have congregated in little Chinatowns in the United States and Europe with no other crime than gambling to divert them—a fact that gave creators of Fu Manchu and other racist movies good resources for American entertainment. A vast majority of the Chinese in these Chinatowns were landless laborers from the province of Kwangtung (Canton). Their style of living was peculiar to American eyes, but they were living as a majority of Chinese tradesmen and laborers have lived in China for untold centuries. Consequently, separation of married partners, even to the extent fantasied by some American reporters of the communes, would hardly have evoked an American kind of horror among the Chinese.

The actual reality of the commune in China is as different from the sensational Western reports as it is complex. It came into being via several stages. The rural land reform of 1950–1952 redistributed land expropriated from the landlords. But that was a temporary step, even though it seemed at the time to be the fulfillment of a long cherished vision first pronounced by Dr. Sun Yat-sen. The land distribution was followed in 1953–1956 by the reorganization of all privately owned land into agricultural cooperatives. And finally, in 1958, the process of rural communization began and was soon completed.

Paralleling the communization in the villages was the "Five Antis" movement of 1952 and later the Joint Public–Private Management order of 1955–1956 which communized the urban areas, and in effect made owners of industries and business and their employees joint participants, as in rural communes. The urban organizations are called street revolutionary committees and each is under the overall management of a committee of the same name.

A Rural Commune

The communes in rural China have become much more solidly the basic building blocks of the larger Chinese society today. Take the Mei Lung Commune west of Shanghai, for example. It consisted, in 1972, of 6,034 households, had a population of 24,000, and possessed 1,415 hectares of cultivated land (about 4,000 acres). Like all other communes, it was subdivided, into thirteen production brigades and 156 production teams. It had five factories employing 800 workers which produce light farm implements, agricultural medicine, clothing, furniture, and glass fibers; a broadcasting station; an institute of agricultural technology; a major health station with a full time M.D.; a clinic with a barefoot doctor in every production brigade; and a resident health worker in every production team. There were also two middle schools; thirteen primary schools; an animal farm to raise fish, pigs, cows, Angola rabbits; and incubators for raising chickens. Beside the two small towns within the confines of the commune, seven of the brigades each had their own stores.

The most interesting feature of the commune is that the boundaries of the production brigades and teams were drawn along village and kinship lines. The Lung Nan Production Brigade No. 4 is a fair illustration. In 1972 there were 350 households in this brigade. Each of its seven production teams was a village predominantly inhabited by people of one surname. The village names bore witness to this: (1) *Kao* Chia T'ang, (2) *Hsu* Chia T'ang, (3) *Chang* Chia Tsai, (4) *Liu* Chia Ch'iang, (5) *Lu* Chia Pang, (6) *P'an* Chia Pang, and (7) *Chuang* Chia T'ang.

Liu Chia Ch'iang,[17] the No. 4 Production Team, had 212 members and fifty-two households of which three were Hsus, ten were Lus, and four were Shans, and the rest, Lius.

We had an afternoon's visit at the home of Comrade Liu Lin-hsing, who was the accountant of his production team. Lin-hsing and his wife were both twenty-eight years old and were both graduates of junior high school. They had two sons aged six months and three years. They lived in two fairly large rooms, one a bedroom and the other used as a kitchen and livingroom combined. In the bedroom were two large beds, Lin-hsing sharing one with the three-year-old son while his wife shared the other with the six-month-old baby.

It turned out to be something of a surprise to us to learn that Lin-hsing's home was slightly less than one-third of a larger residence. His home was separated from the main portion of the residence by a hall-corridor. In this part lived his parents (aged fifty and forty-six), his younger brother (twenty-five) and wife (twenty-six) and their child (two), and his three unmarried brothers (aged twenty-two, nineteen, and sixteen). The entire residence had been built as a family enterprise five years before, but two years later he and his married younger brother decided on *fen chia,* a traditional term for family division.

Why did they decide to *fen chia?* "Oh, our interests are different, we differed in food tastes. . . . When grandma took one grandchild to bed, the mother of the other grandchildren felt jealous . . . so grandmother suggested *fen chia* . . . to reduce conflict *(chian shao mao tun)*" (here Lin-hsing used the revolutionary term "contradiction" instead).

How would the situation have been different before the revolution? "Not too much," Lin-hsing responded. "After some sons are married, *fen chia* usually followed. More freedom that way, some want to eat better than others. . . . If family members were in harmony with each other, they remained together till the youngest sibling is married. . . . If not *fen chia* occurs sooner."

Comrade Huang, our guide who accompanied us on this visit, offered the opinion that *fen chia* did not occur in his part of the country (Hupei Province) as frequently as this. But my wife, who was born and raised in Hupei, and I, a native of Manchuria, did not agree with the comrade.

Who took care of the parents after *fen chia?* "If parents can manage their own cooking, children will underwrite their expenses. If they are too feeble to do so, the earning sons will take turns supporting them (in five-day, ten-day, or one-month shifts). If parents can walk they come to son's home to eat. If not, sons of daughters-in-law will send food over to parents."

Our inquiries at other communes near Peking—and near Fan Yu (capital of Kwangtung Province), Wuhan, Shenyang, and Tientsin —gave us some variation but not a drastically different picture. So the traditional cleavages in the kinship organization, as we noted in Chapter 5, remain active after the revolution. But the old kinship village ties remain the basic building blocks in the new and larger social organization, with one all-important difference. Land, the chief rural means of production, is no longer privately owned. Brothers, even after *fen chia,* continue to be linked by the larger network of the commune and through it, the nation. Two of the most important ingredients in this new situation are a new pattern of communication and the work-point system. But before we discuss these we shall have a brief look at an urban commune.

An Urban Commune

A good example of such an urban organization is the Szu P'ing Street Revolutionary Committee of the Yang P'u Ch'u (county), which formed part of the Shanghai Municipality, and which my family and I visited in 1972. It consisted of nine subdivisions each called a "new village", according to our informants. These were: Cha Tien New Village, Yu T'ien New Village, T'ung Chi New Village, Kung Chiao New Village, and five Anshan New Villages numbered three to seven.

These "villages" are not all new. For example the T'ung Chi New Village centers in a university of that name established long before 1949. In 1972 it had more than a hundred buildings including science halls, dormitories, and faculty residences. The Cha Tien New Village centers in the Cha Pei Electricity Company which also came into being long before 1949. In 1972 it had more than forty-six buildings including the plants, dormitories, and residences. The same is true of Kung Chiao New Village, which centers in a prerevolutionary public bus company and, in 1972, had forty-eight buildings. On the other hand the five Anshan New Villages were all built up since 1953, on what had been swamps, graveyards, and farm land where only thirty or forty families lived.

In other words, the Szu P'ing street organization—which occupied more than two square kilometers, had a total of 1,072 separate buildings, and was made up of nearly half a million people—was founded by pulling together old and existing groups that included intellectuals as well as newly formed groups predominantly catering to workers.

Within this giant "street" organization were seven high schools with 7,000 pupils, thirteen primary schools with 12,000 pupils, eight child care centers and kindergartens with over 1,000 toddlers, and in addition to one central shopping arcade and its five branches, eight factories with some 2,000 workers, a post office, a bank, a hospital and nine health stations, a cultural center, a worker's recreational club, and a Peace Park with a zoo containing lions, tigers, and a small lake for boating.

This street organization is like a rural commune in certain ways. It is under the management of a semielected revolutionary committee. The committee can mobilize every able-bodied resident for special events (such as clearing the streets on March 12, 1971 when Shanghai had two inches of snow). The street organization is subdivided into "lane organizations" *(li lung ke wei hui)* and the latter are subdivided into "immediate neighborhood organizations" *(chu min hsiao chu).* These subdivisions are the counterparts of the production brigades and production teams within each rural commune. Finally, it is similar to the commune in that a degree of local autonomy enables the residents to decide on local issues, such as whether to open up a barber shop.

But the street organization is unlike the rural commune in other significant ways. It is not a joint economic venture. The productive units within it are mostly independent entities each reporting to its own superiors. For example T'ung Chi University is under the Ministry of Higher Education; the major factories are linked to various ministries having to do with production and foreign trade; the buildings belonging to the electricity and public bus companies are controlled by each corporation independently.

Work-Points and the Kinship System

The work-point system is one of the most important ingredients which link the communes to the larger social, economic, and political network. The work-point system operates as follows. For one full day's work, every member of the commune receives work points that are recorded in the work accounts of his commune, according to previously agreed upon criteria differentiating men, women, and adolescents. No one is paid daily, but everyone accumulates work points in a central ledger. The accounts are settled at fixed intervals. The total proceeds of each period are distributed generally in the proportion of about 40 percent for the commune as a whole (for group benefits and improvements) and 60 percent for the individual. The details of settlement vary from place to place, as does also the length of the period of settlement. But the outline given here is roughly applicable to all communes.

There is no question that this work-point system may have important effects on interpersonal relationships. For example, some wives prefer to earn work points instead of having more children who will tie them down in spite of nurseries. Furthermore, the system enables women to view their own labor in terms of some standards other than as wife, mother, or daughter-in-law, so that the magnitude of their contribution becomes economically, and therefore more objectively, measurable. The work-point system is thus a crucial device for the individualization and emancipation of women. It loosens the kinship bonds, and increases the sense of involvement in a larger nonkinship group.

It is interesting that the psychological mechanism described here is echoed in the letter of an American wife to a popular columnist. This woman said that in all of her married years she "felt like a nobody because I was only a 'housewife.' " Her husband made her feel that she should be grateful to him for putting food in her mouth and clothes on her back. However, she now felt better because the home economics department of her state college had published a leaflet in chart form which showed "what a housewife is worth in dollars and cents per week on today's labor market." According to this chart's very modest wage scale (e.g., cooking meals at $2.00 an hour, child care at $.50 an hour, etc.) her work came to about $7,800 a year. So she says,

> Believe it or not, this leaflet gave me dignity. I am no longer feeling like a parasite. Tonight when Mr. Greatheart comes home I am going to greet him like a woman who earns about $8,000 a year because that's what I am.[18]

This American woman's grievance and her way of redressing it illustrate very eloquently one of the basic possible effects of the workpoint system in Chinese communes. In both instances the question is the conversion of the individual from being an appendage of a kinship group into an independent, valuable unit of production in some larger frame of reference. The difference is this. Individual-centered Americans, for whom the control of things is seen as the chief source of security, have allowed economic calculatedness to color most areas of American life. The marital sphere is still a last American sanctuary for sentimentality, but this woman's approach to her problems is probably indicative that pure sentiments are no longer safe even there. Situation-centered Chinese, for whom interpersonal duties, obligations, and privileges are bases for security, have cultivated human feelings to such an extent that laws and their enforcement are always tied to the personal, and business and friendship are ever intertwined. What they need for modernization is the expansion of the economic and impersonal considerations, at the expense of the sentimental and the personal, so as to link individuals in ever wider webs of the national life.[19]

However, situation-centeredness being so deeply embedded in the Chinese way of life, we can safely predict that the power of kinship will not easily disappear.

The reader will recall, in Chapter 3, the story of Wang Hua, who exemplified filial piety. Wang bought a father to whom he could be filial. Now in the August 25, 1979, issue of the *People's Daily* is a story in which the legendary case of Wang Hua came to real life. Chang Kuei-tse and her husband, Chen Fung-Min, who live in Ching An District of Heilungchiang Province, head a family of "three generations under one roof." She is thirty-seven, a collector for the district's electricity company, and her husband is a technician at the district's scientific research institute. They have four children but no living parents. In the fall of 1974 Chang, in the routine of her work, encountered a couple named Wang and Chiang, who were artisans and who were childless but too old to work. In addition, the old man had a heart condition which was just then acute. After mutual consultation Chang and her husband decided to adopt the old couple as parents (for him) and parents-in-law (for her). This in spite of the fact that, prior to this event, Chang had taken care of her crippled parents-in-law for eight years before they passed away.

Not only that, on a Sunday in November 1978 (the same report goes on to relate) Chang's home was in a state of celebration. Quite a few well-wishers from the neighborhood came. Why? Chang's younger brother, also adopted, was getting married. Some ten years before, Chang had encountered, one winter night on a street corner, a hungry and shivering teenager weeping quietly. He was an orphan named Kao. She decided to adopt him as a younger brother. Although he later found some blood relatives he remained a member of Chang's household.

Now Kao is employed and self-sufficient. Still Chang helped him to find a fiancée, bought furniture and personally made bedding for him, and arranged new living quarters for him. So although Chang had not sent out wedding invitations, well-wishers kept coming because "people wanted to congratulate this deeply affectionate and highly moral older sister."

The story goes on to relate how Wang the grandfather was now well and served as a "bank" for the four grandchildren and raised pigs to add to the family income; how Chiang the grandmother was now a storekeeper in a nearby primary school and watched over the youngsters' homework; how Chen the son asked his friends at every opportunity to buy a particular kind of tea from north China because his adopted father loved it; and how Chang and her mother-in-law took care of each other and eagerly shared the household chores.

"The members of this family are all selflessly working and learning for the sake of the Four Modernizations," the writer concluded.

In the October 21, 1980, issue of the *Worker's Daily* there are two letters, both in response to one which had appeared a few days earlier from a girl who described being persecuted by her parents because she wanted to marry someone against their wishes. The first correspondent was entirely on her side, and he invoked the tragedy of Liang Shan-Pe and Chu Yin-t'ai (the characters of a Peking opera who are not unlike the Western Romeo and Juliet) to castigate her old-fashioned parents. He went on:

Our laws since the revolution thirty years ago provide for complete freedom of choice. . . . Generally speaking, in the matter of romance, *seeking the advice of parents is entirely necessary* [italics mine] and differences of opinion are also normal. But if children disagree with their parents, parents have no legal right to interfere.

Under such circumstances, parents are punishable by law if they persist and cause a tragedy.

Parental control of children's marriages is due to the venom of feudalism. Many parents think that they can do anything with their children because they gave birth to the youngsters. There are even some parents who dare to declare, "Never mind if they are forced to suicide, it will be as if we never gave birth to them!" . . . Some obstinate fathers are worse than old Chu [father of Chu Ying-t'ai, the tragic heroine mentioned above]; they would hack short their daughter's hair, peel off their clothes, and beat them and kick them. It is really bad. . . ."

The letter was signed by Ku Pao-hua, employee, Chemical Fertilizer Manufacturing Company, Peking.

However, the second correspondent, Kung Min, from Hunan Province, asks her suffering sister to be more conciliatory toward her parents. Here is how she puts it:

Dear Comrade Fang, Your letter makes me recall my own experiences.

Five years ago I met my husband Chou P'e and we fell in love. I was a nurse in a hospital, he was a miner in a coal mine. Our romance caused many raised eyebrows all around us. They would say, "A lady worker in a hospital is like a flower, she has money and prestige, she can pick and choose easily among the most handsome and eligible young men. Why has she lowered herself to look at a miner—really going downhill."

But Chou P'e's love gave me courage. I ignored all such malignment. However, such pressures moved my parents. They forbade me to have anything to do with Chou P'e. They tried to explain to me so that I would see my erring ways; they asked me not to be guided only by emotion but to think of my own future! They said, "You are the daughter of a cadre, you cannot marry a common miner!" Seeing that I refused to heed them, they also told me that our two horoscopes "clashed" and that the failure of our match was ordained by the gods.

I persisted. Then my parents took several major steps. They got some matchmakers to find other possible mates for me; they hid Chou P'e's letters to me; and they even went to the hospital and collected my monthly salaries to deprive me of my livelihood; their reply to my protest was to beat me mercilessly with a cane. At that the thought of suicide did occur to me. But another thought stopped me. "How meaningless if I die like that!" So I returned from a dead-end street and decided to be courageous. I endured their beating and scoldings. Instead of getting angry I patiently tried to reason with them, by relating to them concrete cases I had heard of all the tragic consequences of parentally dictated marriages. Besides that, I showed special concern for them. My father had a liver ailment. I personally went to get his medicine and bring it to him; without being asked I took it upon myself to do some of the housework so as to lighten my mother's burden. In this way my parents slowly changed their views and eventually agreed to our marriage.

The lesson these experiences taught me is this: We must find the correct responses to parental obstinacy. Most parents who interfere with their children's marriages do so because they believe it is for their children's welfare and happiness. The number of parents who stick to their own views at the expense of their children is really very insignificant. Therefore, if we can make clear to our parents (who are opposed to our choices) the meaning of true parental love, I believe an overwhelming majority of them will change their views."

There is no doubt, as we noted before, that the Communist government wants to reduce the power of kinship in Chinese society. The elimination of clan graveyards, the promotion of cremation, the reduction of funeral and wedding ceremonies and expenses, the use of clan temples as storage space, and the decline of rituals of ancestor worship at home all contribute to this process. The work-point system in the commune is a central ingredient which cannot but erode the core of the kinship system in the long run. But I caution against overestimation of the extent and speed of the change in kinship under communism. The Communist revolution has hastened some changes, but it has been powerless to move in other directions, even with such spectaculars as the Cultural Revolution. Furthermore, many of the apparent changes after 1949 cannot be totally divorced from those which China and the non-Western world had slowly been undergoing under the physical and ideological impact of the West long before that date.

Cadres, the New Communication System, and Social Transformation

In analyzing the foregoing materials one other fact becomes obvious. The traditional class distinction has refused to go away even though, for the society as a whole, inequality because of wealth or income is now minimal. In fact, the salaries of some factory workers are higher than those of some cadre-supervisors and new university teachers.

The objection to nurse Kung Min's marriage to a coal mine worker was entirely rooted in class prejudice, not on the part of her parents only. This in spite of the fact that the very foundation of the new society is supposed to be the farmer and the laborer. In 1972 as my family and I toured China we found everywhere, from the Northeastern Provinces to Canton, signs extolling the proletarian revolution and calling for the rise of the propertyless of the world. At the entrances to all exhibitions, all performing arts arenas, and all public gymnasiums were red banners which said, "Perform for Workers, Farmers, and Soldiers." Such signs have been reduced in number since the fall of the Gang of Four, as we noticed in our most recent visit in 1980, but the emphasis remains.

Yet class distinction is evident not only in cases such as the pressure against Kung Min's marriage to a coal miner, but also in what we learned from students and professionals in China and abroad. One particular experience of our visit in 1980 is most telling. After a daylong visit to Ku Ch'eng, the village south of Kunming, Yunnan, where my wife and I lived for a year during World War II, we invited two villagers to our hotel on the following day for an afternoon's discussion and supper. Villager Chin came with one of his granddaughters, aged eleven, and Feng brought one of her daughters, a farm worker of twenty-four.

We did not realize that our little group would be anything out of the ordinary till dinner time. Ever since we had checked in at the hotel we dined in the main dining hall, which was usually full of white Americans and overseas Chinese. As a rule there were also some traveling cadres in Mao jackets in a section of the hall separated by a movable screen. But on this day as our little group went through the hallway we were at once the object of curious stares from the Whites but especially from the uniformed waitresses. The clothes of our two older guests, especially Feng's blue head cover, the usual attire for all women working in the field in Yunnan, made her village origins unmistakable.

We were seated in a separate and smaller dining room, where a group of cadres in Mao jackets shared another table. The uniformed waitresses, instead of serving us dish by dish as they usually did, laid everything on our table before our arrival. My wife had to guess that the two larger-than-usual pots on a side table a short distance away from ours, one containing rice and the other a mountain of steamed bread, were intended for us. The waitresses simply deserted us until I went out much later and found them. But when they did return we could sense their attitude turn from their usual friendliness to near hostility. Their service degenerated, and they stopped just short of slapping whatever we asked for on the table.

What we did was of course an unusual thing. Our village friends had never seen the inside of such hotels and the hotel people were not accustomed to serving villagers.

Was our experience an unusual one? We think not. In the October 21, 1980, issue of the *People's Daily* was an interesting letter to the editor which bears on this point from another angle. It was from the Interior Affairs Bureau of the Municipality of Shenyang, Liaoning Province, in response to a statement to the press by Comrade Ts'ui Teh-chih, member of the All China People's Congress, while it was in session in Peking. Comrade Ts'ui had expressed concern that "our society has been for many years [during the Cultural Revolution] prejudiced against intellectuals." As an example, Ts'ui cited the instance in which Shenyang Municipal Crematorium had refused to accept the body of associate professor Lai of Liaoning University for cremation and storage, because his salary "was only 79 *yuan* per month, way below the 147 *yuan* minimum level for such a privilege." The letter from the Interior Affairs Bureau offered correction on certain details but did not negate the essentials.

"Comrade Lai died on June 10, 1980," it began.

His body was transported by our bier and cremated in the crematorium under our jurisdiction. In addition the Liaoning University administration also conducted a memorial service for him on June 18 in the auditorium of our Hui Lung Kang Revolutionary Cemetery. According to Regulation No. 24 (1979) of the Municipal Revolutionary Committee, only the ashes of those college faculty members of grade six or higher can be permanently stored in the hall of this cemetery. But Comrade Lai's salary was only seventy-nine *yuan* per month, since he was only recently promoted to the rank of associate professor, and therefore did not qualify. However, the Party committee at Liaoning University petitioned us for an exception in this case. They explained that Lai had been a director of the All China Art and Literature Theory Association and had made significant contributions in the field, including specialized publications. In view of his special circumstances our Bureau approved, on June 16, the storage of his ashes in the hall of our cemetery.

The Kunming hotel episode would not have surprised us before the Communist revolution. At that time inhabitants of cities, especially the intelligentsia and government officials but also the merchants, used to equate villagers and farmers with the ignorant and even the stupid. In the late thirties when some highly educated reformers such as James Yen promoted the rural uplifting movements, we college students used to visit the mud huts and pig sties with curiosity and indulgence. We felt no less superior to them than the foreign missionaries who came to save fallen souls felt to the Chinese as a whole. This was not unnatural in a society that was traditionally divided, as we saw in Chapter 5, between the literati-bureaucrats on the one hand and the rest of the society on the other. But what has happened between the first years after 1949, when Communist officials lived like the common people, and now? Have all the Communist efforts at transforming the society, as epitomized in such slogans as "Serve the People," made little or no difference?

Nor would the Shenyang crematorium regulation have surprised us. In a way of life where the literati-bureaucrats dominated the rest of the society, it was not unnatural for differences in rank among the literati-bureaucrats themselves to reflect highly differentiated privileges. But what has happend to the idea that Chinese officers bear no insignia to distinguish them from the soldiers because the Communist authorities hope to create a truly egalitarian society?

To assess the situation let us look at the pattern of communication since 1949 in comparison with that before it.

Even after the fall of the Ch'ing dynasty in 1910, communication between the central government and the local communities was mainly one-way. The magistrate of each district was appointed from Peking. As the lowest level administrative and judicial official representing the dynasty, he carried out orders from above and occasionally reported to his superiors reactions from below. The local people, for their part, protected themselves from central government encroachment, as we saw in Chapter 7, by settling their own disputes and reducing the impact of its actions as far as possible. The relationship was one of distance from the government instead of identification with it.

The Communist government has created a more thorough nationwide administrative structure through the communes and the Party. It has also instituted work teams *(kung tso tui),* which are periodically dispatched from the provincial central government to the grass-roots level for investigative and persuasive purposes, and the so-called small groups *(hsiao tsu)* in each factory, commune, brigade, or production team, which meet regularly to discuss Maoist precepts and their application to actual life situations.

In addition, the government has utilized old communications media such as the Peking opera and slogans for its own purposes, and it has opened up new communication channels via newspapers, radio, traveling theaters, and now television. Although there were newspapers in China many decades before the Communist revolution, more people can read them now. Radios too were first introduced into China in the twenties, but blaring loudspeakers in outlying rural regions were unknown then. Even the big-character posters *(tatsu-pao)*, which plastered Peking's Tien An Men Square as elsewhere throughout China during the Cultural Revolution, thus gaining worldwide attention, are not entirely new. A French priest who resided and traveled in China before and after the T'aip'ing Rebellion (1850–1864), witnessed, in the city of Han Chuan, Hupei Province, the use of "placards" by the people "to criticize a Government, to call a Mandarin to order. . . . The placards are lively, satirical, cutting, and full of sharp and witty sallies."[20]

After the big-character posters were officially discouraged in 1978, a truly new development in mass communication began to take place —the great volume of letters which now descends on the editorial offices of newspapers. There were always letters to the editors of various newspapers, of course, but nothing like the number and the variety and the boldness of the views expressed since the fall of the Gang of Four.

It is impossible to detail all of the letters that I have seen, but the following is a sample of some of the concerns expressed. Several letter writers in the August 25, 1979, *People's Daily* want more local hotels, public bathhouses, and barbershops; another complains of an insufficiency of reading rooms in the Peking Library, where prospective readers form long waiting lines every day. Other complaints are against rewards for increased food production benefiting only the cadres (*People's Daily*, October 24, 1980); higher level bureaucracy refusing to allow factory workers their duly earned wages for overtime work on the ground that workers' rewards should be spiritual (i.e., patriotic) rather than material (*Shanghai Liberation Daily*, August 16, 1979); overaccumulation of Chinese medicine in some communes and scarcity of the same in others because of inflexibility on the part of higher administrative organs (*People's Daily*, October 20, 1980); and reforestation efforts ordered by cadres being a waste of time and money (*People's Daily*, September 8, 1979).

Throughout these and other letters are implicit or explicit criticisms of cadres on various levels of government for their arrogance, arbitrariness, inflexibility, special privileges, and even corruption. Judging from the letters I have read and other reports, there is an undeniable confrontation taking place between the people and the middle level leadership, i.e., the Party secretaries and cadres (the "Responsible Persons" during the Cultural Revolution) who are the decision makers in communes, factories, hospitals, clinics, schools and universities, and regional and county governments. Although there is a rush now to put all blame on the Gang of Four, in fact what we see is that most of the flaws in the cadre system "appear to be inherited from traditional Chinese bureaucracy. . . . When some leadership cadres are transferred, they bring not only their immediate families, but also secretaries, chauffeurs, and maids and their family members. Others find ways to transfer close to them not only their grown-up children, but daughters-in-law, sons-in-law, and even their sons' fiancées" (*People's Daily,* August 15, 1979). Thus the cadre problem meets the shadow of kinship discussed before.

For observers the danger is to be overly influenced by the mass denunciations of the Gang of Four and to lose sight of the wider historical and cultural context in which these persons operated and the movement they led took place. Previously we noted that the Communist victory in 1949 was but the latest of a series of Chinese responses to Western impact since 1842. We did so by seeing the latest Revolution in the modern Chinese context, but also by lifting our sights in order to perceive the links between different events instead of being blinded by the details of any one of them. If we again do the same we cannot escape the conclusion that the Red Guard phenomenon was part of an ongoing process of reexamination and reintegration to maintain the gains and momentum of a revolutionary movement aimed at transforming an enormous society.

Under Chiang Kai-shek a nationally publicized slogan consisted of these two lines from Dr. Sun Yat-sen's last will:

> The revolution is not yet a complete success,
> Comrades must persevere still more.

Even though Mao's Red Guards were given to enormous and often criminal excesses under the Gang of Four and became counterproductive, can the movement not still be seen as an attempt to encourage comrades to persevere still more?

But Mao's China was much better organized than it had been under his predecessor. Organizations of Chiang's New Life Movement used to send boy scouts and other workers to separate pedestrians on the sidewalks of Nanking so that all should proceed forward on the left, according to Chinese traffic rules; the movement also had camps and training centers for students of different ages. In terms of Chinese history, that kind of "missionary" effort was already a departure from tradition. But Mao's Red Guards were more violent and zealous, and their attacks and excesses were more far-reaching. Depending upon one's point of view, Mao's Red Guards were comparable to members of the American White Citizens Council, the Ku Klux Klan, or to frontier vigilantes; or they might be likened to prison reformers, Protestant evangelists and revivalists, the New Leftists, or even the Women's Christian Temperance Union members led by Carrie Nation, who with hatchet in hand busted up many saloons. The Red Guards were even more drastic departures from China's past.

There is, however, an underlying difference between the Chinese Red Guard phenomenon and the American movements. Most American movements tend to owe their origin to the initiative of bands of individual citizens. At one time or another charges are made that some of these movements are fronts for some larger ideology or for some arm of the goverment (such as the FBI), but there is no evidence that a majority of American organizations are directed by any except the interested citizens themselves. The Chinese Red Guards, however, were instigated by the top echelon of the Communist government. At some point, noncentrally directed Red Guard organizations arose elsewhere in imitation and they might even have appeared to be out of Peking's control. But they were not private organizations; consequently they could be much more easily redirected or called off than could the more spontaneous movements in the United States. From this point of view Thomas Griffith of *Time* magazine was wide of the mark when he characterized the Gang of Four trial as a "phony campaign" because "four is too small a gang" and "everybody knows that many of the bureaucrats who waged the Cultural Revolution still occupy high places" (November 24, 1980). In a situation-centered society correction at the top is far more important than it is in an individual-centered one.

A colossal revolution is still going on in China today. Its achievements are not inconsiderable. In three decades it has not only cleansed China of rats, prostitutes, beggars, and gangsters, but also freed her from epidemics, famine, starvation, and military helplessness. Instead of receiving foreign aid she is giving it, however modestly. Instead of begging for recognition by big powers she is maintaining diplomatic relations in her own terms.

The Soviet Union withdrew its technicians from China in the fifties. But the Chinese industries did not collapse, and all Russian aid was repaid (even for the Korean War). The Chinese built gigantic bridges over the Yangtze River at Chungking, Wuhan, and Nanking, and made membership in the exclusive nuclear club on their own. Many refugees did rush to Hong Kong from China, but no reports described them to be undernourished, emaciated, or raggedly clad. For anyone who knew those sick, starving, and dying Chinese in city streets before 1949 and that China characterized as a "Land of Famine,"[21] the Hong Kong refugees did not seem to be leaving China because of shortage of food.

The enormous purchases of wheat from Australia, Canada, and elsewhere are taken as proof by some of misery under Communism. But three years of crop failure (1959–1961) brought no concomitant starvation, sale of children, mob scenes in the streets, sky rocketing prices of basic food stuffs, and public execution of profiteers that had been common before 1949. The rationing system was efficient enough so that the well-to-do (there are still some who have more than others) could not eat much better or more than the less fortunate. There certainly were shortages, and many families received food and clothing packages through Hong Kong from relatives and friends in the Western world, especially the United States. And other families who received remittances from abroad were accorded the privilege, through award of coupons, of purchasing at stores specially set up with such delicacies as seafood and meats or ginseng[22] in quantities according to the amount of remittance.

In the light of such facts, may not purchases abroad be interpreted as evidence that the Communist government is concerned with food for the people? Can they also not indicate an ability to produce the foreign exchange sorely needed elsewhere? Can they be an attempt to reduce the burden on the rural areas so that more workers might be freed to man factories and build dams? Finally, and even more important, has there been another Chinese government since contact with the West that was both in a position and inclined to take similar steps to feed her citizens?

Of course, a cynical visitor like Simon Leys (pen name of the Frenchman Pierre Rychmans) could observe that the impressive material achievements of China since 1949 have been at the cost of a "prefrontal lobotomy" done on the people.[23] In their situation-centered way of life the Chinese have not been known to condemn conformity or to extol individual freedom. Those attitudes are characteristic of the individual-centered, as we have seen in the foregoing pages, especially Chapter 4. I would not, therefore, agree with Leys. However, may I suggest that the several shifts of the revolutionary winds since 1949 have not encouraged many Chinese to think for themselves? A small illustration will explain what I mean.

My wife and I have been interested in the symbolism of the new Chinese flag. The big star represents the Communist party; but what are the four small stars for? In 1972 the answers we received from "Responsible Persons," other cadres, and guides were: they symbolize labor, farmers, soldiers, and patriotic capitalists or people's capitalists; or they symbolize labor, farmers, people's capitalists, and all other political parties.

On our most recent trip we asked the same question of guides, waiters, taxi drivers, and shop assistants in Wuhan, Peking, and Canton, and of a school teacher and one police official in Kunming, Yunnan. This list includes two men who manned the 1980 Trade Exhibition in San Francisco. The first responses we received were frequently an embarrassed smile or puzzlement. Some said they had not thought about it. Others said they were once told what they symbolized but forgot. One ventured that perhaps the four small stars represented all Chinese. And still others gave us something not dissimilar to the uncertain answers we heard in 1972.

Could it be that the letters to the editors in Chinese newspapers escalated to such an extent because the high leadership now says it is good to do so? Or do they herald fundamental changes in Chinese society and culture in the years to come?

The revolutionary transformation of Chinese social organization and economy is far from complete or self-propelling. What is required is not only change in external arrangements but also psychological reorientation of the individual so that he can satisfy his social needs in ways which are commensurate with the future objectives of the state. The success of such a transformation cannot be assured in advance; some of the spectacular successes of the Peking government have been matched with enormous failures.

However, the American reader who is overly impressed by their successes or failures will do well to reflect on the scene closer at hand.

Slavery was legally abolished in the United States as a result of the

Civil War of 1861–1865. Nearly a hundred years later, the Supreme Court handed down its school desegration ruling. Notwithstanding social, legal, economic, and church efforts as well as massive demonstrations and widespread bloodshed, we are nowhere even remotely near the ideal prescribed by law. Depending upon the holder's optimism or pessimism, current views about the future range from complete integration to inevitable polarization into two separate nations.

Transformation of the psychology and culture of a large and ancient society is a painful and slow process. It may be hurried up somewhat by drastic methods, but its course is bound to twist and turn.

NOTES

1. U.S. Department of Commerce, *Social Indicators 1976*, p. 467. According to the Census Bureau's first 1977 report, the number of people living in poverty was 24,720,000, or 11.6 percent of the population. It was only slightly down from the 1976 figure (11.8 percent) but was greatly reduced from that of 1959 (24.4 percent) (reported in *Chicago Sun-Times*, August 12, 1978).

2. The reader can also gain some notion of this poverty by reading two novels: Pearl Buck's *Good Earth* which portrays conditions in the 1920s, and Lao She's *Rickshaw Boy* which describes the 1920s and 1930s. In the 1930s during the best years of the Nationalist administration the annual per capita income of the Chinese was about U.S. $27. The American per capita income for the years 1930 to 1935 inclusive were: $624, $529, $401, $375, $423, and $472 ("Personal income by states," U.S. Dept. of Commerce, Government Printing Office, Washington, D.C., 1956).

3. In those years many ordinary Chinese and Chinese industries also found refuge or flourished in the Foreign Concessions safe from the ravages of civil wars. Some Westerners have pointed to this to show how these Concessions had "benefited" the Chinese; the argument is not unlike that of how the Mafia has "benefited" some individual Americans and how some American businesses have sought its protection.

4. The deposed boy emperor has given us fascinating details about himself in an autobiography. See Aisin-Gioro Pu Yi, *From Emperor to Citizen: the Autobiography of Aisin-Gioro Pu Yi.*

5. Herlee G. Creel, *Chinese Thought from Confucius to Mao Tze-tung*, p. 241.

6. During and immediately following World War II, China was one of the Big Four, along with Great Britain, the United States, and the Soviet Union.

7. See his statement as reported by Harrison Forman, *Report from Red China.*

8. Ibid., p. 178.

9. Buck, *Land Utilization in China.*

10. Edgar Snow, *Red Star Over China*, p. 216.

11. Many reports from China testify to these and other points. See for example, Jan Myrdal, *Report from a Chinese Village,* and William Hinton, *Fan Shen: A Documentary of Revolution in a Chinese Village.*

12. I fear that corruption on all levels of government in America will escalate if and as inflation becomes worse.

13. One or two Western journalists who have reported on the People's Republic since 1949 have described this to be apocryphal. These journalists are either uninformed or telling an untruth.

14. In this context, Indians, in the persons of Sikh policemen in British uniform, incurred the Chinese epithet, "Running dogs of the British."

15. This psychological background explains why Peking refused American and other foreign offers of help after the giant T'angshan (north China) earthquake of 1976. The Chinese are not unaware of the fact that, for years, boy or girl scouts with tin cans used to collect nickels and dimes on American city streets in the name of disaster relief for the helpless Asians.

16. John K. Fairbank presents a good discussion of this from another point of view. See "The People's Middle Kingdom," *Foreign Affairs,* July 1966, pp. 574–586.

17. *Chia* means home or family, but *ch'iang, t'ang,* and *pang,* which respectively mean wall, pond, and riverbank, were old usages peculiar to the way each village was known.

18. "Ask Ann Landers," *Chicago Sun-Times,* February 9, 1966.

19. For another but similar analysis, see Lucy Jen Huang, *The Impact of the Commune on the Chinese Family, Tempo* monograph.

20. M. Huc, *A Journey through the Chinese Empire,* vol. 2, pp. 76–77.

21. Walter Hampton Mallory, *China, Land of Famine.*

22. The root of a plant traditionally valued by Chinese, Japanese, and Koreans as the best tonic.

23. Simon Leys, *Chinese Shadows.*

CHAPTER 16

World Unrest: Communism and America

The present situation of America, remote as the proposition might at first appear, can be viewed as somewhat analogous to China's when, in consequence of external pressures, the society's internal mechanisms were confronted by problems for which they were not fashioned to deal. America, like China, for many years rejoiced in its isolation from the rest of the world. Insulated from warring Europe and chaotic Asia by two great oceans, Americans were free to shape their own destiny in their own way. The Great Wall psychology was as true of America as it was of China. Then, almost without warning, the walls crumbled, the oceans were reduced to ponds, and geographic distance no longer meant security. Neither people were able to ignore the world any longer; complete freedom of action disappeared forever. In countless ways, the world was making its presence felt in similarly numberless aspects of individual and national life.

In both societies many persons, trapped between the patterns of psychological satisfaction to which they are accustomed and the realities of the present, either despair of the future or point to the past as the only hope. In China the dream is to return to Confucianism; in the United States complete self-reliance and unbridled free enterprise, such as that preached by Milton Friedman, still have appeal to many. Likewise, in both countries some make a fetish of ignoring and retreating from the troubles around them, seeking individual refuge in art, business, entertainment, or scientific inquiry, while others dream of finding a single, simple solution, including the mysteries of some Oriental religion, which overnight would set matters aright. This is what occurs whenever walls are breached.

Here, however, the similarity ends. We must now take into account once again the great difference in the manner of life that was led behind the protective barriers. China's way of life was static. She was the sleeping lion, and the problem was to awaken her and to substitute action for the torpor that had enfeebled her. The American condition is quite the opposite. Americanism is almost synonymous with dynamism. It is no accident that in the history of American life we saw a new optimism, a new vision, an almost ecstatic carefreeness unknown to the rest of the world. The dream of unlimited expansion and unlimited progress, while first recorded in European thought, was given embodiment in the living achievements of American life. For those achievements Americans need apologize to no one, neither to those "artistic" souls here or abroad who have quailed before the specter of "materialism," nor to their own consciences.

The fact is that America is the envy of the world, in spite of the resentment and even hatred against her,[1] particularly of those millions in Asia and Africa who have been so occupied with the problems of survival that, unlike many well-fed bohemians and intellectuals, they find this misnamed materialism very appealing. The American press and the United States information agencies thought they had struck propaganda pay dirt when in 1950 (during the Korean War) the Chinese Communist mission to the United Nations General Assembly went on a buying spree in New York. But Chinese visitors to the United States have always indulged themselves in this fashion, acquiring cameras, household appliances, and autos. Among Chinese students, a description of the ideal life was to live in an American house (for its conveniences), to eat Chinese food (for its delicate satisfactions to the alimentary tract), and to marry a Japanese wife (for her obedience to the master).

Furthermore, far more than her so-called material achievements, American democracy has exercised a still greater attraction to those people who have suffered under warlords, emperors, and despots of all hues and forms. Malfunctions there may be in the American government just as the economic plenitude of America may be purchased in part at the cost of other values, but most of mankind in its misery and subjection would show no hesitation whatsoever if they could exchange their world for the one in which Americans live.

This is one cause of the difficulties that America faces in Asia today. Until not very long ago, the world's non-Western peoples looked upon the achievements of the West with astonishment, fear, and probably envy. But Western ways were not their ways. They did not aspire to take on those ways; they also did not know how. The situation changed greatly and rapidly since World War II. Those who once were overawed now know many of the means by which the West achieves its ends. Those once held in thrall by fear have since discovered cracks in the Western power and have witnessed the spectacle of Western armies being defeated by Asian forces. Those once resigned to envy of the West are now convinced that they are capable of improving their material welfare and terminating their status as inferiors.

The immediate causes of unrest vary from place to place. The goals of organized groups, their methods, and the nature of their leadership also are different. But the basic issues are everywhere the same. The few remaining colonial and semicolonial lands are straining against the chains that have bound them, and the newly independent but economically and politically still weak nations are straining to better themselves in the Western model. It is into the resulting struggle which America has been almost imperceptibly drawn.

The American Dilemma

America has spent billions for the economic recovery of Western Europe and continues to spend billions for its military security. This is done not out of charity or sentiment, but for strategic reasons of self-defense. This would be difficult enough if the problem were confined to Europe, but it is not. The former and present European colonies, protectorates, and spheres of influence are beset by dual pressures that often commingle and coalesce. Native liberation movements and internal revolutions or simple struggles for power frequently are penetrated by Communists so that, as the chief exponent of the fight against communism, America becomes labeled as the abettor and even the inheritor of imperialism—and with good reason. After unsuccessfully aiding the French to crush the Vietnamese independence fighters, America simply slipped into the former colonial master's shoes and Americanized the war in Vietnam. In the process she tried to keep in power first the playboy emperor Bao Dai, then the dictator Diem, and finally the military men Thieu and Ky and their generals, some of whom had actually fought on the side of the French against their own countrymen. Would the American people have tolerated as heads of their government men who had collaborated with their enemies?

Furthermore, even where Communist penetration is nonexistent or nominal, America often feels that it is necessary to take the side of the colonial power or some other despot for other political purposes. For example, America has yet to indicate by some deed or policy statement that she really shares the feelings of African peoples concerning the totalitarian brutalities practiced by the government of the Republic of South Africa against Blacks.

To Americans, these things may be explicable in terms of the anti-Communist struggle. To other peoples of the earth they are not that clear-cut. Many feel that the charges emanating from Moscow do not appear to be at variance with the facts of their daily lives. It does not do much good for America to make the defense that she has proved her good faith by freeing the Philippines, just as it will cause little stir for Russia to describe the good life of the Uzbek minority within her borders. The Philippines and Uzbekistan do not concern the Egyptian fellahin, the Namibian rebels, the Iranian militants, or the Chinese peasant. But discontented peoples bent on improving their life situation are not likely to decline the call of any ism which promises to see to their needs and shows *immediate* signs of fulfilling its pledge.[2]

In this regard the United States suffers from certain disadvantages of historical accident. Except for the Chinese, Asians and Africans have had no experience with Soviet imperialism. But they are only too well acquainted with European imperialism. As we noted in Chapter 15, by the 1930s even the Chinese, whose capital the Russians once occupied together with the United States and six other foreign powers, did not consider Russia to be a significant threat. This picture has not changed; Western Europeans were the last colonial masters, and the Americans are supporting them and opposing Russia.

With such a background, America has become an easy prey to enemy propaganda, whenever she appears to side with the present and former colonial powers. It has not been difficult for Communists to shift the onus of the past onto America while the Soviet Union has run up the banners of peace and plenty, freedom and equality, and anticolonialism and international justice which were once the rightful possession of America, the land that first gave them national expression. Even the Soviet occupation of Hungary, later of Czechoslovakia, and now of Afghanistan angered Americans much more than it impressed the Asians. Instead, the Vietnamese situation was much more real to them, and its much greater and more extensive brutalities were not, as they could see too, all created by the Viet Cong and

Hanoi. I doubt if any amount of American explanation will convince the next several generations of Asians that the United States does not have a double standard where non-European peoples are concerned.

It is this that makes possible the "initiative" which many observers claim to be enjoyed by the Communists since the conclusion of World War II. The philosopher, F. S. C. Northrop, expressed this concern in the following vein:

> The Communists have done their best to make the time in which we live a desperate and tragic one. For how tragic it is that these glorious civilizations which are Asia and Islam, now in resurgence, cannot draw at their leisure in their own way upon the equally glorious civilization of the Hebrew-Christian, Greco-Roman, modern liberalized West, and even upon Karl Marx's original thought, without having their hands and our hands forced by Moscow and Peking Communists.[3]

But Northrop would do well to recall first that the forcing of hands began when the industrialized West expanded at no little expense of the rest of the world. The conditions that this expansion either fostered or contributed to did not allow Asia and Islam to draw at their "leisure" upon Western ways. The needs and pressures of the time were not conducive to a slow metamorphosis, Moscow or no Moscow. Long before Borodin appeared in Canton, many Chinese had learned the lesson of action—and action now, not tomorrow—from Europe and America. They had been to school, as Americans say, in the college of hard knocks prior to any postgraduate courses they may have taken in either Leninist or capitalist theory. Sun Yat-sen, who was introduced to Western ideas at an English mission school in Hawaii and who looked to America as the prototype of what he hoped China might one day be, called for a new China based on his Three People's Principles—nationalism, democracy, and a decent livelihood—many years before Lenin detrained at St. Petersburg.

The real American difficulty is not that Communists have seized the "initiative," but that the international world as the Americans knew it has drastically changed without their permission, exactly as —over a century before—the international world as the Chinese knew it had drastically changed without asking for their advice. Before 1842 the Chinese were used to being known as the "civilized" people by "barbarians" who eagerly sought Chinese ways and maintained tributary relations with them. Americans have held a position of superiority—separate, benevolent, and stern. Theirs is a paradise for the select few. They distribute alms to the poor and the wretched. And like the good guy in a good Western movie, they may be unwillingly pushed into the shoes of the sheriff who then proceeds to clear out the troublemakers so that all the people in the little frontier town live happily ever after.[4] The Chinese were rudely awakened from their reverie when they found themselves powerless in the face of external developments; they had no alternative but to change their ways. Americans have yet to see more clearly the handwriting on the international wall.

How much has the international world changed since the nineteenth century? One good indication is to be found in the impotence of arms superiority. The military conflicts between China and the West since the mid-nineteenth century were usually called "wars" but I do not think most people realize what puny affairs they really were. In the Opium War of 1840–1841 the British forces used no more than a few ships, the chief of which was the H.M.S. *Volage,* a pinnace—a light sailing vessel largely used as a tender.[5] In the Franco-British expedition of 1857–1858, the invading forces consisted of fewer than ten thousand men. But they were able to occupy Canton, then went all the way north, captured T'ientsin forts, and invaded Peking to raze the emperor's summer palace to the ground.[6]

The most revealing of these wars was the Boxer Rebellion of 1900 that led to the flight of the Empress Dowager and the Emperor from Peking and the subsequent occupation of the capital by the armed forces of seven Western powers (including the United States) and Japan. The treaty of 1901 gave the various powers more Foreign Concessions and more trading ports and rights to proselytize in all China than all the other Unequal Treaties before it. In addition it also gave the victors rights to station garrisons in the Legation Quarters in Peking, and an indemnity of over half of the United States federal budget at the time.[7] To force the Celestial Empire with her then four hundred million people into such an abject surrender, the Allied Forces marched to Peking with a total of about twenty thousand men,[8] and the entire war took less than a year.

The contrast between this and American experiences in Vietnam sixty years later is simply too startling to escape our attention. In the latter situation, over half a million American men, with ultramodern weapons and uncontested, massive air and naval support, failed to crush the Viet Cong's and North Vietnam's will and ability to fight. What led a giant China to capitulate so easily and so soon before the small Allied Forces was not simply the inferiority of her weapons and organization but her people's psychological demoralization vis-à-vis the West. Those were the days when Western power was reacted to by the rest of the world with fear, awe, envy, and more reluctantly, respect.

The Japanese first experienced how a weak nation could hurt a militarily and industrially superior power when Chiang Kai-shek, in spite of numerous defeats and retreats, simply refused to surrender —thereby tying up some three million Japanese occupation and fighting soldiers in China. This expenditure of men and equipment contributed significantly to Japan's eventual downfall. If more Americans had recognized the significance of the Japanese experience and later the Korean War as lessons for the future, perhaps they would have objected more vigorously and much sooner to American involvement in Vietnam. But they did not.

The prestige of any individual vis-à-vis his fellow human beings depends upon how far the latter voluntarily concede and defer to him because of their unquestioned acknowledgment of his superiority. If he has to go around waving a big stick or bundles of money and *demanding that they recognize his superiority,* his prestige is nonexistent. A nation's prestige among other nations operates in exactly the same fashion; unfortunately, most Americans have yet to understand this.

This then is the American dilemma. She was used to being left alone. But the shrinkage of distances made the two oceans and the Monroe Doctine lose their significance as isolating devices. She was also used to helping whomever she chose, or missionizing and intervening wherever she wished. She had the initiative; now all this is forever changed. The militancy of the once pliant peoples has now altered the picture; they refuse to be grateful for small favors. They not only are dissatisfied with the status quo but do not want to wait for things to evolve. They will even blackmail America by threatening to invite Soviet aid or to espouse communism. The United States no longer has the initiative as to where and when she wishes or does not wish to help. She must go where the fire is; and fires seem to break out, unexpected to her, almost anywhere.

America's Alternatives

Given a way of life which centers in the individual, it was inevitable that the momentous change in China led to American efforts to uncover the guilty in the American government who "lost" China. We know that to blame a few officials or the State Department for the spread of Communist power throughout the world, and particularly communism's victory in China, is not the least bit different from placing all the blame upon Hoover and the GOP for the depression of the thirties.[9] But "What do we do now?" is a question that has often evoked only confusing answers.

That the American confusion is by no means restricted to governmental circles became clear to me one day in the spring of 1950 when I heard an address which the late Dr. Hu Shih, China's former ambassador to the United States and one of her most distinguished scholars, delivered before the Executives' Club of Chicago. The most interesting portion of his speech, which had been preceded by a five-minute standing ovation, occurred when he made his concluding points. First, he said, America should never recognize the Communist regime in China. At this, wild applause broke out. And second, Dr. Hu continued, America should make a sizable enough increase in the economic and military aid extended to Chiang's Nationalist government and armed forces for the recapture of China. This was received with complete silence.

The precipitous waning of enthusiasm for Dr. Hu's advice is explicable not only by the possibility that these businessmen did not see in the Kuomintang the model of rectitude they might have wished. Most Americans supported the cooperation with Franco and Tito without investigating too closely the condition of their public morality, to say nothing of the divergence of their politico-economic convictions from those of America or from one another. But aid to Franco and Tito was part of a holding operation whose economic and military costs could be measured with some accuracy. Dr. Hu's proposition opened wide the door to commitments whose nature and end no man could foresee. Its virtue, that of positive action, was in the minds of Dr. Hu's auditors outweighed by its accompanying encumbrance, the prospective cost.

If all-out war with the People's Republic of China was unthinkable, what then were the alternatives? There were only three, as follows: (a) to uphold and encourage the Nationalist regime as the present and future government of China; (b) to contain Communist China; and (c) to make a positive attempt at conciliation with the Peking regime.

In retrospect American actions vis-à-vis the People's Republic came in three stages roughly corresponding to these alternatives. The contrasting reactions of Chicago's top businessmen to Dr. Hu's two points expressed a dilemma presented by the first alternative.

Negativism—don't recognize the Communist government—is emotionally satisfying but impractical in the long run because it doesn't lead to concrete results. But the positive course taken on that premise was unacceptable because it would have required military involvement of a magnitude far greater than what happened later in Vietnam.

The fact that Dr. Hu's audience ceased to be enthusiastic about his second proposition shows that our top executives were not, even at that early date, unwise to the dangers of American military involvement on the Asian continent. However, given the emotional need for superiority, America inevitably took to the second alternative—containment. The tragic events of Vietnam and the follies of Dulles's domino theory are behind us. They need not detain us here. The intricate story of how Americans got into that quagmire through three presidents has been elegantly told by David Halberstam.[10]

What remains to be clarified is the fact that the containment policy was founded on two false premises. The first is that the diffusion of ideological communism, either of the Soviet variety or the Chinese variety, can be perpetrated or prevented by physical force. The spread of Christianity in Europe was not stopped by Roman opposition. On the opposite side, Christianity failed to convert a majority of Asians in spite of the pressure of Western military force and social, political, and educational infiltration. One fundamental lesson anthropology teaches us is that the diffusion of any aspect of culture is not a haphazard matter. The incoming elements will only take root if they fit in with the recipient society's needs based in its psychocultural context that we have called in this book its way of life.

The other false premise of containment is that the Chinese have been, and still are, expansionist. Westerners, with their immediate past of three hundred years of colonialism, not unnaturally projected their way of thinking into Chinese behavior. There is no question that various Chinese emperors embarked on wars of conquest to enlarge their empires. But there are two characteristics which made the Chinese situation very different from Western colonialism.

As we noted before, the Chinese as a whole have never been adventurous and their pattern of mutual dependence made them centripetal. Emigration tended to be a last resort, as defense against natural calamities or ravages of war that were completely beyond their control. Consequently, military conquests by Chinese leaders were neither preceded nor followed by rushes of Chinese settlement in the conquered territories. This was true of the most extensive empires of

Han, T'ang, Ming, and Ch'ing no less than in the case of the seven naval expeditions under the eunuch admiral Cheng. The Mongol Empire included nearly all of Asia and about half of Europe, but we do not even have writings of Chinese travelers in Europe to match the fascinating story of Marco Polo in China. The Chinese, in spite of their large numbers, have never led nor ever massively supported their rulers in conquest and colonization outside of China's borders.

The other characteristic is that the Chinese rulers always differentiated between territories within their empire and those of tributary states. Chinese rulers did not tolerate rebellion within the boundaries of their empires, but they usually left other states along China's borders to manage their own affairs more or less in their own way so long as they did not make trouble for China and *acknowledged their subordinate position in a tributary relationship with the imperial court.* At one time or another Vietnam (formerly Annam), Thailand (formerly Siam), and Burma, among many others, were in such a relationship with China. Periodically, the rulers of these kingdoms sent ambassadors bearing tribute to the Chinese capital with credentials or letters showing that they looked up to the Chinese court for guidance, authority, or protection. The details varied from country to country but in a number of instances, the emperor of China was even asked to grant the tributary king a seal of rulership as the basis (or additional basis) for his authority over his own country. The Chinese seal, which for higher offices can be as large as a foot square, was the essential badge of power for all Chinese officials in China. The Chinese emperor has a special seal different from all the rest.

In some instances, this tributary relationship was wholly voluntary on the part of the subordinate state. According to *Sung Shu* or *History of the Liu Sung Dynasty* (ca. A.D. 513) even successive Japanese rulers asked to be confirmed in their titles by the Chinese court.[11] In the case of Siam, the relationship was much more continuous and lasting. At the beginning of the Ming dynasty (ca. A.D. 1378) a ruler of Siam was granted a Chinese seal of office bearing the inscription "Seal of the King of Siam." When Burma invaded Siam, killed that king and took the Crown Prince prisoner, the new king (the younger son of the Crown Prince) took office (ca. A.D. 1400) and specifically petitioned the Ming emperor for a new seal (because the old seal was lost in the war) in the following terms:

> As the head of scores of follower states, Siam cannot mobilize her armed forces except when she possesses a seal from heavenly dynasty.[12]

As a rule the tributary emissaries were entertained in the imperial capital lavishly for several days, at the end of which time they went back to their respective countries with the Chinese emperor's return gifts. Between A.D. 1736 and A.D. 1820 there were no less than twenty-three such tributes from Siam alone, each involving a minister with an entourage of ten or more, a large collection of gifts sepa-. rately to the Chinese emperor and empress, and a sea and land journey of not less than eight or nine months each way. The tributary gifts from Siam in the year A.D. 1787 were especially numerous. They included, for the emperor, one male elephant and one female elephant, six rhinoceros horns, two European blankets, ten bolts of European calico, three hundred catties of elephants' tusks, three hundred catties of teakwood, ten spreads of peacock feathers, and so forth, and, for the empress, about half in number or weight of each of all the items except the elephants.[13] The Chinese records were not too explicit about the return gifts, which usually included various kinds of silk. There is even evidence that at some point the Chinese ruler was a little wary about these ceremonial gestures of subordination. One Ming emperor sent an edict (ca. A.D. 1375) to tell "Siam and other tributary nations not to present tributes any more since the cost and trouble were great."

These exchanges, however, were never followed up by extensive Chinese colonization or missionization in any of the tributary countries. If the Chinese had been as interested in emigration and proselytism as the Europeans for the last ten centuries, their numbers in the South Seas and in the Western world would have been many, many times what they actually are today.[14]

China's relationship with her tributary countries was primarily a matter of prestige and little else. This fact explains why the first ambassadors from Western countries were treated as tribute-bearing emissaries, and why Emperor Ch'ien Lung issued the imperial edict to the English ambassador beginning with something like, "His Imperial Majesty's domains want nothing from the barbarian countries. . . ."

Of course, lack of expansionist tendencies in the past does not preclude China from having them in the future. Besides, the Chinese under Western pressure have had to accept many non-Chinese ways for self-defense, from universal education to a Communist government. But the point is that the Chinese, in contrast to Western peoples, were historically nonexpansionist and have acted cautiously in military ventures even under communism.[15] Furthermore, even if the Chinese Communist government tries its hand in the art of subversion in lands distant from China it still must be seen essentially as a response to the West. A parallel is found in that some American Blacks want separate facilities in schools, dormitories, and classes. The Blacks did not invent segregation. They demand it in self-defense, or at least wish to warm their hands on that symbol of white superiority to get even if nothing else.

But the fact that the Chinese are not really expansionist is less important than the American need to create some particular threat and to restore her once powerful American Great Wall. This was the true reason for containment. The psychological forces in its support were so strong that they delayed any serious American consideration of the third alternative—a positive attempt at conciliation with the People's Republic of China—till all hope of American success in Vietnam seemed out of sight.

The events following former President Nixon's initiative in 1972 did not lead to diplomatic normalizations between the two countries until 1979, in spite of a whole stream of American visitors to China, including former President Gerald Ford, in the eight intervening years. The obvious reason for this long delay was Peking's insistence on the three preconditions for normalization, namely: (1) derecognition of Taiwan; (2) termination of the mutual security treaty with Taiwan; and (3) withdrawal of remaining United States military personnel on Taiwan. But it is interesting that, shortly after he was nominated to be United States ambassador to the U.N. by the then President-Elect Carter, Andrew Young spoke in favor of normalizing relations with Vietnam. The reason? America needs "a strong Vietnam" that could become an independent Marxist state like Yugoslavia, to serve as "a buffer against Chinese expansionism." So the containment psychology lives on.

In the 1953 version of this book I wrote:

> Those who favor recognition usually do so in the expectation that this would be the first step toward disrupting the Peiping-Moscow alliance. Mao, such persons contend, can be transformed into an Asiatic Tito. There are reasonable grounds for hoping that China, unlike Russia's European satellites, is not and will not become a Soviet puppet. But anti-Western feeling has been so great in China that we cannot reasonably expect that any Chinese government could now re-embrace the West with the fervor of a Tito.

That was before the Sino-Soviet split. That split baffled some observers and gave undue hope to others for a quick United States–China rapprochement. I was right in projecting the split but I was wrong in stating that Peking would not warm up to Washington so abruptly as she has been doing since normalization of diplomatic relations in 1979. Could anyone have imagined a few years ago that Coca-Cola will now be bottled and distributed in China?

Consequently, the China Council of The Asia Society, in a recent issue of its newsletter (Winter 1979–80) declared: "In the 1980s, American encounters with China promise to be increasingly substantive and complex. Long-term scholarly exchanges, increased trade and tourism, and direct personal contact at many levels have already altered many American perceptions of China."

I have no doubt about the increasingly "substantive and complex" exchange activities to come but I must sound a note of caution about the "altered . . . American perceptions of China." The reason the United States for so long refused to pursue a more realistic course vis-à-vis China goes straight to the heart of the American way of life. That way of life, as we have seen in the foregoing chapters, is marked by the fear of inferiority. Individual Americans defend themselves against this fear by acquisition of wealth and by continuous victories over others in business, in religion, in race, and even in male-female relationships. Americans may talk about equality, but what they want is to be more equal than others. Therefore, on the national level the main American stumbling block against establishing and then carrying out a realistic China policy is the fear of surrender of superiority, which is, for the egocentric man, equivalent to acknowledging his own inferiority. It is precisely this American emphasis on her national superiority that is being challenged, not merely by the Chinese, but by most Asians and Africans. The following complaint did not come from a Chinese, but from a Hindu whose homeland has been on friendly terms with the United States and is one of the principal Asian recipients of American aid.

I recently returned from a five-month visit to India and the Southeast Asian countries and there I was once more made aware that one of the main causes of the resentment against the Western powers is their arrogant assumption that the "white fathers" know what is good for the backward Asian peoples, and that the decisions of the Western powers should be liked, and if not liked, then lumped by the Asians. It is this attitude of

the Western nations which has put the Asian democracies' backs up—
even though on an ideological basis they are with the Western democracies. . . . These criticisms were not advanced by Communists or fellow
travelers who are engaged every hour in maligning the Western democracies, and particularly the United States, but by those Asians who have
read Thomas Jefferson, Abraham Lincoln, and Franklin D. Roosevelt,
who know of America's past history and her heritage. . . .

There are 500,000,000 persons in the free countries of Asia. They live
for the most part in countries lately freed from Western domination.
They are struggling to maintain their newly achieved independence,
freedom, and democratic government in a world in which Communism
threatens to overwhelm them. . . . What does all this add up to? Simply
this: that Asians can no longer be ignored. They refuse to be treated as
step-children or second-class citizens of the world. Further, that to ignore
the dynamic developments in the newly freed Asian countries would be
to court disaster in the cold, and in some areas not so cold, war. . . . The
United States used to have a very large reservoir of good will among the
Asian people. Though that reservoir has been greatly depleted, it is not
too late to replenish it. If the Western democracies want the Asian democracies as friends and allies, then let them be accepted and treated as
equals, with no mental reservations. It has to be friendship with no holds
barred, or perhaps there will be no friendship at all.[16]

The historical record of America's emergence from a colonial status and the lessons of American family life should have taught
Americans that there is no people and no individual more touchy
about national or personal rights or more eager to assert them than
those who are newly independent or are aspiring to be so. Yet Americans find this Asian and African insistence on equality to be hardly
tolerable. Despite the heritage of which Singh spoke, Americans do
have serious "mental reservations" about recognizing in others the
equality they demand for themselves.

The recognition of a former inferior's equality is interpreted necessarily by the self-reliant man as detracting from his superior position. What he must do is to combat his fear and reassure himself of
his own importance through external signs: popular acclaim, residence in restricted neighborhoods, membership in exclusive clubs,
and other indications which not infrequently take the form of outright violence inflicted upon the impudent inferiors to keep them in
their places. On a national plane, the fear of becoming inferior is less
allayed by economic aid than by force of arms.

With this in view it becomes understandable why, since World

War II, the total American aid to Western Europe was two and one half times that for all East Asia, but that our *annual* armament expenditure is now many times that of aid to all foreign countries for all the post-World War II years combined.[17] For if it is a question of aid, Americans would far prefer to give to Europe than to Asia or Africa. Europeans, being white, are still superior to Asians and Africans, though inferior to Americans. But when it is a question of aid or force, Americans really do not care to give themselves a choice at all.

Outside of arms, Western superiority vis-à-vis the East is sometimes also defended under a veil of "love" for China and the Chinese. Holders of such views hate what communism has done to that "wonderful" and "traditional" country and its ancient institutions, and are really "sorry" for the hapless and suffering Chinese. Some years ago the *New Yorker* magazine featured a long article most of which seemed to be a report of the opinions of a European Catholic priest, Father LaDany. The magazine quoted a long excerpt from an essay of the good priest, according to whom all changes brought about by the Communist revolution are bad except, in a residual way, those resulting from reactions to the revolution, where the "real" Chinese values occupied a central place.

It is wonderful to walk around the hills of Hong Kong or roam in the picturesque Mediterranean streets of Macao and look from either place at the hills beyond, for one does not see there any curtain, iron or bamboo. . . . Away from the Peking daily press, one sees beyond the hills a wonderful land . . . where from the time of Confucius philosophers have been discussing good government, where lawyers had worked out a legal system comparable to that of the Romans, where Buddhist philosophy found a fertile soil in the speculative mystical Taoist mind . . . where the rhythm of life was different from that of any other country, where a foreigner could feel at home once he had mastered the language, sonorous, musical, strong and delicate . . . where the storyteller in the market place recited to the rhythmic accompaniment of the castanets endless stories from the Three Kingdoms, where each one knew the village from which his ancestors had come and many simple folk could trace the family tree back for centuries. . . . Looking at her in this mood, one is not inclined to see in China of today the dark blotches, the terror, the millions of youths toiling painfully in the border lands, the handful of wicked men in command, the superhuman, or subhuman, labor of the masses. Once a year one wants to look at China, wonderful even today, and at that China only. . . . There are true and not merely fictitious values in China as she is now. Communism, like every terrifying power in history, from the Pharaohs, to Hitler, has its values, order, creativeness, dynamism, tenacity, and idealism, however distorted. It also creates values by reaction, as a challenge to thought and to a search for other solutions. China the wonderful is there in the "reactionaries," men of culture who strive to salvage the Chinese heritage even at the risk of their lives. It is also there deep in the reality of their daily life.[18]

The reader can easily appreciate the Alice in Wonderland world that Father LaDany shares with all his kindred souls. But is the Father LaDany kind of mental picture of China rare among Americans today? I hope so but am not sure.

Two years ago my wife and I were invited to a luncheon by the wives of some educators and businessmen, to brief them on China. They and their husbands were soon to take a three-week tour of the People's Republic. The ladies were busy studying guidebooks, short histories of China, and geography. They knew that tips were out in China, but what gifts should they give their guides in appreciation? And how could they avoid offending their Chinese hosts and hostesses?

Among the materials they were studying was a long letter from a friend of one of the ladies who had a China connection, who claimed to speak Chinese fluently. The letter is too lengthy to quote in full, but some excerpts follow:

> I am thrilled for you and wish I was packing for China instead of Switzerland. It was an emotional trip for me two years ago for I was actually seeing the sights and streets of my childhood. . . . I am sure you have been deluged with suggestions so the following may be very repetitive. . . . Glue—take a small bottle or tube, . . . as most the stamps are glueless and their glue is awful. Paper matches—they have only the bulky little wooden matches and they are hard to carry. (You can gauge the sophistication and standard of living of a country by their matches.) Bob . . . reports that most underdeveloped countries have wooden matches.

The correspondent went on to list some other items to bring, from tea bags and instant coffee to soap and Kleenex. She concluded with what she meant by her "emotional" relationship with China:

> Since we were there for business purposes they (the Chinese) were far more anxious for us to see modern China but my interest was in the old since I had tender memories of tap dancing with my sisters at the Altar of

the Sky at the Temple of Heaven so I insisted on several sentimental journeys.

My fellow anthropologists will agree with me that the author of this letter is not a reliable source on China and the Chinese. Her relation with the Chinese is not unlike that between many a white hunter in Africa and his "beaters," or even his victims whose stuffed heads adorn his living room walls at home. But her advice was seriously studied by highly placed Americans about to visit China.

While revision of American perceptions of China remains problematic, one fact is clear. Those who wish to change or to prevent change in Asia by force, and those who hope that Asia will slowly meander its ancient way are both hopelessly out of date.

Asians, Africans, and Pacific Islanders too do not care to be patient curios waiting for the admiring glances of the West, nor do they want to be told that only the Soviet Union or the United States know what is best for them. That era has long passed. What the Soviet Union and the United States—two of the three most powerful nations on earth—must understand is the importance of cultivating voluntary cooperation on the part of their weaker or have-not brethren with whom they hope to live in peace and to work together constructively, or whose development they hope, each in its own way, to guide.

For this purpose, both the United States and Russia have to make realistic assessments not only of what they need but also what Asians and Africans need; not only what they see as right or wrong, but also what Asians and Africans see as right or wrong; not only to analyze their own fears and anxieties but also the fears and anxieties of Asians and Africans; not only to mind their own security and status drives but also the security and status drives of Asians and Africans.

Powerful and prosperous nations must make efforts not to aggravate the inferiority feelings of the less powerful and the less prosperous nations, just as it is wise for the rich people in any society to avoid inciting inferiority feelings or resentment among the poor. When we used our enormous air power with the express purpose of pounding the North Vietnamese into submission and forcing them to come to the conference table to participate in what we described as "unconditional discussion,"[19] it reminded one of the biblical story of David and Goliath. The Western world has always admired little David because he vanquished the giant instead of submitting to him despite the obvious disparity in their relative strengths. The self-reliant man can justly be proud of his own achievements in the spirit of little David against overwhelming odds. But did it seem possible that the leaders of North Vietnam or other non-Western nations were totally ignorant of the story of David and Goliath? Was it rational for Americans to expect themselves to act as fearless Davids while at the same time expecting others to submit like faint-hearted cowards?

The Enemy Within

The preceding analysis does not mean that aid extended through UNRRA, AID, the Peace Corps, and other agencies has been useless, or that American advisers to premiers and farmers have not been helpful. Yet this framework cannot be given real substance unless there is a critical change in the American outlook. Otherwise aid to the rest of the world will be too small to be effective, the American attitude will be too overbearing to be palatable, and America's resources will be chiefly consumed in the production of weapons.

However, although the problem of America's relationships with other nations is great, it pales when compared with the danger from within the American society itself. Ever since the rise of communism in Russia, Americans have not merely been the chief architect for international alliances against communism; they have also defined the danger from within as Communist infiltration of government, labor, education, and the arts. This American preoccupation with the menace of communism becomes apparent when we contrast it to the lack of a Communist scare in Japan after World War II.

For its own imperialist purposes, a Japanese government under the military allied itself with anti-Communist Nazi Germany and Fascist Italy at the time of World War II. It invaded Manchuria and attempted to conquer China on that platform. But since she has divested herself of military imperialism, Japan seems far less concerned with communism next door and at home than does her senior ally, the United States. Why then are Americans so fearful of communism?

I suggest that the answer lies in a well-known psychological mechanism. Human beings are likely to be most fearful of that which is most attractive to them. The Roman emperors were once fearful of Christianity; they used to throw the Christians to the lions. The Catholic church was once terribly afraid of Protestants; it used to persecute them under the Holy Inquisition and burn the heretics at the stake. But the Romans became Christians, and the Catholic church has now liberalized its canons and steered its liturgies away from Latin, and is being pressed from within on questions such as the use of the "pill" and marriage for priests and nuns. On the other hand, the Chinese who have never persecuted the missionaries except for one brief mob outburst in 1900, have successfully resisted conversion. Could it be that Americans are most fearful of communism or totalitarianism because this type of ideology offers something most attractive to them?

I find it hard to answer this question in the negative; and the foregoing analysis of the individual-centered way of life seems to lend support to my answer.

The immediate needs of the discontented Chinese since 1842 were of two kinds. Their material need was not of a sort that "agrarian reformers" could wholly rectify. Its source was in the overbearing cost of government. The psychological need was for a renewed sense of national dignity and individual self-respect. The people either supported or acquiesced in the Communist victory because the Communists met the first of these needs by reducing taxes and eliminating graft. They fulfilled the second need by giving a majority of the downtrodden a voice and a sense of involvement in the larger Chinese world, and by humiliating and expelling all Westerners regardless of whether these Westerners as individuals had or had not contributed to the well-being of the Chinese.[20]

The sources of discontent in the West are of a different and more complex kind. As I have remarked in several connections throughout this book, the primary cause of American discontent is that fragmentation of family and community life and isolation of the individual which are direct consequences of the emphasis placed upon individual self-reliance. Though at its extreme in America, this discontent is common to the people of all Western nations. Detached from the primary groups and isolated from close ties with fellow human beings, the Western individual has turned to the conquest of the physical environment or to the search for eternal Truth and God for status and security. This orientation has found expression in pursuits as dissimilar on their surface as utopian writings, scientific inquiry, exploration of unknown frontiers on earth and in space, gigantic commercial and colonial empires or worldwide establishments and crusades to spread the Word or to save souls. But none of these endeavors is permanently satisfying to the individual because none can fulfill the deeply felt need for close and lasting human associations and that sense of purposefulness in life which only those associations can provide.

It is, I believe, the restoration of a sense of belonging and the provision of a purpose in life which is the fundamental attraction of totalitarianism to Westerners.

Not unnaturally, Westerners hold the view that Communism's appeal is economic in origin. This to a limited extent is undeniably true. There is, for example, evidence that Western Europeans voted for Communist slates in alarming numbers in the first postwar years[21] and that this number has declined somewhat as European recovery progressed. In this sense, Marshall Plan aid was money well spent and those programs, such as the Schuman Plan, whose goal was the economic stability of Europe were of some importance. But in regard to the Communist parties themselves, it must be seriously questioned that this loss of voting strength has in any way altered their goals, dimmed the loyalty of their true ideological supporters, or canceled their attraction for the isolated individual looking for a cause. Whether in Asia or the West, men who are searching for a way out of economic distress or struggling to free themselves of oppression will swell the ranks of any movement that offers them hope. But once their basic objectives are reached, the Chinese tend again to be content and find little or no need to give further active support to such movements. That tendency, as we saw in the last chapter, is the basic stumbling block to the future of ideological communism in China, and is the very tendency the Chinese leaders are endeavoring to overcome. Most Westerners, however much their lives are bettered economically still suffer from an emotional vacuum which they can fill only by continued espousal of the cause and continued efforts to achieve new conquests in its name.[22]

In the Marxian interpretation of history and in its doctrinal elaborations by Lenin, Stalin, and Engels, we come closer to the primary appeal of communism. The fact that Marxism is, in the first instance, economic is only incidental to the fact that it also provides answers, certainty, and direction to life. It gives meaning not only to history but to the day-to-day life of the believer. Communism provides him with a faith he can avow, and in that avowal it assures him he is joining not simply the ranks of an ordinary political party but by this very act becomes himself the chosen instrument of history and a director of mankind's destiny. In brief, the believer has restored to him that focus and sense of purposefulness and identity which he has been deprived of by the isolation of the individual in Western society. Further, communism, despite widespread belief to the contrary, does not ask this individual to break with what is most fundamental in Western culture. Communism, as I have already suggested, is in fact the latest culmination of tendencies and attributes that are much deeper in the mainstream of Western life than is commonly supposed.

To begin with, let us quote first from the personal histories of three well-known former Communists and then from a study of a single Western Communist party to see if in these individual testimonials and this group study we do not see further corroboration of much that has concerned us throughout this book. *The God That Failed* consists of autobiographical essays by six individuals—Arthur Koestler, Ignazio Silone, Richard Wright, André Gide, Louis Fischer, and Stephen Spender—on their committal of faith to communism and their eventual disillusionment. In this volume we read:

KOESTLER: I became converted because I was ripe for it and lived in a disintegrating society thirsting for faith. . . . I was ripe . . . as a result of my personal case-history, thousands of other members of the intelligentsia and the middle class of my generation were ripe for it, by virtue of other personal case-histories; but, however much these differed from case to case, they had a common denominator: the rapid disintegration of moral values, of the pre-1914 pattern of life in postwar Europe, and the simultaneous lure of the new revelation which had come from the East. . . . To say that one had "seen the light" is a poor description of the mental rapture which only the convert knows. . . . There is now an answer to all questions, doubts and conflicts are a matter of the tortured past—a past already remote, when one had lived in dismal ignorance in the tasteless, colorless world of those who *don't know.* Nothing henceforth can disturb the convert's inner serenity—except the occasional fear of losing faith again, losing thereby what makes life worth living. . . . Both morally and logically the Party was infallible. . . . Renegades from the Party were lost souls, fallen out of grace; to argue with them, even to listen to them, meant trafficking with the Powers of Evil. . . . (We were) the only righteous men in a crooked world. . . . Those who were caught by the great illusion of our time, and have lived through its moral and intellectual debauch either give themselves up to a new addiction of the opposite type, or are condemned to pay with a life-long hangover.[23]

SILONE: The phenomenon which most impressed me, when I arrived at the age of reason, was the violent contrast . . . between family and private life . . . and social relations. . . . For me to join the Party . . . was not just a simple matter of signing up with a political organization; it meant a conversion, a complete dedication. . . . One had to change one's own name, abandon every former link with family and friends. . . . The Party became family, school, church, barracks; the world that lay beyond it was to be destroyed and built anew. The psychological mechanism whereby each single militant becomes progressively identified with the collective organization is the same as that used in certain religious orders and military colleges, with almost identical results. Every sacrifice was welcomed as a personal contribution to the "price of collective redemption." . . . Anyone who thinks he can wean the best and most serious-minded young people away from Communism by enticing them into a well-warmed hall to play billiards, starts from an extremely limited and unintelligent conception of mankind. . . . The day I left the Communist Party was a very sad one for me, it was like a day of deep mourning, the mourning for my lost youth. . . . I carefully avoided . . . ending up in one of the many groups and splinter groups of ex-Communists . . . as I know well the kind of fate which rules over these . . . and makes little sects of them which have all the defects of official Communism—the fanaticism, the centralization, the abstraction. . . . But my faith in Socialism . . . has remained more alive than ever in me. . . . It has gone back to what it was when I first revolted against the old order; a refusal to admit the existence of destiny, an extension of the ethical impulse from the restricted individual and family sphere to the whole domain of human activity, a need for effective brotherhood, an affirmation of the superiority of the human person over all the economic and social mechanisms which oppress him. . . . There has been added to this . . . a feeling of reverence for that which in man is always trying to outdistance itself, and lies at the root of eternal disquiet.[24]

WRIGHT: I was meeting men and women . . . who were to form the first sustained relationships of my life. . . . It was not the economics of Communism, nor the great power of trade unions, nor the excitement of underground politics that claimed me; my attention was caught by the similarity of the experiences of workers in other lands, by the possibility of uniting scattered but kindred peoples into a whole. . . . Here at last, in the realm of revolutionary expression, Negro experience could find a home, a functioning value and role. . . . I had made the first total emotional commitment of my life. . . .

(Of the trial of an erring Party member, Wright reports:) The trial began in a quiet, informal manner. The comrades acted like a group of neighbors sitting in judgment upon one of their kind who had stolen a chicken. Anybody could ask and get the floor. . . . Yet the meeting had an amazingly formal structure of its own, a structure that went as deep as the desire of men to live together. . . . A member of the Central Committee . . . rose and gave a description of the world situation. . . . He painted a horrible but masterful picture of Fascism's aggression in Germany, Italy, and Japan. . . . It was imperative that here be postulated against what or whom Ross's crime had been committed. . . . The next speaker discussed the role of the Soviet Union as the world's lone workers' state. . . . Not one word had been said of the accused. . . . An absolute had first to be established in the minds of the comrades so that they could measure the success or failure of their deeds by it. Finally a speaker came forward and spoke of Chicago's South Side, its Negro population, their suffering and handicaps, linking all that also to the world struggle. Then still another speaker . . . described the tasks of the Communist Party on the South Side. At last, the world, the national, and the local pictures had been fused into one overwhelming drama of moral struggle in which everybody in the hall was participating. . . . This presentation . . . enthroned a new sense of reality in the hearts of those present, a sense of man on earth. With the exception of the church and its myths and legends, there was no agency in the world so capable of making men feel the earth and the people upon it as the Communist Party. Toward evening the direct charges against Ross were made, not by the leaders of the Party, but by Ross's friends, those who knew him best! . . . No one was terrorized into giving information against him. They gave it willingly. . . . The moment came for Ross to defend himself. . . . He stood trembling; he tried to talk and his words would not come. . . . His personality, his sense of himself, had been obliterated. Yet he could not have been so humbled unless he had shared and accepted the vision that had crushed him, the common vision that bound us all together. "Comrades," he said . . . , "I'm guilty of all the charges. . . ." No one prodded him. . . . No one tortured him. No one threatened him. He was free to go out of the hall and never see another Communist. But he did not want to. He could not. The vision of the communal world had sunk down into his soul and it would never leave him until life left him. He talked on, outlining how he had erred, how he would reform.[25]

Since the remaining three contributors were never active members of the Communist party, although they, too, were caught up in its promise, I shall not quote from their reminiscences.[26] It is sufficient to say that the remaining accounts are as revelatory as the preceding, deviating only in that the writers were "worshippers from afar." If it is objected that these men are artists or intellectuals, and therefore not typical Communists, I say again, that the artist or the intellectual of renown is the mirror of his society and the articulate voice of millions whose discontent, needs, and responses are no less real because they are not verbalized.

The group study, an analysis of the Communists party's organization and operation in France, is by A. Rossi and entitled *A Communist Party in Action*. In this work, Rossi shows how party membership provides one and all with the satisfactions so eloquently described by their more famous former brethren. Says Rossi:

> This act (of becoming a Party member) . . . is analogous not to the act by which one joins other political parties but to the act by which one joins a church, i.e., while it is not necessarily irreversible, it binds the individual for so long as he remains a member, to a *way of life*—a way of life, furthermore, so different from other ways of life that no man can make the adjustments necessary for it without giving up, in most cases once and for all, a part of his personality. . . . However up-to-date its organization and tactics, the Party ministers to its members' primitive—or, if you like, basic—need to *belong*. . . . The Party asserts control over every department of their lives, and recognizes no dividing line between the political and the personal. The militant, therefore, either subordinates himself and all his interests to the Party, or invites certain consequences that are sure to give him pause. The Party is a movement to which he belongs, a community in which he lives, and a way of life in which he participates. It is the supreme reality. . . . The Party is . . . less a party than an ecclesia. . . . It possesses certain characteristics which Georges Sorel, when he found them in the socialist and working-class movements in their early days, regarded as repetitions of the mores and tendencies of the early Christian communities. The Party, like the "evangelical" socialism of which Sorel wrote, ministers to certain deep-seated needs— both of the masses and of their elites. . . . The Communism of the Communist Party is a *societas perfecta,* with its own values, its own hierarchy, and its own mores—a society-within-a-society which regards itself as destined to destroy the society it is within. Your true Communist thinks of himself as already a citizen of another polity, as subordinated to its laws even as he awaits the time when he can impose them upon others. The Party is the model-in-miniature of the new society, and it is all the easier to recognize as such because that new society already lives and has its being over a sixth of the earth's surface. . . . The Party comes to be at once the militant's family, his way of life, and his fatherland; and Party "spirit" comes to be his supreme value, which he must cultivate and nourish incessantly. . . . The proletariat is what matters, because its historical mission is to represent the general interest. The Communist Party, as the party of the proletariat, is the unique bearer of the nation's mission and thus, ultimately, of the mission of all mankind; so that the Party, at the apex of the pyramid, speaks and acts for them all.[27]

It is commonly assumed that all of this represents something uniquely and radically different in Western society. Rossi speaks of "a new kind of party" that is producing "a new kind of Frenchman."

However, I want to cite a few sentences from a study much like Rossi's of the revolutionary party of Robespierre, a party consisting largely of the middle class, not the proletariat, that in its power at the time of the French Revolution bore unmistakable resemblances to the subject of Rossi's inquiry. I refer to Crane Brinton's *The Jacobins* a pioneer scientific examination of a revolutionary group in Western society.

In the doctrines of Rousseau, the philosophic father of Jacobinism, Brinton notes that the "general will" was the expression of divine law, and

> If the individual does not share in the mystic loyalty of the general will, if he sets his will against that of a society, it is a proof that he is not in a state of grace. His is a will to evil. But no man is free in doing evil. To prevent him is to free him, and release his free will, which is that of the society. The Jacobins of Limoge . . . put it clearly: "Is it not to be in reality the friend of one's brothers to force them, in a manner of speaking, to accept the cup of salvation which is offered them in the name of reason and humanity?" Robespierre said more neatly: "The revolutionary government is the despotism of liberty against tyranny."[28]

What, in its final consequences, is the distinction between Rousseau's "general will" and Marx's "will of history"? And how far is it from the concept that the Jacobins are the vehicle of the general will to the thesis that the Bolsheviks are the bearers of the will of history? Or from the doctrine that therefore "the revolutionary government (the Jacobins) is the despotism of liberty against tyranny" to the contention that "the dictatorship of the proletariat" (the Bolsheviks) is likewise "the despotism of liberty against tyranny"? We may say of the Communists, as Brinton did of the Jacobins, "with upright hearts and clear consciences, they could proceed to the Terror."

Nor should we be surprised to find that in the Jacobin clubs, as in the Communist party, "grace, sin, heresy, repentance, regeneration have their place." The prototype of the trial of Ross in Richard Wright's narrative occurred time and again within the Jacobin clubs. Says Brinton, "Sessions were held to determine the orthodoxy of the whole membership of a society. . . . A member of the Lyons society writes of these in terms that make equally clear how far these were tests of conscience and of ability to withstand a common inquisition: 'This tribunal of the conscience of man and the justice of the people is terrible indeed, but it is also just. The most practiced audacity, the most refined hypocrisy disappeared before the watchful and penetrating eyes of the sound members of the society and of the numerous citizens who filled the gallery.' " It is also in keeping with the preceding that "Robespierre and his more sincere followers conceived themselves to be the small band of the elect . . ."; that there was an "insistence on inner, emotional conviction of righteousness"; that the "Jacobins did not feel of their opponents that they were wrong . . . but that they had sinned." It appears that Rossi's new kind of Frenchman is not new at all, either in his adopted country or elsewhere in the West.[29]

I have devoted this much attention to the Jacobins, to the ways of Western Communist parties and to the emotions and beliefs of the followers to show that communism, in America as well as Europe, is not a distinctly new phenomenon but one that is rooted in the Western way of life. It is all there: the great abstractions, the absolutes, the struggle between good and evil, the doctrine of infallibility. From these come missionary zeal, self-righteousness, martyrdom, persecution, and the refusal to compromise. The use of religious terminology and concepts in either the "godless" Russia of the twentieth century or the "godless" France of 1789 is neither fortuitous nor an artificial transfer of the religious emotion to secular affairs. It is the product of what is inherently Western.

It is not by chance that, having forsaken the Communist theology by which he would once have rescued all mankind from sin, Whittaker Chambers and others in a similar position would tell us that our salvation now depends on following them into another orthodoxy to which they have been converted. To those who possess the inner light, the final truth, their fellows live in darkness, and it is the mission of the righteous to save all men from the error of their ways. It was fitting that it was Rossi's friends who testified against him, for who could be more interested in restoring him to the path of the elect, of helping him to expiate his sins and erase his guilt, than his friends?

Similarly, the officials of the Holy Inquisition, in addressing themselves to those being tried for religious heresy, were careful to explain that they acted not as the persecutors but as the friends of the accused. They did not wish to burn them for their sins, but rather to restore them to a state of grace. If this proved impossible, if sinners were unwilling to be saved, then naturally the stake was their fate. In the Jacobins' efforts to preserve the "purity" of their clubs and of their members' thoughts, in the periodic "cleansing" of the Communist hierarchy and of the Communist rank and file, are we confronted by phenomena essentially different from one another?

Just as the wish to impose one's own abstract principles on others gives rise to persecution and purges, so do these abstractions and the organizations founded to advance them appeal to the isolated individual by restoring to him a sense of purposefulness in life that makes it possible for him to become the type of man commonly called "the enemy within." Whatever may have been his particular "case history," as Koestler called it, Klaus Fuchs, the atomic scientist who delivered vital secrets to the Soviet Union not for material rewards but to assist the cause to which he belonged, was such a man. Said Gordon Dean, chairman of the Atomic Energy Commission, of this case:

> Fuchs is the type of man who . . . apparently owes his allegiance to nothing that ordinary humans owe theirs to. He is going to make his own decisions regardless of any rules he purports to operate under. What do you do with a man like that? Usually he is a very intelligent man. He is an independent man. He is an idealist of some kind. He might be a Communist idealist, but he is an idealist of some kind. You don't usually spot this kind in a (security) check.[30]

Although Dean is right in summing up the security problem presented by men like Fuchs ("an idealist of some kind"), it is erroneous to assume that they owe their "allegiance to nothing that ordinary humans owe theirs to." Ordinary Westerners do give allegiance to other causes because of what are fundamentally the same compulsions that directed Fuchs to give his loyalty to communism. The danger that Fuchs and his comrades present is the obverse of the coin that makes others who possess similar but differently directed compulsions a point of strength in Western society. Out of his study of the Fuchs case and others like it, Alan Moorehead concluded, "The seat of treason in each case is the same: the inner conviction of the accused that what he is doing is right."[31]

It is this inner conviction—precisely the same Jacobinian "inner, emotional conviction of righteousness" that Brinton noted—that upheld the early Christians in their struggles and sent missionaries to the ends of the earth, that supported the great Western scientists who advanced new concepts and made possible revolutionary inventions, and that sustained numberless others through lifelong trials that the average Chinese would back away from at his earliest opportunity. The conditions that create the so-called enemy within have been present in the West for centuries and cannot be wholly dealt with by security checks of their end product. Such precautions are indeed necessary in these critical times, but the crucial and as yet unanswered question is how are we to develop a preventive more far-reaching than loyalty boards and one that will see us through tests yet to come?

Koestler concluded that he and others became "ripe" for communism because they lived in a "disintegrating society thirsting for faith." As the answer to communism, Rossi suggested that France reestablish "the moral foundations of national unity" where "the bonds of community have grown weak" by "an attempt to persuade the masses of men to accept an ideal other than that which the Communists have offered." I submit that this is partly so; the bonds of community are indeed weak, but not for the reasons that Rossi has offered, nor is the route to safety in the direction that Rossi and others would take us. Rossi says we must reestablish our moral foundations in the *political* community. Silone would have us affirm "the superiority of the human person over all *economic and social* mechanisms which oppress him." (Italics mine.) Their common ground is plain enough, call it what you will. The answer to communism, they and many others say, is a new or rejuvenated ideal, a militant faith to believe in, a spiritual rebirth, a new individualistic and moral foundation for political, economic, and social life. What they want is more of the same.

At this point some readers may see, as my friend Stuart Gerry Brown did, an inner contradiction in this analysis. If what communism has to offer fits so well with what the individual-centered man needs, why has the American Communist party never attracted more than perhaps a hundred thousand members?

The answer is not complex. Totalitarianism cannot function unless there are two sides: there must be leaders determined to impose their wills and ideas on others and there must also be followers who are, for whatever reason, eager to relate to the leaders emotionally, to carry out their wills with enthusiasm and to submit to their dictates voluntarily. This totalitarianism may be found in different human arenas: interpersonal, economic, therapeutic, religious, or political. We know political totalitarianism well, Fascist or Communist. But is a cult group which requires of its believers unquestioned total submission to its leader, tenets, and rituals not a form of totalitarianism in action?

Being individual-centered, Americans grow up wishing to buck authority no matter where, and ready to compete with each other by all means. They tend, therefore, each to go his or her separate ways, "to go into business on my own."

What we have in America as a result are, instead of a tendency for one totalitarian establishment to control all or most of the society, a galaxy of totalitarian establishments each with its absolute leader, supreme or only truth, and rituals which assert control of every department of their willing followers' lives. Being members of such a group gives the individual-centered person a warm relationship with others (sociability), purpose and certainty (security), and a strong sense of being the chosen and the only righteous ones against the outside crooked or fallen world (status).

How else can we explain the proliferation of cults from the milder ones such as the Dharma Realm Buddhist Monastery and University at Ukiah and the Nyingma Institute in Berkeley and Sonoma to the more militant such as the Unification Church of Rev. Sun Myung-Moon, Synanon, the Church of Scientology, and the People's Temple, made notorious by the tragedy in Jonestown? As we pointed out before, not all ardent supporters of such movements are the poor and ignorant. Many of those active in the Buddhist monasteries and Moon's Unification Church who obey their masters with extreme postures of obeisance are highly educated holders of graduate degrees from major American universities.

In addition to such competing totalitarian establishments, another aspect of American life fits the pictures as well. This is increasing interpersonal violence in our midst: rape, murder (especially motiveless murder), assault on the elderly and the handicapped, and even mayhem against caged animals in zoos.

The usual view is that these are works of the mentally deranged or the misguided minority. That view reminds me of what the psychiatrist David G. Hubbard, Director of Aberrant Behavior Center in Dallas, Texas said a few years ago about airplane hijackers. These men are schizophrenic paranoics, he said. They are suffering from a sense of failure, for example, inadequate masculinity. But after also claiming that "the hijacker is unique, he should be treated as such" the psychiatrist admitted that there are an estimated eight million Americans with the psychiatric syndrome he described.[32] Add to the above the estimated one million cases of incest and several million cases of battered children and physically abused wives a year[33], and we obtain a situation that is no longer marginal to the individual-centered way of life, but fundamental.

Some clinicians may see violence as an attention getting device by its perpetrators. But as one self-reliant individual's decision to force his private will on some victim, interpersonal violence is but the smallest building block of totalitarianism on a national scale.

Interpersonal violence is not confined to societies with any particular way of life. But its quantity and variety are not universal. Unless we appreciate the link between it and the psycho-cultural factors underlying totalitarianism, and develop our preventive work from that premise, we will have no hope ever of reducing it any more than we can prevent future Jonestowns.

However, when all is said, are cults and interpersonal violence safety valves which prevent the American society from turning totalitarian from within?

I have tried to show that, for lack of a better word, Western spirituality is a consequence of the individual's detachment from the primary groups. This spirituality is responsible both for the material magnificence of Western culture and also for its recurring determination to destroy what it has created. It is this committal to the abstract which is responsible for a government of laws and a bill of rights, but it also makes it possible for the West to kill millions of men in the name of the salvation of mankind. It is the doctrine of absolute evil that enables the West to be so relentless in its attack upon social ills but, in its complement as the belief in absolute good, leads Westerners into imposing their particular brand of the good upon each other and upon other peoples of the world.

And I wish to say further that the purposelessness and insecurity of the liberated individual will not be redressed with any degree of permanence by a restoration or reaffirmation of "faith," be it political, economic, or moral. The road that begins in individualism and self-reliance travels surely and directly to the totalitarian state. Paradoxical though this seems to be, the present direction of Western society is proof enough of its validity. In pursuing self-reliance, the individualist societies undermine kinship and community ties, prevent intimacy among human beings except in the marital sphere, consciously attack all customs and traditions, and glorify instability and change. If there is no longer the unity of the primary group, there is the unity of the Communist party or the Hitler Youth Corps, or the yippie colony, or a Manson family, or a People's Temple, or a secret society for anti-Establishment, or the Ku Klux Klan, or the crime syndicate. If direction is no longer provided by custom and tradition, there is the demagogue to point the way. If instability and change leave us without anchorage, the police state is ready to assign us a place and a number in the scheme of things. If, in sum, we do not "belong," if we are purposeless and insecure, Big Brother is ready to admit us to his society, solve our problems for us, and otherwise provide us with what we desire. He grants us the opportunity for emotional release in gigantic parades, monstrous rallies, and organized violence. He gives us the fanatical "faith" the Western spirit craves: the absolutes, the abstractions, a sense of mission and infallibility, the symbols to hate and the symbols to love. He asks but one price, and this price millions have proved themselves ready to pay: the surrender of personal freedom.

Extreme individualism thus ends by destroying the liberty it intended to defend, and Western society as a whole wrecks itself against the rocks upon which it builds. With the advent of ultimate weapons, Western men now hold the potentiality of destroying the world with them in this process. It is indeed ironic that Americans, having jointly with other Westerners broken down Japanese and Chinese doors and foisted their presence on the Asians, had to use the atom bomb on the Japanese and for long have thought they needed containment or antiballistic missiles to "protect" themselves against the Chinese. Those who believe in destruction will surely project their own belief onto others.

The Communist appeal to the West and to China is thus of two different kinds, though, in the most fundamental sense, communism has found its source of strength in a response to what was, in each case, the basic weakness of the society. However, despite the fact that the Communists have triumphed in China while they have at least been brought to a temporary standstill in the West, I cannot but believe that in the long run the West, by way of the irrevocable polarization of its individual-centered peoples behind major or minor causes, stands in more serious danger of succumbing to communism or some other brand of totalitarianism than does China.

The Chinese are not motivated by abstract principles. They believed themselves to be superior to others, but never saw themselves as the chosen people who alone would live while all others would perish. They do not see the world or mankind as irreparably divided between the absolutely good and the absolutely evil, the completely just and the completely unjust. The Chinese do not commit themselves to one god—be that god a religious deity, a philosopher of dialectical materialism, or a little father in Moscow or Peking. They lack the zeal of the missionary—be that missionary a preacher of Christianity or Marxism—to carry the one message of truth to the unenlightened, much less to enforce that message upon the disinterested or unwilling. National militancy, class struggle, inevitable war, unconditional surrender—all of these are ideas that fit the Western pattern of life but which are in fact wholly alien to the Chinese. If the Chinese believe that there is sin, it is the unforgivable fault of setting son against father, group against group, and insisting that one man, class, race, religion, or nation must drive another to ruin and construct the future upon the wreckage.

Why these things are so has been the subject of this book. The Chinese have their place. They belong. They, therefore, do not give themselves irrevocably to gods or heroes, nor do they seek the infinite or attempt to exercise total control over the finite. The fundamental impulse of the Chinese is to live and let live and thus preserve what they cherish most—the solidity of human relations within the primary group, and the assurance that human relations beyond it will help and not endanger it. Between the individual and the totalitarian state, protecting the freedom of the former and warding off the impositions of the latter, stands this primary group and all those institutional bulwarks of men and custom which arise out of it and are associated with it. But in the West, as every year passes, between the individual and his freedom and the state and its authority there is less of this type of protection. It is just this bulwark of human solidarity that individualism and self-reliance have succeeded in weakening and even destroying. And it is upon these troubled ruins that totalitarianism arises.

It is true that the superstructure of such a totalitarianism has already established itself in China. Mass demonstrations, persecution, leader worship, slogan shouting, vigilante-type bands invading the cities—all the drummed up enthusiasms of Western political movements in general and totalitarian parties in particular are being utilized by the Chinese Communists. Probably many Chinese are more easily captivated by such techniques than they would otherwise have been if they had not been introduced to them during the preceding century of Western influence. Neither must we underestimate the determination of the Communist elite, a trained and dedicated leadership group in the Western pattern, and the amount of influence which it can exert during this period of transition. The turbulence of the last thirty years in China under communism is a certain indication that the Chinese are beginning to draw some of the Western-type battle lines as they have never done before, or are resisting them.

But of this we may be certain: the wholesale transformation of a society, particularly one that has through two millennia proved itself doggedly resistant to fundamental change, cannot occur without a persistent willingness of the society's members to cooperate *actively* in the effort. A Hitler or a Stalin cannot run a nation singlehandedly. Each must be supported by millions of fervent devotees who are willing to die for the hero and his cause. And it is precisely this unalterable devotion to a cause, particularly the cause of radical and total change, that the average Chinese lacks. Having satisfied his immediate social needs in primary groups with which he is tied in a network of duties, obligations, and privileges, he sees no reason to strain himself further and he has little time and fervor for anything else.

To transform this attitude into one of permanent militancy requires more than tinkering with the social machine which has produced the Chinese-type man and his way of life. It requires instead the total destruction of that machine and the creation of a new one whose end product would be the Western-type man—isolated, insecure, purposeless, and therefore perpetually in search of something to which he can belong and for which he can fight. This means that to succeed wholly in the Western mode the Communists would have to destroy what the Chinese value most, the kinship and local loyalties. This, as we saw in the last chapter, the Chinese leaders are not doing. Instead the basic building blocks of the new Chinese society— the commune—is still rooted in kinship and local ties. But the communes are far more actively linked with each other and with the larger national state via many features including new modes of production, distribution, communication, ideological exercises, and work assignments away from home.

The Chinese Communist leadership, in spite of twists and turns, seems to sense that if they hope to build a lasting Communist government and society, they must exercise their power in a way that is commensurate with the Chinese reality rather than Stalinist theory. It seems inevitable that communism will be a vastly different thing in China than it is in the West.[34]

The solidarity of the primary groups and the institutions and attitudes associated with them which are the consequences of the Chinese way of life are the true barriers to the growth of totalitarianism in China. But the West as a whole and America in particular cannot present this defense in depth. Within the West the path to totalitarianism has already been cleared, a path which the Chinese Communists have yet to open. Great armies and their deployment in worldwide conflicts are no answer to the fundamental threat, for these wars are themselves the final tragic evidence of Western insecurity and purposelessness and can only speed the day of totalitarian victory—whether that totalitarianism be the dictatorship of a Hitler, a Stalin, or an unknown who is now waiting off stage for his grand entrance.

Dire warnings from politicians and publicists against creeping or galloping socialism and impassioned appeals to return to the ways of the fathers will not deter the onward march of totalitarianism. For the individual's search for emotional security and purpose began when the self-reliant ways of the fathers undermined the primary and communal groups. And unless social cohesion is restored through those institutions then these aimless individuals will surrender *en masse*—despite their heritage of political liberty, despite constitutions, and despite noble sentiments—to the totalitarianism which gives them, in exchange for their freedom, that purposefulness and emotional security for which they yearn and which a society of extreme individualism denies them. The danger is neither distant nor abstract. It is with us now and it is concrete. And it cannot be ended or appreciably reduced by voting for one political party or another. The danger must be faced and fought where it begins—in the primary groups.

Thus together the peoples of China and America may yet prevent the success of totalitarianism: the Chinese by not entirely surrendering their pattern of mutual dependence within the primary groups and the Americans by rejuvenating those fundamental social units. The task of the Chinese is one of resistance to totalitarianism through the preservation of that basic source of strength which has for centuries been the stabilizing factor in Chinese life. The task of the Americans is resistance through a reduction of self-reliance and a concomitant increase of mutual dependence among men.

NOTES
1. Here we need to note that resentment or hatred is not incommensurate with envy.
2. In discussing the appeal of communism to Westerners we shall see that there is another kind of "discontent" and another variety of "needs" that communism purports to salve and fill.
3. Northrop, "The Mind of Asia."

4. This American psychology of preserving innocence of intent by the denial of the desire for power has been elegantly documented by William H. Blanchard in *Aggression American Style*. However, this same denial of the desire for power was not uncommon among Europeans in their colonial conquests. Thus a Frenchman wrote in the 1959 edition of the *Encyclopedia Britannica* about French conquest of Vietnam: "Nguyen Anh succeeded in organizing a counterrevolution in the south and, with the help of a French bishop . . . and a number of French officers, defeated the Tay-Son. . . . In 1802, under the name of Gia-Long, [he] became emperor of unified Vietnam (Annam). Gia-Long's policy of friendship with France, however, was abandoned by his successor Ming-Mang (1820–41) and Tu-Duc (1848–83), who began a terrible persecution of Christians. This led to intervention and eventually to conquest by France in the latter half of the 19th century and thus to a long period of French rule before Vietnam recovered its independence after World War II" (Hubert Deschamps, "Vietnam," *Encyclopedia Britannica*, p. 145A).

5. See Sir Richard Dane, "China and the So-called Opium War," *The Asiatic Review* 25 (1929):611–624, and G. E. Gaskill, "A Chinese Official's Experiences During the First Opium War," *The American Historical Review* 39 (1933):82–86.

6. Yen-yu Huang, "Viceroy Yeh Ming-ch'en and the Canton Episode (1856–1861)," *Harvard Journal of Asiatic Studies* 6 (1941):37–127.

7. The indemnity China agreed to pay the powers was U.S. $333 million at 4 percent interest, in thirty-nine annual installments. The United States federal budget for that year was $590 million.

8. Ten thousand Japanese with twenty-four guns; four thousand Russians with sixteen guns; three thousand British with twelve guns; two thousand Americans with six guns; eight hundred French with twelve guns; three hundred Germans and Italians. See Rev. Frederick Brown, *From T'ientsin to Peking with the Allied Forces*. Rev. Brown was a Methodist Episcopal missionary in T'ientsin, hired by the British Intelligence Unit of the British Expeditionary Force. For a comprehensive view of the Boxer Rebellion see Chester C. Tan, *The Boxer Catastrophe*.

9. The reader interested in the role of American involvement in China prior to Communist assumption of power will do well to read Tang Tsou, *America's Failure in China, 1941–50*.

10. Halberstam, *The Best and the Brightest*.

11. *Sources of Japanese Tradition*, compiled by Ryusaku Tsunoda, William Theodore de Bary, and Donald Keene, pp. 9–11. This took place in spite of the fact that Chinese forces never set foot in Japan.

12. Fu-yi Li, *"Chung Kuo Wen Hua Tui T'ai Kuo Ti Ying Hsiang"* [The influence of Chinese civilization on Thailand] in Sun-sheng Ling et al., *Chung T'ai Wen Hwa Lun Chi*, [*Collected essays on Chinese-Thai Civilizations*], pp. 236–237. Siam is another country where Chinese soldiers never set foot.

13. Ibid., pp. 63–64.

14. For a fuller exposition of the facts, see Francis L. K. Hsu, "The Myth of Chinese Expansionism," *Journal of Asian & African Studies* 13, nos. 3–4 (1978):184–195.

15. John K. Fairbank, "New Thinking about China," *Atlantic Monthly*, June 1966, pp. 77–78.

16. J. J. Singh, "How to Win Friends in Asia," *The New York Times Magazine*. (Singh was at the time the president of the Indian League of America.)

17. From 1949 to 1968 aid to East Asia was $6,638,134,000; aid to Europe, $15,227,546,000, *Operations Report*, Data as of December 31, 1967, Agency for International Development, Washington, D.C., p. 43. Estimated special defense support for South East Asia operations for the years 1965–68 are respectively as follows: $103,000,000; $5,812,000,000; $20,133,000,000; $26,547,000,000. Total national defense budget for the same respective years are: $45,973,000,000;

$54,179,000,000; $67,457,000,000; $77,373,000,000, *The Budget in Brief, Fiscal Year 1970.* In 1979 the defense budget was increased to $117,700,000,000. The estimated defense budgets for 1980 through to 1983 are $130,400,000,000, $146,200,000,000, $165,500,000,000, and $185,900,000,000, *The Budget in Brief, Fiscal Year 1981.* In 1978 all foreign aid came to $2,097,900,000, or about 2 percent of the 1979 defense budget. However, only about 8 percent of that amount went to Europe ($165,000,000), some 20 percent to East Asia ($452,100,000) and the bulk of it to the Middle East ($1,480,800,000), *U.S. Statistical Abstracts, 1980.*

18. "A Reporter at Large: The China Watchers," *The New Yorker,* February 17, 1966, pp. 106 and 108.

19. This American psychology continued to unfold itself as the second edition of this book went to press. Two years after the Paris conference began, following the cessation of U.S. bombing of North Vietnam, Defense Secretary Laird was to say that partial resumption of that bombing was our way to "shock" Hanoi into meaningful negotiations. Then President Nixon ordered the Cambodian invasion which was, according to White House officials at Key Biscayne, Florida, to "convince Hanoi . . . that the United States was not entirely predictable" (reported in *Sunday Star-Bulletin and Advertiser* [Honolulu], May 17, 1970).

20. The Reverend John Hayes, an American Presbyterian missionary who was born in China and who spent ten months in Chinese prison in 1951, had a clear view of this. In an interview with *U.S. News and World Report* (March 13, 1953) after his release, he described the soldiers who arrested him as "play acting." Thirty soldiers were dispatched to put him in jail. "Is the whole country run like that?" asked the interviewer. "No", responded Hayes. "They were out there to make a demonstration of the fact that the new Government could throw an American in jail whenever it wanted to . . ." (p. 36).

21. Monsieur Paul Dumard, the French tool- and diemaker who votes Communist is quoted as follows: "Hell, I have to work under any system. I got my family to think of. The kids need shoes and the wife needs a coat. Where the hell do you think I can get the money? What the workers want is a good standard of living and more opportunities for themselves and their kids.

"I don't care if the workers get a good standard of living under capitalism or socialism. It doesn't make any difference to me. I don't want a revolution; I just want change. It's none of my business what workers do in other countries. They don't concern themselves about me; why the hell should I concern myself about them? Let them fight their own battles, and I'll fight mine.

"But nothing I say is going to make any difference.

"All I want is to enjoy myself in this life. For all I know it may be the only one I have. When you're dead, maybe you've had it. Hell, I don't know. All I want is to have a good life, that's all. Is that too much?" (From *The Politics of Despair* by Hadley Cantril, pp. 221-222.)

22. For a penetrating analysis of this problem, see Philip E. Slater, *The Pursuit of Loneliness: American Culture at the Breaking Point.*

23. From *The God That Failed* (1949) edited by Richard Crossman: Abridgment of pp. 17, 20, 23, 24, 34-35, 55-56 by Arthur Koestler. Copyright 1949 by Richard Crossman; reprinted by permission of Harper & Row, Publishers, Inc.

24. From *The God That Failed* (1949) edited by Richard Crossman: Abridgment of pp. 96, 98-99, 113-114 by Ignazio Silone. Copyright 1949 by Ignazio Silone; reprinted by permission of Harper & Row, Publishers, Inc.

25. From *The God That Failed* (1949) edited by Richard Crossman: Abridgment of pp. 117-118, 155-156 by Richard Wright. Copyright 1944 by Richard Wright. Reprinted by permission of Harper & Row, Publishers, Inc.

26. Later works by one-time Communists speak in the same vein. For example,

"For most converts, Communism satisfies deep needs: it gives them a purpose, a program of action, a reason for living. . . . After a time the Communist may have no friends except in or near the Party, and leaving the Party can mean a terrible loneliness. In spite of this, most people break away—there are several times as many ex-Communists in this country as there are Communists—but those who remain are strengthened in their faith. If a person cannot bring himself to leave the party because life outside it seems unbearable, then his faith grows big enough to justify his staying in." Granville Hicks, *Where We Came Out,* p. 90.

27. From A. Rossi, *A Communist Party in Action* (New Haven, 1949). Lest anyone think this is a situation symptomatic of social illnesses confined to France, he is invited to examine *Report on the American Communist* by Morris L. Ernst and David Loth. The conclusion of Ernst and Loth based on the case histories of three hundred Communists is in no essential way different from those of Rossi.

28. Crane Brinton. *The Jacobins: An Essay in the New History* [1930], p. 215.

29. Brinton did not end his inquiry into the characteristics of revolution and revolutionaries with his study of the Jacobins. In a later publication, *The Anatomy of Revolution,* he undertook to determine what "uniformities" there might be among revolutions. For this purpose, he studied in addition to the French Revolution of 1789, the English revolution of the 1640s, the American Revolution, and the Russian Communist revolution. Among his conclusions about *all four,* is: "Our revolutionists are convinced that they are the elect, destined to carry out the will of God, nature, or science. . . . The opponents of these revolutionists are not just political enemies, not just mistaken men, grafters, logrollers, or damned fools; they are sinners, and must not merely be beaten—they must be wiped out. Hence the justification of the guillotine and the firing squad. For our revolutionists display that vigorous intolerance which in the logic of the emotions, as well as in that of the intellect, follows perfectly on the conviction of being absolutely, eternally, monopolistically right. If there is but one truth, and you have truth completely, toleration of differences means an encouragement to error, crime, evil, sin. Indeed, toleration in this sense is harmful to the tolerated, as well as very trying on the tolerator. As Bellarmine said, it is a positive benefit to obstinate heretics to kill them because the longer they live the more damnation they heap upon themselves. . . . Perhaps the most important uniformity in our four revolutions is that as gospels, as forms of religion, they are all universalist in aspiration and nationalist, exclusive in ultimate fact. They end up with a God meant indeed for all mankind, but brought to mankind, usually a not altogether willing mankind, by a Chosen People. . . . (And American) Manifest Destiny is by no means the palest of the gods. . . . What separates these revolutionaries from traditional Christianity is most obviously their insistence on having their heaven here, now, on earth, their impatient intent to conquer evil once and for all" (p. 214 and pp. 216–217 of the revised edition).

30. From a copyrighted interview in *U.S. News & World Report,* November 24, 1950.

31. Alan Moorehead, *The Traitors,* p. 214.

32. See Hsu, "Kinship is the Key," *The Center Magazine,* pp. 4–14.

33. Ray E. Helfer and C. Henry Kempe, eds., *The Battered Child,* pp. 24–25. In Marin County, California alone there are reportedly 360 cases of abused wives each month, according to Robert F. Thomas, Executive Director of Family Service Agency of Marin at San Rafael (*San Francisco Chronicle,* February 27, 1980).

34. For a further analysis of how Chinese behavior under Communism is rooted or has deviated from its Chinese mold, see Francis L. K. Hsu, "Chinese Kinship and Chinese Behavior" in Ping-ti Ho and Tang Tsou, eds., *China in Crisis,* vol. I, pp. 579–608. Godwin C. Chu and Francis L. K. Hsu, eds., *Moving A Mountain: Cultural Change in China.*

Purpose and Fulfillment

Whereof what's past is prologue; what to come,
  In yours and my discharge.
                              ANTONIO IN *The Tempest*

We have now come to the end of our comparative examination of two contemporary peoples, each the inheritors, makers, and participants of a great historical civilization. At the core of each civilization is a particular way of approaching men, gods, and things. The Chinese way certainly predated Confucius and Mencius who systematized, expounded, and added to it. But Americans often forget that their way has a history that is nearly as long. Plato, Socrates, and other thinkers demonstrated, dramatized, and enriched it.

Some sociologists may see the individual-centered American way of life I have presented as characteristic of the urban or industrial society, while the situation-centered Chinese way as characteristic of the rural or peasant society. Furthermore, some sociologists even hypothesize that as modernization and industrialization gather steam in rural or peasant societies, their way of life will also move in the individual-centered direction.[1]

I find it difficult to agree with this position. If that were true, the problem of inducing industrialism in the so-called underdeveloped societies would have been an easy proposition. All the industrially advanced countries need do is to provide and install the factories and these would then be self-perpetuating. Those involved in foreign aid have found a totally different reality. It was human beings who created, sustained, and escalated industrialism, not vice versa. Toward this end the individuals involved not only have to desire the results of industrialization but also develop a way of looking at the world in which control of things comes before their relationships with each other. Modern conditions of production, once under way, will certainly exert some influence over human behavior, but to see the former as the genesis of the latter is to put the cart before the horse.

Certainly this was not the sequence of events which unfolded itself in the history of the West. The germ of the American individual-centered way of life even predated the ancient Greeks and Romans, Christianity and the Renaissance, not to speak of the Reformation and the Industrial, French, and American revolutions. That germ is to be found in the Western version of the primeval Flood legend.

As punishment for the wickedness of men, God decided to flood the earth and kill all except the chosen man Noah and his immediate family. Noah made an ark into which he packed his wife, his three sons and their wives, together with seven pairs of all "clean" and one pair of all other animals to escape the disaster. When the flood subsided, they landed on Ararat. After thanking the Lord by appropriate rituals, Noah and his wife apparently lived for a while with their sons and their wives together. Then Noah drank the wine he had made and, while under the influence of liquor, he masturbated in his tent. Ham, seeing his father engaged in self-eroticism, told his two brothers about it; they were all disgusted with Noah. Some kind of quarrel ensued, and Noah then played favorites by blessing Shem and Japheth, cursing Ham, and condemning Ham's son Canaan to be the slave of Shem and Japheth.[2] Then the sons and their wives all went their own separate ways.

When the flood came, Noah was six hundred years old and his own father Lamech had died five years before. But we have no indication as to what happened to his widowed mother. In those legendary times people lived for a very long time. Lamech died when he was seven hundred and seventy-seven and Noah did not die until he was nine hundred and fifty. Is it not possible that Noah's mother might have survived his father for a little over five years? The fact is that neither he nor the narrator of the legend concerned themselves with her.

Noah and his group did not return to the soil where they were born and lived before the flood came. After it subsided they did not even make any gesture in that direction, nor did Noah think about his father's or mother's graveyard back home. Furthermore, Noah and his sons did not remain together long. They quarrelled and then separated. And the source of trouble which caused their dispersion was drunkenness and sexuality. The legend of Noah's approach to the flood and its aftermath thus inevitably set the tone of the husband-wife dominated kinship system of the individual-centered Western man.

The contrast between the Western version of the legend and its Chinese counterpart is truly startling. The Chinese account is briefly as follows:

Emperors Yao and Shun (said respectively to have reigned 2357–2258 B.C. and 2258–2206 B.C.) were great and moral rulers. In Yao's old age a terrible flood devastated the country. Yao appointed a certain Kun to control the flood but Kun was unsuccessful. Yao decided to resign and offered the throne to the able and popular man Shun as his successor. Emperor Shun exiled Kun because he had failed to control the flood and appointed the exile's son Yu in his place. Yu worked for many years, in the course of which he went all over the country, and succeeded in finally eradicating the flood. During his tours of duty he passed by his own house three different times, but he did not enter it even once. After his success, Yu was offered the throne by a grateful Emperor Shun.

The Chinese legend did not name any chosen person (as Noah was) to be favored by God and spared from the disaster; instead all Chinese were to be saved from it. The Chinese legend did not carry the theme that the Chinese (or some one group among them) should take refuge in a boat or flee the country to somewhere else; instead they remained where they were born and lived. There was no question of sons going in different directions from their fathers; instead Yu worked hard to succeed where his father had failed, thus not only vindicating his father's name but also giving honor to his ancestors. Finally, by not even once visiting his wife during his many years of work, Yu put his larger duty before matters of his own heart.

The legend of Yu's approach to the flood and its aftermath thus also inevitably set the standard for the father-son dominated kinship system of the mutually dependent Chinese.

Whether there was such a historically verifiable flood or Noah or Emperor Yu is not the question here. The important thing is that over the centuries each people made, embellished, and continued to tell the same myth in their own image. Westerners obviously are in tune with Noah's and his sons' lack of concern for kinship continuity and ancestors, just as the Chinese must have found nonindividualistic approaches of emperors Yao, Shun, and Yu agreeable. Being rootless, Westerners have always tended to seek causes (ideal, social, or supernatural) to fight for, to entrench themselves in, and to act as bases for expansion by proselytization or force.[3] Being tied to kinship and locality, the Chinese have always been reluctant to emigrate and unimpressed by abstraction, social ills, utopia, and gods except to the extent of safeguarding the integrity and interests of their primary human groups.

However, the Chinese, along with many other non-Western peoples, are no longer able to continue their own way of life as they had developed and lived it over the centuries. The Chinese survived the Mongol and Manchu conquests and their way of life flourished in spite of the conquerors. But they have not found an efficient answer among their traditional tools to meet the challenge of modern times. The Western world is today the arbiter of mankind's fate. It is paradoxical that the reaction against Western physical domination has gone far to complete the conquest of the world by Western culture. To ensure its own survival, the rest of the world has been obliged to imitate the West, by inviting Western assistance or by reshaping, on their own, the traditional institutions and the individual in the Western model—democratic or totalitarian or a composite of the two.

In this process of utilizing Western methods, instilling Western beliefs, and achieving Western goals, a majority of non-Western peoples suffer from diverse growth and transformation pains and, to varying extents, have also been compelled to align themselves with one or another of the warring factions of the West. This has occurred at a time when the internal divisions of the West are more serious and its instruments of war more devastating than ever before in history. No "neutralist" or "third force" position can save the non-Western nations from the destruction certain to ensue if Western tensions erupt into a third world war. Whatever their political status, the destiny of the world's peoples is at present more intimately bound to that of the West than at any previous time.

As the leader of one of the Western factions and still the most powerful nation on earth, America has a responsibility to the world the equal of which has never befallen any country. Even those bent on isolationism cannot but agree that a good deal of external responsibility is unavoidable, any more than can non-Western nations hope to escape involvement in what is essentially a Western struggle. Yet America cannot effectively exercise or implement her responsibility to others if she does not first recognize her responsibility to herself. Since the race toward worldwide disaster can be checked only within Western society, America—as the strongest among the coalition of free nations within that society—must point the way toward meeting the West's internal problems.

Within nations these problems appear as individual or group

struggles—crimes of passion, economic strife, racial violence, religious persecution, political irreconcilability, and the like. Between nations they erupt as recurrent wars and almost perpetual preparations for war. These are the negative consequences of a way of life founded on extreme individualism. It is natural therefore that it is in America, the land where European individualism became complete self-reliance, that the individual's emotional security is the most precarious. The positive effects of self-reliance are to be found in America's wealth and power, and so far these reserves have served to mitigate the insecurity that results from the individuals' isolation from each other. Should the tensions and fears that this isolation produces find release in another world conflict, then we are apt to be confronted by a crisis in the American way of life such as was but hinted at during the Great Depression.

Physical destruction can be repaired if there is the will to do so, and the principal danger is, therefore, psychological. Being given to absolutes, the self-reliant man is most in tune with the extreme view of the world that recognizes only two sides, one good and one evil, and that the destruction of one will mean the automatic success of the other. This was the implicit or explicit promise which sustained the fervor and sacrifices for World Wars I and II, after both of which allies became enemies and enemies became allies. Today we are back at exactly the same old game again. Other than the possibility that the United States, China, and Russia, in whatever combination, would be equally exhausted by a new war, there is no reason to suppose that a similar situation would not be produced in the next postwar period as a warring world of hostile states realigned once more and prepared itself for another conflict. Such considerations seem to have occupied an important place in the mind of General MacArthur when during his congressional testimony in early 1950 he said:

> . . . With the scientific methods which have made mass destruction reach appalling proportions, war has ceased to be a sort of the roll-of-the-dice to determine . . . which should be the winner and dictate the terms. (Modern warfare) . . . has outlawed the very basic concepts . . . upon which war was used as a final word when politics failed to settle international disputes. It is inherently a failure now. The last two wars have shown it. The victor had to carry the defeated on his back.
>
> If you have another world war, you are going to get such destruction and destructiveness. I think it was a philosopher who said . . . only those will be happy that are dead . . . (*Life*, May 14, 1951).

The way out of this war cycle as well as the way to confront our domestic social problems is not through the imaginary escape hatch of exchanging a "materialistic" orientation toward life for a more "spiritual" one. It is not Asian spirituality that has produced harmony in the situation-centered Chinese society. Nor will the situation be improved by pointing out that modern physicists who probe the atom and the ultimate nature of the universe have reached conclusions increasingly resembling certain mystical teachings of Asia.[4] It was not a materialistic orientation that has produced the Western systems of abstract, theoretical thought—whether scientific, philosophic, or religious—which underlie Western material success. The true dichotomy is not between a material or spiritual emphasis but between the central importance attached to human relationships in the one, resulting in the mutual dependence of men, and the attempt to escape them in the other, generating the need for control of things as the isolated individual's defense against his fellow men. In turning away from the human group, the individualist Westerners also seek emotional security in quests more truly spiritual than anything the Chinese have known. These are the factors which propelled self-reliant Americans to build a nation that baffles, and is the envy of, most of the world; their nation embodies the apparent paradox of extreme idealism flourishing among supposedly crass materialists. The cynical, the envious, and the honestly puzzled miss the nexus which explains both phenomena: the individual's detachment from intimate relationship with other human beings.

Throughout the foregoing chapters we have avoided the question: Which of the two ways of life is better? And for what? After this intensive examination of the contrasting civilizations the two peoples have respectively built for themselves, I ask the indulgence of my readers for engaging in a bit of value judgment. If we assume, as I think we must, that civilizations exist for men and not vice versa, then the question becomes one of which way of life is more generative of human good.

What is human good? I think that it must be something more than sheer existence. For if sheer existence is the basic human good, then we might as well all be oysters.

I submit that the human good includes at least the following two minimum components. The first is freedom from physical suffering, the most common forms of which are hunger and malnutrition,[5] others being bodily harm due to natural disaster and illness. The second is freedom from psychological insecurity, especially fear of fellow human beings and crippling anxiety about one's place among them, and from boredom.

The Chinese way of life has failed so badly with reference to the first component that traditional China was justifiably categorized as a land of famine. By contrast, the American way of life, through its superb economic, engineering, and bio-medical achievements, still leads mankind in its battle against all that ails the body, and for physical fitness.

The usual view of the problems facing America today centers in the economic: recession, inflation, and energy. But these are all within the competence of the American genius. I have no doubt that in time American economic strength will reassert itself. As for energy, it need not be a problem at all. If Americans drive a little less and conserve a little more, the United States will become not only self-sufficient but an exporter of energy as well as technology.

Where the American way has failed badly is with reference to the second component of human good. Despite its spectacular successes in the field of entertainment, which pleases the senses, and in extending the frontiers of knowledge, which enriches the mind, boredom is common. When human beings are purposeless they are bound to be bored. To defend themselves against boredom they will have to seek new pleasures or find new enemies, including imaginary ones. Isolation of the individual and scarcity of intimate relationships are correlated with acute fears and anxieties, which propel many to be hostile toward their fellow men or to seek aspirations so high that they cannot fulfill them, or can only fulfill them at the cost of breaking themselves or others. That is why there is so much vandalism, senseless murder, and mayhem not only among the poor and the underprivileged, but also among the affluent and the well-placed. Most Americans no longer dare to walk alone in parks and scenic spots, even in broad daylight. Girls and young children are told to beware of their male relatives. Homes in cities and most suburbs are defended by fancy security devices and have especially become prisons for the elderly. The human environment has become so unpredictable that America may justifiably be called a land of mistrust.[6]

All the great principles of human conduct propounded by Confucius, Mencius, Chu Hsi, Wang Yang-ming, and Tseng Kuo-fan have failed to enable a majority of Chinese in traditional China to derive an adequate livelihood free from crop failures and epidemics. On the other hand, all the great discoveries and inventions by Pythagoras, Louis Pasteur, Thomas Edison, Alexander Graham Bell, and Henry Ford have failed to enable a majority of Americans to open their hearts to, and be free from fear of, their fellow human beings.

The Chinese, by way of the school of hard knocks, have slowly come to realize that they can no longer stand up in the world by going back to their traditional ethical principles. It took them over one hundred years of humiliation, near-chaos, or repeated and bloody struggles against internal and external foes before they came to the present situation which promises to make further progress possible.

The road ahead is not all smooth. There will be relapses. Recent press reports of prostitution in Peking, and of misuse of government power for private gain elsewhere, are but a few examples. There will be further ideological twists and turns. The fall of the Gang of Four will by no means be the last of revolutionary ups and downs. Will the Chiang Ai-chen murder spree we saw in Chapter 2, the bomb explosion in a Peking railway station which killed ten people and injured scores of others by a disgruntled man (reported in the American press in early November, 1980), and the shooting death of a branch Party secretary in Changteh, Hunan Province (*Hunan Daily,* October 20, 1980) portend more violence in the days and months ahead? The announcement by Vice-Premier Teng of his gradual retirement seems to portend an orderly succession of power, but the Chinese have yet to solve their basic problems of population control and of making significant progress in their drive toward the Four Modernizations while avoiding the pitfalls that beset the industrially advanced West. But Chinese leaders, and a majority of the Chinese, seem determined to change direction.

Most Americans, on the other hand, have yet to realize the need to alter any of the fundamental tenets of the American way of life. They look to intensification of self-reliance, more physical welfare provisions and safeguards, deeper penetration of the individual psyche by way of psychoanalysis, and heightened satisfaction of the senses, including the sexual, as elements of human progress.[7] They refuse to see that such activities may lead to greater exacerbation of the many problems which ail the society. I have even seen in print, and heard said more than once, that violence and fear of fellow human beings is one of the prices we have to pay for living in a free society.

All human beings must live in association with other human beings. They need to relate to each other in terms not merely of how *useful* one is to the other, but more importantly of how much *feeling* one has for the other. Usefulness is a matter of skills and it can be achieved, for a majority of mankind, by training. It may even be improved or made possible by legislation, as when Blacks and other minorities are admitted under Fair Employment laws to apprenticeships or jobs formerly reserved for Whites. But feeling is not so easily trained in the same sense as are skills, for it is a matter of the heart. It certainly cannot be improved or made possible by legislation, for even the most thorough laws and enforcement agencies are simply powerless to make harmonious couples out of unloving spouses. In fact, such measures often worsen the situation by generating exactly opposite results.

Self-reliant Americans, being overly zealous of their privacy, are more able to relate to each other through *usefulness* than by way of *feeling,* since the former requires opening one's heart far less than does the latter. The resulting loneliness and isolation of the individual make up the Western, and particularly American, condition many writers have mistaken for the human condition.

But loneliness and isolation of the individual are not the only pitfalls of a society held together principally by the usefulness of its members rather than by their feeling for each other. Mistrust, hatred, violence, and separatism are its other bitter fruits. Under the circumstances the well-known remedies for America's ills—increased productivity, elimination of poverty, and equality among the races—are simply not good enough. By all means try to eliminate poverty and right the racial wrongs. But these will not begin to come about, and these will not cure the ills even if they come about, unless something more fundamental is recognized and squarely faced first.

This fundamental something is that our relationship with our fellow human beings is more of a key to peace or violence among human beings and between human groups, and to happiness or misery for the individual, than is our control over things. Therefore when concerned Americans speak of improving the quality of the life of the individual, they should be thinking of *improving the quality of interpersonal life for the individual instead.*

If the control of material wealth continues to be the individual's principal investment in emotional security, Whites will be unable to surrender any substantial part of that wealth for the betterment of Blacks and the poor, and as Blacks and the poor become more affluent they will be just as reluctant to surrender any substantial part of their wealth for the benefit of other Blacks and other poor. Besides, those who pin their faith on wealth as the panacea for human problems should reflect on the case of Nazi Germany and imperial Japan. At the height of their industrial and military powers, did the Germans and the Japanese live in peace among themselves or among the family of nations?

How to modify a way of life predicated on self-reliance so as to allow more weight to interpersonal relationships is extremely problematic. Human beings switch to new models of automobiles much more easily than they will agree to change their basic ways of seeing men, gods, and things. Some early twentieth-century Chinese reformers unrealistically talked about complete westernization of China. Their present-day American counterparts will be equally disappointed if they hope for simple American incorporation of any significant lessons from the East. Each people is tied to its long past which cannot but play an important part in any change—evolutionary or revolutionary.

But many Americans, especially the young, are already seeking a change in their way of life. In the sixties they sought change by way of negative and destructive acts on campuses and in the streets. Such demonstrations had abated by the seventies but other manifestations which began during that period have continued in force. Little communelike groups in which the members keep no private property are not rare today in the country. Sensitivity experiments in which participants are encouraged to touch each other under certain guises are still common. The Living Theatre in which nude or nearly nude actors and members of the audience merge in hugging each other has played to full houses.

The late pop-rock-soul blues singer, Janis Joplin, preached a gospel of supremacy of feeling over intellect. "Being an intellectual," Janis said, "creates a lot of questions and no answers. You can fill your life up with ideas and still go home lonely. All you really have that really matters are feelings. That's what music is to me." *Newsweek* magazine (February 24, 1969), which gave this quote, also reported that Joplin had been "making more converts per capita than Billy Graham." Joplin and Elvis Presley are now dead, but what they represented is still offered by numerous rock groups and by many evangelists, each enjoying a sizable following.

These happenings, seen in conjunction with the widespread phenomena of antiwar sentiments and of youths discarding the comforts and status symbols of their well-to-do homes to lead socially amorphous but physically and psychologically intimate lives among

strangers, all point to but one direction: the need of the young to relate to each other and to the rest of the world not by wealth and superiority but by opening up their hearts, not by what one can do for the
other, but by what one is to the other. This is what young Americans
really mean when they want to be "true" and "undisguised" and
make their lives meaningful.

The key to discover and implement mechanisms for developing
greater depth and permanency in human relationships for society as
a whole must be sought in the cradle of human development: the
family. We need first and foremost a reassessment of our kinship system. Toward this end we need to divert a fraction of the colossal national wealth to design and carry out basic researches.

The traditional American view is that the primary duty of members of Congress is to make more laws. But laws are role manifestations. We voice often enough such sentiments as "you can't legislate
family harmony" or "racial brotherhood". We must realize that we
can't legislate obedience to law either. Isn't it time then for our lawmakers, together with our president and his Cabinet, to produce
fewer new laws and devote more of their creative energies to new
ways of modifying our society's affective pattern, so that more people
will obey the laws already on the books and fewer will break them or
search for legal loopholes? We need to break the vicious circle of
more laws, more laws violated, more investigation and persecution
of lawbreakers and more laws to prevent breaking of newly enacted
laws.

Toward this end our leaders in government and education can do
many things. But I hope they will be farsighted enough to give due
weight to the fundamental and long-term goals of our nation. A few
years ago the *Reader's Digest* carried an article (May 1977:96–100)
condensed from *Newsweek* entitled "We've Got Too Much Law." In
it were authoritative testimonies and statistics to indicate how our
courts are clogged by mounting increases in the number of cases
pending before them. The article concluded that one way to reduce
the burden is to decriminalize certain kinds of behavior such as personal use of marijuana.

Without arguing about what behavior should be decriminalized, I
see such steps as merely palliative. They are attractive to those who
demand immediate action but not helpful in the long run. Decrimi-
nalization of some behavior will soon be overtaken by the necessity
to criminalize other and new forms of behavior. To get at the root of
the matter we have to reduce or rechannel the psychic need and so-

cial inducement to violate laws. For this we must go back to the family and primary education.

Since the family is the primary arena of human development, can't our officials promote public interest in, and sponsor systematic scholarly inquiries on, new designs for the family which will strike a happy medium between stability requirements and those of progress?

Then, since nurseries and grade schools mold our youngsters at an early age and provide the opportunity for close cooperation with parents, innovation must involve the schools and the parents. For they can reinforce or nullify each other. We need a new approach to, and a new formula for, parent-teacher cooperation. For example, can't our officials help us, by public hearings and working committees, to examine the question of what and how non-Western reading materials may be integrated with benefit into our preschool and primary grade curricula, and how we can induce parents to accept that they are far more responsible for their children's behavior than are the teachers in schools?

In our universities we have departments of economics and government as well as of business management, but I know of no department of the family. Our government has departments of education, housing and urban development, treasury, and labor, but not of family. If the family is so important to us why not have an independent and prestigious unit devoted to the family in all major universities and in our government?

In all these researches and deliberations one point of reference should be held firmly before us. Civilizations—whether they provide philosophies, space exploration, moral rules, profits, air conditioning, or clean sheets—exist for men, be they men or women, old or young, White or Black, plumber or professor; but not vice versa. No civilization, or any aspect of it, is worthwhile which shows signs of running amok so that the physical or psychological well-being of a majority of humans has to be sacrificed in its name.

Consequently, our researches and deliberations must not, as is so often the fashion of the day, take the requirements of industrialization and the modern political state as absolute ends so that human beings have to be trained toward meeting them. Instead we should address ourselves to the much more important problem of how human beings can develop and sustain feelings for each other as fellow human beings instead of as tools, despite the requirements of industrialization and a modern political state. Or we must attempt to re-tailor industrialization and a modern political state so that their requirements will not interfere with the genesis and maintenance in human beings of feelings for each other as fellow human beings.

To facilitate the new researches and new deliberations let us appeal to the self-reliant man's self-interest. Self-reliance is a great ideal, but the conditions of life in which this ideal has served its ends effectively have changed. No ideal can operate without a social context. Honesty is certainly a fine ideal, but it is not always the best policy in diplomacy. We need a new social framework in which our cherished idea can reasonably work without leading to unwanted consequences.

The achievement of this new social framework cannot be dependent upon altruism, for no man is that altruistic. But the self-reliant man should see that it is in his own interest or the interest of his children and his children's children for him to support efforts to find a new social framework for peace within the United States and between the United States and the rest of the world. The cornerstone of this new social framework is that man liberate himself from the magical mode of thinking in human affairs. Man used to pray or recite incantations for rain where he now builds huge dams, and engage priests and witch doctors to cure illnesses where he now makes use of the X-ray and penicillin. Thanks to Western contributions to the natural sciences, the world has gradually emerged from this premodern notion of the magical nature of the physical universe.

But man continues to react magically about human behavior and human relations.[8] He considers it utter foolishness to build a skyscraper on sand but he still insists on building empires or alliances by forcing unwilling peoples to do his bidding. He would not think of cheating on the aircraft or rockets he constructs by slipping in inferior chrome, but he still tries to pull the wool over the eyes of other humans by denying them their due, and by giving out half-truths through misleading advertisements or propaganda efforts in intrasocial and international designs.

Above all, he is still addicted to the magic of words in human affairs.[9] Lovers under the moonlight can whisper a lot of magical words to each other. But these words will retain their magic only if there is substance in their relationship as lovers. No amount of words can substitute for the magic of true love. Not recognizing this basic principle governing human behavior, man still thinks he can change a saucepan into a spade because he calls it a spade, a dictatorship into democracy by calling it a democracy, or a lot of irreligious frivolities into religion by calling it worship of God.

It is necessary for us to realize and recognize that in human affairs no less than in the physical world everything has a price and we cannot get anything for nothing. The price may be money, energy, heartache, misery, revolution, war, or outright death; and it may be paid by ourselves or the future generations to come but it cannot be evaded forever. In family affairs men and women who show no respect and consideration for their own parents cannot later expect their own children to treat them with respect and consideration. In international affairs countries that have ruthlessly oppressed or enforced their superiority over other countries can hardly expect mercy or love from their former inferiors once the shoe is on the other foot. The United States, as the most illustrious and the richest descendant of Europe, is paying and will be paying through the nose, not in money alone, for the generations of international misdeeds perpetrated by its ancestors. The modern day racial violence in the United States is but a partial payment for the three hundred years of slavery enjoyed by our forebears. And if the Blacks get carried away by their present hatred of the Whites and give themselves to enormous excesses, they or their children will in the same way be paying for such excesses later.

Even the self-reliant man needs to realize that no one has a permanent tenure in life. In that sense we are all transients, and what we need is a pleasant journey through this world, free from physical and psychological suffering, for ourselves and our descendants yet to come. To achieve this, it is essential that we make it pleasant for others while there is still time. And, toward the end of our individual journeys, even the self-reliant man needs the assurance that it is not the end of everything. If he can feel that what he has done with his life will not entail undue payments on the part of his children and his children's children, will he not have lived with a sense of purpose and died with a feeling of fulfillment?

NOTES

1. One sociologist, William Goode, does caution against this oversimplified hypothesis even though he sees incompatibility between industrialization and the Chinese type of kinship system (see William J. Goode, *World Revolution and Family Patterns,* pp. 369–371).

2. The passage concerning Noah's self-eroticism is generally deleted or changed into more neutral statements in the modern versions of the Bible containing such expressions as "and became drunk and lay uncovered in his tent. And Ham . . . saw the nakedness of his father, and told his two brothers outside." If these newer statements were correct, it will become a great puzzle as to why the brothers should be so very ashamed of their father's naked body, and why Noah should be so very angry with Ham, who merely told his two brothers about his nakedness, which they covered with a garment.

3. Lest it be thought that proselytization came with the Judeo-Christian tradition, the reader should note the following actions of Alexander the Great (356–323 B.C.) during his retreat from India, as described by the anthropologist, Prince Peter of Greece and Denmark:

> Undeterred, yet deeply shaken by the incomprehension surrounding him, Alexander persisted in his views. After the ordeals of retreat from the Beas and the terrible crossing of Gedrosia (the Baluchistan desert), on arrival in Susa he organised the marriage of ten thousand of his followers to Iranian maidens. And at Opis, in Mesopotamia, on his way to Babylon and his premature end, he gave one last, vast banquet, in which all joined him in a symposium and the drinking of a "loving cup" to the union of mankind and universal *amonia* (concord).
>
> ("The importance of Alexander the Great's Expedition for the Relations Between East and West," a paper delivered at Amsterdam Institute of the Tropics, 1965, p. 7.)

No Chinese imperial conqueror throughout the centuries did anything remotely resembling these episodes.

4. Fritjof Capra, *The Tao of Physics,* and Gary Zukov, *The Dancing Wu Li Masters.*

5. Sex deprivation is, of course, also a form of physical suffering. But I do not know of any society, or a section of it, which suffers from sex deprivation other than on a voluntary basis.

6. By describing America as a land of mistrust we do not, of course, mean that all Americans are suspicious of each other, exactly as we do not imply that all Chinese were hungry because China was a land of famine.

7. Such trends are clearly still gathering speed in the United States. The importance given to physical well-being and pleasure is evident wherever we turn. The intense public attention on the inner secrets of the mind is indicated by the popularity of psychoanalysis but especially of psychoanalytic novels such as C. P. Snow's *The Sleep of Reason,* and Philip Roth's *Portnoy's Complaint.* We have not only Masters and Johnson's research to tell us that homosexuals can get just as much pleasure out of sex as anyone else (*Homosexuality in Perspective,* Boston, 1979) but also a couple in the nude who bill themselves as "Sexperts" to advertise their pictorial sex manual *Behind Closed Doors* (*San Francisco Sunday Examiner and Chronicle,* February 17, 1980). The More University of Lafayette, California is called "More" because its founders believe it offers "more sensuality" and "more of everything else." Its one-day "Basic Sensuality" course includes a live demonstration of an hour-long female orgasm. The demonstration is performed by a "skilled male instructor" who uses both hands to manipulate a female instructor. Sue Baranco, dean of More's Sensuality Department, says she had a three-hour orgasm while serving as a live model for the demonstration (*Honolulu Advertiser,* December 30, 1978). There are even "experts" who maintain that incestuous relations are a sound means of communication between parents and children.

8. The popularity of UFO believers in the United States is indicative of the reality of this mode of thinking and the extreme to which it will go. But characteristically the UFO devotees believe that "living" creatures from other planets and not ghosts and spirits are manning the "crafts" from outer space.

9. In a way, this is the underlying assumption of those who see better communications or more research on communication as the means for mitigating or solving problems of our time. But no amount of clarification of meaning between parents and children, Blacks and Whites, and different nations can respectively reduce the generation gap, the racial tension, and the international struggles if the two sides in each conflict harbor irreconcilable goals.

A Brief
Chronology
of China
and the West

by Vera Y. N. Hsu

WESTERN WORLD

CHINA

| BC | |
| 2000 | |

NEOLITHIC AGE
HSIA (*ca.* 1994–)

Farming
Rice cultivation, domestication of horses, pigs, and other animals
Cultivation of wheat and millet
Potter's wheel
Sericulture

BRONZE AGE
Minoan civilization spreads from Crete to Tiryns, Mycenae, Argos (2000–1400)
Cities and towns of stone and brick
Irrigation, woolen industry, extensive commerce with coined money and credit. Horse and war chariot
Egypt and Babylonia already with highly developed alphabetic writing

SHANG (*ca.* 1766– or *ca.* 1523–)
Copper
Pictographic writing developed
Bronzes
Ancestor worship, oracle bones for divination

Code of Laws of HAMMURABI (1750)
Apex of Cretan civilization, extensive trade with Egypt (1600–1500)
Egyptian New Kingdom (1580–1090)
Highly developed city life

1500

Bronze vessels and weapons

City life with specialized trades, commerce by barter and cowrie shells

IKHNATON (1375–1358)

Records kept on bones and books of bamboo slips

MOSES, Jewish tribes revolt in Egypt (1225–)
Movement of Peoples of the Sea (1200)
End of Hittite Kingdom. Fall of Troy

WESTERN WORLD

IRON AGE

Greek colonies established in the islands and Asia Minor (1000–500)

Kingdoms of Israel and Judah established by the Hebrews (933)

Assyrian Empire. Nineveh sacked (933–625)

Carthage founded

Rome founded (753)

Hebrew Prophets

BUDDHA (536–483)

Roman Republic (510–)

War between Athens and Sparta (431–404)

SOCRATES

PLATO

ARISTOTLE

ALEXANDER THE GREAT (336–)

Struggle between Rome and Carthage

BC
1000

500

CHINA

CHOU W. (*ca.* 1122– or *ca.* 1027–)
Feudalism

The Odes

The History
CHOU E. (*ca.* 770–)
Interstate warfare and diplomacy

Iron Age   Written law code (*ca.* 536)

LAOTZE
CONFUCIUS
MOTZE
MENCIUS   CHUANGTZE

CH'IN (*ca.* 221–) Unification of China, Great Wall
Imperial system of government established
HAN W. (206–) SSU-MA CH'IEN *Record of History*
WU-TI sends CHANG CH'IEN (he went about 138–126) to Central Asia. China occupies "Silk Route"

Conquest of Korea	100	JULIUS CAESAR. Julian Calendar (*ca.* 45)
Confucianism proclaimed as state philosophy		Silk to Rome from China
MING-TI sends armies under PAN CH'AO to the		Reign of HEROD as King of Judea (31–4)
Caspian—China's farthest penetration west		Birth of CHRIST (*ca.* 4)
HAN E. (25–)	AD	Golden Age of Roman literature
		Roman Empire at its widest extent
Buddhism from India		
Beginning of Taoist cult	100	Spread of Christianity
Invention of paper and porcelain		
Use of compass		
THREE KINGDOMS: WEI–SHU–WU (220/222–	200	MARCUS AURELIUS
263/286)		Christianity founded amid persecutions
TSIN W. (265–317) Barbarian invasions		
E. (318–420)		

CHINA	AD	WESTERN WORLD
	300	Mayan Empire Council of Nicaea (325) ST. AUGUSTINE
Mass migration to central and south China Spread of Taoism and Buddhism "EPOCH OF SOUTH AND NORTH" (420–589) Chinese pilgrims to India—Cultural contacts	400	Rome taken over by Germanic tribes
Sinicization of northern invaders Cultural and economic development of south China	500	JUSTINIAN's law code (533) Silkworms to Constantinople from China (544) Spread of Islam
SUI (589–) Grand canal to Ch'angan built China reunified; Great Wall rebuilt T'ANG (618–) Examination system Influx of Near Eastern trade and religion (Zoro- astrianism, Manicheanism, Islam)	600	

700

Moslem conquest of Spain (711–715)
Moslems defeated at Poitiers by Franks (732)

LI PO
TU FU } China's most widely known poets

Rise of Frankish culture, CHARLEMAGNE THE GREAT (768–814)

800

BASIL I, Byzantine emperor, restores power of empire and resists Moslems (867–886)
ALFRED THE GREAT, first king of England (871–899)

Chinese culture transforms Japan

900

OTTO I THE GREAT, reunited Holy Roman Empire (936–973)
HUGH CAPET, ruler of Paris area: first of Capetian kings of France (987)

PERIOD OF FIVE DYNASTIES (907–)
Disorder
LIAO (KHITAN) dynasty established
Footbinding of women; printing (movable type)
SUNG N. (960–)

1000

Danish conquest of eastern England (1014–1016)
CANUTE master of Denmark, Norway, and England (1017–1035)
Eastern and Western churches separated (1054)
Norman conquest of England (1066)

Use of paper money and development of commercial enterprise; use of gunpowder
Ocean-going ships

CHINA

WESTERN WORLD

AD	CHINA	WESTERN WORLD
1100	Urbanization Neo-Confucian upsurge SUNG S. (1127–) Neo-Confucianism synthesized by CHU HSI (1130–1200)	First Crusade (1099) Height of Inca civilization in Andes (1100) Crusades: (1147–1149), (1189–1192), (1202–1204), (1218–1221), (1228–1229), (1248–1254), (1270) Universities founded at Paris and Oxford (1200)
1200	YUAN (1279–) Mongols: KUBLAI KHAN	Magna Carta (1215) MARCO POLO sets out for China (1217) Height of Aztec civilization in Mexico (1250) "Model" parliament in England (1295)
1300	Introduction of Judaism, Islam, Christianity, and Lamaism Military roads tie Europe and Asia together MING (1368–)	Hundred Years' War (1337–1453) DANTE Black Death (1348) Italian Renaissance
1400	Despotic rule; final development of imperial government system	CHAUCER Gutenberg Bible printed LEONARDO DA VINCI

	Western History	Chinese History
1500	Discovery of the Americas (1492) Reformation (1541) SHAKESPEARE (1564)	YUNG LO sends CHENG HO exploring and conquering as far as Africa First contacts with modern Western world (Portuguese and Dutch) Coastal attacks by Japanese pirates
1600	Beginning of western colonial and missionary expansion on worldwide scale (1600) Arrival of the Pilgrims (1620); Mayflower Compact Harvard College founded (1636)	Corn, sweet potato, tobacco from America Jesuits bring Christianity and science CH'ING (1644–) (Manchu) KANG HSI dictionary
1700	Industrial Revolution (*ca.* 1750) FRANKLIN experiments with electricity (1752) War for Independence (1775–1783) Birth of U.S.A. (1783 or 1787)	CH'IEN LUNG—greatest extent of empire Suzerainty over Tibet, Tarim Basin, Inner and Outer Mongolia and Manchuria Rapid population increase and considerable internal migrations
1800	French Revolution (1789–1815) NAPOLEON Latin American Independence (1800–1850) Monroe Doctrine (1823); EMERSON, MELVILLE Civil War (1861–1865) ABRAHAM LINCOLN NICHOLAS II, tsar of Russia (1894–1917) Age of Colonialism, Asia, Africa (1800–1900)	The "Opium War" (1839–1842) (England) Arrow War (1856–1860) (France and England) Christianity; T'aip'ing Rebellion (1850–1864) Sino-French War (1884–1885) Sino-Japanese War (1894–1895)

WESTERN WORLD

		CHINA

WESTERN WORLD

Open Door Policy (for China) (1899)
Age of Urbanization in America

First World War (1914–1918)
Russian Revolution. U.S. enters the war (1917)

League of Nations

Great Depression (1929)
GANDHI

FRANKLIN D. ROOSEVELT (1933–1945)
Rise of HITLER (1934)
Second World War (1939–1945)

AD
1900

1910

1920

1930

CHINA

Hundred Days' Reform (1898); Boxer Uprising

Warlord period

Republican Revolution (1911) SUN YAT-SEN
FIRST REPUBLIC (1912–) YUAN SHIH-K'AI
Literary renaissance—HU SHIH
Student movement, beginning May 4, 1919

Communist party formed (1920)

SECOND REPUBLIC (1928) CHIANG KAI-SHEK
Nationalist party tutelage (1928–1948)

Industrialization; currency; modern banking
Japanese invasion of all China (1937–)
Sino-Japanese War (1937–1945)

Independence of former colonies

1940

Japan attacks Pearl Harbor (1941)
First atomic bomb dropped on Hiroshima (1945)
United Nations (1945)
Twilight of colonialism. Indian independence (1947)

Abolition of Unequal Treaties (1942)
World War ends (1945)
Civil War (1946–)

1950

Cold War (1945–)
Korean War (1950–1953)

PEOPLE'S REPUBLIC (1949) MAO TSE-TUNG

Growth of Marxism; land reform; collective farms
First Five-Year Plan (1953)
Constitution of 1954
The "Hundred Flowers" Campaign (1957)
Great Leap (1958)

1960

Beginning of U.S. involvement in Vietnam (1961)
Assassination of JOHN F. KENNEDY (1963)
Student unrest; black militancy
Peace movement
Israel–Arab War (1967)
First human heart transplant (1967)
Assassinations of MARTIN LUTHER KING and ROBERT KENNEDY (1968)
First man on the moon (1969)

Sino-Soviet rift
First atomic test
Cultural Revolution (Red Guards)
Fall of LIU SHAO-CHI (1968) and purge of many others

CHINA	AD	WESTERN WORLD
	1970	

WESTERN WORLD

OPEC countries begin to demand higher prices (1971)
Vietnam Peace Agreement (1973)
Watergate; NIXON forced to resign (1974)
Worldwide energy crisis
CARTER wins presidency (1976)
First test tube baby (1978)
AYATOLLAH KHOMEINI assumes power in Iran (1979)
Egypt and Israel sign peace treaty at White House (1979)
Pioneer II returns data on Saturn
Iranian militants take U.S. hostages (November 1979)
Abrogation of U.S.–Taiwan Treaty upheld by Federal Court
USSR invades Afghanistan
Spectacular rise of gold prices from U.S.$226 in 1978 to $524 in 1979

CHINA

PRC admitted to the UN (1971)
RICHARD NIXON visits China—Shanghai Communique—(1972)
(Up to 1975 PRC has diplomatic relations with 140 nations including Philippines)
Cultural Revolution II: Anti-Confucius and Lin Piao
Riot at Tien An Men Square (1976)
HUA KUO-FENG new premier (1976)
Chairman MAO dies (1976), HUA succeeds him
Fall of Gang of Four
TENG HSIAO-PING returns to power (1977)
Big-character posters at Peking's "Democracy Wall"
China and Japan establish diplomatic relations (1978)
U.S. and China establish diplomatic relations (1979)
TENG state visit to U.S. (1979)
"Four Modernizations"
Brief Chinese invasion of Vietnam
Conclusion of People's Congress (July 1979)
China condemns Cultural Revolution
Leading dissident WEI CHING-SHENG (Wei Jing Sheng) sentenced

First launching of ICBM
Many cultural, technical and educational exchanges between the U.S. and the PRC
Trial of Gang of Four

1980

Recession in the U.S.
Zimbabwe, new African nation with black majority rule
UN General Assembly demands return of all Arab land. Israel Knesset votes to make Jerusalem its new capital (July 1980)
RONALD REAGAN elected president

References

Aisin-Gioro, Pu Yi
  1964   *From Emperor to Citizen: The Autobiography of Aisin-Gioru Pu Yi.* 2 vols. Peking: Foreign Language Press.

Anonymous
  1966   *My Secret Life.* New York: Grove Press.

The American Bankers Association
  1967   *Banking, A Career for Today and Tomorrow.* Prepared by the Personnel Administration and Management Development Committee, New York.

Barnes, H. E.
  1939   *Society in Transition.* New York: Prentice-Hall. (2nd ed. 1952.)

Bateson, Gregory
  1942   "Some Systematic Approaches to the Study of Culture and Personality." *Character and Personality* 11:76–82. Reprinted in D. G. Haring, *Personal Character and Social Milieu.* New York: Syracuse University Press, 1949, pp. 110–116.

Battle, Ronald H., and Kenney, John P.
  1966   "Aggressive Crime." In *The Annals of the American Academy of Political and Social Science.* Vol. 364. (Special issue on "Patterns of Violence.")

Bennis, Warren G., and Slater, Philip E.
  1964   *The Temporary Society.* New York: Harper Colophon Books.

Bergsma, Lily Chu
  1977   *A Cross-cultural Study of Conformity in Americans and Chinese.* San Francisco: Rand Research Associates.

Bernstein, Carl, and Woodward, Bob
  1974   *All the President's Men.* New York: Simon and Schuster.

Bettelheim, Bruno
  1966   "Violence: A Neglected Note of Behavior." In *The Annals of the*

American Academy of Political and Social Science. Vol. 364. (Special issue on "Patterns of Violence.")

Billington, Ray Allen
1966   *America's Frontier Heritage.* New York: Holt, Rinehart and Winston.

Blanchard, William H.
1978   *Aggression American Style.* Santa Monica, California: Goodyear Publishing Co.

Blenker, Margaret
1965   "Social work and family relationships in later life with some thoughts of filial maturity." In *Social Structure and the Family: Generational Relations,* edited by Ethel Shanas and Gordon F. Streib. Englewood Cliffs, New Jersey: Prentice-Hall.

Block, Herbert
1952   *The Herblock Book.* Boston: Beacon Press.

Bolles, Blair
1952   *How to Get Rich in Washington.* New York: W. W. Norton.

Boorstin, Daniel J.
1965   *The Americans: The National Experience.* New York: Random House.

1973   *The Americans: The Democratic Experience.* New York: Random House.

Brademeier, Harry, and Toby, Jackson
1960   *Social Programs in America.* New York: John Wiley and Sons.

Brinton, Crane
1930   *The Jacobins: An Essay in the New History.* New York: Russell and Russell.

1938   *The Anatomy of a Revolution.* New York: W. W. Norton. Revised 1952. Englewood Cliffs, N.J.: Prentice-Hall. Revised and expanded 1965. New York: Vintage Books.

Brogan, D. W.
1941   *U.S.A.: An Outline of the Country, Its People and Institutions.* London and New York: Oxford University Press.

Brown, Frederick
1902   *From T'ientsin to Peking with the Allied Forces.* London: C. H. Kelly.

Brown, Stuart Gerry, ed.
1950   *The Social Philosophy of Josiah Royce.* Syracuse, New York: Syracuse University Press.

1952   *The Religious Philosophy of Josiah Royce.* Syracuse, New York: Syracuse University Press.

Bryan, Dawson
    1952   *Building Church Membership through Evangelism.* Nashville, Tenn.:
            Abingdon-Cokesbury.

Bryce, James
    1910   *The American Commonwealth.* New York: Macmillan.

Buck, J. L.
    1937   *Land Utilization in China.* Chicago: The University of Chicago
            Press.

Buck, Pearl S.
    1930   *Good Earth.* New York: John Day.

    1941   *Of Men and Women.* New York: John Day.

Cantril, Hadley
    1958   *The Politics of Despair.* New York: Basic Books.

Capra, Fritjof
    1976   *The Tao of Physics.* Boulder, Colorado: Shambhala Publications.

Castro, Josui de
    1952   *The Geography of Hunger.* Boston: Little, Brown and Co.

Centers, Richard
    1949   *The Psychology of Social Classes.* Princeton: Princeton University
            Press.

    1953   "Social Class, Occupation and Imputed Belief." *American Journal
            of Sociology* 58 (May):546.

Chang, Eileen
    1956   *Naked Earth.* Hong Kong: The Union Press.

    1955   *The Rice-Sprout Song.* New York: Charles Scribner's Sons.

Chen, Chung-min
    1977   *Upper Camp: A Study of a Chinese Mixed Cropping Village in Taiwan.*
            Nanking, Taiwan: Institute of Ethnology.

Ch'en, Shou-yi
    1961   *Chinese Literature: A Historical Introduction.* New York: Ronald Press
            Co.

Chin, Ai-li S.
    1966   *Modern Chinese Fiction and Family Relations: Analysis of Kinship, Mar-
            riage and the Family in Contemporary Taiwan and Communist Stories.*
            Cambridge, Mass.: M.I.T. Center for International Studies.

China Reconstructs 27, no. 10, Oct. 1978.

Chow, Yung-teh
    1966   *Social Mobility in China: Status Careers Among the Gentry in a Chinese
            Community.* New York: Atherton Press.

Chu, Ch'en-lou
  1967   "Civic Organizations." In Lung Kuan-hai, *A Social Survey of the Kuting District of Taipei City,* 1967, pp. 115–128.

Chu, Godwin C.
  1966   "Culture, Personality and Persuability." *Sociometry* 29:169–174.

  1977   *Radical Change through Communication in Mao's China.* Honolulu: The University Press of Hawaii.

  1978   *Popular Media in China: Shaping New Cultural Patterns.* Honolulu: The University Press of Hawaii.

Chu, Godwin C., and Hsu, Francis L. K.
  1980   *Moving a Mountain: Cultural Change in China.* Honolulu: The University Press of Hawaii.

  1981   "Integration in China: The Post Mao Years." In *China's New Social Fabric,* edited by Godwin C. Chu and Francis L. K. Hsu, in press.

Chu, Godwin C., and Chu, Leonard L.
  1979   "Letters to the Editor: They Write in China." *East-West Perspectives.* Journal of the East-West Center (summer).

Chung Kuo Fu Nu [Chinese Women], a magazine. No. 6, June 1, 1963.

Clark, Kenneth
  1963   "The Blot and the Diagram." *Encounter.* January.

Clark, Margaret and Anderson, Barbara Gallatin
  1967   *Culture and Aging: An Anthropological Study of Older Americans.* Springfield, Ill.: Charles C. Thomas.

Codere, Helen
  1955   "A Genealogical Study of Kinship in the United States." *Psychiatry* 18:(1).

Cohen, Myron
  1978   "Family Partition and Contractual Procedure in Taiwan." In *Chinese Family Law and Social Change in Historical and Comparative Perspective,* edited by David C. Buxbaum. Seattle: University of Washington Press.

Commager, Henry Steele
  1950   *The American Mind.* New Haven: Yale University Press.

  1974   "The Significance of Watergate." In *Britannica Book of the Year, 1974,* pp. 709–710. Chicago: Encyclopedia Britannica.

Congressional Quarterly, July 7, 1967.

Creel, Herlee G.
  1953   *Chinese Thought from Confucius to Mao Tze-tung.* Chicago: University of Chicago Press.

Crook, Isabel, and Crook, David
    1966   *The First Years of Yangyi Commune.* London: Routledge and Kegan Paul.

Crossman, Richard, ed.
    1949   *The God That Failed.* New York: Harper and Row.

Cuber, John F., and Harper, Robert A.
    1948   *Problems of American Society: Values in Conflict.* New York: Henry Holt.

Cumming, Elaine, and Schneider, David
    1961   "Sibling Solidarity: A Property of American Kinship." *American Anthropologist* 63:498–507.

Dane, Sir Richard
    1929   "China and the So-called Opium War." *The Asiatic Review* 25: 611–624.

de Lone, Richard
    1979   *Small Futures: Children, Inequality, and the Limits of Liberal Reform.* For the Carnegie Council on Children. New York: Harcourt, Brace & Jovanovich.

De Tocqueville, Alexis
    1947   *Democracy in America.* Translated by Henry Reeve. New York and London: Oxford University Press.

Deakin, James
    1966   *The Lobbyists.* Washington, D.C.: Public Affairs Press.

Der Ling, Princess
    1911   *Two Years in the Forbidden City.* New York: Moffat Yard and Co.

Deschamps, Hubert
    1959   "Vietnam." In *Encyclopedia Britannica,* pp. 145–145b.

Di Renzo, Gordon, ed.
    1977   *We the People: American Character and Social Change.* Westport, Conn.: Greenwood Press.

Dickens, Charles
    1967   *American Notes. For General Circulation.* Boston: Ticknor and Fields.

Eberhard, Wolfram
    1967   *Guilt and Sin in Traditional China.* Berkeley: University of California Press.

Eddy, Nathan B.; Halback, H.; Isbell, Harris; and Seevers, Maurice H.
    1965   "Drug Dependence: Its Significance and Characteristics." *Bulletin of WHO* 32L721–33.

Edgerton, Clement, trans.
    1939   *The Golden Lotus (Chin Ping Mei).* London: Routledge.

Ernst, Morris L., and Loth, David
    1952   *Report on the American Communist.* New York: Henry Holt.

FBI
    1978   *Uniform Crime Report.* Washington, D.C.: Superintendent of Documents, U.S. Government Printing Office.

Faber, Doris
    1979   *The Presidents' Mothers.* New York: St. Martin's Press.

Fadhlan, Ibn
    1948   "The Vikings Abroad and at Home." In *A Reader in General Anthropology,* edited by Carleton S. Coon. New York: Henry Holt.

Fairbank, John King
    1966   "New Thinking about China." *Atlantic Monthly* (June) pp. 77–78.

    1966   "The People's Middle Kingdom." *Foreign Affairs* (July).

    1979   *The United States and China.* Cambridge: Harvard University Press.

Feuerwekker, Albert
    1968   "Comments" on "Nineteenth-Century China: The Disintegration of the Old Order and the Impact of the West" by Kwang-ching Lin. In *China in Crisis,* Vol. I, Book 1, edited by Ping-ti Ho and Tang Tsou. Chicago: University of Chicago Press.

Fifth Moon Exhibition
    1970   *Five Chinese Painters.* Taipei, Taiwan.

Foerster, Norman, ed.
    1934   *American Poetry and Prose.* New York, Boston: Houghton Mifflin.

Forman, Harrison
    1945   *Report from Red China.* New York: Henry Holt.

Freud, Sigmund, and Bullitt, William C.
    1967   *Thomas Woodrow Wilson, 28th President of the United States: A Psychological Study.* Boston: Houghton Mifflin.

Friedman, Milton
    1980   (Report on the Political Storm in Britain Due to Friedman's Theories of Economics), *San Francisco Chronicle,* March 7.

Fromm, Erich
    1941   *Escape from Freedom.* New York: Holt, Rinehart and Winston.

Fuchs, Lawrence H.
    1967   *The Peace Corps and American National Character.* New York: Meredith Press.

Gallin, Bernard
    1966   *Hsin Hsing, Taiwan: A Chinese Village in Change.* Berkeley: University of California Press.

Garrity, John
  1952   "The Truth About the 'Drug Menace.' " *Harper's* 204 (February):27–31.

Gaskill, G. E.
  1933   "A Chinese Official's Experiences during the First Opium War." *The American Historical Review* 39:82–86.

Goode, William J.
  1963   *World Revolution and Family Patterns.* New York: Free Press of Glencoe.

Goodman, Walter
  1963   *All Honorable Men: Corruption and Compromise in American Life.* Boston: Little, Brown and Co.

Gorer, Geoffrey
  1948   *The American People.* New York: W. W. Norton. (Revised 1964.)

Grover, Robert
  1961   *The One Hundred Dollar Misunderstanding.* New York: Ballantine Books, Inc.

Gulick, Sidney L.
  1937   *Mixing the Races in Hawaii.* Honolulu: The Hawaiian Board Book Rooms.

Halberstam, David
  1972   *The Best and the Brightest.* New York: Random House.

Hao, Keng-sheng
  1967   *"Keng Sheng Hsiao Chi"* [A small autobiographical note on Keng Sheng]. *Chuan Chi Wen Hsueh* [Biographical Literature]. Vol. 11, No. 4.

Harris, Frank
  1963   *My Life and Loves.* New York: Grove Press.

Helfer, Ray E., and Kempe, C. Henry, eds.
  1968   *The Battered Child.* Chicago: University of Chicago Press.

Henry, Jules
  1963   *Culture Against Man.* New York: Random House.

Herring, Edward Pendleton
  1936   *Public Administration and the Public Interest.* New York: McGraw-Hill Book Co.

Hicks, Granville
  1954   *Where We Came Out.* New York: Viking Press.

Hill, Jennie-Keith
  1968   *The Culture of Retirement.* Ph.D. dissertation, Northwestern University.

Hinton, William
  1967   *Fan Shen: A Documentary of Revolution in a Chinese Village.* New York:
         Monthly Review Press.

Ho, Ping-ti, and Tsou, Tang, eds.
  1968   *China in Crisis.* Vol. 1, Books 1 and 2. Chicago: University of Chi-
         cago Press.

Hsia, Chih-ts'ing
  1961   *A History of Modern Chinese Fiction 1917–1957.* New Haven: Yale
         University Press.

Hsu, Francis L. K.
  1943   "The Myth of Chinese Family Size." *American Journal of Sociology*
         48:555–562.

  1949   "China." In *Most of the World,* edited by Ralph Linton. New
         York: Columbia University Press.

  1952   *Religion, Science, and Human Crises.* London: Routledge and Kegan
         Paul.

  1953   *Americans and Chinese: Two Ways of Life.* New York: H. Schuman.

  1963   *Clan, Caste and Club.* Princeton, New Jersey: Van Nostrand and
         Co. (Japanese translation of Clan, Caste and Club, Tokyo:
         Baifukan, 1971.)

  1968   "Chinese Kinship and Chinese Behavior." In *China in Crisis,* Vol.
         1, Book 1, edited by Ping-ti Ho and Tang Tsou. Chicago: Uni-
         versity of Chicago Press.

  1968   "Psychological Anthropology: An Essential Defect and Its Rem-
         edy." Paper presented at the 1968 annual meetings of the Ameri-
         can Anthropological Association, Seattle, Washington.

  1971   "Psychological Homeostasis and *Jen:* Conceptual Tools for Ad-
         vancing Psychological Anthropology." *American Anthropologist* 73:
         23–44.

  1971   *Under the Ancestors' Shadow: Kinship, Personality and Social Mobility in
         China.* Stanford: Stanford University Press.

  1973   "Kinship is the Key." *The Center Magazine* 6:4–14.

  1974   *China Day by Day.* New Haven, Conn.: Yale University Press
         (with Eileen Hsu-Balzer and Richard Balzer).

  1975   *Iemoto: The Heart of Japan.* New York: Halsted Press.

  1977   "Review of *Childhood in China,*" edited by William Kessen. *Ameri-
         can Journal of Sociology* 83 (September):521–524.

  1977   "Individual Fulfillment, Social Stability and Cultural Progress."
         In *We, the People: American Character and Social Change,* edited by
         Gordon J. Di Renzo. Westport, Conn.: Greenwood Publishers.

1978   "The Myth of Chinese Expansionism." *Journal of Asian and African Studies* 13:184–195.

Hu, Shih
1953   "Ch'an (Zen) Buddhism in China: Its History and Method." *Philosophy East and West* 3:3–24.

Huc, M.
1857   *A Journey Through the Chinese Empire.* Vol. 2. New York: Harper and Brothers.

Huang, Lucy Jen
1962   *The Impact of the Commune on the Chinese Family. Tempo* monograph. Santa Barbara, California.

Huang, Yen-yu
1941   "Viceroy Yeh Ming-ch'en and the Canton episode (1856–1861)." *Harvard Journal of Asiatic Studies* 6:37–127.

Hyneman, Charles
1950   *Bureaucracy in a Democracy.* New York: Harper.

Janis, Irving L., and Field, Peter B.
1956   "A Behavioral Assessment of Persuability: Consistency of Individual Differences." *Sociometry* 19:241–259.

Jewell, Edward Alden
1939   *Have We an American Art?* New York: Longmans, Green & Co.

Johnston, Richard W.
1952   "Death's Fair-haired Boy." *Life.* June 23.

Jones, James
1951   *From Here to Eternity.* New York: Charles Scribner and Sons.

Judelle, Beatrice
1969   "Child Population Study: National Toy Market Analysis." *Toys and Novelties* (12th report). Chicago: Harbrace Publications.

Kahl, Joseph A.
1953   *The American Class Structure.* New York: Rinehart.

Kammen, Michael
1972   *People of Paradox: An Inquiry Concerning the Origins of American Civilization.* New York: Alfred Knopf.

Keniston, Kenneth
1960   *The Uncommitted: Alienated Youth in American Society.* New York: Dell Publishing Co.

The Kerner Report
1968   Report of the National Advisory Commission on Civil Disorders. New York: Bantam Books.

Kessen, William, ed.
1975   *Childhood in China*. New Haven, Conn.: Yale University Press.

Kroeber, A. L.
1944   *Configurations of Culture Growth*. Berkeley: University of California Press.

La Dany, Father
1966   "A Reporter at Large: The China Watchers." *The New Yorker.* February 12, pp. 41–109.

Lao She (Shu, Ch'ing-ch'un)
1945   *Luo Tuo Hsiang-Tzu*. Translated by Evan King as *Rickshaw Boy*. New York: Reynal and Hitchcock.

Lasch, Christopher
1979   *The Culture of Narcissism: American Life in an Age of Diminished Expectations*. New York: W. W. Norton.

Laski, Harold J.
1948   *The American Democracy*. New York: Viking Press.

1960   "Religion, Value-Orientation, and Intergroup Conflict." *The Journal of Social Issues* 12:14–15.

Lattimore, Owen
1945   *Solution in Asia*. Boston: Little, Brown and Co.

Lau, Sui-kai
1979   "The People's Commune as a Communication Network in the Diffusion of Agritechnology." In *Moving a Mountain: Cultural Change in China,* edited by Godwin C. Chu and Francis L. K. Hsu. Honolulu: The University Press of Hawaii.

Leys, Simon
1977   *Chinese Shadows*. New York: Viking Press.

Levy, Howard S.
1966   *Chinese Footbinding: The History of a Curious Erotic Custom*. New York: Walton Rawls.

Lew, Timothy Tinfang
1923   "China in American School Textbooks." Special Supplement of the *Chinese Social and Political Science Review* (July):1–154.

Lewin, Kurt
1948   *Resolving Social Conflict*. New York: Harper and Brothers.

Lewis, John W.
1966   "Political Aspects of Mobility in China's Urban Development." *American Political Science Review* 60 (December):899–912.

Li, Fu-yi
1958   *"Chung Kuo Wen Hua Tui T'ai Kuo Ti Ying Hsiang"* [The influence

of Chinese civilization on Thailand]. In Sun-Sheng Ling et al., *Chung T'ao Wen Hwa Lun Chi* [Collected essays on Chinese-Thai civilizations]. Taipei.

Lin, Yutang
1935   *My Country and My People.* New York: John Day.

Lindesmith, Alfred R.
1947   *Opiate Addiction.* Bloomington, Indiana: Principia Press.

Link, Henry C.
1936   *The Return to Religion.* New York: Macmillan.

Lipset, Seymour M.
1963   *The First New Nation: The U.S. in Historical and Comparative Perspective.* New York: Basic Books.

Lo, Kuan-chung
Ming Dynasty (1368–1644) *The Romance of the Three Kingdoms.* Translated (partially) by C. H. Brewitt-Taylor. Shanghai: Kelly and Walsh

Lowe, C. H. (Chuan-hua)
1934   *Facing Labor Issues in China.* London: Allen. (This book was first published by the Institute of Pacific Relations.)

Lu, Hsün (Chou, Shu-jen)
1941   *Ah Q Cheng Chuan (The True Story of Ah Q).* Translated by Wang Chi-chen, in *Ah Q and Others.* New York: Columbia University Press.

Lubell, Samuel
1965   *The Future of American Politics.* 3d. rev. ed. New York: Harper & Row.

Lung, Kuan-hai
1967   *Tai Pei Shih Ku T'ing Ch'ü She Hui Tiao Ch'a Pao Kao (A Social Survey of the Kuting District of Taipei City).* Taipei: Department of Sociology, National Taiwan University.

Lynes, Russell
1964   "Dining at Home." In *The American Heritage Cookbook and Illustrated History of American Eating and Drinking.* New York: Simon and Schuster.

Mackerras, Colin, and Hunter, Neale
1967   *China Observed.* Melbourne: Nelson.

Mallory, Walter Hampton
1926   *China, Land of Famine.* New York: American Geographic Society.

Masters, William, and Johnson, Virginia
1979   *Homosexuality in Perspective.* Boston: Little, Brown and Co.

Mazour, Anatole G., and Peoples, John M.
   1964   *Men and Nations: A World History.* New York: Harcourt, Brace and World.

Mead, Margaret
   1949   *Male and Female.* New York: W. Morrow.

Mendelowitz, Daniel M.
   1970   *A History of American Art.* New York: Holt, Rinehart and Winston.

Miller, Donald E.
   1966   "Narcotic Drug and Marijuana Controls." Paper presented at National Association of Student Personnel Administrators Drug Education Conference, Washington, D.C., November 7–8.

Miller, Henry
   1961   *Tropic of Cancer.* New York: Grove Press.

Mills, Ted
   1978   *Quality of Work Life: What's in a Name?* A pamphlet issued by The American Center for Quality of Work Life, Washington, D.C.

Moorehead, Alan
   1952   *The Traitors.* New York: Scribner's.

Munch, James E.
   1966   "Marijuana and Crime." *United Nations Bulletin on Narcotics* 18 (April–June):15–22.

Myrdal, Gunnar
   1944   *An American Dilemma.* New York: Harper and Brothers.

Myrdal, Jan
   1965   *Report from a Chinese Village.* New York: Pantheon Books.

Needham, Joseph (with the collaboration of Wang Ling)
   1954   *Science and Civilization in China.* Cambridge: Cambridge University Press. Volume 1: Introductory Orientations.

   1956   Volume 2: *History of Scientific Thought.*

   1959   Volume 3: *Mathematics and the Sciences of the Earth.*

   1962   Volume 4: *Physics and Physical Technology.* Part I, *Physics.*

   1965   Volume 4: *Physics and Physical Technology.* Part II, *Mechanical Engineering.*

Needham, Joseph (with the collaboration of Wang Ling and Lu Gwei Djen)
   1971   Volume 4: *Physics and Physical Technology.* Part III, *Civil Engineering and Nautics.*

Needham, Joseph (with the collaboration of Lu Gwei Djen)
   1974   Volume 5: *Chemistry and Chemical Technology.* Part II, *Spagyrical Discovery and Invention: Magistries of Gold and Immortality.* (Parts I, III,

IV, V and VI are in preparation, but parts III, IV and V will appear before part I, according to Needham.)

Volume 6: *Biology and Medicine* (projected for the future).

Northrop, F. S. C.
1946   *The Meeting of East and West.* New York: Macmillan.
1952   "The Mind of Asia." *Life,* December 31.

Nowell, Iris
1979   *The Dog Crisis.* New York: St. Martin's Press.

Parker, E. C.; Barry, David W.; Smythe, Dallas W.
1955   *The Television Radio Audience and Religion.* New York: Harper.

People's Republic of China
1974   *Peasant Paintings from Huhsien County.* Peking: People's Fine Arts Publishing House.

People's Republic of China
1968   *Rent Collection Courtyard: Sculptures of Oppression and Revolt.* Peking, Foreign Language Press.

Philpott, H. M.
1943   "Conversion Techniques Used by the New Sects in the South." *Religious Education* 38:174–179.

Pike, Bishop James
1967   "Tax Organized Religion." *Playboy.* 14(April).

Portisch, Hugo
1966   *Red China Today.* Chicago: Quadrangle Books.

Putnam, Carleton
1961   *Race and Reason: A Yankee View.* Washington, D.C.: Public Affairs Press.

1967   *Race and Reality: A Search for Solutions.* Washington, D.C.: Public Affairs Press.

Pye, Lucian
1968   *The Spirit of Chinese Politics: A Psychocultural Study of the Authority Crisis in Political Development.* Cambridge, Mass.: The MIT Press.

Rice, Berkeley
1968   *The Other End of the Leash: The American Way with Pets.* Boston: Little, Brown and Co.

Riesman, David
1950   *The Lonely Crowd.* New Haven: Yale University Press.

Rossi, A.
1949   *A Communist Party in Action.* New Haven: Yale University Press.

Roth, Philip
1968   *Portnoy's Complaint.* New York: Random House.

Salinger, J. D.
  1951 *The Catcher in the Rye.* Boston: Little, Brown and Co.

Sarris, Andrew
  1978 "Film Criticism in the Seventies." *Film Comment* 14 (January).
  1980 "Praise the Year and Pass the Decade." In Films in Focus Series,
          The Village Voice. January 14.

Schneider, David
  1968 *American Kinships: A Cultural Account.* Englewood Cliffs, New Jersey: Prentice-Hall.

Schneider, Louis, and Dornbusch, Sanford M.
  1958 *Popular Religion: Inspiration Books in America.* Chicago: University of Chicago Press.

Schwartz, Benjamin
  1951 *Chinese Communism and the Rise of Mao.* Cambridge: Harvard University Press.

Shanas, Ethel
  1963 "The Unmarried Old Person in the United States: Living Arrangements and Care in Illness, Myth and Fact." Paper prepared for the International Social Science Seminar in Gerontology, Markaryd, Sweden, August, 1963.

Sheridan, James E.
  1966 *Chinese Warlord: The Career of Feng Yü-hsiang.* Stanford: Stanford University Press.

Shih, Nai-an
  1948 *All Men Are Brothers.* Translated by Pearl S. Buck. New York: John Day.

Singh, J. J.
  1952 "How to win friends in Asia." *The New York Times Magazine,* September 28.

Skinner, William G.
  1965 "Marketing and Social Structure in Rural China, Part III." *Journal of Asian Studies* 24 (May):363–399.

Slater, Philip
  1970 *The Pursuit of Loneliness: American Culture at the Breaking Point.* Boston: Beacon Press.

Smith, Henry Nash
  1950 *Virgin Land: The American West as Symbol and Myth.* New York: Vintage Books.

Snow, C. P.
  1968 *The Sleep of Reason.* New York: Scribner's.

Snow, Edgar
1938   *Red Star Over China.* New York: Random House.

Spindler, L., and Spindler, G.
1958   "Male and Female Adaptations in Culture Change." *American Anthropologist* 60:217–233.

Stavrianos, Leften S., et al.
1964   *A Global History of Man.* Boston: Allyn and Bacon.

Steffens, Lincoln
1931   *The Autobiography of Lincoln Steffens.* New York: Harcourt, Brace and Co.

Sun, E-Tu Zen
1965   "Wu Ch'i-chun: Profile of a Chinese Scholar-Technologist." *Technology and Culture* 6:394–406.

Sussman, Marvin B.
1965   "Relationships of Adult Children with Their Parents." In *Social Structure and the Family: Generational Relations,* edited by Ethel Shanas and Gordon F. Streib. Englewood Cliffs, New Jersey: Prentice-Hall.

Tan, Chester C. (T'an, Ch'un-lin)
1955   *The Boxer Catastrophe.* New York: Columbia University Press.

Tawney, Richard H.
1960   *Religion and the Rise of Capitalism.* New York: Harcourt, Brace and Co.

Taylor, G. R., ed.
1949   *The Turner Thesis: Concerning the Role of the Frontier in American History.* Boston: D. C. Heath.

Truman, David B.
1951   *The Government Process: Political Interests and Public Opinion.* New York: Knopf.

Ts'ao, Chan
1929   *The Dream of the Red Chamber.* Translated by C. C. Wang. Garden City, New York: Doubleday, Doran, and Co.

Tsou, Tang
1963   *America's Failure in China, 1941–50.* Chicago: University of Chicago Press.

1968   "Revolution, Reintegration, and Crisis in Communist China: A Framework for Analysis." In *China in Crisis,* Vol. 1, Book 1, edited by Ping-ti Ho and Tang Tsou. Chicago: University of Chicago Press.

Tsou, Tang, ed.
1968   *China in Crisis.* Vol. 2. Chicago: University of Chicago Press.

Tsunoda, Ryusaku, de Bary, William T., and Keene, Donald
  1958   *Sources of Japanese Tradition.* New York: Columbia University Press.

Tuchman, Barbara
  1972   *Notes from China.* New York: Collier Books.

Turner, Frederick J.
  1920   "The Significance of the Frontier in American History." In F. J. Turner, *The Frontier in American History.* New York: Henry Holt.

U.S. Bureau of the Census
  1979   *Divorce, Child Custody and Child Support.* Washington, D.C.: Superintendent of Documents, U.S. Government Printing Office.

U.S.–China People's Friendship Association
  1977   *Peasant Paintings from Huhsien County of the People's Republic of China.* Chicago.

U.S. Department of Commerce
  1977   *Social Indicators 1976: Selected Data on Social Conditions and Trends in the United States.* Washington, D.C.: Superintendent of Documents, U.S. Government Printing Office.

U.S. Government
  1967   *The Challenge of Crime in a Free Society.* Reported by the President's Commission on Law Enforcement and Administration and Justice. Washington, D.C.: U.S. Government Printing Office.

  1967   *Crime and Its Impact: An Assessment.* The President's Commission on Law Enforcement and Administration of Justice, Washington, D.C.: U.S. Government Printing Office.

  1967   *Hearings before a Subcommittee of the Committee on Appropriations.* House of Representatives. February 8.

  1969   *The Budget in Brief, Fiscal Year 1970.* Executive Office of the President, Bureau of the Budget. Washington, D.C.: U.S. Government Printing Office, January 15.

  1980   *The Budget in Brief, Fiscal Year 1980.* Executive Office of the President, Bureau of the Budget. Washington, D.C.: U.S. Government Printing Office.

Walker, C. Lester
  1946   "The China Legend." *Harper's* (March) p. 239.

Warner, Lloyd and Associates
  1949   *Democracy in Jonesville: A Study in Equality and Inequality.* New York: Harper.

Weber, Max
  1952   *The Religion of China.* Glencoe, Illinois: The Free Press.

White, William Charles
    1942   *Chinese Jews: A Compilation of Matters Relating to the Jews of K'aifeng Fu.* 3 Vols. Toronto: University of Toronto Press.

Whyte, William H., Jr.
    1956   *The Organization Man.* New York: Simon and Schuster.

Williams, Robin M.
    1970   *American Society, a Sociological Interpretation.* New York: Knopf.

Wolfgang, Marvin E.
    1967   "The Culture of Youth." Office of Juvenile Delinquency, Welfare Administration, U.S. Department of Health, Education, and Welfare. Reprinted in *Task Force Report: Juvenile Delinquency and Youth Crime.* President's Commission on Law Enforcement and Administration of Justice. Washington, D.C.: U.S. Government Printing Office.

Wu, Ch'eng-en
    1930   *Western Journey.* Partially translated by Helen M Hayes in *The Buddhist Pilgrim's Progress.* New York: E. P. Dutton.

    1943   *Western Journey.* Partially translated by Arthur Waley in *Monkey.* New York: John Day.

Young, Kimball and Mack, Raymond
    1962   *Sociology and Social Life.* 2d ed. New York: American Book Co.

Zukov, Gary
    1975   *The Dancing Wu Li Masters.* New York: Morrow.

Name Index

Acheson, Dean, 224
Adams, Samuel, 373
Adams, Sherman, 219–220, 225
Albright, Ivan LeLorraine, 23
Alcott, A. Bronson, 97
Alsop, Joseph, 7–8
Anderson, Barbara, 340
Anderson, John, 229, 235

Bacall, Lauren, 176
Baker, Bobby, 220
Baldwin, James, 32
Ball, George W., 224
Balzer, Richard, 238
Bao Dai, Emperor, 441
Barth, John, 124
Bateson, Gregory, 77
Beatty, Warren, 176
Beethoven, Ludwig Von, 393
Bell, Alexander Graham, 482
Bellow, Saul, 32
Bennett, Joan, 176
Bergman, Ingrid, 184
Bettelheim, Bruno, 362
Black, Shirley Temple, 176
Blanton, Smiley, 283
Block, Herbert, 225
Bolles, Blair, 221
Booth, John Wilkes, 206
Borodin, Michael, 443
Brando, Marlon, 176
Brinton, Crane, 463–464
Brown, Claude, 124
Brown, Stuart Gerry, xxviii, 466
Bruce, Robert, 104
Bryan William Jennings, 233
Buchannan, Frank, 223
Buck, John L., 310, 316
Buck, Pearl, 61
Bullitt, William C., 184
Buttons, Red, 176

Calvin, John, 409
Canyon, Steve, 359
Capote, Truman, 125
Carlsen, Henrik Kurt, 181
Carlyle, Thomas, 31
Carnegie, Dale, 217
Carson, Rachel, 124
Carter, Billy, 224
Carter, Jack, 229–230
Carter, Jimmy, 174, 450
Chang Ch'ien, 189, 395
Chang, Eileen, 41, 44
Chang Hen-sui, 41
Chang Tso-lin, 183
Chang Wen Tien, 44
Ch'en Tu-hsui, 324
Cheng Ho, Admiral, 29, 448
Chiang Ch'ing (Madame Mao), 177
Chiang Ching-Kuo, 184
Chiang Kai-shek. See Subject Index
Chiang Kai-shek, Madame (Mei-ling
   Soong), 415
Chiang T'ai King (Lu Shang), 246
Ch'ien Chung-shu, 44
Ch'ien Lung (emperor), 449
Chichester (English adventurer), 335
Chopin, Frederick, 393
Chou En-lai, 137, 322
Chou Yang, 45
"Christian General." See Feng Yu-hsiang
Chu Cheng, 196
Chu, Godwin C., 41
Chu Hsi, 482
Clark, Kenneth, 23
Clark, Margaret, 340
Cleveland, Grover, 233
Cohen, Myron, 151
Cole, Thomas, 22
Columbus, Christopher, 104
Connally, John B., 233
Coolidge, Calvin, 218

Cooke, Dwight, 284
Cooper, D. B., 178, 348
Cooper, Gary, 384
Copley, John Singleton, 22
Cromier, Robert, 84

Davies, Jordan, 24
Da Vinci, Leonardo, 19
Davenport, Marcia, 5
Davis, Sammy, Jr., 176
Davis, Stuart, 22
de Castro, Josui, 300
de Kooning, Willem, 23
Deakin, James, 221
Dean, Gordon, 465
Der Ling, Princess, 189, 212
Dewey, John, 97-98, 224
Diem, Ngo Dinh, xxiv, 441
Dietrich, Marlene, 176
Diggs, Charles C. (U.S. Representative), 220
Dodds, Gilbert, 283
Doré, Henri, 245
Douglas, Melvin, 176
Dostoevski, Feodor, 32
Dulles, John Foster, 447

Ebert, Roger, 125
Edgerton, Clement, 32
Edison, Thomas, 483
Eggleston, Sir Alexander, 8
Eikerenkoeter, Frederick J. (Rev. Ike), 284
Eisenhower, David Dwight, 219, 234
Emerson, Ralph Waldo, 135, 378
Engels, Frederick, 457
Escobar, 23

Faber, Doris, 184
Fa Hsien, 395
Falwell, Jerry, 280
Faulkner, William, 32
Feng Yu-hsiang, 183, 227
Fischer, Louis, 458
Flood, Daniel J. (U.S. Representative), 220
Ford, Gerald, 450
Ford, Henry, 483
Fosdick, E., 287
Franklin, Benjamin, 104
Freud, Sigmund, 76, 87, 131, 184
Friedman, Milton, 380
Froebel, Frederick Wilhelm August, 97
Fromm, Erich, 366
Fuch, Klaus, 465

Gallin, Bernard, 199
Garrison, William Lloyd, 373
Gide, Andre, 458
Giles, Herbert A., 32
Goethe, 31

Gogh, Vincent Van, 19
Goldberg, Arthur J., 224
Goldfine, Bernard, 219-220, 225
Goodman, Ellen, 341
Goodman, Walter, 221
Gorer, Geoffrey, 78, 130
Graham, Billy. *See* Subject Index
Green, Arthur, 25
Grover, Robert, 32
Gulick, Sidney, 261

Halberstam, David, 228, 447
Hao Keng-sheng, 82
Harris, Frank, 38, 39
Hart, Henry H., 32
Hawthorne, Nathaniel, 32
Hayes, John, 474
Hayes, Wayne (U.S. Representative), 178, 221
Hayworth, Rita, 184
Hearst, William Randolph, 189
Hemingway, Ernest, 32, 365
Henri, Robert, 23
Henry, Jules, 341
Herlihy, James, 124
Hersey, John, 32
Hesse, Hermann, 118-119
Heyerdahl, Thor, 124
Hitler, Adolf. *See* Subject Index
Ho, Ping-ti, 329
Hoffman, Hans, 22
Homer, Winslow, 19
Hoover, Herbert, 367
Hope, Bob, 383
Hsiung, S. I., 32
Hsu, Penny, 67
Hsu-Balzer, Eileen, 311
Hsu Wen-ch'ang, 1
Hsuan Hua, 285
Hsuan Tsang, 395
Hu Shih, 231, 446-447
Hu Tsung-nan (general), 151
Hubbard, David G., 463
Hughes, Howard, 178
Hurley, Patrick J., 411
Hyneman, Charles S., 217

Jefferson, Thomas, 377
Jewell, Edward Alden, 24
Johnson, Louis A., 21
Johnson, Lyndon B., 184, 220, 228
Jones, E. Stanley, 287
Jones, James (novelist), 124

Kant, Immanuel, 409
Katzenbach, Nicholas, 229
Kelleher, Edward, 361
Keniston, Kenneth, 345
Kennedy, John F., 179, 206, 364

Kennedy, Robert, 176, 206, 234, 364
Kensett, John, 22
King, Martin Luther, Jr., 206, 364
Kinsey, Alfred C., 361–362
Koch, Edward I., 178
Koo, Wellington, 192–193
Koestler, Arthur, 458, 465–466
Kropotkin, Peter Alexeivich, 409
Kuhn, Franz, 32
Kung, H. H., 189, 308
Kuniyoshi, Yasuo, 23
Ky, Nguen Kau, 441

Lao She (Shu She-yü), 42
Lasch, Christopher, 6
Laski, Harold J., 358
Latourette, K. S., 271
Lattimore, Owen, 200
Lenin, 377, 457
Lewin, Kurt, 358
Lewis, Sinclair, 32
Leys, Simon (Pierre Rychmans), 436
Li Shi-mao, 29
Li Hung-chang, 167
Li Yü, 374
Lichtenstein, Roy, 22
Liebman, Joshua, 123
Lin Tse-hsu, 191
Lin Yutang, 375
Lincoln, Abraham, 104, 206
Liu Kuo-sung, 28
Lloyd, Harold, 99
Lo Kuan-chung, 32
Locke, John, 409
London, Jack, 32
Lu Gwei Djen, 384
Lu Hsün (Chou Tso-jen), 42

MacArthur, Douglas, 480
MacDonald, Betty, 125
MacFadden, Bernard, 335
Mackerras, Colin, 252
Magee, J. Ralph (bishop), 278
Mailer, Norman, 32
Manchester, William, 125
Mann, Thomas, 32
Mao Tse-tung. *See* Subject Index
March, Frederic, 176
Marin, John, 22, 123
Marsh, Reginald, 23
Marx, Karl. *See* Subject Index
Massie, Robert K., 125
McCarthy, Eugene, 176, 229
McCarthy, Joseph, 367
McCormack, Robert R., 189
Melville, Herman, 32
Mencius, 22, 483
Mendelowitz, 23
Miller, Henry, 32

Miller, Jeanne, 126
Montaigne, 104
More, Sir Thomas, 134
Morse, Samuel F. B., 22
Mozart, Wolfgang, 393
Murphy, George, 176
Myrdal, Gunnar, 206

Nation, Carrie, 373, 434
Needham, Joseph, 384, 385, 387–388, 391–392, 398
Newman, Paul, 176
Nixon, Richard M., 176, 184, 229, 233, 450
Noland, Kenneth, 23

O'Keeffe, Georgia, 387
Oswald, Lee Harvey, 178–179
Oursler, Fulton, 123
Overstreet, Harry, 123

Pa Chin, 43
Parr, Jack, 176
Paganini, Nicolò, 393
Paine, Thomas, 377
Pan Ch'ao, 395
Pasteur, Louis, 483
Peale, Norman Vincent, 123, 283, 287
Pestalozzi, Johann Heinrich, 97
Plaff, William, 284
Plato, 381
Polo, Marco, 448
Pollock, Jackson, 22, 124
Proxmire, William, 217
Pythagoras, 483

Randall, Clarence, 129
Rasheed, Hakeem Abdul, 284
Rawlings, Marjorie K., 32
Ray, Elizabeth, 178, 221
Reagan, Ronald, 177, 341
Rhyne, Charles S., 224
Reinhardt, Ad, 23
Riesman, David, 121, 132–134, 136
Roberts, Oral, 279
Robespierre, Maximilien François de, 377, 463
Romney, George, 224
Roosevelt, Eleanor, 414
Roosevelt, Franklin D., 218, 233
Roosevelt, Franklin D., Jr., 224
Roosevelt, Theodore (Teddy), 184
Rossi, A., 462–463
Rossner, Judith, 38
Rousseau, Jean J., 97, 377, 463
Rusk, Dean, 229
Russell, Beatrice Jane, 288
Russell, Bertrand, 125

Salinger, J. D., 90
Sarris, Andrew, 126
Schulze, Franz, 24–25
Sculley, Frank, 124
Sheen, Fulton, 124, 287
Shen Ch'ung-wen, 42
Shulman, Max, 38, 124
Shun (emperor), 478
Siemanowski, Raymond, 25
Silone, Ignazio, 458
Skinner, Cornelia Otis, 125
Sloan, John, 23
Smith, Adam, 378, 409
Smith, Gerald L. K., 373
Smith, H. Allen, 125
Smith, Hannah, W., 287
Snow, Edgar, 151
Solzhenitsyn, Alexander, 8
Soong, T. V., 189, 308
Spann, Willie, 178
Spender, Stephen, 458
Spiegel, John P., 363
Spillane, Mickey, 368
Stalin, Joseph, 458, 470, 471
Steele, Max, 124
Steffens, Lincoln, 221, 224
Stern, Susan, 7
Stuart, Gilbert, 22
Sully, Thomas, 22
Sun Myung-Moon, 467
Sun Yat-sen. *See* Subject Index

Taeuber, Irene, 60–61
Talese, Gay, 38
Talmadge, Herman, 220
Tanguy, Yves, 22
T'ao Chu, 227
Tchelitchew, Pavel, 22
Temple, Shirley. *See* Black, Shirley Temple
Teng Hsiao-ping (Deng Xiao-ping), 329, 483
Teng T'uo, 44
Thatcher, Margaret, 380
Thieu, Nguyen Van, 441
Trotsky, Leon, 377
Troyat, Henri, 125
Trueblood, Elton, 287
Truman, Harry S., 101, 220

Tseng Kuo-fan, 482
Tsou Tang, 329
Tu Fu, 189
Tuchman, Barbara, 63–64
Twain, Mark (Samuel Langhorne Clemens), 32, 131

Van Dyck, Sir Thomas, 19
Van Dyke, Dick, 19, 176
Vaughn, Harry, 220
Velikovsky, Immanuel, 124

Wainwright, Jonathan, 178
Waley, Arthur, 47
Wallace, George, 235
Wang Ch'ung, 227
Wang Ling, 384
Wang Yang-ming, 482
Ward, Angus, 416
Warhol, Andy, 22, 123
Warner, Lloyd, 157
Washington, George, 104
Weber, Max, 319, 324
Wen T'ien-hsiang, 237
Werkmeister, Andreas, 391
Whistler, James McNeill, 23
White, William Charles, 271
Whitman, Charles, 364
Whitman, Walt, 37
Whyte, William H., Jr., 136
Willis, William, 335
Williams, Ted, 190
Willkie, Wendell, 232
Wilson, T. Woodrow, 184
Wolfe, Thomas, 6, 32
Wood, Grant, 20, 23, 28
Wright, Richard, 458
Wyeth, Andrew, 19, 23

Yang, Chi-sheng, 134
Yao (emperor), 478
Yen Hsi-shan, 183–184
Young, Andrew, 450
Yu (emperor), 478
Yuan Shih-kai, 379, 410
Yueh Fei, 180
Yung Chung-ching, 189

Subject Index

Abscam, 221
Actors and actresses, attitudes toward, 176–178
Adultery, 21
"Advancement in Officialdom" (a Chinese game), 187, 292
After the First Death (Robert Cromier), 84
Aggression, causes of, 300–301. *See also* Alcoholism; Sex crimes; Violence
Alienation of the youth, 346. *See also* Juvenile delinquency; Narcotics addiction
All Men Are Brothers, 29, 227
Alliluyeva, Svetlana, 125, 307
American Civil Liberties Union (ACLU), 230, 395
American Federation of Labor, 395–396
American way of life: as distinguished from European, 121–123, 127; in art and literature, 124–126; self-reliance versus individualism in, 121–122, 128, 137; factors producing, 128–131. *See also* Individual-centeredness; Mutual dependence; Self-reliance
Analects, 264, 378
Ancestor worship, 248–253
Anti-Catholicism, 359–360. *See also* Religious persecution
Anti-Semitism, 359–360
Art: as projective screens of culture, 17; American and European, 20–25; Chinese traditional, 25; Chinese, since 1949, 26–28; Chinese and Western traditions compared, 19–29
Art of Real Happiness, The (Norman Vincent Peale and Smiley Blanton), 283
Asia Society, 451
Assassination, 206–207, 364
Assembly line (first started in Chinese porcelain works), 295
Association of Odd Fellows, 395
Associations. *See* Clubs

Atheism, 403. *See also* Religion
Autobiographies, popularity of, in America, 125
Autobiography of Lincoln Steffens, The, 221

Babbitt (Sinclair Lewis), 32
Baha'i, 253
Best and the Brightest, The (David Halberstam), 228
Bible, 243, 264–265, 279
Big-character posters, 432
Biographies, popularity of, in America, 125
Black separatism, 358. *See also* Desegregation
Blow-Up, 125
Bolsheviks, 367, 416, 463
Bonnie and Clyde, 125
"Born-again" Christians, 279
Boxer Uprising, 263, 410–411, 444
Breaking Away, 126
Buddha, 240–242, 255, 262, 274
Buddhism, 254–255, 264, 283, 285; Chinese opposition to, 261–262; Western approach to, 274–275
Bureaucracy: and scholarship, 157; rewards in, 188–189, 292–293; power of, 190–191; and religion, 194–195. *See also* Government career
Burial (as filial obligation). *See* Funeral
Business in America, 306–310
Business in China, 293–299; relations of, with government, 304–305

Cargo Cult, 285
Carnegie Council on Children, 161
Catcher in the Rye, The (J. D. Salinger), 90–91, 119
Catholicism, 272–273; reasons for Chinese preference for, 275–276
Challenge of Crime in a Free Society, The (President's Commission on Law En-

forcement and Administration of Justice), 362
Ch'eng Huang (district god), 445
Chi Kung Chuan (The True Story of Chi Kung, the Mad Monk), 227
Chiang Kai-shek, 167, 172-173, 180, 181, 184, 189, 191, 192, 193, 194, 233, 245, 305, 308, 374, 410, 415, 445
Ch'ien Lung (emperor), 449
Children's literature: in America, 83-84; in Taiwan, 85
Child's environment, Chinese and American, 79-92
Chin Ping Mei. See *Golden Lotus, The*
China's Destiny (Chiang Kai-shek), 185
Chinatown, 317-318
Ch'ing Ming (Chinese version of Easter), 251
"Ch'ing Ming Shang Ho" (Spring Festival on the River), 28, 394
Chocolate War, The (Robert Cromier), 84
"Christian General." See Feng Yu-hsiang
Christianity, 253-254, 271, 281; Chinese mercenary attitude toward, 272-273. See also Religion; Supernatural; Mr.
"Chu Divorces His Wife, Mr.," 166-167
Chu Tsai-yü (prince), 391-392, 398
Chung Kuo Ching Nien Tang (Chinese Youth Party), 173
Church, secularization of, in America, 286-289
Cities, in China and America, 312-313
Class, social, 156-163; re-emergence of, under Communism, 429-431
Clubs, 371; *See* Common Cause; *and other free associations by name*
Colonialism: as reason for Communism in Asia, 414-416; America's burden of, 441-443
Comic books, 343-344
Commerce, Chinese (three types of selling), 295
Committees of Correspondence, 373
Common Cause, 230, 280, 395
Communes, 199, 419-420
Communication: problems of, 126-127; between people and government in China, 205, 431-433
Communism, 439-472; intellegentsia's support of, 321-322; background to rise of, in China, 405-412; changes in China under, 418-437; appeal of, to Americans, 458-466; and individualism, 469
Communist Party, American, 466-467
Communist Party in Action, A (A. Rossi), 461-462
Competitiveness: Chinese, 158-159, 320; American, 322-323

Compromise (as a restrictive influence on Chinese science), 389-390
Concubinage, 10; justification for, 50, 242-243
Conformity, 133-137
Confucian temple, 104, 396
Confucianism, 378-379; and education, 95; as non-religion, 264. See also Government
Confucius, 255, 264, 378-379, 482
Conspicuous consumption, 314-316
Contentment, multiple effects of, 384-394
Corruption, 209-216. See also Government; Industrialization
Creativity, social and cultural constraints on, 17
Crime, 360-368, 467-468; and sin, 258
Crusading spirit, Chinese lack of, 373
Cults, 285; proliferation of, 467-468
Cultural Revolution, 44-45, 432-433. See also Red Guard; Gang of Four
Culture and personality, 77, 141-143

Dating, 49-73; American, 56-58; Chinese, 57-60
"Daughters of the American Revolution" (Grant Wood), 20, 23, 28
David and Goliath, 455-456
"Dear Abby" letters, 51-54, 149
"Dear Ann Landers" letters, 424-425
Death of a President, (William Manchester), 125
Democracy, appeal of, to the non-Western world, 440
Desegregation, 353, 359
Dharma Realm Buddhist University, 285, 467
Divination, 244-246
Divorce, 148-149, 153-156. See also Marriage; Weddings
Dogs. See Pets
Domino theory, 103, 447
Dragon God, 231, 242, 256
Dream of the Red Chamber, The (Hung Lo Meng), 29-30, 44, 243
Drug addiction. See Narcotics addiction
Dry parents, 153
Dynastic cycle, 406-407

Earth God, 242, 256, 276
Economic competition, failure of, to divide men in China, 320-328
Economy: American, 307-308; Chinese, 305, 320-323
Education. See Schools
Eikerenkoeter, Frederick J., 284
Elmer Gantry (Sinclair Lewis), 29
Emigration, Chinese lack of interest in, 303-304
Emotionality, 12, 22

Emperors: relations with Chinese people, 187–188; power of, 226–227; opposition to, 382
Empire building (in American government), 216–217. *See also* Government
Empress Dowager, 212, 444
Encyclopaedia Britannica, 99–100
Entrepreneurs in China, 297–298
Ethnocentrism (in American education), 98–108
Examination, imperial, 95, 210
Explorers, Chinese, 394–395
Expressionism, 22
Extroversion, 13

Fair Employment Practices Act, 259
Family: American and Chinese, 79–92; American and English, 122–123; kinds of, 155–156; under Communism, 253
Family division: in traditional China, 302–304; under Communism, 421–422
Fatalism, 106
Federal Bureau of Investigation (FBI), 221
Fen chia. See Family division
Feng Yu-hsiang (the "Christian General"), 183, 227
Fiction: depiction of love in, 29–40; modern Chinese, 42–46
Filial piety: Chinese tales illustrating, 81–82; the twenty-four examples of, 81, 85; duties of, 314–316; as a channel of competition, 320–321. *See also* Family; Parent-child relationship
Five relationships (in Confucian doctrine), 378
Flood myth, 477–479
Footbinding, 374–376
Forbidden City (Peking), 171
Friends of Animals, Inc., 310
From Here to Eternity (James Jones), 34, 37, 124
Fu Manchu, 98, 419–420
Funeral: as a filial obligation, 1–2; exorbitant cost of, in traditional China, 314$ 316

Gambling, 317–318
"Game of Life" (an American game), 292
Gang of Four, 7, 26, 45, 63, 67, 177, 321, 432, 433, 483. *See also* Red Guard
Gay Liberation movement, 3, 383
General Motors, 189, 308
Generation gap, 115, 343–351, 376
Genghis Khan, 103
Gentry, 200–204. *See also* Government
Geography of Hunger, The (Josui de Castro), 300
Geriatrics, 339–340. *See also* Old age
Ghost-Dance Cult, 285

Global History of Man (L. Stavrianos et al.), 101
God That Failed, The (Arthur Koestler et al.), 459
Gods, 242, 243, 245, 345
God's Little Acre, 37
Golden Fleece Award, 217
Golden Lotus, The (Chin Ping Mei), 31, 36–38, 211–212
Golden Mean, 381
Government: prestige of, 187–196; local, in China, 196–205; local, in America, 204–207; attitudes toward, 205–207; and imperial examinations, 209–210; corruption in Chinese, 209–216, 226–228; corruption in American, 216–225; and business, 218–220, 304–306; and revolt, schism, and reform, 225–245; and unions in China, 323–325; and unions in America, 325–328; and Confucianism, 378–381
Graduate, The, 126
Graham, Billy, 3, 280, 362
Grapes of Wrath, The (John Steinbeck), 29
Great Cultural Revolution. *See* Cultural Revolution
Great Leap, 7, 8, 418–419
Great Train Robbery, The, 178
Great Wall psychology, 439, 450
Greatest Story Ever Told, The (Fulton Oursler), 124
Gresham's Law, 288
Guilds, 196–197, 294, 298, 397
Gulliver's Travels (Jonathan Swift), 359, 390
Gun lobby, 229

Hakeem, Church of, 294
Han dynasty, 231, 395, 448
Han Pa (drought-giving spirit or god), 256
Han Yu, 262
Handicraft shop in China, 292–293
Hao Ch'iu Chuan (The Story of an Ideal Marriage), 31
Hare Krishna sect, 283, 285
Hawaii: Protestant and Catholic missionaries in, 260–261; religion of the Chinese in, 273–274
Heroin. *See* Narcotics addiction
Hero worship, 170–185
Hinduism, 253, 283
Hitler, Adolf, 185, 470, 471
Hitler Youth Corps, 185, 468
Homes, 78–79
Homosexuality, 34, 67
How to Get Rich in Washington (Blair Bolles), 221
Huang Ti (Yellow Emperor), 384
Hui kuan (Chinese community clubs), 397
Human good, 481–482

"Hundred Flower Bloom" movement, 321
Hurley, Patrick J., 411
Husband-wife relationship. *See* Marriage

I, A Woman, 126
I am the Cheese (Robert Cromier), 84
I'll Cry Tomorrow (Lillian Roth), 125
Immaculate conception, belief in, 22, 257
Imperialism. *See* Colonialism
In Cold Blood (Truman Capote), 124
In Search of the Historical Jesus, 281
Inclusiveness, 115–117
Individual-centeredness, 12, 17, 40, 88,
     156, 357, 383, 388, 425; in art and fic-
     tion, 46; and love, 51, 54; and attitudes
     toward career women, 62; and repression
     of sex, 63; and diffused sexuality, 67;
     and school, 102; and social class, 159;
     and hero worship, 172, 179; and sex
     crimes and violence, 260–264; and reli-
     gion, 285, 289; and music, 294; and eco-
     nomic life, 309; and juvenile delin-
     quency, 350; and racial relations, 359;
     and social change, 377; and God, 389;
     and nationalism and Communism, 405;
     and Communist Party membership in
     America, 466; and tendency to invite to-
     talitarianism, 469
Individualism, 45; in England, 121–122;
     and American self-reliance, 131–132. *See
     also* Self-reliance; American way of life
Industrialization, lack of, in China, 297–
     301, 312–320; Max Weber's theory of,
     319–320
Infanticide, 79–80, 374
Inner-direction, 133, 136
Inner-self, 125, 127
Inquisition, 404, 464
"Inscrutable" versus "unpredictable," 401
Insecurity, 364–366
Institute of Human-Animal Relationship,
     310
Intelligentsia: economic foundation of, 321–
     322; in America, 459
Interracial marriage. *See* Marriage, inter-
     racial
Introversion, 13
Islam, 253, 259, 271–272. *See also* Moslems
Isolation: social and psychological, 12–13;
     Chinese and American, 439–440

Jacobins, The (Crane Brinton), 463–464
Japanese, 406–407, 415
Jesus Christ, 255, 257, 260
Jews: in China, 270–271, 289–290; in Nazi
     Germany, 353, 412
Jones, Jim, 467
Jonestown (Guyana). *See* People's Temple
Joplin, Janis, 603

Judaism, 253–254, 264
Juvenile delinquency, 343–351, 376

Kerner Report, The, 351, 353–354, 357
Kinship, 89–91, 372, 382; and commune
     organization, 421–422, 425; changes in,
     under Communism, 428, 433; as a bar-
     rier to Communism, 471–472
Kitchen God, 241–243
Kon Tiki (Thor Heyerdahl), 124
Koran, 264
Kramer vs Kramer, 126
Ku Klux Klan, 373, 395, 434, 468
Kungts'antang (Communist Party), 199
Kunming (Yunnan), 429, 430, 436
Kuomintang (Nationalist Party), 199, 200,
     406

La Dolce Vita, 126
Labor-management relations: in China,
     323–324; in America, 325–328
Lady Chatterly's Lover (D. H. Lawrence), 36
Land of Famine (Walter Hampton Mallory),
     435
Landlord-tenant relations, 321–323
Lao Tze, 255, 257. *See also* Taoism
Land reform, 321–323, 412–413
Law: Chinese concept of, 377–378; and sci-
     ence, 390. *See also* Legalists
League of Women Voters, 373
Leaves of Grass (Walt Whitman), 37
Legalists, 379–380. *See also* Law
Li (propriety), 388
Life is Worth Living (Fulton Sheen), 124, 287
Lin Piao, 379
Lin Tse-hsu, 191
Literature. *See* Fiction
Living Theatre, The, 485
Lo! the Former Egyptian (H. Allen Smith),
     124
Lobbyists, The (James Deakin), 221
Long March, 151
Look Homeward Angel (Thomas Wolfe), 31
Looking for Mr. Goodbar (Judith Rossner),
     38, 124
Love: in fiction, 29–46; in American and
     Chinese culture, 49–60. *See also* Marriage
Love Trilogy, The (Pa Chin), 43
Low Man on a Totem Pole (H. Allen Smith),
     124
Lun Heng (Wang Ch'ung), 227

Ma Tsu, 243
Madame Sarah (Cornelia Otis Skinner), 125
Magic Mountain, The (Thomas Mann), 31
Main Street (Sinclair Lewis), 32
Majong. *See* Gambling
Manchild in the Promised Land (Claude
     Brown), 125

Manchukuo, 408
Mandate of Heaven, 230-231, 246, 418
Manhattan, 126
Manson Family, 468
Mao Tse-tung, 104, 174, 188, 247, 413, 433
Marital life: American, 144-145; Chinese, 146-152
Marriage, 149-152; inter-racial, 355-357. *See also* Love
Marriage of Maria Braun, The, 126
Marshall Plan, 358
Martyrs, 382-383
Marx, Karl, 409, 443, 458, 463
Marxism, 416, 458-459, 469-470
Masculinity, 364-365
Material achievements, 440
Material-spritual dichotomy, 468-469
Mature Mind, The (Harry Overstreet), 124
May 30 Affair, 323. *See also* Labor-management relations
Medicare, 341
Meeting of East and West, The (F. S. C. Northrop), 385
Mein Kampf (Adolf Hitler), 185
Memoir of An Ex-Prom Queen (Max Shulman), 38
Memoirs of Hecate County (Edmund Wilson), 37
Men and Nations: A World History (Mazour and Peoples), 100
Mencius, 22, 379, 482
Mercy League, 310
Midnight Cowboy (James Herlihy), 124
Military in China, 158
Min Sheh Tang (People's Socialist Party), 173
Ming Dynasty, 134, 231, 382, 448-449
Missionary zeal, 257-263, 268; lack of, among Chinese, 255-257
Mohists, 380
"Monopoly" (American game), 292
Monotheism: characteristics of, 253-254, 258-259; Chinese approach to, 271-276
Monroe Doctrine, 445
Moral Majority, 280
Mormons, 135
Morphine. *See* Narcotics addiction
Moslems, 262
Mount Olympus, 243
Movies, 125-126
Music, 390-394
Musicians, treatment of, in China and the West, 282-283
Mutual dependence, 113-117; as a factor in bureaucratic corruption, 213-214; between this and other worlds, 247; in economic life, 299, 304; as a factor in failed industrialization, 313-314, 316, 320; in

landlord-tenant relations, 321; in competition and advancement, 325; in old age, 342; in parent-child relations, 347; deleterious consequences of, 372; in Confucianism, 380, 389; under Communism, 405, 447; as a barrier to totalitarianism, 471
My Life and Loves (Frank Harris), 38-39
My Secret Life, 38-39

Narcissism, 7
Narcotics addiction, 345
National Association for the Advancement of Colored People (NAACP), 395
National character, 132-133
Nationalism, 404
Nazism, 185, 412
Negro. *See* Race relations
Nepotism: in China, 213; in America, 216
Never on Sunday, 126
New Deal, 228-229, 232-233
New Life Movement, 185, 433
New Year's Eve (Chinese), 242, 251, 273
Newsfront, 126
Ngo pu (evil-type supplementary instruction), 95-96
Nicholas and Alexandra (Robert K. Massie), 125
Noah, 257, 477-478
North Dallas Forty, 125
Northern Expedition, 410
Northern Ireland, 404
Northrop, F. S. C., 214-215, 385-386, 389, 443
Novels. *See* Fiction
Nu Wa, 257

Of Mice and Men (John Steinbeck), 21
Old age, 335-342
Old Man and the Sea, The (Ernest Hemingway), 365
One Hundred Dollar Misunderstanding (Robert Grover), 35-36
Opera, Chinese, 41-42
Opium. *See* Narcotics addiction
Opium War, 191, 444
Opportunism, 400-401
Oppression in China, 406-408
Orchestra Rehearsal, 126
Organization Man, The (William H. Whyte, Jr.), 135-136
Organization, voluntary, Chinese lack of, 394-399
Other-direction, 134-135

Painting, 19-29
Pao Kung An (The Story of His Eminence Pao), 227
Parent-child relationship, 79-92, 108, 110-

113, 121, 122, 130, 156; exclusiveness of, 86-87; mutual dependence in, 113-117; under Communism, 422. *See also* Schools
Peace Corps, 373
Peace of Soul (Fulton Sheen), 124
Peer Group, 111-112, 114-115
People's Temple, 284-285, 467, 469
Personality, 76-92; and culture, 77, 141-142
Pets, 309-310
Philosophy, Chinese, 378-382
Phrenology, 244-245
Pike, James, 289
Pinocchio, 85
Playbooks that Teach Your Child to Dress, 83
Polytheism, 253, 258, 259; and Chinese attitude toward Christianity, 272-273; Western approach to, 274
Poor People's March, 228, 358
Popular education: in traditional China, 41-42; under Communism, 43-45
Pornography: in painting, 20-21; in fiction, 29-40; Chinese and Western, 38-40
Power of Positive Thinking (Norman Vincent Peale), 124, 190, 287
Predicament of Modern Man, The (Elton Trueblood), 287
Prejudice. *See* Race relations
Pressure groups, 194, 229
Primogeniture, 313
Privacy, 78-79, 89
Prohibition, 361, 433
Prostitution, 62, 364-365, 434, 462-463
Pu Yi, Aisin-Gioro (Henry Pu Yi): as last ruler of the Ch'ing (Manchu) dynasty, 189; as emperor of the puppet regime of Manchukuo, 408
Puritanism, 63-65

Race relations, 103-104, 129-130, 351-352; tensions in, 355-356, 358, 359-360, 376, 453
Red Cross, 373
Red Guard, 137, 321, 329, 369; as missionary effort, 433-434
Reincarnation, 246, 247, 406
Religion, 105-108; in China and the West, 253-266; Chinese attitude toward, 270-273, 290-291; American intolerance in, 270; American approach to, 278-287. *See also* Supernatural, the; Polytheism; Monotheism; Pantheism
Religious persecution, 259-262
Repression (in art), 21-22
Researches into Chinese Superstitions (Henri Doré), 245-246
Revolution: and American way of life, 128-130; of 1911, in China, 244, 379, 410;

absence of, in Chinese history, 377-384; French, 463
Rickshaw Boy (Lao She), 43
Romance, 49-63; under Communism, 63-70
Romance of the Three Kingdoms, The, 31-32
Romantic love, 51. *See also* Love

Salvation Army, 395
Santa Claus, 108; Black version of, 358
Schools, 92-108. *See also* Parent-child relationship
Science, Chinese lack of, 384-394
Science and Civilization in China (Joseph Needham), 384
Science of Living Institute. *See* United Church
Scientology, Church of, 476
Sea Around Us, The (Rachel Carson), 124
Secret societies, 397-398
Self-expression (in American and Chinese children), 93-94, 98
Self-reliance, 108-117, 148-149, 152; and English individualism, 121-122, 128, 130-131; and corruption, 217, 222, 233; and religion, 254, 276, 278, 280-281, 283; and economic life, 293, 305-306, 308-309; and industrialization in China and America, 319-320, 321; and labor unions, 238, 326; and old age, 335, 339, 342; and generation gap, 343; and juvenile delinquency, 346-347, 349; and identity-seeking, 349; and race relations, 351-352, 359; and violence, 365-366; and China's weaknesses, 372, 376; and religion, 388-389; and America's foreign relations, 468, 469, 471; and America's future, 472, 480-481; counter-balance to, 484-485, 487, 489. *See also* American way of life; Individual-centeredness
Self-sufficiency (as distinguished from individualism and self-reliance), 128-129
Sex, repression of, 22, 63; Chinese attitude toward, 22; in Chinese fiction, 31-33; pornographic, 33; in American and Chinese fiction, 33-40; in literature and erotica, 39, 44-45
Sex crimes, 360-368
Sexes, relations between, 49-73, 174-175; and attitudes toward love, 49-59; in public life, 56-57, 59-63; role of middle man in, 54-55. *See also* Painting; Fiction
Sexuality: in Western Painting, 22-23; in Chinese and Western literature, 29-40, 45; in public life, 56-63; and individual-centered way of life, 67
Shadow plays, 42
Shen shih. See Gentry
Shout, The, 125

Shun (emperor), 477–478

Sino-Soviet relations, 451–452

Situation-centeredness, 17, 136–137; in pornographic fiction, 39–40; in art and fiction, 46; and love, 51, 54; and romance, 63–64, 65; and relationship between the sexes, 67; and social class, 159, 163, 168; and hero worship, 172, 177, 179, 180; and associations, 398; under Communism, 405, 418; and communes, 425, 481. *See also* Mutual dependence

Six Arts *(Liu Yi)*, 391, 402

Snake Pit (Mary Jane Ward), 125

Snow White and the Seven Dwarfs, 85

Social dancing, 60

Social needs, 108–110; Chinese and American patterns of, 110–115

Society for the Prevention of Cruelty to Animals (SPCA), 373, 396

Sojourners, 397

Son of Heaven, 194

Soul, Chinese concept of, 246–248; and "rescuing" versus "saving," 257–258

South Africa, Republic of, 129, 352

"Southeast the Peacock Flies," 149

Spirit world, 240–251, 400. *See also* Supernatural, the

Spirituality: alleged Oriental, 297; and individual isolation, 468–469

Spiritual-material dichotomy, fallacy of, 297

Stalinism. *See* Marxism

Steppenwolf (Hermann Hesse), 119

Steve Canyon, 99

Story-telling in China, 41–42

Strange Romance of the Beautiful Pair, The (Yu Chiao Li), 31

Strange Stories from a Chinese Studio (Liao Tsai Chih Yi), 31

Success, attitudes toward, 165–170; and hero worship, 170–171

Sun Yat-sen, 167, 264, 332, 398, 410, 418, 420, 433

Supernatural, the: American attitudes toward, 239–240, 276–289; Chinese attitudes toward, 239–247, 271–273; relativistic and absolutistic views of, 255–256. *See also* Ancestor worship; Spirit world

Supreme Ruler of Heaven, 240–241, 389

Synanon, 467

T'aip'ing Rebellion, 263, 410, 432

Tale of the Mirrored Flower (Ching Hua Yuan), 29, 390

Tale of Two Cities, A (Charles Dickens), 30

T'ang dynasty, 41, 134, 395, 448

Taoism, 254–255, 270, 380; as political safety valve, 382

Temple of Heaven, 67, 171

"10", 126

Thailand (Siam), 448–450

Thematic Apperception Test (TAT), 138

Theology, 264–266

Thomas Woodrow Wilson: A Psychological Study (William C. Bullitt), 184

Three Peoples' Principles *(San Min Chu Yi)*, 410, 443

Three Principles Youth Corps, 185

Thy Neighbor's Wife (Gay Talese), 38

Tolstoy (Henri Troyat), 125

Tom Jones (Henry Fielding), 30

Tonkin Resolution, 229

Torrent, The: A Trilogy (Pa Chin), 43

Totalitarianism, 471–472. *See also* Communism, appeal of, to Americans

Toy industry in America, 84

Tradition, influence of, on the Chinese, 372–377

Tradition-direction, 134

Treaty of Nanking (1842), 191

Tree of Wooden Clogs, The, 125

Tropic of Cancer (Henry Miller), 34–36

Truck Stop Congregation, 279

True Story of Ah Q, The (Lu Hsun), 42–43

True Story of Chi Kung, The, 31, 227

True Story of His Eminence Pao, The, 31, 227

Twelve Tests of Character (E. Fosdick), 287

Twenty Letters to a Friend (Svetlana Alliluyeva), 125

"Twenty-Four Examples of Filial Piety," 81, 85

Two Adolescents, 37

Ulysses, 125

Under the Sea Wind (Rachel Carson), 124

Unidentified Flying Object (UFO), 395

Unification Church, 467

Unitarian Church, 277

United Church, 284

Universal Life Church, 282

Utopia (Thomas More), 227

Valley of Decision, 5–7

Van Impe, Jack, 279

Violence, 360–368; insecurity as common cause of, 364, 377; as building block for totalitarianism, 468

Virgin Birth: in the Bible, 22; in Taoism, 22, 257

Viet Cong, 444

Vietnam, 444, 448

Vietnam War, 228–229, 278, 447

Watergate, 229

Way of life, 12–13; and national character types, 132–134

Wealth of Nations, The (Adam Smith), 378

Weathermen, 7
Weddings, 243, 316
Wen God, (epidemic-giving god), 255–256
West, impact of, on China, 406–410
Western Chamber, 31
Western Paradise, 240–241, 247. *See also*
   Supernatural, the; Religion
White Citizens Council, 395, 434. *See also*
   Race Relations
White racism, 351–352
Women's Christian Temperance Union, 433
Work-point system, 424–425; and kinship
   system, 428

Worlds in Collision (Immanuel Velikovsky),
   124

Yangtze River, 1, 174, 178, 416
Yearling, The (Marjorie K. Rawlings), 32
Yin and *yang,* 257, 387
*Yu Chiao Li (The Strange Romance of the Beauti-
   ful Pair),* 31

Zebra Derby, The (Max Schulman), 123
Zen Buddhism, 285
Zeus, 243